STUDENT ENCYCLOPEDIA
OF AFRICAN LITERATURE

STUDENT ENCYCLOPEDIA OF

African Literature

DOUGLAS KILLAM AND
ALICIA L. KERFOOT

GREENWOOD PRESS
Westport, Connecticut • London

Library of Congress Cataloging-in-Publication Data

Killam, G. D.
   Student encyclopedia of African literature / Douglas Killam and Alicia L. Kerfoot.
      p. cm.
   Includes bibliographical references and index.
   ISBN 978–0–313–33580–8 (alk. paper)
  1. African literature (English)—Encyclopedias.   2. African literature (English)—
Bio-bibliography—Encyclopedias.   3. African literature—Encyclopedias.   4. African
literature—Bio-bibliography—Encyclopedias.   5. Authors, African—Biography—
Encyclopedias.   6. Africa—In literature—Encyclopedias.   I. Kerfoot, Alicia L.   II. Title.
   PR9340.A52K65   2008
   820.9'9603—dc22
   [B]   2007035356

British Library Cataloguing in Publication Data is available.

Library of Congress Catalog Card Number: 2007035356
ISBN: 978–0–313–33580–8

First published in 2008

Greenwood Press, 88 Post Road West, Westport, CT 06881
An imprint of Greenwood Publishing Group, Inc.
www.greenwood.com

Printed in the United States of America

The paper used in this book complies with the
Permanent Paper Standard issued by the National
Information Standards Organization (Z39.48–1984).

10   9   8   7   6   5   4   3   2   1

CONTENTS

LIST OF ENTRIES   vii

GUIDE TO RELATED TOPICS   xv

PREFACE   xxv

THE ENCYCLOPEDIA   **1**

SELECTED BIBLIOGRAPHY   325

INDEX   329

LIST OF ENTRIES

Abrahams, Lionel
Abrahams, Peter
Abruquah, Joseph Wilfred
Achebe, Chinua
Acholonu, Catherine Obianuju
Adair, Barbara
Adedeji, (Alu)Remi Aduke
Adichie, Chimamanda Ngozi
Africa Is People
African Child, The
African Image, The
African Tragedy, An
African Writers Series
African-American Literature
African-British Literature
African-Canadian Literature
African-Caribbean Literature
Afrika, Tatamkhulu Ismail
Age of Iron
Aidoo, Ama Ata
Aiyejina, Funso
Ajayi, Christie Ade
Ajayi, Tolu(walogo)
Ajose, Audrey
Akassa You Mi: A Historical Drama
Aké: The Years of Childhood
Akello, Grace
Akenhaten: Dweller in Truth
Alford, Gwen
Alkali, Zaynab
All for Love: A Novel
All for Oil
Aluko, T(imothy) M(ofolorunso)
Amadi, Elechi
Amriika
Anduru, Agoro
Angira, Jared
Aniebo, I.N.C.
Anowa

Anthills of the Savannah
Anthologies
Anyidoho, Kofi
Apartheid
Armah, Ayi Kwei
Arrow of God
Arrowheads to My Heart
Atta, Sefi
Awoonor, Kofi (Nyedevu)
Bâ, Amadou Hampâté
Bâ, Mariama
Bacchae of Euripides, The
Baderoon, Gabeba
Bandele-Thomas, Biyi
Bavino Sermons
Beatification of Area Boy, The
Beautyful Ones Are Not Yet Born, The
Beggar, The, The Thief and the Dogs, and
    Autumn Quail
Bekederemo, J(ohn) P(epper) Clark
Ben, in the World
Ben Jelloun, Tahar
Ben-Abdallah, Mohammed
Beti, Mongo (pseudonym of Alexandre Biyidi)
Bikoroa Plays, The
Biography and Autobiography
Bitter Eden
Bitter Fruit: A Novel
Black, Stephen
Black Atlantic
Black Consciousness in South
    Africa
Black Docker, The
Blackburn, Douglas
Blackheart
Blame Me on History
Blanket Boy's Moon
Blay, J. Benibengor
Blind Moon

Blood Knot, The
Bloodlines
Bloom, Harry
Boehmer, Elleke
Boesman and Lena
Boetie, Dugmore
Book of Secrets, The
Bosman, H(erman) C(harles)
Boundaries
Brettell, N.H.
Brew, (Osborne Henry) Kwesi
Breytenbach, Breyten
Brink, Andre
Broken Reed
Brutus, Dennis
Bukenya, Austin
Burger's Daughter
Butler, Frederick Guy
By the Sea
Cairo Trilogy
Call Me by My Rightful Name
Call Me Woman
Camara Laye
Campbell, Roy(ston)
Captain's Tiger, The
Carnival of Looters, A
Casely-Hayford, Adelaide
Casely-Hayford, Gladys
Casely-Hayford, Joseph Ephraïm
Censorship
Chaka
*Chaos Theory of the Heart and Other Poems
    Mainly since 1990*
Chedid, Andrée
Cheney-Coker, Syl
Children of Gebelawi
Chimombo, Steve
Chingono, Julius
Chinodya, Shimmer
Chinweizu
Chipamaunga, Edmund
Chipasula, Frank
Chraïbi, Driss
Clayton, Cherry
Cloete, (Edward Fairlie) Stuart (Graham)
Clouts, Sydney (David)
Cochlovius, Karen
Coetzee, J(ohn) M(axwell)
Collector of Treasures, The

Collen, Lindsay
Combrinck, Lisa
Concubine, The
Conservationist, The
Conton, William (Farquhar)
Cook, Méira
Cope, Jack (Robert Knox)
Couchoro, Félix
Couto, Mia
Cripps, A(rthur) S(hearly)
Cry, the Beloved Country
Cugoano, Ottobah
Cullinan, Patrick (Roland)
Currey, Ralph Nixon
Dadié, Bernard
Dance in the Sun, A
Dance of the Forests, A
Dangarembga, Tsitsi
Dangor, Achmat
Daughter of Mumbi
Daughters of Twilight
De Graft, Joe (Joseph Coleman)
Death and the King's Horseman
Dedan Kimathi
Dei-Anang, Michael Francis
Detained: A Writer's Prison Diary
Devil on the Cross
Dhlomo, H(erbert) I.E.
Dhlomo, R(obert) R(olfes) R(eginald)
Dib, Mohammed
Diescho, Joseph
Dikobe, Modikwe (pseudonym of Marks
    Rammitloa)
Dilemma of a Ghost, The
Diop, Alioune
Diop, Birago
Diop, Cheikh Anta
Diop, David
Divorce, The
Djoleto, (Solomon Alexander) Amu
Down Second Avenue
Drama
Drum
Dry White Season, A
Du Plessis, Menán
Duodu, Cameron
Dusklands
Easmon, R(aymond) Sarif
Echeruo, Michael J.C.

Echewa, T. Obinkaram
Edufa
Efuru
Egbuna, Obi B(enedict)
Ekwensi, Cyprian
Emecheta, Buchi
Enekwe, Ossie
Eppel, John
Equiano, Olaudah
Essop, Ahmed
Experience, The
Eye of the Earth, The
Fagunwa, D(aniel) O.
Fall, Malick
Famished Road, The
Farah, Nuruddin
Fatunde, Tunde
Feminism and Literature
Fettouma, Touati
Fiawoo, Ferdinand Kwasi
Fisherman's Invocation, The
Fitzpatrick, (Sir) J. Percy
Fixions and Other Stories
Foe
Fools and Other Stories
Footprints in the Quag
Forest of a Thousand Daemons, The
Foriwa
Fragments
From a Crooked Rib
Fugard, Athol
Fugard, Sheila Meiring
Garuba, Harry
Gay and Lesbian Sexuality in
    Literature
Ghanem, Fathy
Gibbon, Perceval
*Girl Who Killed to Save: Nongquase the
    Liberator, The*
Gods Are Not to Blame, The
God's Bits of Wood
God's Step-Children
Going down River Road
Gordimer, Nadine
Grain of Wheat, A
Grass Is Singing, The
Gray, Stephen
Great Ponds, The
Guest of Honour, A

Gunny Sack, The
Gurnah, Abdulrazak
Gwala, Mafika Pascal
Haarhoff, Dorian
Hakim, Te[a?]wfiq (Husayn) al-
Hammer Blows
Head, Bessie
Healers, The
Heavensgate
Helena's Hope, Ltd
Hello and Goodbye
Henshaw, James Ene
Heroes
Hope, Christopher (David Tully)
House Gun, The
House of Hunger
Houseboy
Hove, Chenjerai
Hussein, Ebrahim N.
I Will Marry When I Want
*Ibadan: The Pankelemes Years, a Memoir
    1946–1965*
Idanre
Ike, (Vincent) Chukwuemeka
Imbuga, Francis
In the Ditch
In the Fog of the Season's End
In the Heart of the Country
Incidents at the Shrine
Instant in the Wind, An
Interpreters, The
Iroh, Eddie
Iyayi, Festus
Jabavu, Noni (Helen Nontando)
Jacobson, Dan(iel)
Johnson, Lemuel A.
Jonker, Ingrid
Jordan, A(rchibald) C(ampbell)
Journey Within, The
Joys of Motherhood, The
July's People
Ka, Aminata Maiga
Kagame, Alexis
Kahiga, Samuel
Karodia, Farida
Karone, Yodi
Katiyo, Wilson
Kayira, Legson
Kente, Gibson

Kgositsile, Keorapetse
Kibera, Leonard
Kimenye, Barbara
Konadu, (Samuel) Asare
Kongi's Harvest
Kourouma, Ahmadou
Kunene, Daniel P.
Kunene, Mazisi (KaMdabuli)
Kurunmi
Kuzwayo, Ellen
La Guma, Alex(ander)
Labyrinths
Ladipo, Duro
Laing, B(ernard) Kojo
Lament for an African Pol
Landlocked
Langbodo
Last Harmattan of Alusine Dunbar, The
Lessing, Doris
Letters to Martha
Life & Times of Michael K
Likimani, Muthoni
Limits
Lion and the Jewel, The
Lipenga, Ken
Literary Criticism
Literary Theory
Little Karoo, The
Livingstone, Douglas
Looking on Darkness
Looming Shadow, The
Lubega, Bonnie
Lubwa P'chong
Maclennan, Donald (Alasdair Calum)
Madanhire, Nevanji
Maddy, Yulisa Amadu (Formerly Pat
    Yulisa or Pat Maddy)
Madmen and Specialists
Mafeking Diary of Sol T. Plaatje, The
Mafeking Road
Magaia, Lina
Magona, Sindiwe
Mahfouz, Naguib
Maina Wa Kinyatti
Man of the People, A
Man Who Lost His Shadow, The
Manaka, Matsemela
Mangua, Charles
Mapanje, Jack

Marabi Dance, The
Marechera, Dambudzo
Marriage of Anansewa, The
Marshall, Bill Okyere
Martha Quest
Master of Petersburg, The
Matigari
Mattera, Umaruiddin Don
Matthews, James
Maunick, Edouard
Mazrui, Ali A.
Mbuli, Mzwakhe
McLoughlin, Timothy O.
Mda, Zakes (Zanemvula Kizito Gatyeni)
Memmi, Albert
Meniru, Theresa Ekwutosi
Mezu, S(ebastian) Okechukwu
Mhlophe, Gcina
Mhudi
Miller, Ruth
Millin, Sarah Gertrude
Mine Boy
Mission to Kala
Mnthali, Felix
Modisane, William "Bloke"
Mofolo, Thomas (Mopoku)
Moore, Bai T(amia) J(ohnson)
Mopeli-Paulus, A(twell) S(idwell)
Motsisi, (Karobo Moses) Casey "Kid"
Mphahlele, Es'kia (Ezekiel)
Mpina, Edison
Mtshali, (Oswald) Mbuyiseni
Mugo, Micere Githae
Mulaisho, Dominic
Mungoshi, Charles
Munonye, John
Muntu
Muriel at Metropolitan
Mutloatse, Mothobi
Mutswairo, Solomon
Mwangi, Meja
Myth, Literature, and the African World
Mzamane, Mbulelo (Vizikhungo)
Nagenda, John
Nakasa, Nat(haniel Ndazana)
Napolo Poems
Nazareth, Peter
Nazombe, Anthony
Ndebele, Njabulo (Simakahle)

Ndhlala, Geoffrey
N'Djehoya, Blaise
Ndu, Pol Nnamuzikam
Nervous Conditions
Neto, Agostinho
Ngara, Emmanuel
Ngcobo, Lauretta
Ngema, Mbongeni
Ngubiah, Stephen N.
Ngugi wa Thiong'o
Nicol, Abioseh
Nicol, Mike
Night of Darkness
Nightwatcher, Nightsong
Njami, Simon
Njau, Rebeka (aka Marina Gashe)
Nkosi, Lewis
No Bride Price
No Longer at Ease
No Sweetness Here
No-Good Friday
None to Accompany Me
Nortje, Arthur
Ntiru, Richard Carl
Nwabueze, Emeka
Nwakoby, Martina Awele
Nwankwo, Nkem
Nwapa, Flora
Nyamfukudza, Stanley
Nyamubaya, Freedom
Nzekwu, Onuora
Obafemi, Olu
Oculi, Okello
Of Chameleons and Gods
Ofeimun, Odia
Ogot, Grace (Emily)
Oguibe, Olu
Ogundipe-Leslie, Molara
Ogunyemi, Wale
Oil Man of Obange
Ojaide, Tanure
Okai, Atukwei
Okara, Gabriel (Imomotimi Gbaingbain)
Okigbo, (Ifeanyichukwu) Christopher
Oko, Akomaye
Okome, Onookome
Okot p'Bitek
Okoye, Ifeoma
Okpewho, Isidore

Okri, Ben
Olafioye, Tayo Peter
Old Man and the Medal, The
Oludhe Macgoye, Marjorie
Omotoso, Kole
One Man One Wife
Only Son, The
Onwueme, Tess Akaeke
Onyeama, Dillibe
Ordeal in the Forest
Osadebay, Dennis (Chukude)
Osahon, Naiwu
Osiris Rising
Osofisan, Femi
Osundare, Niyi
Oti, Sonny
Our Sister Killjoy
Ovbiagele, Helen
Owusu, Martin (Okyere)
Oyebode, Femi
Oyekunle, Segun
Oyono, Ferdinand
Oyono-Miha, Guillaume
Palangyo, Peter
Palm-wine Drinkard, The
Paradise Farm
Path of Thunder, The
Paton, Alan (Stewart)
People of the City
Pepetela (pseudonym of Artur Carlos
    Maurício Pestana dos Santos)
Perpetua and the Habit of Unhappiness
Petals of Blood
Peters, Lenrie (Leopold Wilfred)
Plaatje, Solomon T(shekisho)
Plomer, William (Charles Franklyn)
Poor Christ of Bomba, The
Popular Literature
Prince Kagwema (pseudonym of Osija Mwam-
    bungu)
Pringle, Thomas
Prison Literature in South Africa
Prisoners of Jebs
Proper Marriage, A
Qabula, Alfred Temba
Question of Power, A
Rabéarivelo, Jean-Joseph
Rabémanajara, Jacques
Rainmaker, The

Rampolokeng, Lesego
Raw Pieces
Rediscovery
Reign of Wazobia, The
Religion and Literature
Return to Beirut, The
Ripple from the Storm, A
Rive, Richard
River Between, The
Road, The
Roberts, Sheila
Rotimi, Ola
Rubadiri, David
Ruganda, John
Ruheni, Mwangi (pseudonym of Nicholas
    Muraguri)
Ruhumbika, Gabriel
Rui, Manuel
Rumours of Rain
Rungano, Kristina
Saadawi, Nawal el
Salih, Tayeb
Sallah, Tijan M(omodou)
Samkange, Stanlake
Sancho, Ignatius
Saro-Wiwa, Ken(ule Beeson)
Sassine, Williams
Schreiner, Olive (Emilie Albertina)
Scully, William Charles
Season of Anomy
Season of Migration to the North
Seasons of Thomas Tebo, The
Segun, Mabel (Dorothy)
Sekyi (William Essuman-Gwira) Kobina
Sellassie, Sahle
Selormey, Francis
Sembene Ousmane
Senghor, L(eopold) S(edar)
Sepamla, Sipho (Sydney)
Seremba, George
Serote, Mongane Wally
Seruma, Eneriko (pseudonym of
    Henry S. Kimbugwe)
Serumaga, Robert
Shaihu Umar
Sibenke, Ben
Simbi and the Satyr of the Dark Jungle
Sirens Knuckles Boots
Sixth Day, The

Sizwe Bansi Is Dead
Slater, Francis Carey
Smith, Pauline (Janet)
So Long a Letter
Sofola, Zulu
Son of Woman
Song of Lawino
Sons and Daughters
Sony Labou Tansi
Sowande, Bode
Soyinka, Wole
Sozaboy: A Novel in Rotten English
Sport of Nature, A
States of Emergency
Stone Country, The
Story of an African Farm, The
Strong Bread, The
Sutherland, Efua T(heodora)
Sweet and Sour Milk
Taban Lo Liyong
Tahir, Ibrahim
Tejani, Bahadur
Tell Freedom
Themba, (Daniel Canodoise) Can
Things Fall Apart
Thomas, Gladys
Through a Film Darkly
Time of the Butcherbird
Tlali, Miriam
Tomorrow Left Us Yesterday
Trial and Other Stories, The
Trial of Christopher Okigbo, The
Trials of Brother Jero, The
Tsodzo, T(hompson) K(umbirai)
Turbott Wolfe
Tutuola, Amos
Two Thousand Seasons
Udechukwu, Obiora
Ugah, Ada
Uka, Kalu
Ulasi, Adaora Lily
Umelo, Rosina
Valley of a Thousand Hills, The
Vambe, Lawrence
Van der Post, (Sir) Laurens (Jan)
Van Wyk, Christopher
Vassanji, M(oyez) G.
Vatsa, Mamman Jira
Vera, Yvonne

Vilakazi, B(enedict) W(allet)
Visions and Reflections
Vladislavic, Ivan
Voice, The
Wachira, Godwin
Waciuma, Charity
Waiting for the Barbarians
Waiting Laughters
Walk in the Night, A
Wall of the Plague, The
Wangusa, Timothy
War Literature
Watene, Kenneth
Watson, Stephen
Weep Not, Child
Were, Miriam
Whaley, Andrew

Wheatley, Phillis
When Sunset Comes to Sapitwa
Why Are We So Blest?
Wicomb, Zoë
Wilhelm, Peter
Will to Die, The
Williams, Adebayo
Witch-Herbalist of the Remote Town, The
Wrath of Napolo: A Novel, The
Wrath of the Ancestors, The
Yirenkyi, Asiedu
You Can't Get Lost in Cape Town
You Must Set Forth at Dawn
Young Adult Literature
Zeleza, Paul Tiyambe
Zimunya, Musaemura Bonas
Zungur, Sa'ad

GUIDE TO RELATED TOPICS

GENERIC CATEGORIES

African Writers Series
African-American Literature
African-British Literature
African-Canadian Literature
African-Caribbean Literature
Anthologies
Biography and Autobiography

Drama
Literary Criticism
Literary Theory
Popular Literature
Prison Literature in South Africa
War Literature
Young Adult Literature

HISTORICAL PERIODS

Apartheid
Black Atlantic

Black Consciousness in South Africa
Censorship

NOVELISTS

Abrahams, Lionel
Abrahams, Peter
Abruquah, Joseph Wilfred
Achebe, Chinua
Adair, Barbara
Adichie, Chimamanda Ngozi
Ajayi, Tolu(walogo)
Akello, Grace
Alkali, Zaynab
Aluko, T(imothy) M(ofolorunso)
Amadi, Elechi
Aniebo I.N.C.
Armah, Ayi Kwei
Atta, Sefi
Awoonor, Kofi (Nyedevu)
Bâ, Amadou Hampâté
Bâ, Mariama
Bandele-Thomas, Biyi
Ben Jelloun, Tahar
Beti, Mongo (pseudonym of Alexandre Biyidi)
Black, Stephen
Blackburn, Douglas
Bloom, Harry

Boehmer, Elleke
Boetie, Dugmore
Bosman, H(erman) C(harles)
Breytenbach, Breyten
Brink, Andre
Bukenya, Austin
Camara Laye
Casely-Hayford, Joseph Ephraïm
Chedid, Andrée
Cheney-Coker, Syl
Chinodya, Shimmer
Chipamaunga, Edmund
Chraïbi, Driss
Cloete, (Edward Fairlie) Stuart (Graham)
Cochlovius, Karen
Coetzee, J(ohn) M(axwell)
Collen, Lindsay
Conton, William (Farquhar)
Cook, Méira
Cope, Jack (Robert Knox)
Couchoro, Félix
Cripps, A(rthur) S(hearly)
Dadié, Bernard

Dangarembga, Tsitsi
Dangor, Achmat
Dei-Anang, Michael Francis
Dhlomo, R(obert) R(olfes) R(eginald)
Dib, Mohammed
Diescho, Joseph
Dikobe, Modikwe (pseudonym of Marks
    Rammitloa)
Djoleto, (Solomon Alexander) Amu
Du Plessis, Menán
Duodu, Cameron
Easmon, R(aymond) Sarif
Echewa, T. Obinkaram
Egbuna, Obi B(enedict)
Ekwensi, Cyprian
Emecheta, Buchi
Enekwe, Ossie
Eppel, John
Essop, Ahmed
Fagunwa, D(aniel) O.
Fall, Malick
Farah, Nuruddin
Fettouma, Touati
Fitzpatrick, (Sir) J. Percy
Fugard, Sheila Meiring
Ghanem, Fathy
Gibbon, Perceval
Gordimer, Nadine
Gray, Stephen
Gurnah, Abdulrazak
Hakim, Tawfiq (Husayn) al-
Head, Bessie
Hope, Christopher (David Tully)
Hove, Chenjerai
Ike, (Vincent) Chukwuemeka
Imbuga, Francis
Iroh, Eddie
Iyayi, Festus
Jacobson, Dan(iel)
Jordan, A(rchibald) C(ampbell)
Ka, Aminata Maiga
Kahiga, Samuel
Karodia, Farida
Karone, Yodi
Katiyo, Wilson
Kayira, Legson
Kibera, Leonard
Konadu, (Samuel) Asare
Kourouma, Ahmadou
La Guma, Alex(ander)

Laing, B(ernard) Kojo
Lessing, Doris
Likimani, Muthoni
Lubega, Bonnie
Madanhire, Nevanji
Maddy, Yulisa Amadu
Magaia, Lina
Mahfouz, Naguib
Mangua, Charles
Marechera, Dambudzo
Marshall, Bill Okyere
McLoughlin, Timothy O.
Mda, Zakes (Zanemvula Kizito Gatyeni)
Memmi, Albert
Mezu, S(ebastian) Okechukwu
Millin, Sarah Gertrude
Mnthali, Felix
Mofolo, Thomas (Mopoku)
Moore, Bai T(amia) J(ohnson)
Mopeli-Paulus, A(twell) S(idwell)
Mphahlele, Es'kia (Ezekiel)
Mpina, Edison
Mulaisho, Dominic
Munonye, John
Mutswairo, Solomon
Mwangi, Meja
Nagenda, John
Nazareth, Peter
Ndhlala, Geoffrey
N'Djehoya, Blaise
Ngcobo, Lauretta
Ngubiah, Stephen N.
Ngugi wa Thiong'o
Nicol, Mike
Njami, Simon
Njau, Rebeka
Nkosi, Lewis
Nwakoby, Martina Awele
Nwankwo, Nkem
Nwapa, Flora
Nyamfukudza, Stanley
Nzekwu, Onuora
Oculi, Okello
Ogot, Grace (Emily)
Okoye, Ifeoma
Okpewho, Isidore
Okri, Ben
Olafioye, Tayo Peter
Oludhe Macgoye, Marjorie
Omotoso, Kole

Onyeama, Dillibe
Osofisan, Femi
Ovbiagele, Helen
Oyono, Ferdinand
Palangyo, Peter
Paton, Alan (Stewart)
Pepetela (pseudonym of Artur Carlos
    Maurício Pestana dos Santos)
Peters, Lenrie (Leopold Wilfred)
Plaatje, Solomon T(shekisho)
Plomer, William (Charles Franklyn)
Prince Kagwema (pseudonym of Osija
    Mwambungu)
Rabéarivelo, Jean-Joseph
Rive, Richard
Roberts, Sheila
Rubadiri, David
Ruganda, John
Ruheni, Mwangi (pseudonym of Nicholas
    Muraguri)
Ruhumbika, Gabriel
Saadawi, Nawal el
Salih, Tayeb
Samkange, Stanlake
Saro-Wiwa, Ken(ule Beeson)
Sassine, Williams
Schreiner, Olive (Emilie Albertina)
Scully, William Charles
Sellassie, Sahle
Selormey, Francis

Sembene Ousmane
Sepamla, Sipho (Sydney)
Seruma, Eneriko (pseudonym of
    Henry S. Kimbugwe)
Serumaga, Robert
Smith, Pauline (Janet)
Sony Labou Tansi
Sowande, Bode
Soyinka, Wole
Taban Lo Liyong
Tahir, Ibrahim
Tejani, Bahadur
Tlali, Miriam
Tsodzo, T(hompson) K(umbirai)
Ugah, Ada
Uka, Kalu
Ulasi, Adaora Lily
Van der Post, (Sir) Laurens (Jan)
Van Wyk, Christopher
Vassanji, M(oyez) G.
Vera, Yvonne
Vladislavic, Ivan
Wachira, Godwin
Waciuma, Charity
Wangusa, Timothy
Were, Miriam
Wicomb, Zoë
Wilhelm, Peter
Williams, Adebayo
Zeleza, Paul Tiyambe

NOVELS

African Child, The
African Tragedy, An
Age of Iron
Akenhaten: Dweller in Truth
All for Love: A Novel
Amriika
Anthills of the Savannah
Arrow of God
Beautyful Ones Are Not Yet Born, The
Beggar, The, The Thief and the Dogs, and
    Autumn Quail
Ben, in the World
Bitter Eden
Bitter Fruit: A Novel
Black Docker, The
Blackheart

Blanket Boy's Moon
Bloodlines
Book of Secrets, The
Boundaries
Broken Reed
Burger's Daughter
By the Sea
Cairo Trilogy
Call Me by My Rightful Name
Chaka
Children of Gebelawi
Concubine, The
Conservationist, The
Cry, the Beloved Country
Dance in the Sun, A
Daughter of Mumbi

Daughters of Twilight
Devil on the Cross
Dry White Season, A
Dusklands
Efuru
Experience, The
Famished Road, The
Foe
Forest of a Thousand Daemons, The
Fragments
From a Crooked Rib
God's Bits of Wood
God's Step-Children
Going down River Road
Grain of Wheat, A
Grass Is Singing, The
Great Ponds, The
Guest of Honour, A
Gunny Sack, The
Half of a Yellow Sun
Healers, The
Heroes
House Gun, The
Houseboy
In the Ditch
In the Fog of the Season's End
In the Heart of the Country
Instant in the Wind, An
Interpreters, The
Journey Within, The
Joys of Motherhood, The
July's People
Lament for an African Pol
Landlocked
Last Harmattan of Alusine Dunbar, The
Life & Times of Michael K
Looking on Darkness
Looming Shadow, The
Man of the People, A
Man Who Lost His Shadow, The
Marabi Dance, The
Martha Quest
Master of Petersburg, The
Matigari
Mhudi
Mine Boy
Mission to Kala
Muriel at Metropolitan
Nervous Conditions
No Bride Price

No Longer at Ease
None to Accompany Me
Oil Man of Obange
Old Man and the Medal, The
One Man One Wife
Only Son, The
Ordeal in the Forest
Osiris Rising
Our Sister Killjoy
Palm-wine Drinkard, The
Paradise Farm
Path of Thunder, The
People of the City
Perpetua and the Habit of Unhappiness
Petals of Blood
Poor Christ of Bomba, The
Proper Marriage, A
Question of Power, A
Return to Beirut, The
Ripple from the Storm, A
River Between, The
Rumours of Rain
Season of Anomy
Season of Migration to the North
Seasons of Thomas Tebo, The
Shaihu Umar
Simbi and the Satyr of the Dark Jungle
Sixth Day, The
So Long a Letter
Son of Woman
Sozaboy: A Novel in Rotten English
Sport of Nature, A
States of Emergency
Stone Country, The
Story of an African Farm, The
Sweet and Sour Milk
Things Fall Apart
Time of the Butcherbird
Trial of Christopher Okigbo, The
Turbott Wolfe
Two Thousand Seasons
Voice, The
Waiting for the Barbarians
Walk in the Night, A
Wall of the Plague, The
Weep Not, Child
Why Are We So Blest?
Witch-Herbalist of the Remote Town, The
Wrath of Napolo: A Novel, The
Wrath of the Ancestors, The

PLAYS

Akassa You Mi: A Historical Drama
All for Oil
Anowa
Bacchae of Euripides, The
Beatification of Area Boy, The
Bikoroa Plays, The
Blood Knot, The
Boesman and Lena
Captain's Tiger, The
Dance of the Forests, A
Death and the King's Horseman
Dedan Kimathi
Dilemma of a Ghost, The
Divorce, The
Edufa
Foriwa
Girl Who Killed to Save: Nongquase the
    Liberator, The
Gods Are Not to Blame, The

Helena's Hope, Ltd
Hello and Goodbye
I Will Marry When I Want
Kongi's Harvest
Kurunmi
Langbodo
Lion and the Jewel, The
Madmen and Specialists
Marriage of Anansewa, The
Muntu
No-Good Friday
Rainmaker, The
Reign of Wazobia, The
Road, The
Sizwe Bansi Is Dead
Sons and Daughters
Strong Bread, The
Through a Film Darkly
Trials of Brother Jero, The

PLAYWRIGHTS

Acholonu, Catherine Obianuju
Adichie, Chimamanda Ngozi
Aidoo, Ama Ata
Amadi, Elechi
Bandele-Thomas, Biyi
Bekederemo, J(ohn) P(epper) Clark
Ben-Abdallah, Mohammed
Black, Stephen
Blay, J. Benibengor
Brink, Andre
Bukenya, Austin
Butler, Frederick Guy
Chedid, Andrée
Chimombo, Steve
Dadié, Bernard
Dangarembga, Tsitsi
Dangor, Achmat
De Graft, Joe (Joseph Coleman)
Dei-Anang, Michael Francis
Dhlomo, H(erbert) I. E.
Easmon, R(aymond) Sarif
Egbuna, Obi B(enedict)
Enekwe, Ossie
Fatunde, Tunde
Fiawoo, Ferdinand Kwasi
Fugard, Athol

Haarhoff, Dorian
Hakim, Tawfiq (Husayn) al-
Henshaw, James Ene
Hussein, Ebrahim N.
Imbuga, Francis
Kente, Gibson
Ladipo, Duro
Lubwa P'chong
Maddy, Yulisa Amadu
Manaka, Matsemela
Marshall, Bill Okyere
Mda, Zakes (Zanemvula Kizito Gatyeni)
Mnthali, Felix
Mugo, Micere Githae
Nazareth, Peter
Ngugi wa Thiong'o
Njau, Rebeka
Nwabueze, Emeka
Obafemi, Olu
Ogunyemi, Wale
Oko, Akoll1aye
Omotoso, Kole
Onwueme, Tess Akaeke
Osofisan, Femi
Oti, Sonny
Owusu, Martin (Okyere)

Oyekunle, Segun
Oyono-Miha, Guillaume
Rabémanajara, Jacques
Rotimi, Ola
Ruganda, John
Rui, Manuel
Sekyi (William Essuman-Gwira) Kobina
Seremba, George
Serumaga, Robert
Sibenke, Ben
Sofola, Zulu

Sony Labou Tansi
Sowande, Bode
Soyinka, Wole
Sutherland, Efua T(heodora)
Thomas, Gladys
Tsodzo, T(hompson) K(umbirai)
Udechukwu, Obiora
Watene, Kenneth
Whaley, Andrew
Yirenkyi, Asiedu

POETRY COLLECTIONS

Arrowheads to My Heart
Bavino Sermons
Blind Moon
Carnival of Looters, A
*Chaos Theory of the Heart and Other Poems
    Mainly since 1990*
Eye of the Earth, The
Fisherman's Invocation, The
Hammer Blows
Heavensgate
Idanre
Labyrinths
Letters to Martha

Limits
Napolo Poems
Nightwatcher, Nightsong
Of Chameleons and Gods
Raw Pieces
Rediscovery
Sirens Knuckles Boots
Song of Lawino
Valley of a Thousand Hills, The
Visions and Reflections
Waiting Laughters
When Sunset Comes to Sapitwa

POETS

Abrahams, Lionel
Acholonu, Catherine Obianuju
Afrika, Tatamkhulu Ismail
Aidoo, Ama Ata
Aiyejina, Funso
Alford, Gwen
Angira, Jared
Anyidoho, Kofi
Awoonor, Kofi (Nyedevu)
Baderoon, Gabeba
Bandele-Thomas, Biyi
Bekederemo, J(ohn) P(epper) Clark
Ben Jelloun, Tahar
Blay, J. Benibengor
Brettell, N.H.
Brew, (Osborne Henry) Kwesi
Breytenbach, Breyten
Brutus, Dennis
Bukenya, Austin

Butler, Frederick Guy
Campbell, Roy(ston)
Casely-Hayford, Gladys
Chedid, Andrée
Cheney-Coker, Syl
Chimombo, Steve
Chingono, Julius
Chinodya, Shimmer
Chinweizu
Chipasula, Frank
Clayton, Cherry
Clouts, Sydney (David)
Combrinck, Lisa
Cook, Méira
Cope, Jack (Robert Knox)
Couto, Mia
Cripps, A(rthur) S(hearly)
Cullinan, Patrick (Roland)
Currey, Ralph Nixon

Dangor, Achmat
De Graft, Joe (Joseph Coleman)
Dei-Anang, Michael Francis
Dhlomo, H(erbert) I. E.
Dib, Mohammed
Dikobe, Modikwe (pseudonym of Marks
    Rammitloa)
Diop, Birago
Diop, David
Djoleto, (Solomon Alexander) Amu
Duodu, Cameron
Echeruo, Michael J. C.
Enekwe, Ossie
Eppel, John
Fall, Malick
Fugard, Sheila Meiring
Garuba, Harry
Gray, Stephen
Gwala, Mafika Pascal
Haarhoff, Dorian
Hope, Christopher (David Tully)
Hove, Chenjerai
Imbuga, Francis
Johnson, Lemuel A.
Jonker, Ingrid
Kagame, Alexis
Kgositsile, Keorapetse
Kunene, Daniel P.
Kunene, Mazisi (KaMdabuli)
Laing, B(ernard) Kojo
Likimani, Muthoni
Livingstone, Douglas
Lubwa P'chong
Maclennan, Donald (Alasdair Calum)
Maina Wa Kinyatti
Manaka, Matsemela
Mapanje, Jack
Marechera, Dambudzo
Mattera, Umaruiddin Don
Matthews, James
Maunick, Edouard
Mbuli, Mzwakhe
McLoughlin, Timothy O.
Mda, Zakes (Zanemvula Kizito Gatyeni)
Mezu, S(ebastian) Okechukwu
Mhlophe, Gcina
Miller, Ruth
Mnthali, Felix
Moore, Bai T(amia) J(ohnson)

Mopeli-Paulus, A(twell) S(idwell)
Mpina, Edison
Mtshali, (Oswald) Mbuyiseni
Mugo, Micere Githae
Mungoshi, Charles
Mutswairo, Solomon
Nagenda, John
Nazombe, Anthony
Ndu, Pol Nnamuzikam
Neto, Agostinho
Ngara, Emmanuel
Nicol, Abioseh
Nicol, Mike
Nortje, Arthur
Ntiru, Richard Carl
Nyamubaya, Freedom
Oculi, Okello
Ofeimun, Odia
Oguibe, Olu
Ogundipe-Leslie, Molara
Ojaide, Tanure
Okai, Atukwei
Okara, Gabriel (Imomotimi Gbaingbain)
Okigbo, (Ifeanyichukwu) Christopher
Oko, Akoll1aye
Okome, Onookome
Okot p'Bitek
Okri, Ben
Olafioye, Tayo Peter
Oludhe Macgoye, Marjorie
Osadebay, Dennis (Chukude)
Osofisan, Femi
Osundare, Niyi
Oyebode, Femi
Paton, Alan (Stewart)
Peters, Lenrie (Leopold Wilfred)
Plomer, William (Charles Franklyn)
Pringle, Thomas
Rabéarivelo, Jean-Joseph
Rabémanajara, Jacques
Rampolokeng, Lesego
Roberts, Sheila
Rubadiri, David
Rungano, Kristina
Sallah, Tijan M(omodou)
Scully, William Charles
Segun, Mabel (Dorothy)
Senghor, L(eopold) S(edar)
Sepamla, Sipho (Sydney)

Serote, Mongane Wally
Slater, Francis Carey
Soyinka, Wole
Taban Lo Liyong
Tejani, Bahadur
Thomas, Gladys
Udechukwu, Obiora
Ugah, Ada
Uka, Kalu

Van Wyk, Christopher
Vatsa, Mamman Jira
Vilakazi, B(enedict) W(allet)
Wangusa, Timothy
Watson, Stephen
Wheatley, Phillis
Wilhelm, Peter
Zimunya, Musaemura Bonas
Zungur, Sa'ad

SHORT STORY COLLECTIONS

Collector of Treasures, The
Fixions and Other Stories
Fools and Other Stories
Footprints in the Quag
House of Hunger
Incidents at the Shrine
Little Karoo, The

Mafeking Road
Night of Darkness
No Sweetness Here
Tomorrow Left Us Yesterday
Trial and Other Stories, The
You Can't Get Lost in Cape Town

SHORT STORY WRITERS

Aiyejina, Funso
Ajayi, Tolu(walogo)
Anduru, Agoro
Aniebo I.N.C.
Atta, Sefi
Blay, J. Benibengor
Bosman, H(erman) C(harles)
Butler, Frederick Guy
Casely-Hayford, Adelaide
Casely-Hayford, Gladys
Chingono, Julius
Chinodya, Shimmer
Cloete, (Edward Fairlie) Stuart (Graham)
Coetzee, J(ohn) M(axwell)
Conton, William (Farquhar)
Cope, Jack (Robert Knox)
Couto, Mia
Dangor, Achmat
Easmon, R(aymond) Sarif
Egbuna, Obi B(enedict)
Ekwensi, Cyprian
Essop, Ahmed
Gibbon, Perceval
Gordimer, Nadine
Head, Bessie
Jacobson, Dan(iel)
Kahiga, Samuel
Karodia, Farida

Kibera, Leonard
Kimenye, Barbara
Kuzwayo, Ellen
La Guma, Alex(ander)
Lessing, Doris
Lipenga, Ken
Magaia, Lina
Magona, Sindiwe
Mattera, Umaruiddin Don
Matthews, James
Mhlophe, Gcina
Modisane, William "Bloke"
Motsisi, (Karobo Moses) Casey "Kid"
Mphahlele, Es'kia (Ezekiel)
Mungoshi, Charles
Mutloatse, Mothobi
Mzamane, Mbulelo (Vizikhungo)
Nazareth, Peter
Ndebele, Njabulo (Simakahle)
Ngema, Mbongeni
Nicol, Abioseh
Njau, Rebeka
Nyamfukudza, Stanley
Nyamubaya, Freedom
Ogot, Grace (Emily)
Okri, Ben
Rive, Richard
Roberts, Sheila

Ruhumbika, Gabriel
Rungano, Kristina
Saadawi, Nawal el
Seruma, Eneriko (pseudonym of
    Henry S. Kimbugwe)
Smith, Pauline (Janet)
Taban Lo Liyong
Tejani, Bahadur

Themba, (Daniel Canodoise) Can
Tutuola, Amos
Vassanji, M(oyez) G.
Vera, Yvonne
Vladislavic, Ivan
Zeleza, Paul Tiyambe
Zimunya, Musaemura Bonas

SOCIAL AND THEORETICAL FRAMEWORKS

Black Consciousness in South
    Africa
Feminism and Literature

Gay and Lesbian Sexuality in
    Literature
Religion and Literature

PREFACE

The *Student Encyclopedia of African Literature* aims to provide an overview of the major authors and works in African literature from the past, and from our contemporary context. In that sense, it is as up-to-date as possible, with many descriptions of current works. It also provides a good sense of the history of African literature—with entries on such important figures as Olaudah Equiano, Olive Schreiner, and Doris Lessing. The *Encyclopedia* also aims to provide a cultural and social context for the literary works and figures that it details, and to do so includes subject entries on such topics as Apartheid, Feminism and Literature, and War Literature (to name a few). Occasionally these topical entries are subdivided according to geography in order to make the different regional influences clear.

The volume has a total of 598 entries on authors, works, and the above-mentioned subjects. Authors and texts were selected for inclusion based on their relevance to both the history of African literature and the growing scope of this literature in our contemporary context. Topics that have had a major influence on the creation, reading, and understanding of African literature were chosen for the subject entries. Many of the author and subject entries also include critical resources that provide a list of some of the current criticism on the author or subject of note. These resources (sometimes only one or two works) are not available for every author, but are available for most of the subject entries. The individual title entries do not include critical resources. A selected bibliography of critical work on more general themes in African literature is also available at the end of the *Encyclopedia*.

The *Encyclopedia* is organized alphabetically, with an alphabetical list of entries preceding the work. There is also a guide to related topics, which subdivides most of the entries into relevant categories such as "Novelists," "Playwrights," "Poets," etc. Topics, titles, or authors who appear throughout the work are rendered in boldface type as cross-references to indicate their existence elsewhere in the *Encyclopedia*. The authors hope that students are provided with direction and assistance in their reading of African literature through the use of this work. It aims to offer guidance rather than critical commentary, and many of the entries focus on biographical, plot-based, and historical information that will be of use to the student who wishes to research further topics in African literature, or who is merely looking for a place to start his or her reading. The authors also wish to thank the Social Sciences and Humanities Resource Council of Canada for their generous financial support of the *Student Encyclopedia of African Literature*.

A

Abrahams, Lionel (1928–2004)
South African poet, editor, and critic from Johannesburg, South Africa (the subject and locale of much of his writing). Abrahams was educated at Damelin College and the University of the Witwatersrand and his writing was privately tutored by Herman Charles **Bosman.** Abrahams is the editor of seven volumes of Bosman's work (1952–57); several literary journals, including *The Purple Renoster* and *Sesame;* and anthologies of South African writing. Co-founder of Bateleur Press and a champion of new writers, he was awarded two honorary doctorates and the Medal of the English Academy of South Africa.

Abrahams published five volumes of poetry: *Thresholds of Tolerance* (1975), *The Journal of a New Man* (1984), *The Writer in Sand* (1988), *A Dead Tree Full of Live Birds* (1995), and **Chaos Theory of the Heart and Other Poems Mainly since 1990** (2005). Abrahams's poetry covers themes of political, personal, and cultural significance, while his poetic technique focuses on the descriptive, speculative, or argumentative modes; his style is variant and relies on cadence and sound play, with the use of free verse for the most part. Abrahams's autobiographical novel, *The Celibacy of Felix Greenspan* (1977, reissued in North America in 1993), breaks its narrative into eighteen stories that offer a realistic and ironical image of growth from childhood to adulthood. A sequel to the novel was published in 2002 under the title of *The White Life of Felix Greenspan,* and although the two overlap chronologically, *The White Life of Felix Greenspan* looks at the earlier years of Felix's life and ends later than *The Celibacy of Felix Greenspan.* Abrahams's essays also represent important contributions to literary and cultural debate, and are included in anthologies of his work such as that published in honor of his sixtieth birthday, titled *A Reader* (1988), and in a collection of stories, essays, and poems to commemorate Abrahams's seventieth birthday titled *Writer in Stone* (1998).

Abrahams, Peter (1919–)
South African novelist and essayist, born in Vrededorp, Johannesburg. Abrahams attended school and college intermittently before temporarily working as a seaman and then moving to Britain in order to attempt a career as a writer. An assignment in Jamaica resulted in Abrahams moving his family to Kingston in 1959, where he worked as a novelist, editor, and political commentator.

Despite Abrahams's move from South Africa, his fiction returns there as he contemplates issues of race and identity. His early interest in Marxism influenced Abrahams's novels *Song of the City* (1945) and **Mine Boy** (1946), which depict the lives of rural migrant workers who face racial discrimination and alienation in the industrialized city. Abrahams's early writing also includes two volumes of poetry, *Here, Friend* (ca. 1940) and *A Blackman Speaks of Freedom* (1941); a collection of sketches, *Dark Testament* (1942); and a novel about an illegal interracial love affair titled *The Path of Thunder* (1948). This early writing tended to display an optimistic hope for a world without color prejudice and with individual freedom.

In a second stage of his career Abrahams became more concerned with the history and politics of race, with resultant work such as the novel *Wild Conquest* (1950), the essay collection *Return to Coli* (1953), and his autobiography, **Tell Freedom** (1954). *Wild Conquest* is a historical novel that traces the beginnings of racial conflict in South Africa to the Great Trek of 1836 and the struggle between the Afrikaners and the Africans over the fate of the land. *Wild Conquest* ends with a hope that individuals can make a difference against the color prejudice in South Africa, but this hope appears dampened in *Return to Coli,* which Abrahams wrote after he returned to South Africa for six weeks. *Tell Freedom* reinforces Abrahams's role as an author who portrays firsthand experiences of the reality of black South Africa. Following the publication of *Tell Freedom,* Abrahams opens up his setting to that of West Africa and the Caribbean with his works *A Wreath for Udomo* (1956) and *This Island Now* (1966), which foretell the complexity of the movement from colonialism to independence, but Abrahams does continue to produce work set in South Africa, as is his *A Night of Their Own* (1965). Abrahams draws together over a century of black history in Africa, the Caribbean, and North America in his *The View from Coyoba* (1985), which offers an ideal of freedom for blacks from Western cultural influences. *The Coyaba Chronicles: Reflections on the Black Experience in the 20th Century* (2000) is a memoir that explores interracial relationships and the goal of an integrated identity. There are three

major sections of the book: "The World at War," "The Road to Coyaba," and "The Cold War and the Third World." The memoir interweaves the personal with the political, as it also gives accounts of major political and social leaders. This work may have also been published under the title of *The Black Experience in the 20th Century: An Autobiography and Meditation* (2000). One major aspect of Abrahams's work is its influence on other major writers (such as Chinua **Achebe** and **Ngugi wa Thiong'o**) through his example as one of the first black African writers in the 1950s and 1960s. Abrahams offers an important example of how African literature navigates the issues of power, race, and culture in both a historical and a contemporary context.

Abruquah, Joseph Wilfred (1921–[1997?])

Ghanaian novelist. Abruquah went to a Methodist school in what was then the Gold Coast called Mfantsipim School, followed by King's College, London, and Westminster College, London. He began his literary career in 1960s Ghana with his first novel *The Catechist* (1965), which was an autobiographical depiction of the religious atmosphere that he grew up in. Abruquah's second novel, which deals with the loss of African values and culture, is titled *The Torrent* (1968) and follows the character Josiah Afful, who is transformed into a black European by expatriates.

Achebe, Chinua (1930–)

Nigerian novelist, born in Ogidi, Nigeria, and went to school at the local Church Missionary Society primary school, at Government College, Umuahia, and University College, Ibadan. Achebe became a radio producer for the Nigerian Broadcasting Corporation in 1954, and then became the Director of External Broadcasting in 1961 and remained with the corporation until the 1966 massacre of Igbos in northern and western Nigeria. Achebe served in the Biafran diplomatic service after the outbreak of the Nigeria-Biafra war (1967–70), and in 1971 he founded *Okike: Journal of New African Writing.* He continued to supervise the journal while he simultaneously held a number of teaching posts at universities in the United States and at the University of Nigeria, Nsukka. He has been awarded the Nigerian National Merit Award and the Order of the Federal Republic, the Commonwealth Poetry Prize (1974), the Lotus Award for Afro-Asian Writers (1975), the Campion Medal (1996), and the German Booksellers Peace Prize (2002). He is a Fellow, Royal Society of Literature, London (1981); an honorary foreign fellow, a member of the American Academy of Arts and Letters (1983); and an honorary fellow, American Academy of Arts and Sciences (2002). He was the McMillan-Stewart Lecturer, Harvard University (1998), the Presidential Fellow Lecturer, World Bank (1998), and he currently teaches at Bard College as the Charles P. Stevenson, Jr. Professor of Languages and Literature. In 2007 he won the Man Booker International (MBI) prize in honor of his literary oeuvre.

Achebe is the author of five novels: ***Things Fall Apart*** (1958), ***No Longer at Ease*** (1960), ***Arrow of God*** (1964), *A **Man of the People*** (1966), and ***Anthills of the Savannah*** (1987); short-story collections: *Girls at War and Other Stories* (1972); children's stories: *Chike and the River* (1966), *The Drum* (1977), *The Flute* (1977), and *How the Leopard Got His Claws* (with John Iroaganachi, 1976); poetry: *Beware, Soul Brother and Other Poems* (1971; issued in the United States as *Christmas in Biafra and Other Poems,* 1973), which won the 1972 Commonwealth Poetry Prize; essays: *Morning Yet on Creation Day* (1975), *Hopes and Impediments: Selected Essays, 1965–1987* (1988), *Another Africa with R. Lyons* (1998), ***Africa Is People*** (1998), and *Home and Exile* (2000); and political commentary: *The Trouble with Nigeria* (1983).

Achebe depicts and analyzes the impact of European contact on African identity in his writing. He notes how European imperialist mythology constructs Africa, and he works to provide a counter-discourse that takes part in a reconstruction of the African self. Achebe demonstrates his early literary theory in "The Role of the Writer in a New Nation" (*Nigeria Magazine,* no. 81, 1964) and "The African Writer and the English Language" (*Transition* 4, no. 18, 1965), and there are echoes of his theory in his short stories and his novel *Things Fall Apart. Things Fall Apart* counteracts the racist images of Africa found in such fiction as Joyce Cary's *Mister Johnson* and Joseph Conrad's *Heart of Darkness.* Achebe has returned to these early theoretical and literary arguments several times throughout his career, as in his controversial 1975 Chancellor's Lecture on racism in *Heart of Darkness,* his 1989 interview with Bill Moyers (*A World of Ideas,* ed. Betty Sue Flowers, 1989), and his 1993 Ashby Lecture at Cambridge University, England. Thus, there is a connectedness between genres in Achebe's literary production, as he reworks themes and offers new interpretations of literary and political history.

Achebe's novels offer historical and contemporary perspectives, with depictions of the Berlin Conference of 1884–85, as well as the 1960s' superficial decolonization, and the neocolonial atmosphere of today. The novels challenge the racial myths behind the scramble for land and its impact on Africa, and analyze the movement from oral ethnic cultures to literacy and nation-state cultures. Achebe's positioning of literacy demonstrates how writing makes the oral storyteller's art of conserving, interpreting, and transmitting communal history a contemporary one. Writing is thus crucial to social reconstruction, because those who control the narratives of history also control national identity. Recent nonfictional work by Achebe continues to focus on African identity and self-identity as they are accomplished through speech, image, and text. *Another Africa* (1998) is a book of photography by R. Lyons, for which Achebe wrote the introduction. *Africa Is People* (1998) is a Presidential Fellow Lecture for the World Bank Group, presented June 17, 1998, and *Home and Exile* (2000) is an autobiographical reflection on Achebe's and Africa's literary development. Achebe wrote the book from three lectures that he gave as the 1998 McMillan-Stewart Lectures at Harvard University on December 9, 10, and 11, 1998.

Acholonu, Catherine Obianuju (1951–)

Nigerian literary critic, playwright, and poet. Acholonu was born in Orlu, Nigeria, and attended secondary schools in Orlu before obtaining her master's degree and a Ph.D. from the University of Dusseldorf, Germany; she has been a teacher at Alvan Ikoku College, Owerri, since 1978. Acholonu is the author of both plays and poetry that are inspired by the traditional narratives and poetry of her Igbo people. Her poetry includes three books of poems for school children, as well as her better-known poetry collections *Nigeria in the Year 1999* (1985) and *The Spring's Last Drop* (1985). Acholonu's plays include *Into the Heart of Biafra* (1985), based on experiences of the Nigeria-Biafra war; *Trial of the Beautiful Ones* (1985), which incorporates myths and legends; and *The Deal and Who Is the Head of State* (1986), a play that addresses topical issues. Her most controversial critical work is her anthropological study titled *The Igbo Roots of Olaudah Equiano* (1989), in which she maintains that she discovers **Equiano**'s father's surviving descendants. Acholonu also critiques Western feminism in her critical work *Motherism,* which looks at the idea of motherhood in Nigerian cultural affairs. She is also the author of *The African Feminist Challenge in Life and Literature* (1991), and "Motherism: The Afrocentric Alternative" was published in the online

publication *Konch Magazine* (March–April 2002; http://www.ishmaelreedpub.com). Acholonu has also acted as the Senior Special Assistant to the President of Nigeria on Arts and Culture, and has published both a lecture: *Africa in the 21st Century: Towards a Truly Global Literary Canon* (Afa Publications, 2002), which was the keynote lecture to the 2002 Annual Convention of the Association of Nigerian Authors; and a children's work: *To Live as Jesus Lived* (Afa Publications, 2002).

Adair, Barbara (no date of birth available)

A novelist and human rights lecturer in the faculty of Law and then a lecturer at the Graduate School of Public and Development Management at Witwatersrand University in Johannesburg. Adair is also a senior research coordinator at the National Economic and Labour Council (Nedlac), and a part-time senior commissioner at the Commission for Conciliation, Mediation and Arbitration. She has written one novel, *In Tangier We Killed the Blue Parrot* (2004). The novel tells the story of Paul Bowles and Jane Auer, a literary couple living in Morocco during the late 1940s, and Adair explores the minds of the two authors through her research and retelling of their lives.

Adedeji, (Alu)Remi Aduke (1937–)

Nigerian children's writer, born in Okemesi in western Nigeria. She gained her bachelor's and master's degrees, and has taught at the Polytechnic, Ibadan. She is a member of the International Board on Books for Young People (IBBY), and is the associate editor for *Bookbird* in Nigeria. Adedeji began to write books for African children when she found that most books available for young people did not address African culture. Adedeji focuses a great deal of her works on Nigerian folktales that feature the tortoise, although her books do offer a variety of subjects and levels of difficulty. For example, *The Fat*

Woman (1973) contains stories about un-complicated life experiences for young children, while *Dear Uncle* (1986) is meant for older children and contains stories about contemporary Nigerian family life. *Moonlight Stories* (Heinemann, 1999) contains ten short stories based on ancient folktales.

Adichie, Chimamanda Ngozi (1977–)

Nigerian novelist, born in Nigeria (Igbo) specifically Abba, in Anambra State, and grew up in Nsukka. Her father was vice-chancellor at the University of Nigeria, Nsukka, where her mother was also a lecturer. Adichie moved to the United States at the age of nineteen, and attended Drexel University in Philadelphia, then transferred to Eastern Connecticut State University and graduated in 2001 with a bachelor of science in communication and political science. She then went on to complete a master's degree in creative writing at Johns Hopkins University in Baltimore.

Her short stories are mostly about the Nigerian immigrant experience in America; have been published in journals in Canada, the United States, and Great Britain; and have been selected for the Commonwealth Broadcasting Association award as well as the BBC short story award. Adichie was short-listed for the Caine Prize for African Writing 2002 and was a runner-up in the Commonwealth Short Story Award 2002. Her story set during the Nigerian civil war won the 2003 PEN/David Wong short story award, and she also received the O. Henry Award in 2003. Her second novel is set in Biafra during the Nigerian civil war (1967–70). *Purple Hibiscus,* her first novel, was short-listed for the Orange Prize and was winner of the Hurston/Wright Legacy award for debut fiction, and the 2005 Commonwealth Writers' Prize for First Best Book. She was a Hodder Fellow at Princeton University for the 2005–2006 academic year.

Purple Hibiscus is about a young girl (Kambili) who both admires and feels intimidated by her father, who is an influential person in the community. When Kambili and her brother visit their aunt in a different town, their eyes are opened to the diversity of human existence while their exposure to different opinions regarding family and religion result in changes for both them and their family. Adichie's second novel is titled *Half of a Yellow Sun* (2006) and portrays the lives of three characters caught up in the Biafran struggle to build an independent republic in Nigeria. Already widely acclaimed, *Half of a Yellow Sun* deals with the impact of the end of colonialism, class, and race on individual identity, morality, and human relationships. Adichie has also written a play, *For Love of Biafra* (1998), a collection of poems titled *Decisions* (1998), and a number of her short stories, essays, and poems have been published in prominent literary journals, magazines, and newspapers such as *Wasafiri, New York Times, Virginia Quarterly Review,* and the *Guardian.*

Africa Is People (1998)

Chinua **Achebe**'s Presidential Fellow Lecture for the World Bank Group, presented June 17, 1998. In it he recalls his invitation to the Organization for Economic Cooperation and Development (OECD) in Paris in 1989, and his realization that the wealthy countries of the world wished to imagine African countries into economic cooperation based solely on fictional assurances. It is at this point that Achebe recalls saying "Africa is not fiction. Africa is people, real people." He goes on to appeal for a greater awareness of the realities in Africa, and not to assume or fabricate knowledge based on oppressive stereotypes.

African Child, The (1954)

A novel by **Camara Laye,** translated from the French (*L'Enfant noir,* 1953), and also published in English as *The Dark Child* (1954). One of francophone Africa's earliest novels, it also achieved renown in an

English translation. *The African Child* is a first-person, semiautobiographical tale whose narrator remains nameless for much of the novel. Born to a respected family of blacksmiths, the young boy is raised first near the mountainous region of Guinea, where he learns his people's traditions, the magic of the forge and of snakes. After traditional initiation rights the growing boy goes to the capital city, Conakry, enrolls in French schools and lives with his uncle. School is difficult, and causes him to grow distant from his traditions, as he becomes more French in outlook. The story also details beliefs, stories, and traditions of the Malinke people. *The African Child* has long been popular with African, European, and American audiences. Many readers praise its sensitive, lyrical style; others criticize it for failing to portray or protest the French colonial presence in Guinea at that time. Still others suggest that a reading informed by Malinke or Mande sources shows that a middle-ground interpretation is best of all.

African Image, The (1962)

A study by Ezekiel (now Es'kia) **Mphahlele.** It is the first study by a black critic of the presentation of Africans in fiction by Europeans and by white South Africans. Mphahlele addresses the wider, pressing issues (in its time) of the value and implications of Africans pursuing and gaining a "European" education. The book opens serious critical discussion of an emerging African literary tradition and the place of this writing in the educational agendas of African countries. Mphahlele also addresses the issue of negritude in the wider context of problems of education that face postindependence African countries.

African Tragedy, An (1928)

A novel by R.R.R. **Dhlomo.** This simple, moralistic tale of the disasters that befall urbanized Africans represents the first time African hardships were depicted in a realistic way. It is the story of Robert Zulu, whose life is brutalized by the evil conduct of life in the mines. Dhlomo, who worked on the mines, was well equipped to comment on the subject. It is a classic example of literature inspired by mission education.

African Writers Series

Begun in 1962 by Heinemann Educational Books in London. Chinua **Achebe** was the Series Editor for the first one hundred works and held the title of the Founding Editor afterward. The series introduced many to new writing in the form of plays, poetry, and autobiography in addition to the novels, and it became known as "the orange series" due to the color of the covers. Van Milne (the first Heinemann editor) began the series with reprints of novels by Chinua Achebe, followed by **Ngugi wa Thiong'o**'s first novel and autobiographies by Kaunda, Odinga Odinga, Nelson Mandela, and Olusegun Obasanjo.

Following Van Milne as editor was Keith Sambrook, who along with Chinua Achebe, focused on publishing more new work by African writers who were not able to find a place for their work in the general publishing markets of Britain, America, or English-speaking Africa. Because of this focus on new work by African authors, the series was known for its major role in the publication of new writers in paperback, and occasionally in hardcover as well. A majority of the demand that the Heinemann Educational Books met was the need for new educational textbooks due to the new universities and secondary schools that were founded after independence and required African writers for the curriculum.

In 1967 James Currey became the editor of the series and the work of Ayi Kwei **Armah** and Tayeb **Salih** was published, while Achebe's insistence on the publication of work despite controversial treatment of sex, religion, or politics made the series even more important to African literature as a whole. In 1972 (at number 100 in the series)

Ngugi briefly took over editorship from Achebe, but Aig Higo (Managing Director in Ibadan), Akin Thomas (in Ibadan), Henry Chakava, Simon Gikandi, and Laban Erapu (in Nairobi) took on larger roles when Ngugi found that the editorship was encroaching on his creative writing. The headquarters for the series in Ibadan, Nairobi, and London worked to make the editorial process fair, and whenever an editor backed a book with reports from his readers and his own judgment the book was accepted. In fact, the editors agreed almost completely about the novel and short story choices, although poetry was more based on individual choice, and plays were best judged by those who could imagine the feasibility of their performance, not only in the theater but also in communities across Africa and despite police forces in South Africa. In addition to this ability to imagine the work that would best represent African literary needs, editors like James Currey (who made the work of South African writers in exile available) and David Philip (who found ways of helping writers like Alex La Guma to avoid South African Customs) helped to make writing available to the African public that might not have otherwise appeared.

Many people were encouraged by the willingness of the series to receive manuscripts, and although most were turned down, they were all sent out for report and the reports were made available to the authors. In the 1970s Alan Hill was chairman, and he supported the growth of publication as talent also grew. In one year twenty-two works were published, and for many other years about fifteen were published. The series was also economically well off, and it managed to gain the cooperation of authors like Bessie **Head,** by being open to their opinions about their own work. The series also gained literary prestige, as critics looked to it first for new African writing, and it sold around 80 percent of its books in Africa, around 10 percent in North America, and 10 percent in Britain and worldwide.

However, after this successful high point the series suffered greatly when in April 1982, the Nigerian foreign exchange plummeted and sales dropped while debts piled up—accountants began to call for the closure of the series. James Currey and Keith Sambrook started up their own imprint in 1984, while in the mid-1980s Heinemann had four different owners and was able to continue to print about three new titles per year under the editorial leadership of Adewale Maja-Pearce and Abdulrazak **Gurnah,** and with the help of John Watson, who helped to sell the series in the United States. The series boasted 270 books when it experienced problems in the mid-1980s, including titles by the African Nobel Prize winners, Wole **Soyinka,** Nadine **Gordimer,** and Naguib **Mahfouz.** The series continues to influence African literature with publications like M. G. **Vassanji**'s *The Gunny Sack* and Shimmer **Chinodya**'s *Harvest of Thorns,* and with poems like those collected in *The Chattering Wagtails of Mikuyu Prison,* which discusses Jack **Mapanje**'s imprisonment without trial in Banda's Malawi. The series also debuted authors like **Sony Labou Tansi** to an English audience, and Wangui wa Goro translated Ngugi's *Matigari* from Gikuyu for publication by the series.

UK Harcourt Education has also published a Junior African Writers Series (JAWS) created in an effort to help children learn English. The books are categorized in age-appropriate levels, and there is also a teacher's handbook. The African Writers Series is also available integrated within Literature Online, which offers users the ability to cross-search 350,000 other literary works and critical and reference material support. Information about the online service and the Web site advertising the service can be found at: http://www.umi.com/products_pq/literature/chadwyck/african_writers_ser.pdf and http://www.umi.com/products_pq/descriptions/african_writers_ser.shtml. The electronic database also boasts Arabic literature in translation, and author biographies. When it is complete the African Writers Series online will contain the entirety of the original print series (including accompanying text by the author, introductions, notes, glossaries, other editorial material, and illustrations), depending on the availability of copyright.

Another index of the works in the series can be found at http://www.geocities.com/africanwriters/AuthorsA.html

Further Reading

Clarke, Becky. "The *African Writers Series—* Celebrating Forty Years of Publishing Distinction." *Research in African Literatures (Bloomington, IN)* 34, no. 2 (2003): 163–74.

Hill, Alan. "The *African Writers Series." Research in African Literatures* 2 (1971): 18–20.

Kibble, Matt. "The *African Writers Series* Reborn: An Electronic Edition." *Wasafiri: The Transnational Journal of International Writing* 46 (2005): 66–68.

Low, Gail. "In Pursuit of Publishing: Heinemann's *African Writers Series." Wasafiri: The Transnational Journal of International Writing* 37 (2002): 31–35.

Maja-Pearce, Adewale. "Publishing African Literature: In Pursuit of Excellence: Thirty Years of the Heinemann *African Writers' Series." Research in African Literatures* 23, no. 4 (1992): 125–32.

Moore, Gerald. "A Comment on 'The African Writers Series.'" *Research in African Literatures* 2 (1971): 21–25.

Okyerefo, Michael Perry Kweku. "The Cultural Crisis of Sub-Saharan Africa as Depicted in the African Writers Series: A Sociological Perspective." Frankfurt: Lang, 2001. (*European University Studies, XII:* Sociology, 348): 208.

Unwin, Vicky, and James Currey. "The 'African Writers' Series' Celebrates 30 Years." *Southern African Review of Books* 5, no. 2 (1993): 3–6.

African-American Literature

Despite African presence in North America before the transatlantic slave trade, African-American literature begins with the oral performances of the African slaves. Because literacy was outlawed for slaves due to the slaveowners' fear of uprising and rebellion, written African-American literature does not appear until the eighteenth century. The first written literature emerges from the northern and eastern United States where, as Darwin Turner notes, slaves had some exposure to education. The first written African-American literature is poetic, with works such as Lucy Terry's "Bars Fight, August 28, 1746" (1746), and Jupiter Hammon's "An Evening Thought: Salvation by Christ, with Penitential Cries" (1760), along with the more well-known Phillis **Wheatley,** who was a slave of a Boston tailor, and who wrote elegies and devotional lyrics that were published in 1773 under the title *Poems on Various Subjects, Religious and Moral.* Hammon and Wheatley demonstrate the difficulties of writing in slavery, as they both extol the importance of proper behavior in order to gain some voice regarding the inhumanity of slavery. Later in the eighteenth century African-American literature gained predominance, with a number of autobiographical narratives of slavery that were promoted by the abolitionists. Some important examples are Olaudah **Equiano**'s *The Interesting Narrative of the Life of Olaudah Equiano; or, Gustavus Vassa, the African Written by Himself* (1789), which is extremely transatlantic in its conception and can also be classed as African-British literature; Frederick Douglass's autobiography, *Narrative of the Life of Frederick Douglass, an American Slave* (1845); and Martin Robinson Delany's *The Condition, Elevation, Emigration, and Destiny of the Colored People of the United States* (1852).

The problems arising from a combination of African heritage and American nationalism are tackled in many of the nineteenth-century African-American novels, plays, and poetry. These works combine feelings of independence, anger, and historical maltreatment with a wish to be accepted by the dominant white society. Issues regarding slavery and miscegenation are represented in the first African-American novel-length book, William Wells Brown's *Clotel; or, The President's Daughter* (1853), and in his play *The Escape* (1858), while slavery is represented as a form of organized economic theft in Martin Delany's *Blake; or, The Huts of America* (1861–62). Racism in relation to economics in America is broached in Frank Webb's *The Garies and Their Friends* (1857), while at the turn of the nineteenth century Charles Waddell Chestnutt's *The House behind the Cedars* (1900) explores the attempt by a near-white mulatto to pass as white, and *The Marrow of Tradition* (1901) considers what the resurgence of racism following the brief progressive period after the Civil War means for African-Americans. The Baptist minister Sutton Griggs published five novels from 1899 to 1908 that started out in support of "race patriotism" (*Imperium in Imperio,* 1899), and finished with an aim to find racial reconciliation (*Pointing the Way,* 1908). In her novel *Iola LeRoy* (1892) Ellen Watkins Harper discusses the caste question, and she also gained success with her abolitionist poetry. Another successful writer from this period is Paul Laurence Dunbar, who gained acclaim for his comic dialect verse, aesthetic use of his black heritage, and his romanticism—but not until after William Dean Howell recommended him to the readers of *Lyrics of Lowly Life* (1896). Dunbar's concern with African-American heroes in his work (e.g., Frederick Douglass and Ethiopia) contrasts with his use of self-abuse, the combination of which predates a similar effect in the negritude poetry of the twentieth century.

An African-American middle class and intelligentsia surfaced at the turn of the nineteenth century, which led to a large emigration of African-Americans to the cities and a political leadership under W.E.B. DuBois and James Weldon Johnson, who also influenced the literary scene and encouraged a greater realization of African-American consciousness that helped lead to the Harlem Renaissance of the 1920s and 1930s. Harlem appealed to a large number of intellectuals from America, Africa, and the African diaspora with the result being a community of musicians and writers. Alain Locke petitioned for "the New Negro" (*The New Negro,* 1925) to participate in American civilization, while Harlem artistic production was defined by a pride in African heritage. Important works coming out of the Harlem Renaissance are Countee Cullen's *Color* (1925) and *The Ballad of the Brown Girl* (1927), Jean Toomer's *Cane* (1923), Langston Hughes's *The Weary Blues* (1926) and *Not without Laughter* (1930), and Claude McKay's *Home to Harlem* (1928) and *Banjo* (1929).

During the depression era, African-American writing turned more specifically to issues of racism and oppression, with works such as *Black Thunder* (1936) by Ama Bontemps, which is about a Virginian slave rebellion; Zora Neale Hurston's satirical *Moses, Man of the Mountain* (1939); *Native Son* (1940) by Richard Wright, a novel that tackles violence and psychological oppression; and Ralph Ellison's *Invisible Man* (1952) that deals with issues of identity and social acceptance in relation to the negation of an African-American existence by the larger white society. The Pulitzer Prize was awarded to an African-American for the first time during this era, when poet Gwendolyn Brooks won for *Annie Allen* (1949). Brooks's later works include *1917—In the Mecca: Poems* (1968), *A Capsule Course in Black Poetry Writing* (1975), and *1917—Beckonings: [Poems]* (1975). James Baldwin tackled topics like homosexuality and race relations in works such as *Go Tell It on the Mountain* (1953), *Giovanni's Room* (1956), *Another Country* (1962), and *The Fire Next Time* (1963). Lorraine Hansberry's *A Raisin in the Sun* (1959) was applauded by established theater critics, despite the fact that it was thought politically naive by many black critics.

The 1960s and 1970s saw the rise of the civil rights and **Black Consciousness** movements, both of which led to the attempt to define a black aesthetic through literary production. Eldridge Cleaver's *Soul on Ice* (1967) and Malcolm X's *Autobiography of Malcolm X* (1965) are closer examples of the emerging black aesthetic than the popular politics of Martin Luther King Jr. Other works that explore a black aesthetic are *Dutchman* (1964) by Imamu Amiri Baraka (formerly LeRoi Jones) and Toni Morrison's *The Bluest Eye* (1970), as well as Alex Haley's *Roots* (1976), a popular work that successfully combines fiction with black history and genealogy to explore the place of African-Americans in America. Also important in this period was novelist Claude Brown, who recorded his experiences of growing up poor in Harlem in his 1965 bestseller *Manchild in the Promised Land.* The book reached a wide audience and exposed the masses to inner-city black culture. Brown also published *The Children of Ham* (1975), and died in Manhattan on February 2, 2002. Playwright Ed Bullins's career began in 1965 with the production of *How Do You Do, Dialect Determinism (or The Rally),* and *Clara's Ole Man* at the Firehouse Repertory Theatre in San Francisco. He later became the Resident Playwright and Associate Director at Robert Macbeth's New Lafayette Theatre in Harlem, New York, where Bullins ran the Black Theatre Workshop. Other important novelists include Ishmael Reed; Gloria Naylor (*The Women of Brewster Place,* 1982); John Edgar Wideman (*Philadelphia Fire,* 1990); and Toni Cade Bambara, editor of an anthology of essays, poems, and stories titled *The Black Woman* (1970), and author of *The Salt Eaters* (1980) and *If Blessing Comes* (1987). Also of note are dramatists Charles Fuller (*A Soldier's Play,* 1982) and August Wilson (*Fences,* 1987),

who appeal to a broader audience, as do Ntozake Shange's books *For Colored Girls Who Have Considered Suicide, When the Rainbow Is Enuf* (1975) and *Sassafrass, Cypress, and Indigo* (1982).

Starting in the 1970s, African-American women's writing has progressively grown and become increasingly popular and critically acclaimed. In 1993 Toni Morrison won the Nobel Prize for literature, and other African-American women writers also deal with the difficult perspective that comes out of being oppressed as blacks, as women, and as black women. Of importance are authors like Alice Childress (1920–94) who had a career in the theater as actor, director, and playwright. Her plays include *Florence* (1949), *Wedding Band: A Love/Hate Story in Black and White* (1972), *Mojo: A Black Love Story* (1970), and *Moms: A Praise Play for a Black Comedienne* (1987). Childress is also the author of a number of novels, among them *Those Other People* (1989) and *A Hero Ain't Nothin' but a Sandwich* (1973). She also wrote the screenplay for the 1978 film based on *A Hero Ain't Nothin' but a Sandwich.* Also of note is Lucille Clifton, whose 1969 book, a collection of poetry entitled *Good Times,* was published to critical acclaim. Clifton became a writer in residence at Coppin State College in Baltimore, Maryland, in 1971, and remained at Coppin until 1974, during which time she produced two further books of poetry, *Good News about the Earth* (1972) and *An Ordinary Woman* (1974). Clifton's later poetry collections include *Next: New Poems* (1987), *Quilting: Poems 1987–1990* (1991), and *The Terrible Stories* (1996). *Generations: A Memoir* (1976) is a prose piece celebrating her origins, and *Good Woman: Poems and a Memoir: 1969–1980* (1987) collects some of her previously published verse. Clifton's many children's books include *All Us Come Cross the Water* (1973), *My Friend Jacob* (1980), and *Three Wishes* (1992). She also wrote an award-winning series of books featuring events in the life of Everett Anderson, which include *Some of the Days of Everett Anderson* (1970) and *Everett Anderson's Goodbye* (1983). Another popular writer of the 1970s, Octavia Butler (a science fiction writer), received a "genius grant" from the John D. and Catherine T. MacArthur Foundation in 1995. Butler's most popular work is *Kindred* (1979), a novel about a black woman from 1976 southern California who time-travels back to before the Civil War. More recently, Barbara Chase-Riboud (a Carl Sandburg Prize–winning poet and author of four historical novels: *Sally Hemings, Valide: A Novel of a Harem, Echo of Lions,* and *The President's Daughter*) is a winner of the Janet Heidinger Kafka Prize and received a knighthood in arts and letters from the French government in 1996. Born and raised in Philadelphia, Chase-Riboud has received many fellowships and honorary degrees. Another more recent writer, Michelle Cliff, was born in Jamaica and grew up there and in the United States. She is the author of novels (*Abeng, No Telephone to Heaven,* and *Free Enterprise*), short stories (*Bodies of Water*), prose poetry (*The Land of Look Behind* and *Claiming an Identity They Taught Me to Despise*), as well as much criticism. Cliff is also the editor of a collection of the writings of the southern American social reformer Lillian Smith entitled *The Winner Names the Age.*

In contemporary African-American women's writing like Maya Angelou's *I Know Why the Caged Bird Sings* (1969), Toni Morrison's *The Bluest Eye,* and Alice Walker's *The Color Purple* (1982) and *The Third Life of Grange Copeland* (1970), there is an emphasis on the complexity and constructedness of gender, rape, other violent abuse against women, as well as a focus on the way that such black female experiences fit into a larger picture of race relations and national identity in America. Recent works by such authors as Marita Golden and Jamaica Kincaid continue such a tradition. Golden's writing includes novels such as *Long Distance Life* (1989), *A Woman's Place* (1986), *And Do Remember Me* (1992), *The Edge of Heaven* (1998), and *After: A Novel* (2005). Golden's nonfiction includes three anthologies she has edited: *Wild Women Don't Wear No Blues: Black Women Writers on Love, Men and Sex* (1993), *Skin Deep: Black and White Women on Race* (1995, with Susan Richards Shreve), and *Gumbo: A Celebration of African American Writing* (2002, with E. Lynn Harris). Kincaid's recent works include novels such as *The Autobiography of My Mother* (1996), *Mr. Potter* (2002), and nonfiction works such as *Talk Stories* (2001), which is a collection of the columns Kincaid wrote for the *New Yorker*'s "Talk of the Town" column, and *Among Flowers: A Walk in the Himalaya* (2005). African-American feminist scholars have also greatly developed the study of African-American literature and culture through their analysis of the effects of Eurocentrism and the place of African-American women's writing in the postmodern era.

The foundations of African-American literature as a literature of self-assertion and self-definition within a Eurocentric society continue to grow and develop, and African-American authors continue to explore and express what it means to be African-American. Recently, popular literature by authors such as California Cooper, Eric Dickey, Lynn Harris, Terry McMillan, Omar Tyree, and Zane (to name a few) has come to the forefront, and works such as *Sap Rising* (2001) by Christine Lincoln, *Miracle at St. Anna* (2002) by James McBride, *Just as I Am* (1994) by E. Lynn Harris, and *The Fall of Rome* (2002) by Martha Southgate deal with important issues in African-American culture. Eric Dickey's most recently published works are *Thieves' Paradise* (2002), *The Other Woman* (2003), *Naughty or Nice* (2003), *Drive Me Crazy* (2004), and *Genevieve* (2005). Percival Everett was the winner of the Honors PEN/Oakland-Josephine Miles Award for Excellence in Literature in 1997 for *Big Picture* and has also published such works as *God's Country* (2003), *Erasure* (2001), and *Glyph* (1999). E. Lynn Harris is the author of popular novels such as *Not a Day Goes By* (2000), *Any Way the Wind Blows* (2001), and *A Love of My Own* (2002). His short story "Money Can't Buy Me Love" was published in *Got to Be Real: Four Original Love Stories* (2000), and he also has work published in *Gumbo: A Celebration of African American Writers* (2002), which he also co-edited with Marita Golden. Hannah Crafts's *The Bondwoman's Narrative* (2002), found and published by Henry Louis Gates Jr., offers an early narrative (ca. 1855–59) of a fugitive slave brought to life from a manuscript that Gates bought and defends as an authentic example of early African-American women's writing. Similarly important are Z. Z. Packer's collection of short stories *Drinking Coffee Elsewhere* (2003), and Edward P. Jones's historical novel *The Known World: A Novel* (2003), which is set in Virginia before the Civil War, won the 2004 Pulitzer Prize for Fiction. Wanda Coleman is a nationally recognized performance poet who is the author of many books of poetry and prose, including *Bathwater Wine* (1998), *Imagoes* (1983), *Heavy Daughter Blues* (1987), *A War of Eyes and Other Stories* (1988), and *African Seeping Sickness: Stories and Poems* (1990). In addition, within the last thirty years three African-Americans have won the Pulitzer Prize for drama: Charles Gordone, for *No Place to Be Somebody,* Charles Fuller, for *A Soldier's Play,* and August Wilson for *Fences* and *The Piano Lesson.*

Further Reading

Bascom, Lionel C., ed. *Renaissance in Harlem: Lost Voices of an American Community.* New York: Bard, 1999.

Bigsby, C.W.E. *The Second Black Renaissance: Essays in Black Literature.* Westport, CT: Greenwood Press, 1980.

Billingslea-Brown, Alma. *Crossing Borders through Folklore: African American Women's Fiction and Art.* Columbia: University of Missouri Press, 1999.

Carroll, Rebecca. *I Know What the Red Clay Looks Like: The Voices and Vision of Black American Women Writers.* New York: Carol Southern Books, 1994.

———, ed. *Swing Low: Black Men Writing.* New York: Carol Southern Books, 1995.

Coser, Stelamaris. *Bridging the Americas: The Literature of Paule Marshall, Toni Morrison and Gayle Jones.* Philadelphia: Temple University Press, 1995.

Dickson-Carr, Darryl. *The Columbia Guide to Contemporary African American Fiction.* New York: Columbia University Press, 2005.

Diedrich, Maria, Henry Louis Gates Jr., and Carl Pedersen, eds. *Black Imagination and the Middle Passage.* New York: Oxford University Press, 1999.

Ervin, Hazel Arnett, ed. *African American Literary Criticism, 1773 to 2000.* New York: Twayne, 1999.

Favor, Martin. *Authentic Blackness: The Folk in the New Negro Renaissance.* Durham: Duke University Press, 1999.

Gabbin, Joanne V. *Furious Flowering of African American Poetry.* Charlottesville: University Press of Virginia, 1999.

Gates, Henry Louis Jr. *Loose Canons: Notes on the Culture Wars.* New York: Oxford University Press, 1992.

———. *The Signifying Monkey: A Theory of Afro-American Literary Criticism.* New York: Oxford University Press, 1988.

Givens, Archie, ed. *Spirited Minds: African American Books for Our Sons and Our Brothers.* New York: W. W. Norton, 1997.

———, ed. *Strong Souls Singing: African American Books for Our Daughters and Our Sisters.* New York: W. W. Norton, 1998.

Golden, Marita, ed. *Wild Women Don't Wear No Blues: Black Women Writers on Love, Men and Sex.* New York: Doubleday, 1993.

Jenkins, McKay. *The South in Black and White: Race, Sex, and Literature in the 1940s.* Chapel Hill: University of North Carolina Press, 1999.

Kubitschek, Missy Dehn. *Claiming the Heritage: African-American Women Novelists and History.* Jackson: University Press of Mississippi, 1991.

Montgomery, Maxine Lavon. *The Apocalypse in African American Fiction.* Gainesville: University Press of Florida, 1996.

Mullane, Deirdre, ed. *Crossing the Danger Water: Three Hundred Years of African-American Writing.* New York: Anchor Books, 1993.

Peterson, Carla L. *"Doers of the Word": African-American Women Speakers and Writers in the North (1830–1880).* New York: Oxford University Press, 1995.

Posnock, Ross. *Colour and Culture: Black Writers and the Making of the Modern Intellectual.* Cambridge: Harvard University Press, 1998.

Rogers, Lawrence R. *Canaan Bound: The African-American Great Migration Novel.* Chicago: University of Illinois Press, 1997.

Soitos, Stephen. *The Blues Detective: A Study of African American Detective Fiction.* Amherst: University of Massachusetts Press, 1996.

Taylor, Carole Anne. *The Tragedy and Comedy of Resistance: Reading Modernity through Black Women's Fiction.* Philadelphia: University of Pennsylvania Press, 2000.

Wintz, Cary D. *Black Culture and the Harlem Renaissance.* Houston: Rice University Press, 1988.

Wonham, Henry B. *Criticism and the Color Line: Desegregating American Literary Studies.* New Brunswick: Rutgers University Press, 1996.

Worley, Demetrice A., and Jesse Perry Jr. *African American Literature: An Anthology.* Lincolnwood, IL: NTC Publishing Group, 1998.

Zafar, Rafia. *We Wear the Mask: African Americans Write American Literature, 1760–1870.* New York: Columbia University Press, 1997.

African-British Literature

Writing by African-British authors began in the eighteenth century and has flourished since the mid-twentieth century. African-Caribbean writing is associated more with West Indian-British literature, except rap and dub poetry, which demonstrates a connection with African oral tradition.

Slave narratives make up the majority of the early published work of African-British writers in the eighteenth and nineteenth centuries. The most well-known slave narratives published in Britain are Briton Hammon's *A Narrative of the Uncommon Sufferings, and Surprizing Deliverance of Briton Hammon, A Negro Man* (1760); Ukawsaw Gronniosaw's *A Narrative of the Most Remarkable Particulars in the Life of James Albert Ukawsaw Gronniosaw, an African Prince, as Related by Himself* (ca. 1770); Ignatius **Sancho**'s *Letters of the Late Ignatius Sancho, an African* (1782); Ottobah **Cugoano**'s *Thoughts and Sentiments on the Evil and Wicked Traffic of the Slavery and Commerce of the Human Species* (1787); and Olaudah **Equiano**'s *The Interesting Narrative of the Life of Olaudah Equiano; or, Gustavus Vassa, the African, Written by Himself* (1789). A later narrative is that of Peter Thomas Stanford's *From Bondage to Liberty: Being the Life Story of the Rev. P. T. Stanford* (1889). Female writers also expressed their experiences as slaves. Mary Prince published her autobiography in 1831, and a version edited by Thomas Pringle is entitled *The History of Mary Prince, a West Indian Slave,* while Mary Seacole's *Wonderful Adventures of Mrs. Seacole in Many Lands* was published in 1857. The narratives of these authors express the tyranny and cruel violence of slavery, and the hypocrisy of so-called Christian enslavers who were prospering because of slave labor. Writers born in Africa, like Gronniosaw, Equiano, and Cugoano, relate their memories of childhood in Africa, and their writing expresses strong nationalistic and abolitionist aims. In contrast, Mary Seacole expresses a patriotism that is in line with her British upbringing and her inheritance as the daughter of a Scottish army officer and a free Jamaican black woman.

In their historical contexts, these autobiographies are even more influential because in the eighteenth and nineteenth centuries the question of whether black people were human was still being seriously posed, and slaves were treated as human cargo. Thus the focus by these authors on the fact that they have written what will ultimately be a product for sale and exchange is heightened when they make sure to emphasize authorship, like

Equiano does when he includes in the title that the book is "written by himself."

In their definition of self as unique from the Western culture that usually defines identity, the early slave narratives anticipate the themes of African literature in the 1950s and 1960s, when African identity is affirmed, rather than seen as a negative of Western culture. In a similar manner to later African-British authors, Equiano undermines the dominant racist attitude toward color by explaining that in Igbo society the European skin pigment is thought of as different and strange. Equiano's romanticization of his mother also anticipates the focus on maternity in later negritude writing, and demonstrates the importance of the mother in many African societies.

More modern African-British authors of renown include Buchi **Emecheta**, Ben **Okri**, Gabriel Gbadamosi, and Ernest Marke, who emigrated to Britain as a stowaway in 1917 and worked at several different jobs until he could publish his autobiographical work *In Troubled Waters* (1975). Buchi Emecheta has written several novels and children's stories, and is originally from Lagos, but moved to Britain in 1962. She has a sociology degree from the University of London, and uses her sociological knowledge to write about female characters that are in search of self-fulfillment in the midst of male and racial oppression. Emecheta has written about such sociological concepts as culture clash, population control, polygamy, immigration, maternity, the role of the female, and slavery in such works as *Second Class Citizen* (1974), *The Joys of Motherhood* (1979), *The Slave Girl* (1977), *Gwendolen* (1989), *The Rape of Shavi* (1983), *Destination Biafra* (1982), and *The New Tribe* (2000), which follows the challenges facing a black child adopted by a white family, while *Kehinde* (1996) follows the self-development of the heroine in the very different contexts of African beliefs about reincarnation and European beliefs about abortion.

Ben Okri was born in Nigeria, but moved to Britain in 1978, where he went to university. His work comprises the novels *Flowers and Shadows* (1980); *The Landscapes Within* (1981); *The **Famished Road*** (1991), which won the Booker Prize; *In Arcadia* (2002); and a collection of short stories, ***Incidents at the Shrine*** (1986). Okri explores themes like postindependence, nationalism in Nigeria, and Africa's neocolonial history, Okri's treatment of which is emphasized by the image of the *abiku,* the child spirit of West African mythology who cycles through birth and death in order to pain his parents. The primary influence for this cyclical image also comes from the way that Wole **Soyinka** treats the repetitive nature of evil in his poems "Abiku," "Death in the Dawn," and "Idanre."

Poet and playwright Gabriel Gbadamosi was born in 1961 to Irish/Nigerian parents and was educated at Cambridge. Gbadamosi has published poems in *The New Poetry 1968–1988* (1988) and *The Heinemann Book of African Poetry in English* (1990), and his plays, which experiment with a combination of Western and African dramatic theories, include such titles as *No Blacks, No Irish; Shango; Abolition; Eshu's Faust;* and a television play titled *Friday's Daughter. Eshu's Faust* is an experimental play that retells the Faust story through the Yoruba trickster god Eshu and was initially produced at King's College, Cambridge, in 1992. Much of Gbadamosi's work has been made possible through fellowships and Arts Council grants, especially a Winston Churchill Fellowship, which allowed him to travel to West Africa to study indigenous drama. Gbadamosi also won the first Richard Imison Memorial Award, sponsored by the *Times,* for a radio drama called *The Long, Hot Summer of '76* (ca.1993–94) about the Notting Hill Carnival. Among Afro-British writers, there are many who are also academics, including E. B. Asibong who is the author of a book of poetry, *Infolding* (1979), and Abdulrazak Gurnah, who is a teacher of literature at the University of Kent, Canterbury, and has published seven novels: *Memory of Departure* (1987), *Pilgrims Way* (1988), *Dottie* (1990), *Paradise* (1994), *Admiring Silence* (1996), *By the Sea* (2001), which is narrated by Saleh Omar, an elderly asylum-seeker living in an English seaside town, and *Desertion* (2005), which was short-listed for the 2006 Commonwealth Writers Prize.

Rap and dub poetry came to the forefront in the inner city of the 1970s and 1980s, when racial tension and poor job prospects resulted in much antiestablishment literature. The poetry is greatly influenced by the spoken word and oral performance, and can be composed of anything from word play in rap form to carefully composed rhythmic patterns and rhetorical devices that derive from oral poetry. Most often, rap and dub poetry is self-published, like Rauf Adu's *The Rise and Rise of General Gun* (1981), or appears in anthologies like *News for Babylon* (ed. James Berry, 1984), *Angels of Fire: An Anthology of Radical Poetry in the '80s* (eds. Sylvia Paskin, Jam Ramsay, Jeremy Silver), *Apples and Snakes* (1984), and David Orme and Martin Glynn's *Doin Mi Ed In: Rap Poems* (1993). Some rap and dub authors have had their work published by mainstream publishers, including Milton Smalling, John Agard, Linton Kwesi Johnson (who coined the expression *dub poetry* and chose to start his own recording label [LKJ Records] in 1981 so as not to rely on major recording companies),and Benjamin Zephaniah. Also available are online databases of material, such as the "Roots Archives"—a database of Jamaican Roots Reggae Albums from 1970–1985, which can be found at http://www.roots-archives.com/about/.

Initial (first-generation) dub and rap poetry is characterized by defiant verse that reminds one of the slave narratives, negritude poetry, South African resistance poetry of the 1970s and 1980s, and the Nigerian Afro-beat of Fela Anikulapo-Kuti since the 1970s. This defiant tone is apparent in works like Milton Smalling's *Living on the Edge of Paradise* (1982), *Fighting Spirit* (1983), and *The Battlefield* (1986); Linton Kwesi Johnson's *Inglan Is a Bitch* (1980); and John Agard's *Mangoes & Bullets: Selected and New Poems 1972–84* (1985) and *Laughter Is an Egg* (1990).

Radical revolutionary views have more recently been tempered by apparent improved inner-city conditions, the rise of a black middle class, and black representation in government. For example, Linton Kwesi Johnson's earlier poem, "Di Great Insohreckshan," chronicles the riots by Afro-Caribbean Britons in 1981, while his more current "Mi Revalueshanary Fren" turns instead to Eastern Europe. Another example is Benjamin Zephaniah's work, which demonstrates his movement toward a more middle-class stance if you compare *Dread Affair* (1984) and *Job Rocking* (in *Black Plays: Two,* ed. Yvonne Brewster, 1989) to *Talking Turkeys* (1994), which is an ironical critique of a number of more current issues like fox hunting ("A Killer Lies"), multiculturalism ("Multi-Culture"), and the environment ("Solidarity"). Zephaniah has most recently published titles such as *A Little Book of Vegan Poems* (2000), *Wicked World* (2000), *Refugee Boy* (2001), *Too Black, Too Strong* (2001), *We Are Britain!* (2002), and *Chambers Primary Rhyming Dictionary* (2004). Martin Glynn's "Machoman" discusses the issue of growing violence in Western society, while *A Caribbean Dozen: Poems from Caribbean Poets* (1994) by John Agard and Grace Nichols (which includes Afro-British poets) and Nichols's *Give Yourself a Hug* celebrate Caribbean life, rather than focusing on a literature of protest, and thus are outside of the dub and rap category.

In one sense, it could be said that despite amazing literary accomplishments, African-British writing continues to exist under the strictures that those authors of the eighteenth-century slave narratives experienced. As antiestablishment writing becomes integrated into the critical and cultural majority, it also turns to more conventional forms of protest that tend to stall progress. Continued change and acknowledgment of literature outside of the critical canon is needed to make the voices of Great Britain's ethic minorities heard.

Further Reading

Adi, Hakim. *History of Communities in Britain: African and Caribbean.* London: Wayland, 2005.

Anyekachi Wambu, ed. *Empire Windrush: 50 Years of Writing about Black Britain.* Phoenix, 1999.

Baker, Houston A., Manthia Diawara, and Ruth H. Lindeborg, eds. *Black British Cultural Studies: A Reader.* Chicago: University of Chicago Press, 1996.

Berry, James. *News for Babylon: The Chatto Book of West Indian-British Poetry.* London: Chatto, 1984.

Blake, Ann, Leela Gandhi, and Sue Thomas, eds. *England through Colonial Eyes in Twentieth-Century Fiction.* New York: Palgrave, 2001.

Braithwaite, E. R., and Anyekachi Wambu. *Hurricane Hits England: An Anthology of Writing about Black Britain.* New York: Continuum, 2000.

Bryan, Beverley, Stella Dadzie, and Suzanne Scafe, eds. *The Heart of the Race: Black Women's Lives in Britain.* London: Virago, 1985.

Dabydeen, David, and Paul Edwards, eds. *Black Writers in Britain, 1760–1890.* Edinburgh: Edinburgh University Press, 1991.

Gilroy, Paul. *The Black Atlantic: Modernity and Double Consciousness.* Cambridge: Harvard University Press, 1993.

———. *There Ain't No Black in the Union Jack: The Cultural Politics of Race and Nation.* London: Hutchinson, 1987.

Head, Dominic. *The Cambridge Introduction to Modern British Fiction, 1950–2000.* Cambridge: Cambridge University Press, 2002.

Husband, Charles, ed. *"Race" in Britain: Continuity and Change.* London: Hutchinson, 1982.

Innes, C. L. *A History of Black and Asian Writing in Britain.* Cambridge: Cambridge University Press, 2002.

Mirza, Heidi Safia, ed. *Black British Feminism: A Reader.* London: Routledge, 1997.

Newland, Courttia, and Kadija Sessay, eds. *IC3: The Penguin Book of New Black Writing in Britain.* London: Penguin, 2001.

Owusu, Kwesi, ed. *Black British Culture and Society: A Text Reader.* London: Routledge, 2000.

Phillips, Caryl, ed. *Extravagant Strangers.* London: Faber, 1997.

Phillips, Mike, and Trevor Phillips. *Windrush: The Irresistible Rise of Multi-Racial Britain.* London: HarperCollins, 1998.

Procter, James. *Dwelling Places: Postwar Black British Writing.* Manchester: Manchester University Press, 2003.

———. *Writing Black Britain, 1948–1998.* Manchester: Manchester University Press, 2000.

Richardson, Alan, and Debbie Lee, eds. *Early Black British Writing.* Boston: Houghton Mifflin, 2003.

Rushdie, Salman. *Imaginary Homelands: Essays and Criticism 1981–1991.* London: Granta, 1992.

Sandhu, Sukhdev. *London Calling: How Black and Asian Writers Imagined a City.* London: HarperCollins, 2003.

African-Canadian Literature

African-Canadian literature, like African literature, developed from the European invasion of African civilizations and the slavery and dispersal of African people to North and South America that resulted from that invasion, followed by the colonial and postcolonial mistreatment of their descendants. Both African-Canadian literature and African literature are thus concerned with the retelling and recovering of narratives from this history of resistance and perseverance. The influence of the development of language on both African and African-Canadian cultures is also apparent, with the impact of Africanized Englishes (Creole discourses that arose from colonialism and the slave trade) being the mapping of African grammar and speech patterns onto traditional British forms. In the introduction to her book *She Tries Her Tongue, Her Silence Softly Breaks* (1989), African-Canadian author Marlene Nourbese Philip speaks of this transatlantic complication of language in terms of the way that it fractures traditional English literary meaning and highlights the tension between the written and the oral, especially in African literature. M. Nourbese Philip tackles similar issues in her other poetry publications *Thorns* (1980) and *Salmon Courage* (1983); among her other publications are *Coups and Calypsos: A Play* (2001), *A Genealogy of Resistance and Other Essays* (1997), *Caribana: African Roots and Continuities: Race, Space and the Poetics of Moving* (1996), *Urban Confections: Race, Crimes and Immigration* (1994), *Showing Grit: Showboating North of the 44th Parallel* (1993), *Frontiers: Essays and Writings on Racism and Culture, 1984–1992* (1992), *Looking for Livingstone: An Odyssey of Silence* (1991), and *Harriet's Daughter* (1988).

African and African-Canadian literatures also have similar founding texts, specifically those of Baptist David George and Methodist Boston King, who both escaped slavery in America to become religious leaders. Both men were black loyalists who settled in Nova Scotia in 1783, and later traveled with other black Nova Scotians to Sierra Leone where George dictated his memoir *An Account of the Life of Mr. David George, from Sierra Leone in Africa . . .* (1793), and where King published an autobiographical article titled "Memoirs of the Life of Boston King, a Black Preacher, Written by Himself during His Residence at Kingswood School" (1798). Both works detail the spiritual and physical trials these men experienced as they sought to escape the terrors of slavery and the disappointments of racial prejudice. These works also reiterate the themes of those earlier Anglo-African works, *Letters* (1782) by Ignatius **Sancho,** *Thoughts and Sentiments*

on the Evil of Slavery (1787) by Ottobah **Cugoano,** and the *Interesting Narrative* (1789) by Olaudah **Equiano.**

Although there are common cornerstones to African and African-Canadian literature, the two genres have developed uniquely due to different cultural climates, and especially due to Canada's antiblack immigration laws, which were in effect until 1967. Afro-Canadians during this period of segregation from Africa continued to assert their connections to Africa through, for example, the naming of black Christian denominations—assigning titles like "African Baptist" or "African Methodist Episcopal" or "African Orthodox." African-Canadians in Montreal, Toronto, and Cape Breton in the 1920s demonstrated their support for a black nationalist and pan-Africanist movement when they praised Jamaican racialist Marcus Garvey's Universal Negro Improvement Association.

The ideal of *Afrocentrism,* which calls for an attention to African identity in the education of black African descendants, is a strong surviving element of Pan-Africanism (which calls for spiritual and national solidarity between people of black African descent) in African-Canadian literature. Algerian psychologist and black liberation theorist Frantz Fanon develops such pan-Africanist and black nationalist thought in his works *Peau noire, masques blancs* (1952; *Black Skin, White Masks,* 1967) and *Les Damnés de la terre* (1961; *The Wretched of the Earth,* 1963). Fanon has influenced such African-Canadian authors as Austin Clarke, whose essay *Public Enemies: Police Violence and Black Youth* (1992) draws attention to the black perspective of white Canadians' "polite" racism, and whose short fiction *Nine Men Who Laughed* (1986) depicts Canadian immigrants as pseudo-slaves. More recent publications by Clarke (which are concerned with similar themes) include *The Polished Hoe* (2002), and *Pigtails 'n' Breadfruit: The Rituals of Slave Food, A Barbadian Memoir* (1999). Dionne

Brand's works *Primitive Offensive* (1982), *Chronicles of the Hostile Sun* (1984), and *No Language Is Neutral* (1990), which was nominated for the 1990 Governor-General's Award for poetry, all tackle neocolonialism in different forms. Dany Laferrière's *Comment faire l'amour avec un nègre sans se fatiguer* (1985; *How to Make Love to a Negro,* 1987) calls to mind Fanon with language that deals with interracial sex, while Maxine Tynes's book *Borrowed Beauty* (1987) explores Pan-Africanism through racially aware poetry. The religious context to Pan-Africanism is also apparent in African-Canadian literature in that the literature encourages an anti-Occident Islam (as in Laferrière's *Comment faire l'amour avec un nègre sans se fatiguer*—Laferrière's recent writings include *Je suis fatigue* [2001], and *Le cri des oiseaux fous* [2000], for which he won the Prix Carbet des Lyceens in 2002), refers to African deities (as in writings by Brand and Nourbese Philip), and also contains elements of Rastafarianism (the faith instigated in Jamaica that accepts the late Haile Selassie I of Ethiopia as the messiah and Africa as the Promised Land) in some works of dub or oral-performance poets. Baha'i Frederick Ward offers a different view in his novels *Riverlisp* (1974), *Nobody Called Me Mine* (1977), and *A Room Full of Balloons* (1981), which argue for the spiritual unity of humanity.

Also an inspiration for Afro-Canadian writers is Africa itself, which is demonstrated in such works as Nourbese Philip's novel *Looking for Livingstone: An Odyssey of Silence* (1991), which questions imperialism and its ethnocentricity, and Charles R. Saunders's fantasy novels *Imaro* (1981), *Imaro II: The Quest for Cush* (1984), and *Imaro III: The Trial of Bohu* (1985) follow the stories of an African hero who has the strength of Hercules. Similarly, Djanet Sears dramatizes her character's uncovering of self and of Africa in her play *Afrika Solo* (1990). Sears has won Stratford Festival's 2004 Timothy Findley Award, and has published other important plays, such as *Harlem Duet* (1997), and *The Adventures of a Black Girl in Search of God* (2003), which was short-listed for a 2004 Trillium Book Award. Lawrence Hill's *Some Great Thing* (1992) is set in Winnipeg, but black francophone Cameroon is portrayed in opposition to a Canada that is inclined to hate. Lawrence Hill's other works include *Black Berry, Sweet Juice: On Being Black and White in Canada* (2001), *Any Known Blood* (1997), *Women of Vision: The Story of the Canadian Negro Women's Association, 1951–1976* (1996), *Trials and Triumphs: The Story of African Canadians* (1992), and *The Book of Negroes* (2007).

Syl Cheney-Coker's novel *The Last Harmattan of Alusine Dunbar* (1990) relates part of African-Canadian history with a magic realism twist, as it follows the lives and efforts of black loyalist pioneers in the mythical village of Malagueta to build a nation. A similar theme can be found in Cheney-Coker's *Concerto for an Exile* (1973), which characterizes Nova Scotia as an indicator of insanity. Other important works by Syl Cheney-Coker include *The Blood in the Desert's Eyes* (poems, 1990) and *The Graveyard Also Has Teeth* (1980). African-Canadian literature has been encouraged and inspired by writers like Jojo Chintoh, who was part-founder of the Toronto-based journal *Black Images* (1972–74), and Harold Head, who edited the anthology of African-Canadian literature *Canada in Us Now* (1976), a work that is concerned with recovering the relationship between artist and community.

Many Africans uphold African-Canadian anthologies and bibliographies, even if they were only residents of Canada for a short time. F.E.M.K. Senkoro is from Kenya, and has only published a small amount of lyrics in English, while Nigerian (Biafran) writer Samuel Udochukwo Ifejika speaks out against materialism in post–civil war Nigeria in his novel *The New Religion* (1973). South African poet Arthur **Nortje** describes his residence in Canada in *Dead Roots* (1973, published post-humously), which contains twenty metaphorical poems about Canada, and South African author Rozena Maart won the 1992 Journey Prize for her story "No Rosa, No District Six" (*Fireweed* 32, 1991). Ghanaian-Jamaican poet Kwame Dawes, whose book of poems *Progeny of Air* (1994) won the Forward Poetry Prize for best first collection, also lived in Canada for a short time. Three African authors of international acclaim have resided in Canada. Paul Tiyambe **Zeleza** from Zimbabwe-Malawi is the author of two fiction collections, **Night of Darkness** (1976) and *The Joys of Exile* (1994), and a novel, *Smouldering Charcoal* (1992), and his most recent short story, "Blood Feuds," appears in *The Picador Book of African Stories* (2000), edited by Stephen Gray. From South Africa, and African National Congress representative, Archie Crail was nominated for a Governor-General's Award in 1992 for his collection of short stories, *The Bonus Deal* (1992), while Molara **Ogundipe-Leslie** is an academic and poet from Nigeria, and is the author of an important work in Anglo-African women's poetry *Sew the Old Days and Other Poems* (1985).

Jane Tapsubei Creider is another African-born African-Canadian writer whose novel is titled *The Shrunken Dream* (1992), as is Zimbabwean Yvonne **Vera,** whose works include *Why Don't You Carve Other Animals?* (1992), *Nehanda* (1993), *Without a Name* (1994), *Under the Tongue* (1996), *Butterfly Burning* (1998), *Opening Spaces: An Anthology of Contemporary African Women's Writings* (1999), and *The Stone Virgins* (2002). South Africans Dee September, Nonqqba ka Msimang, and Kwanza Msingwana are also African-born authors who are Canadian. September is the author of the book of poems *Making Waves* (1979), while Msimang's short story "Lady in Waiting" won a prize from the Swedish International Development Agency in 1985, and Msingwana's stories are pub-lished alongside others in *Only Mountains Never Meet* (1993).

Nonblack African authors have also contributed to the proliferation of African-Canadian literature, including the South Asian author Réshard Goal (pseudonym Ved Devajee), who was born in London, partially educated in South Africa, and describes South Africa in his novels *Price of Admission* (1970), *Nemesis Casket* (1979), and *Cape Town Coolie* (1990). Similarly, Farida **Karodia** (who is South African-South Asian) has four fictional works that follow Mozambican and South African issues: *Daughters of the Twilight* (1986), *Coming Home and Other Stories* (1988), *A Shattering of Silence* (1993), *Boundaries* (2004), and *Other Secrets* (2000), which was nominated for the International IMPAC Dublin Literary Award. M. G. **Vassanji,** who is Kenyan-South Asian, is concerned with depicting East Indian-East African life in his books: *The **Gunny Sack*** (1989), *No New Land* (1991), *Uhuru Street: Short Stories* (1992), *The **Book of Secrets*** (1994), *Amriika* (1999), *The In-between Life of Vikram Lall* (2003), and *When She Was Queen* (2005). In *Distance of Distinct Vision* (1992), Zimbabwean-Chinese artist Laiwan captures her African identity in art and language, while historian Bridglal Pachai (South African-South Asian) describes his search for freedom and happiness in South Africa and Nova Scotia in his memoir, *My Africa, My Canada* (1989).

It is clear that African-Canadian and African literature share a similar past and thus similar philosophies and topics of interest, as well as authors. Afro-Canadian literature would not be the same without the participation of African writers, and there are many anthologies of African-Canadian literature: Liz Cromwell's anthology *One Out of Many: A Collection of Writings by 21 Black Women in Ontario* (1975); *Canada in Us Now,* edited by Harold Head; *Other Voices: Writings by Blacks in Canada* (1985) by Lorris Elliott; Ann

Wallace's *Daughters of the Sun, Women of the Moon: Poetry by Black Canadian Women* (1990); Ayanna Black's *Voices: Canadian Writers of African Descent* (1992) and her *Fiery Spirits: Canadian Writers of African Descent* (1994). Pieces by George and King are in George Elliott Clarke's anthology *Fire on the Water: An Anthology of Black Nova Scotian Writing*, 2 vols. (1991–92), while works by Syl Cheney-Coker, Kofi **Awoonor,** and Niyi **Osundare** are placed against works by Brand, Nourbese Philip, and Claire Harris in a special issue of *Prism International* 22, no. 4 (1984). Useful bibliographies include "Contemporary Canadian First Nations Writers and Writers of Colour: A Working Bibliography" (*West Coast Line* 28, nos. 1–2, 1994) by Lisette Boily, and *Bibliography of Literary Writings by Blacks in Canada* (1986) and *Literary Writings by Blacks in Canada: A Preliminary Survey* (1988) by Lorris Elliott (useful more for initial research as it is now outdated and somewhat inaccurate). Historical material can be found in "African Canadians: The Peoples of Canada: An Encyclopedia for the Country" (typescript, 1993) by James W. St. G. Walker.

Further Reading

Algoo Baksh, Stella. *Austin C. Clarke: A Biography.* Toronto; Barbados: ECW; University of the West Indies Press, 1994.

Baugh, Edward. "Friday in Crusoe's City: The Question of Language in Two West Indian Novels of Exile." *ACLALS-Bulletin* 5, no. 3 (1980): 1–12.

———. "Friday in Crusoe's City: The Questions of Language in Two West Indian Novels of Exile." In *Language and Literature in Multicultural Contexts,* ed. Satendra Nandan. Suva. Fiji: University of South Pacific, 1983, 44–53.

Bialas, Zbigniew, and Kowalczyk-Twarowski, Krzysztof, eds. and introduction. *Ebony, Ivory & Tea.* Katowice, Poland: Wydawnictwo Uniwersytetu Slaskiego, 2004, 228–42.

Birbalsingh, Frank. "Austin Clarke: Caribbean-Canadians." In *Frontiers of Caribbean Literatures in English,* ed. Frank Birbalsingh. New York: St. Martin's Press, 1996, 86–105.

Black, Ayanna, ed. *Fiery Spirits: Canadian Writers of African Descent.* Toronto: HarperCollins, 1994.

———, ed. *Voices: Canadian Writers of African Descent.* Toronto: HarperCollins, 1992.

Braziel, Jana Evans. "From Port-au-Prince to Montréal to Miami: Trans-American Nomads in Dany Laferrière's Migratory Texts." *Callaloo: A Journal of African-American and African Arts and Letters* 26, no. 1 (2003): 235–51.

———. "Trans-American Constructions of Black Masculinity: Dany Laferrière, le Nègre, and the Late Capitalist American Racial Machine-désirante." *Callaloo: A Journal of African-American and African Arts and Letters* 26, no. 3 (2003): 867–900.

Brown, Lloyd W. "The West Indian Novel in North America: A Study of Austin Clarke." *The Journal of Commonwealth Literature* 9 (1970): 89–103.

Brydon, Diana. "Caribbean Revolution and Literary Convention." *Canadian Literature* 95 (1982): 181–85.

Butling, Pauline. "Dionne Brand on Struggle and Community, Possibility and Poetry." In *Poets Talk: Conversations with Robert Kroetsch, Daphne Marlatt, Erin Mouré, Dionne Brand, Marie Annharte Baker, Jeff Derksen, and Fred Wah,* eds. Pauline Butling and Susan Rudy. Edmonton: University of Alberta Press, 2005, 63–87.

Cameron, Elspeth. "Who Is Marlene Nourbese Philip and Why Is She Saying All Those Terrible Things about PEN?" *Chatelaine* 63, no. 11 (1990): 86–87+.

Carr, Brenda. "To 'Heal the Word Wounded': Agency and the Materiality of Language and Form in M. Nourbese Philip's *She Tries Her Tongue, Her Silence Softly Breaks.*" *Studies in Canadian Literature* 19, no. 1 (1994): 72–93.

Clarke, Austin. "In the Semi-Colon of the North." *Canadian Literature* 95 (1982): 30–37.

———. "An Interview with LeRoi Jones." In *Conversations with Amiri Baraka,* ed. Charlie Reilly. Jackson: University Press of Mississippi, 1994, 36–50.

———. "Some Speculations as to the Absence of Racialistic Vindictiveness in West Indian

Literature." In *The Black Writer in Africa and the Americas,* ed. Lloyd W. Brown. Los Angeles: Hennessey & Ingalls, 1973, 165–94.

Clarke, George Elliott. "Clarke vs. Clarke: Tory Elitism in Austin Clarke's Short Fiction." *West Coast Line* 31, no. 1) (1997): 110–28.

———. "Harris, Philip, Brand: Three Authors in Search of Literate Criticism." *Journal of Canadian Studies* 35, no. 1 (2000): 161–89.

———, ed. *Fire on the Water, Volumes One and Two.* Porter's Lake, Nova Scotia: Pottersfield Press, 1991.

———, ed. *Odysseys Home: Mapping African-Canadian Literature.* Toronto: University of Toronto Press, 2002.

Courcy, Nathalie. "Le Goût des jeunes filles de Dany Laferrière: Du chaos à la reconstruction du sens." *Présence Francophone: Revue Internationale de Langue et de Littérature* 63 (2004): 84–94, 243.

Craig, Terrence. "Interview with Austin Clarke." *World Literature Written in English* 26, no. 1 (1986): 115–27.

Cramer, Laura Ann. "Exploring Voice and Silence in the Poetry of Beth Cuthland, Louise Halfe and Marlene Nourbese Philip." In *(Ad)dressing Our Words: Aboriginal Perspectives on Aboriginal Literatures,* ed. Armand Garnet Ruffo. Penticton, BC: Theytus Boks, 2001, 125–34.

Cuder-Domínguez, Pilar. "African Canadian Writing and the Narration(s) of Slavery." *Essays on Canadian Writing* 79 (2003): 55–75.

Dabydeen, Cyril, ed. *A Shapley Fire: Changing the Literary Landscape.* Oakville, Ontario: Mosaic Press, 1987.

Deloughrey, Elizabeth. "From Margin to the (Canadian) Frontier: 'The Wombs of Language' in M. Nourbese Philip's *She Tries Her Tongue, Her Silence Softly Breaks.*" *Journal of Canadian Studies* 33, no. 1 (1998): 121–44.

Deslauriers, Pierre. "African Magico-Medicine at Home and Abroad: Haitian Religious Traditions in a Neocolonial Setting: The Fiction of Dany Laferrière and Russell Banks." In *Mapping the Sacred: Religion, Geography and Postcolonial Literatures,* ed. Jamie S. Scott (introduction) and Paul Simpson-Housley. Amsterdam: Rodopi, 2001, 337–53.

Dickinson, Peter. "Duets, Duologues and Black Diasporic Theatre: Djanet Sears, William Shakespeare and Others." *Modern Drama* 45, no. 2 (2002): 188–208.

Dorscht, Susan R. Rev. of *Grammar of Dissent: Poetry & Prose,* ed. Carol Morrell. *Canadian Ethnic Studies* 29, no. 1 (1997): 188–91.

Essar, Dennis F. "Dany Laferrière, 'Primitive' Writer: A Haitian Esthetic." In *Haïti: Ecrire en pays assiégé/Writing under Siege,* eds. and introduction Marie-Agnès Sourieau and Kathleen M. Balutansky. Amsterdam: Rodopi, 2004, 423–57.

Fabre, Michel. "Changing the Metropolis or Being Changed by It: Toronto West Indians in Austin Clarke's Trilogy." *Recherches Anglaises et Nord-Américaines* 24 (1991): 129–35.

Fraser, Kaya. "Language to Light On: Dionne Brand and the Rebellious Word." *Studies in Canadian Literature/Etudes en Littérature Canadienne* 30, no. 1 (2005): 291–308.

Fumagalli, Maria Cristina. "'The Smallest Cell Remembers': *She Tries Her Tongue, Her Silence Softly Breaks* and Marlene Nourbese Philip's Journey Back to Africa." *EnterText: An Interactive Interdisciplinary E-Journal for Cultural and Historical Studies and Creative Work* 3, no. 2 (2003): 162–79. http://people.brunel.ac.uk/~acsrrrm/entertext/home.htm.

Gallou, Claire. "Speaking the Unspeakable: Marlene Nourbese Philip's Poetry and the Creation of a New Caribbean Identity." *Paroles Gelées: UCLA French Studies* 20, no. 2 (2003): 60–66.

Garvey, Johanna X. K. "'The Place She Miss': Exile, Memory, and Resistance in Dionne Brand's Fiction." *Callaloo: A Journal of African-American and African Arts and Letters* 26, no. 2 (2003): 486–503.

Godard, Barbara. "Deterritorializing Strategies: Nourbese Philip as Caucasianist Ethnographer." In *Ebony, Ivory & Tea,* eds. Zbigniew Bialas and Krzysztof Kowalczyk-Twarowski. Katowice, Poland: Wydawnictwo Uniwersytetu Slaskiego, 2004, 228–42.

Goddard, Horace L. "The Immigrants' Pain: The Socio-Literary Context of Austin Clarke's Trilogy." *ACLALS Bulletin* 8, no. 1 (1989): 39–57.

Goldman, Marlene. "Mapping the Door of No Return: Deterritorialization and the Work of Dionne Brand." *Canadian Literature* 182 (2004): 13–28.

Hall, Phil. "The Continent of Silence: Marlene Nourbese Philip." *Books in Canada* 18, no. 1 (1989): 1.

Hamner, Robert D. "Overseas Male: Austin Clarke's *Growing Up Stupid under the Union Jack*." *College Language Association Journal* 36, no. 2 (1992): 123–33.

Harris, Claire. "Poets in Limbo." In *A Mazing Space: Writing Canadian Women Writing*, eds. Shirley Neuman and Smaro Kamboureli. Edmonton: Longspoon /Newest, 1986, 115–25.

Henry, Keith S. "An Assessment of Austin Clarke, West Indian-Canadian Novelist." *College Language Association Journal* 29, no. 1 (1985): 9–32.

Hunter, Lynette. "After Modernism: Alternative Voices in the Writings of Dionne Brand, Claire Harris and Marlene Philip." *University of Toronto Quarterly* 62, no. 2 (1992/1993): 256–81.

Johnson, Erica L. "Unforgetting Trauma: Dionne Brand's Haunted Histories." *Anthurium: A Caribbean Studies Journal* 2, no. 1 (2004): 27 paragraphs.

Kidnie, Margaret Jane. "'There's Magic in the Web of It': Seeing beyond Tragedy in *Harlem Duet*." *Journal of Commonwealth Literature* 36, no. 2 (2001): 29–44.

Kinnahan, Linda A. *Lyric Interventions: Feminism, Experimental Poetry, and Contemporary Discourse*. Iowa City: University of Iowa Press, 2004.

Knowles, Ric. "Othello in Three Times." In *Shakespeare in Canada: "A World Elsewhere?,"* ed. Diana Brydon (preface and afterword) and Irena R. Makaryk (preface and introduction); Jessica Schagerl (appendix). Toronto: University of Toronto Press, 2002, 371–94.

Lacovia, R. M. "Migration and Transmutation in the Novels of McKay, Marshall, and Clarke." *Journal of Black Studies* 7 (1977): 437–54.

Lima, Maria Helena. "'Beyond Miranda's Meanings': Contemporary Critical Perspectives on Caribbean Women's Literatures." *Feminist Studies* 21, no. 1 (1995): 115–28.

MacDonald, Joyce Green. "Finding Othello's African Roots through Djanet Sears's *Harlem Duet*." *Approaches to Teaching Shakespeare's Othello*, eds. Peter Erickson and Maurice Hunt. New York: Modern Language Association of America, 2005, 202–8.

Mahlis, Kirsten. "A Poet of Place: An Interview with M. Nourbese Philip." *Callaloo: A Journal of African Diaspora Arts and Letters* 27, no. 3 (2004): 682–97.

Mehan, Uppinder. "The Art and Activism of M. Nourbese Philip." *Paragraph* 15, no. 2 (1993): 20–23.

Morrell, Carol, ed. *Grammar of Dissent: Poetry and Prose by Claire Harris, M. Nourbese Philip, and Dionne Brand*. Fredericton, New Brunswick: Goose Lane Editions, 1994.

Ramraj, Victor. "Temporizing Laughter: The Later Stories of Austin Clarke." In *Short Fiction in the New Literatures in English: Proceedings of the Nice Conference of the European Association for Commonwealth Literature and Language Studies*, ed. Jacqueline Bardolph. Nice, France: Faculté des Lettres et Sciences Humaines de Nice, 1989, 127–31.

Sarbadhikary, Krishna. "Weaving a Multicoloured Quilt: Marlene N. Philip's Vision of Change." *International Journal of Canadian Studies* 10 (1994): 103–18.

Saul, Joanne. "'In the Middle of Becoming': Dionne Brand's Historical Vision." *Canadian Woman Studies/Les Cahiers de la Femme* 23, no. 2 (2004): 59–63.

Saunders, Leslie. "Austin Clarke." In *Profiles in Canadian Literature*, ed. Jeffrey M. Heath. Vol. 4. Toronto: Dundurn, 1982, 93–100.

———. "Marlene Nourbese Philip's 'Bad Words.'" *Tessera* 12 (1992): 81–89.

———. "'The Mere Determination to Remember': M. Nourbese Philip's Stop Frame." *West Coast Line* 31, no. 1 (1997): 134–42.

Thompson, Dawn. "Looking for Livingstone in Marlene Nourbese Philip's *Looking for Livingstone*." In *Writing a Politics of Perception: Memory, Holography, and Women Writers in Canada*. Toronto: University of Toronto Press, 2000, 63–78.

Uppal, Priscila. "Recovering the Past through Language and Landscape: The Contemporary English-Canadian Elegy." PhD diss., York University, Toronto, 2004.

Vevaina, Coomi S. "Searching for Space: A Conversation with M. Nourbese Philip." Interview. *Open Letter* 9, no. 9 (1997): 15–26.

Wiens, Jason. "'Language Seemed to Split in Two': National Ambivalence(s) and Dionne Brand's

'No Language Is Neutral.'" *Essays on Canadian Writing* 70 (2000): 81–102.

Williamson, Janice. "Blood on Our Hands: An Interview with Marlene Nourbese Philip." *Paragraph* 14, no. 1 (1992): 18–19.

———. "Writing a Memory of Losing That Place." In *Sounding Differences: Conversations with Seventeen Canadian Women Writers.* Toronto: University of Toronto Press, 1993, 226–44.

African-Caribbean Literature

Despite the connections between Africa and the Caribbean archipelago, and the fact that much of the population of the Caribbean is of African descent, there are some major cultural differences that surround any connection between African and Caribbean literature. Most of these differences have to do with the way that slavery and colonialism deteriorated African cultural identity over a period of hundreds of years, and the way that the distance between the Caribbean and Africa allowed for a quite different cultural development, in addition to the fact that in the Caribbean a multicultural society has resulted in the reinvention of culture on many levels. African identity is more like a foundation upon which Caribbean identity has formed and interacted with, and it could be said that it is one of the foundations that helped many African-Caribbeans overcome poverty and oppression. George Lamming discusses this issue of the importance of Africa to West Indian literature and identity in his 1966 article "Caribbean Literature: The Black Rock of Africa," which was published in *African Forum: A Quarterly Journal of Contemporary Affairs.* Lamming analyses the history and foundations of Caribbean literature and attempts to understand the way that African heritage is treated in Caribbean works by authors such as Vera Bell, Eric Roach, and Derek Walcott, as well as in works by white and Indo-Caribbean authors such as Geoffrey Drayton, Samuel Selvon, and V. S. Naipaul. Lamming concludes that the focus of Caribbean literature on decolo-nization and the reformation of inequality and poverty associated with African identity causes Caribbean literature to be very focused on Africa.

Now, forty years after Lamming's article was published, the African roots of Caribbean writing have been closely explored, as have been the roots of Caribbean language. Linguists have found that Caribbean Creoles are a combination of Dutch, English, Spanish, or French with African, or in some cases, Indian words as well. Now it is important that these Creoles are analyzed and that conventions are established for their preservation, and in order to make it easier for authors to use them in a literary sense (who have had to establish their own spelling and usage conventions). In this sense, too, the Caribbean Creoles offer a distinct connection between African and Caribbean cultures, and Caribbean authors such as Merle Collins, *Angel* (1987), note that a knowledge of the influence of African language on Creole languages is important.

Other cultural connections to Africa are apparent in the performance cults and symbolic languages of the Shango of Trinidad and the Jamaica-based Rastafarian religion and culture, and the focus on African religious traditions like African gods, obeah, and in Haiti *voudou.* Such traditions were originally broken up and made to go into hiding due to the separation of those with common language and cultures by slaveholding plantation owners. Keeping in mind that people from a number of the West African coastal and inland areas were conveyed to the Caribbean during the slave trade, cultural connections between African and Caribbean communities that are generally indicated are an Igbo culture in Barbados, an Ashanti/Coromantee culture in Jamaica, and a Yoruba culture in Trinidad. Storytelling traditions also derive from African roots, and stories like the Anancy tales of the Akan people, which were retold in colloquial English as "Nancy stories" in the Caribbean, have also been retold in such works as Andrew Salkey's *Anancy's Score* (1973). Also important is the tradition of orature, specifically folktales, storytelling, and musical and poetical performance. Within oral tradition ritualistic storytelling, mythological and folktale characters like the West African Watermaid, musical forms like calypso and reggae, as well as the rhythms of performance poetry all contribute to a Caribbean identity that has its roots in the oral traditions of Africa. Calypso, for example, has its beginning in satirical African songwriting, and as Gordon Rohlehr and Hollis Liverpool (the Mighty Chalkdust) note, the form began in Trinidad due to the resistance of African-Caribbean people against colonialism. Similarly, oral culture in Jamaica reflects the African influences that provide the backbone for contemporary oral poetry, reggae, dub, which focus on a construction and explanation of selfhood that is based on the *griot* customs of West Africa. Such influences are seen in poets such as Louise Bennett, Jean "Binta" Breeze, Michael Smith, John Agard, Mutaburuka, and Linton Kwesi Johnson, who reflect the importance of the oral to Caribbean culture as a whole, and even the written literature demonstrates a reliance on oral culture derived from African heritage.

Although it is influenced greatly by European forms, African elements of Caribbean theater and drama include things like satirical comedy, masking, music and dance, and Creole language. For example, Derek Walcott (of St. Lucia) uses the tradition of masking in *Dream on Monkey Mountain* (1972) and *Tijean and His Brothers* (1972), and Creole-speaking Caribbean peasants are featured in his early work as well. Walcott's poetry is also of note, and in his poem "A Far Cry from Africa" (*In a Green Night*, 1962) he represents the attempt of middle-class Caribbeans to understand their links to both Africa and Europe. Derek Walcott's recent poetry includes *Tiepolo's Hound* (2000) and *The Prodigal* (2004), while his recent plays are *The Haitian Trilogy* (2002) and *Walker and the Ghost Dance* (2002), and he has also written a nonfiction book titled *What the Twilight Says* (1998). Similarly, African elements are included in *An Echo in the Bone* (1985) by Dennis Scott (of Jamaica) and in the unpublished "I, Lawah" by Rawle Gibbons (of Trinidad), which has played a role in the growth of Carnival theater. Gibbons's published works are *A Calypso Trilogy* (1999) and *No Surrender: A Biography of the Growling Tiger* (1994). Carnival theater is derived from traditional European festivals, but it is also distinctly African in its cultural, political, as well as formulaic history. One can observe such political traditions in a work like *Bellywoman Bangarang*, which is staged by the women's theater company from Jamaica, Sistren, and which makes use of masking and improvisation that includes occurrences from the actors' daily lives in black working-class Kingston.

Written literature has also explored and drawn attention to African-Caribbean associations. George Lamming's character Fola in *Season of Adventure* (1970) is against participation in a ceremony of souls, only to uncover her African heritage through it, while other Caribbean authors and scholars like O. R. Dathorne (*The Scholar Man*, 1964), Neville Dawes, Denis Williams (*Other Leopards*, 1963), Oliver Jackman (*Saw the House in Half*, 1974), and Kamau Brathwaite spent time in Africa when they were young. Brathwaite's work, specifically, added to a cultural understanding of the relationship of Africa to the Caribbean, and is of great importance to the Barbados, due to the fact that official Barbadian culture disregarded African survivals for quite a long time. Brathwaite's *The Arrivants* (1973) is an epic poetic trilogy that follows his characters from Africa to the "New World" to England, and he further explores the connection in essays on topics like the African tonal quality underlying the way that English-language Christian hymns are sung in small Barbadian religious meetings, on how people might march behind a military band with an African rhythm, and on the character of Caribbean cultural identity, which Brathwaite investigates in *Contradictory Omens* (1974). Brathwaite's works of the 1990s include *The Zea Mexican Diary* (1993), *Shar: The Hurricane Poem* (1990), and *Trench Town Rock* (1994). In 1998 he received the Casa de las Américas Prize for his poem "MR," and he also received the 1998 Pride of Barbados Award for literature. Brathwaite's recognition of the influence of African tradition on Barbadian cultural identity, albeit hidden underneath the dominant European influence, along with the similar recognition of poets like Bruce St. John (whose Barbadian Creole performance poetry includes the influence of African tonality), has helped to make the importance of such African cultural influences known. Also of importance to this exploration of African identity is M. Nourbese Philip's "Discourse on the Logic of Language" (*She Tries Her Tongue, Her Silence Softly Breaks*, 1989), in which she discusses the relationship between the silencing of slaves for speaking their own language and the difficulties that the poet experiences when attempting to overcome the barriers of English. M. Nourbese Philip's other poetry includes *Thorns* (1980) and *Salmon Courage* (1983), while her nonpoetic works are *Coups and Calypsos: A Play* (2001), *A Geneology of Resistance and Other Essays* (1997), *Caribana: African Roots and Continuities: Race, Space and the Poetics of Moving* (1996), *Urban Confections: Race, Crimes and Immigration* (1994), *Showing Grit: Showboating North of the 44th Parallel* (1993), *Frontiers: Essays and Writings on Racism and Culture, 1984–1992* (1992), *Looking for Livingstone: An Odyssey of Silence* (1991), and *Harriet's Daughter* (1988). Lorna Goodison (of Jamaica) calls up the African

etymology of Jamaican place-names (as well as other cultural and historical influences on Jamaica, other than African ones) in her poem "To Us All Flowers Are Roses" (*Selected Poems*, 1992), and other recent publications by Lorna Goodison include *Guinea Woman: New and Selected Poems* (2000) and *Travelling Mercies* (2001). The Barbadian voice is evident in the works of African-American Paule Marshall (who was born in New York to Barbadian parents), who tells the story of an African-American woman who discovers a sense of her African ancestry on the island of Carriacou through dance and ritual in *Praisesong for the Widow* (1983). Paule Marshall's most recent published work is *The Fisher King* (2000).

Jamaican novelist Erna Brodber captures the intricacy of Caribbean identity through her descriptions of African as well as European-based folk traditions as influential in the life of a young woman growing up in a small town in Jamaica in *Jane and Louisa Will Soon Come Home* (1980). Other works by Brodber are *Myal* (1988) and *Louisiana* (1994). In Earl Lovelace's novel *The Wine of Astonishment* (1982) he follows the lives of Spiritual Baptists in the village of Bonasse, and makes conclusions about community solidarity and a shared history through the tradition of African storytelling. In his play *Jestina's Calypso* (1984), Lovelace depicts the struggles of Jestina, who labors against the negative stereotyping of female beauty by men who value the fair-skinned Western ideal of femininity based on racism and colonialism. In 1997 Lovelace's *Salt* (1996) won the Commonwealth Writers Prize (Overall Winner, Best Book).

The interaction between African and Caribbean cultures is a good example of the way that African consciousness is of importance to a number of literary forms from many places that both rely on African heritage and define it. Caribbean culture is a combination of many elements from world cultures, as they have defined and been transformed by Caribbean culture, one of the most central elements being African culture. The Caribbean connection with Africa continues to fuel new and creative literature, drama, and poetry as it is inspired by the symbolic importance of Africa and African people as cultural survivors of racism and colonialism.

Further Reading

Alexander, Simone A. James. "Healing and Reconciliation in Paule Marshall's *The Fisher King*." *Network 2000: In the Spirit of the Harlem Renaissance* 11 (2003): 11–20.

———. "Kamau Brathwaite: A Selected Bibliographical Update, 1990–2002." *ALA Bulletin: A Publication of the African Literature Association* 28, no. 1 (2001): 55–65.

Balderston, D. *Encyclopedia of Latin American and Caribbean Literature 1900–2003*. London: Routledge, 2004.

Baugh, Edward . "Lorna Goodison." In *Twentieth-Century Caribbean and Black African Writers,* ed. and introduction Bernth Lindford. Third Series. Detroit: Gale, 1996, 85–95.

———. "Lorna Goodison in the Context of Feminist Criticism." *Journal of West Indian Literature* 4, no. 1 (1990): 1–13.

Birbalsingh, Frank. "Lorna Goodison: Heartease." In *Frontiers of Caribbean Literatures in English,* ed. and introduction Frank Birbalsingh. New York: St. Martin's Press, 1996, 152–66.

Bobb, June. "'No Choice but to Sing': Symbolic Geographies and Lorna Goodison's Wild Women." *Sargasso* 10 (2001): 31–38.

Breslin, Paul. "Derek Walcott's 'Reversible World': Centers, Peripheries, and the Scale of Nature." *Callaloo: A Journal of African Diaspora Arts and Letters* 28, no. 1 (2005): 8–24.

Cartwright, Keith. "Notes toward a Voodoo Hermeneutics: Soul Rhythms, Marvelous Transitions, and Passages to the Creole Saints in *Praisesong for the Widow*." *Southern Quarterly: A Journal of the Arts in the South* 41, no. 4 (2003): 127–43.

Chevannes, Barry. *Rastafari and Other African-Caribbean Worldviews*. London: Macmillan Press, 1995.

Cobb, Michael L. "Irreverent Authority: Religious Apostrophe and the Fiction of Blackness in Paule Marshall's *Brown Girl, Brownstones*." *University of Toronto Quarterly: A Canadian Journal of the Humanities* 72, no. 2 (2003): 631–48.

Dabydeen, David. "Derek Walcott in Conversation with David Dabydeen." *Wasafiri: The Transnational Journal of International Writing* 42 (2004): 37–41.

Dalleo, Raphael. "Another 'Our America': Rooting a Caribbean Aesthetic in the Work of José Martí, Kamau Brathwaite and Edouard Glissant." *Anthurium: A Caribbean Studies Journal* 2, no. 2 (2004): 20 paragraphs.

Dash, J. Michael. *The Other America: Caribbean Literature in a New World Context*. Charlottesville: University of Virginia Press, 1998.

de Caires Narain, Denise. *Contemporary Caribbean Women's Poetry: Making Style*. London: Routledge, 2002.

Demirtürk, Lâle. "Postcolonial Reflections on the Discourse of Whiteness: Paule Marshall's *The Chosen Place, the Timeless People*." *CLA Journal* 48, no. 1 (2004): 88–102.

Eppert, Claudia. "(Un)Learning Home: Paule Marshall's *Praisesong for the Widow*, Emmanuel Levinas, and an Ethics of Reading for Alterity." In *Bridges across Chasms: Towards a Transcultural Future in Caribbean Literature,* ed. and introduction Bénédicte Ledent. Liège, Belgium: Liège Language and Literature, English Department, Université de Liège, 2004, 169–83.

Gibbons, Rawle. "'Band Meet Band': Carnival and Text in a Production of Walcott's *Drums and Colours*." In *Caribbean 2000: Regional and/ or National Definitions, Identities and Cultures,* eds. Lowell Fiet and Janette Becerra, 95–105. San Juan: Sargasso/Caribe—Facultad de Humanidades, Universidad de Puerto Rico, 2000.

———. "Theatre and Caribbean Self-Definition." *Modern Drama* 38, no. 1 (1995): 52–59.

Habekost, Christian. *Verbal Riddim: The Politics and Aesthetics of African-Caribbean Dub Poetry*. Atlanta: Rodopi, 1993.

Hodges, Hugh. "Start-Over: Possession Rites and Healing Rituals in the Poetry of Lorna

Goodison." *Research in African Literatures* 36, no. 2 (2005): 19–32.

James, Cynthia. "Reconnecting the Caribbean-American Diaspora in Paule Marshall's *Brown Girl, Brownstones* and Erna Brodber's *Louisiana*." *CLA Journal* 45, no. 2 (2001): 151–70.

Jenkins, Lee M. *The Language of Caribbean Poetry: Boundaries of Expression.* Gainesville: University Press of Florida, 2004.

John, Catherine A. *Clear Word and Third Sight: Folk Groundings and Diasporic Consciousness in African Caribbean Writing.* Durham, NC: Duke University Press, 2003.

Johnson, Beverly A. "Revolutionary Solutions: Challenging Colonialist Attitudes in the Works of Paule Marshall." *CLA Journal* 45, no. 4 (2002): 460–76.

Josephs, Kelly Baker. "Versions of X/Self: Kamau Brathwaite's Caribbean Discourse." *Anthurium: A Caribbean Studies Journal* 1, no. 1 (2003): 34 paragraphs.

Keizer, Arlene R. *Black Subjects: Identity Formation in the Contemporary Narrative of Slavery.* Ithaca, NY: Cornell University Press, 2004.

Lamming, George. "Caribbean Literature: The Black Rock of Africa." *African Forum: A Quarterly Journal of Contemporary Affairs* 1, no. 4 (1966): 32–52.

Macarie, Gilles. "'Not His, but Her Story': The Place of Women in Derek Walcott's Poetry." *Commonwealth Essays and Studies* 26, no. 1 (2003): 71–74.

MacDonald, Joyce Green. "Bodies, Race, and Performance in Derek Walcott's *A Branch of the Blue Nile*." *Theatre Journal* 57, no. 2 (2005): 191–203.

Moffett, Joe W. "'Master, I Was the Freshest of All Your Readers': Derek Walcott's *Omeros* and Homer as Literary Origin." *Lit: Literature Interpretation Theory* 16, no. 1 (2005): 1–23.

Puri, Shalini. *The Caribbean Postcolonial: Social Equality, Post-Nationalism, and Cultural Hybridity.* New York: Palgrave Macmillan, 2004.

Reichardt, Ulfried. "Diaspora Studies and the Culture of the African Diaspora: The Poetry of Derek Walcott, Kamau Brathwaite and Linton Kwesi Johnson." In *Diaspora and Multiculturalism: Common Traditions and New Developments,* ed. Monika Fludernik. Amsterdam: Rodopi, 2003, 287–327.

Stanford, Ann Folwell. *Bodies in a Broken World: Women Novelists of Color and the Politics of Medicine.* Chapel Hill: University of North Carolina Press, 2003.

Thieme, John. "Caliban's New Masters: Creolizing Archetypes in Kamau Brathwaite's Arrivants Trilogy." *Commonwealth Essays and Studies* 5 (2003): 27–39.

Welsh, Sarah Lawson. *The Routledge Reader in Caribbean Literature.* London: Routledge, 1996.

Williams, Claudette May. *Charcoal & Cinnamon: The Politics of Color in Spanish Caribbean Literature.* Gainesville: Board of Regents of the State of Florida, 2000.

Yeh, Michelle. "Interview with Derek Walcott." *Literary Imagination: The Review of the Association of Literary Scholars and Critics* 4, no. 3 (2002): 294–302.

Afrika, Tatamkhulu Ismail (1921–2002)

Afrika is the adopted name of a South African poet and novelist who was born in Egypt and brought to South Africa by his parents when he was still a young child. Afrika's first novel, *Broken Earth* (1940), was published while he was serving in the South African forces. While in active service in North Africa, he was taken captive and held as a POW for three years. When Afrika returned to South Africa, he took up anti-**apartheid** activism as a member of the (then outlawed) African National Congress and was arrested by the minority white South African government in 1964, the same year he converted to Islam. When the government declared the traditionally black District Six, Cape Town, a white area, Afrika strongly opposed the decision in his role as a founding member of the Al-Jihaad organization, and in 1987 he was banned from writing and public speaking for five years.

Despite the ban, this is when Afrika began to write again. His poetry about prison and the oppression of apartheid was first published in literary magazines such as *Contrast* and *New Coin* and were then collected in *Nine Lives* (1991) and *Dark Rider* (1992). Afrika gained much recognition from the South African literary establishment for his work as well, with a CNA Debut Prize (1991), the English Academy of Southern Africa's Olive Schreiner Prize (1992), Thomas Pringle Award (1991 and 1993), and the SANLAM Literary Award (1994). After a majority elected democratic government was established, Afrika published a second novel, *The Innocents* (1994), a series of four novellas called *Tightrope* (1996), a novel about his experiences as a POW titled *Bitter Eden* (2000), and [five] further collections of verse, *Maqabane* (1994), *Flesh and the Flame* (1995), *The Lemon Tree and Other Poems* (1995), *Turning Points* (1996), and *Mad Old Man under the Morning Star* (2000). He wrote an unpublished novel titled *Lizard on the Wall* in 2002, and *Mr. Chameleon* (2000) is the title of Afrika's unpublished autobiography. A tribute and selection of fifty poems from Afrika's previous eight collections of verse was published under the title *Nightrider* in 2003, after he was hit by a car and subsequently died from his injuries in 2002. Afrika's nonmaterialistic lifestyle and dedication to the representation of South African social issues resulted in a literature that speaks for all levels of South African society in a lyrical and inspired manner.

Age of Iron (1990)

A novel by J. M. **Coetzee.** Elizabeth Curren, a retired classics lecturer who is dying of cancer, narrates the novel during the years 1986–89. These years cover the South African state's claim to absolute power and the resistance of black youth. Curren searches for redemption, and even considers lighting herself on fire outside of Parliament, but decides to focus her attentions on a young black man who is set on ignoring her. Curren's narrative is a letter to her daughter in America, which she gives to an alcoholic to deliver who keeps her company in the final days of her life.

Aidoo, Ama Ata (1942–)

Ghanaian playwright, poet, novelist, short-story writer, and critic, born at Abeadze Kyiakor, near Dominase, in Ghana. Aidoo attended the Wesley Girls' High School at Cape Coast in the Central Region of Ghana and gained a bachelor's at the University of Ghana, Legon (1964). She produced her first two plays while still an undergrad, after she participated in the School of Drama writers' workshops, and after graduation she took the creative writing program at Stanford University in the United States. Since then, Aidoo has taught as a research fellow at the Institute of African Studies, University of Ghana, worked as a lecturer at the University of Cape Coast, Ghana, and has been a visiting lecturer at various universities in Africa and the United States. Aidoo was also Secretary for Education in the military government of Flt. Lt. Jerry Rawlings in the early 1980s, but since her resignation she has lived in exile, first as a freelance writer in Zimbabwe, and then as a lecturer in the United States. *Changes: A Love Story* (1991) is Aidoo's second novel, which won a Commonwealth Writers Prize and was rereleased by Harcourt Education in 2004.

Aidoo is an extremely versatile writer, as she has published novels, short stories, drama, poetry, and young adult literature. Aidoo's published dramatic works include *The **Dilemma of a Ghost*** (1965) and ***Anowa*** (1970), while her short-story collections are titled ***No Sweetness Here*** (1970) and *The Girl Who Can and Other Stories* (1996), and her first novel, ***Our Sister Killjoy*** (1977) is a fiction told in four sections, and in a verse-prose style. Aidoo's poetry collections include *Someone Talking to Sometime* (1985) and *An Angry Letter in January* (1992), while her works for young adults are *The Eagle and* the Chickens and Other Stories (1989) and Birds and Other Poems (1989).

Aidoo analyzes the place of the individual in the history of colonialism and neocolonialism in Africa, and as a black African feminist she also takes into account the oppression of modern African women in two of her most well-known essays: "No Saviours," which was published in The New African as an introduction to Ghanaian novelist Ayi Kwei **Armah**'s The Beautyful Ones Are Not Yet Born, and "To Be an African Woman Writer—Overview and Detail," which was published in Criticism and Ideology (1988), edited by Kirsten Holst Petersen. Aidoo also emphasizes the oral roots of African literature (especially storytelling) in her dramatic works, because the idea of generic division is a particularly Western idea that does not apply to the storyteller's combination of poetry, acting, and narrative plot. As a result, Aidoo's work is a combination of community involvement, music, and dance that draws attention to community support. This focus on traditional form results in Aidoo's ideal future of an African literature that will renew its emphasis on verbal discourse.

Aiyejina, Funso (1949–)

Poet and short-story writer, born in Ososo, Edo State, Nigeria, and holds a bachelor's degree from the University of Ife, a master's from Acadia University, Nova Scotia, Canada, and a doctorate from the University of the West Indies, Trinidad. He taught at the University of Ife (now Obafemi Awolowo University) and since 1990 has taught at the University of the West Indies in Trinidad. In 1995–96, he was Fulbright Lecturer in Creative Writing at Lincoln University in Jefferson City, Missouri.

Short fiction by Aiyejina has appeared in Okike; his poetry has been published in many journals, including Opon Ifa, Okike, West Africa, Greenfield Review, and Trinidad and Tobago Review; his stories and plays have been broadcast over the radio in Nigeria and England; and his work appears in a number of anthologies. Aiyejina's first book of poems, A Letter to Lynda (1988), explores indigenous idioms and images and won the Association of Nigerian Authors Prize in 1989. The Legend of the Rockhills and Other Stories (1999) won Best First Book, Africa, for the Commonwealth Writers Prize in 2000, and Aiyejina has also published a second anthology of poems under the title of I, The Supreme (2005).

Ajayi, Christie Ade (1930–)

Nigerian children's writer, born in Ile-Oluji, Nigeria, and educated in Nigeria, the UK, and the United States. Her main concern has been with the learning needs of Nigerian children and with developing basic vocabulary and reading skills in preschoolers. Her titles include Ade, Our Naughty Little Brother (1975), Emeka and His Dog (1982), and a host of others.

Ajayi, Tolu(walogo) (1946–)

Nigerian poet and writer of fiction. Ajayi was born in Ijebu-Ode, Ogun State and went to school in Nigeria and at the University of Liverpool Medical School in the UK, where he gained his MD in 1970. He then worked as a specialist in psychiatry at Memorial University of Newfoundland, Canada. His novels include The Year (1981), The Lesson (1985), and The Ghost of a Millionaire (1990). His short story "Family Planning" from Eyes of the Night (1992) won the 1990 BBC World Service short story competition, and his other compilation of short stories is titled After a Bad Moon (1995). His collections of poetry include Images of Lives (1992) and Motions and Emotions (1993).

Ajose, Audrey (date of birth not available)

Ajose is from Nigeria and is the author of the popular young adult books Yomi's Adventures (1964) and Yomi in Paris (1966).

Akassa You Mi: A Historical Drama (2001)

A play by Ola **Rotimi.** Performed first in 1977, this play portrays the Koko King of Nembe's (Nigeria's) attack of the Royal Niger company at Akassa in 1895. The Nembe people saw the attack as a necessary reaction for their economic survival after the British took their land and inflicted suffering and poverty upon them. The British saw it as a rebellion.

Aké: The Years of Childhood (1981)

Wole **Soyinka**'s autobiography of the first ten years of his childhood, which begin before World War II and end when he starts grammar school. Soyinka provides striking images of his parents and of the atmosphere of Aké. Soyinka is extremely successful at evoking the internal feelings of childhood, and despite some criticism directed at his construction of conventional society, Aké is greatly admired.

Akello, Grace (date of birth not available)
Akello is from Uganda; she has been the minister of state for gender, labor, and social development in the Ugandan government since 1999, and has been a member of Parliament since 1996. She also is the founder of the Nile Book Service, which sends textbooks to African schools. She is most known for her book My Barren Song or Dar es Salam, published in Tanzania in 1979. She is also the author of Iteso Thought Patterns in Tales (1981) and Self Twice-Removed: Ugandan Woman (CHANGE International Reports: Women and Society), 1982.

Akenhaten: Dweller in Truth (1985)

A historical novel by Naguib **Mahfouz,** translated from Arabic into English in 1998. In an attempt to recreate the events that led to the political and religious split of Egypt, the character Meriamun speaks with the members of Akhenaten's court including his high priest, his chief of security, and his queen Nefertiti. The reader is meant to interpret this information and decide alongside Meriamun what sort of politician and religious icon Akhenaten really was.

Alford, Gwen (date of birth not available)
Alford is from Nigeria. Her collection of poetry titled The Journey Inside (2001) is her first collection and covers issues such as religion, what it means to be a mother, race, search for self-identity, and activism.

Alkali, Zaynab (1950–)
Nigerian novelist, born in Biu, Nigeria, took undergraduate and graduate degrees in English at Bayero University, Kano, and has taught English and African literature at Bayera University and the University of Maiduguri. Among Alkali's novels are the Association of Nigerian Authors award winner for prose fiction in 1985, The Stillborn (1984), and The Virtuous Woman (1987), both of which depict the condition of women in patriarchal African cultures. The protagonists, Li in The Stillborn and Nana Ai in The Virtuous Woman, are examples of African women that counter those of colonial literature, in which African women suffer the alienation of racism and sexism, and of earlier Nigerian novels in which women are defined only by their domestic roles. Despite their counter-narratives these characters are still defined (in the end) by patriarchal institutions. Zaynab is also the author of a collection of short stories titled Cobwebs and Other Stories (1995/1997) and is co-editor of Vultures in the Air: Voices from Northern Nigeria (1995) with Al Imfeld. Her short story "The Vagabond" (1993) was published in The Heinemann Book of African Women Writers (1993, edited by Charlotte Bruner). Zaynab won a prize for the best short story of the year in 1997, and in April 2001 she received the region's highest title available to women: Magiran Garkida.

All for Love: A Novel (2005)

A novel by South African novelist and short-story writer Dan **Jacobson**. In this historical novel set in Europe before World War I, Jacobson portrays the affair of Princess Louise (daughter of the Belgian king) and a lieutenant in the Austrian army named Geza Mattachich. They are not discreet and are banished from Vienna to endure exile and imprisonment. Jacobson narrates the tale in a third-person voice, and offers historical footnotes and excerpts from the memoirs of the Princess and the lieutenant.

All for Oil (2000)

A play by J. P. Clark **Bekederemo**. This play depicts the dispossessed people of the Niger Delta region, who fail to benefit from the resources of the region or the independence they received forty years ago. Specifically, the story follows the history of the Oil Rivers Protectorate and the Royal Niger Company to criticize the actions of the Nigerian ruling class in regard to the oil crisis in the Niger Delta.

Aluko, T(imothy) M(ofolorunso) (1918–)

A Nigerian novelist, Aluko was also an engineer and town planner who began in the Nigerian public service as a colonial officer in 1950 and was a permanent secretary in the Ministry of Works and Transport by 1966 when he left civil service. In 1963 Aluko was awarded the title of Officer, Order of the British Empire (OBE); in 1964 the title of Officer, Order of the Niger (OON); and in 1976 he took his doctorate in municipal engineering.

Aluko's first novel, *One Man One Wife* (1959), deals with the battle between Christians and traditionalists in southern Nigeria. He followed this with a satire of the colonizer's plans for rural economy and assimilation titled *One Man, One Matchet* (1964), which displays Aluko's detailed understanding of Yoruba society. He is also the author of

Kinsman and Foreman (1966), *Chief the Honourable Minister* (1970), *His Worshipful Majesty* (1973), *Wrong Ones in the Dock* (1982), *A State of Our Own* (1986), and *Conduct Unbecoming* (1993). *My Years of Service* (1994) is Aluko's autobiography of his experiences as a university teacher and engineer.

Amadi, Elechi (1934–)

Nigerian novelist and playwright, born in a small village near Port Harcourt in Rivers State, Nigeria, and is from the Ekwerre people of eastern Nigeria. Amadi was educated at Government College, Umuahia, and studied mathematics and physics at University College, Ibadan (B.Sc. Hons. 1959). He has had a career as a teacher and principal, a soldier, a civil-service administrator, and writer-in-residence at Rivers State College.

Amadi's three novels, *The* **Concubine** (1966), *The* **Great Ponds** (1969), and *The Slave* (1978), make up a trilogy that focuses on the role of religion in social and traditional community existence. In these works, individual identity is lost due to ancestral rules, and in many of his works Amadi depicts the loss of individual relationships within an established community. Amadi is also the author of *Estrangement* (1986) and five plays: *Isiburu* (1973), *The Road to Ibadan* (1974), *The Dancer of Johannesburg* (1977), *Peppersoup* (1977), and *The Woman of Calabar* (2002). He has also published *Speaking and Singing* (2003), which is a collection of essays and poems, and a collection titled *Elechi Amadi at 55: Poems, Short Stories, and Papers* was edited by W. Feuser and Ebele Eko and published in 1989. Amadi's narrative of his participation in the Nigeria-Biafra war as a Federal Army officer, as well as a Biafran prisoner, is published in his nonfictional work *Sunset in Biafra* (1973). Amadi is also the author of *Ethics in Nigerian Culture* (1982), and is a Fellow of the Nigerian Academy of Education (2003) and a Member of the Order of the Federal Republic (2003).

Amriika (1999)

A novel by M. G. **Vassanji.** Beginning in the late 1960s in America, Vassanji tells the story of a student from Dar es Salaam named Ramji, who moves to America. Ramji is active in antiwar protests, seeks spiritual meaning, and gets involved in revolutionary activities that haunt him later in the novel, when he is faced with a crossroads of past and present.

Anduru, Agoro (1948–92)

Tanzanian short-story writer. Born in a village on the eastern shores of Lake Victoria in what is now Tanzania, Anduru was educated at local schools. He tells the story of his education and partial deafness in "Without Despair," which is one of the narratives in *A Bed of Roses and Other Writings* (1989). Anduru trained and worked as a radio journalist, and his first short stories were published in the 1970s in Tanzania's weekly newspaper *Sunday News.* His writings, including *Temptation and Other Stories* (1981) and *This Is Living and Other Stories* (1982), depict everyday city life in Tanzania, and uncover superficiality, materiality, and immorality in an attempt to appeal for honesty, decency, loyalty, friendship, and love. Agoro published an article on sign language in the year of his death (1992), titled "The Development of Sign Language in Tanzania," in *East African Sign Language Seminar, Debre Zeit, Ethiopia, August 20–26, 1990* (Helsinki: Finnish Association of the Deaf, 40–41).

Angira, Jared (1947–)

Kenyan poet. Angira studied commerce at the University of Nairobi and edited the literary magazine *Busara,* in which some of his early poetry first appeared. His poetry collections include *Juices* (1970), *Silent Voices* (1972), *Soft Corals* (1973), *Cascades* (1979), *The Years Go By* (1980), *Tides of Time: Selected Poems* (1996), and *Lament of the Silent & Other Poems* (2004). Angira offers humorous satire about the arrogance and delusions of those in power—especially politicians, in works such as "An Evening Liberetto" and "No Coffin, No Grave." Many of Angira's poems also portray feelings of disillusionment due to betrayed hopes for independence, and they also demonstrate his use of poetry to encourage political mobilization against the elite. Angira is currently the Chairman of the Kenya Organisation of Writers Association.

Aniebo, I.N.C. (1939–)

Born in Awka in Anambra State of Nigeria, Aniebo joined the Nigerian army after his secondary education. He was a commissioned officer before he joined the Biafran army as one of its pioneer officers. Discharged from the army after the Nigeria-Biafra war (1967–70), he went to the United States for his undergraduate and graduate degrees. He is currently a teacher of creative writing at the University of Port Harcourt, Nigeria.

In the 1960s Aniebo began to publish short stories in journals, magazines, and newspapers, some of which were later collected in *Of Wives, Talismans and the Dead* (1983) and *Man of the Market: Short Stories* (1994). *Rearguard Actions* (1998) is a collection of eight short stories about the Nigerian civil war and the terrible experiences of people during that time. Aniebo's novels include *The Anonymity of Sacrifice* (1974) and *The Journey Within* (1978). *The Anonymity of Sacrifice* is one of the earliest novels about the Biafran conflict, and it narrates the story of two soldiers fighting on the Biafran front in a manner that uncovers the anonymity of "the unknown soldier" and makes the war more tangible as an individual experience. *The Journey Within* focuses on traditional Igbo life and values, and those characters that resist the confusion between African and European values are the most positive ones for Aniebo. Aniebo focuses on the themes of conflict and infidelity in marriage, human relationships, the cultural conflict between

Africa and Europe, and the superficiality of social structures.

Anowa (1970)

A play by Ama Ata **Aidoo.** The play takes as its inspiration a traditional Ghanaian legend about a woman who disobeys her parents and marries the man she loves. Aidoo investigates the need for compromise and truthfulness in relationships through the characters of Anowa and her lover Kofi. The play comments on the effects of individuality when Anowa and Kofi refuse to associate with one another or the rest of the community, and commit suicide instead.

Anthills of the Savannah (1986)

A novel by Chinua **Achebe.** Set in the imaginary West African country of Kangan, which strongly resembles Nigeria, the novel continues Achebe's examination of political conditions in a representative postcolonial country initiated in *A Man of the People* (1966). Achebe portrays the effect of military rule on a country where democratic processes are undermined, political unrest is replaced by self-serving autocrats, and where constitutional processes are suspended. Achebe rejects international finance capitalism as a reason for Kangan's political problems, and through the experiences and musings of his principal characters he illustrates that the problem is a lack of leadership. The novel is a study of how power corrupts and of how in the end this power destroys itself. The novel demonstrates Achebe's convictions about the role of stories and storytelling that counteracts the forces that threaten oral wisdom with technology.

Anthologies

EAST AFRICA

One of the leading anthologists in East Africa is David Cook, who edited *Origin, East Africa: A Makerere Anthology* (1965),

Poems from East Africa (1971) with David **Rubadiri,** and *In Black and White: Writings from East Africa with Broadcast Discussions and Commentary* (1976). Writers such as **Ngugi wa Thiong'o,** Jonathan Kariara, and John **Ruganda** benefited from Cook's magazine for the Department of English at Makerere University titled *Penpoint,* and from their inclusion in Cook's anthologies. The first East African poetry anthology to contain poems influenced by African literary traditions (as well as experimental ones) was edited by Lennard Okola in 1967 and was titled *Drum Beat: East African Poems. Faces at Crossroads: A "Currents" Anthology* (1971), *Singing with the Night: A Collection of East African Verse* (1974), and *The Debtors: Plays from East Africa* (1977) were edited by Professor of Literature at Egerton University Chris L. Wanjala, who also edited *Attachments to the Sun* (1980) with Douglas Blackburn and Alfred Horsfall. The Students' Book Writing Scheme of the East African Literature Bureau published the first three of Wanjala's anthologies, along with Robert Green's *Just a Moment, God! An Anthology of Verse and Prose from East Africa* (1970), S. N. Waititu and Y. G. Obasa's *Sleepless Nights* (1975), and Peter Waithaka and Sam Mbure's *Flashpoints* (1976). Poets such as Bahadur **Tejani,** Jared **Angira,** and Arnin Kassam, who would go on to publish poems in further anthologies, were introduced in editor Arthur Kemoli's *Pulsations: An East African Anthology of Poetry* (1974), which was published as part of the Book Writing Scheme. Kemoli's anthology also contained some rural popular culture poetry from poets associated with the National Teachers' College, Kyambogo, Uganda, whose work was chosen from the student magazine *Nanga,* and was edited by British author Denis C. Hills.

Government and other professional institutions sometimes also publish anthologies. For example, *The Stranger and Other Stories*

(1989), *Chameleon's Second Delivery* (1985), and *The Winner and Other Stories* (1994) were published by the Kenya Institute of Education. Poetry collections from Kenyan schools such as *Youthful Voices* (1992), *Search for a New Tomorrow* (1993), and *The Secrets of Wisdom* (1994) were edited and published by the British Council, Nairobi. East African Educational Publishers has also produced several anthologies, including *Boundless Voices: Poems from Kenya* (1988), edited by Arthur I. Luvai, and *Tender Memories: Poems and Short Stories* (1989), edited by A. Luvai, W. Kabira, and M. Muluka, while Longman Kenya has published *An Anthology of East African Poetry* (1988), edited by A. D. Amateshe. Heinemann Kenya has also published a number of anthologies.

East African authors who appear most in anthologies are Ngugi wa Thiong'o, Joseph Kariuki, John Ruganda, David Rubadiri, Jared Angira, Grace **Ogot,** Jonathan Kariara, Joseph G. Mutiga, **Taban** Lo Liyong, Samuel N. Mbure, and Benjamin Onyango Ogntu. For example, Jonathan Kariara's poetry appears in *Origin, East Africa,* and *Modern African Prose* (1964), and he co-edited *Introduction to East African Poetry* (1977) with Ellen Kitonga. Poetry by Joseph G. Mutiga appears in *Drum Beat* and *Origin, East Africa,* while *Modern Poetry from Africa* (1963), edited by Ulli Beier and Gerald Moore, contains poetry by Joseph Kariuki. The collection *Nexus* contains poetry by Samuel Mbure, whose work has also been broadcast in the African Poetry program of the Voice of Kenya.

Less recent works like *East African Literature: An Anthology* by Zettersten (1983) and the Longman *Anthology of East African Short Stories* (1988) set a precedent for more recent collections in their focus on the diversity of genres and authors, as well as a combination of both political and personal themes. A culmination of this kind of precedent can be seen in such collections

as *Half a Day and Other Stories: An Anthology of Short Stories from North Eastern and Eastern Africa* (2004). This anthology contains contributions from writers such as Naguib Mahfouz, Eneriko Seruma, Peter Nazareth, Ngugi wa Thiong'o, Fatmata Conteh, Nawal El Saadawi, and M. J. Vassanji. Similarly, a short story collection that focuses on women's writing from East Africa is *Words from a Granary,* edited by Violet Barungi (2001). Other publications, like Angela Smith's *East African Writing in English* (1989), have a more general focus, and also include an overview of the varied roles of the novel, poetry, and drama in East Africa. Collections of interviews, essays, and nonfictional writing also play a role in East African anthologies. *Winging Words* (2004) by Ezenwa Ohaeto is a collection of interviews with African writers and critics, while *Gathering Seaweed: African Prison Writing* (2002) bases its collection on a specific kind of description common to prose, poetry and plays, and includes contributions from Steve Biko, Breyten Breytenbach, Kenneth Kaunda, and Nelson Mandela.

Recent East African poetry anthologies are numerous. A focus on the dialogic aspect of poetry is apparent in Kimani Niogu's *Reading Poetry as Dialogue: An East African Literary Tradition* (2004), as it not only draws on the Gikuyu and KiSwahili verse forms gungu, kmondo, and gi candi, but also includes English translations alongside the original languages. The focus on the importance of the poetry as a verbal art form thus comes across as a part of this anthology. Other new works are collections of poetry such as Margorie Oludhe Macoye's *Make It Sing & Other Poems* (1998), and Edouard Maunick's *It and Island—Poems of the Same Passion* (2002), which focus on individual authors. Editors Okot Benge and Alex Bangirana's *Uganda Poetry—Anthology 2000* (2000) combines established poets with new ones in its compilation and brings together different voices to represent the rich diversity of Ugandan poetry.

SOUTH AFRICA

Because of the settlement of an English-speaking population in South Africa as early as the eighteenth century, the first examples of anthologies appear around 1820 when settlers began to establish printing and publishing businesses. Robert Greig and Thomas **Pringle** were instrumental in the early formation of anthology, and by 1828 R. J. Stapleton published a selection of works from periodicals titled *Poetry of the Cape of Good Hope. The Poetry of South Africa* (1887), edited by Alexander Wilmot, is a good example of an early anthology despite its colonial prejudice. In contrast, Francis Carey **Slater**'s *Centenary Book of South African Verse* (1925) was the first anthology to focus more on poetic traditions from an indigenous perspective and was followed by the *New Centenary Book of South African Verse* (1945). Then came an anthology edited by Roy Macnab and Charles Gulston titled *South African Poetry: A New Anthology* (1948), which was more ambitious and was the first to include a black poet in the work of H.I.E. **Dhlomo.**

The progress of poetic form after World War II is demonstrated in Guy **Butler**'s *A Book of South African Verse* (1959) and Jack **Cope** and Uys Krige's *Penguin Book of South African Verse* (1968). Cope and Krige's anthology includes translations of Afrikaans and black poetry, which is a diverse approach that many anthologies take up. For example, Johan van Wyk et al. take this approach in their *SA in Poësie/SA in Poetry* (1988), as does Stephen **Gray** in the *Penguin Book of Southern African Verse* (1989). *Seven South African Poets* (1971), edited by Cosmo

Pieterse, *Black Voices Shout!* (1974), edited by James **Matthews,** *A Century of South African Poetry* (1981) by Michael Chapman, *The Return of the Amasi Bird: Black South African Poetry 1891–1981* (1982), edited by Tim Couzens and Essop Patel, and *Voices from Within,* edited by Chapman and Achmat **Dangor** (1982), all focus on the work of noteworthy black poets. **Apartheid** in South Africa also provides a theme for many anthologies, such as Ampie Coetzee and Hein Willemse's *I Qabane Labantu: Poetry in the Emergency/Poësie in die Noodtoestand* (1989) and Ari Sitas's *Black Mamba Rising* (1986). Anthologies that focus on women's writing include such works as *Siren Songs* (1989) by Nohra Moerat and *Breaking the Silence* (1990) by Cecily Lockett. More recent South African poetry anthologies reflect the continuation of such earlier foundations. Robert Beold has edited an anthology titled *It All Begins: Poems from Postliberation South Africa* (2003), while Ingrid De Kok and Gus Ferguson edited *City in Words: An Anthology of Cape Town Poems* (2001). Michael Chapman is the editor of *New Century of South African Poetry* (2002), while Arja Salafranca and Alan Finlay are the editors of *Glass Jars among Trees: Prose and Poetry* (2003). Editor Zolani Mkiva has collected poetry from *The Railway Magazine,* written in the late nineteenth and early twentieth centuries by railway workers, in the anthology titled *Railway Poetry* (2001). Forging into the virtual form of poetry, Mike Cope is the editor of "A Virtual Anthology of Some South African Poetry," which can be found at http://www.cope.co.za/Virtual/virtual.htm. Other recent South African poetry anthologies are *Seasons Come to Pass: A Poetry Anthology for Southern African Students,* edited by Es'kia **Mphahlele** with Helen Moffet (2002), and *Operations and Tears: A New Anthology of Malawian Poetry* (2004), which is a collection that harkens back to the years of major political change in Malawi between 1992 and 1994.

Short-story anthologies emerged and developed in a similar manner to poetry anthologies, as an early focus on European and colonial concerns gave way to a more balanced approach with an inclusion of indigenous authors and critiques of the social and political atmosphere. Thus, E. C. Parnwell focuses on colonial aims and ideals in his *Stories of Africa* (1930), while H. C. **Bosman** and C. Bredell in their *Veld-Trails and Pavements* (1949) and Richard **Rive** in his *Quartet: New Voices from South Africa* (1963) demonstrate a change of emphasis. A large number of short-story anthologies are produced for the educational market in South Africa, but a more generally directed anthology is *A Century of South African Short Stories* (1978), edited by Jean Marquard. Marquard's anthology contains a balanced selection of texts, and Martin Trump revised it in 1994. Anthologies that focus on the publication of black writing include works such as *Forced Landing, Africa South: Contemporary Writings* (1980), edited by Mothobi **Mutloatse,** and *Hungry Flames and Other Black African Short Stories* (1986), edited by Mbulelo **Mzamane.** *Sometimes When It Rains* (1987), edited by Ann Oosthuizen, *One Never Knows: An Anthology of Black South African Women Writers in Exile* (1989) by Lindiwe Mabuza, and *Raising the Blinds: A Century of South African Women's Stories* (1990) by Annemarie van Niekerk focus on the publication of women's writing. A more current anthology of women's writing is that of Margaret Daymond, Dorothy Driver, Sheila Meintjes, Leloba Molema, Chiedza Musengezi, Margie Orford, and Nobantu Rasebotsa, who are the editors of *Women Writing Africa: The Southern Region* (2003). Along the lines of the political and literary are collections such as *Writing South Africa: Literature, Apartheid, and Democracy, 1970–1995,* edited by Derek Attridge and Rosemary Jolly (1998), and *Contemporary Jewish Writing in South Africa: An Anthology,* edited by

Claudia Bathsheba Braude (2002). Another recent anthology, edited by Nadine Gordimer but contributed to by authors worldwide, is *Telling Tales* (2004), which is a collection of short stories from twenty-one writers sold to raise funds for the fight against HIV/AIDS in southern Africa.

The anthology *Six One-Act Plays by South African Authors* (1949, no editor) marked the beginning of the dramatic anthology market, and was produced after the Federation of Amateur Theatrical Societies of South Africa held a competition for inclusion in it. In the 1960s and afterward drama was revitalized in South Africa, and resultant anthologies include works such as *Contemporary South African Plays* (1979) by Ernest Pereira; *Theatre One* (1978), *Theatre Two* (1981), and *Market Plays* (1986) by Stephen Gray; *South African People's Plays* (1981) by Robert Kavanagh; Temple Hauptfleisch and Ian Steadman's *South African Theatre: Four Plays and an Introduction* (1984); and Duma Ndlovu's *Woza Afrika!* (1986). Recent additions to this category of anthology include Stephen Gray's *South African Plays* (1993) and *More Market Plays* (1994), collected by John Kani.

Cross-genre anthologies of note include *Towards the Sun* (1950), edited by Roy Macnab; Nadine **Gordimer** and Lionel **Abrahams**'s *South African Writing Today* (1967); and Stephen Gray's *Writer's Territory* (1973). Translations of African authors are included in Andre **Brink** and J. M. **Coetzee**'s *A Land Apart* (1986), while David Bunn and Jane Taylor depict the convergence of politics and art in *From South Africa: New Writing, Photographs and Art* (1987). Specialist anthologies of note are *Reconstruction: 90 Years of Black Historical Literature* (1981), edited by Mothobi Mutloatse; *LIP from Southern African Women* (1983), edited by Susan Brown et al.; and Seagang Tsikang and Dinah Lefekane's *Women in South Africa: From the Heart* (1988).

Other anthology topics that have emerged of late are those that focus on critical essays, popular stories, travel, folklore, and juvenile writing (just to name a few). Many of the anthologies published before 1990 focus on social and political issues associated with apartheid, and these concerns continue to characterize many recent anthologies with postapartheid narratives.

SOUTH-CENTRAL AFRICA

An anthology of Rhodesian poetry titled *Rhodesian Verse: 1888–1938* was published in 1938 by John Snelling, followed by his *A New Anthology of Rhodesian Verse* in 1950. Included in the 1938 anthology is the poetry of A. S. **Cripps,** who speaks of the need for the inclusion of black poets in anthologies, and demonstrates the Rhodesian tendency to resist English modernism in his introduction to the anthology. In contrast, *Poetry in Rhodesia: 75 Years,* published by D. E. Finn in 1968, includes poetry by both black and white writers collected from periodicals like *Rhodesian Poetry* and *Two Tone.* More current anthologies such as *Under the African Skies: Poetry from Zambia* focus on the landscape of contemporary South-Central Africa. Among the many poets included in the collection are Sekelani Banda, Wilmont Benkele, Jennifer Carol, Cheela Chilala, Malama Katulwende, Mercy Khozi, and John Njovu.

New Writing in Rhodesia (1976) is T. O. **McLoughlin**'s anthology of poetry, short stories, and a play, which focuses heavily on black authors. McLoughlin published another anthology of short stories by A. S. Cripps, Doris **Lessing,** Charles **Mungoshi,** and Tsitsi **Dangarembga,** as well as less well-known authors, in *The Sound of Snapping Wires* (1990). Kizito Muchemwa offers a selection of black poets writing in English in his *Zimbabwean Poetry in English* (1978), while Mudereri Kadhani and Musaemura Bonas **Zimunya** published their anthology

And Now the Poets Speak (1981) after (and in celebration of) Zimbabwean independence, while *Songs That Won the Liberation War* (1982) is Alec Pongweni's compilation of Shona and English translation songs that were sung by guerillas and popular musical groups during the liberation war. The collection of short stories from Zimbabwe, *Writing Still: New Stories from Zimbabwe* (2003), continues the tradition of country-based anthologies. It also contains the 2004 Caine Prize–winning short story "Seventh Street Alchemy" by Brian Chikwava. The concern in the anthology is with postindependence Zimbabwe and the issues that arise out of that independence. The placement of poetry alongside plays or short stories continues to be popular in contemporary anthologies. *Short Writings from Bulawayo* and *Short Writings from Bulawayo 2* (2003, 2005), edited by Jane Morris, place stories, poems, and nonfiction pieces that evoke Zimbabwe's second city and its rural surroundings alongside one another. *The Unsung Song: An Anthology of Malawian Writing in English,* edited by Reuben Chirambo (2001), acts as an introduction to contemporary Malawian literature through short stories, poetry, and literary essays. Working with the theme of HIV/AIDS in southern Africa is *Nobody Ever Said AIDS: Poems and Stories from Southern Africa,* edited by Nobantu Rasebotsa, Meg Samuelson, and K. Thomas. This work includes twenty stories and twenty-four poems from forty-two southern African writers regarding the issue of HIV/AIDS. Some of the writers are well known, and others are debuted in the anthology. A lack of Malawi drama induced Mufunanji Magalasi to produce a collection of new plays that would bring modern Malawian drama to a larger audience. The collection contains nine plays by five dramatists and is called *Beyond the Barricades* (2001).

The *Mambo Book of Zimbabwean Verse in English* (1986) by Colin and O-Lan Style offers English translations of Shona and

Ndebele poetry as well as poems by both black and white poets writing after 1950, and a sampling of the poetry that was available to Snelling. Poetry in English and translated into English from Angola, Botswana, Lesotho, Malawi, Mozambique, Swaziland, Tanzania, Zambia, and Zimbabwe is compiled in Musaemura Bonas Zimunya's *Birthright: A Selection of Poems from Southern Africa* (1989). Norm Kitson edited the Zimbabwean Women Writers organization's publication of its members' English poems and short stories in *Anthology* (1994), and it has also published anthologies in Shona and Ndebele. Anthologies of essays and criticism include works such as Doris Lessing's *Time Bites: Views and Reviews* (2004), which contains essays on a wide variety of themes, and A. M. Yakubu's *Sa'adu Zungur: An Anthology of the Social and Political Writings of a Nigerian Nationalist* (1999).

WEST AFRICA

Many West African poetry anthologies offer a selection of materials that have already been published. Some examples of this kind of anthology include *Modern Poetry from Africa* (1963 and new editions), edited by Gerald Moore and Ulli Beier; Kojo Senanu and Theo Vincent's *A Selection of African Poetry* (1976); and Wole **Soyinka**'s *Poems of Black Africa* (1975). In his *West African Verse* (1965), Donatus Nwoga organizes his anthology of published poets based on early foundational poets and more modern ones, which tends to break the material into a study of the movement from colonial to postcolonial in West Africa. A demonstration of the interaction between poetry and social and political statements is apparent in Nwoga's anthology with selections from poets such as Dennis **Osadebey** and Gladys **Casely-Hayford,** while self and social awareness through technically masterful poetry is apparent in selections from L. S. **Senghor,**

Soyinka, Lenrie **Peters,** and Christopher **Okigbo.** A more recent work with similar concerns is Tanure Ojaide's *The New African Poetry: An Anthology,* which is also edited by Tijan M. Sallah.

Anthologies in West Africa are also often compiled based on country, as is Kofi **Awoonor** and G. Adali-Mortty's *Messages: Poems from Ghana* (1971), which focuses on more well-known poets and offers a selection that highlights social and political satire. A more recent collection of Ghanaian poetry is *Face to Face,* which was edited by the Goethe Institute, Accra, in 2004. It is a collection of both short stories and poetry from twelve younger or previously unpublished writers from Ghana. It was inspired by a literary workshop and creative writing competition on the subject of HIV/AIDS that was judged by writers Esi Sutherland-Addy and Amma Darko from Ghana, and writers Lutz van Dijk and Norman Ohler from Germany.

There is a focus on new poets in anthologies published in the 1980s such as *Summer Fires* (1983) and *The Fate of Vultures* (1989), which were initiated by the BBC, and the Nigerian works *Voices from the Fringe* (1988), edited by Harry **Garuba,** and *Rising Voices* (1991), edited by David Cook, Olu **Obafemi,** and Wumi Raji. The collective nature of these last two anthologies demonstrates the way that the anthology form can point to communal narratives and identities. In addition, the publication of these anthologies allowed poets to be involved throughout the publication process, which results in a more collaborative effort. Literary associations show a similar attention to the involvement of authors in the publication processes of their own works, and the critical interaction that happens throughout the production of an anthology is an important part of its literary function. *A Melody of Stones: An Anthology of New Nigerian Writing* (2003) carries the tradition of Nigerian anthology into the twenty-first century. It is edited by Femi

Osofisan, Remi Raji, and Veronica Uzoigwe, and published by the PEN Nigeria Centre.

Recent anthologies of African literature focus on poetry and drama (similar to earlier ones), and women's writing has benefited from the anthology form. *Contemporary African Plays,* edited by Martin Banham and Jane Plastow, includes six plays by authors such as Wole Soyinka, Percy Mtwa, Mbongeni Ngema, Barney Simon, and Ama Ata Aidoo. *Post-Colonial Plays: An Anthology,* edited by Helen Gilbert, mixes well-known texts with unpublished ones to address issues such as race and class relations, gender and sexuality, and political corruption. Contributions to an anthology of women's writing titled *Unwinding Threads: Writing by Women in Africa* were selected and edited by Charlotte H. Bruner as part of the African Writers Series in 1983. A more recent women's writing anthology, *Opening Spaces: An Anthology of Contemporary African Women's Writing,* similarly features short stories by women (selected by Yvonne Vera). It brings together stories by writers from all over Africa that address daily life and contemporary issues. The anthology features women writers such as Ama Ata Aidoo, Melissa Tandiwe Myambo, Norma Kitson, Veronique Tadjo, Farida Karodia, and Gugu Ndlovu. Recent short-story anthologies such as *Under African Skies: Modern African Stories,* edited by Charles R. Larson, and the *Picador Book of African Stories,* edited by Stephen Gray (2000), also demonstrate the importance of the short-story anthology for both classic works and unpublished material. Other recent general African anthologies collect past material, such as *Empire Writing: An Anthology of Colonial Literature 1870–1918* (1998), which is edited by Elleke Boehmer.

Anyidoho, Kofi (1947–)

Ghanaian poet, born in Wheta in the Volta Region of Ghana and was educated at the University of Ghana, Legon (BA), Indiana University (MA), and the University of Texas (PhD). Anyidoho taught primary, middle, and secondary school in Ghana before moving into a university career. He is currently a Professor of Literature in the English Department as well as Director of the School of Performing Arts of the University of Ghana. He has received several awards for his poetry, including the Valco Fund Literary Award, the Langston Hughes Prize, the BBC Arts and Africa Poetry Award, the Fania Kruger Fellowship for Poetry of Social Vision, Poet of the Year (Ghana), and the Ghana Book Award. He was elected a Fellow of the International Academy of Poets in 1974. Some of his poems have been translated into Italian, German, Dutch, and Slavic.

Anyidoho's poetry has been published in many journals and anthologies, and his five published books of poetry are *Elegy for the Revolution* (1978), *A Harvest of Our Dreams* (1985), *Earthchild* (1985), *Ancestral-Logic and Caribbean Blues* (1993), and *Praise Song for the Land* (2002), which includes a CD with readings of the poems. Anyidoho's major themes are public, political, and social concerns, and his poetry is deeply influenced by the traditions and culture of the Ewe people of Ghana. The poetry is elegiac and uncovers the connections, in a traditional African ontological context, between tragedy and comedy, life and death, and sorrow and joy. In his poetry Anyidoho reacts to the dehumanization and torture that characterizes the European colonization of Africa and its peoples, and to the lack of moral rectitude of many postindependence African leaders. He makes his preoccupation with the plight of postindependent Africa explicit in "House-Boy" (in *A Harvest of Our Dreams*): "The dreams of Fanon's wretched of the earth / condense into storms in our mourning sky." Anyidoho is also the editor of a collection of essays titled *Beyond Survival: African Literature and the Search for New Life,* with Abena P. A. Busia and Anne V. Adams (1998). The collection has a literary focus, but also offers a thesis about the role of African-heritage writers in current crises for African peoples as a whole. Another critical work by Anyidoho is *Fontomfrom: Contemporary Ghanaian Literature, Theatre and Film,* which he co-authored with James Gibbs (2000). He has also recently published an article in *Africa Today* titled "The Back without Which There Is No Front" (9/22/2003).

Apartheid

In the South African Nationalist Party electoral platform of 1948, D. F. Malan suggested to the all-white electorate the policy of *apartheid,* which called for the separation of ethnic groups in the Union of South Africa. The Nationalist Party's success due to the apartheid platform meant that white South Africa was ensured control over natural resources like gold, diamonds, and uranium; over the Cape sea route; and domination over the black, "coloured" (what the government called those of mixed race), and Asian minorities.

Due to these obviously undemocratic proceedings, in 1961 South Africa was expelled from the British Commonwealth, and was defined as a republic by an all-white referendum that year. Dr. Hendrik Verwoerd and Nationalist Party prime ministers after him made sure to solidify white control over, as the party defined them, the "non-whites" or "non-Europeans." Such oppression and racism resulted in political unrest that erupted in violence, as in the Sharpeville massacre (1960), the Soweto uprising (1976), and township violence throughout the republic in the 1980s. By the early 1990s, however, many factors contributed to the unfeasibility of apartheid, including years of economic sanctions, a sports boycott, guerilla warfare led mainly by Umkhonto we Sizwe from the military wing of the African National Congress, the Soviet bloc disintegration, and the end of the Cold War. In April 1994 the first all-race elections were held in South Africa, and were won by

ANC leader Nelson Mandela, signifying the end of apartheid.

Because of apartheid's discrimination based on skin color, all South African experiences were not the same, and so it was not possible for there to be a cohesive national South African literature. White South Africans were economically and socially well-off, while the oppression and totalitarian government of a police-state were applied to Africans, coloreds, and Asians. In spite of possibilities for unification that came out of the nonracial slant of the Congress movement and the focus on the oppressed in the **Black Consciousness** movement of the 1970s, one of the cultural results of segregation was the growth of different subliteratures that only became more different as oppression and **censorship** became more marked.

Black South African writing during the apartheid era focused, to a great extent, on the affliction of black communities and how they could retaliate against the subjugation of the apartheid government. Early attempts at resistance through literature, like the work of Sol T. **Plaatje** and others, helped to lay a cornerstone for a future black South African literature, but such early attempts were inhibited by the tactics of colonial government. A unique black South African literature began to emerge out of these early forms in the 1950s, and especially in the periodical press with publications like *Drum* magazine, *Golden City Post,* and *The Classic* that published short stories and articles, which appealed to a wide black urban public. These periodicals also served to help start writers' careers, like those of Bessie **Head,** Arthur Maimane, Todd Matshikiza, James **Matthews,** Bloke **Modisane,** Casey **Motsisi,** Es'kia **Mphahlele,** Nat **Nakasa,** Lewis **Nkosi,** Henry Nxumalo, and Can **Themba.** However, the exile that many authors were sent into after the Sharpeville massacre and the continued repressive attitude of the government led to a decline in such innovative writing by the 1960s.

By the 1970s resistance to the government was rejuvenated by the black labor movement brought about by the Durban strikes of 1973, and the advent of the Black Consciousness movement (led by Steve Biko), which brought about the 1976 Soweto uprising. When the Black Consciousness organizations were banned in 1977, and the labor movement was required to sift through repressive legislation in order to make progress, the literary scene came to the forefront as a vehicle for resistance to apartheid. Out of this era came *Staffrider* magazine and the *Staffrider* Series, which were collections of stories, novels, books of poetry, and anthologies that were based on the material that first appeared in the magazine. This use of literature to voice resistance by focusing on black cultural and social heritage had always been a goal of the Black Consciousness movement, but it also led to the development of writing that addressed issues outside of resistance as well, and appealed to readers across the townships of South Africa and abroad. New publishing and distribution networks were developed that included the dissemination of materials to do with literacy, education, popular history, and literature through book clubs, youth organizations, and street-to-street selling instead of bookshops. This kind of networking and publishing brought writers and readers together in a way that focused on popular culture.

Black Consciousness writing began with the poetry of Sipho Sepamla, Mongane Serote, and Mafika **Gwala** (as the most significant writers), rather than with prose. After the Soweto uprising Sepamla turned chiefly to prose and to the direction of cultural projects; Serote dealt with the psychology of activism in the poetry that he wrote from exile; Gwala formed writers' groups in the township of Mpumalanga where he continued to write; and first publications were put out by poets like Christopher **van Wyk** and Achmat **Dangor.** Performance poetry like that of Ingoapele Madingoane also became important to the reconstitution of the oral poet, and as a form that successfully combined literature and activism. Although novels like those that came out of the Soweto uprising were of importance to black African literature during the apartheid era (e.g., Miriam **Tlali**'s *Amandla,* Mongane **Serote**'s *To Every Birth Its Blood,* Sipho **Sepamla**'s *A Ride on the Whirlwind,* Mbulelo **Mzamane**'s *The Children of Soweto,* and Mothobi **Mutloatse**'s *Mama Ndiyalila*), the short story was the strongest form of black South African prose. The short story was a form that had a political message (as in the stories of Mtutuzeli Matshoba) but was also concerned with the "rediscovery of the ordinary," as Njabulo **Ndebele** has described the pattern he noticed in Joel Matlou's stories, so that literary resistance developed into a kind of resistance that also explored identity and looked toward the future of black South African culture. Part of this forward-looking aspect was also an understanding of the history of black literature that came to be of importance as apartheid was coming to a close. Such an historical understanding was brought about by both an academic and grassroots interest in oral traditions, in the rerelease of foundational texts like those of Plaatje and H.I.E. **Dhlomo,** and in a celebration of what was called the "*Drum* decade."

By the 1980s a popular culture for the people based on the role of literature was developing into what would be known by the mid-1980s and during the tearing down of the regime in the 1990s as the "people's culture." The renewal of organized political resistance headed by the United Democratic Front and the Congress of South African Trade Unions (which both identified with the exiled liberation movement led by the African National Congress) during this era led to the repositioning of black literature. For example, poets like Mzwakhe **Mbuli** (who called for African National Congress–oriented political platforms) were characterized as "people's poets," while black workplace audiences were inspired by the worker poetry and plays that characterized township writers. Also of note is the fact that despite the importance of anti-apartheid literature as a literature of black readers and writers, on an international scale much antiapartheid literature is associated with white South African writers like Alan **Paton,** Nadine **Gordimer,** Athol **Fugard,** or J. M. **Coetzee,** who are themselves aware of the difficult role of the writer who attempts to represent the lives and experiences of subaltern others.

Just as apartheid defined South African writing during its predominance on the political scene, so postapartheid writing is influenced and defined by the political past and experiences after apartheid that led to a more forward-looking perspective. Postapartheid writers focus both on the past, the impact of the past on the present, and the new challenges and promises of the postapartheid era. Joanne Fedler's *The Dreamcloth* (2005) tells the story of a journalist who returns home to Johannesburg in 1994 to deal with her family's past secrets. André Brink deals with postapartheid issues through magical realism and fantasy in his books, for example, *Imaginings of Sand* (1996), *Devil's Valley* (1999), *The Rights of Desire* (2001), *The Other Side of Silence* (2003), *Before I Forget* (2005), and *Praying Mantis* (2005). Farida Karodia tells a story of family troubles during the apartheid era in *Other Secrets* (2000), while K. Sello Duiker (1974–2005) explores the complex social issues that young people face in contemporary South Africa in *Thirteen Cents* (2001) and *The Quiet Violence of Dreams* (2002). Zakes Mda's debut novel *Ways of Dying* (1995) focuses on the continued problems and pain that must be overcome in the postapartheid era, while in *The Heart of Redness* (2000), Mda tells a story about the experiences of those under colonial rule in South Africa, and the importance of the past and personal ancestry to such experiences. Similarly, in *The Madonna of Excelsior* (2002) Mda moves from the 1970s to the present, and follows the transition of South Africa from apartheid to democracy,

demonstrating a hopeful vision of the ways that cooperation can overcome individual conflicts. J. M. Coetzee's *Disgrace* (1999) tackles the portrayal of racial relationships in postapartheid South Africa, while something like *The Smell of Apples* (1993) by Mark Behr looks back both to childhood and to the context of apartheid in the 1970s. In addition to chronicling the hopeful, authors also have begun to deal with the realities of change. In her article titled "South Africa's Black Writers Explore a Free Society's Tensions" in the *New York Times* (June 24, 2002), Rachel Swarns notes that "over the last two years, black writers have begun to examine the world that has emerged since white rule ended in 1994. And in their novels the friction between blacks and whites that has long dominated South African literature takes a back seat. On centre stage now are the awkward adjustments of the post-apartheid era" (Swarns, http://www.nytimes.libaccess.lib.mcmaster.ca; accessed June 24, 2006). Some of the tensions that Swarn notices authors like Phaswane Mpe and his book *Welcome to Our Hillbrow* (2001) dealing with are the return of those who were living in exile during apartheid, the fight to maintain African traditions, the influx of immigrants from nearby countries who come to South Africa to look for work, mental illness, AIDS, homosexuality, Westernization, and continued political corruption. Similarly, in their introduction to a special issue of *Modern Fiction Studies,* "South African Fiction after Apartheid," David Attwell and Barbara Harlow (2000, 3) note that the fields of:

> South African literature since 1990 [are] the experiential, ethical, and political ambiguities of transition: the tension between memory and amnesia. It emphasizes the imperative of breaking silences necessitated by long years of struggle, the refashioning of identities caught between stasis and change, and the role of culture—or representation—in limiting or enabling new forms of understanding.

The focus is both on the past as something that defines the present, and the need to recover issues and voices that have been repressed or discouraged in the past but will contribute to the future of South African literature.

Further Reading

Alexander, Neville. "The Politics of Language Planning in Post-Apartheid South Africa." *Language Problems and Language Planning* 28, no. 2 (2004): 113–30.

Attwell, David, and Barbara Harlow, eds. and introduction. *Special Issue: South African Fiction after Apartheid. MFS: Modern Fiction Studies* 46, no. 1 (2000).

Ballantine, Christopher. "Re-Thinking 'Whiteness'? Identity, Chance, and 'White' Popular Music in Post-Apartheid South Africa." *Popular Music* 23, no. 2 (2004): 105–31.

Barnard, Rita. "Bitterkomix: Notes from the Post-Apartheid Underground." *South Atlantic Quarterly* 103, no. 4 (2004): 719–54.

———, ed. and Grant Farred, ed. and introduction. "After the Thrill Is Gone: A Decade of Post-Apartheid South Africa." *South Atlantic Quarterly* 103, no. 4 (2004): 589–605.

Chambers, David L. "Civilizing the Natives: Marriage in Post-Apartheid South Africa." *Dædalus: Journal of the American Academy of Arts and Sciences* 129, no. 4 (2000): 101–24.

Davis, Geoffrey V. "'The Now Is in Our Hands': Innovation and Reorientation in Post-Apartheid South African Drama." *Anglophonia: French Journal of English Studies* 7 (2000): 165–77.

———. *Voices of Justice and Reason: Apartheid and Beyond in South African Literature.* Amsterdam: Rodopi, 2003.

Diala, Isidore. "Interrogating Mythology: The Mandela Myth and Black Empowerment in Nadine Gordimer's Post-Apartheid Writing." *Novel: A Forum on Fiction* 38, no. 1 (2004): 41–56.

———. "Nadine Gordimer, J.M. Coetzee, and Andre Brink: Guilt, Expiation, and the Reconciliation Process in Post-Apartheid South Africa." *Journal of Modern Literature* 25, no. 2 (2001): 50–68.

Dimitriu, Ileana. "The End of History: Reading Gordimer's Post-Apartheid Novels." *Current Writing: Text and Reception in Southern Africa* 15, no. 1 (2003): 17–37.

Feurle, Gisela. "Madam & Eve: Ten Wonderful Years: A Cartoon Strip and Its Role in Post-Apartheid South Africa." In *Cheeky Fictions: Laughter and the Postcolonial,* ed. and introduction Susanne Reichl and Mark Stein. Amsterdam: Rodopi, 2005, 271–86.

Gallagher, Susan Vanzanten. "The Backward Glance: History and the Novel in Post-Apartheid South Africa." *Studies in the Novel* 29, no. 3 (1997): 377–95.

Graham, Shane. "The Truth Commission and Post-Apartheid Literature in South Africa." *Research in African Literatures* 34, no. 1 (2003): 11–30.

Green, Michael. "Translating the Nation: Phaswane Mpe and the Fiction of Post-Apartheid." *Scrutiny2: Issues in English Studies in Southern Africa* 10, no. 1 (2005): 3–16.

Horrell, Georgie. "Post-Apartheid Disgrace: Guilty Masculinities in White South African Writing." *Literature Compass* 2, no. 1 (2005): 1–11.

Irlam, Shaun. "Unraveling the Rainbow: The Remission of Nation in Post-Apartheid Literature." *South Atlantic Quarterly* 103, no. 4 (2004): 695–718.

Joseph-Vilain, Mélaine. "Magic Realism in Two Post-Apartheid Novels by André Brink." *Commonwealth Essays and Studies* 25, no. 2 (2003): 17–31.

Kamwangamalu, Nkonko M. "The Language Policy/Language Economics Interface and Mother-Tongue Education in Post-Apartheid South Africa." *Language Problems and Language Planning* 28, no. 2 (2004): 131–46.

———. "Language, Social History, and Identity in Post-Apartheid South Africa: A Case Study of the 'Colored' Community of Wentworth." *International Journal of the Sociology of Language* 170 (2004): 113–29.

Lebdai, Benaouda. "J. M. Coetzee's *Disgrace*: Post-Apartheid Questioning of Reconciliation." *Commonwealth Essays and Studies* 23, no. 1 (2000): 27–33.

Lenta, Margaret. "Goodbye Lena, Goodbye Poppie: Post-Apartheid Black Women's Writing."

ARIEL: A Review of International English Literature 29, no. 4 (1998): 101–18.

McKinney, Carolyn. "'A Little Hard Piece of Grass in Your Shoe': Understanding Student Resistance to Critical Literacy in Post-Apartheid South Africa." *Southern African Linguistics and Applied Language Studies* 22, nos. 1–2 (2004): 63–73.

Moslund, Sten Pultz. *Making Use of History in New South African Fiction: An Analysis of the Purposes of Historical Perspectives in Three Post-Apartheid Novels.* Copenhagen: Museum Tusculanum, 2003.

Pechey, Graham. "The Post-Apartheid Sublime: Rediscovering the Extraordinary." In *Writing South Africa: Literature, Apartheid, and Democracy, 1970–1995,* ed. and introduction Derek Attridge and Rosemary Jolly. Cambridge: Cambridge University Press, 1998, 57–74.

Reef, Anne. "Representations of Rape in Apartheid and Post-Apartheid South African Literature." In *Textual Ethos Studies or Locating Ethics,* eds. Anna Fahraeus (introduction) and AnnKatrin Jonsson. New York: Rodopi, 2005, 245–61.

Samin, Richard. "'Burdens of Rage and Grief': Reconciliation in Post-Apartheid Fiction." *Commonwealth Essays and Studies* 23, no. 1 (2000): 19–26.

Spitczok von Brisinski, Marek. "Rethinking Community Theatre: Performing Arts Communities in Post-Apartheid South Africa." *South African Theatre Journal* 17 (2003): 114–28.

Stiebel, Lindy. "The Return of the Native: Lewis Nkosi's Mating Birds Revisitied in Post-Apartheid Durban." In *Still Beating the Drum: Critical Perspectives on Lewis Nkosi,* ed. and introduction Lindy Stiebel and Liz Gunner. New York: Rodopi, 2005, 167–81.

Stotesbury, John A. "Urban Erasures and Renovations: Sophiatown and District Six in Post-Apartheid Literatures." In *Babylon or New Jerusalem? Perceptions of the City in Literature,* ed. and preface Valeria Tinkler-Villani. Amsterdam: Rodopi, 2005, 259–70.

Visser, Irene. "How to Live in Post-Apartheid South Africa." *Wasafiri: The Transnational Journal of International Writing* 37 (2002): 39–43.

Waal, Margriet van der. "The Universe Is Made of Stories, Not Atoms: Narrative Constructions of Identity in Post-Apartheid Fiction." *CDS Research Report* 23 (2005): 93–107.

Wasserman, Herman. "Re-Imagining Identity: Essentialism and Hybridity in Post-Apartheid Afrikaans Short Fiction." *Current Writing: Text and Reception in Southern Africa* 12, no. 2 (2000): 96–112.

Wisker, Gina. "Redefining an African Sky: South African Women's Writing Post-Apartheid." *Kunapipi: Journal of Post-Colonial Writing* 24, nos. 1–2 (2002): 140–54.

Worsfold, Brian. "The Anti-Apartheid Liberal and Post-Apartheid Cultural Resistance: A Critical View of Nadine Gordimer's *The House Gun.*" In *Postcolonialism and Cultural Resistance,* ed. Jopi Nyman and John A. Stotesbury. Joensuu, Finland: Faculty of Humanities, University of Joensuu, 1999, 253–59.

———. "Post-Apartheid Transculturalism in Sipho Sepamla's *Rainbow Journey* and J. M. Coetzee's *Disgrace.*" In *Towards a Transcultural Future: Literature and Society in a "Post"-Colonial World,* ed. Geoffrey V. Davis, Peter H. Marsden, Bénédicte Ledent, and Marc Delrez. New York: Rodopi, 2005, 89–94.

Armah, Ayi Kwei (1939–)

Ghanaian novelist, born to Fanti-speaking parents in Sekondi-Takoradi, the twin harbor city and capital of the Western Region of Ghana. He had his early education at Achimota School, near Accra. He then worked as a Radio Ghana scriptwriter, reporter, and announcer. At the age of nineteen he went to the United States as a scholarship student and acquired postgraduate degrees from Harvard and Columbia. Armah focuses his literary work on the retrieval of the African past for the reinvention of postcolonial Africa. He has taught at universities in North America, including Massachusetts and Wisconsin, and is a resident of Dakar, Senegal, where he combines the writing of fiction with professional translation and university teaching in literature and creative writing. Armah is a scholar, a critic, a university professor, essayist, poet, and short-story writer, but he is known for his novels—of which he has written seven: *The **Beautyful Ones Are Not Yet Born*** (1968), which uncovers government corruption; ***Fragments*** (1970), written in the autobiographical mode about postcolonial African society (represented by Ghana); ***Why Are We So Blest?*** (1972), a portrayal of the contemporary world that examines postcolonial African leaders' preference for European culture; ***Two Thousand Seasons*** (1973), which portrays the African past; *The **Healers*** (1978), a fictional recreation of Akan society; ***Osiris Rising*** (1995), which uses the Isis-Osiris myth cycle to tell a story of love, death, and the promise of creative renewal in modern Africa; and *KMT: In The House of Life, An Epistemic Novel* (2002), which is a historical novel whose narrator translates hieroglyphic texts that were left by Egyptian scribes a millennia ago.

In an essentially autobiographical article, "One Writer's Education" (*West Africa,* August 1985), Armah identifies himself not simply as an Akan, an Ewe, a Ghanaian, and a West African, but "most significantly as an African." Like his compatriot Ama Ata **Aidoo,** he sees Africa as a "community without unity," and his writing, particularly in *Two Thousand Seasons,* insists on a community with unity. Despite Western influences on his style, all of Armah's works express concerns that are uniquely African, and he is able to successfully synthesize style and subject matter.

Further Reading

Lorentzon, Lief. "Ayi Kwei Armah's epic we-narrator. (Postcolonial African Writers)." *Critique: Studies in Contemporary Fiction* 38, no. 3 (1997): 221–34.

Ode Ogede. *Ayi Kwei Armah: Radical Iconoclast: Pitting Imaginary Worlds against the Actual.* Athens: Ohio University Press, 2000. Ogede's goal is to provide an unbiased picture of the thematic and stylistic route Armah has traveled in his development as one of Africa's most gifted and revolutionary novelists.

Petrie, Paul R. "The Politics of Inspiration in Ayi Kwei Armah's *The Healers.*" *Critique: Studies in Contemporary Fiction* 38, no. 4(1997): 279–88.

Wright, Derek. "Ayi Kwei Armah and the Significance of His Novels and Histories." *IFR: International Fiction Review* 17, no. 1 (1990): 29–40.

Arrow of God (1964; rev. 1974)

A novel by Chinua **Achebe.** The novel develops the theme, initiated in Achebe's first novel, ***Things Fall Apart*** (1958), of the impact on Igbo traditional life of British imperial-colonial rule. Set in eastern Nigeria during the period of the entrenchment of colonial rule, it tells the tragic story of Ezeulu, chief priest of the god Ulu, who in trying to reconcile the demands of his god and his quest for personal power brings calamity on himself, his family, and his clan. A clear narrative, highly allusive English, and the use of local imagery and folk literary materials characterize Achebe's style. His vision is neutral, ironic, and tragic in a novel that deals with problems of traditionalism under stress from Western concepts and ideals.

Arrowheads to My Heart (1999)

A collection of poems by Tayo Peter **Olafioye.** These poems explore the political and literary implications of national identity, as well as personal interpretations of the self in everyday life, and satirical observations of California life embedded in Nigerian traditional imagery.

Atta, Sefi (1964–)

Born in Lagos Nigeria, and grew up there. Sefi has worked as an accountant in the United Kingdom and the United States, and graduated from a creative writing program at

Antioch University in Los Angeles. Her short stories have won awards from the Red Hen Press, Zoetrope, the Commonwealth Broadcasting Association, and the BBC. She has won the BBC's African Performance Competition for plays twice, and in 2002 the first part of her novel *Everything Good Will Come* was short-listed for the MacMillan Writers Prize for Africa. *Everything Good Will Come* (2004/2005) is a novel about a friendship between two Nigerian girls who deal with the traditional system in two different ways during the military rule of the 1970s. Sefi has also published a number of online short stories, in addition to short stories in *The Penguin Book of New Black Writing in Britain* (2000), *Best of Carve Magazine* (2002), *Crab Orchard Review* (2004), and *Roar Softly and Carry a Great Lipstick* (2004).

Awoonor, Kofi (Nyedevu) (1935–)

Awoonor, who was previously known as George Awoonor-Williams, is a Ghanaian poet, novelist, and critic, who was born in Wheta Ghana, studied at Achimota School, the University of Ghana, the University of London, and at the State University of New York at Stony Brook, where he gained a PhD in English and Comparative Literature. After he held the positions of Chair of the Department of Comparative Literature at SUNY Stony Brook and head of the Department of English and Dean of the Faculty of Arts at University of Cape Coast, Awoonor was appointed Ghana's ambassador to Brazil in 1985 and to Cuba in 1989, and has also served as Ghana's representative in the United Nations. He has acted as a contributing editor to *Transition* and he received the National Book Council Award for poetry in 1979.

Awoonor uses traditional Ewe folklore and poetry in his work. His first volume of poetry, titled **Rediscovery** (1964), was followed by *Night of My Blood, Messages: Poems from Ghana* (a co-edited volume of Ghanaian poetry), and his novel *This Earth,*

My Brother (all 1971). Awoonor also published two short plays, *Ancestral Power* and *Lament* (1972), before returning to poetry with his third volume *Ride Me, Memory* (1973), and a translation of Ewe oral poetry by Henoga Vinoko and Komi Ekpe in *Guardians of the Sacred Word* (1974). Arrested for aiding a political fugitive on his return from the United States to Ghana, Awoonor's experience as a prisoner in Ghana's Ussher Fort Prison is visible in works that followed such as *The House by the Sea* (1978) and *Until the Morning After: Collected Poems* (1987). His poetry deals with larger social topics such as the effects of colonialism, political corruption, and national identity, but does so in a very personal manner. Awoonor's physical and psychological separation from his early life in Africa and the Western influences upon his life come through in *Night of My Blood*, while in *Ride Me, Memory* he portrays his experiences in the United States and the connections he finds between the sufferings of African-Americans and Africans. In *The House by the Sea* Awoonor depicts his travels through America, his return to Ghana, his imprisonment, and his hopes for the future, while in *This Earth, My Brother* he returns to many of the themes emphasized in his poetry—especially that of political corruption following Ghanaian independence. Upset by the hypocrisy of a corrupted postindependence Ghana, Awoonor attempts to reconcile expectations and realities in *This Earth, My Brother*, while in his second novel, *Comes the Voyager at Last* (1992) he tells a mythic tale of the return of a slave from the New World to his native land. He has also published *The Latin American & Caribbean Notebook* (1993), a collection of poetry woven with the rhythmic and metaphorical power of Ewe and other African traditions, and *Herding the Lost Lamb* (2002), another book of poetry. He is a recipient of the National Book Council Award for poetry (2001) and served as President of the African Literature Association (1998–1999).

Awoonor offers a critical perspective in *The Breast of the Earth: A Critical Survey of Africa's Literature, Culture and History* (1975), which comprises essays on African writers, music, oral literature, art, and politics that mirror Awoonor's own focus on African traditional culture in his poetry and fiction. He is also the author of political commentary: *The Ghana Revolution: A Background Account from a Personal Perspective* (1984), *Ghana: A Political History from Pre-European to Modem Times* (1990), and *Africa: The Marginalised Continent* (1994).

Further Reading

Elimimian, Isaac. *Theme and Style in African Poetry.* Lewiston, NY: Edwin Mellen Press, 1991.

Kolawole, Mary. "Kofi Awoonor as a Prophet of Conscience." *African Languages and Cultures* 5, no. 2 (1992): 125–32.

McKoy, Sheila Smith. "'This Unity of Spilt Blood': Tracing Remnant Consciousness in Kofi Awoonor's *Comes the Voyager at Last.*" *Research in African Literatures* 33, no. 2(2002):194–209.

B

Bâ, Amadou Hampâté (1901–91)

Bâ was born in Bandiagara, Mali, to a Fula Muslim family, and was brought up to adhere to the Muslim teachings of mystical master Tierno Bokar. He went to a francophone primary school and worked in colonial administration as junior clerk. While involved with the French colonial research institute based in Dakar (IFAN), Bâ searched for ethnographic texts and worked with colonial historians and ethnographers to produce publications on this material. He became Director of the new Malian Institute for Research in Human Sciences and an Ambassador to UNESCO in the 1960s. His understanding of the importance of old age and oral tradition led him to edit, transcribe, and translate texts from Fula in collaboration with his colleagues (*Koumen,* 1961, with Germaine Dieterlen; *Kaîdara,* 1968, with Lilyan Kesteloot). He also wrote and published some of the traditional myths in *Njeddo Dewal* (1985). Bâ's novel is titled *L'Etrange destin de Wangrin* (1973; trans. *The Fortunes of Wangrin,* 1999), and depicts the humorous travels of an interpreter who turns out to also be a thief. Later in his life Bâ returned to Abidjan to focus on teaching an Islam faith that is in conversation with other religious beliefs from around the world. He also wrote *Amkoullel, L'enfant peul* (1991), an autobiography that also uses his ethnographic knowledge.

Further Reading

Austen, Ralph A. "From a Colonial to a Postcolonial African Voice: *Amkoullel, l'enfant peul.*" *Research in African Literatures* 31, no. 3 (2000): 1–17.

Grodz, Stanislaw "Towards Universal Reconciliation: The Early Development of Amadou Hampâté Bâ's Ecumenical Ideas." *Islam and Christian Muslim Relations* 13, no. 3 (2002): 281–302.

Harrow, Kenneth W. "Under the Cover of the Way: A Feminist Reading of Hampâté Bâ's *Kaîdara.*" *Research in African Literatures* 31, no. 3 (2000): 18–26.

Bâ, Mariama (1929–81)

Senegalese novelist writing in French. Bâ's first novel drew international attention when it was published in 1979, just two years before her death. The literary quality of that first novel, *Une si longue lettre* (**So Long a Letter,** 1981) is added to its pioneering nature, as Bâ was among the very first female novelists from sub-Saharan Africa to explore the experience of Muslim African women (another Senegalese writer, Aminata Sow-Fall, produced her novel *La Grève des Bàttu; The Beggar's Strike,* 1981, in the same year). Despite Bâ's insistence that *So Long a Letter* was not closely autobiographical, the outline of its heroine's life does follow Bâ's own. Born in Dakar, Senegal, the daughter of a civil servant (later, Senegal's first minister of health), Bâ married a parliamentarian, from whom she separated after bearing nine children. A primary schoolteacher and later schools inspector, Bâ became a prominent activist in Senegalese women's associations. *So Long a Letter* won the first Noma Award in 1980 for writing published in Africa and soon appeared in more than a dozen translations. Bâ died, after a long illness, shortly before the publication of her second novel, *Un chant écarlate* (1981; *Scarlet Song,* 1986). *Scarlet Song* deals with cross-cultural marriage and follows the difficulties of a young Frenchwoman, Mireille, as she adjusts to an African value system and deals with the inability of her Senegalese husband, Ousmane, to find cultural unity in their marriage.

Further Reading

Azodo, Ada Uzoamaka. *Emerging Perspectives on Mariama Bâ: Postcolonialism, Feminism, and Postmodernism.* Trenton, NJ: Africa World, 2003.

Dubek, Laura. "Lessons in Solidarity: Buchi Emecheta and Mariama Bâ on Female Victim(izer)s." *Women's Studies: An Interdisciplinary Journal* 30, no. 2 (2001): 199–223.

Gueye, Medoune. "Reading the Postcolonial Paradigm in Mariama Bâ and Simone Schwarz-Bart: Resistance and Negotiation." *Bridges: An African Journal of English Studies/Revue Africaine d'Etudes Anglaises (Bridges)* 9 (2003): 105–26.

Reyes, Angelita. *Mothering across Cultures: Postcolonial Representations.* Minneapolis: University of Minnesota Press, 2002.

Bacchae of Euripides, The (1973)

This play by Wole **Soyinka** was commissioned by the National Theatre of Great Britain in 1971 and was adapted in 1973. It depicts a fifth-century Hellas that suffers from slave labor and state-controlled Eleusinian mysteries that can only be solved by the cathartic and democratizing force of Dionysus (a foreign god who is the younger brother of the Yoruba deity Ogun in this version of the play). Humor juxtaposed with brief references to Nietzsche and Frazer subtly hints at the Afro-Asiatic roots of Greek civilization. The conclusion Soyinka reaches about the martial puritanism of Attica is equally analogous to contemporary Nigeria's state corruption.

Baderoon, Gabeba (1969–)

Gabeba grew up in Crawford, Athlone, and attended Livingstone High School in Claremont. She received a doctorate in English and Media Studies from the University of Cape Town, with a thesis on images of Islam in South African media and art. She has published on the topic of representations of Islam, and has lectured in universities in South Africa, Europe, and the United States. Gabeba is the author of three collections of poetry, *The Dream in the Next Body* (2005), *The Museum of Ordinary Life* (2005), and *A Hundred Silences* (2006). Her poetry also appears in the anthology *Ten Hallam Poets* (2005), and in translation in the compilations *Poetry on the Road* (2005) and *Weltklang—Nacht der Poesie* (2005). *The Dream in the Next Body* contains poems written while Gabeba lived in Cape Town, Sheffield, and a university town in Pennsylvania. The poems capture individual moments that hold both specific and wider resonations.

Bandele-Thomas, Biyi (1967–)

Also known as Biyi Bandele, this Nigerian poet, playwright, and novelist was born in Kafanchan, northern Nigeria, studied drama at Obafemi Awolowo University, Ile-Ife (1987–90), and lives in London, writing and working for several periodical publications and the BBC. Bandele-Thomas is the author of a collection of poetry, *Waiting for Others* (1989), which won the British Council Lagos

Award; six plays, *Rain* (1989), winner of the International Student Playscript Competition, *Marching for Fausa* (1993), *Resurrections* (1994), *Two Horsemen* (1994), which was selected as the Best New Play at the London New Play Festival in 1994, *Death Catches the Hunter*, and *Me and the Boys* (1995); three novels, *The Man Who Came in from the Back of Beyond* (1991), *The Sympathetic Undertaker and Other Dreams* (1991), and *The Street* (1999); and several plays for radio and television. In 1997 his stage adaptation of Chinua **Achebe**'s ***Things Fall Apart*** was performed in Leeds and London. He is also the author of an adaptation of Aphra Behn's *Oroonoko,* which was presented by the Royal Shakespeare Company in 1999.

Bandele-Thomas's satirical novels depict the corruption and militarism of contemporary Nigerian politics, and the interconnectedness of his stories draws the reader into a labyrinth-like narrative. Bandele-Thomas's characters struggle with reality and attempt to understand their moral identities in *The Man Who Came In,* which incorporates multiple narratives and deals with political and military violence, and *The Sympathetic Undertaker,* which is in some senses a continuation of the first novel. In *The Street,* Bandele depicts a multiracial community in Brixton, South London. The book follows a group of characters, in the midst of which is Nehushta, who develops her relationship with her father after he awakes from a long coma. Despite a tendency toward pessimism in his plays and novels, Bandele-Thomas also offers an underlying hope for an end to human suffering.

Further Reading

Ehling, Holger. "Biyi Bandele-Thomas: Coming Out Grinning." *Matatu: Journal for African Culture and Society* 23–24 (2001): 91–95.

Kehinde, Ayo "A Parable of the African Condition: The Interface of Postmodernism and Postcolonialism in Biyi Bandele-Thomas's Fiction." *Revista Alicantina de Estudios Ingleses* 16 (2003): 177–90.

Bavino Sermons (1999)

Poems by Lesego **Rampolokeng.** In these poems Rampolokeng considers the damage caused by power-hungry people throughout time, in South Africa, and in the world. He turns the violence of Soweto into poetic images that hope for survival.

Beatification of Area Boy, The (1995)

A play by Wole **Soyinka.** Set in an area outside a street market, we encounter a number of characters in vignettes dramatizing street crime and other social problems during the Nigeria-Biafra war (interspersed with satirical songs). Soyinka subtitled the play "A Lagosian Kaleidoscope" because of the nature and scale of its depiction of Nigerian life under the military regimes of the 1980s and 1990s. The play premiered in Britain while Soyinka was living in self-imposed exile.

Beautyful Ones Are Not Yet Born, The (1968)

In Ayi Kwei **Armah**'s first novel, the bodily and moral corruption of Accra fascinates and repels "the man," a railway clerk who refuses bribes and faces the resentment of his wife and colleagues as a result. Accra is characterized by the fading nationalist ideals of Kwame Nkrumah, the continued poor quality of life for the majority, and the excessive consumption of goods by the upper classes (especially the minister Koomson). "The man" and his friend "the Teacher" become disillusioned, and "the Teacher" chooses to live his life in seclusion.

Beggar, The, The Thief and the Dogs, and Autumn Quail (2000)

Three novels by Naguib **Mahfouz.** These short novels are set in 1950s postrevolutionary Egypt and depict the country as it adapts to change. The stories all hold relevance for their contemporary context, and comment in one way or another on the Egyptian government. *The Beggar* tells the story of a man who has a number of affairs and becomes disconnected from his family as a result. It highlights the danger of believing that actions do not hold consequences, and the alienation that can result from such an approach. *The Thief and the Dogs* portrays a thief who is released from prison after the revolution, only to cause his own destruction through his attitude of blame. *Autumn Quail* takes as its subject the purge following the revolution, the victim of which is the corrupt official portrayed in this story.

Bekederemo, J(ohn) P(epper) Clark (1935–)

Nigerian poet and playwright; originally published under the name of J. P. Clark. Born of both Urhobo and Ijo ancestral origins, Bekederemo received his early education at the Native Administration School and the prestigious Government College in Ughelli, and his bachelor's degree in English at the University of Ibadan, where he edited various magazines, including the *Beacon* (1956–) and *The Horn* (1957–). When he graduated Bekederemo worked as an information officer in the Ministry of Information in the old Western Region, as features editor of the *Daily Express*, as a research fellow at the Institute of African Studies, University of Ibadan, and a professor of English at the University of Lagos until his retirement in 1980. In 1982 he founded, with his wife Ebun Odutola (a professor and former director of the Centre for Cultural Studies at the University of Lagos), the Pec Repertory Theatre in Lagos. Since his retirement Bekederemo has held visiting professorial appointments at several institutions, including Yale and Wesleyan University in the United States.

Bekederemo's poetic works are *Poems* (1961), a set of forty lyrics that treat various themes; *A Reed in the Tide* (1965), poems that speak of the poet's indigenous African background and his travel experience in America and other places; *Casualties: Poems 1966–68* (1970), a depiction of the violence of the Nigeria-Biafra war; *A Decade of Tongues* (1981), seventy-four poems, all except "Epilogue to Casualties" (dedicated to Michael Echeruo) previously published; *State of the Union* (1981), which explores sociopolitical events in Nigeria; *Mandela and Other Poems* (1988), which deals with aging and death; *A Lot from Paradise* (1999), which looks to the past and contains twenty-five poems divided into two sections; and *Of Sleep and Old Age* (2004), poems about aging, death, dying, and questions of religion. The development of Bekederemo's poetic voice is visible in his early stage of trial and experimentation, exemplified by such juvenilia as "Darkness and Light" and "Iddo Bridge"; his imitative stage, in which he appropriates such Western poetic conventions as the couplet measure and the sonnet sequence, exemplified in such lyrics as "To a Fallen Soldier" and "Of Faith"; and his individualized stage, in which he attains the maturity and originality of form visible in such poems as "Night Rain," "Out of the Tower," and "Song." Bekederemo's poetic themes include violence and protest (*Casualties*), institutional corruption (*State of the Union*), the beauty of nature (*A Reed in the Tide*), European colonialism ("Ivbie" in *Poems*), and humanity's inhumanity (*Mandela and Other Poems*), and he draws his imagery from an interweaving of indigenous African and Western literary traditions. In addition, Bekederemo is the author of an autobiography in poetic form that describes his childhood by the Niger Delta, titled *Once Again a Child* (2004).

Bekederemo's dramas include *Song of a Goat* (1961), a tragedy in the Greek classical mode in which the impotence of Zifa, the protagonist, causes his wife Ebiere and his brother Tonye to have an illicit affair that results in suicide; *The Masquerade* (1964), a sequel in which Dibiri's rage leads to the death of his suitor Tufa; *The Raft* (1964), in which four men drift down the Niger aboard a log raft; *Ozidi* (1966), an epic drama rooted in Ijaw saga; *The Boat* (1981), a prose drama that documents Ngbilebiri history; *All for Oil* (2000), which tells the story of the deprived inhabitants of the Niger Delta region; and *The Wives Revolt* (1991), a comedy that represents wives against husbands in an argument over a compensation fee paid by the oil company. Bekederemo's plays draw heavily from the Greek classical mode (especially the early ones), employ fantastical stage devices (such as the disintegration of the raft on the stage in *The Raft*), and challenge and engage the audience with their poetic quality and their combination of foreign and local imagery.

Bekederemo's other works include his translation of the *Ozidi Saga* (1977), an oral literary epic of the Ijaw; his critical study *The Example of Shakespeare* (1970), which discusses his aesthetic views about poetry and drama; his journalistic essays in the *Daily Express, Daily Times,* and other newspapers; and his travelog *America, Their America* (1964), which criticizes American society and its values. As one of Africa's preeminent and distinguished authors, Bekederemo continues to be an important international figure in literary affairs. In 1991 he received the Nigerian National Merit Award for literary excellence, received an honorary doctorate from the University of Benin, and saw the Howard University publication of *The Ozidi Saga* and *Collected Plays and Poems 1958–1988.*

Further Reading

Okpewho, Isidore. "The Art of *The Ozidi Saga.*" *Research in African Literatures* 34, no. 3 (2003): 1–26.

Ben, in the World (2000)

Doris **Lessing**'s sequel to her novel *The Fifth Child.* In this sequel Ben Lovatt explores his role in the world, and investigates whether a similar fear of him as that he grew up with exists in the world. In his journey, which takes him to France, Brazil, and the Andes, he meets with people who are sympathetic and people who take advantage of him. Lessing portrays Ben's journey as one that searches for identity and leads to disaster.

Ben Jelloun, Tahar (1944–)

Novelist, essayist, and poet writing in French, Ben Jelloun was born in Morocco and raised in Fès, Tangiers, and Rabat, where he read philosophy. A member of the leftist Union of Moroccan Students who staged the 1965 student uprising, he was drafted into the army after the Moroccan government reintroduced compulsory military service as a means to subdue rebellious youth. He wrote his first poem, "L'Aube des dalles," while in El Hajeb's and Ahermoumou's military barracks between 1966 and 1967. When he returned to civilian life in 1968, he accepted a teaching position in Tétouan; later he was transferred to Casablanca, where he wrote the draft of his first novel, *Harrounda* (1973), and contributed to Abdellatif Lâabi's literary journal *Souffles.* Since 1971, the date of the publication of *Hommes sous linceul de silence,* he has lived in Paris. He is the author of an anthology of Moroccan poetry, *La Memoire future: Anthologie de la nouvelle poésie du Maroc* (1976), short stories, and poems, but he is best known for his novels, including *Moha le fou, Moha le sage* (1978), *La Prière de l'absent* (1981), and *La Nuit sacrée* (1987; *Sacred Night,* 1989), for which he was awarded the Prix Goncourt.

The exile and solitude he experienced both in Morocco and France influence Ben Jelloun's work. *La Reclusion solitaire* (1976), *La Plus haute des solitudes* (1977), and *Hospitalité française* (1984) explore the isolation and alienation of immigration from North Africa to France over the last thirty years. In *L'Ecrivain public* (1983) and *L'Enfant de sable* (1985; *Sand Child,* 1987), characters' alienation from themselves causes solitude and anguish. Solitude is also at the center of *Jour de silence ... Tanger* (1990), the story of a forgotten elderly man. Ben Jelloun critiques gender relationships in Maghrebi societies in all of his work, from his first novel *Harrounda* through to *Les Yeux baissés* (1991) and a recent collection of short stories, *Le Premier amour est tojours Ie dernier* (1995). Ben Jelloun is also the author of *Le Racisme tel qu'explique a ma fille* (*Racism, as Explained to My Daughter,* 1998), and *Islam Explained* (2004), both informative and important works of explication.

Ben Jelloun reaches beyond the Moroccan experience in some of his recent novels, which deal with human dignity and social justice on a larger scale. *L'Homme rompu* (1994) is dedicated to Indonesian novelist Pramoedya Ananta Toer and deals with the theme of corruption; the short stories of *L'Ange aveugle* (1992) depict life in the south of Italy; while *Les Raisins de la galére* (1996) tackles injustice and intolerance. *Corruption* (1996) is a tale of modern-day morality that follows Mourad, a Moroccan man whose honesty goes unappreciated until he finally gives in to the temptation of corruption; *La nuit de l'erreur* (1997) builds on folklore and imagination by merging the traditions of the tale and the novel; *Cette aveuglante absence de lumière* (*This Blinding Absence of Light,* 2002) describes the desert concentration camps in which King Hassan II of Morocco held his political enemies; while *Last Friend: A Novel* (2006) is a story of friendship and betrayal between two young men, and is set in twentieth-century Tangier.

Ben-Abdallah, Mohammed (1944–)

Ghanaian dramatist. Of mixed North African and Ghanaian descent, Mohammed Ben-Abdallah was born in Kumasi. He was educated and had early work experience in Accra, Kumasi, and Legon; later he went abroad to earn postgraduate qualifications in theater at the Universities of Georgia and Texas in the United States. He returned in 1982 with a doctorate, already a playwright and director, to teach at the School of Performing Arts, University of Ghana, Legon. During the next ten years he held ministerial-level offices in culture and education in the Rawlings government and was the first Chair of the National Commission on Culture. In office he did not hesitate to implement programs he believed in, even though they were controversial or unpopular.

Ben-Abdallah's roles as a playwright, teacher, and political activist cannot be disassociated from one another, as his concerns embrace classroom, national, and continental issues. He is the author of children's plays based on Ananse stories; as a pan-Africanist he draws on the work of Frantz Fanon; and he encourages the use of African languages. Ben-Abdallah's plays analyze historical, political, and social issues in a controversial and sometimes scandalous mode. *The Trial of Mallam Ilya* (1987) takes place in recent Ghanaian history; *The Verdict of the Cobra* (1987) explores regional tensions; *The Witch of Mopti* (1989) depicts supernatural power; *The Fall of Kumbi* (1989) draws on the controversy about the origin of the Ashanti nation; *Ananse and the Golden Drum: A Play for Children* (1994) focuses on young adult folklore. Ritual, dance, music, and storytelling conventions provide the structure of Ben-Abdallah's work and connect it to a national tradition. He supports an authentic African theater, which he believes should have meaning for its target audience and should deconstruct barriers through a broad social appeal as well.

Ben-Abdallah's later plays are indicative of the passage of time and of his experience in government. He bases *Land of a Million Magicians* (1993), which he wrote and directed for a summit of the Non-Aligned Movement, loosely on Bertolt Brecht's *Good*

Woman of Setzuan. A character-narrator, an emphasis on the variety of national cultural traditions, and a main central issue (in this instance strategies for development) are characteristic of Ben-Abdallah's techniques for theatrical emphasis. He also emphasizes the contrast between a performed and published play as the version for production has an upbeat ending, while the published text has a downbeat ending.

Beti, Mongo (1932–2001)
(pseudonym of Alexandre Biyidi)
Novelist writing in French. Educated in Cameroon and France, Beti taught in French *lycées* until 1994. Publicly critical of Ahmadou Ahidjo and Paul Biya, the first two presidents of Cameroon, he was permitted to visit his country only briefly in 1961 and 1991. It is useful to look at Beti's literary production in two parts: before independence in 1960 and after. In the preindependence period he published a short story, "Sans haine, sans amour" (1952), and a novel, *Ville cruelle* (1954), under the pen name of Eza Boto, and as Mongo Beti, *Le Pauvre Christ de Bomba* (1956; The **Poor Christ of Bomba,** 1971), *Mission terminée* (1957; **Mission to Kala,** 1964), and *Le Roi miraculé* (1958; *King Lazarus,* 1960). These anticolonial novels portray young men who attempt success on their own terms in a society that teaches useless knowledge in French schools for unproductive travel, rather than traditional African values. The role that these works played in the mounting opposition to colonialism made them important international works and literary models. Beti, along with Ferdinand **Oyono**, also influenced the trend toward realism in the African novel in French during this period.

Between 1960 and 1994, Beti taught and lived in Rouen, where he published his pamphlet *Main basse sur le Cameroun* (1972), which was critical of Cameroon's lack of freedom, one-party system, and the relationship between government and French profiteers. Beti returned to fiction when his pamphlet was seized by the French authorities, and in 1974 he published *Perpétue ou L'habitude du malheur* (**Perpetua and the Habit of Unhappiness,** 1978), in which the life of a bright young girl is a metaphor for the fate of the Cameroonian populace under Ahidjo. *Remember Ruben* (1974; trans. 1980) recalls Ruben Um Nyobé, a national hero killed in 1958, while in *La Ruine presque cocasse d'un polichinelle* (1979; *Lament for an African Pol,* 1985) young revolutionaries succeed in deposing an unfit chief. In *Les Deux Mères de Guillaume Ismaël Dzewatama, futur camionneur* (1983) and *La Revanche de Guillaume Dzewatama* (1984), a white woman encourages her husband and his son to resist the corrupt regime, but this optimism disappears in *L'Histoire du fou* (1994), which lacks any hope that the government can fix Cameroon's problems. Beti also published a number of articles that uncovered corruption and injustice in Camroon in the journal he edited between 1978 and 1991 titled *Peuples noirs, peuples africains. Trop de soleil tue l'amour* was published in 1999, and *Branle-bas en noir et blanc* in 2000, both of which have been called "texts inspired by the rediscovery of the land of his birth, in what might be called a powerful third phase of his literary production" (Ambroise Kom, "Remember Mongo Beti [1932–2001]. [In Memoriam: Mongo Beti]," *Research in African Literatures* [33, no. 2 (2002): 2]). Not long before his death, Mongo Beti worked with a group of educators to establish a radio station, Radio Alternance, to promote creativity and freedom of expression. *Remember Mongo Beti* (2003) is a memorial by Prof. Ambroise Kom, and *Mongo Beti parle* (2001) is a conversation held with Ambroise Kom and recorded for publication before Mongo died.

Bikoroa Plays, The (1981, 1985)
A collection of three plays by John P. Clark **Bekederemo.** The plays included in this

collection are *The Boat, The Return Home,* and *Full Circle.* They were first performed in 1981 and in 1985 at the University of Lagos and the National Theatre of Nigeria. *The Boat* unfolds Ngbilebiri history in the form of prose drama, while *The Return Home* is set in the 1920s, and *Full Circle* is set in the 1950s.

Biography and Autobiography

EAST AFRICA

Biography and autobiography comprise texts such as prison diaries, travel narratives, letters, and accounts of childhood and the impact of European ideology on African identity. In East Africa, these types of narratives are important in relation to the interaction between politics and instructional texts. Biographies of import from an earlier period are those such as the account of Ham Mukasa of Buganda written by Ugandan Catherine Sebuliba and published in *The Uganda Journal* (23, no. 2) in 1959, and the description of Mwalimu Julius Kabarage Nyerere in *Freedom and After* (1963) by Tom Mboya. Early autobiographies include those such as Permenas Githendu Mockerie's *An African Speaks for His People* (1934) and Mugo Gatheru's *Child of Two Worlds* (1964). More recently, Waris Dirie's *Desert Flower: The Extraordinary Life of a Desert Nomad* (2001) outlines the life of a child born into a traditional family of tribal desert nomads in East Africa. Aidan Hartley's *The Zanzibar Chest* (2003) tells of the author's family and his childhood and adulthood as a journalist in Africa. Joseph Mungai writes of his life as a medical researcher and former vice-chancellor of the University of Nairobi, as well as his work with HIV/AIDS. Meena Alexandre's *Fault Lines: A Memoir* honors the tenth anniversary of the postcolonial writer, with a foreword by **Ngugi wa Thiong'o** (2003), while on a more biographical note Parviz

Morewedge's *The Scholar between Thought and Experience: A Biographical Festschrift in Honor of Ali A. Mazrui* (2001) honors Mazuri's work and focuses on his multifaceted treatment of cultural studies. A biography of Ngugi wa Thiong'o, simply titled *Ngugi wa Thiong'o,* puts his work in context and traces his career in relation to the way that he has shaped culture in East Africa through the 1960s to 1980s and beyond.

Political autobiographies are numerous, and some important examples include Bildad Kaggia's *Roots of Freedom, 1921–63* (1975), Jomo Kenyatta's *Suffering without Bitterness* (1967), which describes Kenya's fight for freedom, and trade unionist Harry Thuku's *An Autobiography* (1970). Tom Mboya's *Freedom and After* (1963) describes his experience in Kenyan politics, while J. M. Kariuki gives an account of his goal of a free Kenya and his experience during his detention in 1953 in his *"Mau Mau" Detainee* (1963). Waruhiu Itote's *Mau Mau General* (1967), Joram Wamweya's *Freedom Fighter* (1971), Gakaara wa Wanjau's *Mwandiki wa Mau Mau ithaamrio-ini* (Gikuyu, 1983; *Mau Mau Author in Detention,* 1988), and Henry Muoria's *I, the Gikuyu and the White Fury* (1994) also deal with the Mau Mau theme.

NORTH AFRICA

Recent works like *Walking through Fire: A Life of Nawal El Saadawi* (translated by Sherif Hetata, 2002), and *Daughter of Isis: The Autobiography of Nawal El Saadawi* (1999), as well as Tawfiq (Hussayn) al-Hakim's *The Prison Life: An Autobiographical Essay* (translated by Pierre Cachia in 1993) are important North African works in the category of autobiography and biography.

SOUTH AFRICA

Due to the social and political climate of the twentieth century in South Africa, autobiography became an important form of literature that dealt with issues of **apartheid,** race, class, language, and religion (among others). Works such as Peter **Abrahams's** *Tell Freedom* (1954), Ezekiel (Es'kia) **Mphahlele's** *Down Second Avenue* (1959), and Bloke **Modisane's** *Blame Me on History* (1963) demonstrate the importance of autobiography in South Africa. More recent autobiographies of note are Alan **Paton's** *Towards the Mountain* (1980) and *Journey Continued* (1988), Nelson Mandela's *Long Walk to Freedom* (1994), and J. M. **Coetzee's** *Boyhood: Scenes from Provincial Life* (1997).

Diaries and travel narratives form the vast majority of early writing in South Africa, much of which was written by colonists. R. Raven-Hart's collection of early travel narratives *Before van Riebeeck: Callers at South Africa from 1488 to 1652* (1967) offers a collection of works from Bartholomeu Dias's first sighting of the Cape of Good Hope to Jean-Baptise Tavernier's 1549 settlement of the Cape for a month. Rev. Erasmus Smit's journal of 1815 (*Dag Verhaal van Eerw*) was published in 1956 and describes his interactions with the Cape Bushmen at Toornberg, although Smit does not demonstrate a cultural respect for the /Xam language and customs. Also important is the narrative of //Kabbo, a /Xam man who narrated his story to Wilhelm Bleek, who in turn recorded it in a biased but culturally important form in *Specimens of Bushmen Folklore* (1911). Journals of settlers are also an important element of the colonial period, especially the British settlers who immigrated to the Cape Colony in 1820. Some of these narratives include *The Reminiscences of an Albany Settler* (1871) by H. H. Dugmore, *Reminiscences of a South African Pioneer* (1913) by W. C. **Scully,** *Settler's Heritage* (1954) by Francis Carey **Slater,** and *Chronicle* (vols. 1 and 2, 1946 and 1949) by Jeremiah Goldswain.

Autobiographies also exist as a result of the Anglo-Boer war (1899–1902), and the social and political discourses that arose from it. Some narratives that reflect on the war are *The Petticoat Commando; or, Boer Women in Secret Service* (1913) by Johanna Brandt, *Commando: A Boer Journal of the Boer War* (1929) by Deneys Reitz, Afrikaans poet Totius's (pseudonym of D. F. du Toit) war diary *Vier-en-sestig dae te velde. 'n Oorlogsdagboek* (*Sixty-four Days in the Battlefields: A War Diary*, 1977), and *Met die Boere in die veld* (*With the Boers in the Battlefields*, 1937) by Boer cowgirl Sarah Raal. Sol T. **Plaaje** also published his contemplations of the war in his **Mafeking Diary of Sol T. Plaatje** (1973, 1999), while Winston Churchill's *London to Ladysmith via Pretoria* (1900) offers the story of his capture and escape during the Boer war. Slightly later autobiographies are also reflexive of their social and political contexts, as are medical doctor Louis Leipoldt's *The Bushveld Doctor* (1937), and Afrikaaner Uys Krige's *The Way Out* (1946), which describes his escape from German capture in 1944.

In 1948 the Afrikaner Nationalist takeover resulted in less Afrikaans autobiography, and a growth in travel narratives that continued until the 1970s. There was a focus on the adventure of discovery in English-language works such as Laurens **van Der Post's** *Venture to the Interior* (1952), *The Lost World of the Kalahari* (1958), and *The Heart of the Hunter* (1961), and T. V. Bulpin's *The Ivory Trail* (1954). Other autobiographies focus on the political climate and what that means for individual identity, some examples of which are M. E. Rothman's *beskeie deel: 'n Outobiografiese vertelling* (*The Measure of My Days: An Autobiographical Narration*, 1972), and Alan Paton's **Cry, the Beloved Country** (1949), *Towards the Mountain* (1980), and *Journey Continued* (1988). Other autobiographies of note include *Light on a Dark Horse* (1951) by Durban-born poet Roy **Campbell,** *The South African Autobiography* (1984) by William **Plomer,** and *Karoo Morning* (1977) and *Bursting World* (1983) by Guy **Butler.**

A different sort of narrative is captured in the orally transmitted *Paulina Dlamini: Servant of Two Kings,* which was edited by H. Filter and S. Bourquin in 1986 and is the autobiography of a Zulu woman who was servant to Cetshwayo (a Zulu king) and later converted to Christianity. Township life is caught on paper by Godfrey Moloi in his *My Life: Volume One* (1987; rewritten as *My Life: Volumes One and Two,* 1991). Violent social and political unrest is expressed in Charles Hooper's *Brief Authority* (1960), and in Rian Malan's *My Traitor's Heart* (1990), while the colored Afrikaans voice is represented in autobiographical works of fiction such as Abraham Philips's *Die verdwaalde land* (*The Lost Land,* 1992) and A.H.M. Scholtz's *Vatmaar: 'n Lewwddagge verhaal van 'n tyd wat nie meer is nie* (*Take It: A Lively Story of a Time That Is No More,* 1995).

Autobiographies by South African women focus on either the development of an individual self, or the way that individual identity interacts with social and political concerns. Such works include Sarah Gertrude **Millin**'s *The Night Is Long* (1941) and *The Measure of My Days* (1955), Noni **Jabavu**'s *Drawn in Colour: African Contrasts* (1960) and *The Ochre People: Scenes from a South African Life* (1963), Petronella van Heerden's *Kerssnuitsels* (1962), Eve Palmer's *The Plains of the Camdeboo* (1966), Ellen **Kuzwayo**'s ***Call Me Woman*** (1985), Lynn Freed's *Home Ground* (1986), Emma Mashinini's *Strikes Have Followed Me All My Life* (1989), and Sindiwe **Magona**'s *To My Children's Children* (1990) and *Forced to Grow* (1992). Goonarathnam Goonam's *Coolie Doctor* (1991) depicts her difficult position as an Indian Durbanite in apartheid South Africa. Similarly, Winnie Mandela's *Part of My Soul* (1985), Helen Joseph's *Side by Side* (1986), Nonna Kitson's *Where Sixpence Lives* (1987), and Mary Benson's *A Far Cry* (1989) all provide strong antiapartheid images. Many autobiographies of important South African black leaders are the result of collaborative efforts, as are *Freedom for My People: The Autobiography of Z. K. Matthews: Southern Africa 1901 to 1968* (1981), *Let My People Go* (1962) by Albert Luthuli, and *Long Walk to Freedom* (1994) by Nelson Mandela.

Childhood plays an important role in many South African autobiographies. For example, in Peter Abrahams's *Tell Freedom* Abrahams depicts his childhood experiences as a poor colored Afrikaans boy and his journey to self-realization as an author, while other narratives that depict childhood experiences of apartheid include *Down Second Avenue* by Ezekiel Mphahlele, "*Buckingham Palace,*" *District Six* (1986) by Richard **Rive,** *Kaffir Boy: Growing out of Apartheid* (1986) by Mark Mathabane, *Memory Is the Weapon* (1987) by Don **Mattera,** *Coolie Location* (1990) by Jay Naidoo. Afrikaans author F. A. Venter focuses on place in his depiction of his childhood on a farm in *Kambro-kind* (*Kambro Child,* 1979), while Athol **Fugard** also depicts place when he describes Port Elizabeth in *Cousins: A Memoir* (1994). Similarly, Chris Van Wyk writes of the former trade union leader Bill Jardine's childhood in Johannesburg in his *Now Listen Here: The Life and Times of Bill Jardine* (2004). Chris Van Wyk has also written a childhood memoir about himself and his family and the impact of apartheid race politics on their community in his *Shirley, Goodness and Mercy—A Childhood Memoir* (2004). Other recent biographies include *Arthur Kenneth Nortje: Poet and South African* by Craig McLuckie, *Sindiwe Magona: The First Decade* by Siphokazi Koyana (2004), Maureen Rall's *Peaceable Warrior: The Life and Times of Sol Plaatje* (2003), J.D.F. Jones's *Teller of Many Tales: The Lives of Laurens Van Der Post* (2002), *Mandela Dead and Alive 1976–2001* (2001) by Edouard J. Maunick, and Laura Jones's *Nothing Except Ourselves: The Harsh Times and Bold Theater of South Africa's Mbongeni Ngema* (1994).

Social and political themes are an important part of most South African autobiographies. Along with the representations of the oppressive apartheid regime in works like Bloke Modisane's *Blame Me on History,* and Naboth Mogatle's *Autobiography of an Unknown South African* (1971), there are also works like Trevor Huddleston's *Naught for Your Comfort* (1956), which depicts township life and working conditions there in the 1950s, as well as those that depict working life in the factories, as does Alfred Temba **Qabula**'s *A Working Life: Cruel beyond Belief* (1989). Narratives of political dissidence include those of ANC politician Carl Niehaus, who relates the story of his negative reaction to his conservative Afrikaan's upbringing in *Om te veg vir hoop* (*To Fight for Hope,* 1993), and Beyers Naudé's *My land van hoop* (*My Land of Hope,* 1996), which tells of the religious leader's opposition and resultant house arrest. Ashwin Desai's *We Are the Poors: Community Struggles in Post-Apartheid South Africa* (2002) demonstrates that the sociopolitical autobiography of the past continues to be of importance in today's context. Similarly, Mike Nicol tells of Cape Town past and present when he returns to the city after a sojourn in Berlin in his *Sea-Mountain, Fire City: Living in Cape Town* (2001), and Letlapa Mphahele's *Child of This Soil: The Life of a Freedom Fighter* (2002) tells of a different personal experience and existence. On a more historical note, Pauline Smith's diaries are published under the title of *Secret Fire: The 1913–1914 South African Journal of Pauline Smith* (1997).

Some autobiographies are published in fragmented forms, due to the early death or political persecution of the authors. Such texts include the writing that Can **Themba** and Nat **Nakasa** did for *Drum* magazine in the 1950s, as well as Themba's *The Will to Die* (1972) and Nakasa's *The World of Nat Nakasa* (ed. Essop Patel, 1993). Also of note is Alex La Guma's journal of his experiences under apartheid, titled *Liberation Chabalala: The World of Alex **La Guma*** (1993), and the posthumously published writings of Bessie Head titled *A Woman Alone* (1990, ed. Craig Mackenzie). Peter Abrahams has published an autobiography under the title of *The Black Experience in the 20th Century: An Autobiography and Meditation* (2000), while Breyten Breytenbach's *Dog Heart* acts as his 1999 memoir. Stephen Gray's biography on Herman Charles Bosman is titled *Life Sentence: A Biography of Herman Charles Bosman* (2005), and Gillian S. Eilersen's *Bessie Head Thunder behind Her Ears: A Biography* (1996) offers more information about that great author. Walter Saunders is the author of a biography on Douglas Livingstone titled *For Douglas Livingstone: A Reminiscence* (1996), while Stephen Gray is the author of a collection of biographical essays titled *Free-lancers and Literary Biography in South Africa,* which describes the biographical pursuit of the subject and the practical work of Gray as a literary biographer. The collection includes essays on Douglas Blackburn, Stephen Black, Sipho Sepamla, and Richard Rive—and shorter pieces on such authors as Bessie Head, Etienne Leroux, and Mary Renault.

Exile is also a formative theme in South African autobiography, as Breyten **Breytenbach**'s diary of his excursion to Africa on a ninety-day visa from exile in Paris titled *Seisoen in die paradys* (1976; *A Season in Paradise,* 1980), his *Return to Paradise* (1993), and his prison memoir, *True Confessions of an Albino Terrorist* (1984) demonstrate. Es'kia Mphahlele similarly published a work about his experience of self-imposed exile in *Afrika My Music* (1984), which follows his work *Down Second Avenue* and explains his decision to return to South Africa.

SOUTH-CENTRAL AFRICA

There have been several published narratives of the experiences of Europeans in Zimbabwe since the middle of the nineteenth century, most of which treat their subjects as scientific exploration or as religious or colonial stories of the "civilization" of the land and people. Missionary narratives by David Livingstone and hunting narratives by Frederick Courtenay Selous are most prominent in these categories, although their influences are also of note. Influences on Livingstone and Selous include William Charles Baldwin's *African Hunting* (1863), the translation of Edward Mohr's *To the Victoria Falls of the Zambesi* (1876), missionary Thomas Morgan Thomas's *Eleven Years in Central South Africa* (1873), and Frank Oates's *Matabeleland and the Victoria Falls* (published posthumously in 1881). A comparison between the published books and unpublished letters and journals was made possible by the Oppenheimer series of the late 1940s. Examples of note are *The Matabeleland Journals of Robert Moffat* (the letters and journals of John and Emily Moffat), *The Matabele Mission* (both 1945), and *The Northern Goldfield Diaries of Thomas Baines* (1946). The private journals and letters tend to reflect more doubt about colonial identity than the published works do, and a similar doubt is apparent in letters written by members of the Jesuit Zambesi mission in *Gubulawayo and Beyond,* ed. M. Gelfand (1968), as well as the reports and letters that appear in *Journey to Gubuluwayo,* ed. R. Roberts (1979).

The occupation of Mashonaland by the British South Africa Company in 1890 resulted in autobiographies of settlers, administrators, and soldiers who saw themselves in a positive light as the founders of Southern Rhodesia. Such works include R. Blennerhassett's and L. Sleeman's *Adventures in Mashonaland* (1893), *How We Made Rhodesia* (1896) by A. G. Leonard, *Scouting on Two Continents* (1927) by F. R. Burnham, *Melina Rorke: Told by Herself* (1939), and *Great Days* (1940) by Frank Johnson. One contrasting text is *The Old Transport Road* (1914) by Stanley Portal Hyatt, because it mourns the death of romance, rather than praising progress.

Black autobiography in English was mediated by white transcriptions of oral narrations in the early period. H. Rider Haggard and Bertram Mitford published narratives, as did A. A. Campbell in *Mlimo* (1911). Domestic concerns became more common in white narratives later in the century, however, with settlers' poverty as the focus in autobiographies like Hylda Richards's *Next Year Will Be Better* (1952) and Daphne Anderson's *The Toe-Rags* (1989), which look back at the 1920s and 1930s. Autobiographical works by Doris **Lessing** deal with similar issues, particularly in her *Under My Skin* (1994), which details her family's ruin during the period. Lessing's autobiography also points to autobiographical elements that appear in her series of novels *Children of Violence,* while her book *Going Home* (1957) depicts her final visit to Rhodesia, and *African Laughter* (1992) charts her return to her childhood home after Zimbabwean independence allows her return.

In the 1960s several politicians used the autobiographical form to express their views publicly. After the collapse of federation, white liberals like Sir R. Welensky in his *Welensky's 4000 Days* (1964) and Sir R. Tredgold in his *The Rhodesia That Was My Life* (1968) used autobiography to represent alternatives to violent racial polarization. Supporters of independence also used the autobiographical form, as in Brigadier A. Skeen's *Prelude to Independence* (1966), while work like Nathan Shamuyarira's *Crisis in Rhodesia* (1965) represents one of the first from a Rhodesian modern nationalist position, a position held with authority due to his involvement in events from his perspective as editor of *The African Daily News* from 1956 to 1963. Ndabaningi Sithole provides a similar point of view in his semiautobiographical *African Nationalism* (1968), which represents his experiences to demonstrate the oppression of blacks in Rhodesia. Judith Todd's *The Right to Say No* (1972) and Peter Niesewand's *In Camera* (1972) both provide the perspective of radical white protesters who were persecuted for their actions. Important black autobiographies from Rhodesia include *An Ill-fated People* (1972) and *From Rhodesia to Zimbabwe* (1976) by Lawrence **Vambe,** the nationalist autobiography of Didymus Mutasa titled *Rhodesian Black behind Bars* (1974), Stanislaus Made's account of the struggle for education that blacks had to experience in *Made in Zimbabwe* (1980), Maurice Nyagumbo's memories of the southern African black resistance as seen from the point of view of a migrant worker and then nationalist leader in *With the People* (1980), and Joshua Nkomo's journey from a traditional spiritual position to his political career in trade unionism and eventual role as Zimbabwe's vice-president in *Nkomo: The Story of My Life* (1984).

Since independence, autobiographies of note include Kenneth Skelton's story of his experiences as Anglican bishop of Matabeleland (and his opposition to UDI) in *Bishop in Smith's Rhodesia* (1985), the violence of Rhodesian troops during the liberation war described by Bruce Moore-King in his *White Man, Black War* (1988), which fails to exhibit an understanding outside of his settler ideology, and the torn identity of a white child growing up in Rhodesia in Peter Godwin's *Mukiwa* (1996). Alexandra Fuller's *Don't Lets go to the Dogs Tonight: An African Childhood* (2002) tells of her experience growing up in a family of white farmers in southern Africa, while Peter Fraenkel's *No Fixed Abode* (2005) relates vividly the author's childhood in a middle-class Jewish family that is forced to emigrate from Germany to Zambia in 1939. In biography, Stephen Chan tells the life of Robert Mugabe from his roots as a freedom fighter to his eventual role as a virtual dictator in a land torn by HIV/AIDS, famine, and corruption in *Robert Mugabe: A Life of Power and Violence* (2003). Other prominent biographies include Flora Veit-Wild's *Dambudzo Marechera: A Source Book on His Life and Work* (2002), and her work with Anthony Chennells on *Emerging Perspectives on Dambudzo Marechera* (1999). In addition, David Pattison chronicles the life of Dambudzo Marechera in *No Room for Cowardice: A View of the Life and Times of Dambudzo Marechera* (2002). Several biographies on Arthur Shearly Cripps also exist, including Owen Sheers's *The Dust Diaries* (2004), and John Robert Doyle's *Arthur Shearly Cripps* (1975).

Many novels by authors from South-Central Africa also incorporate autobiography into fiction. The autobiographical content of Stanlake **Samkange**'s *The Mourned One* (1975) is noted by Terence Ranger in *Are We Not Also Men?* (1995), and autobiographical elements can be seen in fiction from Ndabaningi Sithole's *The Polygamist* (1972) to Shimmer **Chinodya**'s *Dew in the Morning* (1982).

WEST AFRICA

Early autobiographies in West Africa are represented by Ignatius **Sancho**'s *Letters of the Late Ignatius Sancho, an African* (1782) and Olaudah **Equiano**'s *The Interesting Narrative of the Life of Olaudah Equiano; or, Gustavus Vassa, the African, Written by Himself* (1789). The written autobiographical form is not notable in West Africa again until the mid-twentieth century, when nationalist leaders against British rule wrote about themselves. Examples include Kwame Nkrumah's *Ghana* (1957), Obafemi Awolowo's *Awo: The Autobiography of Chief Obafemi Awolowo* (1960), *My March through Prison* (1985), and *The Travails of Democracy and the Rule of Law* (1987), Ahmadu Bello's *My Life* (1960), Anthony Bnalimo's *Fugitive Offender* (1965), and Nnamdi Azikiwe's *My Odyssey* (1970). David Akpode Ejoor's memoir is based on his experience as a soldier in the Nigeria-Biafra war (1967–70), which was an event that inspired many memoirs. Nigerian diplomat John Mamman Garba's autobiography, *The Time Has Come* was published posthumously in 1989, while fellow Nigerian Simeon Adebo is the author of *Our Unforgettable Years* (1983) and *Our International Years* (1988), Joe Garba (also Nigerian) is the author of *Diplomatic Soldiering* (1987), while *Flashback* (1989) was written by Nigerian jurist Akinola Aguda. Liberian diplomat C. L. Simpson wrote *The Symbol of Liberia* in 1961.

Common subjects for West African biographies are political heads of state. Peter Omati's *Kwame Nkrumah: The Anatomy of an African Dictatorship* (1970), L. H. Ofosu-Appiah's *The Life and Times of Dr. J.B. Danquah* (1974), and Kwame Anthony Appiah's *In My Father's House* (1992) all take Nkrumah and his contemporaries as their subject. Biographies of note on Nigeria and its inhabitants include *Ahmadu Bello, Sardauna of Sokoto, Values and Leadership in Nigeria* (1986) by John Paten, *Gowan* (1985) by J. Elaigwu, *A Right Honourable Gentleman: The Life and Times of Alhaji Sir Abubakar Tafawa Balewa* (1991) by Trevor Clark, and *Prince of the Niger* (1992) by Chidi Amuta and about Babangida. In contrast, a religious leader is the subject of Ismail Balogun's *The Life and Works of Othman don Fodia* (1975), as is E. A. Ayandele's *Holy Johnson, Pioneer of African Nationalism (1836–1970)* (1970), while C. O. Taiwo follows the life of educator Henry Carr in *Henry Carr: An African Contribution to Education* (1975). The Nigerian civil war is depicted in Frederick Forsyth's biography of Emeka Ojukwu, titled *Emeka* (1982), and in Olusegun Obasanjo's *Nzeogwu* (1987), which is a biography of Chukuma Nzeogwu. Dele Olojede and Onukaba Adinoyi-Ojo tell the story of a Nigerian journalist killed by a parcel bomb in 1986 in their book *Born to Run: The Story of Dele Giwa* (1987), while Jean Boyd

depicts a female subject in *The Caliph's Sister: Nana Asma'u 1793–1865, Teacher, Poet and Islamic Leader* (1987), as does Justus Akinsanya in *An African "Florence Nightingale": A Biography of Chief (Dr.) Mrs. Kofoworola A. Pratt* (1987).

Childhood also plays a major role in the autobiographies of West African writers. Nigerian Mabel **Segun**'s *My Father's Daughter* (1965), Nobel laureate Wole **Soyinka**'s *Aké: The Years of Childhood* (1981; translated into Yoruba by Akinwumi Isola [2005?]), and Robert Wellesley Cole of Sierra Leone's *Kossoh Town Boy* (1960) are just a few examples. Other autobiographies cover life experiences beyond childhood, such as Nigerian Buchi **Emecheta**'s *Head above Water* (1986). In addition, Chinua Achebe has written *Home and Exile* (2000), which is an autobiographical reflection on both his and Africa's literary development. John Pepper Clark Bekederemo's autobiography is written in poetic form by the author, who describes growing up by the Niger Delta in *Once Again a Child* (2004). Tayo Olafioye's *Grandma's Sun: Childhood Memoir* (2000) is the author's semifictional autobiography written in the third person and following that tradition of earlier fictional autobiographies.

The struggle for education is an important part of many West African biographies, including *Chinua Achebe: A Biography* (1997) by Ezenwa-Ohaeto, which follows **Achebe**'s early education and rise as a literary figure. Tijan Sallah and Ngozi Okonjo Iweala have written a biography on Chinua Achebe titled *Chinua Achebe: Teacher of Light* (2003), which is intended for the general reader. June Milne traces the life of Kwame Nkrumah in *Kwame Nkrumah: A Biography* (2000), which contains new information relating to Nkrumah's time spent in Guinea after the 1966 Ghanaian military coup. *Emerging Perspectives on Niyi Osundare* by Abdul Rasheed N'allah (2005) explores the background of the Nigerian poet, and how he began his career. *WS: A Life* *in Full* by Kwesi Kwaa Prah (2004) is a picture biography of Wole Soyinka, which was published in honor of this seventieth birthday in 2004. Other popular biographical subjects in West Africa are Nnamdi Azikiwe, Kwarne Nkrumah, Obafemi Awolowo, and Ladoke Akintola. Other biographies of note are *Akintola: The Man and the Legend* (1982) by Victor Ladipo Akintola, which depicts the life of Nigerian politician Samuel Ladoke Akintola (who was assassinated in 1966) and *Isará: A Voyage around "Essay"* (1989) by Wole Soyinka, which uses fictional techniques to describe its nonfictional subject. *Akintola: The Man and the Legend* provides the political context at the time of preindependence and the nationalist movement in West Africa, while also delineating the complexity of Akintola's position in that context. Soyinka's *Isará: A Voyage around "Essay"* blurs fact and fiction in an attempt to emphasize the importance of narrative in historical identity. The result is that characters and events are portrayed more symbolically than historically correct, which in turn allows Soyinka the freedom to explore the importance of narrative to history.

Trevor Shoonmaker has edited a biography titled *Black President: The Art and Legacy of Fela Anikulapo-Kuti* (2003), which is essentially a tribute to the artistic nature and dedication to justice of Fela Anikulapo-Kuti. Another recent political biography is *Bola Ige: The Passage of a Modern Cicero* by Ayo Banjo (2003). It is a memorial to Chief BolaIge that contains individual tributes, literary essays, and creative responses to BolaIge's life and work. Other recent biographies are that of Ben Okri by Robert Fraser and titled *Ben Okri: Towards the Invisible City* (2002), and Sandra L. Richards's *Ancient Songs Set Ablaze: The Theatre of Femi Osofisan* (1999), which acts as a study on the life and work of Femi Osofisan. On a more political note, Onookome Okome's *Before I Am Hanged: Ken Saro-Wiwa—Literature, Politics, and Dissent* offers a full-length study of Kenule Saro-Wiwa's judicial murder in 1995 (1999), while Craig W. McLuckie and Aubrey McPhail's biography *Ken Saro-Wiwa: Writer and Political Activist* (1999), and Ojo-Ade Femi's *Ken Saro-Wiwa: (A Bio-Critical Study)* (1999) deal with similar issues. Also of note is Mary Ebun Modupe Kolawole's *Zulu Sofola: Her Life and Works,* which was published in 1999.

Bitter Eden (2000)
A novel by Tatamkhulu Ismail **Afrika.** Based on his own experiences as a prisonor-of-war during World War II and his capture in North Africa, Afrika's novel portrays the complex emotional journeys of the men who become physically close in a male-only camp. The men see themselves as heterosexual, but they forge profound relationships with one another as Afrika depicts the details of camp life and the impact of the war.

Bitter Fruit: A Novel (2003)
A novel by Dangor Achmat. The characters in this novel come to a realization that history remembers even when people try to forget. Set in South Africa, the character Mikey goes in search of his past when he learns that he may be the product of his mother's rape by a white police lieutenant. He uncovers the history of his grandfather's battle with colonialism in India, and turns to revenge in an attempt to obtain social order.

Black, Stephen (1880–1931)
South African dramatist and novelist, Black was born in Claremont, Cape Town, and was educated at Saint Saviour's Upper Boys' High School and at Diocesan College. He won many athletic awards and the Rhodes Prize for Literature (1904). He wrote three novels and worked as a journalist, but he is best known as a dramatist.

Black worked as an actor-manager and wrote popular plays with which he and his company toured from the Cape to what was then Rhodesia. Although many of the texts have been lost, the Africana Collection of the South African Library, Cape Town, and the Johannesburg Public Library's Strange Collection retain unpublished texts. Three of his most significant plays are *Love and the Hyphen* (1908, rev. 1928–29), *Helena's Hope, Ltd* (1910), and *Van Kalabas Does His Bit* (1916) because they demonstrate Black's inquisitiveness, his ear for dialogue, and his theatrical and comic timing. The plays are satires of all layers of Cape society, and they also provide a record of social mores and contemporary interracial relations. Black lived in London between 1913 and 1915 and France from 1918 to 1927, marketing his work, writing, and negotiating foreign rights for his repertoire. He toured refurbished versions of his plays in South Africa from 1916 to 1917 and again in 1928 with a new company.

Further Reading

Cartwright, M. F. "Stephen Black 1880–1931: A Chronology." *English in Africa (EinA)* 8, no. 2 (Sept. 1981): 91–94.

Gray, Stephen. "The Comic Theatre of Stephen Black in South Africa." *Kunapipi* 4, no. 1 (1981): 62–74.

———. "The First Night of Stephen Black's Love and the Hyphen." *Quarterly Bulletin of South African Library* 35 (1980): 26–40.

———. "Stephen Black, Man of Letters." *Contrast: South African Literary Journal (Contrast)* 17, no. 4 (1989): 73–80.

———. "Stephen Black and Love and the Hyphen (1908–1928)." *Critical Arts: A Journal of Cultural Studies* 2, no. 1 (1981): 51–59.

Black Atlantic

The term *black Atlantic* has come into popular usage and academic discussion recently, but what it represents (the common cultural aspects of the areas around the Atlantic Ocean where those of African descent live) is not a recent concept. The areas encompassed under the heading of black Atlantic include the Caribbean, a large portion of North America, most of sub-Saharan Africa, a number of areas in Latin America, and many places in Western Europe. These areas were quite distinct and despite some trade links and a small amount of migration, they did not become clearly connected until the fifteenth century, when in the mid-1400s the Portuguese, Spanish, and other countries began to send explorers (like Columbus) to the "New World." The most important development in the creation of a black Atlantic happened in 1516 when the European slave trade began; this forced movement of black Africans into North and South America and the Caribbean resulted in the large Afro-diasporic population of these areas. In addition, the more recent movement of a small amount of Afro-diasporic peoples to different parts of Europe from the Americas, Caribbean, and Africa has added to the black Atlantic cultural area.

Cultural and community development in the black Atlantic was characterized by the diversity of African heritages that were brought together, interactions with native populations, and a refusal to accept the dominant European cultures. Such cultural development also affected coastal and (to a lesser extent) interior African regions, where the reciprocal movement of people and ideas across the black Atlantic began intermittently in the sixteenth to eighteenth centuries and became more frequent in the nineteenth century as the directions of the interactions became more varied as intellectuals from across the black Atlantic lived or met one another in London or Paris, and also traveled throughout the different transatlantic regions. These black Atlantic interactions were characterized, for example, by Caribbean theorists like Frantz Fanon who influenced pan-African political thought, or by Harlem Renaissance poets like Langston Hughes who influenced the West African philosophy of negritude. European and white "New

World" cultures were also influenced by the black Atlantic interactions, as the definition of the European self depended very much on the imagined black other.

In spite of these connections and interactions many scholars did not study the regions of the black Atlantic in relation to one another, but focused on their separate attributes and quite often studied white literature and culture as separate from black literature and culture. However, in his 1993 book *The Black Atlantic* sociologist and cultural theorist Paul Gilroy drew attention to this lack of attention (which many scholars were starting to understand as a misrepresentation) by naming the interconnected areas the "black Atlantic" and discussing the possibility of speaking of these places as one collective space due to the network of interactions that exist across the area. In addition, Gilroy argues that it is impossible to think about either white or black culture in the Atlantic without one another due to the way that black culture defines itself in the face of white culture's repressive or racially defined societies. Gilroy also stresses that in his configuration of the black Atlantic there is no one center, nor is Africa the sole originator of black Atlantic culture, rather, he suggests that each area (in a number of different ways) influences all other areas. Gilroy's idea and term have proven to be very useful for talking about an important social relationship. In the study of literature the term *black Atlantic* builds a more complex picture, as writers from past and present and from various parts of the black Atlantic can be discussed alongside one another, and influences between cultures and eras can produce very productive readings based on the idea of a black Atlantic. In such a configuration the interconnected relationship between authors and artists is stressed, and the labeling of any one writer as "African" or "Caribbean," for example, is impossible because of all of the interrelated influences that are representative of a black Atlantic culture.

Although Gilroy's book has both been praised and criticized, it is a very clear fact that the concept of the black Atlantic will continue to be a useful way of looking at the connections and cultural similarities of Africa, America, the Caribbean, and Europe. One of the major criticisms of Gilroy's work is that he does not pay enough attention to Africa as the source and cornerstone of many of the traditions of importance in these black Atlantic countries, and although it is obvious that so many combinations of cultures and ideas cannot have one clear center, Africa is of great importance to the formation of a black Atlantic culture. In any case, the fact remains there is an interconnected cultural formation that covers four continents and is not based only on white or black culture, but is a unique combination of the cultures that have come in contact across the Atlantic Ocean since the fifteenth century, have expanded throughout the twentieth, and will continue to grow in relation to one another in the future. The concept of the black Atlantic is not only of importance in the academic world, but in mainstream culture as well. One example of such importance is the Web site http://www.blackatlantic.com, which is an archive of interdisciplinary material that helps the viewer understand the ways that the idea of the black Atlantic has been constructed.

Further Reading

Austerlitz, Paul. "Mambo Kings to West African Textiles: A Synesthetic Approach to Black Atlantic Aesthetics." In *Musical Migrations: Transnationalism and Cultural Hybridity in Latin/o America, Volume I,* ed. Frances R. Aparicio, Cándida F. Jáquez, and María Elena Cepeda. New York: Palgrave Macmillan, 2003, 99–113.

Braxton, Joanne M., and Maria I. Diedrich, eds. *Monuments of the Black Atlantic: Slavery and Memory.* Münster: LIT, 2004.

Brydon, Diana. "Detour Canada: Rerouting the Black Atlantic, Reconfiguring the Postcolonial." In *Reconfigurations: Canadian Literatures and*

Postcolonial Identities/Littératures canadiennes et identités postcoloniales, ed. Marc Maufort and Franca Bellarsi. Brussels: Peter Lang, 2002, 109–22.

Carney, Judith. "Out of Africa: Colonial Rice History in the Black Atlantic." In *Colonial Botany: Science, Commerce, and Politics in the Early Modern World,* ed. Londa Schiebinger and Claudia Swan. Philadelphia: University of Pennsylvania Press, 2004, 204–20.

Chrisman, Laura. "Beyond Black Atlantic and Postcolonial Studies: The South African Differences of Sol Plaatje and Peter Abrahams." In *Postcolonial Studies and Beyond,* ed. Ania Loomba, Suvir Kaul, Matti Bunzl, Antoinette Burton, and Jed Esty. Durham, NC: Duke University Press, 2005, 252–71.

Davis, Geoffrey V. *Voices of Justice and Reason: Apartheid and Beyond in South African Literature.* Amsterdam: Rodopi, 2003.

Dayan, Joan. "Paul Gilroy's Slaves, Ships, and Routes: The Middle Passage as Metaphor." In *Sisyphus and Eldorado: Magical and Other Realisms in Caribbean Literature,* ed. Timothy J. Reiss. Trenton: Africa World, 2002, 187–99.

DeCorse, Christopher R., ed. *West Africa during the Atlantic Slave Trade: Archaeological Perspectives.* London: Leicester University Press, 2001.

DeLombard, Jeannine Marie. "Turning Back the Clock: Black Atlantic Literary Studies." *New England Quarterly: A Historical Review of New England Life and Letters* 75, no. 4 (2002): 647–55.

Desai, Gaurav. "Gendered Self-Fashioning: Adelaide Casely Hayford's Black Atlantic." *Research in African Literatures* 35, no. 3 (2004): 141–60.

Eburne, Jonathan P., and Jeremy Braddock, eds. "Introduction: Paris, Modern Fiction, and the Black Atlantic." *MFS: Modern Fiction Studies* 51, no. 4 (2005): 731–40.

Elmer, Jonathan. "The Black Atlantic Archive." *American Literary History* 17, no. 1 (2005): 160–70.

Fulani, Ifeona. "Erzulie's Daughters: Black Women Reconfiguring the Black Atlantic." *Dissertation Abstracts International, Section A: The Humanities and Social Sciences* 65, no. 9 (2005): 3373–74.

Gilroy, Paul. "The Black Atlantic as a Counter-culture of Modernity." In *Theorizing Diaspora: A Reader,* ed. Jana Evans Braziel and Anita Mannur. Malden: Blackwell, 2003, 49–80.

Gruesser, John Cullen. *Confluences: Postcolonialism, African American Literary Studies, and the Black Atlantic.* Athens: University of Georgia Press, 2005.

Jakubiak, Katarzyna. "Between a Failure and a New Creation: (Re)reading Yusef Komunyakaa's "The Beast & Burden" in the Light of Paul Gilroy's Black Atlantic." *Callaloo: A Journal of African Diaspora Arts and Letters* 28, no. 3 (2005): 865–81.

Loeffelholz, Mary. "Edmund Clarence Stedman's Black Atlantic." *Victorian Poetry* 43, no. 2 (2005): 189–204.

Newman, Judie. "Black Atlantic or Black Athena? Neo-Slave Narratives in Contemporary Fiction." *Foreign Literature Studies/Wai Guo Wen Xue Yan Jiu* no.1 (2005): 64–71.

Piot, Charles. "Atlantic Aporias: Africa and Gilroy's Black Atlantic." *South Atlantic Quarterly* 100, no. 1 (2001): 155–70.

Rutledge, Rebecka Rychelle. "Metaphors of Mediation: Race and Nation in Black Atlantic Literature." *Dissertation Abstracts International, Section A: The Humanities and Social Sciences* 62, no. 6 (2001): 2107.

Wong, Edlie L. "Fugitives and Foreigners: Compulsory Mobility and Homemaking in the Early Black Atlantic." *Dissertation Abstracts International, Section A: The Humanities and Social Sciences* 65, no. 2 (2004): 511.

Black Consciousness in South Africa

The crackdown on many opponents of **apartheid** after the Sharpeville massacre in 1960 led, in a sense, to the Black Consciousness movement as the first organized opposition to apartheid. The movement was a philosophical, cultural, and somewhat political one, and it came to the forefront at the segregated universities and theological colleges by the end of the 1960s. In South Africa, the Black Consciousness movement was the most influential and important movement against apartheid in the 1970s.

The Black Consciousness movement was based upon a philosophy and ideology developed first by urban students who had been most influenced to white culture, and had an expressed desire to reconnect with their African heritage in search of self-identity. Others in the intellectual community also understood the need to build a black community in the face of the oppression and division caused by apartheid. Students of the younger generation were in search of new ways of opposing apartheid through action, and felt that the civil protest and focus on education of the black organizations of the past had not accomplished enough in the protest against apartheid. The Black Consciousness movement influenced people and sought support through groups such as the South African Students' Organization (founded in 1969), the Black People's Convention (1972), Black Community Programmes (1973), the Black Women's Federation (1975), and the South African Students' Movement (which espoused a more Black Consciousness focus after 1972).

The political backgrounds of those involved in the Black Consciousness movement were varied, and this diversity helped to build psychological solidarity as a group in the face of the destructive effects of apartheid. Black Consciousness also focused on the need to undermine the South African government, the fight against assimilation, an awareness and pride in African heritage, and it aimed to free blacks from the repressive restrictions forced upon them due to apartheid. Despite varying political backgrounds, those who supported Black Consciousness did have the same ideas and outlooks to one extent or another, and the movement drew attention to the division between the impoverished black community and the wealthy white community that was so marked in South Africa. The movement demonstrated how the separation between white and black was a tool of the white government to control the black population through a devaluing of African heritage, and it maintained that the goal of liberation was one that black people should take up for themselves through the voicing of their own perspectives rather than relying on the sympathetic white community. Certain values were also encouraged in relation to psychological and political freedom (especially by the most famous leader of the movement, Steve Biko), such as a humanist and community-based attitude (including education and community programs), the rejection of all things commercial or consumer-based, and the rediscovery and awareness of black cultural history—all in order to fight against the influence of the West on black South African identity.

These values also extended to the need for the building of black unity and community for all of those who were oppressed in South Africa because of their skin color, which included Africans, those labeled "coloured" by the government (those of mixed race), and Indians. Only those black people who were part of the apartheid system (as Homeland leaders, councilors, or businessmen) were excluded from this ideal of unity, and people in the black community banded together for political and social change.

Cultural forms like prose literature, fine art, drama, music, and poetry were major components of the Black Consciousness movement. Black art in the 1970s focused on the message of unity, and worked to spread the message of a common black cultural identity. The creative production of cultural material in this period was unique and experimental in that the artists had to rely on their own resources, because the material from before the Sharpeville massacre of 1960 had been banned. The literature focused on political messages both in content and the effects of form, and writers in the 1970s saw themselves as a major part of the movement to undermine white domination. In this sense, politics were a fundamental component of art and literature, which was seen as containing major possibilities for social liberation due to the repression of other forms of political acts, and a way to cement the shared identity of the black community. Not only did artists' work demonstrate their own commitment to the Black Consciousness movement, it was also a way to reach out to readers, listeners, or viewers who were not currently involved. This relationship between reader and writer was one that was stressed in much literature and art of the period, and Black Consciousness authors felt that they were the mouthpiece of the ordinary person, as they expressed the oppression and pain of living under apartheid and looked for ways of solving such issues. In turn, this focus on the reader led to a more accessible literature for wider audiences, and a favoring of forms like plays and performance poetry over the written word. Simultaneously, the use of African languages was discouraged because it was associated with the politics of the apartheid government, who relied on language as one way of dividing the population based on ethnic background. Instead, those involved in the Black Consciousness movement focused on the use of an English associated with the townships' use of *flytaal* patois, and emphasized that grammatical correctness was not necessary.

There was also a call for a new way of critically understanding black writing, as the mainly white literary critics of the period did not adequately understand or judge the importance of black writing. Instead, the critics focused on European-based criteria for what was considered good art, and there was no understanding of local or township-based lifestyles and cultural heritage. As a result, one of the aims of the Black Consciousness movement in relation to literary criticism was to define what should be aesthetically pleasing in African literature. Much of this criteria focused on traditional and oral literature, and the inheritance of forms like the *imbongi* (the precolonial praise poet) were stressed as the basis for contemporary black poetry.

The focus on forms of literature available to a wide variety of the black public was one that was of utmost importance for the Black Consciousness emphasis on the building of a community of resistance. The result was that instead of catering to Western audiences overseas, black performers, writers, and artists focused on the messages they were to convey to black audiences and readers. The result of this emphasis was hoped to be a new community identity that was related directly to the aims of the Black Consciousness movement, and would change ideas of subjectivity throughout the community through a joint effort for change.

Black Consciousness continued to be the major form of political opposition throughout the 1970s, and was a great encouragement for the cultural and political production of black literary and artistic materials in the period. In this combination of the political and culture the movement was responsible for a great deal of visible opposition that led to things like the Soweto uprising of 1976–77 as well as important works of literature and theater by important authors like Mongane Wally **Serote,** Mtutuzeli Matshoba, Miriam **Tlali,** Matsemela **Manaka,** Mafika Gwala, and Sipho **Sepamla.** The predominance of the Black Consciousness movement lessened when in the 1980s nonracial groups like the United Democratic Front and the movement of the black trade unions into the political and cultural arenas came onto the scene, but despite its lessened importance in the 1980s the Black Consciousness movement's influence and effect remains of note to this day. It gave rise to a number of authors, drama groups, and literary journals (like *Staffrider*) that have had a huge effect on the direction in which South African literature and art has developed.

Further Reading
The University of Fort Hare Library's online catalog includes a history of the library, which notes that the Steve Biko Letters and

Lennox Papers are held in their Africana collection (the Howard Pim Library). The library also holds the collections of the African National Congress (including a chronology of the ANC and Thabo Mbeki's speech at the March 1996 opening of the Archives), Pan Africanist Congress of Azania, AZAPO and the Black Consciousness Movement, the A. C. Jordan Papers, as well as the Lovedale Press Records (http://www.ufh.ac.za/).

Brown, Duncan. "Black Consciousness, Tradition and Modernity: Ingoapele Madingoane's 'Black Trial.'" *Current Writing: Text and Reception in Southern Africa* 9, no. 1 (1997): 1–26.

Collins, Patricia Hill. *Black Feminist Thought: Knowledge, Consciousness, and the Politics of Empowerment.* New York: Routledge, 2000.

Farred, Grant. "It's an X-Thing: The Culture of Black Nationalism in Contemporary South Africa." In *Reading the Shape of the World: Toward an International Cultural Studies,* ed. Henry Schwarz and Richard Dienst. Boulder, CO: Westview Press, 1996, 144–63.

Frank, Heike. *Role-Play in South African Theatre.* Bayreuth, Germany: Thielmann & Breitinger, 2004.

Gaylard, Rob. "Beyond Protest: The Legacy of Black Consciousness in Njabulo Ndebele's *Fools and Other Stories.*" *English Studies in Africa: A Journal of the Humanities* 45, no. 1 (2002): 31–44.

Gqola, Pumla Dineo. "Contradictory Locations: Blackwomen and the Discourse of the Black Consciousness Movement (BCM) in South Africa." *Meridians: Feminism, Race, Transnationalism* 2, no. 1 (2001): 130–52.

Jones, Gavin. "'The Sea Ain't Got No Back Door': The Problems of Black Consciousness in Paule Marshall's *Brown Girl, Brownstones.*" *African American Review* 32, no. 4 (1998): 597–606.

Lee, Soo-Hyun "The Bluest Eye: Tragic Aspects of Black Consciousness of the Self." *Studies in Modern Fiction* 9, no. 1 (2002): 195–217.

Mitchell, Michele. *Righteous Propagation: African Americans and the Politics of Racial Destiny after Reconstruction.* Chapel Hill: University of North Carolina Press, 2004.

Steadman, Ian. "Race Matters in South African Theatre." In *Theatre Matters: Performance and Culture on the World Stage,* ed. Richard Boon and Jane Plastow. Cambridge: Cambridge University Press, 1998, 55–75.

Ward, Brian. *Just My Soul Responding: Rhythm and Blues, Black Consciousness, and Race Relations.* Berkeley: University of California Press, 1998.

Black Docker, The (1986)

Sembene Ousmane's first novel (translated from the French *Le Docker noir,* 1956). It follows the struggles of a Wolof immigrant from Senegal named Diaw Falla as he writes novels and works on the docks in Marseilles. A French author steals Falla's manuscript under the auspices of showing it to a publisher, and she is killed when Falla violently confronts her in Paris. Sembene's novel vividly describes the personal and social struggles of the African immigrant experience in France, and the work is partially autobiographical as it relates to Sembene's own experiences as a dockworker in Marseilles.

Blackburn, Douglas (1857–1929)

Blackburn, a novelist, was a left-wing British journalist who lived in the Transvaal Republic and Natal between 1892 and 1908. Blackburn's seven novels include a trilogy, *Prinsloo of Prinsloodorp: A Tale of Transvaal Officialdom by Sarel Erasmus* (1899), *A Burgher Quixote* (1903), and *I Came and Saw* (1908), which is a subtle satire of the Transvaal Boers in their contests with British imperialism. *Kruger's Secret Service, by One Who Was in It* (1900) is an ironic and scathing portrait of the Rand and criticism of Cecil Rhodes militarism. *Richard Hartley, Prospector* (1904) parodies the colonial adventure romance, while Blackburn's *Leaven: A Black and White Story* (1908), the first "Jim Comes to Joburg" (about rural-urban migration), exposes mining capitalist exploitation, colonial violence, and the negative influence of the "civilizing mission" on Africans. *Love Muti* (1915) portrays an interracial relationship, while *Secret*

Service in South Africa (1911) is the title of Blackburn's autobiography.

Further Reading

Gray, Stephen. "Piet's Progress: Douglas Blackburn's Satire on the Foundation of the Transvaal." *English Studies in Africa: A Journal of the Humanities (ESA)* 24, no. 1 (1981): 25–36.

Rice, Michael. "Douglas Blackburn's *A Burgher Quixote.*" *Kunapipi (Kunapipi)* 8, no. 1 (1986): 70–86.

Shum, Matthew. "The Content of the Form: Romance and Realism in Douglas Blackburn's *Leaven.*" *English in Africa (EinA)* 21, nos. 1–2 (1994): 93–102.

Blackheart (2004)

Lesego **Rampolokeng**'s first novel. Influenced by Rampolokeng's poetic voice, *Blackheart* provides a flowing psychological and social narrative that combines world events with surreal images. Although it portrays violence and enclosure that echoes apartheid South Africa, it does not stick to one time or setting, and explores the implications of a global self.

Blame Me on History (1963)

The autobiography of Bloke **Modisane.** The author reflects on his life before leaving South Africa for exile in England. He left his job as a reporter for *Drum,* and muses on his life in Sophiatown, the black township in Johannesburg where he grew up. He remembers incidents from his own life, the murder of his father, buried in a coffin bearing the son's name. The narrative conveys the cosmopolitan character of life in the township and reveals the ambivalence that Modisane felt for it and for the white world that attracted him but punished him. The text succeeds in conveying Modisane's difficulties in understanding himself and the world under apartheid.

Blanket Boy's Moon (1953)

A novel by Atwell Sidwell **Mopeli-Paulus.** The novel, written in collaboration with Peter Lanham, was a popular success for its dramatization of the causes and prosecution of ritual medicine murder in rural Lesotho and for its depiction of the township life of migrant workers in Johannesburg. Mopeli-Paulus records the nature of Lesotho life and customs, the policies and practices of the British administration, and the unwholesome conditions in which migrant mine workers found themselves.

Blay, J. Benibengor (1915–)

Ghanaian writer of fiction, poetry, and drama. Most of Blay's many novelettes, stories, plays, and books are published under his own imprint, Benibengor Book Agency (Aboso), or by Stockwell (Ilfracombe, England). Born in Half Assini, Western Ghana, he was educated at the Regent Street Polytechnic, London. In 1958, he was elected a member of the Ghanaian National Assembly and later became Minister of Arts and Culture under President Kwame Nkrumah, who wrote an introduction to his book of verse *Ghana Sings* (1965).

Blay's books deal with tradition and change in postcolonial Ghana with a heavily moralistic slant. Because his books follow the European and Onitsha market chapbook romance formula, they have appealed to a wide range of the reading public since the early 1940s. The novelettes include *Emelia's Promise and Fulfilment* (n.d., ca. 1944), *Dr. Bengto Wants a Wife* (1953), *After the Wedding* (1967), and *The Story of Tata* (ca. 1976). The collections of stories include *Be Content with Your Lot* (1947, a collection of his early stories), *Operation Witchcraft* (1956), and *Tales for Boys and Girls* (1966). Of the several volumes of verse, *Thoughts of a Youth* (1967) combines the texts of *Immortal Deeds* (1940), *Memoirs of the War* (1946), and *King of the Human Frame* (1947) in one volume. He also published a biography entitled *Legend of Kwame Nkrumah* (1973).

Further Reading

Benibengor Blay, J. *Earlier Poems.* Aboso, Ghana: Benibengor Book Agency, 1971.

"Biographical Information on J. Benibengor Blay." In *Ghana Association of Writers: Annual Writers' Congress 1973.* Accra: Ghana Association of Writers, 1973.

Blind Moon (2003)

Poems by Chenjerai **Hove.** These poems express Hove's fascination with the way that poetry can create both bodies and landscapes. He deals with the suffering and violence of Zimbabwe in terms of the inextricable connections between political violence, the landscape, and individual human experience.

Blood Knot, The (1961)

A play by Athol **Fugard.** The action of the play portrays the interaction between two "coloured" (mixed-race) half-brothers, one of whom is dark-skinned and the other light-skinned enough to "pass for white" and the conflict between their ideas about their future. The lighter-skinned brother, Morrie, is serious and wants to save money to buy a farm. Zachariah is desperate to meet a woman. Following Morrie's advice to begin with a pen pal, Zachariah enters a prolonged communication with Ethel, a white woman. He lies about their condition and invites Ethel to visit them. Finally he must confront the fact of his dark skin. The tensions and disappointments of the play are mitigated when, later, Ethel writes to Zachariah to tell him she is engaged to another man. The brothers return to their former life.

Bloodlines (2001)

A novel by Elleke **Boehmer.** Boehmer portrays the relationship between two women who are brought together through history. The background for the novel is the new South Africa, and personal issues regarding voice and reunion resonate with this setting.

Bloom, Harry (1913–81)

South African journalist and novelist. He was educated at the University of the Witwatersrand and worked as an advocate in Johannesburg until his self-imposed exile to England in 1963. His first novel, *Transvaal Episode* (originally published as *Episode,* 1956), depicts an uprising in the fictional township of Nelstroom in the aftermath of the 1952–53 African National Congress defiance campaign. The novel was banned because the South African authorities believed it had the potential to disturb race relations and endanger the safety of the state, and Bloom was denied an exit permit to travel to England to receive the British Authors' Club Prize for the best novel of 1956 for *Episode.* Bloom finished his second novel, *Whittaker's Wife* (1962), while he was serving a three-month detention in prison. He also wrote the book for *King Kong: An African Jazz Opera* (1961), the tragedy of a boxer from the black ghetto, which reached a multiracial audience both locally and internationally.

Further Reading

Erb, Cynthia. "King Kong in Johannesburg: Popular Theatre and Political Protest in 1950s South Africa." In *East of West: Cross Cultural Performance and the Staging of Difference,* ed. Claire Sponsler and Xiaomei Chen. New York: Palgrave, 2000, 143–65.

Kearney, J. A. "Harry Bloom's Transvaal Episode: Unbanned and Unread?" *English in Africa* 24, no. 2 (1997): 69–85.

Boehmer, Elleke (1961–)

South African novelist Boehmer was born in South Africa of Dutch parents and educated there and, as a Rhodes Scholar, at Oxford University. Boehmer now lives in Britain and teaches at the School of English at Leeds University. She is the author of three novels and one critical work: *Screens against the Sky* (1990) and *An Immaculate Figure,* both set in South Africa; *Colonial and Post-Colonial Literature* (1995), a history of the writing of empire and of writing that grew out of opposition to it; and *Bloodlines* (2001), which explores the story of two women who are brought together by history, and whose developing friendship is set against the background of a new South Africa.

As a feminist writer, she portrays women's stories in particular and defines what she has referred to as a largely male southern African literary context. In *Screens against the Sky* the passivity of the central character is shown to be as much a product of her white consciousness as of her exclusion in gendered terms from a male public and political world. In *An Immaculate Figure* she portrays a character who is a victim of her white vision; she exposes men who manipulate her and use her beauty to further their material aspirations. Some recent anthologies and works of history and literary history Boehmer is author and editor of are *Empire Writing: An Anthology of Colonial Literature 1870–1918* (1998), *Stories of Women: Gender and Narrative in the Postcolonial Nation* (2005), *Scouting for Boys: A Handbook for Instruction in Good Citizenship* (2005), and *Empire, the National, and the Postcolonial, 1890–1920: Resistance in Interaction* (2002).

Further Reading

Daymond, M. J. "Bodies of Writing: Recovering the Past in Zoe Wicomb's *David's Story* and Elleke Boehmer's *Bloodlines*." *Kunapipi: Journal of Post Colonial Writing* 24, nos. 1–2 (2002): 25–38.

Boesman and Lena (1969)

A play by Athol **Fugard** in which a "coloured" (mixed-race) couple are evicted from their shantytown home. They travel from place to place with their possessions on their backs. The action of the play (performed on a totally empty stage) is confined to a night of confrontation between Boesman and Lena, and of fear when an old African who shares their campfire dies unexpectedly. The play explores poverty and homelessness, the apparent need of the oppressed to oppress in turn, and the importance of claiming personal freedom.

Boetie, Dugmore (1920–66)

Boetie published only one book, the autobiographical novel *Familiarity Is the Kingdom of the Lost* (1969). The novel is a picaresque narrative based on Boetie's life from the 1920s to the 1950s. Orphaned after murdering his abusive mother, the picaro inhabits the extreme margins of black South African urban township life in various roles, as a thief, con man, and perpetual prisoner. Boetie's novel offers political criticism of the cruelty of the laws regulating African urban labor and the inferior status of African soldiers fighting in World War II, and offers very individual solutions—such as survival through cunning manipulation. Unlike a later generation of **Black Consciousness** writers, Boetie does not focus on his African identity. Instead the book demonstrates the influence of American popular culture (films, comics, and jazz) on Boetie's work. The playwright Barney Simon edited the text and, in an epilogue, questions the autobiographical nature of the book.

Further Reading

Edgecombe, R. S. "Dugmore Boetie's Picaresque Novel." *World Literature Written in English* 29, no. 2 (1989): 129–39.
Titlestad, Michael. "Sounding Out Discourse: Pilgrims and Vagrants." *Current Writing: Text and Reception in Southern Africa* 14, no. 2 (2002): 135–54.

Book of Secrets, The (1994)

A novel by M. G. **Vassanji**. Pius Fernandes is a retired Goan teacher living in Dar es Salaam. He stumbles upon the diary of Alfred Corbin, an English colonial officer in East Africa. The diary, written in 1913 but found in 1988, reveals for Fernandes secrets that lead him into a contemplation of his community's history in East Africa, its colonial tensions, and his own achievements and failures. The novel focuses on excerpts from Corbin's diary and Fernandes's comments on them. Through the diary Fernandes learns of the relationship between the Shamsi community of Kikono, a border town between Kenya and Tanganyika, and its colonial masters. It reveals his own link with that community as he comes to terms with his unrequited love for a pupil, Rita, whose life touches the lives described in the diary. Some of the diary's secrets unravel to clarify incidents and histories of the community, but there are others that remain unresolved. The action of the novel spans almost a century and takes the reader through the colonial confrontation in East Africa, its diverse communities, its aspirations at independence, and its ideas of modernity.

Bosman, H(erman) C(harles) (1905–51)

Bosman was born in a bilingual (English and Afrikaans) home outside Cape Town. He spent most of his life in Johannesburg where he had a public-school education and trained as a teacher at the University of Witwatersrand. His only posting was to the remote Groot Marico district on the Botswana border, an akra devastated by the Anglo-Boer war. This became the locale of most of the 150 short stories on which his reputation is based.

In 1926 he was sentenced to hang for having killed his stepbrother but was reprieved. As recorded in his memoir, *Cold Stone Jug* (1949), he served his prison term until released in 1930. In the same year his first story was published under the title of "Makapan's Caves," which employs his frequent narrator, Oom Schalk Lourens, who also appears in *The Touleier*. In London in the late 1930s he produced stories such as "Mafeking Road," which displays the power of empire and its effects on colonized people. During World War II he was editor of a pro-United Party newspaper in Pietersburg in the Northern Transvaal, which is the setting of his novels *Jacaranda in the Night* (1947) and *Willems-*

dorp (not published until 1977). The novels are a critique of Afrikaner exclusivity as the Nationalist Party rose to power and initiated the **apartheid** era. Although Bosman died too soon to be categorized as an antiapartheid writer, his handling of such crucial issues as the injustice of the Immorality Act (which forbade so-called mixed relationships) and of the migrant labor system enforcing population dispersals represented his generally antisegregationist views. The only collection of his work Bosman put together himself was *Mafeking Road* (1947). It contains twenty-one stories that have come to enjoy classic status, although not published until as late as 1963. *Makapan's Caves and Other Stories* (1987), edited by Stephen **Gray,** is a cross-section of Bosman's short fiction.

Further Reading

Abrahams, Lionel. "Mr Bosman: A Protege's Memoir of Herman Charles Bosman." *English in Africa* 28, no. 2 (2001): 11–47.

Anderson, Mitzi. *Herman Charles Bosman—The Prose Juvenilia.* Pretoria, South Africa: Unisa Press, 1998.

Lenta, Margaret. "White South African and Latter-Day Bohemian: Two Editions of Herman Charles Bosman." *Current Writing: Text and Reception in Southern Africa* 15, no. 1 (2003): 109–22.

MacKenzie, Craig. "Bosman's 'Voorkamer' Stories: A Reconsideration." *Current Writing: Text and Reception in Southern Africa* 12, no. 1 (2000): 75–90.

Mynhardt, Patrick. *Herman Charles Bosman 1905–2005: A Centenary Selection.* Johannesburg, South Africa: Wits University Press, 2005.

Snyman, Salome. "Herman Charles Bosman's 'Louis Wassenaar': A Case of Writer's Block or Exemplary Metafiction?" *English in Africa (EinA)* 30, no. 1 (2003): 71–86.

New Editions

Jacaranda in the Night. Human & Rousseau (2000).
Old Transvaal Stories. Human & Rousseau (2000).

The Rooinek and Other Boer War Stories. Human & Rousseau (2000).

Cold Stone Jug: Anniversary edition. Human & Rousseau (1999).

Idle Talk: Voorkamer Stories (i): Anniversary edition. Human & Rousseau (1999).

Mafeking Road & Other Stories: Anniversary edition. Human & Rousseau (1998).

Willemsdorp: Anniversary edition. Human & Rousseau (1998).

Boundaries (2003)

A novel by Farida **Karodia.** Despite the change that has occurred in most of the new South Africa, the town of Vlenterhoek in Karoida's novel is behind the times. The novel follows the events that lead to Vlenterhoek's gradual change and widening of horizons. Those events include the return of a character to the town after living in Canada for a long time, the taping of an elaborate TV commercial in the town, and the construction of a resort at the town's mineral springs.

Brettell, N. H. (1908–91)

Brettell emigrated to Zimbabwe (then Rhodesia) in 1930. Two volumes of poetry, *Bronze Frieze* (1950) and *Season and Pretext* (1975), established him as a significant southern African poet, and he also wrote an autobiography, *Side-Gate and Stile* (1981), and a volume of *Selected Poems* (1994) appeared posthumously. Brettell is also the author of an article titled "Rhodesian Poetry of a Decade or So" in *Arts Rhodesia* (1978), and he won Rhodesia's PEN literary prize twice (1972 and 1978).

Brettell's small number of works means that he has been less well-known, although poet Douglas **Livingstone** spoke of Brettell as "the undoubted giant of poetry in southern Africa, and probably this continent." Brettell's voice is ambivalently melancholy, his diction latinate but leavened with Zimbabwean and English dialect, and his varied stanza forms rigorously controlled.

Further Reading

Hacksley, Gregory. "I, You and Cymbeline: An Exploration of Shakespeare's Influence in the Poetry of Noel Brettell." *Shakespeare in Southern Africa: Journal of the Shakespeare Society of Southern Africa (ShSA)* 15 (2003): 29–37.

Brew, (Osborne Henry) Kwesi (1928–)

Ghanaian poet. Born of a Fante family in central Ghana, Kwesi Brew was brought up after the death of his parents by a British guardian. He had his early education in Ghana and was among the first bachelor's graduates from the University College of the Gold Coast in 1951. He later served both colonial and independent governments in district commissions, and after independence in diplomatic posts in Europe.

At college Brew participated in college literary activities. After graduation he won a British Council poetry competition in Accra, and his poems appeared in the Ghanaian literary journal *Okyeame*. His *Shadows of Laughter* (1968), a collection of Brew's early poetry, reveals a thematic interest in the value of the individual in contrast to that of society as a whole. In some poems he depicts rituals of traditional African life. *African Panorama and Other Poems* (1981) portrays rural and urban life. His collection *Return of No Return* (1995) pays tribute to the American writer Maya Angelou. Brew is the author of *The Clan of the Leopard and Other Poems* (1996).

Breytenbach, Breyten (1939–)

South African poet, prose writer, and painter Breytenbach was born in Bonnievale in the Western Cape and studied fine art at the University of Cape Town. He left South Africa for Paris in the early 1960s, and when he married a Vietnamese woman he was not allowed to return. He co-founded Okhela (Zulu for "ignite the flame"), a resistance group fighting **apartheid** in exile. In 1975, on a trip to South Africa, he was betrayed, arrested, and sentenced to nine years of imprisonment for high treason. He was released in 1982 and he returned to Paris and lived alternately in Paris and Gorée, Senegal. His work includes numerous volumes of poetry, novels, and essays, some of which are written in Afrikaans, and translated into English. He has won five CNA (Central News Agency) Awards. Breytenbach recently returned to South Africa to teach creative writing at the University of Natal.

Breytenbach's writing reveals an artist's constant search for his own identity. Breytenbach also provides an accurate insight into the inhuman conduct of totalitarian regimes on individuals. His poetry and prose offer a distinctive combination of skepticism and a celebration of life. In his poetry images of surreal worlds connect to the brutal realities of apartheid. Breytenbach's recent publications include *Dog Heart* (a memoir, 1999), *Lady One* (2001), and *Word Work* (1999).

Further Reading

Jacobs, J. U. "Mapping a Heartland: Breyten Breytenbach's 'Zone of Bastardization' in *Dog Heart*." *Current Writing: Text and Reception in Southern Africa* 15, no. 2 (2003): 91–105.

Lutge-Coullie, Judith, and J. U. Jacobs, eds. *A.K.A. Breyten Breytenbach: Critical Approaches to His Writings and Paintings*. Amsterdam: Rodopi, 2004.

Pedri, Nancy. "The Verbal and Visual Mirrors of Postcolonial Identity in Breyten Breytenbach's *All One Horse*." *Journal of Literary Studies/ Tydskrif vir Literatuurwetenskap* 18, nos. 3–4 (2002): 295–312.

Sienaert, Marilet. *The I of the Beholder—The Identity Formation in the Art of Breyten Breytenbach*. Roggebaai, South Africa: Kwela Books, 2002.

Brink, Andre (1935–)

A South African novelist, playwright, and essayist, Brink was born in Vrede, a small town in the Orange Free State, into an Afrikaans family. His father's work as a magistrate meant the family moved every four or five years during his childhood. His parents were supporters of the ruling Nationalist Party. Brink graduated from Potchefstroom University in 1959 with master's degrees in both English and Afrikaans, did postgraduate work at the Sorbonne in the early 1960s, and gained a doctorate at Rhodes University, Grahamstown, where he taught for thirty years. In 1991 he became Professor of English at the University of Cape Town. He has been the recipient of many literary prizes, both within and outside South Africa, the most notable being the Martin Luther King Memorial Prize, the Prix Médicis Étranger, and the South African CNA (Central News Agency) Award, which he has received three times (for both English and Afrikaans works). His work has twice been on the short list for the Booker Prize (for *An **Instant in the Wind*** and ***Rumours of Rain***). He was awarded the Légion d'Honneur in 1982 and made an Officier de l'Ordre des Arts et des Lettres by the French government in 1987. His works have been translated into more than twenty languages. He was nominated three times for the Nobel Prize for Literature. In postapartheid South Africa, Brink is a strong supporter of the ANC and the government of national unity.

In Europe Brink was exposed to contemporary trends in European literature; moreover, it radicalized his politics, partly because of the Sharpeville massacre, which occurred during his time abroad. In the mid-1960s he and a number of other South African writers formed the *Sestigers* ("1960-ers") movement, which sought to meld techniques of European experimental writing with traditional Afrikaans realism. His writing during this period, which was solely in Afrikaans, tended to avoid the sociopolitical realities of South Africa in its attempt to become more cosmopolitan and experimental. The student revolts in Paris in 1968 led to his reassessment of his notion of the responsibilities of the writer in society.

His return to South Africa marked a different approach to his writing, and Brink began to explore his complex relationship with the Afrikaner in **apartheid** South Africa. His first openly political novel, *Kennis van die Aand* (1973), caused a sensation within rigidly conservative Afrikaans society for its political and sexual content. The novel was banned in 1974 under the new censorship laws that were applied for the first time to an Afrikaans work. Cut off from his Afrikaans readership, Brink translated the novel into English as ***Looking on Darkness*** (1974). Brink makes political statements based on his method of translation. In *A Chain of Voices* (1982) Brink uses English for the black characters and Afrikaans for the Afrikaner characters, so that the characters literally do not understand each other. In his more recent works Brink writes in both languages simultaneously.

Since the 1970s, Brink has based his novels within a South African political context. His work attempts to rethink and revise Afrikaner history in order to understand the present in *An Instant in the Wind* (1976), *A Chain of Voices, The First Life of Adamastor* (1993), and *On the Contrary* (1993). He explores the nature of political action or inaction in *The Wall of the Plague* (1984), ***States of Emergency*** (1988), and *An Act of Terror* (1991); exposes what he sees as both the positive and negative aspects of the Afrikaner in *Rumours of Rain* (1978) and *A **Dry White Season*** (1979); and considers the role of the writer or artist within a repressive political regime in *Looking on Darkness* (1974). *Imaginings of Sand* (1995/1996) depicts South Africa as it makes the transition to democracy; in *Devil's Valley* (1999) a crime reporter and failed husband and father moves to the Devil's Valley—home for 160 years to a sect of Boers shut off from the rest of the world; *Rights of Desire* (2000) depicts a romance between a young woman and an older man against the backdrop of postapartheid South Africa; and

The Other Side of Silence (2002) tells the story of Hanna, who escapes an orphanage in Bremen, only to join a boatload of young women transported to the male settlers of South West Africa in the early twentieth century. Experimentation with form is evident in many of his novels, some of which have been described as postmodernist. A prolific writer, Brink is the author of seventeen novels, a number of plays and short stories, and numerous translations of literary works into Afrikaans. An edition of his critical writings was published as *Mapmakers: Writing in a State of Siege* in 1983, and he is the author of *Jan Vermeiren: A Flemish Artist in South Africa* (2000).

Further Reading

Bernstein, Neil W. "Revisiting Ovid's Philomela: Silence, Revenge, and Representation in Andre Brink's *The Other Side of Silence.*" *Classical and Modern Literature: A Quarterly* 24, no. 2 (Fall 2004): 11–27.

Dixon, Shelley. "'Stories or History'?: Female Counter Narratives in Andre Brink's *Imaginings of Sand.*" *AUMLA: Journal of the Australasian Universities Language and Literature Association* 101 (2004): 39–70.

Joseph-Vilain, Melanie. "Andre Brink and the Afrikaner Heritage." *Commonwealth Essays and Studies* 27, no. 1 (Autumn 2004): 26–37.

Broken Reed (2005)

A novel by Sophia Mustafa. Sophia Mustafa's final novel, published in Tanzania after her death in 2005. It tells the story of a Muslim woman named Nureen, who struggles through Indian independence, growing up in Africa, and an arranged marriage to her Pakistani cousin. It charts Nureen's emotions through these events and in relation to feelings of enclosure, freedom, and affection.

Brutus, Dennis (1924–)

A South African poet, Brutus was born to South African parents in Zimbabwe (then Rhodesia), and as a young child moved with them to South Africa. He received his bachelor's degree at the University of Fort Hare in 1947, after which he taught in schools for fourteen years and became a supporter of the struggle against **apartheid.** During an eighteen-month term in the prison on Robben Island his first volume of poems, ***Sirens Knuckles Boots*** (1963), was published in Nigeria. In 1966 he left South Africa with his family on an exit permit, and lived in London and the United States, while also traveling to campaign against apartheid. Brutus played a crucial role in the decision by the International Olympic Committee to exclude South Africa from the Olympic Games. He has taught at Northwestern University, the University of Texas, and the University of Pittsburgh, where he is currently an emeritus professor.

Since his first book, Brutus has written many more, including **Letters to Martha** and Other Poems from a South African Prison (1968), *Poems from Algiers* (1970), *Thoughts Abroad* (1975), *Strains* (1975), *China Poems* (1975), *Salutes and Censures* (1984), *Airs and Tributes* (1989), *Still the Sirens* (1993), *Leafdrift* (2005), edited by Lamont B. Steptoe, and *Remembering Soweto 1976* (2004). *A Simple Lust* (1973) and *Stubborn Hope* (1978) are collections that also contain previously unpublished poems. Brutus's poetry combines the radical and the traditional, and he treats the ugliness of oppression and the need for resistance with a lyrical, meditative, and analytical tone. After his experience in prison his style becomes more colloquial. His poems represent his struggle between human love and love of his country. Brutus came to be regarded outside South Africa as one of the most powerful voices from the land of apartheid.

Within South Africa itself Brutus is still not well known. His work was not allowed to appear in school texts and anthologies in the later years of apartheid.

Further Reading
Laws, Page R. "'Shaped by the Cages That Kept Us': The Prison Poetry of Etheridge Knight and Dennis Brutus." *Middle Atlantic Writers Association Review* 13, no. 2 (December 1998): 78–87.

McLuckie, C. W., and P. J. Colbert, eds. *Critical Perspectives on Dennis Brutus*. Colorado Springs: Three Continents Press, 1995.

Bukenya, Austin (1944–)
A Ugandan novelist, poet, and playwright, Bukenya was born in Masaka, Uganda, educated in Uganda, Tanzania, and the UK, and has taught at Makerere University and at Kenyatta University, Kenya. Bukenya's satirical novel *The People's Bachelor* (1972) criticizes the extravagance and pretentiousness of the African elites, as does his play *The Bride* (1984). Bukenya's research on oral literature is titled *Understanding Oral Literature* (1995); he is the author of *A Guide to East African Poetry* (1978), and is the assistant editor of *Thirty Years of Bananas (New Drama from Africa S.)* (Oxford University Press, 1993).

Burger's Daughter (1979)
A novel by Nadine **Gordimer.** As the title suggests, Rosa Burger struggles to define herself as separate from her father Lionel, a dedicated worker for racial justice in South Africa who died as a martyr imprisoned by the racist regime. Unable to abandon the principles of a lifetime as Burger's daughter in order to achieve personal happiness, Rosa eventually accepts her role as her father's successor. This novel provided the focus of one of the greatest legal cases against South African **censorship.**

Butler, Frederick Guy (1918–2001)
A South African poet, dramatist, short-story writer, historian, autobiographer, and critic, Butler was born and educated in the Eastern Cape town of Cradock. Butler evokes the

harsh beauty of the Karoo and records his upbringing in the first of his three volumes of autobiography, *Karoo Morning* (1977). In 1938 he graduated from Rhodes University and received his master's in English the following year. In 1940 he married Jean Murray Satchwell, but left South Africa in August to fight in World War II. Butler received his Honours degree in English from Brasenose College, Oxford in 1947, and his eight years as student and soldier are chronicled in the second volume of his autobiography, *Bursting World* (1983). On his return to South Africa he lectured in English at the University of the Witwatersrand. In 1951 he moved to Grahamstown as Senior Lecturer at Rhodes, and a year later was made Professor and Head of English. He retired in 1987, when he was appointed Emeritus Professor and Honorary Research Fellow. Butler received honorary doctorate of literature degrees from the universities of Natal, the Witwatersrand, South Africa, and Rhodes.

His early plays on the encounter between Boer and Briton, *The Dam* (1953), which received the Van Riebeeck Tercentenary Foundation Award, and *The Dove Returns* (1956), were performed with the support of the National Theatre Organization. Another play, *Demea,* was begun in the 1950s, but because it called for a nonracial cast, it could not be performed before 1990. Eastern Cape history, particularly the 1820 Settlers, provide the inspiration and subject matter for much of Butler's literary work. For the 150th anniversary celebrations in 1970 *Richard Gush of Salem* (1982) was performed, like the earlier Settler play, *Take Root or Die* (1970), and *Cape Charade or Kaatjie Kekkelbek* (1968), at the newly built Rhodes Theatre.

Butler's work aims to distinguish and synthesize the two strains of "Europe" and "Africa." Butler represents Africa as a place where white English-speakers strive to come to terms with themselves and their beliefs, and as a state of mind in which the poetic

imagination tries to find a locus, an idea he also explores in the third volume of his autobiography, *A Local Habitation* (1991). Butler's poetry struggles to reconcile contending forces and to be true to experience, which results in a combination of tension, serenity, and naturalness.

By the Sea (2002)

A novel by Abdulrazak **Gurnah.** A man from Zanzibar seeks refuge in Britain from the atrocities committed by the Zanzibar government. Gurnah vividly portrays the negative experience of a refugee in Britain at the end of the twentieth century. The man, Rajab Shaaban, unexpectedly meets the son of the man he was named after in England (Latif Mahmud), and the drama between the two families takes a major part of the narrative.

C

Cairo Trilogy (1956–57)

Naguib **Mahfouz**'s three novels published in 1956–57 follow the life of a Cairo family through three generations from 1917 to 1944. Egyptians regard the hero of *Palace Walk,* Ahmad Abd al-Jawad, and his wife Amina as archetypal figures. In *Palace of Desire,* attention focuses on their sons, the sensual Yasin and the intellectual Kamal (who is an autobiographical portrait of Mahfouz). In *Sugar Street* the grandchildren grow up and are drawn into the conflict between the Muslim Brotherhood and the Communists. These books, in which Mahfouz says he set out to write "a history of my country and of myself," are generally regarded as his greatest work.

Call Me by My Rightful Name (2003)

A novel by Isidore **Okpewho.** Set during the 1960s in America and Africa, this novel narrates the strange story of Otis Hampton, who suddenly starts to chant in an indecipherable language. When he discovers that the chant is a Yoruba family chant from Nigeria, Otis journeys there and is led to the exact place where his ancestor was enslaved before he could complete an ancient rite. Otis finds his relations, lives in the village for two years, learns the language, and completes the rite that his enslaved ancestor couldn't. He then returns to America and becomes involved in the civil rights movement.

Call Me Woman (1985)

The autobiography of Ellen **Kuzwayo.** The book reveals the resilience of its author, her struggle to overcome personal adversity and to become a community leader. Her own search for a place to call home is juxtaposed with the wider history of displacement experienced by black people in South Africa. The personal trauma of a disastrous marriage and separation from her sons is doubled by the trauma of detention without trial, but she also insists on the typicality of her experience. The book celebrates the achievements of black women in South Africa in the face of their double exclusion (as women and as blacks). Feminist critics have explored the tensions and ambiguities in Kuzwayo's attempt to define a feminist position while at the same time subscribing to what appear to be rather stereotypical views of femininity and womanhood.

Camara Laye (1928–80)

This Guinean novelist who wrote in French was born in Kouroussa, Upper Guinea, in what was then French West Africa. (Laye's first or given name is in fact Laye, and his family name is Camara, but he always referred to himself as "Camara Laye.") He was born into a lineage of Malinke (or Mande) blacksmiths and goldsmiths, and during his childhood in Kouroussa and in his mother's birth village of Tindican, he absorbed the traditional and not yet heavily French-influenced culture of his people. He attended both the Koranic and the local French elementary school in Kouroussa, and at age fourteen he traveled to Conakry, the distant coastal capital of Guinea, to pursue vocational studies in motor mechanics. In 1947, aged nineteen, he traveled to Paris to continue studies in mechanics, where he also worked at the Siruca automobile factory, in Les Halles food market, and took further course work in engineering and toward the *baccalauréat.*

In 1953 he published his first novel, *L'Enfant noir* (*The African Child,* 1954). It is the autobiographical story of a Guinean boy's life from his earliest childhood in the village of Kouroussa through his development in Conakry until his departure for France. The book won the Prix Charles Veillon in 1954, and was followed quickly by the very different *Le Regard du roi* (1954; *The Radiance of the King,* 1956). This second book concerns a white man, Clarence, who seeks his fortune in Africa, but fails. He then embarks on a search for recognition by the African king. In 1956 Camara Laye returned to Africa, first to Dahomey (now Benin), then Gold Coast (now Ghana), and then to newly independent Guinea, where he held a series of government posts. In 1965 he left Guinea for Dakar, Senegal, due to political troubles, and never returned. In 1966 he published his third novel, *Dramouss* (*A Dream of Africa,* 1968). It continues the autobiographical account of *L'Enfant noir,* but also contains a political critique of the corrupt Guinean regime. In 1978 Laye's fourth and final work appeared: *Le Maitre de la parole—Kouma Lafôlô Kouma* (*The Guardian of the Word,* 1980). Here, the author positions himself as the recorder and translator of the month-long 1963 narration by the traditional Malinke *griot* (traditional storyteller) Babou Conde of the famous Soundiata (or Sundiata or Sunjata) story: that of the legendary thirteenth-century founder of the powerful empire of Old Mali. Camara Laye died in Dakar of a kidney infection in 1980.

L'Enfant noir is widely recognized as a landmark in contemporary African writing. It is widely taught, read, translated, and critiqued in several languages. *Le Regard du roi* has attracted nearly as much critical attention—James Kirkup's recent English translation of *The Radiance of the King* includes an introduction by Toni Morrison. Though his life's literary output was small, Laye is an important pioneering figure in African literature in European language.

Further Reading

Butler, Thorpe. "Devolution as Salvation in Laye Camara's *The Radiance of the King.*" *Griot: Official Journal of the Southern Conference on Afro American Studies* 19, no. 1 (2000): 32–39.

King, Adele. *Rereading Camara Laye.* Lincoln: University of Nebraska Press, 2002.

Morrison, Toni. "On 'The Radiance of the King.'" *New York Review of Books* 48, no. 13 (August 9, 2001): 18–20.

Campbell, Roy(ston) (1901–57)

Campbell is South Africa's most widely recognized poet. He is known as a critic, autobiographer, and controversialist. Born in Durban in 1901 into the family of a wealthy physician, he was educated there before sailing for Oxford in 1919 to attempt admission to Merton College, where he hoped to read English. He was not successful and so he went to London, where he associated with the literary and artistic world of the capital. In 1922 he met and married the painter Mary Garman; the couple moved to the Welsh village of Aberdaron, where Campbell completed a long and extraordinary poem, *The Flaming Terrapin* (1924).

With the success of *The Flaming Terrapin*, Campbell returned to South Africa in 1924 where he founded South Africa's first bilingual literary and political journal, *Voorslag.* The journal's attacks on the color bar, as **apartheid** was then known, embarrassed its financial backer, and he forced Campbell's resignation as editor. It was during the period of artistic and political engagement when he worked on *Voorslag* that Campbell wrote many of the lyrics he was to publish in *Adamastor* in 1930. These are poems that depict white South African racial attitudes as not just morally wrong but also politically suicidal. Before his return to Europe at the end of 1926 he also wrote the long satire, *The Wayzgoose* (1928), an attack on white South African mediocrity and complacency.

On their return to England, the Campbells rented a cottage in Kent in 1927 and that same year met Vita Sackville-West, with whom Mary Campbell had an affair. This is the background to *The Georgiad* (1931), the long satirical poem attacking Sackville-West and all her friends. Of more lasting poetic value than *The Georgiad* was the next volume of verse he published, *Adamastor,* which confirmed his status as a poet of high talent.

In 1928 Campbell moved to France, where he published *Flowering Reeds* (1933), which demonstrates the French influence. He moved to Spain in 1933, where he finished an autobiography, *Broken Record* (1934), and revised the sonnet sequence he wrote in his last year in France, which was published as *Mithraic Emblems* in 1936. The Campbells moved to Portugal in 1937, where he wrote a long poem in defense of Franco's Nationalists. It was published as *Flowering Rifle* (1939), and with the appearance of this five-thousand-line poem Campbell's relations with his fellow writers in English (already strained by *The Georgiad*) were finally broken. *Flowering Rifle* convinced all who read it that Campbell was a fascist, and he was never able to fully free himself of this perception.

During World War II, he began a translation of the poems of St. John of the Cross, which he published in 1951, the same year that he published an additional autobiography titled *Light on a Dark Horse: An Autobiography (1901–35)* (1952). Campbell also wrote war poems about his service in the British forces in East Africa during the war, which he published as *Talking Bronco* (1946). After the war he lived in Portugal, where he was killed in car crash.

Further Reading

Akerman, Anthony. "Dark Outsiders: Writing the Dramatic Life of Roy Campbell." *English in Africa* 30, no. 1 (May 2003): 5–20.

Chapman, Michael. "Campbell Then and Now: The Case of the Politically Incorrect Poet." *English in Africa* 30, no. 1 (May 2003): 21–33.

Coullie, Judith Lutge. "The Race to Be a Hero: Race and Gender in Roy Campbell's *Light on a Dark Horse.*" *Scrutiny2: Issue in English Studies in Southern Africa* 6, no. 2 (2001): 3–16.

Taylor, Dora. "Unbroken Record: A Study of Roy Campbell." *English in Africa* 29, no. 2 (October 2002): 31–36.

Captain's Tiger, The (1998)

A play by Athol **Fugard.** Subtitled "A Memoir for the Stage," this work depicts an Author, his younger self who is a servant called the Captain's Tiger on a steamship, and the Tiger's relationship with the character he is writing, Betty Le Roux. The author recalls this period of his life and his interactions with his character—who insists on being real despite his imagination of her. The play is somewhat autobiographical in that Betty's narrative—told in detail as part of the plot of the play—is that of Fugard's mother, Elizabeth Magdalena Katerina Potgieter.

Carnival of Looters, A (2000)

Poems by Tayo Peter **Olafioye.** Olafioye explores the meaning of nationhood in this volume of poetry, published first in his home nation of Nigeria. He captures a feeling of loss and nostalgia for his home, anger at the "looters" who are tearing it apart, and personal feelings of love and desire that interlock with the theme of nationhood. He calls for the use of poetry to understand the idea of the nation, and to effect political change.

Casely-Hayford, Adelaide (1868–60)

A prose writer, Casely-Hayford was born of Fanti and English parents and studied in Sierra Leone and England and later lived in Sierra Leone. As one of Africa's pioneer writers in English, she and Mabel Dove Danquah were among the first to reach an international audience. Casely-Hayford used her influence as the wife of the distinguished diplomat Joseph Ephraïm Casely-Hayford to benefit Africa in general and African women in particular, especially in women's education. Her story "Mista Courifer," discovered by Langston Hughes and anthologized in *An African Treasury* (1960), is a lightly ironic portrait of a Sierra Leone elitist who apes everything British; it and the autobiographical *Reminiscences* (1953) reveal a sense of herself as African that was unusual in a Creole culture that privileged its British heritage.

Further Reading

Cromwell, Adelaide M. *An African Victorian Feminist: Adelaide Smith Casely Hayford 1868–1960.* London: Frank Cass, 1986.

Desai, Gaurav. "Gendered Self-Fashioning: Adelaide Casely Hayford's Black Atlantic." *Research in African Literatures* 35, no. 3 (Fall 2004): 141–60.

Hunter, Lucilda, ed. *Mother and Daughter: Memoirs and Poems by Adelaide and Gladys Casely-Hayford.* Freetown: Sierra Leone University Press, 1983.

Casely-Hayford, Gladys (1904–50)

A poet and short-story writer, Gladys Casely-Hayford was born in Ghana but was taken early to England for medical care and was educated in Europe. She returned to Freetown, Sierra Leone, in 1926 to help her mother, Adelaide **Casely-Hayford,** with her girls' vocational school. In the 1930s she spent a few years in Europe, joined a Berlin jazz group, and traveled in the United States. She was, like her parents, a pioneer West African writer, and intensely aware of herself as

African. That awareness informs the language and rhythms of such poems as "Rejoice" and "Nativity," which celebrate blackness. Although she was not widely published before her death, during the 1960s her poems were often anthologized. She also wrote poems in Krio, some of which were published as *Take Um So* (1948), a pamphlet.

Further Reading

Hunter, Lucilda, ed. *Mother and Daughter: Memoirs and Poems by Adelaide and Gladys Casely-Hayford.* Freetown: Sierra Leone University Press, 1983.

Casely-Hayford, Joseph Ephraïm

(1866–30)
Lawyer and politician from the Gold Coast, he is the author of the novel *Ethiopia Unbound* (1911), which is one of the first texts of fiction produced in English in West Africa. His book is a defense of black people and critical of Christianity, a religion dominated by white people, despite the fact that its origin can be, according to him, traced back to Ethiopia. *Ethiopia Unbound* is the story of Kwamankra and his friend Whitely who move from London to the Gold Coast. The author constructs a satirical presentation of the colonial milieu. Stories and songs, sometimes in Fanti, are included in the narration as are poems in Victorian English. It is an African literary landmark, and the work of a distinguished intellectual. Biographies on Joseph Ephraïm Casely-Hayford include Isaac S. Ephson's article in *Gallery of Gold Coast Celebrities 1632–1958* (1969), and L. H. Ofosu-Appiah's *Joseph Ephraim Casely Hayford: The Man of Vision and Faith* (1975).

Censorship

EAST AFRICA

Although censorship in East Africa has historically been politically motivated, the early 1970s did see a moral response to sexual content in popular fiction and a debate about its effect on human behavior, which led the Tanzanian government to temporarily ban Osija Mwambungu's (**Prince Kagwema's**) novel *Veneer of Love* (1975), Charles **Mangua's** *Son of Woman* (1971), and David G. Maillu's books. The banning of works is the most common kind of censorship, and there are many examples of it. For example, **Ngugi wa Thiong'o's** and Ngugi wa Mirii's play *Ngaahika Ndeenda (I Will Marry When I Want)* was banned until 1994, while Ngugi's play *Maitu Njugira (Mother Sing for Me)* was not allowed to be publicly performed by the Kamiriithu Theatre Group in 1982, and Kamiriithu's people's theater was later demolished by police. Ngugi's novel (written in the Gikuyu language) *Matigari* (1986) was removed from the Kenyan market in 1987, and around the same time Joe **De Graft's** *Muntu,* Alamin Mazrui's Swahili play *Kilio cha Haki (The Cry for Justice)* and students of Nairobi School's *Kilio (The Cry)* were also banned from participating in any public or political action.

In addition to the banning of texts, censorship is also present in the form of imprisonment or detention of authors. *Transition* magazine editor Rajat Neogy was detained and put on trial by President Milton Obote in the late 1960s, and despite the fact that Neogy was cleared, *Transition* was no longer published in Uganda. The omission of some authors from the school curriculum can also be defined as censorship, and in the 1980s in Kenya "literature" as a subject in the school system became conflated with "English," resulting in the removal of several local books (in 1988 Ngugi wa Thiong'o's books were removed) that had been required texts.

The effect of outside competition also censors East African works in the sense that they are not able to compete with more dominant cultures. The Kenya National Theatre ran into this kind of censorship when its foreign management clashed with the Ministry of Social Services over the inclusion of Kenyan plays in the repertoire. The foreign administration of the theater finally allowed two Kenyan plays to run for eight days, while two foreign shows ran for thirty-one days. Publishers' choices also determine what kind of literature will be available to the East African market, and much of what is published is popular literature, and popular Western literature that does not represent East African literature with serious themes or more "literary" aims. In addition, publishers are far more unlikely to publish new indigenous authors whose work would add to the growth of East African literature.

In addition to all of these forms of censorship, there is also the problem of self-censorship, which refers to the decision some authors make not to publish their work because of inevitable persecution. Again, a reliance on foreign publishers, donors, and theater owners results in self-censorship when adherence to foreign traditions or artistic ideas is required for fiscal operation. Currently, censorship on the Internet has become an issue in areas like Ethiopia, where in May 2006, Web sites and blogs criticizing the government became mysteriously unavailable. In a similar testament to continued censorship in Ethiopia, in November 2005, newspaper editors and the leadership of the main opposition coalition were arrested after they protested against the results of the May 15 legislative elections, and a number of journalists working for the independent press were also arrested in 2006 for defamation cases going back to the end of the 1990s. In the Sudan, authorities closed the *Khartoum Monitor* newspaper for a day, after an argument involving two articles about the clashes that took place between internally displaced persons and Sudanese security forces in Soba Eradi IDP camp in May 2005.

Censorship has been undermined in East Africa through various forms including satire, humor, and allegory, and in a certain sense it has in turn fueled rather than dampened the production of literature. For example, Ngugi wrote **Devil on the Cross** while he was in prison for publishing *Ngaahika Ndeena* in 1978, while other works like Francis **Imbuga**'s play *Betrayal in the City* (1976), John **Ruganda**'s *The Floods* (1980), Cyprian Karamagi's novel *Bulemu the Bastard* (1980), and Wahome Mutahi's *Three Days on the Cross* (1991) demonstrate subversive reactions to censorship.

NORTH AFRICA

In North Africa similar censorship problems exist. In Tunisia, for example, "a large number of books are banned in the country, websites are blocked, state media are totally dominant, private media exercise strict self-censorship and dissident voices are thrown into prison" (*Afrol News,* February 2, 2005, http://www.afrol.com/articles/15503). *Afrol News* also reports that the International Publisher's Association (IPA) and PEN Norway and the Norweigian section of International PEN encouraged the EU to adopt a plan to tackle Tunisia's censorship problems, and gave them a list of books banned by the Tunisian government.

SOUTH AFRICA

In South Africa, the Publications Act of 1974 (which became effective in April 1975) controls the staging of public entertainment, and the production and distribution of books and films. Before 1975 the Suppression of Communism Act (1950) and the Publications and Entertainment Act (1963) were the means of censorship, while the Internal Security Act (1976) later joined these acts to allow the state to suppress literature they defined as Communist or as published by an outlawed organization (like the African National Congress). In addition to these restrictive laws was the set of laws that held in place the **apartheid** legislation, which together resulted in extensive governmental control and censorship throughout the 1950s and 1960s. Many authors were banned and went into exile, and even the works of those who went into exile were banned so that they were not available in South Africa. In fact, under these strict laws many publishers and writers incurred large financial losses, while readers were prohibited from reading important works. For example, in 1976 there were 1,141 publications (including things like films) deemed "undesirable" out of the 1,944 that were submitted. After 1976 censorship only increased due to the Soweto uprising. This kind of censorship resulted in a sort of isolation for South Africa, as scholars and authors like Dennis **Brutus,** Todd Matshikiza, James **Matthews,** Es'kia **Mphahlele,** Nat **Nakasa,** and Lewis **Nkosi** were made silent. Committees set up by the Publications Act reviewed books, films, and entertainments, and the act also had a Directorate of Publications, and a Publications Appeal Board. The role of the committees was to examine publications submitted by publishers, the police, the general public, or customs officers and to decide whether the publication should be banned without hearing evidence. The directorate then conveyed the findings to the necessary people, and if the publication was determined to be objectionable it could be an offense both to distribute and to possess it. The definitions of what could be found undesirable under the Publications Act were detailed in section 47(2), which included indecency, obscenity, blasphemy; to bring "any section of the inhabitants of the Republic into ridicule or contempt"; to be "harmful to the relations between any section of the inhabitants of the Republic"; or to be "prejudicial to the safety of the State, the general welfare, or the peace and good order." In addition, despite the fact that the act allowed for an appeal against the decision of a publications committee, many writers refused to comply with the system by utilizing the appeals process (although some appeals were allowed).

Andre **Brink**'s *Kennis van die Aand* (***Looking on Darkness,*** 1974) was the first Afrikaans literature to be banned (in 1973). In 1977 Ètienne Leroux's *Magersfontein, O Magersfontein* (1976) was banned despite the fact that it was a Central News Agency (CNA) winner and while it was banned it won the Hertzog Award. Breyten **Breytenbach**'s *And Death White as Words* (1978) was banned while he was in prison. Despite the suppression of these works, it was mainly works by black authors that were affected by censorship. Miriam **Tlali**'s ***Muriel at Metropolitan*** (1975) was banned because it was seen to contain negative remarks about Afrikaners, Sipho **Sepamla**'s collection of poems *The Soweto I Love* (1977) and Gibson **Kente**'s play *Too Late* (1975) were also banned. Meanwhile, the play *Confused Mhlaba* by Khayalethu Mqayisa failed on appeal, and eight out of the first thirteen volumes of *Staffrider* were banned, and with them works by Mtutuzeli Matshoba, Mothobi **Mutloatse,** Daniel P. **Kunene,** Mbulelo **Mzamane,** and Mongane Wally.

When, in 1979, André Brink's *A **Dry White Season*** (1979) and Nadine **Gordimer**'s ***Burger's Daughter*** (1979) were banned, there was a public uproar that resulted in an appeal by the directorate against its own committees. *A Dry White Season* was secretly published and distributed by mail in an attempt to escape censors, and it tackled the subject of deaths in detention in order to raise Afrikaner political consciousness. Gordimer's text was accused of attacking the Republic of South Africa, and was banned under all categories of the act. Gordimer countered with *What Happened to Burger's Daughter* (1980), which criticized censorship in specific terms. Eventually J.C.W. van Rooyen, chair of the Publications Appeal Board in 1980, had to deal with the uproar that was caused by the banning of major texts. Some changes were made under van Rooyen's supervision, including a call for a more realistic interpretation of the criteria, a definition of "undesirability" based on the "probable reader" rather than the general public, and the creation of an expert committee to decide literary merit. The results were that texts were not banned based on passages out of context; there was more lenience toward the expression of political complaints by black writers; the banning of issues of literary journals before they were released was no longer allowed; and less literary works were banned, while ones that had been banned were published again. Instead, there was a turn to the regulation and censorship of resistant political groups and of the media.

The goal of censorship in South Africa was to assist apartheid policies by containing political debate and the impact of literary imagination. Due to this agenda, authors and artists were persecuted while publishing and academic work was hindered. In 1990 F. W. de Klerk brought in changes that turned the government away from greater control, and currently the censorship laws are under revision. In spite of these changes, censorship continues to be a problem in South Africa. The *Freedom of Expression Institute* in Johannesburg recently released a report on the growth of self-censorship in South Africa, citing the example of a documentary on South African President Thabo Mbeki that was pulled from broadcast in May 2006. The press release states: "given the content of the documentary, the decision to pull the documentary at the very last minute has the look and the feel of self-censorship" (http://allafrica.com/stories/200605260781.html).

SOUTH-CENTRAL AFRICA

The focus of censorship in South-Central Africa, specifically in Zimbabwe, has historically been obscenity and indecency in literature and film. This focus on obscene or indecent material continued into the 1990s, and one explanation of the earlier censorship is a settler agenda associated with both moral expectations and protection from the corruption of Western influences. The focus of censorship changed slightly during the UDI (Unilateral Declaration of Independence) period (1965–79) in Rhodesia, when the government created laws to control the press (in particular) and the censorship board banned literature that focused on the oppression and goals of the black majority (due to an anxiety created by civil war between settlers and African nationalism groups).

From 1912 (when the Obscene Publications Act was created) until 1932 the official censors were the town police in Bulawayo and Salisbury. The 1912 act was created in order to prevent the publication, marketing, dissemination, and possession of any obscene print material. The production and importation of such products carried the heaviest fine (up to 250 pounds), while the fine for possession was ten pounds. In 1914 censorship focused on communications with foreign countries through mail or other means (specifically Germany) and was cited as a security measure. The government continued this focus on national security after World War I, as in the late 1920s a controller of censorship was introduced by the Ministry of Defence who monitored postal services, radio, newspapers, books, and photography. Censorship continued to be associated with defense as World War II brought about new legislation from 1939–45.

Film began to be censored starting in 1917, as the government agreed to be led by the Transvaal censorship board in the matter. The Transvaal board sent its lists of films acceptable for European audiences and acceptable for "coloured persons and natives" to the Zimbabwean government weekly. The American Board of Missions also controlled access to films for black residents by 1927, and even more legislation to control access to material was brought about through the Entertainments Control and Censorship Act (1932), which especially limited access to the lower classes and to the black population. The focus of the 1932 board of censors was on new technology and material available in metropolitan centers, and the focus on banning material that criticized or satirized draws attention to a religious and racially based motivation.

After World War II the Southern Rhodesian government used censorship mainly against the press. Initially set up to censor Communist literature, the Subversive Activities Act (1950) later prohibited more than that accused of Communism. In fact, in the early 1960s it brought legal action against any newspaper, editor, or author who created "alarm and despondency." As the UDI began to fall apart in 1965 censors given power through the Emergency Powers (Control of Publications) Act went into newspaper offices and censored the papers as they were being set. Some papers responded with blank spaces, but that too was censored. In 1966 these regulations were found by the Constitutional Council to breach the Bill of Rights, and in 1967 the Censorship and Entertainment Control Act was issued to replace the former censorship laws; this was the foundation for censorship until independence. Throughout the 1970s a great number of books and magazines were censored for sexual or nationalist content, as the board of censors appointed by the Minister of Law and Order regularly created lists of banned material.

Despite the fact that the 1967 act was technically in place until three years after independence, in 1980 a major change occurred in policy, as many books by Zimbabwean authors that had been banned during UDI were unbanned. For the first time the Zimbabwean public had access to works by authors such as Canaan Banana, Wilson **Katiyo,** Doris **Lessing,** Charles **Mungoshi,** Garikai Mutasa, Solomon **Mutswairo,** Stanlake **Samkange,** Ndabaningi Sithole, Lawrence **Vambe,** Thomas Mapfumo, and Frederick Zindi. A return to censorship occurred in 1981 when

Black Sunlight by Dambudzo **Marechera** was banned because of obscenity, and although it was unbanned in 1982 after appeal, the instance foreshadowed future inclinations.

Beginning with the Censorship and Entertainment Control Amendment Act of 1983, censorship has returned to the focus it demonstrated in 1912, as it penalizes indecent or obscene works and especially sexual content in visual material. There are fewer books banned for sexual content than had been in the preindependence era, and almost none have been banned for political content since 1980. For example, in 1996 a Zimbabwean film titled *Flame* was questioned because of its sexual content and not its political message, while later that year the board attempted to ban works displayed by the gays and lesbians of Zimbabwe at the Zimbabwe International Book Fair.

Despite these actions, there was a concerted effort throughout the 1980s to release books that were banned during UDI, especially those with a political message, but also those that were previously thought to be obscene.

WEST AFRICA

Journalists and other media outlets are targeted for censorship in West Africa, as there is a greater amount of illiteracy and the reading public tends to prefer newspapers and other periodicals. The censorship of journalists involves extreme actions like harassment, physical abuse, arrest and incarceration without trial, death threats, murder, and occasionally, family members are held in the absence of the journalists themselves. For example, in 1984 Charles Gbenyon (editor-in-chief of Liberian Television) was murdered in President Samuel Doe's mansion, and Nigerian investigative journalist Dele Giwa (editor-in-chief of *Newswatch*) was murdered by parcel bomb in 1986.

Nigerian journalists Dan Agbese, Ray Ekpu, and Yakubu Mohammed of *Newswatch* magazine were all detained in April 1994 (and later given a presidential pardon) after they interviewed a retired brigadier-general who criticized the military regime. The harassment in Ghana encouraged journalists to keep silent, until in 1991 and 1992 there was outspoken opposition from the Ghana Journalist Association when the state-owned *Daily Graphic* threatened eleven outspoken critics with transfer. In Sierra Leone the government introduced a law (repealed in 1993) that reduced their thirty-six newspapers to eleven, and journalists like Ibrahim Seaga-Shaw (editor of *New Oracle*) were arrested and interrogated. Journalists from foreign countries were also subjected to censorship techniques, as in the case of Geraldine Brooks. In April 1994 Brooks (a reporter for the *Wall Street Journal*) was turning up material for a story on the violence in Ogoniland, Nigeria, related to that associated with Ken **Saro-Wiwa**'s execution, when she was arrested, held for several days, and then deported. Two CNN journalists were also deported in the same year.

Publishing and media outlets are subject to censorship techniques like confiscation of their publications, the production of fake editions that are supportive of the government, restrictive licensing laws, proscription, short-term closure, and police siege. Legislation aimed at restricting freedom of the press included Ghana's licensing laws of 1963, 1973, and 1989; Nigeria's Official Secrets Act of 1962, decrees 4 (1984) and 43 (1993); Liberia's decree 88A of 1984; and Sierra Leone's press guidelines of 1994, as they contained strict registration mandates and vetoes on specific publications. The advent of what was called *guerilla journalism* began when entire editions of Nigerian periodicals like the *News* and *Tell* were seized at multiple times in 1993 and 1994, and the response of the *News* was to replace its publication for a short period (and published in differing locations) with *Tempo*. In Senegal a regional conference on censorship and West African Music was held in 2005. Journalists gathered to share and compile information on the status of censorship and auto-censorship in many other countries and continents (http://www.freemuse.org/sw8980.asp). Similarly, the West African Journalists Association (WAJA) has recently shown concern over the levels of censorship in the Gambia, Nigeria, and Sierra Leone, citing lack of independence of media monitoring commissions, a lack of protection for the confidentiality of sources, and requirements for media outlets to register with governments (http://www.ifex.org/en/content/view/full/28201/?PHPSESSID). In Nigeria the ability to prohibit material has been used widely, and in 1994 nineteen newspapers and magazines were banned. Out of those nineteen ten were run by the Concord Group, which is owned by Moshood Abiola, who is commonly regarded as the winner of the 1992 presidential elections, and who was detained when election results were annulled by the military.

Further Reading

North Africa

Gafaiti, Hafid. "Between God and the President: Literature and Censorship in North Africa." *Diacritics: A Review of Contemporary Criticism* 27, no. 2 (1997): 59–84.

South Africa

Anthonissen, Christine. "Challenging Media Censoring: Writing between the Lines in the Face of Stringent Restrictions." In *Re/Reading the Past: Critical and Functional Perspectives on Time and Value*, ed. J. R. Martin and Ruth Wodak. Amsterdam: Benjamins, 2003, 91–112.

de Lange, Margreet. "Censorship and Literature in a Democratic South Africa." In *The Search for a New Alphabet: Literary Studies in a Changing World*, ed. Harold Hendrix, Joost Kloek, Sophie Levie, and Will van Peer. Amsterdam: Benjamins, 1996, 135–39.

de Lange, Margreet, and Ampie Coetzee. *The Muzzled Muse: Literature and Censorship in South Africa*. Amsterdam: Benjamins, 1997.

Drewett, Michael. "Aesopian Strategies of Textual Resistance in the Struggle to Overcome the Censorship of Popular Music in Apartheid South Africa." In *Censorship and Cultural Regulation in the Modern Age,* ed. Beate Müller. Amsterdam: Rodopi, 2004, 189–207.

Grobler, G.M.M. "Creative African-Language Writing in South Africa: Writers Unshackled after Apartheid?" *South African Journal of African Languages/Suid-Afrikaanse Tydskrif vir Afrikatale* 15, no. 2 (1995): 56–60.

Higgins, John. "From Academic Analysis to Apparatchik Thinking: A Reply to André du Toit." *Pretexts: Literary and Cultural Studies* 12, no. 2 (2003): 191–97.

Jaygbay, Jacob. "Self-Censorship in African Scholarship and Scholarly Publishing." *Journal of Scholarly Publishing* 29, no. 2 (1998): 112–17.

Kabeer, Naila. "Selective Rights, Collective Wrongs: Women, Body-Politics and the Development Agenda." *Index on Censorship* 24, no. 4 (1995): 32–42.

Kistner, Ulrike. "The Elided Performative: The Human Rights Commission's Inquiry into Racism in the Media." *Pretexts: Literary and Cultural Studies* 10, no. 2 (2001): 195–217.

Merrett, Christopher. "The Banning and Unbanning of *Africa Today* in South Africa." *Africa Today* 39, nos. 1–2 (1992): 3–4.

Mungai, Anne, and Alison Preston, trans. "Responsibility and Freedom of Expression." In *African Experiences of Cinema,* ed. Imruch Bakari and Mbye B. Cham. London: British Film Institute, 1996, 65–66.

Ngugi wa Thiong'o. "License to Write: Encounters with Censorship." *Comparative Studies of South Asia, Africa and the Middle East* 23, nos. 1–2 (2003): 54–57.

Ssali, Ndugu Mike. "Apartheid and Cinema." In *African Experiences of Cinema,* ed. Imruch Bakari and Mbye B. Cham. London: British Film Institute, 1996, 83–101.

Trabold, Bryan P. "Writing Space, Power, and Strategies of Resistance in Apartheid South Africa: The Story of the 'Weekly Mail' and 'New Nation.'" *Dissertation Abstracts International, Section A: The Humanities and Social Sciences* 64, no. 8 (2004): 2871–72.

South-Central Africa

Ambler, Charles. "Popular Films and Colonial Audiences in Central Africa." In *Hollywood Abroad: Audiences and Cultural Exchange,* ed. Melvyn Stokes and Richard Maltby. London: British Film Institute, 2004, 133–57.

West Africa

[Author unknown.] "Soyinka 'Silenced?'" *West Africa,* no. 3914 (September 1992): 1819.

Korpe, Marie. *Shoot the Singer!: Music Censorship Today*. London: Zed Books, 2004.

Chaka (1931)

A novel by Thomas **Mofolo,** translated from the Sesotho (*Chaka,* 1925). The result of prolonged research by its writer, the chronicle of the life of Shaka, a notable Zulu king, is a landmark in South African fiction. Mofolo describes the rise and fall of Chaka, whom he presents as a noble figure fatally lured by the desire for power. A relentless and despotic leader, Shaka subjugates most of the neighboring tribes. The price of this success is a pact in which he agrees to kill his wife. The tyrant's inevitable downfall is linked to his life; his enemies as well as his own brothers (who he initially wrested the chieftainship from) threaten him. The brothers eventually kill him, thus solemnizing the evil he has sown. Mofolo's psychological and philosophical insights into Shaka are unique.

Chaos Theory of the Heart and Other Poems Mainly since 1990 (2005)

This final work by Lionel **Abrahams** includes seventy-five poems, including those that have been published elsewhere and some new ones.

Chedid, Andrée (1920–)

Novelist, poet, and playwright writing in French, born in Egypt of Lebanese descent. She wrote the first of twenty volumes of verse while she was a student at the American

University in Cairo. She has also written ten novels as well as a number of plays, of which the best-known is *Bérénice d'Egypt* (1981). Chedid won the Grand Prix of Belgium in 1975 for her whole body of work, three French prizes for her poetry, and the Prix Goncourt for the short story. In 1991, the journal *Sud* devoted an issue to her entitled *Andrée Chedid, Voix multiple.*

Chedid defies geographic, temporal, and linguistic barriers, as her fiction flows easily between France and Egypt. Her novels include *Sommeil délivré* (1952; *From Sleep Unbound,* 1983); *Le Sixième jour* (1960; *The Sixth Day,* 1987), also a film, *La Maison sans racines* (1985; *The Return to Beirut,* 1989); and *L'Enfant multiple* (1989; *The Multiple Child,* 1995). Recently Chedid has published in French *Le message: Roman* (2000), *Petite Terre, Vaste Rêve* (2002), *Poursuites : [poèmes]* ([dessins de] Xavier; préface de Jörge de Sousa Noronha, 2003), and *Rythmes: Poèmes* (2003). Recent English translations include *The Prose and Poetry of Andrée Chedid: Selected Poems, Short Stories, and Essays,* translated by Renée Linkhorn (1990); *Selected Poems of Andrée Chedid,* translated and edited by Judy Cochran (1995); *[Green Integer #37] Fugitive Suns: Selected Poetry: A Bilingual Edition,* translated by Lynne Goodhart and John Wagner (1999), which is her first English-language collection of poetry from throughout her career; and *Territories of Breath* (*Territoires du soufflé*), translated and edited by Judy Pfau Cochran (2002).

Further Reading

Bancquart, Marie-Claire, and Michael Bishop, trans. "Andrée Chedid, Venus Khoury-Ghata, and Martine Broda." *Studies in Twentieth Century Literature* 26, no. 1 (Winter 2002): 228–36.

Cochran, Judy Pfau. "Andrée Chedid: Poet of Flesh and Destiny." *Antemnae Review* (October 4, 2002): 93–102.

Cheney-Coker, Syl (1945–)

Poet and novelist Cheney-Coker was born in Freetown, Sierra Leone. He studied at the universities of Oregon and Wisconsin in the United States, and in 1988 was a visiting writer in the International Writing Program at the University of Iowa. He works as a journalist in Freetown.

Cheney-Coker's four volumes of poetry, *The Road to Jamaica* (1969), *Concerto for an Exile* (1973), *The Graveyard Also Has Teeth* (1980), and *The Blood in the Desert's Eyes* (1990), derive from the Creole culture of Sierra Leone, where the images, patterns, and techniques of indigenous African oratory are far less influential than those of European culture. As a result, African themes such as the slave trade and its consequences for the people of Sierra Leone, his own Creole roots, the destruction of the natural environment, and the internecine wars of independent Africa are paired with references to Greek mythology, Goya, Breughel, Shakespeare, Blake, and Vivaldi. Cheney-Coker's only novel, *The **Last Harmattan of Alusine Dunbar*** (1990), won a Commonwealth Writers Prize and is an account of the history of Sierra Leone in the magic realist style.

Further Reading

Bertinetti, Paolo. "Reality and Magic in Syl Cheney-Coker's *The Last Harmattan of Alusine Dunbar.*" In *Coterminous Worlds: Magical Realism and Contemporary Post-Colonial Literature in English,* ed. (and introduction) Elsa Linguanti, Francesco Casotti, and Carmen Concilio. Amsterdam: Rodopi, 1999, 197–207.

Whyte, Philip. "Gender and Epic in Syl Cheney-Coker's *The Last Harmattan of Alusine Dunbar.*" *Commonwealth Essays and Studies* 26, no. 1 (Autumn 2003): 53–60.

Children of Gebelawi (1959; trans. 1981)

This work by Naguib **Mahfouz** is an allegorical novel in five parts, four of whose heroes relive in a Cairo alley the lives of Adam, Moses, Jesus, and Muhammad. The fifth represents the scientist, whose activities bring about the death of their ancestor Gebelawi. The novel has been banned ever since its serialization in 1959 because many consider it to be blasphemous. Mahfouz claims that it is deeply religious.

Chimombo, Steve (1945–)

Malawian poet and playwright, born in Zomba and educated at Zomba Catholic Secondary School. He studied at the University of Malawi, the University of Wales, and at Columbia University, where he completed a PhD. He is Professor of English at Chancellor College, Malawi.

Chimombo is the author of three plays, *The **Rainmaker*** (1978), *Wachiona Ndani?* (1983), which is particularly popular in Malawi, and *Sister! Sister!* (1995), but is better known as a poet. His ***Napolo Poems*** (1987) was nominated for a Commonwealth Poetry Prize and draws on oral tradition surrounding the legendary characters Mbona and Napolo, while *Python! Python!* (1992), is an epic poem. Chimombo published *A Referendum of the Forest Creatures* (1993) in response to political developments in Malawi, while *The "Vipya" Poem* (1996) commemorates the sinking of the *M. V. Vipya* in Lake Malawi in 1946. He has also written a short novel, *The Basket Girl* (1990), *Napolo and the Python: Selected Poetry* (1994), *The Wrath of Napolo: A Novel* (2000), and *The Bird Boy's Song: Retold by Steve Chimombo* (2002).

Chimombo's verse struggles to help both poet and nation survive unbroken under an oppressive political dispensation. He has also published literary criticism, including *A Bibliography of Oral Literature in Malawi: 1860–1986* (1987), *Malawian Oral Literature: The Aesthetics of Indigenous Arts* (1988), and *The Culture of Democracy: Language, Literature, the Arts, and Politics in Malawi, 1992–1994* with Moira Chimombo (1996).

Further Reading

Nazombe, Anthony. "Chimombo's Use of the M'bona Myth in *The Rainmaker*." *Journal of Humanities* 1 (1987): 37–53.

Chingono, Julius (1946–)

Chingono is a Zimbabwean writer of poetry, and more recently short stories. He has published five books of poetry, including *Chipo Changu, Mureza weRudo, Ruvimbo,* and two English books *Kazwi* and *Flag of Rags.* Chingono has also published poetry in various literary magazines and anthologies such as *Chirimo, Electra, Parade, Revival,* and the *Mambo Book of Zimbabwean Verse.* His first short story, titled "Maria's Interview," was published in Irene Staunton's short-story collection *Writing Still* (2003). Most of Chingono's poetry involves social commentary and a concern for those who have difficult lives.

Chinodya, Shimmer (1957–)

Chinodya, a fiction writer and poet, was born in Gweru, Rhodesia (now Zimbabwe), and educated at Goromonzi High School and at the then University of Rhodesia, where he studied English literature and trained as a school teacher, and at the University of Iowa in the United States, where he gained a master's degree in fine art. Some of his poems were published in T. O. McLoughlin's *New Writing in Rhodesia* (1976) and Kizito Muchemwa's anthology *Zimbabwean Poetry in English* (1978), but his first major publication was a collection of loosely related tales, *Dew in the Morning* (1982). In *Dew in the Morning,* Chinodya describes growing up in colonial Rhodesia and expresses the sights and sounds of rural life in Africa, where memorable peasant characters struggle to survive in a harsh environment. In his first novel, *Farai's Girls* (1984), he once again explores the theme of growing up in Rhodesia, this time against the background of a guerilla war of liberation. His novel *Harvest of Thorns* (1989) portrays life in the Rhodesia of the

1950s as well as the liberation war of the 1960s and 1970s, and fuses Western and African modes of expression. The experiences of a protagonist who eventually becomes a guerilla fighter, but who finds that he has nothing when the war is over, link the various segments of the novel together. *Harvest of Thorns* won the 1990 Commonwealth Writers Prize for the Africa region and has since been translated into German. Chinodya has also written five children's books in the series *Traditional Tales of Zimbabwe;* a film script, *Everyone's Child* (1996); a collection of short stories about political, religious, and other relevant issues titled *Can We Talk and Other Stories* (1998); and texts for schools, all of which reveal a writer keen to introduce students to a literature and culture rooted in Africa but open to the influences of the wider world.

Further Reading

Calder, Angus. "The New Zimbabwe Writing and Chimurenga." *Wasafiri: Journal of Caribbean, African, Asian and Associated Literatures and Film* 22 (1995): 35–42.

Chinweizu (1943–)

Nigerian poet and critic. Born in Eluama-Isuikwato in eastern Nigeria, Chinweizu studied mathematics and philosophy at the Massachusetts Institute of Technology and American studies and history at the State University of New York, Buffalo, before undertaking postdoctoral research in economics back at MIT. This background enabled him to carry out an interdisciplinary exploration of Africa's contemporary political, economic, and cultural condition, an exploration that centers with passionate intensity on the continent's despoliation by the West. He continued to focus on this topic while working as a journalist from the 1980s onward for newspapers such as the Lagos *Guardian* and *Vanguard,* which has led him to be identified as Nigeria's most celebrated polemicist.

The West and the Rest of Us (1975) is a historical account of Western domina-

tion of the developing world, especially of Africa. The book critiques Africa's governing elites and argues for the dissolution of dominant Eurocentric values and a reconstruction of African society through the establishment of pan-African political and economic unity. Chinweizu's most influential work, *Toward the Decolonization of African Literature* (1980), is a compilation of a series of essays published in *Okike* in the 1970s and co-authored with Onwuchekwa Jemie and Ihechukwu Madubuike. In this work Chinweizu and his colleagues dissect the analytical weaknesses and prejudices of "Eurocentric" critics of African literature. Chapters on African fiction and poetry distinguish between works that the three authors see as tied to Eurocentric models and works they regard as authentically African, while another chapter of note is that on oral storytelling techniques. Both Chinweizu's poetry, collected in *Energy Crisis* (1978) and *Invocations and Admonitions* (1986), and his stories, collected in *The Footnote* (1981), frequently reiterate the destructive social and cultural transformations inflicted on Africa by the West. The essay collection *Decolonising the African Mind* (1987) contains some astringent analysis of Africa's economic malaise, along with harsh criticism of other African writers. *Anatomy of Female Power* (1990) inverts progressive recognitions of women's oppression under patriarchy and identifies women as tyrants over men.

Further Reading

Chowdhury, Kanishka. "Afrocentric Voices: Constructing Identities, (Dis)Placing Difference." In *Race-ing Representation: Voice, History, and Sexuality,* ed. Kostas Myrsiades and Linda Myrsiades. Lanham, MD: Rowman & Littlefield, 1998. 17–41.

Chipamaunga, Edmund (1938–)

Zimbabwean novelist Chipamaunga was born in Chivhu in what was then Rhodesia, and educated at Daramombe Primary, St. Mary's Secondary, and St. Augustine's High School, and at the University of Rhodesia, where some of his poems were published in the student magazine *Opus*. He has been headmaster at schools in Zimbabwe, and during the 1980s served as Zimbabwe's ambassador to the United States and Kenya. His first novel, *A Fighter for Freedom* (1983), explores the causes of the Zimbabwean liberation war and the way it was prosecuted by blacks and whites. The narrative combines nineteenth-century realism and the fantasy of the African folktale, while it also disproves colonial myths that portray blacks as childish cowards incapable of planning a war, with a protagonist whose military exploits and legendary stature recall the heroes of the Hollywood Western. Chipamaunaga's second novel, *Chains of Freedom* (1997), explores the theme of betrayal in postindependence Africa as greed and corruption multiply in Zimbabwe, and he is also the author of *Feeding Freedom* (2000). Chipamaunga's writing explores themes and concerns central to an understanding of the Zimbabwean experience.

Chipasula, Frank (1949–)

A Malawian poet, Chipasula was born in Luanshya, Zambia. He started writing at the age of fifteen. He began a degree in English at the University of Malawi, but completed it in exile at the University of Zambia. Chipasula also gained postgraduate degrees at Yale and Brown universities in the United States, and teaches black studies at the University of Nebraska at Omaha.

Visions and Reflections (1972) was the first book of verse published by a Malawian. It was followed by *O Earth, Wait for Me* (1984), *When My Brothers Come Home* (1985), ***Nightwatcher, Nightsong*** (1986), and *Whispers in the Wings* (1991). Malawi's most eloquent literary opponent of the Banda regime, Chipasula's poems embody his understanding of literature's powers of precognition and of the poet's task as witness to oppression. They criticize the former Banda regime, blending an exile's love and anger with fundamental optimism. Chipasula also edited *The Heinemann Book of African Women's Poetry* with Stella Chipasula in 1995.

Chraïbi, Driss (1926–)

Moroccan novelist writing in French. Born in El Jadida, Morocco, Chraïbi attended Koranic school before going through the French educational system in Morocco. He studied chemistry in 1945 at university in Paris, France. After graduation he began a postgraduate course in neuro-psychiatry, but abandoned his studies to travel throughout most of Western Europe. He has worked as a chemical engineer, journalist, photographer, night watchman, laborer, and producer with French radio. Chraïbi made an impact on francophone literature with his first autobiographical novel, *Le Passé simple* (1954; *The Simple Past,* 1990), which attacks Islam and patriarchy and the way women are treated in a traditional, taboo-laden society. In his next novel, *Les Boucs* (1955; *The Butts,* 1983) he condemns racism in France, and draws on his experience as a laborer to show how Maghrebi immigrant workers are discriminated against by their host community. In *Succession ouverte* (1962; *Heirs to the Past,* 1972), Chraïbi offers a sequel that tempers the strong statements he made in his first novel. *La Mère du printemps* (1982; *Mother Spring,* 1989) and *Naissance à l'aube* (1986, *Birth at Dawn,* 1990) interpret the history of Morocco and its Berber inhabitants, and celebrate their culture and allegiance to Islam. Chraïbi continues to explore many themes related to the Maghreb, its history and culture, in a language that is somber, humorous, and satirical. In 1985 an English translation by Robin A. Roosevelt of *Flutes of Death: A Novel,* was published, while *L'Homme du Livre* (1995), dedicated to his father, celebrates the life of the Prophet. With *L'Inspecteur Ali* (1991) Chralbi began a series of detective novels in which an eponymous Moroccan police inspector solves cases, not always in Morocco. For example, the inspector travels in *L'Inspecteur Ali et la CIA,* and in *L'Inspecteur Ali à Trinity College,* when he goes to Cambridge to find out who murdered a Moroccan princess studying there. The first volume of Chraïbi's memoirs, titled *Vu, lu, entendu* was published in 1998, as was an English version of *Muhammad,* translated by Nadia Benabid. Chraïbi has also published some children's titles, including *L'âne Khal invisible* (2000) and *L'âne Khal à la télévision* (2000).

Further Reading
Dejean de la Batie, Bernadette. "Manifestations of Serail Mentality in Driss Chraïbi's Detective Stories: Arab-Muslim Masculinity Portrayed, Displayed and Caricatured." *Nottingham French Studies* 41, no. 2 (Autumn 2002): 80–89.

Oteng, Yaw. "Is the Other Elsewhere? Culture as a Dialectic of Identities in Driss Chraïbi's *Mother Spring." Chimeres: A Journal of French Literature* 25, no. 2 (Spring 2001): 13–22.

Spleth, Janice. "Driss Chraïbi's Mother Comes of Age." In *African Novels in the Classroom,* ed. and introduction Margaret Jean Hay. Boulder, CO: Rienner, 2000, 63–74.

Clayton, Cherry (date of birth unknown)
Clayton is the author of *Leaving Home* (1994). She is a feminist critic, was a lecturer at the University of Guelph in 2000, and has written a great deal on African women's writing.

Cloete, (Edward Fairlie) Stuart (Graham) (1897–1976)
South African novelist and short-story writer Cloete was born in Paris to a Scottish mother and a South African father, educated privately by a governess, then at schools in England and France, and served in World War I.

A prodigious writer of the epic, action-packed adventure story, Cloete wrote fourteen novels, of which the best remembered now are *The Curve and the Tusk* (1952), *Rags of Glory* (1963), set during the Anglo-Boer war, and *How Young They Died* (1969). He produced eight short-story collections, among which are *The Soldiers' Peaches and Other African Stories* (1959), *The Silver Trumpet and Other African Stories* (1961), and *The Writing on the Wall and Other African Stories* (1968).

Further Reading
Reckwitz, Erhard. "History as Romance, Tragedy and Farce: Narrative Versions of the Anglo-Boer War." In *Telling Stories: Studies in Honour of Ulrich Broich on the Occasion of His 60th Birthday,* ed. Elmar Lehmann and Bernd Lenz. Amsterdam: Gruner, 1992, 163–87.

Taylor, Dora. "They Speak of Africa VI." *English in Africa* 29, no. 2 (October 2002): 62–66.

Clouts, Sydney (David) (1926–82)
A South African poet, Clouts was born in Cape Town and educated at the South African College School and the University of Cape Town (BA, 1950). After service in World War II, he worked as an insurance clerk, a bookseller, and an editor and later manager for the International Press Agency, Cape Town. He emigrated to London in the early 1960s, but visited South Africa on reading and lecture tours in 1974 and 1980. His poems were widely published and anthologized, and he won the Olive Schreiner Prize and the Ingrid Jonker Prize for *One Life* (1966), which is incorporated in his posthumous *Collected Poems* (1984).

Clouts received considerable critical notice in the 1960s and 1970s. Although his poetry covers a comprehensive range of themes, his main concerns are with problems of perception, aesthetic experience, the art of poetry, the mystery of existential being, and the "African" reality. He ascribes to poetry a unique transcendent power.

Further Reading

Goddard, Kevin. "Sydney Clouts's Poetry." *English in Africa* 19, no. 2 (1992): 15–34.

Joubert, Susan. "The Unresolved Shibboleth: Sydney Clouts and the Problems of an African Poetry." *Theoria: A Journal of Studies in the Arts, Humanities and Social Sciences* 75 (1990): 87–106.

Cochlovius, Karen (Date of birth unknown) South African author Cochlovius is a freelance geologist who works all over southern Africa. Her only novel is titled *Desert Varnish* (2003), and follows a young African geologist who is digging a tunnel for the Lesotho Highlands Water Scheme in southern Africa.

Coetzee, J(ohn) M(axwell) (1940–)
A South African novelist and critic, Coetzee was born in Cape Town and educated at the University of Cape Town, where he studied English and mathematics, and the University of Texas at Austin, where he gained a PhD with a dissertation on Samuel Beckett. He worked as a lecturer at the State University of New York at Buffalo (SUNY) and then returned to South Africa in 1971. He has been in the Department of English at the University of Cape Town since 1972 and holds the title of Arderne Professor of English Language and Literature.

Coetzee's first novel, *Dusklands* (1974), was announced as the first modern South African novel by one reviewer, but it is more accurately the first postmodern South African novel. Ten more novels have followed: *In the Heart of the Country* (1977), a critique of colonial pastoral writing; *Waiting for the Barbarians* (1980), in which he begins to deal with contemporary political conditions in South Africa in an allegorical mode; *Life & Times of Michael K* (1983), which portrays one of the inarticulate victims of **apartheid,** a harelipped gardener who attempts to return his dying mother to the Karoo as civil war threatens Cape Town; *Foe* (1986), in which he tests the limits of the discourses of postmodernism, postcolonialism, and feminism and the possibility of talking about victims of colonization without speaking for them; *Age of Iron* (1990), the self-reflexive narrative of a marginal woman; *The Master of Petersburg* (1994), set in St. Petersburg and narrated by Dostoevsky; *Disgrace* (1999); *The Lives of Animals,* which is edited and introduced by Amy Gutmann (1999); *Elizabeth Costello: Eight Lessons* (2003); and *Slow Man* (2005).

Coetzee consistently refuses to comment on the meaning of his novels, or to declare overtly his political affiliations. Since the late 1980s there has been a growing body of theoretically informed criticism produced by critics within and outside South Africa that locates the novels in postmodern and postcolonial contexts. A 1990 bibliography lists approximately five hundred items of commentary on Coetzee, including books, anthologies, journal articles, reviews, and interviews. The volume of critical commentary on Coetzee's works continues to escalate, and Coetzee is the recipient of numerous awards: for *Dusklands,* the Mofolo-Plomer Prize; for *In the Heart of the Country,* the CNA (Central New Agency) Award; for *Waiting for the Barbarians,* the Geoffrey Faber Prize, James Tait Black Memorial Prize, the University of Cape Town Book Award, and the CNA Award; for *Life & Times of Michael K,* the Booker-McConnell Prize, the Jerusalem Prize, the Prix Femina Étranger and the CNA Award; for *Age of Iron,* the *Sunday Express* Book of the Year award and the University of Cape Town Book Award; for *Master of Petersburg,* a Commonwealth Writers Prize, and for *Disgrace* the 1999 Booker Prize. Coetzee received an honorary Doctorate of Letters from the University of Strathclyde in 1985 and from the State University of New York at Buffalo in 1989. In 1988 he was nominated for the Nobel Prize and elected Fellow of the Royal

Society of Literature and, in 1990, was made an honorary Fellow of the Modern Languages Association of America. Coetzee won the 2003 Nobel Prize for Literature, and his *Lecture and Speech of Acceptance, upon the Award of the Nobel Prize, delivered in Stockholm in December 2003* was published in 2004.

Coetzee is also a literary critic, a translator, a commentator on popular culture, and a reviewer; he has published approximately two hundred items in these various fields. *White Writing: On the Culture of Letters in South Africa* (1988) is a collection of critical essays about the European invention of South Africa, and in a similar vein, he has published *Giving Offense: Essays on Censorship* (1996), *Stranger Shores Essays 1986–1999* (2001), *The Humanities in Africa (Die Geisteswissenschaften in Afrika)* (2001), and a chapter in *Ebony Ivory & Tea*, which is edited by Krzysztof Kowalczyk Twarowski, titled "The Novel in Africa." *Doubling the Point: Essays and Interviews* (1992) gathers his major critical writing from 1970 to 1990; each of its eight sections is introduced with an interview between Coetzee and the editor, David Attwell, who describes the book as in a sense Coetzee's autobiography. Coetzee's autobiographical memoir, *Boyhood: Scenes from Provincial Life,* was published in 1997, and a second installment titled *Youth* was published in 2002.

Further Reading

Attridge, Derek. *J. M. Coetzee and the Ethics of Reading: Literature in the Event.* Chicago: University of Chicago Press, 2004.

Attridge, Derek, and Peter D. McDonald, eds. "M. Coetzee's *Disgrace.*" Interventions: *International Journal of Postcolonial Studies* 4, no. 3 (2002): 315–468.

Clarkson, Carrol "'Done Because We Are Too Menny': Ethics and Identity in J. M. Coetzee's *Disgrace.*" *Current Writing: Text and Reception in Southern Africa* 15, no. 2 (2003): 77–90.

Head, Dominic. *J. M. Coetzee.* Cambridge: Cambridge University Press, 1997.

Kossew, Sue. *Critical Essays on J. M. Coetzee.* New York: G. K. Hall, 1998.

Monson, Tamlyn. "An Infinite Question: The Paradox of Representation in *Life & Times of Michael K.*" *Journal of Commonwealth Literature* 38, no. 3 (2003): 87–106.

Splendore, Paola. "'No More Mothers and Fathers': The Family Sub-Text in J. M. Coetzee's Novels." *Journal of Commonwealth Literature* 38, no. 3 (2003): 148–61.

Yeoh, Gilbert. "Love and Indifference in J. M. Coetzee's *Age of Iron.*" *Journal of Commonwealth Literature* 38, no. 3 (2003): 107–34.

Collector of Treasures, The (1977)

Short stories by Bessie **Head.** The issues arising in the village of Serowe, Botswana, include the impact of Western civilization on the traditional way of life, the irresponsible attitudes of men in the village, and the hardships endured by women. Some of the stories are retellings of traditional tales, while others attempt to capture the contemporary mix of gossip, local lore, and oral history that constitutes the cultural fabric of the largely oral community of Serowe.

Collen, Lindsay (1948–)

Novelist and political activist Collen was born in Umtata, Transkei, South Africa. Collen studied at the University of Witwatersrand and the London School of Economics, and lived in New York and the Seychelles before settling in Mauritius, where she has lived since 1974. She has worked (among other things) as a teacher, nurse's assistant, typesetter, layout artist, and adult literacy teacher, but she is foremost a political activist. She is the author of five novels, *There Is a Tide* (1990), *The Rape of Sita* (1993), *Getting Rid of It* (1997), *Mutiny* (2001), and *Boy* (2004), which won the 2005 Commonwealth Writers Prize for Best Book for the Africa Region. *The Rape of Sita* was banned in Mauritius because religious fundamentalists considered the book's title blasphemous (it uses the name of a sacred Hindu deity), and it also won the 1994 Commonwealth Writers' Prize for the Africa Region.

Combrinck, Lisa (1967–)

Combrinck is a poet who was born in Cape Town and graduated from the University of Cape Town with a degree in English. She has worked as an arts and education reporter in Cape Town, an assistant editor for the *Southern African Review of Books,* lectured in English at Vista University, and was based in the Communications Unit of the President's Office in Pretoria. Combrinck is a former vice-president of the Congress of South African Writers, and an executive member and Chair of the Literature Panel of the National Arts Council of South Africa. Her poetry has been widely anthologized, both in South Africa and internationally. Her first collection of poetry is titled *An Infinite Longing for Love: A Collection of Poetry* (2005).

Concubine, The (1966)

A novel by Elechi **Amadi.** With *The Great Ponds* (1969) and *The Slave* (1978), *The Concubine* forms an epic trilogy. Set in the Niger Delta in precolonial times, the novel portrays rural village life in Erekwi (Ikwerre), where social morality and interaction revolve around ancestor worship and other ideals of local fishing communities. The protagonist Ihuoma is good, beautiful, and dignified, but suffers the curse of the sea god. The supernatural aspect of Ihuoma's character remains hidden from her lovers, who all die soon after marriage. She thus symbolizes fate in a society where European values do not disturb the old truths, and which is orderly and predictable unless the gods are wronged.

Conservationist, The (1974)

A novel by Nadine **Gordimer** and joint winner of the Booker Prize. Mehring, the conservationist of the title, is a wealthy South African industrialist. Pleased with his perception of himself as a preserver of the landscape and traditions of rural South Africa on his hobby farm outside Johannesburg, he in fact actively perpetuates white masculine privilege. Both Mehring and the text itself are haunted by the nameless black man from nearby who has died and is buried on the farm; for Mehring the man symbolizes the uncertainty and lack of control that lie too close to the surface of his carefully ordered life.

Conton, William (Farquhar) (ca. 1925–2003)

Conton, novelist and short-story writer, was born in Bathurst, now Banjul, in the Gambia and had primary education in Gambia, Guinea, and Sierra Leone. He had his secondary and university education in England. Returning to Sierra Leone, he served first as principal of the government secondary school in Bo and for many years afterward as Chief Education Officer of the Sierra Leone government.

The publication of *The African* (1960) places Conton among the first group of modern African writers to emerge in the 1950s and 1960s. *The African* has been translated into Arabic, Russian, and Hungarian and has had two American editions. He also wrote short stories as well as an African history textbook that has been used widely in African schools. *The African* evokes the coming of age of Kisimi Kamara, his initiation into Western education and culture from primary and secondary school in Songhai to university in England, and his determination on his return to Africa to affect the political liberation of his people from British colonial rule. The novel has an obvious political message.

Cook, Méira (1964–)

Cook is the author of poetry, fiction, and essays and was born in Johannesburg, South Africa. Cook obtained her doctorate in Canadian literature from the University of Manitoba and completed a two-year term as a postdoctoral fellow at the University of

British Columbia. She has also been a teacher of creative writing and literature, and a freelance film and arts reviewer and editor. Her two volumes of poetry are titled *Toward a Catalogue of Falling* (1996) and *A Fine Grammar of Bones* (1993), and she has also published a novel titled *The Blood Girls* (1999).

Her most recent work is titled *Writing Lovers: Reading Canadian Love Poetry by Women* (2005).

Cope, Jack (Robert Knox) (1913–91)

A South African novelist, short-story writer, poet, and editor, Cope was born in Natal, South Africa, and attended boarding school in Durban, afterward becoming a journalist on the *Natal Mercury* and then a political correspondent in London for South African newspapers. At the outbreak of World War II he returned to his father's farm and took up creative writing, while working at various jobs. During the following four decades Cope published eight novels, more than one hundred short stories, and three collections of poetry, the last one in association with C. J. Driver. For twenty of those years, beginning in 1960, he edited *Contrast,* a bilingual English and Afrikaans literary magazine. He co-edited *The Penguin Book of South African Verse* (1968) with Uys Krige and, as general editor throughout much of the 1970s, produced the Mantis editions of southern African poets. In 1980 he moved to England, where he published *The Adversary Within: Dissident Writers in Afrikaans* (1982) and his *Selected Stories* (1986).

Cope's first novel, *The Fair House* (1955), considers the Bambata Rebellion of 1906 in an attempt to account for the later racial and political conditions in his country. Later novels, including *The Golden Oriole* (1958), *Albino* (1964), and *The Rain-Maker* (1971), chronicle the white man's destruction of black culture and the ensuing struggle by the blacks to regain their pride and identity. Cope's short stories evoke vivid images of South Africa, and in "A Crack in the Sky" (*The Tame Ox,* 1960) and "Power" (*The Man Who Doubted and Other Stories,* 1967) his moral vision is clear, while his third collection, *Alley Cat and Other Stories* (1973), contains darker themes of alienation and loneliness. Among Cope's main achievements was his influence on South African literature during the 1960s and 1970s, important years in the struggle against **apartheid.**

Further Reading

Gordon, Gerald. "Jack Cope and Contrast." *Contrast: South African Literary Journal* 13, no. 1 (1980): 25–31.

Haresnape, Geoffrey. "Belief in the Song: Jack Cope and South African Poetry in English." *Contrast: South African Literary Journal* 17, no. 3 (1989): 44–52.

Marquard, Jean. "In Conversation with Jack Cope." *Contrast: South African Literary Journal* 14, no. 4 (1983): 29–38.

Maughan-Brown, David. "The Image of the Crowd in South African Fiction." *English in Africa* 14, no. 1 (1987): 1–20.

Couchoro, Félix (1900–68)

Born in Ouidah, a well-known slave trading town on the coast of Dahomey, now Benin, Félix Couchoro attended mission school and received primary education before starting work as a Catholic primary school teacher. In Paris in 1929 he published his novel *L'Esclave,* which was heavily influenced by colonial novels and campaigns for assimilation in Africa. It was nonetheless a pioneering work for its time and Couchoro became a well-respected and active journalist in the Dahomean press, one of the most critical of colonial administration at the time. In 1941 he moved to Togo and became active in the Togolese nationalist movement. He published a second novel locally in 1941 (*Amour de féticheuse*) and a third one in 1950 (*Drame d'amour à Anecho*). These achievements made Couchoro famous within Togo, and because he denounced colonial repression he was forced to flee the Gold Coast in 1954. He returned to Togo after the Nationalist victory in 1960 and started a new career publishing serial novels in the Togolese daily newspaper. He produced eighteen novels that depict a universe of junior clerks, civil servants, traders, and pretty girls, in a style borrowed from popular European fiction, Bible stories, and mixed with French local usage. He had a wide readership in Lomé and represents the closest francophone attempt at a local literary production, part Onitsha, part **Ekwensi,** part Benibengor Blay. His first novel has been reprinted and is now part of the common literary heritage of Benin and Togo.

Further Reading

Dunton, Chris. "Appraisal of a Pioneer." *West Africa* 3699 (1988): 1208.

Salami, Sabit Adegboyega. "Felix Couchoro: A Togolese Novelist of the Onitsha School." *Black-Orpheus: Journal of African and Afro American Literature* 4, no. 2 (1982): 33–45.

Couto, Mia (1955–)

A Mozambican poet and short-story writer, Couto writes in Portuguese. A member of Mozambique's ruling party, Frelimo, Couto was born in Beira and had just begun his journalism career when he was drawn into the war of independence against Portugal under Frelimo. After the war, he became the director of the Mozambique Information Agency (AIM) and editor of the government-owned daily newspaper, *Notîcias.* While in government service, he began to publish short stories and contribute articles to newspapers. He later quit government service to take a degree and pursue a career in environmental biology, but continued to produce radical journalism and fiction. In two collections of his short stories, *Vozes anoitecida* (1986; *Voices Made Night,* 1990) and *Cada homen e uma raea* (1990; *Every Man Is a Race,* 1994), he juxtaposes narrative

motifs and folk magic from oral traditions with events that mirror the social wounds of postwar Mozambique. From the juxtaposition, postwar realities assume the eeriness of folktale while the fantasies of folktale resolve themselves into parables for satiric refigurations of present-day realities. Thus, in "The Day Mabata-bata Exploded" (*Voices Made Night*), the motif of an exploding ox from popular folktale merges into the reality of an ox deliberately stuffed with explosives and ruthlessly left by armed bandits for unsuspecting peasants. Couto's first detective story is titled *Under the Frangipani* (1996, translated 2001), and his novel *Last Flight of the Flamingo* was published in 2005. He was short-listed for the Caine Prize in 2001 for "The Russian Princess," a short story that was published in *The Picador Book of African Stories 2000.*

Other notable work by Couto, yet to be translated into English from the Portuguese, includes *Cronicando* (1991), a collection of journalistic essays originally published in newspapers and magazines; *Terra Sonâmbula* (1992), a novel; and *Estórias Abensonhadas* (1994), a collection of short stories.

Further Reading

Long-Innes, Chesca. "The Psychopathology of Post-Colonial Mozambique: Mia Couto's *Voices Made Night." American Imago: Studies in Psychoanalysis and Culture* 55, no. 1 (Spring 1998): 155–84.

Rothwell, Phillip. "Fuzzy Frontiers. Mozambique: False Borders—Mia Couto: False Margins." *Portuguese Literary and Cultural Studies* 1 (Fall 1998): 55–65.

———. *The Postmodern Nationalist: Truth, Orality, and Gender in the Work of Mia Couto.* Lewisburg: Bucknell University Press, 2005.

Salter-Iglesias, Andres-Xose. "Translating Mia Couto: A Particular View of Portuguese in Mozambique." In *Less Translated Languages,* ed. (and introduction) Albert Branchadell and

Margaret Lovell West. Amsterdam: Benjamins, 2004, 177–87.

Cripps, A(rthur) S(hearly) (1869–1952)

A poet, novelist, and essayist, Cripps came to present-day Zimbabwe as an Anglican missionary in 1901, determined to fight for racial freedom and equality under the overarching power of one God after reading Olive **Schreiner**'s *Trooper Peter Halket of Mashonaland* (1897). Born in Tunbridge Wells, England, and educated at Charterhouse and Trinity College, Oxford, Cripps had published a volume of poetry, *Primavera* (1890) with Lawrence Binyon, and had completed his collection of poetry *The Black Christ* (1902) before he embarked for Africa. The poems in *The Black Christ* appear fairly conventional and hymnal in quality, but are shaped by Cripps's libertarian philosophy, missionary zeal, and transparent love for Africa (especially "The Black Christ," "In Deserto," and "To the Veld").

Besides *The Black Christ,* Cripps published several other volumes of poetry, among them *Titania and Other Poems* (1900); *Lyra Evangelistica: Missionary Verses of Mashonaland* (1909); *Lake and War: African Land and Water Verses* (1917); and *Africa: Verses* (1939). He also published two novels, *The Brooding Earth* (1911) and *Bay-Tree Country* (1913); two collections of folkloric short stories, *Faeryland Forlorn: African Tales* (1910) and *Cinderella of the South: South African Tales* (1918); and an assortment of general prose, including missionary travel journals and pamphlets on political topics. The title of *Bay-Tree Country* invokes the image of white settlers as the wicked who flourish in a desert land like the green bay tree of the Bible, and it uses the forced labor scandal of 1911 as backdrop to criticize the exploitation of indigenous Africans by white settlers, a position further pursued in his essay *An Africa for Africans: A Plea on Behalf of Territorial Segregation Areas and Their Freedom in a Southern African Colony* (1927).

Further Reading

Brown, G. R., A. J. Chennells, and L. B. Rix. *Arthur Shearly Cripps: A Selection of His Prose and Verse.* Gwelo: Mambo, 1976.

Doyle, John Robert. *Arthur Shearly Cripps.* Boston: Twayne, 1975.

Sheers, Owen. *The Dust Diaries.* New York: Faber & Faber, 2004.

Steere, Douglas V. *God's Irregular: Arthur Shearly Cripps. A Rhodesian Epic.* London: SPCK, 1973.

Cry, the Beloved Country (1948)

A novel by Alan **Paton.** The story is simple, but the narrative style creates a fable of social transformation arising out of crime, degradation, death, and despair. The main character, Stephen Kumalo, an aging minister of religion in Ndotsheni, Natal, receives a letter that takes him from the countryside to the slums of Johannesburg in search of his son. The year is 1946, and the Reverend Kumalo encounters for the first time African resistance to white laws in the form of a squatter camp outside Johannesburg and the boycott of subsidized buses due to raised fares. Although Kumalo must return to Natal unable to help his son, who killed a white man in the course of a burglary, the story ends more hopefully when his drought-stricken country receives help from a white man, the father of the man whom Kumalo's son killed.

Cugoano, Ottobah (b.1757)

Cugoano was kidnapped at the age of two from his native Ajumako, in what is now the Central Region of Ghana, and enslaved in the West Indies. Taken to England, educated by one Alexander Campbell, and baptized, he married an English woman and had a family. He was an active member of the London Committee for the Abolition of the Slave Trade, and in 1787 he wrote to Edmund Burke and George III urging them to stop the slave trade. Cugoano's *Thoughts and Sentiments on the Evil of Slavery* (1787) is his firsthand account of his traumatic dislocation from his family, his auction as a slave, what he suffered on the plantations, and his eventual freedom. He assumes a moral position as he censures Western and Christian institutions for condoning and profiting from slavery. In an apparent paradox, Cugoano also affirms the liberating power of formal education and Christianity. He tends in *Thoughts* to censure the negative activities of the church while affirming the positive values of genuine Christianity. Cugoano condemns African slave hunters, "who were the first cause of [his] exile and slavery," but insists that the European is ultimately responsible for the slave trade.

Although *Thoughts* is autobiographical, Cugoano assumes a public voice to speak to the collective experience of black people. Writing is a public act for Cugoano; it is an act of empowerment and a way to raise the voice of the voiceless millions of oppressed black people throughout the world. Cugoano questions the preposterous argument of proslavery advocates that Africans are the descendants of Ham who suffer from Noah's curse and who therefore may be enslaved, and he argues that neither skin color nor texture of hair can determine a person's character and morality.

As a slave narrative, *Thoughts* garnered support for the antislavery movement, and by refuting aspersions about black people and by questioning Europe's imperial quest in Africa, Cugoano's narrative inaugurates a tradition of protest and anticolonial writing.

Further Reading

Bogues, Anthony. *Black Heretics, Black Prophets: Radical Political Intellectuals.* New York: Routledge, 2003.

Carretta, Vincent, ed. *Unchained Voices: An Anthology of Black Authors in the English Speaking World of the Eighteenth Century.* Lexington: University Press of Kentucky, 1996.

Edwards, Paul. "Three West African Writers of the 1780s." In *The Slave's Narrative,* ed. Charles T. Davis and Henry Louis Gates, Jr. Oxford: Oxford University Press, 1985, 175–98.

Cullinan, Patrick (Roland) (1932–)

South African poet and biographer Cullinan was born in Pretoria and attended Charterhouse School and Oxford University in the UK before returning to South Africa where he was for many years a sawmill operator in the Eastern Transvaal. With Lional **Abrahams** he founded the journal *The Bloody Horse: Writings and the Arts* (1980) and the Bateleur Press. Through the journal (the title is taken from a poem by Roy **Campbell**), Cullinan sought to reestablish poetry as art.

Cullinan's poetry collections include *The Horizon Forty Miles Away* (1973), *Today Is Not Different* (1978), *Selected Poems, 1961–1991* (1992), and *Transformations* (1999). Cullinan has also written a novel, titled *Matrix* (2002). The volume *The White Hail in the Orchard* (1984) contains what Cullinan calls "Versions" by which he means translations from the poetry of Eugenio Montale. Cullinan has taught at the University of the Western Cape, and he has also published a biography of Robert Jacob Gordon, a Dutch traveler and soldier, *Robert Jacob Gordon 1743–1795: The Man and His Travels at the Cape* (1992). He also recently published *Imaginative Trespasser: Letters from Bessie Head to Patrick and Wendy Cullinan 1963–1977* (2005), and in April 2003, the republic of Italy conferred the title of *Cavaliere* on him for his translations of Italian poetry in South Africa.

Currey, Ralph Nixon (1907–2001)

South African poet Currey had lived and taught in England since the early 1920s. A veteran of World War II, during which he served in the British Royal Artillery, Currey was born in Mafeking and left South Africa at fourteen to go to school in England and to Wadham College, Oxford.

Currey's poetry derives from his war experience and the challenges of living between two worlds. His four early volumes of poems are *Tiresias and Other Poems* (1940), *This Other Planet* (1945), *Indian Landscape: A*

Book of Descriptive Poems (1947), and *Formal Spring: Translations of French Renaissance Poems* (1950). In addition to these, he has published a dramatic poem for the radio titled *Between Two Worlds* (1947), broadcast a radio feature on the BBC called *Early Morning in Vaaldorp* (1961), edited *Letters and Other Writings of a Natal Sheriff, Thomas Phipson, 1815–1876* (1968), and written a critical study titled *Poets of the 1939–1945 War* (1967). Currey also published poems in journals and anthologies and his *Collected Poems* (2001). *Vinnicombe's Trek* (1989) records the pioneering history of Currey's grandfather who composed simple verse when on horseback. Among other honors and awards, Currey won the Viceroy's Poetry Prize (1945, shared with Anthony Delius) and the South African Poetry Prize (1959). He was elected Fellow of the Royal Society of Literature in 1970.

Further Reading

Bannerjee, Jacqueline. "'Jasper, Marble and Khaki Drill': Service Poets in India." *Literary Half Yearly* (Mysore, India) 14, no. 1 (1973): 65–73.

D

Dadié, Bernard (1916–)

Playwright and novelist writing in French. Born in Côte d'Ivoire, where he spent his youth, Dadié qualified in 1939 as a civil servant in the colonial administration and worked at Dakar's Institut Fondamental d'Afrique Noire until 1947. Upon his return to Abidjan, he became actively involved with his country's independence movement, for which he became the press attaché. His subsequent sixteen-month imprisonment for demonstrating against the colonial power is related in detail in *Carnet de prison* (1981). From 1957 until his retirement from government in 1985, he held many senior ministerial offices, including that of Côte d'Ivoire's Minister for Culture, and not only continued writing but also kept alive his early humanist ideals of social justice and respect for people of all walks of life.

As a student Dadié wrote two plays, one of which, *Assémien Déhylé,* was performed in 1936 in Dakar by fellow students and a year later in Paris, at the 1937 Colonial Exposition. From this time and throughout his literary career, theater remained for him the genre capable of breaking political deadlocks and overbearing government attacks against civil liberties. Particularly noteworthy are *Monsieur Thôgô-Gnini* (1970; trans. 1985), written and performed in Abidjan at the height of the 1963 political unrest; *Béatrice du Congo* (1970), staged at the Avignon Festival in 1971; *Les Voix dans Le vent* (1970); *Iles de tempête* (1973); and *Mhoi-Ceul* (1979).

Versatile in his use of literary genres, Dadié gained literary recognition soon after his liberation from prison with *Afrique debout* (1950), a book of verse that was followed by an autobiographical and no less successful novel, *Climbié* (1956; trans. 1971). Other novels include *Un Nêgre à Paris* (1959; *An African in Paris,* 1994), *Patron de New York* (1964; *One Way: Bernard Dadié Observes America,* 1994), which received the Grand Prix Littéraire d'Afrique Noir, *La Ville où nul ne meurt* (1968; *The City Where No One Dies,* 1986), *Commandant Taureault et ses nègres* (1980), and *Hands* (2003). Dadié has also published traditional tales such as *Le Pagne noir* (1955; *The Black Cloth,* 1987) as well as short stories in *Les Jambes du fils de Dieu* (1980). New editions of *An African in Paris* (2002) and *Monsieur Thôgô-Gnini* (1999) testify to the continuing importance of Dadié's work.

Further Reading

Coundouriotis, Eleni. "Writing Stories about Tales Told: Anthropology and the Short Story in

African Literatures." *Narrative* 6, no. 2 (May 1998): 140–56.

Frederick, Patricia. "Quest and Sacrifice in Two Tales by Bernard Dadié." *Romance Quarterly* 40, no. 4 (Fall 1993): 203–10.

Mudimbe Boyi, Elisabeth, Brian Hollis, trans., and Beverley Foulks, ed. asst. "Bernard Dadié: Literary Imagination and New Historiography." *Research in African Literatures* 29, no. 3, (Fall 1998): 98–104.

Syrotinski, Michael. "'When in Rome . . .': Irony and Subversion in Bernard Dadié's Travel-Writing." *Journal of African Travel Writing* 7 (1999): 66–79.

Dance in the Sun, A (1956)

A novel by Dan **Jacobson,** published in one volume with Jacobson's novella *The Trap* (1955) in 1957. From the beginning the narrative hints at danger or at least profound discomfort when two university students on a hitchhiking vacation in South Africa are forced to look for lodging in an isolated place named Mirredal. When they are grudgingly offered a night's accommodation in a large, rambling, shuttered, overfurnished house, they encounter a family drama involving sexuality and race. The whites' fear and rejection of the sun, a complex symbol, is part of their inability to accept and be part of the African earth itself.

Dance of the Forests, A (1963)

A play by Wole **Soyinka.** This ambitious play was written for Nigeria's independence celebrations, although the organizing committee for that event did not accept it as an official entry. Drawing on Yoruba myth, in particular the attributes associated with specific gods (such as Ogun's combination of creative passion and violence), Soyinka builds a complex plot and employs music, dance, and masquerade in order to comment on the historical basis for Nigeria's contemporary reality. As Forest Head calls ancestors to life to celebrate the present, no idealized version of the past is discovered but rather a legacy of oppression, violence, and martyrdom. An extended flashback establishes parallels between lives from the past and the actions of living characters. The play's vision of Nigeria's future emerges in a series of climaxes that are vividly compelling and yet difficult to interpret.

Dangarembga, Tsitsi (1959–)

A Zimbabwean novelist and dramatist, Dangarembga was educated at the Universities of Cambridge and Zimbabwe, where she studied medicine and psychology, and is best known for her novel **Nervous Conditions** (1988), set in 1960s colonial Rhodesia. A female *bildungsroman*, the novel is a harrowing indictment of sexual and cultural imperialism that exposes the stultifying power of colonial assimilation. In addition to *Nervous Conditions,* which won a Commonwealth Writers Prize, Dangarembga has published a play, *She No Longer Weeps* (1987), about a young student who becomes pregnant in the city. Dangarembga is also known for her film work, most significantly *Kate Kate Zvako* (*Mother's Day*) a short film, which won the Harare International Film Festival in 2004, and *Everyone's Child* (1996).

Further Reading

Creamer, Heidi. "An Apple for the Teacher?: Femininity, Coloniality and Food in *Nervous Conditions.*" In *Into the Nineties,* ed. Anna Rutherford. New South Wales, Australia: Dangaroo Press, 1994, 344–60.

Edson, Laurie. "A Narrative of Ethical Proportions: History, Memory, and Writing in Dangarembga's *Nervous Conditions.*" In *Literature and the Writer,* ed. and introduction Michael J. Meyer. Amsterdam: Rodopi, 2004, 227–41.

Patchay, Sheena. "Transgressing Boundaries: Marginality, Complicity and Subversion in *Nervous Conditions.*" *English in Africa* 30, no. 1 (May 2003): 145–55.

Thomas, Sue. "Rewriting the Hysteric as Anorexic in Tsitsi Dangarembga's *Nervous Conditions.*" In *Scenes of the Apple: Food and the*

Female Body in Nineteenth and Twentieth Century Women's Writing, ed. and introduction Tamar Heller and Patricia Moran. Albany: State University of New York Press, 2003, 183–98.

Dangor, Achmat (1948–)

South African poet and prose writer Dangor was born and educated in Newclare, Johannesburg, and has worked in the business world and for various NGOs. Politically active, he was banned between 1973 and 1978. During the 1970s he was a member of Black Thoughts and in the 1980s of COSAW (the Congress of South African Writers).

Dangor's prose collection *Waiting Jar Leila* (1978) won the Mofolo-Plomer Prize and he has published a play, *Majiet* (1986), and two novels, *The Z Town Trilogy* (1989) and **Bitter Fruit**: *A Novel* (2003), but is best known as a poet. A regular contributor to such publications as *New Nation* and *Staffrider* and well represented in anthologies such as *The Return of the Amasi Bird* (1982) and *Modern South African Poetry* (1984), his two collections are *Bulldozer* (1983) and *Private Voices* (1992), which won the BBC prize for African poetry. In 1997 he brought out *Kafka's Curse: A Novella and Three Other Stories,* another award-winning collection, and *Bitter Fruit: A Novel* was short-listed for the 2004 Booker Prize.

Further Reading

Kruger, Loren. "Black Atlantics, White Indians, and Jews: Locations, Locutions, and Syncretic Identities in the Fiction of Achmat Dangor and Others." *South Atlantic Quarterly* 100, no. 1 (2001): 111–43.

Monier, Hawabibi. "Dialogic Strategies in Waiting for Leila: Canonical, Vernacular, and Political Inspirations; Proceedings of the Conference of the Association of University English Teachers of South Africa, University of the Western Cape, 30 June–5 July 1996." In *AUETSA 96, I-II: Southern African Studies,* ed. Hermann Wittenberg and Loes Nas. Bellville, South Africa: University of Western Cape Press, 1996, 248–52.

Sastry, Sailaja. "Assuming Identities: *Kafka's Curse* and the Unsilenced Voice." *Journal of Literary Studies/Tydskrif vir Literatuurwetenskap* 18, nos. 3–4 (2002): 275–83.

Young, Elaine. "Cursing and Celebrating Metamorphosis: Achmat Dangor's 'Kafka's Curse.'" *Current Writing: Text and Reception in Southern Africa* 12, no. 1 (2000): 17–30.

Daughter of Mumbi (1969)

A novel by Charity **Waciuma.** The Mau Mau emergency in Kenya is the setting for this autobiographical story of childhood and adolescence. Waciuma represents how she learned from her storyteller grandfather to love and respect Kikuyu lore, and from her health-inspector father and her mother, a district counselor, to conciliate cultural differences, even those between the local indigenous "witch doctors" and the practitioners of Western "scientific" medicine. With candor and clarity Waciuma paints an endearing portrait of herself, her family, and the Kikuyu customs that shaped her life.

Daughters of Twilight (1986)

A novel by Farida **Karodia.** Fourteen-year-old Meena narrates the petty daily indignities and major discriminatory acts of **apartheid.** In a two-year period, the Abdul family is forcibly evicted, their education opportunities are downgraded, and they are the targets of the sadistic brutality of some Afrikaner neighbors who know they can act with impunity. The father of the family, a Muslim immigrant, is Asian, the mother "coloured" (mixed race). Meena's beautiful seventeen-year-old sister Yasmin and their grandmother, Nana, have built up a household and family store in an area now reclassified for whites. Dispossessed, harassed, with Yasmin raped and impregnated, they struggle on despite deprivation and empowered by Nana's faith and Meena's hope for a better future.

De Graft, Joe (Joseph Coleman) (1924–78)

Ghanaian dramatist and poet who was born and initially educated in Cape Coast. After gaining a degree in English at University College, Achimota, he returned to Mfantsipim School in Cape Coast as a teacher and became involved in drama. His career was devoted to teaching, but he was also passionately committed to the theater and often combined the two.

From Mfantsipim, de Graft joined with Efua **Sutherland** to set up programs at the Drama Studio in Accra and the School of Music and Drama, Legon. Between 1962 and 1969, he worked not only as a teacher but also as an adaptor, writer, director, and contributor to the national theater movement and the establishment of drama education at the University of Ghana. In 1969 he moved to Nairobi, first to a UNESCO appointment in language teaching and then to a university post in drama. His collection of poems, *Beneath the Jazz and Brass* (1975), was published while he was in East Africa. He returned to Ghana to take up a professorship in 1977, the year before his death.

De Graft's works include **Sons and Daughters** (1964), **Through a Film Darkly** (1970), a more complex drama that de Graft worked on over an extended period and has links with Pirandello; *Muntu* (1977), a wide-ranging historical pageant that incorporates myth, folk songs, drums, storytelling, and formal exchanges, and *Mambo* (produced 1978 but unpublished), which is a response to *Macbeth*. His plays include a concern for the importance of the arts in national life, the damaging effects of racism, and the violence of some African leaders during the 1970s. The affection former students hold for him is a testimony to his commitment as a teacher.

Further Reading

Awooner, Kofi. "The Imagery of Fire: A Critical Assessment of the Poetry of Joe De Graft."

Okike: An African Journal of New Writing 19 (1981): 70–79.

Death and the King's Horseman (1975)

A play by Wole **Soyinka**. According to the author's note, the play is based on events that took place in 1944 in Oyo, Western Nigeria, when British authorities intervened in a traditional burial ritual on the death of the Alafin of Oyo, preventing Alafin's servant (the Master of Horse) from following his master by committing suicide. The British Resident had the Horseman arrested, whereupon the Alafin's son fulfilled the servant's role by killing himself. The play uses these events to reveal not only the strength of Nigerian/Yoruba religious beliefs, but also the arrogance of the British colonial administration as a whole and of the individuals, both men and women, in that administration.

Dedan Kimathi (1974)

A play by Kenneth **Watene.** The action of the play unfolds in Kenya in late 1956, after several years of unequal struggle between the Mau Mau freedom fighters and the colonial military forces. This historical moment parallels a critical point in the life of the protagonist, whose strength, courage, and hope have been stretched to the limit. The admission of vulnerability in such a perspective does not deny Dedan Kimathi the stature of a nationalist hero or the legendary qualities popularly attributed to him. As well, it shows him as a human being endowed with human weaknesses.

Dei-Anang, Michael Francis (ca. 1909–77)

Ghanaian poet, playwright, and novelist Dei-Anang was born at Mampong-Akwapim, Ghana, and attended Achimota College, Ghana, and the University of London before entering the civil service, where he served in several ministries in the colonial and postcolonial periods. He was one of the main pillars in Kwame Nkrumah's African Secretariat, which was mainly concerned with the liberation of the rest of Africa still under colonial rule. He was arrested and detained for two months after the fall of Nkrumah in 1966.

Dei-Anang reveals his interest in the oral poetry and traditional myths and legends of the Akan people in the traditional themes of his poems in English, which were the first creative works by an African to be published in Ghana. His first collection, *Wayward Lines from Africa* (1946) was followed by *Africa Speaks* (1959), which contains a useful introductory essay on African poetry. His poems also appeared in *Okyeame* and *An African Treasury,* an anthology of the 1960s edited by Langston Hughes, who visited Ghana at the time of independence. Dei-Anang's later collections were *Ghana Semitones* (1962) and *Ghana Glory: Poems on Ghana and Ghanaian Life* (1965), the latter co-authored with Yaw Warren and introduced by Kwame Nkrumah. In 1961 the Masquers' Theatre, University of Chicago, produced *Okomfo Anokye's Golden Stool* (1960), a drama in three acts based on an Ashanti legend, and actors from the University of Ghana staged the play again during the silver jubilee celebrations of Asantehene in August 1995. The earlier *Cocoa Comes to Mampong: Brief Dramatic Sketches Based on the Story of Cocoa in the Gold Coast* (1949) is more didactic, and Dei-Anang also wrote critical articles such as "Women Writers of the 20th Century in Ghana, West Africa," which appears in *Folio: Papers on Foreign Languages and Literature* (1978). After 1966, Dei-Anang left Ghana for the United States, where he taught at a college in Brockport, New York.

Detained: A Writer's Prison Diary (1981)

A memoir by **Ngugi wa Thiong'o.** On December 30, 1977 Ngugi was detained for publishing *Ngaahika Ndeenda* (1977; *I Will Marry When I Want,* 1982), an experiment in community theater that portrays the Mau Mau guerillas who fought for Kenyan independence as heroes and patriots and the home guards who resisted them as traitors. The diary discusses the conception and writing of *I Will Marry* and of the ideology behind the Kamiriithu experiment in general. He reflects on his work, his country's social and political history, the personalities that make that history, and a whole range of issues including the language question. He attacks capitalism, neo-colonialism, and imperialism and comments on the novel he was writing while in prison, **Devil on the Cross** (1982), and the character of Wariinga, the novel's female hero. While Ngugi is critical of university intellectuals for their inconsistency ("they talk progressive and act conservative"), he has high praise for the great nationalist J.M. Kariuki, murdered for his populist views in 1975.

Devil on the Cross (1982)

A novel by **Ngugi wa Thiong'o,** translated from the Gikuyu (*Caitaani Muthuraba-ini,* 1980). The novel deals with the effect of the exploitation of Kenyans through the collusion of corrupt Kenyans with the international entrepreneurial comprador bourgeoisie. Related themes Ngugi treats in the novel are the alienation of the people from the land, the destruction of a productive Kenyan peasantry, and the exploitation of labor through the coercive methods of state, church, and police. Ngugi's purpose goes beyond the mere description of these civil and political problems. The experiences of his principal characters, Wangari, Muturi, Gatuiria, and Wariinga, demonstrate what actions can be taken to counteract the oppressive methods of the state and to return the means and rewards of production to the people. Ngugi achieves his effect here (as in his other writings) by a reliance on coincidence, exaggeration, and melodrama, especially in the scenes that satirize Christianity through the depiction of the Devil's Feast. Wariinga, whom Ngugi refers to as "my

Wariinga," is the true hero of the novel. She acts on behalf of the people when she executes a representative of the oppressor class, thus consummating her symbolic role in the novel and revealing Ngugi's contempt for those Kenyans who collude with external oppressors or who see the vicious exploitation of their people and deplore it, but fail to act. The novel was a popular success in Kenya, selling some thirteen thousand copies in three successive printings. It is also estimated that perhaps one hundred thousand people heard the novel when it was read aloud.

Dhlomo, H(erbert) I. E. (1903–56)

A South African journalist, playwright, and poet, Dhlomo was born in Siyamu, Edendale, and educated in the sheltered missionary environment of Adams College, where he eventually graduated as a teacher. Dhlomo took to journalism early in his life, and it is here that he left his mark as one of the most important literary figures of the 1930s and 1940s. In 1937, he became the first African librarian at the Carnegie Bantu Library in Johannesburg. He left for Durban in 1941, where he was appointed as assistant editor of *Ilanga lase Natal (The Natal Sun)*, a position he retained until his death. He was active in the African National Congress, particularly as a driving spirit behind the formation of the Youth League in 1946.

Dhlomo's creative work, written mainly after 1936, articulates his theories on African literature and includes at least nine plays and numerous poems. The **Girl Who Killed to Save**: *Nongquase the Liberator* (1936), the only one of his plays to be published during his lifetime; its subject is the events surrounding the vision of the Xhosa prophet Nongquase, and the subsequent cattle killing of 1857. The play is very much of the "missionary literature" genre, but Dhlomo outgrew such a colonial focus in his later work. Of his poems, the best known is *The **Valley of a Thousand Hills*** (1941), a carefully constructed work that contrasts the harmony of nature and the cruelty of human society. His complete creative output appeared posthumously in *Collected Works* (1985).

In his criticism Dhlomo advocates the use of Western styles, but only as far as they can enhance the existing African tradition. The view that only Africans can truly express the African soul finds expression in his uncompleted play "The Expert," a scathing criticism of white liberalism and missionary intervention in African affairs. Dhlomo's dramas are unwieldy, with a thoroughness and attention to detail more reminiscent of a novel than of theater, which is in line with his own feeling that Africans first had to produce "literary drama" before they could produce plays for the stage. Dhlomo's journalistic essays on African art are among the most valuable pieces of South African literary history.

Further Reading

Butcher, Neil. "Herbert Dhlomo in Perspective." *South African Theatre Journal* 6, no. 2 (1992): 49–63.

Lehmann, Elmar. "Colonial to Post-Colonial South African-Style: The Plays of H.I.E. Dhlomo." In *Imagination and the Creative Impulse in the New Literatures in English*, ed. M. T. Bindella and G. V. Davis. Amsterdam: Rodopi, 1993, 109–22.

Wenzel, Jennifer. "Voices of Spectral and Textual Ancestors: Reading Tiyo Soga alongside H.I.E. Dhlomo's *The Girl Who Killed to Save*." *Research in African Literatures* 36, no. 1 (2005): 51–73.

Dhlomo, R(obert) R(olfes) R(eginald) (1901–71)

South African novelist. Rolfes Dhlomo, the elder brother of H.L.E. **Dhlomo,** was born in Siyamu, Edendale, educated at the Ohlange Institute, and graduated as a teacher from the American Mission Board School in Amanzimtoti. He became a regular contributor to *Ilanga lase Natal (The Natal Sun)*, a bilingual newspaper, and later to a Transvaal newspaper, *Bantu World*. He worked as a mine clerk in Johannesburg before he joined the staff of *Ilanga,* and later he became the editor. Dhlomo is known primarily as the author of a series of Zulu historical novels based on the lives of nineteenth-century African leaders: *U-Dingane* (1936), *U-Shaka* (1937), *U-Mpande* (1938), *U-Cetshwayo* (1952), and *U-Dinizulu* (1968). He also wrote the novella *An **African Tragedy*** (1928), and contributed a number of English short stories to *Sjambok,* a literary journal (1929–31). In 1951, he became the first recipient of the Vilakazi Memorial Award.

The short stories written for *Sjambok* are incisive, with a journalistic style. "The Death of Masaba," written in 1929, reflects an intimate knowledge of mining conditions and provides an historical perspective not to be found in any report or history of the period. The short stories also attempt to present a realistic picture of life, rather than trying to create lasting literary artifacts. Dhlomo returned to the theme of conflict between rural and city life in the Zulu-language *lndlela Yababi (The Evil One)* (1946). Here he looks again at the effects of township life on African morale, but with far greater maturity than in *An African Tragedy* or the *Sjambok* stories. Dhlomo is a writer of note, but his English writing has received little critical attention.

Further Reading

Canonici, N. N. "Elements of Conflict and Protest in Zulu Literature." *South African Journal of African Languages/Suid Afrikaanse Tydskrif vir Afrikatale* 18, no. 3 (August 1998): 57–64.

Loflin, Christine. "Multiple Narrative Frames in R.R.R. Dhlomo's 'Juwawa.'" In *The Postmodern Short Story: Forms and Issues,* ed. (and introduction) Farhat Iftekharrudin, Joseph Boyden, Mary Rohrberger, and Jaie Claudet. Westport, CT: Praeger, 2003, 223–32.

Dib, Mohammed (1920–2003)

Algerian novelist and poet Dib was born in Tlemcen, Algeria. From 1939 to 1951 he worked in a variety of occupations before turning to literature. Expelled from Algeria in 1959 for his outspoken political stance, he settled in France.

Dib's principal writings are in French. They include his trilogy of prerevolutionary Algeria: *La Grande maison* (1952), *L'Incendie* (1954), and *Le Métier à tisser* (1957). These were followed by *Qui se souvient de la mer* (1962; *Who Remembers the Sea,* 1985), *Cours sur la rive sauvage* (1964), *La Danse du roi* (1968), and *Habel* (1977). Dib continued his energetic publication with *Dieu en Barbarie* (1970) and *Le Maître de chasse* (1973); *Les Terrasses d'Orsol* (1985), *Le Sommeil d'Éve* (1989), and *Neiges de marbre* (1990). Dib's other works include *Le Désert sans détour* (1992), *L'infante Maure* (1994), *L'arbre à dires* (1998), *The Savage Night: La Nuit Sauvage* (2001), *Comme un bruit d'abeilles* (2001), and *Simorgh* (2003). He has also published a children's book titled *Salem et le Sorcier* (2000), and a collection of short stories titled *L'hippopotame qui se trouvait vilain* (2002). His first collection of poetry, *Ombre gardienne* (1961), was followed by *Formulaires* (1970), *Omneros* (1975), *Feu beau feu* (1979), *Ô vive* (1987), *Le Cœur insulaire* (2000), *L.A. Trip* (2003), and *L'Enfant-jazz* (1998), for which Dib received Prix Mallarmé.

Further Reading

Ahmad, Fawzia. "Mohammed Dib and Albert Camus's Encounters with the Algerian Landscape." In *Maghrebian Mosaic: A Literature in Transition,* ed. Mildred Mortimer. Boulder, CO: Rienner, 2000, 101–17.

Desplanques, Francois, and Patricia Geesey, trans. "The Long, Luminous Wake of Mohammed Dib." *Research in African Literatures* 23, no. 2 (1992): 71–88.

Hughes, Edward J. "Haunted and Haemorrhaging: The World of Mohammed Dib's *La Nuit Sauvage*." *French Studies: A Quarterly Review* 59, no. 1 (2005): 63–69.

Salhi, Zahia. "Fifty Years of Mohammed Dib's Algerian Trilogy." *Banipal: Magazine of Modern Arab Literature* 14 (2002): 74–75.

Diescho, Joseph (1955–)

A native-born Namibian novelist, Diescho was raised in a rural village near the Roman Catholic mission of Andara in northern Namibia. He graduated in political science and law from Fort Hare University before going on to study in Germany and the United States for his postgraduate degrees.

His two novels, *Born of the Sun* (1988) and *Troubled Waters* (1993), have Namibian settings. *Born of the Sun,* partly autobiographical, is set in the early 1960s and traces the growth of political consciousness in Muronga, who leaves the idyllic village of Kake in eastern Kavango to work in the mines. The work ends with the exiled hero's homecoming still in the distant future. Set in 1974, *Troubled Waters* is a novel that focuses on two young people who are distanced from their roots as a result of political change. The novel portrays a broken tribal society and reveals a profound political understanding. Diescho has also edited a collection of Namibian folktales.

Diescho is the Director of Public Relations at the University of South Africa and has published scholarly papers on government in Africa, including: *Understanding the New Partnership for Africa's Development* (published by the Namibia Institute of Democracy in co-operation with Konrad-Adenauer-Stiftung, 2002), *The Namibian Constitution in Perspective* (1999), "The Effects of Colonialism on the Development of Local Self-Government in Africa" (1996), and *Traditional and Contemporary Forms of Local Participation and Self-Government in Africa,* given at an international conference in Nairobi, Kenya, in 1996, and at Johannesburg in 1997.

Dikobe, Modikwe (1913–)
(pseudonym of Marks Rammitloa)

Novelist and poet Dikobe went to live in Johannesburg at the age of ten, left school without finishing, and attended night classes run by the African Communist Party while working at a variety of jobs. Following the bus boycott (1942) and the squatters' movement (1946), he became involved in the trade union movement. He was detained for three months and then banned in the early 1960s, and as a "listed" person, he could not publish under his own name. He published some journalism and a volume of poetry (*Dispossessed*, 1983), but his reputation as a writer rests on his novel, *The **Marabi** Dance,* begun in the 1950s, finished in 1963, and finally published, after passing through various hands, by Heinemann in 1973. The novel's examination of the urban black working class is displaced in a series of subnarratives, many of which deal with the urban experiences of rural migrants.

Further Reading

Berger, Iris. "Modikwe Dikobe's *The Marabi Dance.*" In *African Novels in the Classroom,* ed. and introduction Margaret Jean Hay. Boulder, CO: Rienner, 2000, 107–14.

Sole, Kelwyn, and Eddie Koch. "*The Marabi Dance:* A Working Class Novel?" In *Rendering Things Visible: Essays on South African Literary Culture,* ed. Martin Trump. Athens: Ohio University Press, 1990, 205–24.

Dilemma of a Ghost, The (1965)

A play by Ama Ata **Aidoo.** The play investigates the requirements for successful interpersonal and intercultural relations. The main character, Ato, a Ghanaian student, is married to a black American woman, Eulalie, and the story examines their illusions about each other's character and culture, focusing on their return to Ghana and their struggle as they face the social, physical, and psychological realities of living in Africa. The play ends with a verbal and physical confrontation between Ato and Eulalie and a sharp observation from Ato's mother about the individual's responsibility to maintain communication with others.

Diop, Alioune (1910–80)

Born in Saint Louis, Senegal, into a Muslim family where French was spoken, Alioune went to French school and received his literary baccalaureat in 1931. He studied philosophy at the University of Algiers, where he met Albert Camus, and found himself in France during World War II. Diop converted to Catholicism and briefly worked in colonial administration at the end of the war.

He created the journal *Présence Africaine* in 1947 with an editorial committee including, among many famous intellectuals, Jean-Paul Sartre, Albert Camus, and Andre Gide. In 1949, he created the publishing house Présence Africaine, which published Aimé Cesaire's *Discours sur le colonialisme* (1955, trans. *Discourse on Colonialism*, 1972). Many of the editorial pieces in the journal were written by Alioune, as well as seminal pieces such as *Niam n'goura* ("Eat in order to live"—Fula proverb) (1947), the definition of his cultural project and his introduction to P. Tempels's *Bantu Philosophy: Niam M'paya* ("Eat in order to fatten"—Fula proverb) (1949). Diop was the driving force behind the movement to organize black intellectuals that started in 1956 with the *Premier Congrès des écrivains et artistes noirs* (First Congress of Black Writers and Artists) and with the creation of the Society of African Culture, which culminated in the Dakar festival of 1966, and of which he was general secretary until his death. Alioune Diop continued to work to keep African intellectuals independent from political pressures, and he initiated the Second World Black and African Festival of Arts and Culture in Lagos in 1977.

Further Reading

Mudimbe, V. Y. *The Surreptitious Speech: "Presence Africaine" and the Politics of Otherness, 1947–1987.* Chicago: University of Chicago Press, 1992.

Nicol, Davidson. "Alioune Diop and the African Renaissance." *African Affairs* 78 (1979): 3–11.

———. "Alioune Diop and the Future Fortunes of FESTAC." *Afriscope* 6, no. 7 (1967): 5.

Diop, Birago (1906–89)

Senegalese gatherer of traditional folktales, poet, and autobiographer. Diop was born in Ouakam, a small village near Dakar. Diop received a mixed traditional and French primary education. In 1920 he traveled north to Saint Louis, Senegal, to attend the renowned lycée Faidherbe. The rich troves of traditional tales, oral histories, and genealogies made an impact on Diop's literary formation. In the late 1920s he traveled to France for one year of military service and then began several years of veterinary training in Toulouse and Paris, where he met L. S. **Senghor,** Léon Damas, and other pioneering francophone literary figures. From the mid-1930s to 1958, Diop traveled across French colonial Africa as a veterinary officer, taking time to collect folktales along the way. From 1960 to 1964, he served as the first Senegalese ambassador to newly independent Tunisia. In 1964 he returned to Dakar and ran a private veterinary practice until his retirement in 1979. From 1979 until his death in 1989 he devoted himself to his memoirs and to leadership in several Senegalese writers' organizations.

Diop started writing poetry in French in 1925, but his public breakthrough was not until 1947, when he published *Les Contes d'Amadou Koumba* (1947), one of the landmark works of contemporary African letters. *Les Contes* is a collection of nineteen stories, all apparently as told to Diop by the family *griot* (traditional storyteller, oral historian, and genealogist) Amadou Koumba, whom Diop met while posted in Kayes, near the intersection of present-day Senegal, Mauritania, and Mali. Diop followed this work with the collections *Les Nouveaux contes d'Amadou Koumba* (1958; *Tales of Amadou Koumba,* 1966, includes texts from both collections of stories), *Contes et lavanes* (1963), the shorter *Contes d'Awa,* and the play *L'os de Mor Lam* (both in 1977). Diop's tales are, like many renderings of traditional oral tales, moral, didactic, and entertaining, and feature animal, human, and supernatural characters such as trickster hares, lazy crocodiles, difficult hyenas, and sharply drawn humans. He presents the bulk of his work as the faithful repetition of traditional tales, but it is clear that he transcribes them, reshapes, and recasts each tale he renders in written form, while preserving their local essence. Critics often address the religious, political, and philosophical dimensions of these seminal collections of West African tales. Diop's tales have been translated into more than a dozen languages and have served functions ranging from the entertainment and instruction of children to the illumination of West African traditions to the illustration of universal human culture.

In comparison to his folktales, Diop's poetry—principally his 1960 *Leurres et lueurs,* a collection of poems dating from 1925—has received less attention. In 1978 he began to publish a remarkable five-volume autobiography or series of memoirs extending from his birth through 1989: *La Plume, raboutée* (1978), *A rebrousse-temps* (1982), *A rebrousse-gens* (1985), *Du temps de . . .* (1986), and *Et les yeux pour me dire* (1989). His memoirs have not received much critical attention, but they are an invaluable resource for students of twentieth-century francophone West African history.

Further Reading

Brewer, Kenneth W. "Political Allegory: Bakhtin, Jameson and Birago Diop's Les Contes d'Amadou Koumba." *Allegory Old and New in Literature, the Fine Arts, Music and Theatre and Its Continuity in Culture,* ed. Marlies Kronegger and Anna-Teresa Tymieniecka. Dordrecht: Kluwer Academy under Auspices of World Institute for Advanced Phenomenological Research and Learning, 1994, 259–64.
Camara, Sana. "Birago Diop's Poetic Contribution to the Ideology of Negritude." *Research in African Literatures* 33, no. 4 (Winter 2002): 101–23.
Coundouriotis, Eleni. "Writing Stories about Tales Told: Anthropology and the Short Story in African Literatures." *Narrative* 6, no. 2 (May 1998): 140–56.
Tcheho, Diop I. C. "The Image of Islam in Selected Tales of Birago Diop." In *Faces of Islam in African Literature,* ed. Kenneth W. Harrow. Portsmouth, NH: Heinemann, 1991, 215–26.

Diop, Cheikh Anta (1923–86)

The work of Cheikh Anta Diop has had a powerful influence on contemporary African thought. He trained as a historian and a nuclear physicist, and Diop was very active in the student nationalist movement in France in the 1950s. Although the Sorbonne did not accept his doctoral thesis in history, it was published and had a great influence on Egyptology, changing the traditional views of a great divide between Egypt and the rest of Africa (*Nation nègre et culture,* 1954). The discussion was continued in the *UNESCO General History of Africa, Volume II,* which presents a balanced view of the discussion on the origins of Ancient Egyptians. *Towards the African Renaissance: Essays in Culture and Development, 1946–1960* (1996) was originally published in French as *Alerte Sous Les Tropiques* (1990) and proceeds from the essays Diop wrote between 1946 and 1960. Diop's speculations have been criticized, but he demonstrated the richness of his hypothesis in many areas, as it stimulated Meroitic studies. During his career as a Professor of History in Dakar and as head of a carbon dating laboratory, he was able to continue his task of building up a cursus (public office) of classical African antiquities, and this legacy is demonstrated in part by the fact that there is an annual Cheikh Anta Diop conference.

Further Reading

Diouf, Mamadou, and Mohamad Mbodj. "The Shadow of Cheikh Anta Diop." In *The Surreptitious Speech: Presence Africaine and the Politics of Otherness, 1947–1987,* ed. V. Y. Mudimbe, Leopold Sedar Senghor (preface), and Christaine Yande Diop (foreword). Chicago: University of Chicago Press, 1992, 118–35.

Spady, James G., and Leandre Jackson, introduction. *Cheikh Anta Diop: Poem for the Living.* Philadelphia: Black History Museum; Umum/Loh, 1997.

Diop, David (1927–60)

Senegalese poet Diop was born in Bordeaux, France, of a Senegalese father and Cameroonian mother. As an adolescent Diop displayed the intellectual verve—and suffered the physical ill health—that characterized his entire short life. His single poetry collection *Coups de pilon* (1956; ***Hammer Blows,*** 1973), in which he articulates a cause that is anticolonialist and pan-Africanist (with its sights ranging beyond Africa to Suez, Hanoi, and Atlanta), confirmed his already significant reputation in francophone African nationalist circles. His reputation was bolstered by his move to Guinea in 1958, which affirmed his support for Sékou Touré's stand against French neo-colonialist hegemony. Diop died tragically, with his second wife and two children, in a plane crash.

Further Reading

Ojo, Samuel-Adeoya. "David Diop: The Voice of Protest and Revolt (1927–1960)." In *Presence Africaine: Revue Culturelle du Monde Noir/ Cultural Review of the Negro World* 103 (1977): 19–42.

Yesufu, Abdur-Rasheed. "Socio-Political Ideology in Poetry: David Diop and Jared Angira." *Journal of English* (Sana'-a, Yemen Arab Republic) 8 (1980): 12–27.

Yesufu, A. Rashid. "A Common Heritage and Predicament: The Implied 'Third World' Motif in Diop's *Hammer Blows.*" *Chandrabhaga: A Magazine of World Writing* 12 (Winter 1984): 6–23.

Divorce, The (1977)

A play by Wale **Ogunyemi.** A full-length comedy, this is one of the most frequently performed English-language plays in Nigeria. The plot, in turns farcical and satirical, deals with a businessman's mistaken belief that his wife is adulterous. The play is at its most attractive when satire and farce combine, as in the portrayal of an incompetent policeman. The houseboy Patrick is a Pidgin-speaking character who is especially popular with audiences. Despite its popularity, the play has attracted criticism on the grounds of male chauvinism.

Djoleto, (Solomon Alexander) Amu (1929–)

A Ghanaian novelist and poet, Djoleto was educated at Accra Academy, St. Augustine's College, and at University College of the Gold Coast. He joined the Ministry of Education in the 1960s as a classroom teacher and education officer and later studied textbook development at the Institute of Education, University of London, returning to Ghana to become an editor of the *Ghana Teachers' Journal.* He is the author of three popular novels, *The Strange Man* (1967), *Money Galore* (1975), and *Hurricane of Dust* (1987), all of which focus on social and economic life. In *The Strange Man* he recounts the life of Mensah in colonial and postcolonial Ghana; *Money Galore* satirizes the corruption at every level of postindependence Ghana; and *Hurricane of Dust* deals with Ghana under military misrule. His poems appear in the anthologies *Voices of Ghana* (1958) and *Messages: Poems from Ghana* (1970) and have been collected in *Amid the Swelling Act* (1992). As a director of Ghana's

Book Development Council and an advisor on educational reform, Djoleto has made an important contribution to Ghana's literary culture. He has also written books for young readers: *Obodai Sai* (1990), *Twins in Trouble* (1991), *The Frightened Thief* (1992), *Girl Who Knows about Cars* (1996), *Kofi Loses His Way* (1995, paperback), and *Akos and the Fire Ghost* (1998).

Further Reading

Abrahams, Cecil. "African Writing and Themes of Colonialism and Post-Independence Disillusionment." *Canadian Journal of African Studies/Revue Canadienne des Etudes Africaines* 12, no. 1 (1978): 119–25.

Down Second Avenue (1959)

Autobiography by Es'kia (Ezekiel) **Mphahlele.** This is his account of growing up in an impoverished family in a black ghetto in South Africa. It is a thoughtful and often angry recreation of the struggle of a sensitive and highly intelligent child to gain an education in conditions that forbid it. The work is highly personalized and focuses on close family life, and it also suggests that the experiences conveyed in it are typical of the experience of a large number of South Africans. The book pays tribute to the resilience of the human spirit and the capacity to prevail against all odds.

Drama

There are several anthologies and collections of African drama that encompass more than one country or area. Helen Gilbert's 2001 *Post-Colonial Plays: An Anthology* offers both well-known plays and previously unpublished ones, with introductions to each play that include information on the author, an outline of the play's performance history, and a summary of its cultural context. *African Drama and Performance,* edited by Conteh Morgan, John and Olaniyan, and Tejumola (2004) is a collection of essays about the study of drama, theater, and performance in Africa from various contributors. Also recent is the Norton Critical Edition of *Modern African Drama,* edited by Biodun Jeyifo (2002), and *Contemporary African Plays,* which contains a selection of six plays from the past twenty-five years of African theater, edited by Jane Plastow and Martin Banham (1999). Under the same title Wole Soyinka, Percy Mtwa, and Ama Aidoo also published *Contemporary African Plays* in 1999.

EAST AFRICA

Rituals, storytelling, dance, and drumming are all important to theater and drama (or *Michezo ya Kuigiza*) in East Africa, where early drama was represented by the court dramatists employed in the Kabaka's palace in Buganda. Contemporary dramatists who carry on the tradition of court drama (in essence) are writers such as Robert **Serumaga,** Byron Kawadwa, Nuwa Sentongo, and Elvania Namukwaya Zirimu. European influences are also apparent due to the use of drama in Christian schools and churches to reinforce English cultural forms. The resultant two dramatic traditions in East Africa are therefore those of English classical theater and indigenous language popular theater. Also important are the Gikuyu-language plays produced in the 1970s by **Ngugi wa Thiong'o,** which helped make Kenyan theater available to more people, and the creation of the Kenya National Theatre, which meant more independent Kenyan drama and less imperialist-based productions.

Political figures, freedom fighters, and those of legendary status form the subject for many plays, such as *Dedan Kimathi* (1974) by Kenneth **Watene,** *The Trial of Dedan Kimathi* (1976) by Ngugi and Micere Githae **Mugo,** and *The Black Prophet* (1982), a play about Elijah Masinde by James Irungu and James Shimanyula. These plays challenge the association of colonialism with progress, and depict the possibilities of freedom from colonial rule. Other works take a more equivocal approach, such as *My Son for My Freedom, The Haunting Past,* and *The Broken Pot,* published by Watene in 1973. *The Trial of Dedan Kimathi* by Ngugi and Micere Githae Mugo is a response to Watene's conservative treatment of historical events in *Dedan Kimathi.*

East African playwrights who write in English include Robert Serumanga, John **Ruganda, Ngugi wa Thiong'o,** Rebeka **Njau,** Francis **Imbuga,** and **Cliff Lubwa P'chong**. Serumaga's English-language plays include *A Play* (1967), *Majangwa: A Promise of Rains* (1974), and *The Elephants* (1971). Ruganda has published *Covenant with Death* (published in *Black Mamba,* 1973), *The Burdens* (1972), *The Floods* (1980), and *Echoes of Silence* (1986) in English, while the English-language plays *The Rebels, The Wound in the Heart,* and *This Time Tomorrow* by Ngugi are collected in *This Time Tomorrow* (1970), and in 1962 Ngugi's *The Black Hermit* (1968) was produced in honor of Ugandan independence. Novelist and journalist Rebeka Njau is the author of *The Scar* (1963), while Francis Imbuga's plays include *The Fourth Trial* (1972), *The Married Bachelor* (1973), *Betrayal in the City* (1976), *Game of Silence*(1977), *The Successor* (1979), *Man of Kafira* (1984), *Aminata* (1988), and *The Burning of Rags* (1989). Ugandan **Cliff Lubwa P'chong** has published *Generosity Kills* and a work inspired by Okot p'Bitek's poem *Song of Lawino* titled *The Last Safari* (1975). Mumbi Kaigwa's *The Voice of a Dream* (2002) is a play made up of true stories collected from the author's fellow country people. It explores East African identity through music, dance, storytelling, and song and was performed at the Festival of Storytelling and Dance (SANDD) that Kaigwa organized in Nairobi. Bill Okyere Marshall has published two plays recently, *Shadow of an Eagle* and *Stranger to Innocence* (both 2003). The focus in East Africa is to develop indigenous theater and to encourage the use of drama as a social and political tool.

SOUTH AFRICA

Stephen **Black** is often referred to as the first English-language South African dramatist, although Shakespearean and Restoration plays were performed by the African Theatre as early as 1801, Black (active from 1908–17 and 1928–29) wrote and produced his own satirical comedies in the style of Sheridan and Wilde with a unique South African emphasis on local references, South African stock characters like the Boer patriarch and the colonial maiden, and the use of South African English. Although Black did not publish his plays, his best-known work includes *Love and the Hyphen* (1908), **Helena's Hope, Ltd** (1910), *The Flappers* (1911), and *The Uitlanders* (1911).

In the 1930s an urban black culture began to emerge, with H.I.E. **Dhlomo**'s founding of the Bantu Dramatic Society in 1932 in order to promote drama with an emphasis on African issues. There are nine of Dhlomo's plays that survive, all of which offer an interpretation of rural tribal history (including Xhosa history) in the contemporary black context. Dhlomo is an important figure in the early critical and theoretical formation of African-centered and noncolonialist drama, and his plays include *The **Girl Who Killed to Save**: Nongqause the Liberator* (the first published play by a black South African), *Ntsikana* (1936), *Cetshwayo* (1936), *Dingane* (1937), *Moshoeshoe* (1937), *The Living Dead, The Pass (Arrested and Discharged), The Workers,* and *Malaria* (1939–41).

The development of theater during the **apartheid** era (1948–90) was dictated by the state-approved companies, who gained extensive funding. In contrast, theater companies that were targeted as resistant struggled to stay alive due to the pass laws, segregation of venues, and censorship. State-approved and funded performing arts councils that followed the National Theatre Organization (1947–61) in 1963 were represented by province, with CAPAB in the Cape, NAPAC in Natal, PACOFS in the Orange Free State, and PACT in the Transvaal. Although they had high performance standards, these theaters reserved dramatic culture for white audiences. In contrast, from the late 1950s and through the mid-1970s many actors and writers promoted an alternative type of theater that was not racially divided. For example, African performers Athol **Fugard,** Gibson **Kente,** and Barney Simon worked together at the Rehearsal Room at Dorkay House, Johannesburg (1961), as a part of the Union Artists and the African Music and Drama Association. In addition, Fugard also collaborated with the Serpent Players in New Brighton township (from 1963), while Robert McLaren set up Workshop '71; Brian Astbury, Yvonne Bryceland, and Fugard opened the multiracial Space Theatre in Cape Town; Barney Simon and Mannie Manim of The Company (1974) and of the Market Theatre (1976) made their stages available to many theatrical programs, while the Junction Avenue Theatre Company was established in 1976. In 1995 the Market Theatre was awarded the American Jujamcyn Award.

One major South-African dramatist is Athol Fugard, who has amassed a large amount of work during his theatrical career. Works of note by Fugard include his early Sophiatown "township" plays, **No-Good Friday** (1958) and *Nongogo* (1959); his investigation of the psychological results of racial division, *The Blood Knot* (1961); his political plays on apartheid themes (workshopped at the Serpent Players) *Sizwe Bansi Is Dead* (1972) and *The Island* (1973), *Statements after an Arrest under the Immorality Act* (1972); the auto-biographical *"Master Harold" . . . and the Boys* (1982); his biography of sculptor Helen Martins titled *The Road to Mecca* (1984); as well as the political dramas *My Children, My*

Africa! (1989), *Playland* (1992), and *Valley Song* (1996). Fugard's works demonstrate a close attunement to the social atmosphere of South Africa, as they interpret for the stage an acute understanding of the nature of human existence and the injustice of apartheid through a sensitive and careful use of South African language that captures the intensity of conflict. Recently, Fugard has published several plays including *The Captain's Tiger* (1998), *Sorrows and Rejoicings* (2001), and *Exits and Entrances* (2004), which portrays Fugard's brief friendship with the Afrikaans actor Andre Huguenet.

Theater practice in South Africa has also been deeply influenced by Workshop '71 (begun by Robert McLaren), which allowed for workshopped productions such as *Crossroads* (an adaptation of *Everyman*) and the prison play *Survival*. Workshop '71 made popular theater more of a reality, especially in the way that it encouraged democratic composition and nonracial theater. Workshop productions by Barney Simon demonstrate a focus on language, social comment, biographical and heavily narrative elements; examples of Simon's work include *Black Dog/In'emnyama* (1984), *Outers* (1985), *Born in the RSA* (1985), and *Score Me the Ages* (1989). Percy Mtwa and Mbongeni **Ngema** worked with Barney Simon to produce *Woza Albert!* (1980), which reflected a performance style that was very reflective of Grotowski's poor theater, as it depended mainly on the actor's body and ability, used many character changes, restricted the use of props, and orchestrated voices in order to create music. Mtwa's *Bopha!* (1986), Ngema's *Asinamali!* (1985), and his musical *Sarafina!* (1987), are also important contributions to South African theater.

In its productions, the Junction Avenue Theatre Company used the experience of Workshop '71 to develop another view of South African history. Their *Fantastical History of a Useless Man* (1976), *Randlords and*

Rotgut (1978), *Sophiatown,* (1986) and *Tooth and Nail* (1989) all explore political elements of South African society such as apartheid (and the end of apartheid), industrial issues, and inner-city Johannesburg.

Other companies took inspiration from the **Black Consciousness** movement of the 1970s and created a more confrontational type of theater that was often the target of state-based harassment. Three such companies were the Theatre Council of Natal (TECON), which was founded in 1969 but was banned after the production of *Antigone in '71;* the People's Experimental Theatre (PET), which was founded in Lenasia in 1973 but was charged with staging revolutionary plays after its first production, that of Mthuli Shezi's *Shanti;* and the Music, Drama and Literature Institute (MDALI), founded in 1972 but forced to close when Molefe Pheto (its leader) was detained.

The "township musical" took hold in the 1970s, a form that had actually begun in 1959 with the production of *King Kong* with an all-black cast. Gibson Kente took up the genre with his shows *How Long?* (1971), *Too Late* (1973), and *Sikalo* (1976), which were performed only for black township audiences. Matsemela **Manaka** and Maishe Maponya were two writers influenced by this genre, and they were also Africanists whose work was closely linked to the Black Consciousness movement. Manaka deals with the social and economic conditions of black dispossession in his early plays, *Egoli* (1979), *Pula* (1982), and *Children of Asazi* (1984). In *Gorée* (1989), *Blues Afrika Cafe* (1990), and *Ekhaya* (1991) Manaka goes on to explore African culture in an attempt to encourage a theater that allows for social reconstruction. Maponya's plays, some examples of which are *The Hungry Earth* (1978), *Umongikazi/The Nurse* (1982), and *Gangsters* (1984), represent the abuses of apartheid in a very direct manner, and they also offer a unique combination of technical aspects like improvisation,

choral singing, gumboot dancing, mime, and the use of multiple roles, which result in an emphasis on performance rather than text. Zakes Mda depicts political issues as they relate to the lives of everyday people in his collections *We Shall Sing for the Fatherland* (1979) and *And the Girls in Their Sunday Dresses* (1993). Plays like the radio production *Banned* (1982) are concerned with the abuses to be found in independent states such as Lesotho, while in *Joys of War* (1989) Mda depicts the topic of armed struggle and its moral implications and social context.

Other important types of theater that developed near the end of apartheid are workers' theater, theater for development, and theater-in-education. Workers' theater saw its beginnings during the states of emergency years (1983–87), and is tied to Natal and the Durban Workers Cultural Local (DWCL). Groups like Junction Avenue worked with factory workers and intellectuals to put on plays such as *The Long March, The Sun Shall Rise for the Workers,* and *Comment.* Zakes Mda and the Marotholi Travelling Theatre in Lesotho are closely linked to the theater for development movement, while in South Africa the movement has made an impact with works such as *Koma* (1986) by Matsemela Manaka, Maishe Maponya's Winterveld project with unemployed squatter-camp youth, and Doreen Mazibuko's *Moments,* which is an analysis of the lead-up to the 1994 elections. Theater-in-education provides a wide spectrum of education-based theater, with programs like the Handspring Puppet Theatre's science-related shows, the performance of *Julius Caesar* by Matsemela Manaka in rural areas (both in Setswana and English), and the production of *Romeo and Juliet* that Market Theatre Laboratory took on tour to the township of Sebokeng.

Both alternative and state theaters reevaluated their positions in South-African society near the end of the apartheid era, when alternative theaters became more mainstream and state-sanctioned theaters marked a decline in attendance due to their outdated political positions. Because apartheid and political opposition framed so much of alternative theater's work, there was a necessary revision of political themes at the end of apartheid, while the state-based theaters had to become nonracial if they were to be politically acceptable. When censorship was lifted those who were exiled could return, and theatrical productions could take place that were previously banned. There were still political components to the reorganization of state and private-sector funding, although opportunities were now available for black writers, performers, and managers due to the reorganized performing arts councils, and indigenous art forms were encouraged. Works that reflect this time of social and political change are Sue Pam-Grant's *Curl Up and Dye* (1989), which deals with the decline of inner-city Johannesburg, and Paul Slabolepzsy's *Mooi St. Moves* (1992), which satirically deals with urban stereotypes.

Other innovated styles in the early to mid-90s include William Kentridge's unique use of puppetry, animated video, and European and African music in his *Woyzeck on the Highveld* (1992), which he produced in collaboration with Handspring Puppet Company. The themes of truth and reconciliation were tackled in the same company's production of Alfred Jarry's *Ubu and the Truth Commission* (1997, scripted by Jane Taylor), which utilized a wide range of media to get its very relevant message across. The Grahamstown Festivals (particularly of 1997 and 1998) demonstrated the success of Brett Bailey and the Third World Bunfight's *iMumbo Jumbo The Days of Miracle and Wonder* and *Ipi Zombi?*, which are amateur township-based performances that utilize ritual and demonstrate the important new directions that theatrical performance is taking.

The evolution of other multimedia theater companies from the late 1980s to today

is also relevant to theatrical development. The African Research and Educational Puppetry Programme, now called arepp: Theatre for Life Trust, was founded in 1987 by Maishe Maponya, Oupa Mthimkulu, Ann Wanless, and Gary Friedman as a community-based educational trust that uses puppetry to provide social life-skills education to disadvantaged communities. The company's first long-term project was called *Puppets against AIDS,* which was an educational puppet show about HIV and AIDS that they took on the road in 1988. The IROKO Theatre Company is a registered charity that was founded in 1996 and uses interactive performances and workshops in oral storytelling, drama, music, and dance to educate and bolster the creative potential and self-esteem of children and young people. The First Physical Theatre Company (1997) works in South Africa to tease together the elements of theater, dance, music, mime, design, voice, song, and movement to heal and transform the lives of South Africans. The South Africa Theatre Exchange began in 2000 through the impetus of Nefertiti Burton. The focus of the Exchange is the development of new work collaboratively created by South African and African-American theater artists and students. The group presented the play *Middle Passage: A Healing Ritual* at the Grahamstown Arts Festival Student Theatre Festival in 2003 and featured students from the Vus'a Bantu Performing Arts Project, and from the African American Theatre Program of the University of Louisville's Department of Theatre Arts. The intention was to join energies from both sides of the Atlantic to honor the Africans who died in the middle passage. Other recent dramatic productions of note are Mbongeni Ngema's *House of Shaka* (2005), which is based on the authorized biography of King Goodwill Zwelithini Zulu, as well as *Sing African Dance* (2005), also by Mbongeni Ngema, which demonstrates the history and spirit of Africa through song and dance in the first pan-African musical play. Published new works of note are also Mda Zakes's *Fools, Bells and the Habit of Eating: Three Satires* (2002), and Lewis Nkosi's *The Black Psychiatrist* (2001). Other new works can be found in editor Anne Fuchs's *New Theatre in Francophone and Anglophone Africa* (1999), dedicated to the memory of playwrights **Sony Labou Tansi** and Matsemela Manaka.

WEST AFRICA

The theoretical work *Drama and Theatre in Nigeria: A Critical Source Book* (1981), edited by Yemi Ogunbiyi, analyzes the boundaries between African ritual and the idea of drama, which may represent a combination of West African rituals performed in the round in a village, and the European structure of theater with an audience, stage, and admission rate. During the postcolonial period, anglophone West African drama was encouraged by independence movements and the cultural transitions that resulted from them. The antecedents for West African drama in English are considered by both Anthony Graham-White in his *The Drama of Black Africa* (1974) and Michael Etherton in his *The Development of African Drama* (1982), while Hubert Ogunde's contribution (in the 1940s) to a professional musical theater that contained both European variety concert and Yoruban *alarinjo* theater traditions is discussed by Ebun Clark in his *Hubert Ogunde: The Making of Nigerian Theatre* (1979). Other critical resources on West African theater include Effiok Bassey Uwatt's *Playwriting and Directing in Nigeria* (2002)—a compendium of interviews with the late Ola Rotimi over the past thirty years; *Ola Rotimi's African Theatre: The Development of an Indigenous Aesthetic* by Niyi Coker (2005); *Poetry, Performance, and Art: Udje Dance Songs of the Urhobo People* by N. C. Durham (2003); and Patrick Ebewo's

Barbs: A Study of Satire in the Plays of Wole Soyinka (2002). Similar works on West African theater are Karin Barber, John Collins, and Alain Ricard's *West African Popular Theatre (Drama and Performance)* (1997); Elaine-Utudjian Saint-Andre's article "New Modes of Writing in West African Drama: Prison Plays from Sierra Leone, Ghana and Nigeria" in *Commonwealth Essays and Studies* 14, no. 1 (Autumn 1991): 70–77; and Chris Nwamuo's article "Henshaw and the Genesis of Literary Theatre in Nigeria" in *The Literary Criterion* 23, nos. 1–2 (1988): 118–30.

Ghanaian Kobina Sekyi wrote one of the best-known early West African plays, *The Blinkards* (1915), which reflects Sekyi's focus on Akan-Fanti culture and traditional values. Efua **Sutherland** was also instrumental in the development of drama after the Ghana became independent in 1957, as she played a part in the Ghana Drama Studio set up by Kwame Nkrumah. The Ghana Drama Studio emphasized cultural identity and contained a touring company that performed plays in the language of the Ashanti (Twi). Sutherland also reinterpreted Euripides's *Alcestis* as *Edufa* (1967), and her *The Marriage of Anansewa* (1975) incorporates the Anansesem tradition of folktales. Nigerian James Ene **Henshaw** was working in Nigeria around the same time that Sutherland was working in Ghana, and he established an English-speaking drama that combined Victorian English theater style with African social comment. There have been many reprints of Henshaw's first volume of plays, *This Is Our Chance: Three Plays from West Africa* (1956), which also included *The Jewel of the Shrine* and *A Man of Character*. Sierra Leone dramatist Raymond Sharif **Easmon** published similarly well-structured plays in his *Dear Parent and Ogre* (1964) and *The New Patriots* (1965). West African drama quite often responds to the history and culture that comprises the backdrop of each generation of playwrights. Playwrights who choose to use the English language still extrapolate from their African heritage, and in this way bring change to the European play. Early West African dramatists created a European play form that spoke against the negative cultural impacts of colonialism. Sekyi used English as well as Fante (and may have produced his play in Fante), and real experimentation with the dramatic form flowered in the 1960s, at the same time as independence.

Novelist, poet, essayist, dramatist and Nobel Prize winner (1986) Wole **Soyinka** is the most famous West African dramatist. Soyinka joined others in his generation of Nigerian playwrights (such as J. P. Clark **Bekederemo,** Ola **Rotimi,** Ime Ikiddeh, Kalu **Uka,** Zulu **Sofola,** Yemi Ajibade, Uwa Udensi, and Wale **Ogunyemi**) many of whom are Yoruba, to create a reputation for Nigeria after independence in 1960. Nigeria has played an important role in the development of drama, as Christ Dunton demonstrates in his *Make Man Talk True: Nigerian Drama in English since 1970* (1992). The university programs played an important role in this growth of drama, as the famous department of theater arts at Ibadan, along with extramural theater companies, tours, and drama groups in schools and colleges all encouraged the growth of theater.

Soyinka and Bekederemo both demonstrate the impact of this university growth, and Soyinka's shrines to Yoruba gods on the Ife campus were a theatrical demonstration of his political and social views on the role of African tradition in modern life. Soyinka's first major work similarly focused on Yoruba mythology, was written for the 1960 Nigerian independence celebrations, and is titled *A Dance of the Forests* (1963). Soyinka uses myth both to teach about the Yoruba world and to critique contemporary Nigerian politics, while he also uses satire and comedy to comment on his anger at false behavior (as he does in *The Jero Plays,* 1973). Soyinka

emphasizes poetry and meaninglessness in *The Road* (1965), while his command of language, juxtaposition of theatrical elements, and ability to produce dramatic tension all add to the success of *Death and the King's Horseman* (1975). Soyinka has also developed critical theory about drama in his critical essays **Myth, Literature and the African World** (1976) and *Art, Dialogue and Outrage* (1988). Ketu Katrak discusses Soyinka's use and definition of tragedy in *Wole Soyinka and Modern Tragedy,* 1986, while *Critical Perspectives on Wole Soyinka,* edited by James Gibbs (1980), and *Research on Wole Soyinka,* edited by James Gibbs and Bernth Lindfors (1993), also offer introductions to Soyinka's work. A new work from Soyinka is *King Baabu* (2002), which is a satirical play concerning the dictatorial political regimes of Africa. J. P. Clark Bekederemo's first play, *Song of a Goat,* was first produced at the Mbari Club in Ibadan. Although traditional elements were visible in *Song of a Goat,* Bekederemo used even more of them in his dramatic adaptation of the Ozidi saga titled *Ozidi* (1966), and he also transcribed and translated the storytelling and community performance tradition of the seven-day Ozidi saga in Orua (the Delta region of Nigeria) in 1977 (*The Ozidi Saga*) and made a film of one performance (titled *Tides of the Delta*) in Orua with Frank Speed in 1964.

Of the same era as Soyinka and Bekederemo is Ola Rotimi, who studied playwriting at Yale, and whose early comedy is titled *Our Husband Has Gone Mad Again* (1974), while his historical dramas are **Kurunmi** (1971) and *Ovonramwen Nogbaisi* (1974). Rotimi's play *If* (1983) broaches the topic of social injustice in politics, while *Hopes of the Living Dead* (1988) follows the rebellion of a leper; *The Gods Are Not to Blame* (1971) offers a retelling of Sophocles's *Oedipus;* and *Holding Talks* (1979) is a satire on the misuse of language. The historical drama was also developed by Wale Ogunyemi, whose play *Ijaye War* (1970) depicts the Ijaye-Ibadan mid-nineteenth-century conflicts, while *Kiriji* (1976) is about the Kiriji war between Ibadan and the Ekiti and Ijesa peoples in the late nineteenth century. In these works, local history and the intricacy of military and social conflicts are brought alive for Nigerian audiences, while other work by Ogunyemi include the music-dramas *Obaluaye* (1972) and *Langbodo* (1979). Ogunyemi's *Queen Amina of Zazzau* (1999) presents a dramatic interpretation of the life of Queen Amina, the ruler of present-day Zaria between 1588 and 1589.

The gap between rich and poor in Nigeria since independence and the growth of capitalism are also the subject of many Nigerian plays. *Morountodun* (1982) by Femi Osofisan and *Farewell to Babylon* (1979) by Bode Sowande are both examples of texts that deal with the Agbakoya farmers' protest (1868–69). Osofisan has been an important figure in Nigerian drama since the 1970s, and his *Morountodun* combines symbolism and social realism with a political, historical, and contemporary outlook of Nigeria. Other plays by Osofisan include *The Chattering and the Song* (1977), *Once upon Four Robbers* (1980), *Midnight Hotel* (1986), and *Esu and the Vagabond Minstrels* (1991). Kale Omotoso also offers realistic plays that deal with social issues, such as *The Curse* (1976) and *Shadows in the Horizon* (1977). Femi Osofisan has also written *African Theatre: Southern Africa* (2004) and *African Theatre: Women* (2002), as well as *African Theatre: Playwrights and Politics* (2001), *The Nostalgic Drum: Essays on Literature, Drama and Culture* (2001), and *African Theatre in Development,* edited with Martin Banham and James Gibbs (1999). Recent plays or new editions by Femi Osofisan include *Major Plays 1: Many Colours Make the Thunder-King, Farewell to a Cannibal Rage, Oriki of a Grasshopper* (2003), *Major Plays 2* (2003), *Esu and the Vagabond Minstrels* (new edition, 2002), *Bishop Ajayi Crowther: The Triumph and Travails of a Putting* (2002),

One Putting, Many Seasons (2001), *Once upon Four Robbers* (new edition, 2001), *One Legend Many Seasons* (2001), *Restless Breed* (4 short plays, 2002), and *Seasons of Wrath* (5 short plays, 2002). Osofisan has also recently mounted a production of *The Trojan Women or The Women of Owu* (2004), which is set in 1821 Yorubaland and follows the lives of a vanquished queen and her daughters, and a production of *Wèsóò Hamlet!* (*The Resurrection of Hamlet*) in 2003. Also of note is Bode Sowande's recent production of *Superleaf* ("*Orin Ata*") (2004).

In the early 1970s Zulu Sofola started to offer a female point of view on cultural issues both on stage and television. Sofola, Tess Onwueme, and Stella Oyedepo are among the best-known female playwrights in Nigeria. Sofola's *The Sweet Trap* (1977) is about rebellious university wives, and Sofola offers a message of choice for middle-class Nigerian women, who she believes have many opportunities open to them, rather than just one political reality. Tess Onwueme works in many genres and offers a feminist message in her works. Recent works by Tess Onwueme include *Riot in Heaven and Acadia Boys: Two Plays* (2005), *NO Vacancy* (a play, 2005), *What Mama Said* (an epic drama, 2003), *The Missing Face* (revised edition, 2002), and *Then She Said It!* (a play, 2000). A recent critical work on Tess Onwueme is Oliver Kamau's *Revolutionary Theatre in Africa: The Example of Tess Onwueme's Plays* (1999). Onwueme has also mounted recent productions of *The Missing Face* (2001), *Shakara* (2004), and *The Reign of Wazobia,* which has been adapted into film (2004). Ghanaian Ama Ata **Aidoo**'s plays *The **Dilemma of a Ghost*** (1965) and ***Anowa*** (1970) are also important works that deal with cross-cultural family issues and demonstrate Aidoo's dramatic focus on the roles of women in modern African society.

The social realist tradition of the 1980s in Ghana is centered around Asiedu **Yirenkyi**

story, and the contest was a continuing success. From 1951 to 1958 more than ninety stories were published by a number of important authors. *Drum* writers produced energetic language that undermined accepted English. Most of the stories were influenced by the identity that the township of Sophiatown produced in reaction to apartheid, and when it was destroyed in 1957 its literary movement was disturbed.

Dry White Season, A (1979)

A novel by André **Brink.** This novel is a companion piece to the earlier ***Rumours of Rain.*** The novels represent the two aspects of the Afrikaner, the **apartheid** apologist in *Rumours of Rain* and the nonconformist Afrikaner in *A Dry White Season.* Both narrators encounter the "dark side of history" when they visit Soweto. The narrator of *A Dry White Season* is a romance author forced to confront reality when his friend, Ben du Toit, involves him in his battle for justice against the authorities by asking him to safeguard his papers. With du Toit's "accidental" death, the narrator (along with the reader) must repeat the dead man's journey from ignorance to enlightenment, increasingly implicated in the machinery of state control.

Du Plessis, Menán (1952–)

South African novelist Du Plessis is a resident of Cape Town, a city whose natural beauty she evokes in both *A State of Fear* (1983) and *Longlive!* (1989). Her political commitment is mirrored in her fictional concern with what constitutes appropriate action in a repressive society. The novels focus primarily on her characters' inner struggle. *A State of Fear* (winner of two South African awards and well received internationally) is a first-person narrative of a teacher who attempts to combat her feelings of isolation in a deeply divided society by sheltering two politically involved pupils. *Longlive!* reflects a clearer engagement with resistance politics, particularly

protests against the 1985 state of emergency; as well it dramatizes some of the conflicts Du Plessis herself has grappled with: the ethical responsibilities of being a white South African, writing in English despite her Afrikaans background, and rejecting the notion of a "female voice" while showing how notions of identity and history are particularly fraught for women of Afrikaans descent.

Further Reading

MacKenzie, Craig, and Cherry Clayton. *Between the Lines: Interviews with Bessie Head, Sheila Roberts, Ellen Kuzwayo, Miriam Tlali.* Grahamstown: National English Literary Museum, 1989.

Miller, Margaret. "Forms of Resistance: South African Women's Writing during Apartheid." *Hecate* 5, no. 1 (1998): 118–44.

Rich, Paul B. "Literature and Political Revolt in South Africa: The Cape Town Crisis of 1984–86 in the Novels of J. M. Coetzee, Richard Rive and Menán Du Plessis." *SPAN: Journal of the South Pacific Association for Commonwealth Literature and Language Studies* 36 (October 1993): 471–87.

Sergeant, Harriet. *Between the Lines: Conversations in South Africa.* London: J. Cape, 1984.

Duodu, Cameron (1937–)

Ghanaian journalist, novelist, and poet, Duodu was born in eastern Ghana and educated at Abuakwa State College. After graduation he worked as a radio journalist for the Ghana Broadcasting Corporation from 1956 to 1960 and edited the Ghana edition of the South African magazine **Drum** from 1960 to 1965 and the prestigious Ghana *Daily Graphic* between 1967 and 1968. His only novel, *The Gab Boys* (1967), describes the aimless, impoverished lives of young men who seem cut off from the modernization taking place in Ghana and reflects Duodu's own frustrations with village life. Two of his poems, "Return to Eden" and "The Stranded Vulture," were published in the anthology *Messages: Poems from Ghana* (1970). After an unsuccessful attempt at election to public office and disillusioned with the Rawlings government, he moved to Britain in the 1980s to work as a freelance journalist. Some critical articles and words by Duodu include an article in the *Index on Censorship* titled "Cape Times" (1986), an article on "Wole Soyinka: His Talent and the Mystery of His Fate" in the *Legon Observer* (1968), "The Literary Critic and Social Realities" in the *Legon Observer* (1969), and several articles in the *Independent* and the *Guardian* regarding current political issues.

Dusklands (1974)

A novel by J. M. **Coetzee.** The first half of the novel is set in the United States, while the second half is set in southern Africa. The two parts seem unrelated but are allegorically connected in their representations of history and ethnography. "The Vietnam Project" is the first part, in which a "mythographer" named Eugene Dawn explains his role in the "New Life Project," a project of psychological warfare against the Viet Cong. The second section comprises "The Narrative of Jacobus Coetzee," which tells a fictional tale of a frontiersman's two journeys into the southern African interior; a fictional "Afterword" by Dr. S. J. Coetzee, Afrikaner historian and (fictional) father of J. M. Coetzee; an appendix containing the only authentic historical document in the novel, the "Deposition of Jacobus Coetzee (1760)," translated from the Dutch by his descendant, J. M. Coetzee; and a "Translator's Preface," which blurs the distinction between historical and fictional events and characters.

E

Easmon, R(aymond) Sarif (1913–)

A novelist, playwright, and short-story writer, Easmon was born in Freetown, Sierra Leone, and was educated in Sierra Leone, Guinea, and at Newcastle University. He worked as a physician in government service until his aversion to corruption led him into private practice, and the themes of corruption and bribery predominate in his writing.

Easmon's first play, *Dear Parent and Ogre* (1964), which won a playwriting competition in *Encounter* magazine, is about the nepotism and bribery prevalent in the Sierra Leone civil service. In his satirical play *The New Patriots* (1965) many of the characters seem preoccupied with living a Western lifestyle and speaking a language akin to Oxford English. His other work includes a novel, *The Burnt Out Marriage* (1967), and a collection of short stories, *The Feud and Other Stories* (1981). Although critics such as Ama Ata **Aidoo** describe his work as dated, it does show a good sense of the comic.

Further Reading

Lautre, Maxine. "A Recorded Interview with Dr. R. Sarif Easmon." *Cultural Events in Africa* (Cambridgeshire, England) 44 (1968): 1–3.

Nagenda, John. "Generations in Conflict: Ama Ata Aidoo, J. C. De Graft and R. Sarif Easmon." In *Protest and Conflict in African Literature,* ed. Cosmo Pieterse and Donald Munro. New York: Heinemann, Africana Publishing Corp., 1969, 101–8.

Echeruo, Michael J. C. (1937–)

Echeruo was born in Okigwi, eastern Nigeria and educated at the universities of Ibadan and Cornell, where he took his doctorate in English literature. He became a lecturer in English at the University of Nigeria, Nsukka, and published poetry and literary criticism regularly in various journals. Echeruo's work has been anthologized widely. Publications of his poetry include *Mortality and Other Poems* (1995), and *Distanced: New Poems* (1975). Echeruo is also the editor of an *Igbo-English Dictionary* (1998) and has published articles on "Christopher Okigbo, Poetry Magazine, and the 'Lament of Silent Sisters'" in *Research in African Literatures* (2004),

"Modernism, Blackface, and the Postcolonial Condition" in *Research in African Literatures* (1996), and "Derrida, Language Games, and Theory" in *Theoria: A Journal of Social and Political Theory* (1995).

Further Reading

Ogbaa, Kalu, ed. *The Gong and the Flute: African Literary Development and Celebration.* Westport, CT: Greenwood Press, 1994.

Echewa, T. Obinkaram (1940–)

Nigerian novelist Echewa was born in Aba, Nigeria, and educated in Nigerian schools and American universities. Echewa has been an associate professor of English at Cheyney College in Pennsylvania, a contributor to *Time* and the *New York Times,* and a writer of stories, poetry, and articles for magazines such as *The New Yorker, America, Newsweek, West Africa,* and *Essence.* His first novel, *The Landi Lord* (1976), awarded the English-Speaking Union Prize, is an exploration of the confrontation between Christianity and European colonizers on one hand and indigenous traditional culture and African people on the other. In his second novel, *The Crippled Dancer* (1986), the intrigues and feuds of village life reflect the tension between truth and falsehood, past and present, and reality and illusion. His third novel, *I Saw the Sky Catch Fire* (1990), is based on the famous women's riot of Aba, in which the colonial forces were challenged and checked. Skillful characterization, succinct images, and an effective use of folk speech contribute to the success of the novels. He has also published children's books, such as *The Ancestor Tree* (1994), and *Mbi, Do This! Mbi, Do That: A Folktale from Nigeria* (ca. 1998).

Further Reading

Brodzki, Bella. "History, Cultural Memory, and the Tasks of Translation in T. Obinkaram Echewa's *I Saw the Sky Catch Fire.*" *PMLA: Publications of the Modern Language Association of America* 114, no. 2 (March 1999): 207–20.

Hale, Frederick. "The Decline of an Erstwhile Contemplative in T. Obinkaram Echewa's *The Land's Lord.*" *Griot: Official Journal of the Southern Conference on Afro-American Studies* 17, no. 1 (Spring 1998): 69–77.
———. "Igbo Values for the World in T. Obinkaram Echewa's *The Ancestor Tree.*" *Journal of African Children's and Youth Literature* 7–8 (1995–97): 39–50.
Wright, Derek. "T. O. Echewa: A Neglected Novelist." In *Contemporary African Fiction,* ed. and introduction Derek Wright. Bayreuth, Germany: Breitinger, 1997, 255–64.

Edufa (1969)

A play by Efua **Sutherland.** Sutherland bases this play on *Alcestis,* and seeks to point out the parallels between the world views of ancient Greece and contemporary Ghana. The Greek play provides inspiration for some scenes in *Edufa,* but at other moments the playwright's Ghanaian local inspiration becomes apparent. Such moments are visible in Sutherland's use of the Chorus, and in the character of Sekyi, who displays a particularly West African sense of humor.

Efuru (1966)

A novel by Flora **Nwapa.** Efuru is a strong woman who is the avatar of the Goddess of the Lake in a traditional African society. She overcomes the social and personal stress of abandonment by two husbands, and returns to her father's home to help her neighbors and celebrate the Goddess of the Lake. Precolonial customs and tradition are successfully interwoven into the narrative of the novel.

Egbuna, Obi B(enedict) (1940–)

A Nigerian novelist, playwright, essayist, and short-story writer Egbuna was born in Ozubulu, Nigeria. As a scholarship student Egbuna studied in Britain, where he became involved in the Black Power movement. His reputation as a writer generated solidarity demonstrations for his release when he was arrested, charged, and jailed for a plot to murder six policemen in 1968.

Egbuna's first major work, *Wind versus Polygamy* (1964; republished with the title *Elina* in 1974), a novel and its stage adaptation, was Britain's entry at the First World Black Festival of Arts in Senegal in 1966. Much of his early writing addresses racial issues; his play *The Anthill* (1965) and especially *Destroy This Temple* (1971), *The ABC of Black Power Thought* (1973), and *Daughters of the Sun and Other Stories* (1970) examine black-white encounters in a variety of forms. He published a second collection of stories titled *Emperor of the Sea* in 1974 and the novel *The Minister's Daughter* in 1975. When he returned to Nigeria in the mid-1970s he became the director of the East Central State Writers' Workshop, a director of East Central Broadcasting's television service, and published a collection of his essays for the newspaper *Renaissance* (Lagos) as *Diary of a Homeless Prodigal* (1978). After a military coup he went to the United States for graduate studies, gaining a master's degree from the University of Iowa and a PhD from Howard University (1986). Egbuna published a collection of stories, *Black Candle for Christmas* (1980), and two novels, *The Rape of Lysistrata* (1980) and *The Madness of Didi* (1980).

Ekwensi, Cyprian (1921–)

A Nigerian novelist, short-story writer, and purveyor of traditional tales, Ekwensi has had a long and successful career as a writer of popular fiction. Born in Minna, Niger State, he trained as a pharmacist and served in the Nigerian Medical Service. Later he became head of features in the Nigerian Broadcasting Services (1957), director of information of the federal Ministry of Information in Lagos (1961–66), and director of Information Services in Enugu (1966). Ekwensi has also held the directorships of Star Printing and Publishing (1975–79) and *Eagle* magazine (1981). He received the Dag Hammarskjold International Award for Literary Merit in 1968.

Ekwensi's first novel, **People of the City** (1954), established him as the first West African author of a major novel in English that marked an important development in African writing. *People of the City* is a novel that recounts the coming to political awareness of a young reporter and band leader in an emerging African country. *People of the City* was followed by *Jagua Nana* (1961), which tells the story of a socially ambitious prostitute. She falls in love with a young teacher whom she agrees to send to law school in England on the understanding that they will marry upon his return. The tragic potential of the arrangement is finally undermined by a contrived happy ending, but not before Ekwensi creates in his heroine one of the most memorable characters in Nigerian literature. *Burning Grass* (1962), subtitled "A Story of the Fulani of Northern Nigeria," portrays the life of nomadic cattlemen through the adventures of Mai Sunsaye and his sons.

Beautiful Feathers (1963) reflects the nationalist and pan-Africanist consciousness of the preindependence days of the 1950s and how the young hero's youthful commitment to this ideal leads to the disintegration of his family, which underscores the proverb implied in the title: "However famous a man is outside, if he is not respected inside his own home he is like a bird with beautiful feathers, wonderful on the outside but ordinary within." Ekwensi responds to the Nigeria-Biafra war in *Survive the Peace* (1976), which interrogates the problematics of survival in the so-called peace. Journalist James Odugo survives the war only to be cut down on the road by marauding former soldiers. Ekwensi wrote *Divided We Stand* (1980) in the midst of the hostilities (though it was published later), and it reverses the received wisdom that unity is strength, showing how ethnicity, division, and hatred bring about distrust, displacement, and war itself.

Jagua Nana's Daughter (1986) revisits the life of the notorious Jagua Nana of the earlier novel in the life of her daughter Liza who, unlike her mother, is an educated professional woman. Liza's affair with an upper-class professional man blossoms into marriage and guarantees her the security and protection she desires. In *King for Ever!* (1992), a satire on the desire of African leaders to perpetuate themselves in office, Sinanda rises to power from humble beginnings and thereafter aspires to godhead. In *Motherless Baby* (2001) Ekwensi tells the story of a young girl who falls in love with a popular band leader, and subsequently has an unwanted child, while in *Gone to Mecca* he follows a young man (Abdul) on his journey to Mecca. *Masquerade Time* (1991) describes a threatening masquerade as seen by a black American boy, while *The Red Flag* (1996) and *The Drummer Boy* (1960) are also young adult books.

Ekwensi owes his moving depiction of contemporary events of social and cultural importance in part to his personal experience as a worker in northern Nigeria. Critical responses to Ekwensi's work have shown mixed feelings because he wrote for a book-buying public in the West that expected certain literary conventions and forms, and the style of his writing was no doubt influenced by these expectations. Ekwensi's characters and plot structure have also been criticized for their lack of depth and consistency, but there is no question that Ekwensi's works are extremely popular. Several decades of readers, both in the West and in Nigeria, have found entertainment and a realistic picture of Nigerian city life in his novels and short stories.

Further Reading

Dossou Yovo, Noel. "Village and City Environment in Ekwensi's Major Works." *Bridges: An African Journal of English Studies/Revue Africaine d'Etudes Anglaises* 8 (1997–98): 17–39.
Rahman Abdur, Umar. "Politics versus Social Reality in Cyprian Ekwenci's *The Beautiful Feathers.*" *Gombak Review: A Biannual Publication of Creative Writing and Critical Comment* 2, no. 2 (1997): 158–71.
Uwakweh, Pauline Ada. "Speaking in Other Words: Female Subversion as Resistance in Ekwensi's *Beautiful Feathers.*" *Literary Griot: International Journal of Black Expressive Cultural Studies* 11, no. 2 (1999): 9–22.

Emecheta, Buchi (1944–)

Nigerian novelist born in Lagos, Nigeria, to Igbo parents. She left Nigeria with her husband in the early 1960s for England, where she worked as a librarian. The marriage eventually collapsed, and Emecheta was left with five children. She took a degree in sociology and also began to write seriously. Her first two novels, *In the Ditch* (1972) and *Second-Class Citizen* (1974), are autobiographical, recording her experience of living in England, specifically London and learning to write. Her next group of novels, *The Bride Price* (1976), *The Slave Girl* (1977), *The Joys of Motherhood* (1979), *Destination Biafra* (1982), and *Double Yoke* (1982), are set in Nigeria. *The Rape of Shavi* (1983) is a futuristic parable about race relations set in a fictional African country. *Head above Water* (1986) is Emecheta's autobiography. *Gwendolyn* (1989, published in the United States as *The Family,* 1990) takes place in Jamaica and London, and *Kehinde* (1994) is set in both London and Nigeria. *The New Tribe* (2000) tells the story of a young black child who is adopted into a white family, and is the only black child in his English town. The book investigates questions regarding Africa and its diaspora, race, identity, and family. Emecheta has also written television plays and children's books.

Emecheta's fiction seeks to account for the situation of African women in a changing world, whether in colonial Nigeria, traditional Igboland, or contemporary London. A strong sociological element characterizes the fiction, which portrays economic, cultural, and political pressures on African women wherever they live. Emecheta has lived in England for more than twenty years, and her perception of African culture has sometimes been seen as puzzlingly hostile, at least in the earlier novels. Western feminists also often see her as a feminist writer, though she herself is hesitant about the term.

Although much of Emecheta's fiction is realist, she often gives her major characters a sense of the spiritual heritage of African culture: this is particularly important in *The Joys of Motherhood* and *Kehinde*. Emechera's conception of tradition is complex, neither accepting nor rejecting entirely: her female central characters seek sustenance from their people's customs, but if that fails them, they will turn to contemporary options.

Further Reading

Pichler, Susanne. "'Grappling in the Contact Zone': Acculturation in Buchi Emecheta's *Gwendolen*." *Commonwealth Essays and Studies* 26, no. 2 (2004): 47–53.

Sen, Nandini C. "*The Joys of Motherhood* and *The Breast-Giver*: A Study of the Twice Colonised Woman: An Analytical Study of Two Novels by Buchi Emecheta and Mahasveta Devi." *Africa Quarterly* 43, no. 3 (2003): 61–71.

Sheldon, Kathleen. "Buchi Emecheta's *The Slave Girl*." In *African Novels in the Classroom,* ed. Margaret Jean Hay. Boulder, CO: Rienner, 2000, 133–44.

Yearwood, Susan. "The Socio-Politics of Black Britain in the Work of Buchi Emecheta." *BMA: The Sonia Sanchez Literary Review* 6, no. 2 (2001): 115–25.

Enekwe, Ossie (1942–)

Nigerian poet, fiction writer, and playwright. He is a graduate of the University of Nigeria and Columbia University, where he was a fellow in the Writing Division (1972–74). He is a professor of theater in the University of Nigeria. He has published a collection of poems, *Broken Pots* (1977); a novel, *Come Thunder* (1984); a nonficional work titled *Igbo Masks* (1987); a one-act play titled *The*

Betrayal (1989); and *The Last Battle and Other Stories* (1996). The Biafran experience is the main theme of his early writing, while in his later work metaphors of liberation dominate his poetic vision. He is dedicated to poetry as an oral art, and his work is characterized by its commitment to human dignity. Enekwe has also published an anthology with Enugu Branch titled *Harvest Time: A Literary/Critical Anthology of the Association of Nigerian Authors* (2001), and he is the editor of *OKIKE*.

Eppel, John (1947–)

A Zimbabwean poet and novelist, Eppel was educated at the universities of Natal and Rhodesia. His first two books were awarded South African literary prizes: the Ingrid Jonker Prize for his volume of poems *Spoils of War* (1989), and the M-Net Prize for fiction for the novel *D.G.G. Berry's Great North Road* (1992). His four further novels are *Hatchings* (1993), *The Giraffe Man* (1994), *The Curse of the Ripe Tomato* (2001), and *The Holy Innocents* (2002), and another two volumes of poetry, *Sonata for Matabeleland* (1995) and *Selected Poems 1996–1995* (2001). Eppel's settings for his writing are Bulawayo and southern Matabeleland. In his prose, city and bush are sites for farces enacted by grotesques and touched by magic realism. His satire is aimed at such various targets as settler nostalgia for Rhodesia, destructive educational systems, political and financial corruption in contemporary Zimbabwe, indifference to Matabeleland's fragile ecology, and Christian fundamentalism that masks a range of public and private immoralities.

Further Reading

Kohler, Peter. "Satire and Testimony in the Late Rhodesian Novel: John Eppel's *D.G.G. Berry's 'The Great North Road.'*" *English in Africa* 20, no. 2 (1993): 67–87.

Meihuizen, Nick. "A Troubled Sense of Belonging: Private and Public Histories in the Poetry of

Isobel Dixon, John Eppel and Don Maclennan." *Scrutiny2: Issues in English Studies in Southern Africa* 7, no. 2 (2002): 63–70.

Saunders, Richard. "John Eppel." *Southern African Review of Books* 38 (1995): 15–16.

Equiano, Olaudah (ca. 1745–97)

Nigerian (Igbo) autobiographer. Equiano's autobiography, *The Interesting Narrative of Olaudah Equiano; or, Gustavus Vassa, the African, Written by Himself* (1789), or *Equiano's Travels*, is an early African account of slavery and the African diaspora. Equiano was born in Essaka, in what is now eastern Nigeria. He was the youngest son of his devoted mother and titled father. He was kidnapped by African slave traders and compares his encounter with African slavery to European slavery. He also focuses on the pain of separation from his family, and the memory of his Igbo childhood informs his narrative. Equiano was determined in all he did, and worked hard to be able to read in English. He was spared continued adversity, but he witnessed and recorded the brutalities endured by other African slaves. The Igbo concept of *chi* or personal fate (a foundation for his Christian faith) hardens him against the various forms of slavery he encounters. He purchased his freedom at the age of twenty-one, continued to travel and trade, and became an effective abolitionist in Britain, where he married Susan Cullen and had two daughters. In his autobiography Equiano demonstrates the atrocities of European slavery. He fought for abolition with enthusiasm and simplicity, arguing for the alleviation of suffering and educating and persuading the British public against slavery. In his lifetime the narrative went through one American and eight British editions and was translated into Dutch, Russian, and German.

Further Reading

Acholonu, Catherine Obianuju. *The Igbo Roots of Olaudah Equiano.* Owerri, Nigeria: AFA, 1989.

Anderson, Douglas. "Division below the Surface: Olaudah Equiano's *Interesting Narrative.*" *Studies in Romanticism* 43, no. 3 (2004): 439–60.

Boelhower, William. "'I'll Teach You How to Flow': On Figuring Out Atlantic Studies." *Atlantic Studies: Literary, Cultural, and Historical Perspectives* 1, no. 1 (2004): 28–48.

Bozeman, Terry S. "Interstices, Hybridity, and Identity: Olaudah Equiano and the Discourse on the African Slave Trade." *Studies in the Literary Imagination* 36, no. 2 (2003): 61–70.

Corley, Ide. "The Subject of Abolitionist Rhetoric: Freedom and Trauma in the Life of Olaudah Equiano." *Modern Language Studies* 32, no. 2 (2002): 139–56.

Nussbaum, Felicity A. *The Limits of the Human: Fictions of Anomaly, Race, and Gender in the Long Eighteenth Century.* Cambridge: Cambridge University Press, 2003.

Potkay, Adam. "Olaudah Equiano and the Art of Spiritual Autobiography." *Eighteenth-Century Studies* 27, no. 4 (1994): 677–92.

Essop, Ahmed (1931–)

South African short-story writer and novelist Essop was born in India and emigrated to South Africa as a child. He was educated at the Johannesburg Indian High School in Fordsburg and at the University of South Africa (BA, 1964) and taught English at schools in Johannesburg.

His first publication was *The Dark Goddess* (1959), which was followed in the 1960s by short stories and poetry published in South African periodicals. He has since published stories in *Staffrider* and in anthologies edited by Stephen **Gray**, Mothobi **Mutloatse**, and Robin Malan. His collection *The Hajji and Other Stories* (1978) received the Olive Schreiner Award, while *Noorjehan and Other Stories* (1990) and *The King of Hearts and Other Stories* (1997) collect further stories. Essop's first novel, *The Visitation* (1980), returns to the setting of the stories of *The Hajji* and was followed by *The Emperor* (1984), and *The Third Prophecy* (2004), which follows Cabinet minister Dr Salman Khan.

Further Reading

Freed, Eugenie R. "Mr. Sufi Climbs the Stairs: The Quest and the Ideal in Ahmed Essop's 'The Visitation.'" *Theoria: A Journal of Studies in the Arts, Humanities and Social Sciences* 71 (1988): 1–13.

Hope, Christopher, and Robyn English. "'Good Books': Ahmed Essop's *The Visitation.*" *English in Africa* 25, no. 1 (1998): 99–103.

Smith, Rowland. "Living on the Fringe: The World of Ahmed Essop." *Commonwealth Essays and Studies* 8, no. 1 (1985): 64–72.

Experience, The (1970)

A novel by Eneriko **Seruma.** The central character in this novel is a black man who resolves to live in a white world, and who learns about himself in the process. His biggest realization is about cultural conflicts, and the novel indicates that the problem is not so much inherent difference as it is superficiality and ignorance.

Eye of the Earth, The (1986)

Poems by Niyi **Osundare.** In his third volume of poems, Osundare represents the ways that nature, the rural landscape, and rural life decay due to the actions of the selfish wealthy who are more concerned about weaponry and profits than the millions who are starving. The poems aim to draw rulers' attention to the need to save the environment.

F

Fagunwa, D(aniel) O. (1903–63)

Nigerian novelist, born in Oke-Igbo, Nigeria. Fagunwa studied at St. Luke's School, Oke-Igbo and St. Andrew's College, Oyo, after which he taught in various institutions in Nigeria. His novels include *Ogboju Ode ninu Igbo lrunmale* (1938), translated from Yoruba into English by Wole **Soyinka** as *The Forest of a Thousand Daemons* (1968), *Igbo Olodumare* (1949; *The Forest of God*, 1984; *The Forest of the Almighty*, 1986), *Ireke Onibudo* (1949), *Irinkerindo ninu Igbo Elegbeje* (1954; *Expedition to the Mount of Thought*, 1994), and *Adiitu Olodumare* (1961). He won the Margaret Wrong Prize for his writing in 1955 and was awarded the MBE in 1959.

Fagunwa is arguably the most widely known writer in the Yoruba language and certainly one of the most widely read. His work has influenced such contemporary Yoruba writers as Amos **Tutuola,** whose stories follow Fagunwa's pattern. Fagunwa's novels follow the pattern of the traditional Yoruba folktale in which the storyteller, aware of his audience and of the didactic function of storytelling in traditional Yoruba communities, narrates his story to a formally educated person, who is requested to write down the story for posterity so that others can learn from it.

The trilogy, *Ogboju Ode ninu Igbo Irunmale*, *Igbo Olodumare*, and *Irinkerindo ninu Igbo Elegbeje,* narrates the heroic journeys of the Yoruba hunters who are his protagonists. *Adiitu Olodumare* and *Ireke Onibudo* record the grass-to-grace life stories of the protagonists for whom the novels are named.

Further Reading

Mojola, Ibiyemi F. " . . . Of Saints and Devils: Women in the Novels of D. O. Fagunwa." *Research in Yoruba Language and Literature* 3 (1992): 30–43.

Smith, Pamela J. "D. O. Fagunwa: The Art of Fabulation in Writing Orality." *Literary Griot: International Journal of Black Expressive Cultural Studies* 3, no. 2 (1991): 1–16.

Smith, Pamela J. Olubunmi. "The Author(ity) of the Text: The Dialectic Tension between Fidelity and Creative Freedom: The Case of Wole Soyinka's 'Free' Translation of D. O. Fagunwa's *Ogboju Ode.*" *Meta: Journal des Traducteurs/ Translators' Journal* 39, no. 3 (1994): 453–59.

Wilkinson, Jane. "Between Orality and Writing: *The Forest of a Thousand Daemons* as a Self-Reflexive Text." *Commonwealth Essays and Studies* 9, no. 2 (1987): 41–51.

Fall, Malick (1920–78)

Senegalese novelist and poet who wrote in French. Malick Fall's literary reputation rests principally on his novel *La Plaie (The Wound)* (1967), first published by Albin Michel, Paris, and republished in 1980 in a limited boxed edition by Nouvelles Éditions Afiicaines, Dakar. He also produced a volume of poems, *Reliefs* (1964), with an introduction by L.S. **Senghor.** Fall worked in the Senegalese Department of Information before embarking on a career as a diplomat.

Reliefs comprises poems written over a long and complex period of Senegalese history, as the country moved from colonial rule to independence. *La Plaie* (translated by Clive Wake in 1973) is one of the celebrated francophone African novels of the 1960s, and is partly autobiographical. The protagonist, Magamou, is drawn to the attractions of the city, is injured in a traffic accident, and survives as a beggar. His wound marks him as an outcast, a status that allows him peculiar insights into society.

Famished Road, The (1991)

A novel by Ben **Okri** and winner of the Booker Prize in 1991. Okri uses images of the road and the *abiku,* the spirit child whose cyclical birth, death, and rebirth is a source of terror and pain for its family, to portray the political transitions in Nigeria and other African countries. *The Famished Road* uses poetic, incantatory, descriptive, and local language to realize its unconventional use of such images. It attentively represents the sociopolitical and economic situations of many African countries, as well as other parts of the world.

Farah, Nuruddin (1945–)

Somali novelist. Farah comes from a nomadic tradition and his studies and employments have been global. Born in Baidoa in the Italian-administered south of Somalia, he grew up in the Ethiopian-ruled Ogaden

and was educated in Ethiopia and Mogadishu and at the Punjab University of Chandigarh (1966–70) and the University of Essex (1974–76). In 1976 his novel *A Naked Needle* (1976) offended Somalian authorities and he could not return under threat of a jail sentence. He spent the next three years in Rome and since 1980 has held positions at universities in Africa, Europe, and North America. He was away from Somalia for twenty years. His writing is preoccupied with the oppression of his country by the clan-based dictatorship of General Siyad Barre, which held power from 1969 until 1991. His novels deal with the collusions of family and state authoritarianisms and of tribalism, Islam, and Marxism and feature pioneering studies of the patriarchal subjection of women in the Horn of Africa. Farah writes in English, but he is Africa's most cosmopolitan, multiliterate, and multilingual writer. Farah was awarded the 1998 Neustadt International Prize for Literature.

His first novel, **From a Crooked Rib** (1970), tells the story of Ebla, an illiterate but independent-minded nomadic woman of the 1950s, and her flight from bartered marriages in a society where a woman's only alternative to being sold by others as a chattel-wife is to sell herself as a prostitute. *A Naked Needle* (his second novel) is more experimental and is set in Mogadishu during the period of Somali political alignment with the USSR that followed Barre's 1969 coup. It was followed by a trilogy, *Variations on the Theme of an African Dictatorship,* comprising the novels **Sweet and Sour Milk** (1979), *Sardines* (1981), and *Close Sesame* (1983). The trilogy is Farah's most artistically mature and complex work.

Farah sets his novel *Maps* (1986) during the 1977 Ogaden war. The novel presents a complex fable of personal, ethnic, and national identity through the relationship between Askar, an orphaned Ogadenese-Somali child, and his adoptive mother Misra, an Oromo woman from the Ethiopian highlands. Farah's seventh novel, *Gifts* (1992), is a love story that places a suitor's offerings against the backdrop of international aid to famine-struck countries. The novel explores the complex psychology of donorship, and the obligations between giver and receiver. *Secrets* (1998) uses myth and metaphor to explore the past and present of characters who are reunited on the eve of civil war. *Links* (2003) is the story of Jeebleh, a Somalian who departs his family in New York to return to civil war–torn Mogadishu where he was born. Farah charts Jeebleh's emotional transformation as he comes to terms with a changed Mogadishu, one that is corrupt and requires great tenacity from its citizens in order to survive. Farah has also published nonfiction in the form of *Yesterday, Tomorrow: Voices from the Somali Diaspora* (2000).

Further Reading

Bardolph, Jacqueline. "Animals and Humanness in Nuruddin Farah's *Secrets*." *Anglophonia: French Journal of English Studies* 7 (2000): 115–21.

Cingal, Guillaume. "Opacity, Otherness and Polysymphony in Nuruddin Farah's *Blood in the Sun*." *Imaginaires: Revue du Centre de Recherche sur l'Imaginaire dans les Litteratures de Langue Anglaise* 10 (2004): 271–81.

Ngaboh-Smart, Francis. "Nationalism and the Aporia of National Identity in Farah's *Maps*." *Research in African Literatures* 32, no. 3 (2001): 86–102.

Woods, Tim. "Giving and Receiving: Nuruddin Farah's *Gifts*; or, the Postcolonial Logic of Third World Aid." *Journal of Commonwealth Literature* 39, no. 1 (2004): 91–112.

Wright, Derek. *The Novels of Nuruddin Farah.* Bayreuth, Germany: Thielmann & Breitinger, 2004.

———, ed. *Emerging Perspectives on Nuruddin Farah.* Trenton, NJ: Africa World Press, 2002.

Fatunde, Tunde (1955–)

Nigerian playwright, gained a bachelor's degree in French from the University of Ibadan and a master's and PhD in France. He teaches, writes, directs plays, participates in trade union activities, and is a journalist; his newspaper columns especially have made him well known as an activist intellectual. He has published five plays: *Blood and Sweat* (1985), first performed in 1983; *No More Oil Boom* (1985), staged in 1984; *No Food, No Country* (1985), performed in 1985; *Oga Na Tief Man* (1986), staged in 1985; and *Water No Get Enemy* (1989), staged in 1988. Fatunde calls the plays unique because they were written for "the general public with minimum level of formal education." Thus plot, characterization, dialogue, and language are highly simplified and predictable. They most often portray a class conflict, followed by a confrontation in which the proletariat act with courage and unity and win morally and/or physically over the bourgeois villains. The dialogue consists of a stepped-down standard English or Pidgin.

Further Reading

Enenche, Hilary. "The Making of Nigerian Agit-Prop Theatre: The Case of Tunde Fatunde." *Presence Africaine: Revue Culturelle du Monde Noir/Cultural Review of the Negro World* 146 (1988): 185–94.

Fioupou, Christiane. "Tunde Fatunde Interviewed." *ALA Bulletin* 20, no. 4 (1994): 9–13.

Feminism and Literature

An acknowledgment of the different experiences of African women outside of male-focused traditional narratives and Western concepts of feminism opens up a space to explore the importance of women's literature to African women's identities. African feminism (also defined as *womanism* by author Alice Walker) is a movement that calls for the equality of African women in the fight against racism, colonialism, and oppression, and an attentiveness to the additional barriers that women must face in the form of political, social, and cultural exclusion. In response to this battle for equality and representation as African women, feminist critics and women authors have drawn attention to a canon of works by African women that better represents African literary history and identity as they relate to the experiences of women.

Current scholarship acknowledges the important role of women in the formation and continuation of these oral traditions in many African cultures. Autobiography is one of the early forms that African women employed to express their identities within the larger historical context. Some early women's autobiographies include Adelaide **Casely-Hayford**'s *Reminiscences* (1953), *The Ochre People* (1963) by Noni **Jabavu,** and *De Tilène au Plateau: une enfance dakaroise* (1975) by Nafissatou Diallo. In the 1960s and 1970s, more women writers published their work, which was being read on a much larger scale. Flora **Nwapa**'s *Efuru* (1966) uses the myth of the watermaid to tell the story of a single woman, while Aminata Sow Fall's series of five novels, starting with *Le Revenant* (1976), offers a critical view of social and political issues through female characters who are dedicated to what they see as the positive elements of African cultural traditions. The oppression of women, as it is related to both cultural traditions and to practices introduced by colonialism, is an issue that has also received a growing amount of attention. Traditional cultural issues such as sexual mutilation, forced maternity, and polygamy, and colonial operations such as economic exploitation, and the undereducation of women in relation to men are uncovered by authors like Ama Ata **Aidoo,** Bessie **Head,** Buchi **Emecheta,** Werewere Liking, and Calixthe Beyala, who work through these issues in a way that moves the fantastical and legendary from oral tradition and into a worldview that focuses on women's perceptions.

The work of Olive **Schreiner** in the late nineteenth century is seminal to the history of South African feminism. Also important is the work of Pauline **Smith,** Bessie Head, Miriam **Tlali,** Gcina **Mhlophe,** and Nadine **Gordimer.** There is a need for a better understanding of a feminism that is appropriate for the role of women in regard to class, race, and the diverse nature of women's experiences in South African society. Recent works that tackle the issue of gender in a class- and race-sensitive way include *Gender, Literature and Religion in Africa* (2005), which focuses on the definition of gender in religious and literary contexts, and *African Gender Studies: A Reader* (2005), which brings an African context to sociological and anthropological conversations about gender. *African Gender Scholarship: Concepts, Methodologies and Paradigms* (2005) also offers a wide range of papers on the issues currently facing feminism in Africa, while *Against Empire: Feminisms, Racism and the West* (2004) by Zillah Eisenstein tackles the relationship between gender, anticolonialism, and empire. Kevin Everod Quashie's *Black Women, Identity, and Cultural Theory: (Un)Becoming the Subject* (2004) studies such authors as Toni Morrison, Ama Ata Aidoo, and Dionne Brand, while Susan Arndt's *Dynamics of African Feminism* (2002) provides feminist criticsm of African women's fiction in order to try and understand the new and changing contexts in African feminist literature.

Further Reading

Amadiume, Ifi. *Male Daughters, Female Husbands: Gender and Sex in an African Society.* London: Zed Books, 1987.

Arndt, Susan. *African Women's Literature: Orality and Intertextuality.* Bayreuth, Germany: Eckhard Breitinger, 1998.

———. "Boundless Whiteness? Feminism and White Women in the Mirror of African Feminist Writing." *Matatu: Journal for African Culture and Society* 29–30 (2005): 157–72.

———, ed. *Dynamics of African Feminism.* Lasmara, Eritrea: Africa World Press, 2002.

Arnfred, Signe, Babere Kerata Chacha, and Amanda Gouws, eds. *Gender, Activism, and Studies in Africa*. Dakar, Senegal: CODESRIA (Council for the Development of Social Science Research in Africa), 2004.

Azuah, Unoma N. "The Emerging Lesbian Voice in Nigerian Feminist Literature." *Matatu: Journal for African Culture and Society* 29–30 (2005): 129–41.

Balfour, Lawrie. "Representative Women: Slavery, Citizenship, and Feminist Theory in Du Bois's 'Damnation of Women.'" *Hypatia: A Journal of Feminist Philosophy* 20, no. 3 (2005): 127–48.

Boehmer, Elleke. *Stories of Women: Gender and Narrative in the Postcolonial Nation*. Manchester, England: Manchester University Press, 2005.

Boyce Davies, Carole. "Feminist Consciousness and African Literary Criticism." In *Ngambika: Studies of Women in African Literature*, ed. Carole Boyce Davies and Anne Adams Graves. Trenton, NJ: Africa World Press, 1986, 1–23.

Bungaro, Monica. "Male Feminist Fiction: Literary Subversions of a Gender-Biased Script." *Matatu: Journal for African Culture and Society* 29–30 (2005): 47–61.

Dandridge, Rita B. "The Race, Gender, Romance Connection: A Black Feminist Reading of African American Women's Historical Romances." In *Doubled Plots: Romance and History*, ed. Susan Strehle and Mary Paniccia Carden. Jackson: University Press of Mississippi, 2003, 185–201.

Eisenstein, Zillah. *Against Empire: Feminisms, Racism and the West*. London: Zed Books, 2004.

Hooks, Bell. *Ain't I a Woman: Black Women and Feminism*. London: Pluto Press, 1982.

Hudson-Weems, Clenora. *Africana Womanism*. Troy, NY: Bedford Publishers, 1993.

Kohrs-Amissah, Edith. *Aspects of Feminism and Gender in the Novels of Three West African Women Writers (Aidoo, Emecheta, Darko)*. Heidelberg: Books on African Studies, 2002.

Le Roux, Elizabeth, et al., eds. *Gender, Literature and Religion in Africa*. Dakar, Senegal: CODESRIA, 2005.

Loots, Lliane. "Voicing the Unspoken: 'Interculturally' Connecting Race, Gender, and Nation in Women's Creative Practice." In *Intercultural Communication and Creative Practice: Music, Dance, and Women's Cultural Identity*, ed. Laura Lengel. Westport, CT: Praeger, 2005, 27–46.

McClaurin, Irma, ed. *Black Feminist Anthropology: Theory, Politics, Praxis and Poetics*. New Brunswick, NJ: Rutgers University Press, 2001.

Moody, Joycelyn. "Naming and Proclaiming the Self: Black Feminist Literary History Making." In *Calling Cards: Theory and Practice in the Study of Race, Gender, and Culture*, ed. Jacqueline Jones Royster and Ann Marie Mann Simpkins. Albany: State University of New York Press, 2005, 107–20.

Ogundipe-Leslie, 'Molara. *Re-Creating Ourselves: African Women and Critical Transformation*. Trenton, NJ: Africa World Press, 1994.

Ogunleye, Foluke. "21st Century Image of Women: A Womanist Reading of Two Nigerian Plays." *South African Theatre Journal* 18 (2004): 112–34.

O'Reilly, Andrea. "In Black and White: African-American and Anglo-American Feminist Perspectives on Mothers and Sons." In *Mother Outlaws: Theories and Practices of Empowered Mothering*, ed. Andrea O'Reilly. Toronto: Women's Press, 2004, 305–27.

Oyewumi, Oyeronke, ed. *African Gender Studies: A Reader*. London: Palgrave, 2005.

———, ed. *African Women and Feminism: Reflecting on the Politics of Sisterhood*. Trenton, NJ: Africa World Press, 2003.

Quashie, Kevin Everod. *Black Women, Identity, and Cultural Theory: (Un)Becoming the Subject*. Piscataway, NJ: Rutgers University Press, 2004.

[Various Authors.] *African Gender Scholarship: Concepts, Methodologies and Paradigms*. Dakar, Senegal: CODESIRA, 2005.

Wehrs, Donald R. *African Feminist Fiction and Indigenous Values*. Gainesville: Florida University Press, 2001.

Fettouma, Touati (1950–)

Fettouma, a francophone novelist of the Maghreb, was born in Azazoa, a small mountainous village in the Kabylia region of

Algeria. Her parents emigrated to France in 1951. She returned to Kabylia in 1975 and remained there for four years, working principally as a librarian in the University of Tiziüouzou in the capital of Kabylia. During this time she witnessed the racism and sexism to which Algerian women are subjected, and on her return to France she wrote about these experiences in her novel *Printemps Désespéré: Vies d'Algériennes* (1984; *Desperate Spring,* 1987), which has also been translated into German and Arabic. The novel is set principally in Kabylia and traces the lives of three generations of Algerian women, from that of the grandmother Sekoura to those of her numerous grandchildren, concentrating particularly on the latter generation. The suffering of women is paramount in this novel, as families force young women to marry partners that they choose for them, husbands beat married women (who exist only through their children) into submission, and career women are subjected to insults because they decide to reject the traditional role assigned to them. Despite the bleakness of these lives, there is hope in the network of women's relationships that provide mutual support and understanding.

Further Reading

Geesey, Patricia. "Identity and Community in Autobiographies of Algerian Women in France." In *Going Global: The Transnational Reception of Third World Women Writers,* ed. and introduction Amal Amireh and Lisa Suhair Majaj. New York: Garland, 2000, 173–205.

Fiawoo, Ferdinand Kwasi (1891–1969)
Ghanaian playwright. Ferdinand Kwasi Fiawoo's formal education in Togoland began late and was interrupted, so it was not until 1928 that the African Methodist Episcopal Zion Church was able to help him travel to the United States to begin undergraduate work. During the next five years he gained three bachelor's degrees and an educational qualification.

From this period came the Ewe *Toko Atolia,* translated by Fiawoo as *The Fifth Landing Stage* in 1943, which remains a significant text in Ghanaian writing for the stage. The plays are also available in *Tuinese* as *Fia Yi Dziehe: Two Plays in Ewe and English* with an introduction by H. Jungraithmayr, translated by H. Jungraithmayr and published by Marburg an der Lahn in 1973. By 1943 Faiwoo was ordained and had returned to the Gold Coast, now Ghana, where he began to play an important role in public life and started work on a PhD. He worked throughout his life to unite Christian education with the best in African culture.

Fisherman's Invocation, The (1978)
Poems by Gabriel **Okara** and winner of a Commonwealth Writers Prize in 1979. Okara uses the image of the riverbank (inspired by the Niger Delta) to connect the thirty-three poems in this volume. The poem "Call of the River Nun" was written before independence in 1957, while the title poem was written after independence in 1963. These poems use Ijaw (Ijo) imagery to express the complexities of building a nation. Other poems in the work include those that deal with war from the Biafran civilian's point of view, love poems, and those that chart cultural conflicts.

Fitzpatrick, (Sir) J. Percy (1872–1931)
South African novelist, son of an Irish lawyer of fallen fortunes who settled in the Cape Colony and became a judge in the Supreme Court. His championship of the *Uitlander* ("foreign") community in the early days of gold mining on the Witwatersrand placed him at the forefront of affairs leading up to and following the Anglo-Boer war. His book *The Transvaal from Within* (1899) rallied English opinion behind their cause.

Fitzpatrick's best-known work, *Jock of the Bushveld* (1907), is about an exceptional dog among the ox-wagon teams plying between the Transvaal and Delagoa Bay (Lourenço Marques/Maputo), an animal story in a social and natural setting in the tradition of *The Jungle Book* and *White Fang* that reflects his admiration for the work of Bret Harte and Mark Twain.

Fitzpatrick first displayed his Anglo-South African attitudes in *Through Mashonaland with Pick and Pen* (1892), an ironic record of Lord Randolph Churchill's tour of Southern Africa. In his collection of sketches *The Outspan: Tales of South Africa* (1897), he anticipated themes to be found in books as different as *Jock* and Joseph Conrad's *Heart of Darkness.*

Further Reading

Cartwright, A. P. *The First South African: The Life and Times of Sir Percy FitzPatrick.* Cape Town: Purnell, 1971.

Cornwell, Gareth. "FitzPatrick's 'The Outspan': Deconstructing the Fiction of Race." *English in Africa* 10, no. 1 (1983): 15–28.

———. "J. P. Fitzpatrick's 'The Outspan': A Textual Source for *Heart of Darkness*?" *Conradiana: A Journal of Joseph Conrad Studies* 30, no. 3 (Fall 1998): 203–12.

Duminy, Andrew, and Bill Guest. *Interfering in Politics: A Biography of Sir Percy FitzPatrick.* Johannesburg: Lowry, 1987.

Nyman, Jopi. *Postcolonial Animal Tales from Kipling to Coetzee.* New Delhi: Atlantic, 2003.

Wessels, Andries. "An Irish Gentleman in Africa: The Ambiguous Political and Cultural Identity of Sir Percy FitzPatrick.(Biography)" *English in Africa,* May 1, 2004.

Fixions and Other Stories (1969)

Short stories by **Taban Lo Liyong.** The stories draw from East African folk tradition. While such stories as "The Old Man of Usumbura and His Misery" and "The Story of Master Hare and His Friend Jumbe Elephant" are wholly original in treatment, critics have often noted correspondences between them and the writing of **Okot p'Bitek** of Uganda and Amos **Tutuola** of Nigeria. As with p'Bitek and Tutuola, Lo Liyong transmutes traditional material into modern applications.

Foe (1986)

A novel by J. M. **Coetzee.** The narrator, Susan Barton, tries to rewrite Daniel Defoe's *Robinson Crusoe* in order to advocate the control of self-representation by both women and colonized people. Susan, who is stranded on Cruso's island and then rescued by a passing ship, narrates her story in letters addressed to Mr. Foe. With the support of Foe Susan moves to London and resides with Friday (whose tongue has been cut out), who she feels she must take care of since Cruso died on the way to England. Susan struggles with Foe over the truthful representation of her story, as he symbolizes the Author who is to turn her story into a book. She also becomes obsessed with the telling of Friday's story until she realizes that "the only tongue that can tell Friday's story is the tongue he has lost." An anonymous narrator brings the story to an end with a description of a wreck that contains the bodies of Foe, Susan, and Friday.

Fools and Other Stories (1983)

Short stories by Njabulo Ndebele, some of which previously appeared in *Staffrider* magazine and were widely read by an African, urban, and politically usurped audience that the stories specifically addressed. The short stories "The Test," "The Prophetess," "Uncle," and "The Music of the Violin" are all set in the mining town of Charterston and follow a middle-class boy as he grows up in a poor community. The title story follows the relationship between a young political activist and a disgraced schoolteacher. The stories provide a nuanced portrayal of life in a South African township under **apartheid,** and consider the realities and possibilities for continued existence and opposition within that context.

Footprints in the Quag (1989)
Short stories by Miriam **Tlali,** published outside South Africa as *Soweto Stories.* The stories portray in detail the agonizing conditions of black women's lives in the city, and use proverbs and idioms from the indigenous Sesotho to draw attention to the importance of traditional culture. The loss of tradition is represented as negative, but the story *"Mm'a-Lithoto"* ("Mother of Bundles") demonstrates the ways that traditions also subordinate women. The stories describe how women are courageous and supportive of one another, as well as secluded and exposed to sexual assault and domestic violence, and they call for gender equality in marriage and a focus on the importance of women's rights.

Forest of a Thousand Daemons, The (1968)
A novel by D. O. **Fagunwa,** translated by Wole Soyinka from the Yoruba (*Ogbojo Ode ninu Igbo Irunmale,* 1938). Like Fagunwa's other novels, *Forest* takes as its outline that of the Yoruba folktale but adds to this Akara-Ogun's journey through the forest of a thousand daemons.

Foriwa (1967)
An Efua **Sutherland** play, performed in the Akan language in 1962. *Foriwa* depicts Ghanaian village life through the story of a West African woman who chooses to court a stranger. The play draws attention to the damage caused by pettiness, and concludes with a more unifying outlook in the community.

Fragments (1970)
A novel by Ayi Kwei **Armah** that portrays Ghana after independence. The primary character, Baako Onipa, gains a creative writing degree but is discouraged by a number of rejections. He cannot meet the financial expectations of his family and Ghanaian society, and support from other characters does not prevent Baako from ending up in a mental health facility. The circular narrative of the novel reflects Baako's grandmother's belief in the circular cycle of life.

From a Crooked Rib (1970)
A novel by Nuruddin **Farah.** The novel follows the adventures of Ebla, a woman who refuses to cater to the traditional role expected of her in Somalian society. She discovers on her travels the violence and corruption of the world, but she also demonstrates her honesty and strength of identity in the face of that world. The novel takes its title from the Somalian proverb: "God created woman from a crooked rib; and anyone who trieth to straighten it, breaketh it." Ebla's resistance to traditional roles results in a self-discovery that is resonant with the proverb.

Fugard, Athol (1932–)
South African dramatist Fugard was born in Middelburg, the son of an English-speaking father and an Afrikaans-speaking mother. After attending school in Port Elizabeth, he began but did not complete a bachelor's course at the University of Cape Town. His position as South Africa's most prominent playwright derives from his ability to turn apparently regional and local themes into more universal metaphors for his deeply felt liberal concern with humanity and his existential struggle to understand his own life.

In the first few years of his creative life Fugard held a variety of short-term jobs such as merchant seaman, writer for the South African Broadcasting Corporation, clerk in the native commissioner's court in Johannesburg, stage manager for the National Theatre Organization, freelance actor-director in Belgium under Tone Brulin, and finally as director of the Rehearsal Room, a performance space at Dorkay House in 1961. In 1964 Fugard settled in Port Elizabeth to become a full-time professional playwright. Since then, except for periodic stints as resident playwright and director at various places in the world, including a very creative period with the Yale Repertory Company, Fugard has remained and continued to work in his "region," namely Eastern Cape Province.

Fugard is influential in both South Africa and in world theater. There are two principal reasons for this. There is his political profile as an opponent of **apartheid.** Both his plays and his experiences with the government and its agencies made him an important witness to the atrocities of racism and bigotry in the country. In the 1990s, as political changes made apartheid an issue secondary to more pressing social and cultural needs, observers have recognized Fugard's role as a technical and thematic innovator in South African, and world, theater.

Fugard's career falls into a number of identifiable periods distinguished by differing working methods and thematic concerns. His first prominent plays were short essays in realism, written for and performed by Fugard and friends in the black townships around Johannesburg. *No-Good Friday* (1977) and *Nongogo* (1977) are exploratory works that depict incidents in the life of a shebeen keeper and a whore, respectively. The first major work was The **Blood Knot** (1963), a play about the dreams of two brothers, one black and the other mixed-race. Set in a single room, it explores the love-hate relationship between two individuals bound together by something more than mere circumstance, and utilizes one other (often offstage) character as a catalyst for the tragic action. This is a pattern he follows with minor variations in virtually all the plays over the years, in *Hello and Goodbye* (1966), *Boesman and Lena* (1969), *The Island* (1974), *Statements after an Arrest under the Morality Act* (1974), *A Place with the Pigs* (1988), *The Road to Mecca,* and *Playland* (both 1994). In the next phase Fugard returned to his home region of Port Elizabeth with what are his most accomplished and enduring works. *Hello and Goodbye* and *People Are Living There* (1969) deal with the angst of the white urban dweller, while *Boesman and Lena* deals with the world of two disenfranchised "coloureds." It is a realistic play set in a barren but identifiable landscape, where it explores the notion of freedom through the struggle of the two itinerants to understand themselves, their relationship with each other, and the world about them.

At the beginning of the 1970s Fugard discovered Grotowsky and began to work through improvisation. The result was a series of highly political workshop productions, including *Orestes* (1978), *Statements after an Arrest under the Morality Act, The Island,* and **Sizwe Bansi Is Dead** (published together in *Statements,* 1974). The latter two works in particular, co-authored with John Kani and Winston Ntshona, did much to consolidate his fame as a political writer.

In 1975 Fugard reverted to scripted plays with the allegorical *Dimetos* (1977), followed by two personal views of apartheid society in *A Lesson from Aloes* (1981) and the compelling and highly autobiographical *"Master Harold" . . . and the Boys* (1982). His concern with personal freedom and the role of the artist inform *The Road to Mecca.* This was followed by *A Place with the Pigs,* and in 1989 he returned to political theater with *My Children! My Africa!* (1990), *Playland,* and the largely workshopped *My Life* (performed 1994). Most recently Fugard has published *Valley Song* (1995), *The Captain's Tiger* (1998), *Sorrows and Rejoicings* (2001), and *Exits and Entrances* (2004). *Exits and Entrances* is about a young playwright and an aging actor, and is a memory play based on Athol Fugard's brief friendship with the celebrated Afrikaans actor Andre Huguenet.

Besides filmed versions of many of the plays, Fugard has also written a number of film scripts, including *The Guest* (1977) and *Marigolds in August* (1982), both filmed by

Ross Devenish. A novel, *Tsotsi,* appeared in 1980 and an autobiographical work, *My Cousin,* in 1995. He has received numerous awards over the years, including the Commonwealth Theatre Award and honorary doctorates from Rhodes University, Yale University, Georgetown University, the University of Cape Town, and the University of the Witwatersrand.

Further Reading

Collins, Michael J. "The Sabotage of Love: Athol Fugard's Recent Plays." In *Twayne Companion to Contemporary World Literature: From the Editors of World Literature Today,* ed. Pamela A. Genova. New York: Twayne; Thomson Gale, 2003, 390–93.

Combrink, Annette L. "External Events and Internal Reality: Fugard's Construction of (Afrikaner) Identity in the Plays of the Nineties." In *Storyscapes: South African Perspectives on Literature, Space and Identity,* ed. (and introduction) Hein Viljoen, Chris Van der Merwe, and Minnie Lewis. New York: Peter Lang, 2004, 55–70.

Foley, Andrew. "Fugard, Liberalism and the Ending of Apartheid." *Current Writing: Text and Reception in Southern Africa* 9, no. 2 (1997): 57–76.

Kruger, Loren. "Seeing through Race: Athol Fugard, (East) Germany, and the Limits of Solidarity." *Modern Philology: A Journal Devoted to Research in Medieval and Modern Literature* 100, no. 4 (2003): 619–51.

Walder, Dennis. *Athol Fugard.* Tavistock, Devon, England: Northcote House Publishers, 2002.

Wertheim, Albert. *The Dramatic Art of Athol Fugard: From South Africa to the World.* Bloomington: Indiana University Press, 2000.

Fugard, Sheila Meiring (1932–)

A South African novelist and poet born in Birmingham, England, Fugard was eight when her parents moved to South Africa. She studied theater at the University of Cape Town, where she began writing short stories. She is married to playwright Athol **Fugard.**

Fugard's first novel, *The Castaways* (1972), won the Olive Schreiner Prize in 1972. The second, *Rite of Passage* (1976), treats race relations in history. A similar intention, "to see history afresh," inspired her book of poems *Threshold* (1975). Her second collection of poetry, *Mythic Things* (1981), emphasizes her continuing interest in fantasy and the mysterious. Her third novel, *A Revolutionary Woman* (1983), is set in the Karoo district of South Africa in 1920 and was inspired by her experience in India in 1981 and by what she learned about Indian history and belief. Fugard has also written critical articles such as "The Apprenticeship Years" in *Twentieth Century Literature: A Scholarly and Critical Journal* (1993), and "A Green Equinox: The Nature of Love in the Fiction of Elizabeth Mavor" in Sheila Roberts's and Yvonne Pacheco Tevis's *Still the Frame Holds: Essays on Women Poets and Writers* (1993).

Further Reading

Daymond, M. J., J. U. Jacobs, and Margaret Lenta, eds. "A Castaway in Africa." In *Momentum: On Recent South African Writing.* Pietermaritzburg, South Africa: University of Natal Press, 1984, 29–31.

Gray, Rosemary. "Sheila Fugard's *The Castaways*: Myth and Psychic Survival." *Commonwealth Essays and Studies* 10, no. 1 (Autumn 1987): 41–48.

G

Garuba, Harry (1958–)

Nigerian poet. Garuba had a nomadic childhood that exposed him to many languages and ethnic groups in Nigeria and fostered in him a cosmopolitan worldview. He attended the University of Ibadan, where he gained his bachelor's and master's degrees and PhD and where he is now a lecturer. He has published a one-act play (*Pantomime for Saint*

Apartheid's Day in *Festac Anthology of Nigerian New Writing,* 1977) and edited *Voices from the Fringe: An ANA Anthology of New Nigerian Poetry* (1988), but he is best known as a poet with a disposition for the tender and the philosophical. The poems in *Shadow and Dream and Other Poems* (1982) explore the metaphor of scars as markers of both historical and contemporary struggles. One of Garuba's strengths as a poet is his ability to translate events—the experience of colonialism, civil war, student activism—into metaphors that are at once specific and general enough to be universal. He has published only one collection, but he is regarded as one of the most outstanding Nigerian poets writing in English. Garuba has also published several critical works, such as "The African Imagination: Postcolonial Studies, Canons, and Stigmatization" in *Research in African Literatures* (2003), "Masked Discourse: Dramatic Representation and Generic Transformation in Wole Soyinka's *A Dance of the Forests*" in *Modern Drama* (2002), "Explorations in Animist Materialism and a Reading of the Poetry of Niyi Osundare" in Abdul-Rasheed, Abiola Irele, and Biodun Jeyifo's *The People's Poet: Emerging Perspectives on Niyi Osundare* (2003), "The Island Writes Back: Discourse/Power and Marginality in Wole Soyinka's *The Swamp Dwellers,* Derek Walcott's *The Sea at Dauphin,* and Athol Fugard's *The Island*" in *Research in African Literatures* (2001), and "Ken Saro-Wiwa's *Sozaboy* and the Logic of Minority Discourse" in Kwame Anthony Appiah and Biodun Jeyifo's *Ogoni's Agonies: Ken Saro-Wiwa and the Crisis in Nigeria* (1998).

Gay and Lesbian Sexuality in Literature

A number of works by African authors deal with gay and/or lesbian sexuality. A textual treatment of gay/lesbian sexuality is visible in works like *Ripple in the Pool* (1975) by Rebeka **Njau,** *Our Sister Killjoy* (1977) by Ama Ata **Aidoo,** and *La Reproduction* (1986) by Thomas Mpoyi-Buatu. In several texts gay/lesbian sexuality is represented as a result of force and oppression, rather than as a viable African category of identity. In contrast, there are a few earlier texts that represent gay and lesbian relationships in a realistic and generally sympathetic manner.

A larger number of texts focus on a negative depiction of gay/lesbian sexuality, and such relationships are more often condemned than portrayed approvingly. Many African states have legislation that also condemns gay/lesbian sexuality, politicians speak out against it, and the press is not always sympathetic. One exception is the African National Congress's Bill of Rights (drafted in 1990 and signed as a Constitution in 1996), which includes a rule against discrimination based on sexual orientation in its equality clause.

There are many texts that characterize gay/lesbian sexuality as oppressive and foreign to Africa. The seduction of reluctant African characters by European gays or lesbians is portrayed in works such as Kole **Omotoso**'s *The Edifice* (1971), Kofi **Awoonor**'s *This Earth, My Brother* (1971), Williams **Sassine**'s *Wirriyamu* (1976), and Jean-Clément Aoué-Tchany's *Du Folklore en enfer* (1990). Wole **Soyinka** characterizes his black American character Joe Golder as a predatory homosexual in *The **Interpreters*** (1965), but he also provides a detailed study of Golder's social psychology as it fits in the thematic development of the novel as whole. Other representations of gay/lesbian relationships are used to demonstrate societal degeneration and to critique corrupt government. Some examples of this kind of treatment are apparent in Mongo **Beti**'s *Remember Ruben* (1974), **Sony Labou Tansi**'s *L'État honteux* (1981), and Bernard Nanga's *Les Chauves-souris* (1980). Mu'azu Hadeja and Sa'ad **Zungur** (Hausa poets) condemn homosexuality because they believe that it undermines the political unity of northern Nigeria, while Wole Soyinka portrays pederasty as an externalized vice associated with the northern emirate courts in his novel **Season of Anomy** (1973). Gay/lesbian sexuality is also portrayed as unnatural in some works that depict imprisonment, such as Gibson **Kente**'s play *Too Late* (1974), James **Matthews**'s story "A Case of Guilt" (1983), and D. M. Zwelonke's *Robben Island* (1973).

Other authors, such as Christopher Okigbo, Yambo Ouologuem, Mariama Ba, Ayi Kwei Armah, David Maillu, Mwangi Gicheru, Taban Lo Liyong, Charles Githae, and **Okot p'Bitek** have also broached the topic of homosexuality, and even those (like Micere Githae-Mugo) who condemn homophobia and relate it to apartheid don't necessarily portray homosexuality as positive. Some sympathetic representations of gay/lesbian sexuality still offer a stereotypical representation in their treatment of the subject, as in *No Past, No Present, No Future* (1973) by Yulisa A. **Maddy** and Yambo Ouologuem's *Le Devoir de violence* (1968; *Bound to Violence,* 1971).

Rebeka Njau's *Ripples in the Pool* depicts a heroine who is psychologically unstable, but who is sympathetic as she is a victim of an oppressive state. In this sense, the text is obvious about its use of the lesbian relationship as a way to further the novel's larger theme. In her book *The Sacred Seed* (2003) Njau demonstrates that the social history of female same-sex relationships in Africa stems from the need for women to maintain economic solidarity, rather than from an infiltration of feminist discourse from the West. In *Our Sister Killjoy,* Aidoo's heroine Sissie is able to connect with the lesbian character Marija, but the characterization of Marija as "other" complicates this representation.

In contrast, Tatamkhulu Afrika's *Bitter Eden* (2002) is a fictionalized account of Afrika's experience as a prisoner of war in World War II, and follows the stories of three men who define themselves as heterosexual, but must attempt to understand the emotional closeness that results from physical proximity and reliance on one another for survival in the male-only camps. Nonfiction works also explore the place of homosexuality in African culture, one of which is *Boy-Wives and Female-Husbands: Studies in African-American Homosexualities* (2001), edited by Will Roscoe and Stephen Murray. This book explores the roots of homosexuality in Africa, and includes an essay by Deborah Amory on the history of homosexual practices in Swahili-speaking societies in Kenya. Another academic book about homosexuality in Africa is *Agenda No. 67: Homosexuality* (2006), edited by Vasu Reddy and published by the Agenda Feminist Media Company, which publishes material that relates to women's issues and concerns in Africa. *Issue 67* focuses on the future of gays and lesbians in Africa, and includes essays by Cheyl Potgieter, Nkunzi Nkabinde, Ruth Morgan, Marius Crous, and Busangowakhe Dlamini.

Further Reading

Arthur, Michael. "Gay Theatres in South Africa: Peter Hayes, Pogiso Mogwera, and Jay Pather." *South African Theatre as/and Intervention,* ed. Marcia Blumberg and Dennis Walder. Amsterdam: Rodopi, 1999, 147–53.

Barnard, Ian. *Queer Race: Cultural Interventions in the Racial Politics of Queer Theory.* New York: Peter Lang, 2004.

———. "The United States in South Africa: (Post)Colonial Queer Theory?" *Postcolonial and Queer Theories: Intersections and Essays,* ed. John C. Hawley. Westport, CT: Greenwood Press, 2001, 129–38.

Desai, Gaurav. "Out in Africa." In *Sex Positives? The Cultural Politics of Dissident Sexualities,* ed. Thomas Foster, Carol Siegel, and Ellen E. Berry. New York: New York University Press, 1997, 120–43.

Dunton, Chris. "The Treatment of Homosexuality in African Literature." In *Homosexual Themes in Literary Studies,* ed. Wayne R. Dynes and Stephen Donaldson. New York: Garland, 1992.

Epprecht, Marc. "The 'Unsaying' of Indigenous Homosexualities in Zimbabwe: Mapping a Blindspot in an African Masculinity." *Journal of Southern African Studies* 24, no. 4 (1998): 631–51.

Heyns, Michiel. "A Man's World: White South African Gay Writing and the State of Emergency." In *Writing South Africa: Literature, Apartheid, and Democracy, 1970–1995*, ed. Derek Attridge and Rosemary Jolly. Cambridge: Cambridge University Press, 1998, 108–22.

Jacobs, J. U. "Cruising across Cultures in the Novels of Antony Sher." *Current Writing: Text and Reception in Southern Africa* 9, no. 2 (1997): 112–31.

Moore, Lisa L. "Lesbian Migrations: Mary Renault's South Africa." *GLQ: A Journal of Lesbian and Gay Studies* 10 (2003): 23–46.

Munro, Brenna Moremi. "Queer Democracy: J. M. Coetzee and the Racial Politics of Gay Identity in the New South Africa." *Journal of Commonwealth and Postcolonial Studies* 10, no. 1 (2003): 209–25.

Noa Ben-Asher, R. Bruce Brasell, Daniel Garrett, John Greyson, Jack Lewis, and Susan Newton-King. "Screening Historical Sexualities: A Roundtable on Sodomy, South Africa, and *Proteus*." *GLQ: A Journal of Lesbian and Gay Studies* 11 (2005): 437–55.

Poirier, Guy. "Masculinities and Homosexualities in French Renaissance Accounts of Travel to the Middle East and North Africa." In *Desire and Discipline: Sex and Sexuality in the Premodern West*, ed. Jacqueline Murray and Konrad Eisenbichler. Toronto: University of Toronto Press, 1996, 155–67.

Shaw, Drew. "Queer Inclinations and Representations: Dambudzo Marechera and Zimbabwean Literature." *Matatu: Journal for African Culture and Society* 29–30 (2005): 89–111.

Smith, Ann. "Queer Pedagogy and Social Change: Teaching and Lesbian Identity in South Africa." In *Lesbian and Gay Studies and the Teaching of English: Positions, Pedagogies, and Cultural Politics*, ed. William J. Spurlin. Urbana, IL: National Council of Teachers of English, 2000, 253–71.

Trengove Jones, Tim. "Fiction and the Law: Recent Inscriptions of Gayness in South Africa." *MFS: Modern Fiction Studies* 46, no. 1 (2000): 114–36.

Ghanem, Fathy (1924–1999)

Egyptian novelist Ghanem worked as a journalist and became editor of the Cairo newspaper *Sabah al-Khair*. His first novel, *The Mountain* (n.d.), satirizes a well-meant attempt to resettle Luxor peasants; in his later novels such as *The Man Who Lost His Shadow* (1966), the background is frequently the "jungle world," as he describes the Cairo press and its Byzantine intrigues and obsessions. Desmond Stewart translated both *The Mountain* and *The Man Who Lost His Shadow* into English. Other novels published by Ghanem are *Set Al-Hosn wal-Gamal* (*The Most Beautiful of All*, 1991) and *Qitt wa Far fil-Qitar* (*A Cat and a Mouse in the Train*, 1995). Some short-story collections by Ghanem include *Ba'd Al-Dhann Ethm, Ba'd Al-Dhann Halal* (*Suspicion Is Often Forbidden, and Sometimes Permitted* 1991), and "*Oyoun Al-Ghoraba*" (*Strangers' Eyes*, 1997). Ghanem was also the Editor-in-Chief of Rose Al-Youssef (1973), a member of the board of Rose Al-Youssef (1981), and a recipient of the State Merit Award for literature in 1994.

Gibbon, Perceval (1878–1926)

A novelist and short-story writer, Gibbon was born at Trelech, Wales, and educated at Old Mill School (London) and the Moravian School (Königsfeld, Germany). After two years' service in the merchant navy, he arrived in South Africa as a journalist shortly before the Anglo-Boer war (1899–1902) and worked as a war correspondent for a syndicate of colonial papers, following which he worked for the *Natal Witness*, the *Rand Daily Mail*, and the *Rhodesian Times*. In the decade before World War I he traveled widely as a correspondent journalist while extending his reputation as short-story writer, novelist, and linguist. A war correspondent at most of the Allied fronts and later a major in the Royal Marines during the war, he was commissioned to write dispatches and an official documentary, *The Triumph of the Royal Navy* (1919). He retired to Guernsey, where he died unexpectedly when at the peak of his literary powers.

Gibbon's African writing embodies the partial acclimatization to Africa of a sensitive Briton steeped in the European tradition. *The Vrouw Grobelaar's Leading Cases* (1905) foreshadows H.C. **Bosman**'s Oom Schalk Lourens tales. *Souls in Bondage* (1904) deals with problems of miscegenation, *Salvator* (1908) is about political intrigue in Mozambique, and *Margaret Harding* (1911) shows a concern with human relationships on a colonial farm and at a nearby TB sanatorium in the Karoo region of South Africa. Some of the stories in *The Adventures of Miss Gregory* (1912) and *The Second-Class Passenger* (1913) have African settings, while those of *Those Who Smiled* (1920) and *The Dark Places* (1926) are wholly Eurocentric.

Renewed interest in Gibbon as war correspondent, feminist, and significant postcolonial author no doubt inspired such projects as John Smallcombe's film *An African Dream* (1988), clearly derived from *Margaret Harding* (reissued in 1983), Janice Honeyman's stage adaptation *The Story of Margaret Harding* (1991), and Brian O'Shaughnessy's radio serial *Margaret Harding* (1996).

Further Reading

de Reuck, Jenny. "Race and Gender: A Study of the Artistic Corruption of Perceval Gibbon's *Souls in Bondage.*" *Journal of Literary Studies/Tydskrif Vir Literatuurwetenskap* 4, no. 1 (March 1988): 38–48.

MacKenzie, C. "The Skaz Narrative Mode in Short Stories by W.C. Scully, Percy FitzPatrick, Perceval Gibbon and Herman Charles Bosman." *Literator* 14, no. 3 (1993): 1–19.

Girl Who Killed to Save: Nongquase the Liberator, The (1936)

A play by H.I.E. **Dhlomo.** Dhlomo depicts the great cattle killing of 1857, which undermined Xhosa resistance to colonial rule. It is informed by a missionary ideology, and sees Nongquase's rejection of tribalism in favor of Christianity as a positive example. The play also portrays Nongquase as the victim of the witchdoctor Mhlakaza and the chief Sarile.

Gods Are Not to Blame, The (1971)

A play by Ola **Rotimi** that reworks Sophocles' *Oedipus* and sets it in a Yoruba royal court in the precolonial period. It is part of a trilogy, and the other works in the trilogy are *Kurunmi* (1969) and *Ovonrameme Nogbaise* (1971). Rotimi's Oedipus withdraws himself from the throne due to his character flaws of impatience, stubbornness, and ethnic distrust. Some critics fail to see how the Greek source is relevant to Yoruba culture.

God's Bits of Wood (1962)

A novel by **Sembene Ousmane**, translated from the French (*Les Bouts de bois de Dieu*, 1960). The novel is set during the French African railway workers' strike of 1947–48. The action takes place in Dakar, Thiès, Bamako, and other villages along the railway line. It portrays the lives of several characters who experience a wide sequence of events, including a women's march, the resistance of the French administrators, and the final settlement of the strike. The book explores the impact of Western technology on Africa, and realistically captures the historical and political significance of the period.

God's Step-Children (1924)

A novel by Sarah Gertrude **Millin,** the first in a trilogy that also includes *King of the Bastards* (1949) and *The Burning Man* (1952). The novels follow a mixed-race ("coloured") family who descend from the Reverend Andrew

Flood and his Khoikhoi wife. Millin's depiction of race is influenced by South African apartheid ideology, and she portrays the descendants of Flood as victims of their heritage, and as a disadvantaged group prone to insanity and inferiority. Despite this misinformed ideology, Millin writes well, and vividly describes the landscape and her characters.

Going down River Road (1976)

A novel by Meja **Mwangi**. The novel is set in postcolonial Kenya, among urban workers employed temporarily on a large construction project. Mwangi focuses in on one particular circumstance in the laborers' existence in order to portray the deplorable labor conditions and the listlessness that they experience with only temporary bursts of solidarity and subversion.

Gordimer, Nadine (1923–)

South African novelist and short-story writer. She was born near Johannesburg, the daughter of Jewish immigrants to South Africa. At eleven years old she was kept home for her health from her formal education. She had a private tutor and was isolated from people her own age until she was sixteen. She attended the University of the Witwatersrand for a year in 1945, but her education as a writer was the intense reading she did as a child and young woman and her growing consciousness of the society in which she grew up, which adopted formal **apartheid** in 1948.

Gordimer has published at least fifteen volumes of short stories, beginning with *Face to Face* (1949) and including two books of selected stories, *Selected Stories* (1975) and *Why Haven't You Written: Selected Stories 1950–72* (1992). Her most recent short-story collections include *Pillage* (2004), *Six Feet of the Country* (2001), and *Loot and Other Stories* (2003), and Gordimer is the editor of *Telling Tales* (2004), an international short-story collection, the profits of which go to

fight HIV/AIDS in southern Africa. She is the author of fourteen novels, including *The Lying Days* (1953), *A World of Strangers* (1958), *Occasion for Loving* (1963), *The Late Bourgeois World* (1966), *A **Guest of Honour*** (1971), *The **Conservationist*** (1974), ***Burger's Daughter*** (1979), ***July's People*** (1981), *A **Sport of Nature*** (1987), *My Son's Story* (1990), ***None to Accompany Me*** (1994), *The **House Gun*** (1998), *The Pickup* (2001), and *Get a Life* (2005), as well as numerous essays on literature and politics, some of which are collected in *The Black Interpreters* (1973), *What Happened to Burger's Daughter; or, How South African Censorship Works* (1980), and *The Essential Gesture: Writing, Politics and Places* (1988). She also collaborated with Lionel **Abrahams** to produce *South African Writing Today* (1967) and with the photographer David Goldblatt for *On the Mines* (1973) and *Lifetimes: Under Apartheid* (1986). This immense body of work spans the period of apartheid from beginning to end. Though she often expresses her knowledge that the white South African writer is extremely handicapped by the limitations of class and race in this period of South African history, she has become known internationally for her consistent attacks on the implications of apartheid. In 1991 she won the Nobel Prize for literature, becoming the third African writer to do so after Nigerian Wole **Soyinka** and Egyptian Naguib **Mahfouz.**

Gordimer has been controversial throughout her career, whether for the rulers of South Africa (who at times banned her work) or for those who find her significance difficult to accept, given that she is a white middle-class African able to write full-time and in security while so many black South African writers had to flee the country or were silenced. Her determination to examine the nature of white identity in the South African context has contributed to the realization in the white world of the nature of apartheid and of the necessity to oppose and destroy it. But she has never placed herself in the company of those who have suffered imprisonment, torture, exile, and death, nor claimed the slightest sharing of experience with black South Africans. For herself, there was no direct involvement in political action beyond her work.

Gordimer's fiction is concerned to examine emotion, physical desire, and political conviction and action. In *The Lying Days* sexual privacy and intimacy are overcast by the Prohibition of Mixed Marriages Act of the early phase of apartheid. This first novel, while charting a very different stage of both South Africa and the female protagonist's white consciousness, has nevertheless important elements in common with her novel of the mid-1990s, *None to Accompany Me.* Sexual desire becomes part of a political landscape in this novel, set in postapartheid South Africa. Black South Africans become much more central as characters in Gordimer's later fiction, and correspondingly, white characters' anxieties about the implications for society of their personal consciences or their political convictions are less important. Vera Stark, the central white female character, has a new dilemma to consider when her daughter fashions her lesbian relationship as a solid, middle-class, professional and personal bond in the mold of old-fashioned bourgeois heterosexual marriage but as contemporary as any two-career relationship, and adopts a black child. Gordimer previously created an equally politically incorrect career for Hillela in *A Sport of Nature,* who pursues political knowledge through sexual connections and lives her antiapartheid politics via her personal life. In *My Son's Story,* Gordimer attempts a mixed-race young male narrative voice, and some reviewers resisted a white writer's transgression of racial boundaries to appropriate identity. But Gordimer has always been a voyager in search of more honesty and equality in human relations. In *The Pickup* (2001) Gordimer narrates the

story of the world's dispossessed through an encounter between a wealthy South African and an illegal alien, while in *Get a Life* (2005) she follows an ecologist in South Africa who is diagnosed with cancer and must deal with the consequences of treatment.

Gordimer often provides politically devastating insights through her observation of personal detail. In her use of the short story form, economy often produces extraordinarily complex layerings of significance as personal and political meet. In "Happy Event," a white couple smile at one another, for example, and in that smile, "Europe, leisure and the freedom of the money they had saved up were unspoken between them" (1978). Middle-class white life, constructing others out of a desire to feel decent, safe, or in control, is set against the realities of black lives in South Africa. Her importance as a writer has been understood mostly to be in her handling of the novel and story forms as political statement: she has developed an idiosyncratic style, moralistic and clear-sighted.

Further Reading
Berg, Mari-Ann. "Self, Other and Social Context: Dialogic Relationships in Nadine Gordimer's *An Image of Success.*" *World Literature Written in English* 37, nos. 1–2 (1998): 156–68.

Brighton, J. Uledi-Kamanga. *Cracks in the Wall: Nadine Gordimer's Fiction and the Irony of Apartheid.* Trenton, NJ: Africa World Press, 2001.

Cook, Ruth McDowell. "Woman's Place in Africa: Nadine Gordimer's 'Flashes of Fearful Insight.'" *Tennessee Philological Bulletin: Proceedings of the Annual Meeting of the Tennessee Philological Association* 40 (2003): 50–59.

Dimitriu, Ileana. "The End of History: Reading Gordimer's Post-Apartheid Novels." *Current Writing: Text and Reception in Southern Africa* 15, no. 1 (2003): 17–37.

Genty, Stephanie. "Genre/Gender in Nadine Gordimer's *The Pickup.*" *Commonwealth Essays and Studies* 26, no. 1 (2003): 83–89.

Kossew, Sue. "'Something Terrible Happened': Nadine Gordimer's *The House Gun* and the Politics of Violence and Recovery in Post-Apartheid South Africa." *Mots Pluriels et Grands Themes de Notre Temps* 13 (2000): (no pagination).

Lee, Hermione. "Nadine Gordimer." In *Writing across Worlds: Contemporary Writers Talk,* ed. Susheila Nasta. London: Routledge, 2004, 315–26.

Moller, Karin. "Writing (on) the Wall: Ethics, Literature, and Nadine Gordimer." *European Journal of English Studies* 7, no. 2 (2003): 165–75.

Monson, Tamlyn. "Conserving the Cogito: Re-reading Nadine Gordimer's *The Conservationist.*" *Research in African Literatures* 35, no. 4 (2004): 33–51.

Newman, Judie, ed. *Nadine Gordimer's* Burger's Daughter: *A Casebook.* Oxford: Oxford University Press, 2003.

Grain of Wheat, A (1963)

Ngugi wa Thiong'o sets this novel in the days leading up to Uhuru celebrations in Kenya. Thiong'o explores the political unrest of the period through his characters' struggle for independence, and their relationships with Kihiga—a revolutionary whom the colonial authorities hang. In this sense he combines political and personal experiences. The outlook of the novel is grim, with a prediction that after independence Kenyans will struggle against one another for political and economic power.

Grass Is Singing, The (1950)

Doris **Lessing**'s first novel. It takes as its theme the political significance of colonial farming in a British colony based on Rhodesia. The farmers, Dick and Mary Turner, fail because they are less cruel than the other farmers. As a result, they and their African servant fall into tragic insanity and ruin. The message implies that English colonialism survived only on the inhumanity and insensitivity of those involved in it.

Gray, Stephen (1941–)

South African critic, anthologist, novelist, and poet. Born in Cape Town, Gray was educated at the universities of Cape Town, Cambridge, and Iowa, and was Professor of English at the Rand Afrikaans University, Johannesburg, before taking early retirement in 1992. Notable among his publications are editions of H. C. **Bosman**'s and Athol **Fugard**'s work, as well as biographical works like *Life Sentence: A Biography of Herman Charles Bosman* (2005), and *Best of Bosman* (2001), three Penguin anthologies of South African stories and poems, and four other volumes of South African drama; he has also published eight novels and a large amount of poetry.

Between 1974 (*It's about Time*) and 1992 (*Season of Violence*) Gray published five volumes of poetry. Many of the poems offer clear, fresh readings of landscape and animal life. A far more troubling subject, however, is the role of the poet in a restricted society, in "a country of words without dialogue" ("Chamber Music at Mount Grace"). He identifies continuities of oppression and of resistance in that history (in the title poem and "In Memoriam: C. Louis Leipoldt" from *Hottentot Venus,* 1979). The rewriting of context, both its recovery and its correction, is the commanding theme of much of Gray's work. In the title poem of *Apollo Cafe* (1990) he chronicles survival in Johannesburg, a city he characterizes as composed of appalling violence and dazzling plenty. In the late 1980s an increasingly brutal environment leads Gray to the harsh, breathless, truncated utterances of *Season of Violence.* After a break from poetry and the opportunity to take a retrospective in the *Selected Poems* (1994), the poems of the mid-1990s like *Human Interest and Other Pieces* (1993) and *Gabriel's Exhibition: New Poems* (1998), show a new range and depth and are less scarred by the immediate present. *Shelley*

Cinema and Other Poems (2006) is a collection of Gray's output over the last seven years, and the long title poem first appeared in *Moving Worlds* (2006).

Schreiner: A One-Woman Play (1983) was successful both in Britain and South Africa. His novels are extremely diverse in form. While an early work such as *Visible People* (1978) is impaired by its caustic humor, *John Ross: The True Story* (1987) is an account of relations between a group of British traders and the Zulu emperor Shaka. *War Child* (1991) is an account of a Cape childhood during World War II, an elegiac work with disturbing undercurrents. Two novels, *Time of Our Darkness* (1988) and *Born of Man* (1989), deal with homosexual relations; the first is a provocative and often moving account of a love affair between a white schoolmaster and a black schoolboy, which Gray powerfully contextualizes in the political situation of the 1970s, and the second employs scandalous comedy to dissect South African attitudes toward sexuality. A more recent novel is *Drakenstein: A Novel* (1994), in which a Johannesburg studio's shoot for a horror movie on location in the Maluti Mountains provides a backdrop for suicide and murder. Recent editions edited by Gray include *Wild Seed* by Herman Charles Bosman (2004), *Herman Charles Bosman: My Life and Opinions* (2003), *Jacaranda in the Night* by Herman Charles Bosman (2000), *Chameleon on the Gallows* by C. Louis Leipoldt (2000), and *Innovation and Derivation: The Contribution of L. & J. G. Stickley to the Arts and Crafts Movement,* edited with Donald A. Davidoff and a foreword by Beverely K. Brandt (1995).

Further Reading

Bethlehem, Louise Shabat. "'Under the Proteatree, at Daggaboersnek': Stephen Gray, Literary Historiography and the Limit Trope of the Local." *English in Africa* 24, no. 2 (1997): 27–50.
Dunton, Chris. "Stephen Gray at Sixty: An Interview and Bibliography of Primary Works." *English in Africa* 28, no. 2 (2001): 49–64.
Gray, Robert W. "Black Mirrors and Young Boy Friends: Colonization, Sublimation, and Sadomasochism in Stephen Gray's 'Time of Our Darkness.'" *ARIEL: A Review of International English Literature* 30, no. 2 (1999): 77–98.
Trengove-Jones, Tim. "Fiction and the Law: Recent Inscriptions of Gayness in South Africa." *MFS: Modern Fiction Studies* 46, no. 1 (2000): 114–36.

Great Ponds, The (1969)

The second novel in Elechi **Amadi**'s trilogy that portrays an Ekwerre village before British colonization. The other two novels are *The* **Concubine** and *The Slave*. *The Great Ponds* follows an argument between two villages over the ponds that ensure their economic, social, and religious survival. The communities are also afflicted by the Spanish influence of 1919, despite the fact that they have not yet been exposed to colonizers. The book explores in detail the complex relationships of the primarily oral community.

Guest of Honour, A (1971)

A novel by Nadine **Gordimer,** set in an unnamed African country at the time of its independence and subsequent fall into authoritarianism and neo-colonialism. This backdrop of the novel is set against the love story between Bray (previously a colonial administrator and the guest of honor at the independence ceremonies) and a white woman named Rebecca. In this sense, the novel combines the personal and the political and questions the interaction between the two.

Gunny Sack, The (1989)

A novel by M. G. **Vassanji** and winner of the Commonwealth Writers Prize. Ji Bai bequeaths a sack with objects from the past in it to her great-nephew Salim Juma in Vassanji's novel about the Indian community in East

Africa. The novel is separated into three sections that reflect Salim's great-aunt Ji Bai, his mother Kulsum, and his love Amina. The objects in the sack recall Salim's family history, as well as his own experiences growing up in Dar es Salaam. Salim's brother Sona interprets their inheritance based on his university education, and his interpretation of the objects is juxtaposed with Salim's throughout the novel.

Gurnah, Abdulrazak (1948–)

Novelist and critic Gurnah was born in Zanzibar and at eighteen moved to England to complete his studies. In 1980–82 he taught at the University of Kano, Nigeria, and in 1982 received his PhD from the University of Kent, Canterbury, where he now teaches English literature. He has published seven novels and has edited *Essays on African Writing: A Re-evaluation* (1993) and *Essays on African Writing: Contemporary Literature* (1995).

Memory of Departure (1987) is a coming-of-age narrative set in an unnamed East African coastal town at the time of independence. The novel's central concerns are coastal culture and how the dynamics of living in a small place influence the formation of a young person. Some autobiographical elements present in his first novel also shape *Pilgrim's Way* (1988), which recounts the experience a Muslim student from Tanzania has in an English provincial town. Racial tensions, questions of belonging, and the making of identity are addressed in *Dottie* (1990), the story of the eponymous black British heroine. *Paradise* (1994), short-listed for the Booker Prize in 1994, fuses myth, storytelling, religions, and East African and European literary traditions to tell of Yusuf's rite of passage. In *Admiring Silence* (1996) a Zanzibari man marries an English woman and writes romantic tales of the Africa he remembers. Only when he returns to Zanzibar does he discover uncomfortable truths about his country and himself. *Desertion* (2005) is

set during a turbulent time in Mombassa's independence from being a British colony in 1899, and also follows a family in Zanzibar in the 1950s. *By the Sea* (2002) tells the story of a man who seeks asylum in Britain from his native Zanzibar's dangerous government.

Further Reading
Callahan, David. "Exchange, Bullies and Abuse in Abdulrazak Gurnah's *Paradise*." *World Literature Written in English* 38, no. 2 (2000): 55–69.

Nasta, Susheila. "Abdulrazak Gurnah." In *Writing across Worlds: Contemporary Writers Talk*, ed. Susheila Nasta. London: Routledge, 2004, 352–63.

Schwerdt, Dianne. "Looking In on Paradise: Race, Gender and Power in Abdulrazak Gurnah's *Paradise*." In *Contemporary African Fiction*, ed. Derek Wright. Bayreuth, Germany: Breitinger, 1997, 91–101.

Whyte, Philip. "Heritage as Nightmare: The Novels of Abdulrazak Gurnah." *Commonwealth Essays and Studies* 27, no.1 (2004): 11–18.

Gwala, Mafika Pascal (1946–)

South African poet and sociocultural critic. Gwala was born in KwaZulu Natal and brought up in Durban. He has spent much of his life in Mpumalanga, a predominantly working-class township near Durban, and has worked as a secondary school teacher, legal clerk, factory worker, publications researcher, and industrial relations officer. He has also lived in Johannesburg and in England, where he did research on adult education at the University of Manchester. He has published two volumes of verse: *Jol'iinkomo* (1977) and *No More Lullabies* (1982). He has also produced short stories and essays, edited a full-length survey of trends in the black community titled *Black Review* 1973, and co-edited *Musha' Zulu Popular Praises* (1991), which includes two praise poems composed by Gwala himself.

Gwala emerged as a significant writer and theorist in the late 1960s and early 1970s, a crucial period for **Black Consciousness.** He was closely associated with the black South African Students Organization, together with such writers as Mongane Wally **Serote,** Mbuyiseni **Mtshali,** and James **Matthews.** He wrote about the political, social, cultural, and emotional needs and aspirations of all those victimized by apartheid. His first volume contains many poems of suffering, anger, and defiance. Throughout his poetry there is a focus on emotions and experiences that makes them liberatory. In his second volume the political focus begins to change; like many others Gwala moved away from Black Consciousness toward a more nonracial socialism. Some of the poems are more militant than those in the earlier volume, but the variety of themes continues.

Further Reading

Gardner, Colin. "Catharsis: From Aristotle to Mafika Gwala." *Theoria: A Journal of Studies in the Arts, Humanities and Social Sciences* 64 (1985): 29–41.

Povey, John. "The Poetry of Mafika Gwala." *Commonwealth Essays and Studies* 8, no. 2 (1986): 84–93.

H

Haarhoff, Dorian (1944–)

Namibian poet and dramatist. Haarhoff was born in Kimberley, South Africa, but has naturalized as a Namibian citizen. He is a prolific and versatile writer who uses Namibian history as a point of departure for discovering a new Namibian identity; his work is also influenced by mythology and Jungian psychology. His poetry has been collected in a number of volumes, of which *Bordering* (1991) and *Aquifers and Dust* (1994) in particular deal with the Namibian experience and explore the physical and psychological frontiers encountered by those who share

his dual history. The poetry is characterized by a vision sometimes wry and ironic, always compassionate. His plays, *Orange* (1988), *Skeleton* (1989), and *Guerilla Goatherd* (1990), display exciting departures from traditional theatrical forms, and they are collected in *Goats, Oranges & Skeletons: A Trilogy of Namibian Independence Plays* (2000). In addition to drama and poetry, Haarhoff is the author of short stories and children's books, including *Desert December* (1992), *Water from the Rock* (1992), *Legs, Bones and Eyes* (1994), and *Grandpa Enoch's Pipe* (2002); he has also published articles and books on writing poetry and on literature, including "Of Monkeys and Human Memory: Teaching Creative Writing" in *Scrutiny2: Issues in English Studies in Southern Africa* (1998), *The Inner Eye: Namibian Poetry in Process* (1997), *Personal Memories: Namibian Texts in Process* (ca.1996), and *The Wild South-West: Frontier Myths and Metaphors in Literature Set in Namibia, 1760–1988* (1992).

Hakim, Te[a?]wfiq (Husayn) al-
(1898–1987)

Egyptian playwright and novelist writing in Arabic. Al-Hakim was born in Alexandria and educated there and at law school in Cairo. Until 1934 he worked as a public prosecutor and a civil servant, after which he concentrated on writing. Although he wrote a few novels, a handful of poems, and essays on arts and literature, he is best known as a playwright. Eleven of al-Hakim's Arabic plays were translated by William Hutchins as *Plays, Preface and Postscripts of Tewfiq al-Hakim,* 2 vols. (1981), and a number of individual plays have been translated as well. *In the Tavern of Life and Other Stories: Metaphysical Tales* was translated by William M. Hutchins in 1998; *The Prison of Life: An Autobiographical Essay* was translated by Pierre Cachia in 1993; and *Return of the Spirit: Tawfiq Al-Hakim's Classic Novel of the 1919 Revolution* was translated by William M. Hutchins in 1990.

Further Reading

Hutchins, William Maynard. *Critical Perspectives on Tawfiq Al Hakim.* Pueblo, CO: Passeggiata Press, 1998.

———. *Tawfiq al-Hakim: A Reader's Guide.* Boulder, CO: Rienner, 2003.

Salama, Mohammad R. "The Aesthetics of 'Pygmalion' in G. B. Shaw and Tawfiq al-Hakim: A Study of Transcendence and Decadence." *Journal of Arabic Literature* 31, no. 3 (2000): 222–37.

Shetawi, Mahmoud al-. "The Treatment of Greek Drama by Tawfiq al-Hakim." *World Literature Today: A Literary Quarterly of the University of Oklahoma* 63, no. 1 (1989): 9–14.

Starkey, Paul. "The Four Ages of Husayn Tawfiq: Love and Sexuality in the Novels of Tawfiq al-Hakim." In *Love and Sexuality in Modern Arabic Literature,* ed. Roger Allen, Hilary Kilpatrick, and Ed De Moor. London: Saqi, 1995, 56–64.

Hammer Blows (1973)

Poems by David **Diop,** translated from the French (*Coups de pilon,* 1956). This book of seventeen poems contains eulogies to African identity that insinuate a negritude position, and argue for violent resistance. They also look toward the future with hope for an Africa without neo-colonialism. Thus the poems both offer harsh criticism and joyful celebration.

Head, Bessie (1937–86)

South African novelist and short-story writer. Head was born in Pietermaritzburg's Fort Napier Mental Institution, where her mother Bessie Amelia Emery (née Birch) was placed after becoming pregnant by a black man. Head grew up in foster care until the age of thirteen, when the welfare authorities placed her in an Anglican mission orphanage in Durban where she received a secondary school education and trained as a teacher. Head found out very soon that teaching did not suit her temperament, so in the early 1960s she moved into the world of journalism and worked in Cape Town and Johannesburg for a newspaper in the famous **Drum** stable. In Cape Town she met and married fellow journalist Harold Head in 1961, and their only child, Howard, was born in 1962. After the break-up of her marriage in 1964 she relinquished South African citizenship and took up a teaching post in Serowe, Botswana. After she lost this job and was declared a refugee Head turned to market gardening and writing, and was granted her Botswanan citizenship in 1979. Plagued by ill health and mental instability, she died in Serowe with six published works and an international reputation.

Head's first work, *When Rain Clouds Gather* (1968), deals with the flight from South Africa of a young black political activist, Makhaya Maseko, his resettlement in Botswana, and his marriage to a Batswana woman. It describes the efforts of Makhaya and Gilbert Balfour, a young English agricultural expert, to establish cooperative farming in a village in southeastern Botswana. It examines the possibility of interracial cooperation and friendship and it incorporates issues real to an independent and developing Africa.

Head's second novel, *Maru* (1971), with its eponymous central character, is a more complex work. The realistic narrative follows Maru and Moleka, who are both in line for the chieftaincy of their tribe and are both in love with a Masarwa woman named Margaret, who is a member of the despised Bushman race who were the slaves of Batswana for generations. There is a surface realism to the novel, and there is an allegorical struggle between human character types. Margaret's racial oppression achieves a universal resonance, and Maru and Moleka become human archetypes whose natures draw them into an unavoidable conflict.

*A **Question of Power*** (1974) is Head's most unusual and difficult novel. Although all three of Head's novels have an autobiographical dimension, *A Question of Power* is the most obviously autobiographical. After a disastrous early life in South Africa, the protagonist Elizabeth leaves on an exit permit for Motabeng village in Botswana, where she engages in co-operative gardening ventures with the local Batswana and an international group of volunteer workers. Here she has a mental breakdown. The narrative switches between her tormented consciousness and the "real world" of the novel—the bustling village life, communal gardening, and the daily activities of Elizabeth and her son. Elizabeth confronts in her consciousness universal powers of good and evil and struggles to attain a sense of human value amid her mental confusion. The novel charts the terrifying course of her breakdown and recovery and ultimately affirms the primary human values of decency, generosity, and compassion.

Head's collection of short stories, *The* **Collector of Treasures** *and Other Botswana Village Tales* (1977), evokes aspects of Botswanan village life, tribal history, the missionaries, religious conflict, witchcraft, rising illegitimacy, and, most important, problems that women in the society encounter. Her social history *Serowe: Village of the Rain Wind* (1981) is composed of a series of transcribed interviews edited and prefaced by the author to constitute a portrait of Serowe village life. The historical novel *A Bewitched Crossroad: An African Saga* (1984) describes the process toward the establishment of the British protectorate of Bechuanaland and tells the story of Sebina, a leader of a clan that is eventually absorbed into the Bamangwato nation.

Some of Head's works appeared posthumously: *Tales of Tenderness and Power* (1989) is a collection of mostly fictional short writings, while *A Woman Alone: Autobiographical Writings* (1990) collects miscellaneous pieces Head wrote in both South Africa and Botswana. Randolph Vigue's *A Gesture of Belonging: Letters from Bessie Head, 1965–1979* (1991) is an important collection of letters interspersed with commentary. *The Cardinals: With Meditations and Stories* (1993) is a previously unpublished novella (which Head wrote in Cape Town in the early 1960s) and a set of shorter pieces.

Further Reading

Brown, Coreen. *The Creative Vision of Bessie Head*. London: Associated University Press, 2003.

Eilersen, Gillian S. *Bessie Head: Thunder behind Her Ears: A Biography*. London: J. Currey, 1995.

Gagiano, Annie. "Memory, Power and Bessie Head: *A Question of Power*." *World Literature Written in English* 38, no. 1 (1999): 42–57.

Ibrahim, Huma. *Bessie Head: Subversive Identities in Exile*. Charlottesville: University of Virginia Press, 1996.

Margree, Victoria. "Wild Flowers: Bessie Head on Life, Health and Botany." *Paragraph: A Journal of Modern Critical Theory* 27, no. 3 (2004): 16–31.

Osei-Nyame, Kwadwo, Jr. "Writing between 'Self' and 'Nation': Nationalism, (Wo)manhood and Modernity in Bessie Head's *The Collector of Treasures and Other Botswana Village Tales*." *Journal of the Short Story in English* 39 (2002): 91–107.

Ward, Alan Ramon. "Using the Heart: The Symbolism of Individual Change in Bessie Head's *Maru*." *International Fiction Review* 31, nos. 1–2 (2004): 19–25.

Healers, The (1978)

A novel by Ayi Kwei **Armah.** This historical novel takes place at the time of the second Asante war (1873–74) in a Fante village called Esuano. It centers around the character Densu, who is falsely charged with the murder of Prince Appia. He escapes to the healer Damfo, who teaches him to turn away from material power, and teaches the historical figure Nkwanta that royal power is oppressive. Densu returns to Esuano, where Appia's mother uncovers a plot to frame him and cuts his trial short. Densu turns down a proposed kingship when he remembers what Damfo taught him about worldly power.

Heavensgate (1962)

Poems by Christopher **Okigbo.** His first full volume of poems, this work is also autobiographical. Okigbo's Western education results in his narrative of return and reconciliation with "mother Idoto" in these poems. Okigbo often comes back to this theme of reconciling his education and his heritage, as the poems display the difficulty of the task.

Helena's Hope, Ltd (1909)

A play by Stephen **Black.** The setting of the play is the title gold mine, where the characters hope to strike it rich. The play follows these characters as the capitalist economy takes hold in twentieth-century South Africa. It ran for six hundred performances and toured South Africa.

Hello and Goodbye (1965)

A play by Athol **Fugard.** This play depicts the interactions between two siblings on the death of their father. Hester Smit visits her brother Johnnie to claim her part of their inheritance, only to find that Johnnie claims their father is very sick, but still alive in the other room. He refuses to let Hester see him, and in the plot that follows Hester looks through a number of old possessions in a fruitless search for money that only leads them both to reminisce about their troublesome childhood. The characters choose definitively to remain alone in their lives, and when Hester leaves Johnnie uncovers the fact that he has feigned the crippled and unemployed identity of his father.

Henshaw, James Ene (1924–)

Nigerian playwright, born in Calabar, Nigeria. He began his writing career in Dublin, with *This Is Our Chance,* written for the Association of Students of African Descent and published, along with *A Man of Character* and *Jewels of the Shrine,* in 1956. These three earlier plays and three of the plays published in *Children of the Goddess* (1964), including the title play, *Magic in the Blood,* and *Companion for a Chief,* emphasize the clash of tradition and modernity. Although *Jewels of the Shrine* is also ironic enough for the conflicts to be played out convincingly, Nigerian critics tend to define Henshaw as a writer for juveniles. In later plays such as *Medicine for Love* (1964) and *Dinner for Promotion* (1967), characterization becomes more rounded, dialogue is more suitable, and comedy adds vitality to the action. In *Enough Is Enough* (1976), about detainees during the Nigeria-Biafra war, increased psychological depth produces intense drama. In *A Song to Mary Charles* (1985), a biographical play about an Irish nun, Henshaw develops an extremely lively and memorable character. Henshaw considers characterization the most important dramatic element.

Further Reading

Bamikunle, Aderemi. "Ene Henshaw and the Beginnings of Popular Plays in Nigeria." *Nigeria Magazine* 53, no. 4 (1985): 84–89.
———. "The Politics of Literary Syllabus: The Marginalization of Ene Henshaw's Plays." *Nigeria Magazine* 53, no. 1 (1985): 77–82.
Nwamuo, Chris. "Henshaw and the Genesis of Literary Theatre in Nigeria." *The Literary Criterion* 23, nos. 1–2 (1988): 118–30.

Heroes (1986)

A novel by Festus **Iyayi** and winner of a Commonwealth Writers Prize. The novel depicts the Nigeria-Biafra war. It is notable for its representation of the war through the eyes of journalist Osime Iyere, who moves from naivety to political awareness. The narrative style is stream-of-consciousness, and the novel suggests that the general public on both sides are victims of a war between classes.

Hope, Christopher (David Tully) (1944–)

South African-born novelist and poet. Born in Johannesburg, he grew up in Pretoria, studied at the universities of Natal and the Witwatersrand, and has been based in London since 1975. Hope is an ambivalent visitor in a postcolonial world.

Hope's first novel, *A Separate Development* (1980), suggests a fantasy autobiography. Harry Mota, a white boy living black, finds unlikely routes through the strict **apartheid** enclaves that enable bizarre but nourishing visions, which mirror his creator's imaginative escape from the banality of white suburbia. *Kruger's Alp* (1984) remains Hope's tour-de-force, and it is a dense and allegorical satire that blends a remaking of Catholic boys' school fundamentalism with the deep history signaled in his title's reference to the exile of an Afrikaner saint (and to his mythical buried millions). Hope followed this with *The Hottentot Room* (1986), the novella *Black Swan* (1987), *My Chocolate Redeemer* (1989), *Serenity House* (1992), *Love Songs of Nathan J. Swirsky* (1994), *Darkest England* (1996), *Signs of the Heart* (1999), and *Heaven Forbid* (2002). Hope's South African phantasmagoria returns in various guises in these works as, necessarily and increasingly, he raids a European hinterland for new material.

A significant body of poetry includes *Cape Drives* (1974), *In the Country of the Black Pig* (1981), and *Englishmen* (1985), a long poem subsequently dramatized by the BBC. He has written books for children such as *Me, the Moon and Elvis Presley* (1999); a good deal of documentary journalism that includes the travel book *Moscow! Moscow!* (1990) and *Brothers under the Skin: Travels in Tyranny* (2003); the early stories in *Private Parts* (1981) reissued with additions as *Learning to Fly* (1990); and a memoir (*White Boy Running,* 1988), which provides an interesting counterpoint to *A Separate Development.*

Further Reading
Wachinger, Tobias. "Happy Occidentalism: Christopher Hope's *Darkest England* and the Concept of a Mission in Reverse." In *Colonies, Missions, Cultures in the English Speaking World: General and Comparative Studies,* ed. Gerhard Stilz. Tubingen: Stauffenburg, 2001, 361–72.

House Gun, The (1998)
A novel by Nadine **Gordimer.** In this novel Duncan Lindgard, one of the young people who share a garden house in postapartheid Johannesburg, shoots another of them—Carl Jespersen—with the "house gun" they keep at the spot. Duncan admits to the crime without admitting to his motivation. The novel focuses on the devastation of his parents, who hire the high-profile lawyer Hamilton Motsamai. Motsamai uncovers the impetus behind Duncan's action, which was not the passionate heterosexual love crime that the courtroom media expect.

House of Hunger (1978)
Stories by Dambudzo Marechera. In these stories Marechera speaks as a student, a poet, an academic, and a nationalist to depict the violence he experienced growing up in Rhodesia, now Zimbabwe. In his stories, Marechera portrays the psychological and physical violence of the struggle for independence, racism, and guerilla warfare in the context of Ian Smith's UDI (Unilateral Declaration of Independence).

Houseboy (1956)
A novel by Ferdinand **Oyono,** translated from the French (*Une vie de boy,* 1956). This novel combines African literary traditions with European ones, and demonstrates Oyono's anticolonialist stance. It is mainly concerned with the portrayal of power relations in the form of a corrupt elite who abuse their power by subjecting more passive characters to violence. Here, it is the French colonial officers who use their power to violently subject the African characters.

Hove, Chenjerai (1956–)
Zimbabwean poet and novelist. Hove is one of the best-known of recent Zimbabwean

writers. He writes in Shona, but he came to prominence first as a poet with *Up in Arms* (1982), *Red Hills of Home* (1985), and, in collaboration with Lyamba wa Kabika, *Swimming in Floods of Tears* (1983). He has most recently published *Rainbows in the Dust* (1998) and *Blind Moon* (2003). However, Hove has also achieved significant success in prose: the first of two English novellas, *Bones* (1988), won the Noma Award and the second, titled *Shadows* (1991), was followed by a collection of essays, *Shebeen Tales* (1994), a novel, *Ancestors* (1996), and a collection of articles written for newspapers titled *Palaver Finish* (2002). As writer-in-residence at the University of Zimbabwe and chair of the Zimbabwe Writers' Union, Hove has been active in the promotion of literature in Zimbabwe. In 1994 he was a visiting professor at Lewis and Clark College in Oregon.

Hove's earlier poems trenchantly support the guerilla war. Often his language is deliberately brutal, as in "Remember Chimoio" (site of a Rhodesian forces massacre). Later, Hove writes more approachable poems that turn to broader issues of unfulfilled political promises and his own role as writer in a chaotic world. Hove's best work, *Bones,* is a moving consideration of the ravages of war on rural folk. Here he combines modernist techniques with repetitive, proverb-like sentences to create a meditation on the destruction of traditional life. *Shadows* extols two young lovers' decision to commit suicide, as their community is rent by violence from both sides in the war. Both novellas finely evoke a beleaguered culture. In *Shebeen Tales,* Hove follows **Ngugi wa Thiong'o** and Ayi Kwei **Armah** in chronicling the conditions of the dispossessed, and indicts the postindependence government for its self-serving "political monologue." *Ancestors* is an evocative tale of a woman who cannot speak or hear, but who manages to communicate the plight of voiceless women when she haunts a man who lives a century later.

Further Reading

Engelke, Matthew. "Thinking about Nativism in Chenjerai Hove's Work. *Research in African Literatures* 29, no. 2 (1998): 23–42.

Oh, Eun Young. "Toward a New Feminist Postcolonial Epistemology: The Reconstruction of Female Subjectivity and Motherhood in *Bones*." *Feminist Studies in English Literature* 6, no. 2 (1998): 183–99.

Thompson, Katrina Daly, introduction and trans. "Chenjerai Hove." *Metamorphoses: Journal of the Five College Seminar on Literary Translation* 10, no. 1 (2002): 362–71.

Hussein, Ebrahim N. (1943–)

Tanzanian dramatist writing in Swahili. He graduated from the theater arts department of the University of Dar es Salaam. Tanzania's preeminent playwright has written *Alikiona (He Got His Just Desserts)* (1970); *Kinjeketile* (1969); *Wakati Ukuta (Time Is like a Brick Wall)* (1971); *Mashetani (Demons)* (1971); *Jogoo Kijijini* and *Ngao ya Jadi* (1976); *Arusi (Wedding)* (1980); and *Kwenye Ukingo wa Thim (At the Edge of Thim)* (1988). He pursued further education in East Germany, returning to teach drama at Dar es Salaam. He later taught at the University of Nairobi.

Hussein has made important contributions to the development of an authentic Tanzanian drama by examining issues of history and national integration (*Kinjeketile, Ngao ya Jadi*); rapid cultural change (*Wakati Ukuta*); social class polarities (*Mashetani*); ethnic chauvinism, greed, and corruption (*Thim*); and cultural and linguistic rejuvenation. He makes innovative use of elements of orature, particularly in *Jogoo Kijijini* and *Ngao ya Jadi.*

Further Reading

Fiebach, Joachim. "Ebrahim Hussein's Dramaturgy: A Swahili Multiculturalist's Journey in Drama and Theater." *Research in African Literatures* 28, no. 4 (1997): 19–37.

Mugo, Micere G. "Gerishon Ngugi, Peninah Muhando, and Ebrahim Hussein: Plays in

Swahili." *African Literature Today* (Freetown, Sierra Leone) 8 (1976): 137–41.

Ricard, Alain. *Ebrahim Hussein: Swahili Theatre and Individualism.* Enugu, Nigeria: Cogito Publishers, 2000.

I

I Will Marry When I Want (1982)

Play by **Ngugi wa Thiong'o** (1977) translated from Gikuyu (*Ngaahika Ndeenda*). The play tells the story of a peasant farmer, Kiguunda, his wife Wangeei, and their daughter Gatoni. A wealthy businessman named Kioi, his wife Jezebel, and their son Muhuumi take advantage of the peasant family. Kiguunda mortgages his farm in order to pay for a Christian wedding between Gatoni and Muhuumi, but when Gatoni becomes pregnant before the wedding it is called off and Kiguunda loses his farm. In this sense, the play calls attention to the exploitation of the peasant people by foreign capitalists who collaborate with the Westernized Kenyan entrepreneurial class. The peasant people who saw the play performed at the Kamiriithu Cultural Centre were inspired by it, and when the authorities saw this they stopped further performances.

Ibadan: The Pankelemes Years, a Memoir 1946–1965 (1994)

Memoir by Wole **Soyinka.** The memoir depicts Soyinka's life as a young dramatist and political activist. He records the events that influenced Nigeria's social and political scene in the 1950s and 1960s. From 1959–65 Soyinka was researching the origins of traditional drama at the University of Ibadan, and witnessed the violence and chaos of the political scene at that time, which he calls *pankelemes*. After independence Soyinka was involved in political events, and the book concludes as he is arrested for an attempt to hold up Ibadan's radio station at the time of the 1964 elections.

Idanre (1967)

Wole **Soyinka**'s first poetry collection. In these poems Soyinka deals with political and personal subjects such as the birth of a still-born child, the appearance of a "born-to-die" spirit child, the harsh violence of the military as civil war advances, and the relationship between artistic inspiration and social realities. He draws from Yoruba myth for this inspiration, and muses on it in his title poem "Idanre."

Ike, (Vincent) Chukwuemeka (1931–)

Nigerian novelist Ike was born in eastern Nigeria and educated at the University of Ibadan and at Stanford in the United States. As an educator, Ike has contributed to the intellectual and cultural development of Africa in important administrative positions at Nigerian universities and at UNESCO and as professor at the University of Jos. His novels include *Toads for Supper* (1965), which is set in a university and deals with love and the inherent problems that married couples from different ethnic backgrounds encounter; *The Naked Gods* (1970), also set in a university, exposes the corrupt practices in the appointment of a new vice-chancellor at Songhai University. In *Expo 77* (1980), secondary school students try to gain admission to the university by cheating in examinations. *Our Children Are Coming* (1990) deals with the problem of youth unrest and student revolt in colleges and universities in Nigeria. In reaction to commissions of inquiry that exclude them, the students set up a counterinvestigation of their own. *The Search* (1991) is the story of the patriotism of a detribalized intellectual, Ola, and his search for Nigerian unity. Ike is also the author of *To My Husband from Iowa* (1996) and *Conspiracy of Silence* (2001). His prose style encompasses dialogue, wit, and satire, which he employs to castigate corruption and the quest for inordinate power. The novels transcend historical, sociological, and political documentation and achieve comedy, tragedy, irony, and metaphor. Ike has also written *How to Become a Published Writer* (1991).

Further Reading

Ezenwa-Ohaeto. "Narrating and Manipulating the Oral Voice in the Novels of Chukwuemeka Ike." *Commonwealth Essays and Studies* 19, no. 1 (1996): 24–30.

Johnson, Alex C. "Sunset at Dawn: A Biafran on the Nigerian Civil War." *African Literature Today* (Freetown, Sierra Leone) 11 (1980): 149–60.

Ugbabe, Kanchana. "The Child Figure in Chukwuemeka Ike's *The Potter's Wheel*." *Okike: An African Journal of New Writing* 27–28 (1988): 67–73.

Imbuga, Francis (1947–)

A Kenyan playwright, novelist, and poet, Imbuga was born in Maragoli, Kenya, where he received his primary and secondary education. He gained his bachelor's and master's degrees from the University of Nairobi and a PhD from the University of Iowa. In the 1970s he traveled to Wales, Ghana, and Nigeria to broaden his theatrical experience, and he has taught literature at Kenyatta University, Nairobi, since 1979.

While still an undergraduate Imbuga began writing dramas for Kenyan television. His television scripts and ten published plays, including a Swahili translation in 1994 of *Betrayal in the City* (1976), have established him as one of Kenya's foremost playwrights. "Kisses of Fate" and *The Fourth Trial* (1972), among his earliest plays, and *The Married Bachelor* (1973), initially published as *Sons and Parents* in 1971 and revised as *The Burning of Rags*, focus on domestic experience. *Game of Silence* (1977) forms a thematic and stylistic transition to the political emphases of later plays: *Betrayal in the City, The Successor* (1979), and *Man of Kafira* (1984) explore the crises of leadership, nepotism, despotism, disillusionment, social unease, and resistance that characterize Africa's postcolonial period.

Since Imbuga draws from well-known events and figures, he deliberately resorts to disguising devices, notably the play-within-play, the figure of the fool, humor, and anagram. Imbuga wrote *Aminata* (1988) for the United Nations Decade for Women Conference held in Nairobi in 1985 and it highlights his identification with some aspects of the women's struggle. Imbuga's novel *Shrine of Tears* (1993), and his poems, which appear in anthologies edited by A. D. Amateshe and A. I. Luvai, operate thematically with his plays.

Further Reading

"Dramatist Francis Imbuga." *Weekly Review* (Nairobi) 27 (1986): 24–25.

Harb, Ahmad. "The Aesthetics of Francis Imbuga: A Contemporary Kenyan Playwright." *The Literary Review: An International Journal of Contemporary Writing* 34, no. 4 (1991): 571–82.

Obyerodhyambo, Oby. "*Of Betrayal in* Betrayal in the City." *The Literary Review: An International Journal of Contemporary Writing* 34, no. 4 (1991): 583–88.

Olaogun, Modupe. "Dramatizing Atrocities: Plays by Wole Soyinka, Francis Imbuga, and George Seremba Recalling the Idi Amin Era." *Modern Drama* 45, no. 3 (2002): 430–48.

Ruganda, John. *Telling the Truth Laughingly: The Politics of Francis Imbuga's Drama* (Sparrow Readers Series, 17) East African Educational Press, 1992.

In the Ditch (1972)

A novel by Buchi **Emecheta.** It follows the narrative of Adah, who must provide for herself and her children after her husband abandons her. They live in a council housing estate in London called "the Ditch," which provides an equivocal community for Adah. The novel has autobiographical elements, which are more fully explained in

Emecheta's autobiography titled *Head above Water* (1986). One of these is the way that Adah escapes the Ditch through resolve and education.

In the Fog of the Season's End (1972)
A novel by Alex **La Guma**. This novel depicts the destruction of lives through apartheid laws, the Sharpeville massacre, the ANC's creation of its armed branch, the Group Areas Act, and the exploitation of mine labor. It comes to the conclusion that only civil war can destroy the fog of the totalitarian system in South Africa, and as the novel comes to a close it sees hope in the training of guerilla freedom fighters.

In the Heart of the Country (1978)
J. M. **Coetzee**'s second novel offers an allegorical rereading of Olive **Schreiner**'s *The Story of an African Farm.* Coetzee's narrator is the psychologically complex Magda, who lives with her father, stepmother, and their servants on an isolated South African farm. Magda refuses to talk to her stepmother, and both craves her father's attention and wishes to kill him. She attempts to find herself but fails to fabricate a continuous internal narrative of self.

Incidents at the Shrine (1986)
Short stories by Ben **Okri**. This collection contains eight stories that sometimes use Pidgin dialogue, are told from differing points of view, and occur both in Africa and elsewhere in the world. They use humor to tackle topics such as traditional African religion, poverty, prostitution, political violence, and isolation.

Instant in the Wind, An (1976)
A novel by André **Brink**. Set in the eighteenth century, Brink retells the legend of the shipwrecked Eliza Fraser and her relationship with an escaped convict who promises to help her in return for his freedom. Brink's character is named Elisabeth Larsson and is a Dutch settler who relies on Adam Mantoor, a black slave who she eventually betrays. Brink emphasizes the fact that both of these characters are enslaved by their contemporary colonial and patriarchal social contexts.

Interesting Narrative of Olaudah Equiano; or, Gustavus Vassa, the African, Written by Himself, The (1789).
See Equiano, Olaudah

Interpreters, The (1965)
Wole **Soyinka**'s first novel. It follows the events in the 1960s leading up to the Nigeria-Biafra war through the lives of a group of male university graduates from Lagos who must interpret their social context and attempt to live in it without losing their honesty. The novel uses complex language and particularly vivid episodic descriptions in order to portray the social context of this group of men.

Iroh, Eddie (1946–)
Nigerian novelist and children's writer Iroh was born in Nigeria and served in the Nigerian army before joining the Biafran War Information Bureau and Reuters News Service during the Nigeria-Biafra war (1967–70). He has worked both in the UK and Nigeria as a journalist and magazine editor.

Iroh belongs to the second generation of Nigerian writers, who wrote about modern Nigerian city life. His first novel, *Forty-Eight Guns for the General* (1976), focuses on the activities of mercenaries who fought in the Nigeria-Biafra war. His second novel, *Toads of War* (1979), shows how a corrupt civil servant tries to protect himself by conscripting the main character, Odim, who knows the civil servant's secrets, into the army. *The Siren in the Night* (1982) is a historical reconstruction of the war that describes Iroh's own experience of intimidation and ethnic loyalties in the aftermath. *Without a Silver Spoon* (1984) is a children's book about a child growing up in a poor family.

Further Reading

Ezeigbo, Theodora-Akachi. "War, History, Aesthetics, and the Thriller Tradition in Eddie Iroh's Novels." *African Languages and Cultures* 4, no. 1 (1991): 65–76.

Iyayi, Festus (1947–)

Nigerian novelist Iyayi was born in Benin City, Nigeria, and studied in Nigeria, the USSR, and England, where he obtained a PhD from the University of Bradford. One of the most politically committed African novelists, Iyayi was dismissed from the faculty of the University of Benin for his revolutionary political and labor activities. His novels include *Violence* (1979), *The Contract* (1982), and *Heroes* (1986), for which he earned a Commonwealth Writers Prize. The novels situate themselves within the framework of class struggle. Iyayi's working-class protagonists begin as innocent individuals but become informed and politically conscious as they are exploited along class lines, and ultimately they champion the cause of the victimized. *Violence* and *The Contract* examine class and gender, while *Heroes* treats the Nigeria-Biafra war as a class-based conflict that leaves the people exploited and stranded on both sides. The collection of short stories *Awaiting Court Martial* (1996) continues his acerbic critique of contemporary Nigerian society.

Further Reading

Ajibade, Kunle. "Festus Iyayi: We Cannot Afford to Fail." *Matatu: Journal for African Culture and Society* 23–24 (2001): 83–89.

Armstrong, Andrew. "Speaking through the Wound: Irruption and Memory in the Writing of Ben Okri and Festus Iyayi." *Journal of African Cultural Studies* 13, no. 2 (2000): 173–83.

Ni-Chreachain, Firinne. "Festus Iyayi's *Heroes*: Two Novels in One?" *Research in African Literatures* 22, no. 1 (1991): 43–53.

———. "How the Present Shapes the Past: Festus Iyayi's *Heroes*—The Nigerian Civil War Revisited." *The Journal of Commonwealth Literature* 27, no. 1 (1992): 48–57.

Udumukwu, Onyemaechi. "Ideology and the Dialectics of Action: Achebe and Iyayi." *Research in African Literatures* 27, no. 3 (1996): 34–49.

J

Jabavu, Noni (Helen Nontando) (1919–)

A South African autobiographer, Jabavu was born in South Africa's Eastern Cape to a distinguished Xhosa family of journalists and educators whose histories she tells in *Drawn in Colour* (1960) and *The Ochre People* (1963). As a teenager, she left South Africa to study in London, where she remained to work as a writer and in television. Jabavu's work reflects her life history, her sense of belonging to "two worlds with two loyalties" in its nostalgic evocation of her rural childhood and exposure of the dehumanization of **apartheid.**

Jabavu's 1955 visit to South Africa provides the point of departure for her writing. *The Ochre People* evokes three different regional cultures: her family home of Middledrift, her uncle's farm at Tsolo, and the urban "locations" of Johannesburg. It combines autobiography with travel writing and broader family, social, and cultural history. Jabavu transcends autobiography to incorporate details of the group experience and to document the breakdown in African family life that results from urbanization. The canvas of *Drawn in Colour* is broader, extending Jabavu's reflections beyond those of a returning exile to include her impressions of Westernization in East Africa. It includes as well her criticism of traditional notions of "a woman's place" and at the same time her refusal of the self-definition *feminist*. These works are precursors to Phyllis Ntantala's account of a similarly privileged early life (*A Life's Mosaic*, 1993), and other contemporary urban women, such as Joyce Sikakane's *A Window on Soweto* (1977) and Ellen **Kuzwayo**'s **Call Me Woman** (1985).

Further Reading

Ayivor, Kwame. "Individualism versus Traditionalism in Four African Novels: Noni Jabavu, Es'kia Mphahlele, Ferdinand Oyono and Kofi Awoonor." *Pretexts: Studies in Writing and Culture* 8, no. 1 (1999): 17–34.

Lenta, Margaret. "Ethnicity and Hybridity: Noni Jabavu Writes against Apartheid." In *Literature of Region and Nation: Proceedings of the 6th International Literature of Region and Nation Conference, 2–7 August 1996*, ed. Winnifred M Bogaards. Saint John: Social Sciences and Humanities Research Council of Canada, with University of New Brunswick in Saint John, 1998, 300–11.

Jacobson, Dan(iel) (1929–)

A South African novelist and short-story writer, Jacobson was born in Johannesburg and began his career as a distinctly South African writer. His early fiction, set in recognizable South African locales, explored not only **apartheid**'s destruction of human lives but also its effects as it resonates in the human psyche, encouraging treachery, paranoia, and denial. His output in those early years was considerable: two novellas, *The Trap* (1955) and *A* ***Dance in the Sun*** (1956), both deal with the ways racism and treachery cripple and restrict the lives of whites, while displacing the powerlessness of blacks. *The Price of Diamonds* (1957), set in Kimberley, the city where Jacobson spent his boyhood, dramatizes events associated with illicit diamond smuggling. *A Long Way from London* (1958) is his first collection of stories, and *No Further West* (1959) is a collection *of* essays about his stay as a fellow at Stanford University. Throughout his career he has published short stories, essays, and critical articles.

Jacobson's first full-length novel, *The Evidence of Love* (1960), is also set partly in Kimberley. Much of the second half of the novel, about the love between a white woman and a "coloured" (mixed-race) man, is set in London. His impressions of London, partly developed in this novel, were more fully expressed in a second collection of essays titled *Time of Arrival* (1964). In 1966 he brought out his last South African novel, *The Beginners,* which follows the lives of two generations of South African Jews. The novel is set variously in South Africa, Israel, and Britain. Jacobson has also published an historical novel titled ***All for Love****: A Novel* (2005), which gives a fictionalized account of a royal scandal set in Vienna at the turn of the last century.

Although he abandoned South Africa after *The Beginners* as a locus for his work, the arid quality of some South African settings is still used his fiction, specifically in *The Confessions of Josef Baisz* (1977), where the characters and the action seem very recognizably South African although the country is named Sarmeda.

Jacobson continued to write essays, some about South African lives and some not. These were collected in *Time and Time Again* (1985). His literary-critical articles were collected in 1988 in *Adult Pleasures: Essays on Writers and Readers.* He returned to South African concerns in the novel *Hidden in the Heart* (1991), in which the protagonist, a man with a propensity for treachery, is an Afrikaner living in London. His ongoing interest in the country of his birth is expounded in *The Electronic Elephant* (1994), a diverse and entertaining account of his travels through southern Africa following the Great North Road into Zambia. Jacobson has also published a memoir about his search for information about his grandfather's life in pre–World War II Lithuania, titled *Heshel's Kingdom* (1997), and has translated Henk van Woerden's *The Assassin: A Story of Race and Rage in the Land of Apartheid* (2001).

Further Reading

Gready, Paul. "Dan Jacobson as Expatriate Writer: South Africa as Private Resource and Half-Code and the Literature of Multiple Exposure." *Research in African Literatures* 25, no. 4 (Winter 1994): 17–32.

Lansdown, Richard. "Weapons of Vicissitude: An Interview with Dan Jacobson." *The Critical Review* 34 (1994): 113–32.

Roberts, Sheila. "On the Doorstep of Africa: Dan Jacobson's *The Electronic Elephant*: A Southern African Journey." *Current Writing: Text and Reception in Southern Africa* 9, no. 1 (1997): 27–42.

———. "A Way of Seeing: Dan Jacobson's *Heshel's Kingdom*." *Current Writing: Text and Reception in Southern Africa* 10, no. 1 (1998): 57–73.

Johnson, Lemuel A. (1941–2002)

A poet, Johnson was born of Sierra Leonean parents in Nigeria and educated in Sierra Leone and in the United States. He was a professor of English at the University of Michigan, Ann Arbor, and also taught in his home country and in Mexico.

Johnson's is a poetic voice both of an individual and of a multitude in its focus on genealogy. Therein lies the strength of *The Sierra Leone Trilogy* (1995), which in its celebration of Johnson's Krio heritage takes us in successive stages back to the poet's youth and the early years of political independence in Africa in the 1960s (*Highlife for Caliban*, 1973); World War II and its legacies in the bodies and minds of West African soldiers such as Corporal Bundu (*Hand on the Navel*, 1978); and finally in *Carnival of the Old Coast* (1995), the centuries of trafficking in human bodies between Africa and the New World (with a few returns to Africa) and beyond that, to biblical times to give voice to "Our Lady of Silences," Hagar, who has a triangular relationship with Abraham and Sarah. The tone is funny, ironic, serious, and tragic in turns in this poetry that, though learned, maintains a fine ear for the rhythm of spoken words as heard in the streets of Freetown, Sierra Leone. Hybridity has never been celebrated with a fuller sense of history and a new cultural and human geography. "How to Breathe Dead Hippo Meat, and Live," the introduction to each volume of the trilogy, and Sylvia Wynter's afterword

to the first volume, "The Poetics and the Politics of *Highlife for Caliban*," provide a sure way to navigate through these poems. Johnson has also written numerous essays on African literature such as "The Dilemma of Presence in Black Diaspora Literature: A Comparativist Reading of Arnaldo Palacios' *Las estrellas son negras*," published in *Afro Hispanic Review* (2002); has written a book titled *Unambiguous Diaspora Slavery/ Ambiguous African Wonders: 11 Ways of Wondering about the Connection* (2000); and has published *Shakespeare in Africa (and Other Venues): Import and the Appropriation of Culture* (1998).

Jonker, Ingrid (1933–65)

A South African poet who wrote in Afrikaans, Jonker was born in the rural area of Douglas, Northern Cape, and educated at a girls' high school in Wynberg, where some of her earliest poetry appeared in the school magazine. She never attended a university.

By the age of sixteen Jonker was corresponding with the poet D. J. Opperman and publishing regularly in family magazines such as *Die Huisgenoot*. Her first book of poems, *Ontvlugting (Escape)* (1956), is characterized by images of death and the passing of childhood. Her second book, *Rook en Oker (Smoke and Ochre)* (1963), won the Afrikaanse Pers-Boekhandel Prize. She became one of the *Sestigers*, a group that included Breyten **Breytenbach**, André **Brink**, Adam Small, and Bartho Smit, and challenged conservative Afrikaans literary conventions. A collection of early poems and poems written at the end of her life, *Kantelson (Toppling Sun)* (1966) was published following her early death by drowning. Her *Versamelde Werke (Collected Works)* (1975, 1983, and 1994) includes her prose, drama, and interviews. Her poems were translated by Jack **Cope** and William **Plomer** and published as *Ingrid Jonker: Selected Poems* (1988), and the Ingrid Jonker

Prize for promising young poets in English and Afrikaans was instituted. At the opening of South Africa's first democratically elected parliament, President Nelson Mandela read "The Child Who Was Shot Dead by Soldiers in Nyanga," a translation of her prophetic poem "Die Kind."

Further Reading

Lytton, David. "Ingrid Jonker Comes to Stratford." *Contrast: South African Literary Journal* (Cape Town, South Africa) 15 (1967): 62–89.

Jordan, A(rchibald) C(ampbell) (1906–68)
South African novelist Jordan was born in Mbokothwana, Transkei, educated at the Lovedale Institution and at St. John's College, Umtata, and gained a PhD at Fort Hare University in 1956. As a result of political pressure, Jordan was forced to leave South Africa on an exit permit in 1961; he settled in the United States, where he was a professor of African languages and literature. *The Wrath of the Ancestors* (1980), Jordan's only novel, originally appeared in Xhosa as *Ingqumbo Yeminyanya* in 1940. His other work includes a collection of African folktales, published posthumously in 1973 as *Tales from Southern Africa,* and a critical study entitled *Towards an African Literature: The Emergence of Literary Form in Xhosa* (1972).

Further Reading

Kwetana, W.M. "A Reconsideration of the Plot Structure of A.C. Jordan's *Ingqumbo Yeminyanya.*" *South African Journal of African Languages/Suid Afrikaanse Tydskrif vir Afrikatale* 7, no. 3 (1987): 77–81.

Neethling, S.J. "On Translating A.C. Jordan's *Ingqumbo Yeminyanya* into Afrikaans." *South African Journal of African Languages/Suid Afrikaanse Tydskrif vir Afrikatale* 17, no. 1 (1997): 18–22.

Nyamende, M.A.B. "Who Really Cares If the Ancestors Are Angry? A.C. Jordan's *The Wrath of the Ancestors 'Ingqumbo Yeminyanya.'*" *South African Journal of African Languages/Suid Afrikaanse Tydskrif vir Afrikatale* 11, no. 4 (1991): 119–24.

Journey Within, The (1978)
A novel by I.N.C. **Aniebo.** It follows the lives of two married couples, set against one another as a good and bad example of a married relationship. Christian and Janet struggle because Janet mimics a European outlook on love and is disappointed by her philandering husband, while Nelson and Ejiaka succeed because they found their marriage on the Igbo expectation of patriarchy. The novel also focuses on the inner lives of the characters and uses the metaphor of the train to demonstrate the winding nature of life and the crossroads of past and present experience.

Joys of Motherhood, The (1979)
A novel by Buchi **Emecheta.** The ironic title of this work refers to the goal of its primary character—Nnu Ego—who fights poverty to give her children a good education that they repay her for with rejection and abandonment. Nnu leaves her village with her selfish husband in the 1930s to become part of the Lgos immigrant community. The background of Nnu's story is the changing landscape of colonial Nigeria, which is moving from a rural to an urban focus.

July's People (1981)
A novel by Nadine **Gordimer.** In this novel Gordimer imagines the violent downfall of the white majority in South Africa. Written before the peaceful transition to majority rule in the 1990s, the narrative explores the implications of revolt for a privileged white family. The Smales escape Johannesburg and take cover in their servant July's rural home, where they subsist thanks to July's family. The tensions that arise and the implications of the discovery of their hiding place makes the Smales's story one that points to the white minority's failure to realize the need for change.

K

Ka, Aminata Maiga (1940–)

Senegalese novelist writing in French. Born in Saint-Louis-du-Sénégal, Ka studied in Senegal, France, and the United States. After living in many countries in Africa, Europe, and North America, she returned to Dakar in 1976. Married to Senegalese author Abdou Anta Ka and mother of a large family, she works with the Ministry of National Education.

Ka began writing in the 1980s, following the deaths of her mother and of fellow writer and friend Mariama **Bâ.** Her first work, published in 1985, consists of two novellas: in *La Voie du Salut,* a promising magistrate is betrayed by the husband she saw as a partner in life and dies from the shock of the betrayal; in *Le Mirair de la vie,* a powerful minister's family is torn apart by opposing social and political visions, while its exploited servant girl commits suicide to defy the "dishonour" of an unjust imprisonment. The novel *En votre nom et au mien* (1989) explores the ramifications of the marriage of a young woman and a wealthy old man. Ka has also published a short story titled *Brisures de Vies (Fragments of Lives)* (1998), and critical material like her essay on "Ramatoulaye, Aissatou, Mireille et . . . Mariama Ba" in *Notre Librairie* (1985).

In all her work Ka emphasizes the victimization of women against the backdrop of a neo-colonial society, whether as high-placed noblewomen or as women whose sincere desire to establish partnerships with men is met with deceit and betrayal. Her tragic stories and incisive political vision assure her place in the tradition of African feminism and women's writing.

Kagame, Alexis (1912–81)

Rwandan philosopher and poet Kagame was born into a family close to the reigning dynasty in Rwanda. He was educated in a seminary and became a Catholic priest in 1941. He started collecting dynastic poetry very early thanks to his access to the royal court. He also translated these texts into French, and his linguistic and ethnographic work is the only written collection of dynastic texts in Rwanda. As a historian his approach was unusual, writing history primarily for his own people. He also wrote poetry in his own language, Kinyarwanda, and produced texts such as *Indyesha birayi,* 1949 (which can be read as a satirical poem of more than two thousand verses, praising pigs instead of cows, so much praised in oral poetry), and even translated some of his poems into French. His major poetic work is *La Divine pastorale* (1952), a long poem in twenty-four cantos, which remains unequalled in the genre of African Christian poetry.

In the 1950s as a professor of theology he produced a synthesis of his works in a thesis on *La philosophie bantu rwandaise de l'être* (1955), a daring attempt to merge Bantu worldviews and classic scholastic philosophy. He completed his poetic and philosophical work by combining history and poetry in his translations of the praise names of Rwandese *armées bovines* (1961). His enormous work has yet to be edited, but he stands as one of the founders of philosophical and religious reflection of African traditions as well as a master of contemporary Rwandese poetry.

Further Reading

Nsengimana, Joseph. *Alexis Kagame, l'homme, la bibliographie thématique et l'esquisse d'analyse de l'oeuvre littéraire.* Ruhengeri: Editions universitaires du Rwanda, 1987.

Nzabatsinda, Anthere. "The Aesthetics of Transcribing Orality in the Works of Alexis Kagame, Writer of Rwanda." *Research in African Literatures* 28, no. 1 (1997): 98–111.

Kahiga, Samuel (1946–)

Kenyan novelist and short-story writer Kahiga was born in the Central Province of

Kenya. He graduated in fine art and design from the University of Nairobi and later studied film production. He has worked as a television producer, a composer, and a contributor to Kenya's *East African Standard*.

At a time when other Kenyan writers were producing their major works of social commitment, Kahiga showed a preference for the personal side of life. *The Girl from Abroad* (1974) and *When the Stars Are Scattered* (1979) are love stories, unusual in African literature, though they also touch on social, cultural, moral, and religious issues. The short stories in *Flight to Juba* (1979) go a step further toward sheer entertainment, while *Lover in the Sky* (1975) has all the characteristics of popular fiction.

Kahiga's once singular interest in themes of universal relevance has made him a model for this kind of writing. His novel *Paradise Farm* (1993) explores humanity's capacity for suffering and compassion, but the seriousness of the subject is subverted to the extent that the book takes the form of a thriller. In an entirely different vein, *Dedan Kimathi: The Real Story* (1990) is a historical novel that offers a reassessment of the Mau Mau movement in Kenya and of one of its most outstanding and controversial personalities.

Further Reading

Simatei, Peter. "Versions and Inversions: Mau Mau in Kahiga's *Dedan Kimathi: The Real Story*." *Research in African Literatures* 30, no. 1 (Spring 1999): 154–61.

Karodia, Farida (1942–)

A novelist and short-story writer, Karodia was born in Aliwal North, South Africa, graduated from Coronationville Teacher Training College in 1961, and taught in Johannesburg and later in Zambia. When the government of South Africa withdrew her passport in 1968, she emigrated to Canada, where she supported herself with teaching and other jobs while studying and writing fiction and radio drama. She returned to South Africa in 1994.

Her first novel, **Daughters of Twilight** (1986), reflects her South African childhood and the limits on education and domicile for nonwhites under **apartheid**. Her collection of short stories, *Coming Home and Other Stories* (1988), shows her skill and versatility in depicting protagonists of various ethnic groups: a Boer girl, a black teacher, a "coloured" (mixed-race) mother, and a white employer. She has also written about Canada, and after a visit to India in 1991 she wrote and filmed *Midnight Embers*, released by Farida Films in 1992. Like Buchi **Emecheta** and Flora **Nwapa**, whose novels describe rape and massacre in the Nigeria-Biafra war, Karodia finds a unique fictional theme in Mozambique. *A Shattering of Silence* (1993) depicts the kidnapping and enslavement of children. *Other Secrets* (2000) tells the story of two sisters living in apartheid South Africa, who must deal with the reduction of opportunity because of racial discrimination, while Karodia's most recent novel *Boundaries* (2003) depicts the return of a woman to South Africa after a long residence in Canada. After her return from exile, Karodia produced a collection of long and short stories set in South Africa, *Against an African Sky and Other Stories* (1995).

Further Reading

Fainman-Frenkel, Ronit. "Ordinary Secrets and the Bounds of Memory: Traversing the Truth and Reconciliation Commission in Farida Karodia's *Other Secrets* and Beverley Naidoo's *Out of Bounds*." *Research in African Literatures* 35, no. 4 (2004): 52–65.

Singh, Jaspal. "Representing the Poetics of Resistance in Transnational South Asian Women's Fiction and Film." *South Asian Review* 24, no. 1 (2003): 202–19.

Versi, Anver. "Not at Home, at Home: Novelist Farida Karodia." *New African* 318 (1994): 39–40.

Karone, Yodi (1954–)

A novelist, Karone was born in France to a Cameroonian family in political exile and spent much of his youth in North Africa, where his father practiced medicine. He obtained university degrees in literature and economics. *Le Bal des caïmans* (1980) is set in Cameroon and based on an actual trial of a revolutionary leader and a bishop during Ahmadou Ahidjo's rule. Their two stories, told in parallel chapters, include descriptions of prison torture and of the politically inspired courtroom proceedings. A similar two-part structure is used in *Le Nègre de paille* (1982), which won the Grand Prix littéraire de l'Afrique noire, to describe the reality and the dream life of a man returning from imprisonment. The next novel, *La Recherche du cannibale amour* (1988), is set partly in Paris and describes the life of an artist. *Les Beaux Gosses* (1988), a story of criminality and corruption in Abidjan, is filled with details of brutal sex and sordid nightlife. Karone's taste for vivid descriptions of violent action shows the influence of one of his masters, Chester Himes, just as his surrealistic scenes show his debt to another acknowledged master, Boris Vian.

Further Reading

Magnier, Bernard. "Romanciers residant a Paris: Entretien avec Yodi Karone." *Notre Librairie: Revue du Livre: Afrique, Caraibes, Ocean Indien* 99 (1989): 197–99.

Sautman, Francesca Canade. "The Race for Globalization: Modernity, Resistance, and the Unspeakable in Three African Francophone Texts." *Yale French Studies* 103 (2003): 106–22.

Katiyo, Wilson (1947–2003)

Novelist and filmmaker Katiyo was born at Mutoko, Southern Rhodesia, now Zimbabwe, and educated at Fletcher High School. Following harassment by the police he completed his education in England. He returned to Zimbabwe at independence but now lives in France. His first novel, *A Son of the Soil* (1976), a narration about decolonization, uses the memories and experiences of the family of the protagonist, Alexio, to show the links between the initial armed resistance to settlers and the Zimbabwean liberation war. In the novel land takes on both political and spiritual dimensions. In the sequel, *Going to Heaven* (1979), the Rhodesian forces brutally murder Alexio's family, and he escapes to England with the help of a white couple. The presence in the narrative of whites who sympathize with the black struggle made the novel a relevant text for the policy of reconciliation that followed Zimbabwean independence. Katiyo gained a wide audience for his work when the national "O" level English examinations chose *A Son of the Soil* as a set text.

Further Reading

Galle, Etienne. "The Probable Young African Hero." *Commonwealth Essays and Studies* 15, no. 1 (1992): 29–35.

Kayira, Legson (ca. 1942–)

Malawian novelist. The facts of Kayira's early life are legendary: a Tumbuka born and educated in Nyasaland (now Malawi), as a young man he walked from there to Khartoum, Sudan, a distance of thirty-two hundred kilometres, to seek opportunities for further education. He was successful and studied in the United States and at Cambridge, England. His first book was the autobiographical *I Will Try* (1965). He has written four novels: The **Looming Shadow** (1968), *Jingala* (1969), *The Civil Servant* (1971), and *The Detainee* (1974).

Kayira's early work was nonpolitical, as he described life in rural Malawi. The tone of the first two novels begins to shift, however, with *The Civil Servant,* in which he deals with social issues such as the export of labor to South Africa. In *The Detainee,* written after a visit to Malawi at the height of the Banda era, he turns to satire. Old Jingala, the hero of the novel of that name, provides a comic portrait of a man whose stopped watch poignantly symbolizes the passing of a whole way of life before the encroachments of central government and party politics.

Further Reading

Henry, Margaret. "Legson Kayira Interviewed." *Cultural Events in Africa* (Cambridgeshire, England) 41 (1968): 1–3.

Jackson, Thomas H. "Legson Kayira and the Uses of the Grotesque." *World Literature Written in English* 22, no. 2 (1983): 143–51.

Kente, Gibson (1932–2004)

A South African composer-arranger and playwright, Kente was born in the Eastern Cape. He revolutionized urban African popular theater through the 1960s.

As a director for Union Artists, Dorkay House, Kente learned the craft of musical theater, producing *Manana, The Jazz Prophet* (1963) and *Sikalo* (1966), a musical that blended African gospel and township jazz. In these plays Kente concentrated on social and communal rather than political issues. In 1967 he formed a company and presented *Life* (1968) and *Zwi* (1970). By 1974 he had three traveling theater companies without state subsidy. Low admission prices and an eclectic and accessible style of theater contributed to his success. From 1973 Kente was greatly influenced by the **Black Consciousness** movement. He was caught between the public's increasing demand for political expression and the authorities' threat of shutting him down. He produced *How Long, I Believe* and *Too Late* (1974–76), political melodramas attacking **apartheid**.

Following his detention and release (1976–77) for attempting to film *How Long,* Kente's work varied from pure entertainment in *Can You Take It?* (1977), a Broadway-style township love story, to *La Duma (It Thundered)* (1978) and *Mama and the Load* (1980), dramatiza-

tions of the conflict between political pressures and family/community solidarity. Some of Kente's plays are gathered together in *South African People's Plays: ons phola hi* (plays by Gibson Kente, Credo V. Mutwa, Mthuli Shezi, and Workshop '71), selected with introductory material by Robert Mshengu Kavanagh (1981). Kente influenced playwrights such as Mbongeni **Ngema**, Matsemela **Manaka**, and Maishe Maponya by creating a form that reflects black experience.

Further Reading

Mshengu. "Gibson Kente '74." *S' ketsh'* (Summer 1974–75): 24–25.

Sebume, Leslie. "Their Love, Their Hate: That's His Life." *Bona* (June 1980): 54–60, 62.

Tshabangu, Mango. "Lifa." *S' ketsh'* (Summer 1972): 12–13.

Kgositsile, Keorapetse (1938–)

A South African poet, Kgositsile trained as a journalist but taught for many years at the University of Dar es Salaam, the University of Nairobi, and the University of Gaborone. He spent most of the 1960s in political exile all over the world, including the United States, where he was in intellectual contact with Es'kia **Mphahlele**, Dennis **Brutus**, both Daniel P. and Mazisi **Kunene**, and others. In the 1970s, he entered the writing program of Columbia University in New York, where he worked for *Black Dialogue* magazine. In 1985, he left Botswana for a long exile when South Africa invaded his host country. His works include *Spirits Unchained* (1969), *For Melba* (1970), *My Name Is Afrika* (1971), *The Present Is a Dangerous Place to Live* (1974), *Places and Bloodstains* (1975), *The Word Is Here* (1980), and *When the Clouds Clear* (1990). A volume of his collected poems, titled *Heartprints* (1980), was published in Germany. He has also published the collected poems *If I Could Sing: Selected Poems* (2002) and *This Way I Salute You: Selected Poems* (2004). He lives in South Africa.

Further Reading

Povey, John F. "Three South African Poets (Brutus, Kgositsile, Mtshali)." *World Literature Written in English* 16 (1977): 263–80.

Rowell, Charles H. "'With Bloodstains to Testify': An Interview with Keorapetse Kgositsile." *Callaloo: A Journal of African American and African Arts and Letters* 2 (1978): 23–42.

Kibera, Leonard (1942–83)

Kenyan novelist and short-story writer Kibera was born at Kibete, Kenya, attended high school at Embu, and studied at the University of California and at Stanford University. He taught at the University of Zambia and at Kenyatta University, Kenya, from 1976 until his death. His first publication was a book of short stories, *Potent Ash* (1968), which he wrote with his brother, Samuel **Kahiga**. The book explores the guilt, betrayal, and failure of the Mau Mau. Several of the stories have been anthologized, especially "The Spider's Web," which points an accusing finger at Kenya's elite for the state of Kenya since independence. His only novel, *Voices in the Dark* (1970), uses dark humor to question why most of the Mau Mau soldiers who fought for independence were forgotten and left to beg and die along the roadside. Kibera has also written several articles of criticism.

Further Reading

Indangasi, Henry. "Fanonist Overtones or Voices in the Dark? A Criticism of *Voices in the Dark* by Leonard Kibera." *Joliso: East African Journal of Literature and Society* (Nairobi, Kenya) 1, no. 1 (1973): 61–66.

Mamudu, Ayo. "Literary Criticism and Theory in the African Novel: Chinua Achebe, Leonard Kibera and Ali Mazrui." *MAWA Review* 7, no. 2 (1992): 71–81.

Kimenye, Barbara (1930–)

Ugandan children's writer and short-story writer. Born in England, Barbara Kimenye studied in a convent in Yorkshire and trained as a nurse in London. On going to East Africa, she changed her profession to journalism and started writing fiction.

Kimenye is best known as a writer of children's adventure stories. Her first publications in this genre were *The Smugglers* (1966), and *Moses* (1967), the first of a series about the escapades of a Kenyan schoolboy named Moses. *The Gemstone Affair* (1978) and *The Scoop* (1978) are addressed to older children. Other titles include *Beauty Queen* (1997), and *Prettyboy, Beware* (1997), as well as *The Modern African Vegetable Cookbook* (1997).

Kimenye's two collections of short stories, *Kalasanda* (1965) and *Kalasanda Revisited* (1966), which contain humorous glimpses of life in a Buganda village, were criticized by F. B. Welbourn for exhibiting a "kizungu [European] imagination," but they have remained popular and are regularly reprinted. One of the stories, "The Battle of the Sacred Tree," has recently been made into a feature film.

Further Reading

Schmidt, Nancy J. "The Writer as Teacher: A Comparison of the African Adventure Stories of G. A. Henty, Rene Guillot, and Barbara Kimenye." *African Studies Review* 19, no. 2 (1976): 69–80.

Konadu, (Samuel) Asare (1932–94)

Ghanaian novelist Konadu was born in Asamang in the Ashanti Region of Ghana and attended local schools and Abuakwa State College in eastern Ghana. He worked as a reporter and for radio before joining the Ghana Information Service in 1951 and later studied journalism in Europe on a Ghana government scholarship. Among the first generation of writers who stormed the Ghanaian market with their own brand of **popular literature** known in neighboring Nigeria as Onitsha market literature, Konadu wrote about life in rural Ghana. The title of his first novel, *The Wizard of Asamang* (1964), reveals his interest in traditional values and his obsession with superstition. A number of popular novels followed, including *Come Back Dora!* (1966), *Shadow of Wealth* (1966), *Night Watchers of Korlebu* (1967), *A Woman in Her Prime* (1967), *Ordained by the Oracle* (1969), and *The Coup Makers* (1994), often incorporating details of the traditional customs and practices of the Akan people of Ghana. He also published popular fiction under the pseudonym Kwabena Asare Bediako, most notably *Don't Leave Me Mercy* (1966) and *A Husband for Esi Ellua* (1967).

Further Reading

Grant, Stephen H. "Publisher for the Many." *Africa Report* 17, no. 1 (1972): 26–27.

Newall, Stephanie. "Making up Their Own Minds: Readers, Interpretations and the Differences of View in Ghanaian Popular Narratives." *Africa: Journal of the International African Institute/ Revue de l'Institut Africain International* 67, no. 3 (1997): 389–405.

Kongi's Harvest (1965)

A play by Wole **Soyinka**. The play portrays the regime of the dictator Kongi, and the attempts of the traditional chief Danlola, his heir Daodu, and the nightclub hostess Sigi to contest that regime. This narrative is a parody of the neo-colonial one-party state in Nigeria, and the play deals with the political and social chaos leading up to the Nigeria-Biafra war. In the 1970 film version Soyinka plays the role of Kongi.

Kourouma, Ahmadou (1927–2003)

A Côte d'Ivoirean novelist, Kourouma was born in Ivory Coast (now Côte d'Ivoire), expelled from secondary school for leading a student strike and inducted in the *tirailleurs* in 1945. Refusing to suppress a mutiny he was sent to Indochina where he became a broadcaster for the French military radio network.

After leaving the army, he studied engineering and became an actuary for insurance companies. He worked briefly in Ivory Coast at the beginning of the 1960s, then in Algeria. Publishers in Paris turned down his first novel, *Les Soleils des indépendances,* in 1964. The Africanized French and the criticism of the new regimes sounded reactionary at the time. It was published in Montreal in 1968 following an award from the journal *Etudes françaises.* Unfortunately the English translation *The Suns of Independence* (1981) is unable to convey the quality of the original. The novel was published in Paris in 1970 and got some scholarly attention for the linguistic creativity in Kourouma's Malinke syntax and the lack of neological restraint. In 1970 Ahmadou Kourouma went back to the Ivory Coast and his play *Tougnantigui, le diseur de vérité* (1973) was not well received by the authorities. Unable to find a job, Kourouma went into exile and became head of the African Insurance School in Yaoundé, Cameroon. In the 1980s he became head of the Reinsurance Company of the Franc Zone, a major economic position qualifying him as one of the leading experts of the insurance business in Africa. His second novel, *Monnè, outrages et défis* (1990), is an epic of "collaboration" over a century of colonial rule and was translated into English as *Monnew: A Novel* by Nidra Poller (1993). His third novel, *En attendant le vote des bêtes sauvages* (1998; translated into English as *Waiting for the Vote of the Wild Animals,* 2001) was shortlisted for literary prizes in France and is the result of his observations of tyranny in Togo, where he lived for several years. His fourth novel was *Allah n'est pas obligé: roman* (2000) and was translated into English as *Allah Is Not Obliged* (2005).

Further Reading

Coates, Carrol F., ed. "Ahmadou Kourouma: Fiction Writer." *Callaloo: A Journal of African American and African Arts and Letters* 23, no. 4 (2000): 1329–66.

Corcoran, Patrick. "'Child' Soldiers in Ken Saro Wiwa's 'Sozaboy' and Ahmadou Kourouma's

'Allah n'est pas oblige.'" *Mots Pluriels et Grands Themes de Notre Temps* 22 (2002).

Doquire-Kerszberg, Annik. "Kourouma 2000: Humour oblige!" *Presence Francophone: Revue Internationale de Langue et de Litterature* 59 (2002): 110–25, 188.

Gray, Stephen. "Ahmadou Kourouma." *Research in African Literatures* 32, no. 1 (2001): 122–23.

Lopez-Heredia, Goretti, and Antonia Diaz, trans. "African Literature in Colonial Languages: Challenges Posed by 'Minor Literatures' for the Theory and Practice of Translation." In *Less Translated Languages,* ed. Albert Branchadell and Lovell Margaret West. Amsterdam: Benjamins, 2004, 165–76.

Ouedraogo, Jean. "Ahmadou Kourouma and Ivoirian Crises." *Research in African Literatures* 35, no. 3 (2004): 1–5.

Waberi, Abdourahman A. "Colossal Kourouma." *Notre Librairie: Revue des Litteratures du Sud* 155–56 (2004): 212–15.

Kunene, Daniel P. (1923–)

South African critic and poet. Born at Edenville in the Orange Free State, Kunene took his bachelor's at the University of South Africa and both his master's and PhD at the University of Cape Town, where he lectured in the department of Bantu languages until 1964, when he left South Africa permanently. In 1976, he became professor of African languages and literature at the University of Wisconsin-Madison. His research focuses on Sesotho literature, especially on Thomas **Mofolo**, whose *Chaka* he translated, and on developing a new methodology for the study of African-language literatures. His scholarly works include *The Works of Thomas Mofolo: Summaries and Critiques* (1967) and *Thomas Mofolo and the Emergence of Written Sesotho Prose* (1989). His creative writings comprise two collections of poetry, *Pirates Have Become Our Kings* (1978) and *A Seed Must Seem to Die* (1981), and a collection of stories entitled *From the Pit of Hell to the Spring of Life* (1986). In *A Seed Must Seem to Die,* born in the aftermath of the Soweto uprising of 1976, the poet mourns the loss of childhood and the deaths of children, but finally suggests that the "seed that must seem to die"—the dead of Soweto—will reappear "Sprouting/Rising/Living!" in celebration of coming liberation. The stories evoke the South Africa of **apartheid** and reveal the resourcefulness with which blacks oppose white control. Kunene has also published an article on "African-Language Literatures of Southern Africa" in *The Cambridge History of African and Caribbean Literature* (2003), and "Speaking the Act: The Ideophone as a Linguistic Rebel" in *Ideophones* (2001, edited by Christa Kilian Hatz). Kunene was also a co-editor for the book *Tongue and Mother Tongue: African Literature and the Perpetual Quest for Identity* with Pamela J. Olubunmi Smith (2002).

Kunene, Mazisi (KaMdabuli) (1930–)

South African poet Kunene was born in Durban and educated at the University of Natal. He left South Africa in 1959 to pursue studies in England. Politically active in the African National Congress and South African National Front, he lived in Lesotho and taught at what is now the National University. He was later a professor of African literature and languages at the University of California, Los Angeles, and in 1993 he returned to South Africa to assume a similar position at the University of Natal, Durban.

Kunene collected and translated his early poetry into English for *Zulu Poems* (1970). Evolving from traditional Zulu literature, the poems reflect the importance of his social and cultural inheritance. With the publication of *Emperor Shaka the Great* (1979), an epic poem inspired by the rise of the Zulu empire, followed by *Anthem of the Decades* (1981), a Zulu epic dedicated to the women of Africa, Kunene earned critical as well as popular recognition. His reputation was further enhanced by the poems collected in *The Ancestors and the Sacred Mountain* (1982). His most recent publications are *Isibusiso sikamhawu* (1994), *Indiba yamancasakazi* (1995), and *Umzwilili wama-Africa* (1996), and he has also contributed critically, with articles such as "Some Aspects of South African Literature" in *World Literature Today: A Literary Quarterly of the University of Oklahoma* (1996). Kunene is a major voice in African literature and an author of international reputation.

Further Reading

Maduka, Chidi. "Poetry, Humanism and Apartheid: A Study of Mazisi Kunene's *Zulu Poems*." *ACLALS (Association for Commonwealth Literature and Language Studies) Bulletin* 7, no. 2 (1985): 11–26.

Masilela, Ntongela. "The Return of Mazisi Kunene to South Africa: The End of an Intellectual Chapter in Our Literary History." *Ufahamu: Journal of the African Activist Association* 21, no. 3 (1993): 7–15.

Reddy, Vasu. "The Writer as Philosopher: Interview with Mazisi Kunene." *South African Journal of African Languages/Suid Afrikaanse Tydskrif vir Afrikatale* 16, no. 4 (1996): 141–44.

Kurunmi (1969)

A play by Ola **Rotimi**. This play is part of a trilogy that also includes *The **Gods Are Not to Blame*** (1968) and *Ovonramenme Nogbaise* (1971). *Kurunmi* portrays an 1858 war between the Yoruba communities of Iyaye and Oyo. This backdrop allows Rotimi to explore the limitations and required characteristics for good leadership. The third play, *Ovonramenme Nogbaise,* follows the British expedition of 1898 led by Sir Ralph Moore against the Kingdom of Benin.

Kuzwayo, Ellen (1914–2006)

A South African autobiographer and short-story writer, Kuzwayo grew up on the farm of her maternal grandparents near Thaba'Nchu in the Orange Free State. After her secondary schooling at Mariannhill in Natal, she went to Adams College in Durban and Lovedale in the Eastern Cape for teacher training. After the publication of her autobiography ***Call Me Woman*** (1985), with its story of community activism and dedication to improving women's lives, she became a spokesperson and role model for black women. Her larger narrative is of the struggle of black women not only to survive but also to break free from traditionally ascribed roles and pursue their own life choices. She places on record the achievements of women who have forged their own paths and rendered valuable service to their communities. *Sit Down and Listen* (1990) is a collection of stories in which Kuzwayo assumes the role of the oral storyteller in order to keep a cultural heritage alive that is in danger of dying out. Several stories demonstrate the value of traditional customs and attitudes, while others examine the plight of women caught between the old and the new or struggling to survive in the city. Kuzwayo has also published *African Wisdom: A Personal Collection of Setswana Proverbs* (1998).

Further Reading

Elder, Arlene A. "'. . . Who Can Take the Multitude and Lock It in a Cage?': Noemia de Sousa, Micere Mugo, Ellen Kuzwayo: Three African Women's Voices of Resistance." *Matatu: Journal for African Culture and Society* 3, no. 6 (1989): 77–100.

Garritano, Carmela J. "At an Intersection of Humanism and Postmodernism: A Feminist Reading of Ellen Kuzwayo's *Call Me Woman*." *Research in African Literatures* 28, no. 2 (1997): 57–65.

Gqola, Pumla Dineo. "Reconsidering Motherhood in the Autobiographies of Ellen Kuzwayo and Emma Mashinini." *Inter Action* 4 (1996): 47–52.

L

La Guma, Alex(ander) (1925–85)

A South African short-story writer and novelist, La Guma was born in District Six, Cape Town, and graduated in 1945 from the Cape Technical College. At the time he was an active member of the Plant Workers Union of the Metal Box Company and was dismissed after organizing a strike for higher wages. He became politically active as a result of his dismissal, joining the Young Communist League in 1947 and the South African Communist Party in 1948. Employed by *New Age* as a reporter in 1955, he began to write short stories critical of the government's policy of racial discrimination.

La Guma's strength is in the short story form. His curiosity about the poverty, despair, oppression, and hopes of humanity combines with a deep concern about the people's suffering and affliction that inhabits the minutest detail of the fictional environment. His first short story, "Nocturne" (1957), reveals his ability to capture atmosphere, speech, and surface meaning. The straightforward narrative of a young man who plans a robbery but is disturbed by classical music streaming in from outside blends event, scene, effective inner dialogue, and moral aim, to make a point about social environment, status, transcendence, and South Africa's racism. La Guma saw his task, in a way, as similar to an African storyteller's, namely to record events as told to him and fashion a narrative both moral and entertaining. An example is the short story "Coffee for the Road" (1965), which reminds the reader that a social practice such as racial discrimination is effective only insofar as it is willingly supported by those victimized by it. The Indian woman who is the protagonist represents the quintessential South African resister, for whom *no* is not a word but a form of action.

In addition to many short stories, La Guma's novels include *A **Walk in the Night*** (1962), *And a Threefold Cord* (1964), *The **Stone Country*** (1967), ***In the Fog of the Season's End*** (1972), and ***Time of the Butcherbird*** (1979). At the time of his death, he was writing another novel, "Zone of Fire." Each novel focuses on something specific, beginning with the social, economic, and political circumstances of the "coloured" (mixed-race) community in *A Walk in the Night*. *And a Threefold Cord* examines the poverty, misery, and loneliness of slum existence that engenders inertia and resignation, while *The Stone Country* portrays humanity imprisoned. *In the Fog of the Season's End* demonstrates the determination to overthrow the state nurtured by that imprisonment. *Time of the Butcherbird* reflects his conviction that only conscious resistance will rid South Africa of the scourge of racism and oppression. "Zone of Fire" imagines the final phase of the protracted struggle for a democratic South Africa.

He also wrote a travel book, *A Soviet Journey* (1978), and a biography of his father, *Jimmy La Guma* (1997). His early journalistic writings and cartoons have been collected in *Liberation Chabalala: The World of Alex La Guma,* edited by Andre Odendaal and Roger Field (1993). Also collected in 1993 were adaptations of La Guma and others' stories in *Deep Cuts: Graphic Adaptations of Stories,* edited by Peter Thuynsma (1993). Cecil Abrahams edited yet another anthology of La Guma's work titled *Memories of Home: The Writings of Alex La Guma* (1991).

Further Reading

Agho, Jude. "Scatology, Form and Meaning in the Novels of Alex La Guma and Biyi Bandele-Thomas." *Neohelicon: Acta Comparationis Litterarum Universarum* 30, no. 2 (2003): 195–208.

Cornwell, Gareth. "*And a Threefold Cord*: La Guma's Neglected Masterpiece?" *Literator: Tydskrif* vir Besondere en Vergelykende Taal en Literatu-urstudie/Journal of Literary Criticism, Comparative Linguistics and Literary Studies 23, no. 3 (2002): 63–80.

Gray, Rosemary. "The Music under the Stone: A Reading of Alex La Guma's The Stone Country." *Commonwealth Essays and Studies* 23, no. 2 (2001): 47–53.

Kane, Baydallaye. "From the Tick to the Brontosaurus: Animal Imagery in Alex La Guma's Novels." *Commonwealth Essays and Studies* 25, no. 2 (2003): 33–44.

Pointer, Fritz. *A Passion to Liberate: La Guma's South Africa—Images of District Six.* Trenton, NJ: Africa World Press, 2001.

Yousaf, Nahem. *Alex La Guma: Politics and Resistance.* Portsmouth, NH: Heinemann, 2001.

Labyrinths (1971)

Poems by Christopher **Okigbo**. The companion volume to *Path of Thunder,* these poems are unoptimistic of the potential for an independent Nigeria. Okigbo explores how the public and the private intertwine, and how corruption and tribalism undermine personal honesty.

Ladipo, Duro (1931–78)

Nigerian dramatist Ladipo came into prominence as a composer of Yoruba folk opera when he wrote a cantata for the 1961 Christmas season that incorporated such traditional instruments as the *bata* drum. It attracted the attention of the German promoter of Nigerian cultures, Ulli Beier, with whose encouragement and guidance he developed a distinctive and highly successful folk opera style. Ladipo found his materials in Yoruba history, and strove for fidelity to Yoruba traditional practice. As a base for his operations he founded the Mbari Mbayo Club at Oshogbo in 1962, to inaugurate which he premiered *Oba M'Oro (Ghost-catcher King).* His most popular achievement by far, however, was *Oba Ko So (The King Did Not Hang),* with which he marked the club's first anniversary, following a year later with *Oba W'Aja (The King Is Dead)* (both published in *Three Yoruba Plays,* 1964). He collaborated with Ulli Beier on several adaptations, which they published using the pseudonym Obotunde Ijimere.

Further Reading

Banha, Martin. "Notes on Eda: A Nigerian Everyman." *Leeds Studies in English* 29 (1998): 49–53.

Hutchison, Yvette. "The Seductive Dance between History and Literature: The Moremi Legend by Historian Samuel Johnson and Playwrights Duro Ladipo and Femi Osofisan." *South African Theatre Journal* 13, nos. 1–2 [Bayreuth African Studies 50] (2000): 31–47.

Ogundeji, Philip A. "Classification and Some Literary Aspects of Duro Ladipo's Plays." *Research in Yoruba Language and Literature* 1 (1991): 20–28.

Ogundeji, Philip Adeodotun. "The Image of Sango in Duro Ladipo's Plays." *Research in African Literatures* 29, no. 2 (1998): 57–75.

Laing, B(ernard) Kojo (1946–)

Ghanaian novelist and poet Laing was born in Kumasi, the capital of the Ashanti Region of Ghana, and gained a master's degree at Glasgow University in 1968. He is the writer of three novels and one volume of poetry.

Search Sweet Country (1986), his first novel, is set in the Ghana of the 1970s and focuses on, among other things, the inability of Ghanaian intellectuals to envision a future for Ghana beyond the corrupt and inept dictatorship of Kutu Acheampong. Laing draws freely from both traditional orature and contemporary world literature to represent his idea of the infinite complexity of perspectives. The second novel, *Woman of the Aeroplanes* (1988), and the third, *Major Gentl and the Achimota Wars* (1992), are also critical of the power-seekers who corrupt all efforts at human progress. *Woman of the Aeroplanes* is a sequel to *Search Sweet Country,* blending the real and the supernatural in an international setting. *Major Gentl and the Achimota Wars* is the partly surreal account of the Wars of Existence, which take place in the year 2020 between Major Gentl of Africa and Torro the Terrible, a hybrid of Europe and Africa. Laing's linguistically innovative poetry is collected in *Godhorse* (1989).

Further Reading

Cooper, Brenda. "Landscapes, Forests and Borders within the West African Global Village." In *Mapping the Sacred: Religion, Geography and Postcolonial Literatures,* ed. Jamie S. Scott and Paul Simpson Housley. Amsterdam: Rodopi, 2001, 275–93.

Lim, Michael. "Written Communities: Ghana and the Fiction of Kojo Laing." *New Literatures Review* 28–29 (1994–95): 46–54.

Maja-Pearce, Adewale. "Interview with Kojo Laing." *Wasafiri: Journal of Caribbean, African, Asian and Associated Literatures and Film* 6–7 (1987): 27–29.

Ngaboh Smart, Francis. *Beyond Empire and Nation: Postnational Arguments in the Fiction of Nuruddin Farah and B. Kojo Laing.* Amsterdam: Rodopi, 2004.

Lament for an African Pol (1985)

A novel by Mongo **Beti**, translated from the French (*Ruine presque cocasse d'un polichinelle,* 1979). Less realist than his previous work, *Remember Ruben* (1974), *Lament for an African Pol* continues the story of two of the characters from *Remember Ruben.* The characters embark on an imaginary journey to a village ruled by a corrupt chief who relies on white missionaries. The message of the imagined journey posits the necessity of revolution to undermine neo-colonialism. A rightful heir replaces the chief, the whites lose their control, and the whole society participates in a revolt that utilizes science and technology.

Landlocked (1965)

Doris **Lessing**'s fourth and final novel of her *Children of Violence* series. In an African post–World War II British colony, Martha Quest becomes disillusioned with the rate of social change and with the Communist group she belongs to. She forms a relationship with a Jewish refugee from Europe, but his anger leads him into self-destruction and away from Martha. She then goes to England, where the novel follows her through a number of sexual, social, and political life experiences. Lessing's major focus is the violent effect of an era of war on her characters.

Langbodo (1979)

Play by Wale **Ogunyemi.** This successful play relies on a large cast to combine dialogue, music, and dance to tell the story of Yoruba writer D. O. **Fagunwa**'s novel, translated by Wole **Soyinka** as *Forest of a Thousand Daemons* (1968). The play uses fantasy to negatively depict the contemporary Nigerian state.

Last Harmattan of Alusine Dunbar, The (1990)

Syl **Cheney-Coker**'s first novel and winner of a Commonwealth Writers Prize. Cheney-Coker's magic-realist narrative follows the fictional West African village of Malagueta as it fights against colonialism from generation to generation. The magician Alusine Dunbar predicted this struggle, and his spirit appears throughout the novel to encourage the Malaguetans. Characters from the town include Sebastian and Jeanette Cromantine, who escaped slavery in North America at the end of the eighteenth century to found Malagueta, the town's military leader Thomas Bookerman, and a woman named Isatu, who returns to Malagueta in hopes of reversing her sterility.

Lessing, Doris (1919–)

A novelist and short-story writer, Lessing was born in Persia but moved with her parents in 1925 to the English colony of Rhodesia (now Zimbabwe), where her father had a farm in Banket, northwest of the capital of Salisbury (now Harare). After moving to Salisbury in

1938, Lessing became involved in the radical political opposition to the racial "colour bar" in the colony and eventually left for London in 1949 with the manuscript of her first novel *The Grass Is Singing* (1950). In her first novel and her early short stories, collected in *African Stories* (1964), Lessing deals with the political and racial problems of colonialism. She also displays a great feeling for the loneliness, failure, and madness of colonial families. In *The Grass Is Singing,* an English couple descend into physical and mental illness as their farm fails, and the wife's erratic treatment of her African "houseboy," alternating abuse with dependence, sets the stage for her murder.

Lessing's major work of African fiction is the series of novels *The Children of Violence,* which appeared in the 1950s and 1960s and traces the development of a rebellious young English colonial woman named Martha Quest, whose life parallels Lessing's. Through the course of several rebellions, beginning in opposition to her mother, Martha Quest ends up in a series of traps and escapes that Lessing treats realistically yet ironically (**Martha Quest**, 1952). Successfully merging personal and political narratives, Lessing traces Martha Quest's progress through a brief loveless marriage to a colonial civil servant (*A **Proper Marriage,*** 1954), a tortured affair with the authoritarian head of a small Communist group (*A **Ripple from the Storm,*** 1958), and a passionate love affair with a Jewish refugee from Poland who is so haunted by the war that he drives himself to destruction (**Landlocked**, 1965). With her naive idealism spent, Martha leaves for London after the war with little hope for an end to white colonial domination.

In her major feminist novel *The Golden Notebook* (1962), Lessing compresses part of the Martha Quest story. The protagonist, Anna Wulf, is an English writer who had earlier lived in an African colony, shared some of the experience of Communism, and written a novel about colonial relationships between blacks and whites. The character of Martha Quest returns in the apocalyptic novel *The Four Gated City* (1969), which ends with massive nerve gas leaks that decimate western Europe and North America and bring about the end of Martha Quest's world.

Though Lessing has gone on to explore madness, science fiction, and political terrorism in more recent novels, her major themes of personal, social, and political disintegration clearly began in her powerful African fiction. Some of Lessing's more recent works include *Mara and Dann: An Adventure* (1999), **Ben, in the World** (2000), *The Sweetest Dream* (2001), *On Cats* (2002), *The Grandmothers* (2003), *Time Bites: News and Reviews* (2004), and *The Story of General Dann and Mara's Daughter, Griot and the Snow Dog* (2005). Lessing's works have also been collected in critical editions like *A Home for the Highland Cattle and, The Antheap,* edited by Jean Pickering (2003).

Further Reading

Crater, Theresa L. "Temporal Temptations in Lessing's *Mara and Dann*: Arriving at the Present Moment." *Journal of Evolutionary Psychology* 25, nos. 3–4 (2004): 190–95.

Majumdar, Nivedita. "The Politics of Authenticity: A Reading of *The Golden Notebook*." *Doris Lessing Studies* 22, no. 2 (2002): 1, 4–8.

Tayeb, Lamia. "Martha's Odyssey: The Motif of the Journey in Doris Lessing's *The Children of Violence*." *Jouvert: A Journal of Postcolonial Studies* 7, no. 2 (2003): 40 paragraphs.

Waterman, David. "Group Allegiance and Coerced Identity: Doris Lessing's The Sentimental Agents in the Volyen Empire." *British and American Studies/Revista de Studii Britanice si Americane* 10 (2004): 61–74.

Letters to Martha (1968)

Dennis **Brutus**'s second volume of poetry. Brutus wrote these poems while he was imprisoned on Robben Island. They vividly portray the prison experience, including fear of torture, solidarity among the prisoners and the wardens, solitary confinement, and the sense of loss that results from a lack of everyday contact with the outside world and loved ones. The title of the work refers to the censorship laws that banned him from publishing anything the authorities deemed seditious, and the poems are obviously not letters but random poems outlining his prison experience.

Life & Times of Michael K (1983)

Booker Prize-winning novel by J. M. **Coetzee**. Michael K is a harelipped gardener who travels with his dying mother to Cape Town in an attempt to fulfill her wish to return there before she dies. His mother dies before arrival, and Michael K buries her ashes on an abandoned farm, digs himself an abode, and grows pumpkins. He is forced into a military camp under the suspicion of providing food for guerilla warriors, and at the camp he refuses sustenance despite the medical officer's efforts. Another section of the novel provides the medical officer's point of view, and he attempts to tell Michael K's story for him. Michael K escapes the camp, and makes Coetzee's allegorical message of escape from history, time, and the influence of others' ideals apparent.

Likimani, Muthoni (ca. 1940–)

Novelist and poet Likimani was born and brought up at Kahuhia Mission, Marang'a District, Kenya, and is the daughter of Levi Gachanja, one of the first ministers of the Kenyan Anglican church. She has worked as a teacher, a nutritionist, a social worker, a broadcaster, and a journalist. She lives in Nairobi, where she owns an advertising and promotion business.

Likimani is the author of the novels *They Shall Be Chastised* (1974) and *Passbook Number F.47927: Women and Mau Mau in Kenya* (1985), the narrative poem *What Does a Man Want?* (1974), a Swahili storybook about children in Kenya called *Shangazi na Watoto*, and *Women of Kenya: 27 Years of Development* (1991). She has written nonfiction on the subject of women in Kenya, and she has represented Kenya at several conferences, including the United Nations Decade for Women Conference in 1985. In 1994 she received the National Council of Women of Kenya (NCWK) award in recognition of exemplary service to women's advancement in Kenya.

Likimani regards *Passbook Number F.47927*, the latter her own identity number during the Mau Mau struggle, as her most important work. The novel, which focuses on the crucial role played by Kenyan women in the Mau Mau insurgency, is a series of self-contained episodes that deal with such injustices as the lack of personal liberty for both men and women forced under penalty of incarceration to carry a passbook, the forced-labor gangs of women used for road building and trench digging, the oppressive detention camps, and the displacement of peasants from their land. *They Shall Be Chastised* deals with the early missionary schools and highlights the problems faced by the indigenous peoples caught between two very different cultures. *What Does a Man Want?* is a satirical view of the contradictions of married life in an African context, including a husband's infidelities, domestic violence, polygamy, prostitution, and the generation gap.

Limits (1962)

Poems by Christopher Okigbo. This volume of poetry is broken into two parts. The first part seeks a poetic identity and voice, while the second part delineates the effects of colonial rule on Africa. A major theme that continues on from Okigbo's first collection, **Heavensgate**, is the attempt to reconcile traditional and Christian beliefs.

Lion and the Jewel, The (1963)

Wole **Soyinka**'s earliest published full-length play. It comically satirizes a schoolmaster,

Lakunle, who values all things Western. He aims to modernize the village of Ilujinle, while the old chief, Baroka, represents the traditional point of view. The two also compete for the love of the beautiful Sidi.

Lipenga, Ken (1954–)

Malawian short-story writer Lipenga was born in the Mulanje district of southern Malawi and educated at Nazombe Primary and Mulanje Secondary Schools, the University of Malawi (BA), the University of Leeds (MA), and the University of New Brunswick, Canada (PhD). He taught at the University of Malawi and later became editor of Malawi's *Daily Times,* the national newspaper. His short-story collection *Waiting for a Turn* (1981) was praised for its accomplished style, humor, and lively intelligence. The title story pressed his comic style into service against the Banda regime: a potential suicide who plans to throw himself off Malawi's highest mountain finds a crowd already waiting with the same idea.

Further Reading

Chimombo, Steve. "'Shreds and Tatters': Lipenga's Short Stories." *Journal of Humanities* 3 (1989):109–27.

———. "Stories on Sapitwa: An Overview of Lipenga's Fiction." *Journal of Humanities* 12 (1998): 77–85.

Literary Criticism

Modern African literary criticism began around the time of World War II, when the theory of negritude was developed by writers such as L. S. **Senghor**, Birago **Diop**, and their West Indian colleague Aimé Césaire. European critics such as Jean-Paul Sartre (who wrote an introduction titled "Black Orpheus" to Senghor's *Anthologie de la nouvelle poésie nègre et malgache de langue française,* 1948) paid attention to what the negritudinist critics were saying and noted the need to judge African literature as more than just the result of European influences. Alioune **Diop**'s founding of the critical magazine *Présence africaine* in 1947 resulted in a new critical focus on French-language writing in Africa and the Caribbean, with the publication of important critical articles like Cheikh Anta **Diop**'s "Nations, négres et culture" and "Of the Marvellous Realism of the Haitians" by Jacques Stephen Aléxis. Starting in 1957, the magazine was also published in English, which made it a key critical text for African writing in English as well. Because negritude encompassed the whole diasporic African culture, it amounted to an early and very important factor in the establishment of a greater understanding of Africa's unique cultural forms.

The negritude movement and the work of European critics such as Ulli Beier, Janheinz Jahn, and Albert Gérard offered a more progressive point of view than most criticism did in the late 1950s and early 1960s, which tended to read African literatures as either exotic (as Dylan Thomas does in his review of Amos **Tutuola**'s The **Palm-wine Drinkard** for the *Observer*) or as an extension of European forms (as A. G. Stock does in his "Yeats and Achebe"). Both ways of reading failed to understand the problems with applying European universal values to texts from African cultures. Despite the problems with criticism that bases a reading of African texts on European influences, there is also an important cultural exchange between colonizer and colonized that must be recognized and analyzed critically. The progress of African writing in colonial languages and that of the vernacular languages of Europe after the disintegration of Latin as a language of empire has been studied by Emmanuel Obiechina, an influential early West African critic, who found that a common appropriative emphasis occurred in the development of various local forms of African English. Obiechina is also known as the first African critic to focus on the popular "market literature" that emerged in the West African market centers, which was inspired both by the oral traditions of African societies and Western pulp fiction and self-help books in self-published texts that appealed to a large number of readers.

Attention to African literature grew in the late 1960s to the early 1980s, as theorists attempted to format a way of analyzing the large amount of new African literature. European, North American, and African critics focused on everything from black diasporic writing as a whole, African and Caribbean writing, continental surveys, regional studies of African writing, studies of individual authors, and studies of African women writers. Some of such works include: Mercer Cook and Stephen E. Henderson's *The Militant Black Writer in Africa and the United States* (1969), Gareth Griffiths's *A Double Exile* (1978), Gerald Moore's *The Chosen Tongue* (1969), Wilfred Cartey's *Whispers from a Continent* (1969), Judith Gleason's *This Africa* (1965), David Cook's *African Literature* (1977), Stephen Gray's *Southern African Literature,* (1979), editors Andrew Gurr and Angus Calder's *Writers in East Africa* (1971), Margaret Laurence's *Long Drums and Cannons* (1968), editor Bernth Lindfors' *Critical Perspectives on Nigerian Literature* (1976), G. D. Killam's *The Novels of Chinua Achebe* (1969) and *African Writers on African Writing* (1973), David Carroll's *Chinua Achebe* (1970), Maryse Condé's "Three Female Writers in Modern Africa," in *Présence africaine* 82, no. 2 (1972), and Lloyd W. Brown's *Women Writers in Black Africa* (1981). The same era saw a growth in critical studies by African critics as well, with works like Oladele Taiwo's *An Introduction to West African Literature* (1967), Eustace Palmer's *Introduction to the African Novel* (1972), Gideon-Cyrus M. Mutiso's *Socio-Political Thought in African Literature* (1974), Ernest Emenyonu's *The Rise of the Igbo Novel* (1978), and F. Abiola Irele's *The African Experience in Literature and Ideology* (1981). Creative

writers also provided critical analysis of African writing in semiautobiographical works and essay collections such as Lewis **Nkosi's** *Home and Exile* (1965), **Ngugi wa Thiong'o's** *Homecoming* (1972), Es'kia **Mphahlele's** *Down Second Avenue* (1959), Richard **Rive's** *Writing Black* (1981), Kofi **Awoonor's** *The Breast of the Earth* (1975), and Wole **Soyinka's** *Myth, Literature and the African World* (1976). Kenyan Simon Gikandi also provides important critical perspectives in his works *Reading the African Novel* (1987) and *Reading Chinua Achebe* (1991).

An African perspective on a unique African aesthetic that simultaneously reflects a multitude of influences and the changing nature of modern African society is presented in texts like Soyinka's *Myth, Literature and the African World,* which analyzes the importance of the Yoruba belief system, while at the same time demonstrating the effect of modernity on African self-expression. Other critics provide a critical analysis that calls for the independence of African texts from an association with European forms. Such critics include **Chinweizu**, Onwuchekwa Jemie, and Ihechukwu Madubuike, whose book on the topic is titled *Towards the Decolonization of African Literature* (1980). This work demonstrates a concern that African writers and critics should aim for a period of decolonization, during which writers could attempt to reconnect with the precolonial foundations of their culture and apply that connection to their own contemporary work, partially through a return to indigenous languages as well. Ngugi wa Thiong'o advocates this return to indigenous language in his book *Decolonising the Mind* (1986), and he is not the only critic to have thought about the implications of language to decolonization. Soyinka also posited the development of Swahili into a pan-African language, but Ngugi has been most committed to the idea and has published plays and novels such as *Devil on the Cross* (1982) and *Matigari* (1986; trans. 1989) in Gikuyu. Other African critics like **Okot p'Bitek** and Lewis Nkosi have argued that despite the need to return to indigenous culture, a variety of languages need to be used in order to make contemporary international connections between different African cultures and to express contemporary reality.

The recuperation of African traditional forms and themes and the development of a unique African aesthetics is not always the focus of African critics, as a number utilized the ideas of structuralism and poststructuralism in the 1980s. Sunday Anozie applies structural analysis to African texts in his *Structural Models and African Poetics* (1981), while Emmanuel Ngara's *Stylistic Criticism and the African Novel* (1982) is a compilation of formalist essays, but in general formalist criticism has not been largely adopted in Africa. Marxist criticism offers an analysis of African texts from a very relevant political and social perspective, wherein the role of the African writer is to reflect on the problems and social realities of his or her community. Such analyses can be seen in Biodun Jeyifo's *The Truthful Lie* (1980), Emmanuel Ngara's *Art and Ideology in the African Novel* (1985), and editor George Gugelberger's *Marxism and African Literature* (1985). The Marxist ideal of direct communication with a wide audience in the face of the oppressive censorship of a number of contemporary African regimes has had an impact on many writers, including Femi **Osofisan** and Kole **Omotoso** in Nigeria, **Sembene Ousmane** in Senegal, Jared **Angira** and Meja **Mwangi** in Kenya, Dambudzo **Marechera** in Zimbabwe, Jack **Mapanje** in Malawi, and Can **Themba** and Maishe Maponya in South Africa. However, the type of Marxism that these authors demonstrate is not necessarily always doctrinaire Marxism, but rather an antiauthoritarianism that can be seen in the way that their literature and art deal with contemporary social issues. Biodun Jeyifo provides a critique of the dominant European Africanist criticism and its effect on the development of an African literary criticism in his article "The Nature of Things" (*Research in African Literatures* 21, no. 1, 1990). Jeyifo focuses his critique on the institutional power that encourages European and American Africanist criticism over African criticism produced within African institutions.

Current African literary criticism, although still subdivided by area or country, also covers more general or subject-based categories. Among such studies are those on the Black Atlantic like Joanna Brooks and John Saillant's *"Face Zion Forward": First Writers of the Black Atlantic, 1785–1798* (2002), Vincent Carretta and Philip Gould's *Genius in Bondage: Literature of the Early Black Atlantic* (2002), Philip Gould's *Barbaric Traffic: Commerce and Antislavery in the Eighteenth-Century Atlantic World* (2003), Alan J. Rice's *Radical Narratives of the Black Atlantic* (2003), Joanne M. Braxton and Maria I. Diedrich's *Monuments of the Black Atlantic: Slavery and Memory* (2004), and *Discourses of Slavery and Abolition: Britain and Its Colonies, 1760–1838,* edited by Markman Ellis and Sara Salih (2004). Other more general criticism continues to focus on surveys of literature or of particular genres or issues like gender, while some encompass more than one area or country in their focus. Alain Ricard has published *The Languages and Literatures of Africa: The Sands of Babel* (2004), which focuses on the dialogue between languages and linguistic consciousness, while Douglas Killam's *Literature of Africa* (2004) provides an introduction to the historical and cultural issues in ten of Africa's most renowned authors. Simon Gikandi and F. Abiola Irele have edited *The Cambridge History of African and Caribbean Literature* (2003), and Pamela J. Olubunmi Smith and Daniel P. Kunene are editors of *Tongue and Mother Tongue: African Literature and the Perpetual Quest for Identity* (2002). Byron

Caminero-Santangelo studies the relationship between African novels and Joseph Conrad's fiction in *African Fiction and Joseph Conrad: Reading Postcolonial Intertextuality* (2004), while Anders Breidlid takes on multiple geographical areas in his study on *Resistance and Consciousness in Kenya and South Africa: Subalternity and Representation in the Novels of Ngugi Wa Thiong'o and Alex La Guma* (2002). Kevin J. Wetmore writes of the influence of Western literature and Greek tragedy on African theater in his book *Athenian Sun in an African Sky: Modern African Adaptations of Classical Greek Tragedy* (2001), while Donnarae MacCann and Yulisa Amadu Maddy analyze *Apartheid and Racism in South African Children's Literature, 1985–1995* (2001), and Bennetta Jules-Rosette studies African writing and identity in France from the early negritude movement to the mid-1990s in *Black Paris: The African Writers' Landscape* (2000). Patricia Hill Collins's *Black Feminist Thought: Knowledge, Consciousness, and the Politics of Empowerment*, Elleke Boehmer's *Stories of Women: Gender and Narrative in the Postcolonial Nation* (2005), and Amal Amireh and Lisa Suhair Majaj's *Going Global: The Transnational Reception of Third World Women Writers* (2000) speak to the continuing importance of feminist criticism in Africa. Other works focus on exile and diaspora, as do Eldred D. Jones and Margorie Jones's *Exile and African Literature: African Literature Today 22* (2000); *Towards the African Renaissance: Essays in Culture and Development, 1946–1960*, translated by Egbuna P. Modum, which is generated from essays by Cheikh Diop; and Isidore Okpewho and Carole Boyce Davies's *The African Diaspora: African Origins and New World Identities* (1999). With a more biographical focus are works like S. Okechukwo Mezu's *Black Nationalists: Reconsidering Du Bois, Garvey, Booker T. and Nkrumah* (1999), A. P. Cartwright's *The First South African: The Life and Times of Sir Percy FitzPatrick* (1971), and Bernth Lindfors's *Blind Men and the Elephant: And Other Essays in Biographical Criticism* (1999). Works that focus on North African criticism are Waïl S. Hassan's *Ideology and the Craft of Fiction* (2003), which undertakes the first sustained interpretation of all of Tayeb Salih's novels and short stories, and Diana Royer's *A Critical Study of the Works of Nawal El Saadawi, Egyptian Writer and Activist* (2001).

EAST AFRICA

The rise of a regional literary scene in the 1960s and 1970s in East Africa paved the way for the development of literary criticism, and writers such as **Okot p'Bitek**, **Taban Lo Liyong**, and **Ngugi wa Thiong'o** helped develop literary criticism with their involvement in journal editing, organization of cultural festivals, and commitment to literary studies at schools and universities. Literary magazines that discussed literature in relation to important social and political contexts bolstered regional criticism. Some of these magazines were *Transition* (originally edited from Uganda and with a focus on the international scene), *East Africa Journal* (with a regional focus), and the university-based *Busara* (Nairobi), *Umma* (Dar es Salaam), and *Dhana* (Kampala). Makerere University in Kampala was the center of critical literary debate for a period in the 1960s, where many East African writers and critics met. New critical emphases were explored by some of these critics in the same period, after they became disillusioned with what was called "Makerere aesthetics" and aimed to focus more on the role that literature could play in postcolonial society. Criticism of the 1960s and 1970s offered a number of approaches, but three in particular were of importance: cultural-nationalist criticism, modernism, and Marxist-nationalism. Cultural-nationalist criticism was instigated by Okot p'Bitek's *Africa's Cultural Revolution*

(1973), which focused on the interaction between oral tradition and written literature, while Taban Lo Liyong took on an avant-garde modernist tone in his criticism, and published critical works such as *The Last Word* (1969) and *Thirteen Offensives against Our Enemies* (1973). Many East African critics agreed with Taban's analysis of negritude, but did not necessarily agree with his assessment of literature as fundamentally fragmentary. Ngugi wa Thiong'o offered a Marxist-nationalist perspective in his works *Homecoming* (1972) and *Writers in Politics* (1981; rev. 1997), which analyze the political contexts of literature in colonial and postcolonial society, as well as the class contexts and authorial ideologies of writers. The issue of language use was also introduced into debate by Ngugi, as he called for an "Afrocentric" literature written in African languages rather than those of the former colonial powers, in his works *Barrel of a Pen* (1983), *Decolonising the Mind* (1986), *Moving the Centre* (1993), and *Penpoints, Gunpoints and Dreams* (1998).

More general studies on East African literature were published in the 1970s and 1980s (although there were also studies of individual authors and thematic collections of essays published). Such general studies included Adrian Roscoe's *Uhuru's Fire* (1977), Chris Wanjala's *For Home and Freedom* (1980), and *The Writing of East and Central Africa* (1984), edited by G. D. Killam. Works of the better-known East African critics include Micere **Mugo**'s *Visions of Africa* (1978), Peter **Nazareth**'s *Literature and Society in Modern Africa* (1972), and editor Chris Wanjala's *Standpoints on African Literature* (1973) and *The Season of Harvest* (1978).

This enthusiastic literary and critical debate in East Africa became less so after the break-up of the East African community in 1976. Almost all of the East African literary magazines went under in the late 1970s, and there was a rising political authoritarianism in Kenya that resulted in the exile of many critical intellectuals. Because of this move away from critical analysis within East Africa, Western universities and academic critics took up an analysis of East African literature and produced works on individual writers such as Ngugi or Okot rather than on the region as a whole. This continues to be the case, in that most works focus on one author rather than taking on a literary region, although as mentioned previously, some critics compare authors from different regions, or offer a region-specific study involving several authors. Current works on/by Ali Mazrui include *Race, Gender and Culture Conflict: Debating the African Condition. Mazrui and His Critics, Volume 1,* edited by Alamin Mazrui and Willy Mutunga; *Governance and Leadership: Debating the African Condition. Mazrui and His Critics, Volume 2,* edited by Alamin Mazrui and Willy Mutunga (2003); *Power, Politics and the African Condition: Collected Essays of Ali Mazrui. Volume 3,* edited by Robert Ostergard, Ricardo Rene Laremont, and Fouad and Falola Kalouche (2004); *Africa and Other Civilizations: Conquest and Counter-Conquest—Collected Essays of Ali A. Mazrui. Volume 2,* edited by Ricardo Rene Laremont and Fouad Kalouche (2002); *Paradigm Lost, Paradigm Regained: The Worldview of Ali A. Mazrui* by Seifuein Adem (2002); and recent works by Mazrui himself include *Political Culture of Language: Swahili, Society and the State* (1999) and *The Power of Babel: Language in the African Experience* (1998).

Other recent works that focus on East African writers are Lindfors Bernth and Bala Kothandaram's *The Writer as Activist: South Asian Perspectives on Ngugi Wa Thiong'o* (2002); Peter Nazareth's *Critical Essays on Ngugi Wa Thiong'o* (2000); Oliver Lovesey's *Ngugi Wa Thiong'o* (2000); Simon Gikandi's *Ngugi Wa Thiong'o* (Cambridge Studies in African and Caribbean Literature) (2000); Derek Wright's *Emerging Perspectives on*

Nuruddin Farah (2002); and *The Novels of Nuruddin Farah* (2004), as well as the combined studies of Ayo Mamudu's "Literary Criticism and Theory in the African Novel: Chinua Achebe, Leonard Kibera and Ali Mazrui" in *MAWA Review* 7, no. 2 (December 1992): 71–81, and Francis Ngaboh-Smart's *Beyond Empire and Nation: Postnational Arguments in the Fiction of Nuruddin Farah and B. Kojo Laing* (2004). In contrast, Eckhard Breitinger focuses on only one country in his *Uganda: The Cultural Landscape* (1999), and Tirop Peter Simatei focuses on the area in general in *The Novel and the Politics of Nation Building in East Africa* (2001).

SOUTHERN AFRICA

Early literary criticism in Southern Africa was dominated by white, masculine, middle-class analyses, and demonstrates the tensions and conflicts that are relevant to a history of literary culture in the area. Critical literature that contemplates the nature of an indigenous literature or literatures, and the inclusion or exclusion of voices based on race, gender, and class, is also an important category that emerges later in Southern Africa.

Assumptions about the value and interaction of English literary traditions with African ones were the focus of much of the early literary analysis in Southern Africa. Books reviews and essays were published by the *Cape of Good Hope Literary Gazette* (1830–35) and the *Cape Town Mirror* (1848–49) that focused on the productivity of creative writing, while Shakespeare was included in the missionary work of teachers at the South African College. English literature was added as a subject for civil service examination in the second half of the nineteenth century, as those teachers headed for the colonies were expected to display knowledge of English writers. Until the 1970s, English-language literary criticism focused on metropolitan centers and demonstrated

a conservative emphasis that mainly resisted political and social contexts. Sol T. **Plaatje's** "A South African's Homage" published in Irsrael Gollancz's tercentenary celebration of Shakespeare, Manfred Nathan's *South African Literature* (1925), and Sidney Mendelssohn's *South African Bibliography* (1910) were all exceptions to this emphasis as they offered a more contextual treatment of South African literature. Es'kia **Mphahlele's** *The African Image* (1962) began an important critical dialogue about the European representation of Africans in literature, and about indigenous African literatures, while the journals *The Bluestocking* (with a target audience of university-educated women) and *The South African Outlook* (which published black critics H.I.E. **Dhlomo** and B.W. **Vilakazi**), as well as antiapartheid magazines like *New Age* and *The Torch,* challenged more conservative academic literary studies of English canonical texts, as did journals such as *The State* (1909–12) and *The Critic* (1932–39), as well as the academic journals *English Studies in Africa* and *Unisa English Studies.*

The critical atmosphere of Southern Africa has changed greatly since the end of the twentieth century due to an interest in poststructuralist, feminist, and other socio-political approaches to literary criticism, as well as the advent of "national" literatures, and the study of postcolonialism. The critical community is presented with a challenge in the work of critics such as Mike Kirkwood, whose essay "The Colonizer: A Critique of the English South African Culture Theory" was published in *Poetry South Africa,* edited by James Polley and Peter **Wilhelm** (1976); and J.M. Coetzee, Stephen **Gray**, and Michael Chapman who all work to uncover the problems with conventional institutional criticism. The state of Southern African literary criticism is debated and represented at both academic and nonacademic conferences, journals published outside of Africa with an interest in African literary studies such as *Ariel, Kunapipi,* and *Research in African Literatures,* as well as journals within Southern Africa such as *Critical Arts, South African Theatre Journal, Current Writing,* and *Pretexts.*

Recent literary criticism coming out of the Southern African area focuses on individual authors, or on the critical development of a specific area of Southern Africa (most often South Africa). Recent works that analyze individual authors or focus on the criticism of one author are abundant. Such is J. U. Jacobs and Judith Lutge-Coullie's *A.K.A. Breyten Breytenbach: Critical Approaches to His Writings and Paintings* (2004), as well as J. Uledi-Kamanga Brighton's *Cracks in the Wall: Nadine Gordimer's Fiction and the Irony of Apartheid* (2001), Corren Brown's *The Creative Vision of Bessie Head* (2003), and Huma Ibrahim's *Bessie Head: Subversive Identities in Exile* (1996). Recent works on J. M. Coetzee include Derek Attridge's *J. M. Coetzee and the Ethics of Reading: Literature in the Event* (2004), Dominic Head's *J. M. Coetzee* (1997), Sue Kossew's *Critical Essays on J. M. Coetzee* (1998), and Coetzee's own critical take on "The Novel in Africa" in editors Zbigniew Bialas and Krzysztof Kowalczyk Twarowski's *Ebony, Ivory & Tea* (2004). A recent work that analyzes Arthur Nortje is Craig McLuckie's *Arthur Nortje: New Critical and Contextual Essays* (2003). Critical works regarding Es'kia Mphahlele include a collection of his essays titled *Es'kia Mphahlele on Education, African Humanism and Culture, Social Consciousness, Literary Appreciation* with a foreword by Don Mattera and edited by Ogube Mphalele, Ramakuela Radithalo, and Thuynsma Ramogale (2003), and Ruth Obee's *Es'Kia Mphahlele: Themes of Alienation and African Humanism* (1999).

Multiple authors are studied in a South African context in Setfan Helgesson's *Writing in Crisis: Ethics and History in Gordimer, Ndebele and Coetzee* (2004), while other works focus more generally on the area. Recent critical works that lean toward one area of Southern Africa in their critical analyses are Martin Trump's *Rendering Things Visible: Essays on South African Literary Culture* (1990); Hein Viljoen, Chris Van der Merwe, and Minnie Lewis's *Storyscapes: South African Perspectives on Literature, Space and Identity* (2004); Sten Pultz Moslund's *Making Use of History in New South African Fiction: Historical Perspectives in Three Post-Apartheid Novels* (2003); Geoffrey V. Davis's *Voices of Justice and Reason: Apartheid and Beyond in South African Literature,* which traces the development of literature in South Africa under apartheid and attempts to identify how writers are now facing the challenge of a new social order (2003); Laura Chrisman's *Rereading the Imperial Romance: British Imperialism and South African Resistance in Haggard, Schreiner, and Plaatje* (2000); *Midfielder's Moment: Coloured Literature and Culture in Contemporary South Africa* by Grant Farred (1999); and Richard Peck's *A Morbid Fascination: White Prose and Politics in Apartheid South Africa* (1997), which uses a wide range of literature to analyze the political culture of white South Africa.

Texts that focus on other Southern African countries include Dorian Haarhoff's *The Inner Eye: Namibian Poetry in Process* (1997), and his *Personal Memories: Namibian Texts in Process* (1996), as well as Robert Muponde and Ranka Primorac's *Versions of Zimbabwe: New Approaches to Literature and Culture* (2005), which considers the relationships between Zimbabwe's literature, history, and politics.

WEST AFRICA

A discussion of West African literary criticism requires first an acknowledgment of the effect of colonialism on the area's literature, especially the incorporation of oral literature into written form and the resultant interest in aesthetic forms at the time of colonization in the nineteenth and early twentieth centuries. Early Western critics of African literature include Gerald Moore, Janheinz Jahn, Ulli Beier, G. D. Killam, Bernth Lindfors, Bruce King, Adrian Roscoe, Charles R. Larson, D. J. Enright, Ronald Christ, Keith Waterhouse, and Anthony West. Many Western critics offered a negative critical perception, wherein Africa lacked a history and culture and therefore its own literary identity, while others offered a more objective perspective that was not as influenced by the colonialist perspective. Those who were influenced by the colonialist perspective used critical forms that emphasized Western rather than any other cultural values, and also criticized African literature's emphasis on particular social issues instead of larger themes.

A number of indigenous West African critics responded to the negative Western criticism with objective and meaningful analyses of African literature that corrected the negative representations that existed in much Western criticism. Some examples of this kind of West African critical work include editor Donatus Nwoga's *West African Verse* (1967), *Wole Soyinka* by Eldred D. Jones (1973), *Culture, Tradition and Society in the West African Novel* by Emmanuel Obiechina (1975), *The Growth of the African Novel* by Eustace Palmer (1979), *The African Experience in Literature and Ideology* by Abiola Irele (1981), *Modern African Poetry and the African Predicament* by Romanus Egudu (1981), and *Structural Models and African Poetics* by Sunday Anozie (1981). Writers also offered critical analysis of their own and others' work in the face of Western-based critiques. Some of such works were *Morning Yet on Creation Day* (1975) and *Hopes and Impediments: Selected Essays, 1965–1987* (1988) by Chinua Achebe, *The Example of Shakespeare* (1970) by J. P. Clark **Bekederemo**, *Myth, Literature and the African World* (1976) by Wole **Soyinka**, *The Breast of the Earth* (1975) by Kofi **Awoonor**, and *The Epic in Africa*

(1979) and *African Oral Literature* (1992) by Isidore **Okpewho**. These and other West African writers and critics drew attention to the need to take into consideration the African cultural consciousness in literary terms, and to consider the impact of colonialism on that consciousness. This kind of criticism then acknowledges the impact of Western critical categories such as Marxism, structuralism, formalism, **feminism**, and even negritude (as well as critics such as L. A. Richards and P. R. Leavis) on African writing, but calls for the negation of racist Western theories about Africa and the praise of traditional cultural values in critical theory.

However, there is not complete agreement among West African critics and writers either. Obi Wali and others debated the implications of the use of a foreign language in African literary discourse after the publication of his article "The Dead End of African Literature" (*Transition*, No. 11, 1963), while Eldred Durasimi Jones aligns himself with formalism and a close reading of individual works in *Literature Today* 1, 1968 (Dan Izevbaye takes a similar position); Abiola Irele prefers sociological analysis; Sunday Anozie focuses on structural analysis; and Omafume Onoge takes a Marxist emphasis. **Chinweizu**, Onwuchekwa Jemie, and Ihechukwu Madubuike are referred to as the *bolekaja* critics (the term alludes to aggressive Yoruba bus conductors), and they offer a critique of African writers and critics for their imitation of Western literary models in their book *Toward the Decolonization of African Literature* (1980), which also calls for a negation of all types of Western literary consciousness.

Postcolonial West African criticism also acknowledges the importance of indigenous publishing to the better availability, and therefore better understanding, of African literary and critical texts. As a result, West African publishers such as the Fourth Dimension in Enugu, New Horn Press in Ibadan, and the

Ghana Publishing Corporation, as well as university presses at Ibadan, Lagos, Ife, and Port Harcourt, all promote West African literary production. West African–edited journals such as *African Literature Today* (edited by Eldred Durosimi Jones and Marjorie Jones), *Okike* (founded by Chinua Achebe), *Nigeria Magazine, ANA Review,* and *Kiabárá* also contribute to indigenous literary production. Outside of Africa, those who contribute to the African literary and critical tradition include the publishers Heinemann, James Currey, Three Continents Press, Hans Zell, Longman, and Africa World Press, and the journals *Research in African Literatures, World Literature Written in English, Journal of Commonwealth Literature, Arid, The Literary Half-Yearly,* and *Kunapipi.*

As with other areas of Africa, West African literary criticism focuses on the analysis of individual authors more often than on the area as a whole. In addition, some West African authors have written criticism that analyzes literature on an African-wide basis. Recent works that focus on a specific area are Karin Barber, John Collins, and Alain Ricard's *West African Popular Theatre (Drama and Performance)* (1997), and Femi Osofisan's *Insidious Treasons: Drama in a Postcolonial State* (2001), which expresses the author's thoughts about the theater profession in Nigeria. Works by critics who are themselves West African include Kofi Anyidoho's *Beyond Survival: African Literature and the Search for New Life* (1998), which he edited with Abena P. A. Busia and Anne V. Adams; Tanure Ojaide's *Culture, Society, and Politics in Modern African Literature: Texts and Contexts* (2002), which investigates the paradoxes and ironies of African literature that is analyzed by African and non-African scholars living outside the continent; Niyi Osundare's *Thread in the Loom: Essays on African Literature and Culture* (2002); and *The Word Is an Egg* (2000), in which Osundare advocates the poetry of performance. Femi Osofisan's

Literature and the Pressures of Freedom: Essays, Speeches and Songs by Femi Osofisan (2001) is similarly both his own work and an analysis of literature in the African context, while in contrast other critics write about specific West African writers. Such texts include works like Ada Uzoamaka Azodo's *Emerging Perspectives on Mariama Ba: Postcolonialism, Feminism, and Postmodernism* (2003); Adelaide M. Cromwell's *An African Victorian Feminist: Adelaide Smith Casely-Hayford 1868–1960* (1986); Chris Nwamuo's article "Henshaw and the Genesis of Literary Theatre in Nigeria" in *The Literary Criterion* 23, nos. 1–2 (1988): 118–30; and Ayo Mamudu's article "Literary Criticism and Theory in the African Novel: Chinua Achebe, Leonard Kibera and Ali Mazrui" in *MAWA Review3* 7, no. 2 (December 1992): 71–81; as well as Francis Ngaboh-Smart's *Beyond Empire and Nation: Postnational Arguments in the Fiction of Nuruddin Farah and B. Kojo Laig* (2004); these works all deal with criticism of both East and West African authors (as mentioned previously). Other works that deal with individual authors in their West African context are Olakunle George's *Relocating Agency: Modernity and African Letters* (2003) (which studies Nigerian authors D. O. Fagunwa, Wole Soyinka, Amos Tutola, and Chinua Achebe); Onookome Okome's *Ogun's Children: The Literature and Politics of Wole Soyinka since the Nobel Prize* (2003); Jeyifo Biodun's *Wole Soyinka: Politics, Poetics, and Postcolonialism* (2003); Onookome Okome's *Writing the Homeland: The Poetry and Politics of Tanure Ojaide* (2002); Molara Ogundipe-Leslie's article "The Poetry of Christopher Okigbo: Its Evolution and Significance" (reprinted in 2000 in a book edited by Uzoma Esonwanne); Tayo Olafioye's *The Poetry of Tanure Ojaide* (2000); and *Tanure Ojaide: Critical Appraisal* (2000), as well as Martin Owusu's *Analysis and Interpretation of Ola Rotimi's* The Gods Are Not to Blame (1998), and Uzoma Esonwanne's editorial collection of *Critical Essays on Christopher Okigobo* (2000).

Literary Theory

Contemporary literary theory has impacted African literary criticism in a variety of ways. The theoretical analysis of African writing has been influenced by works that study colonialist discourse, such as those written by Edward Said, Gayatri Spivak, and Homi Bhabha, and those that respond to the above critics in a materialist sense, such as Fredric Jameson and Leila Ahmed. Abdul JanMohamed's critical work *Manichaean Aesthetics: The Politics of Literature in Colonial Africa* (1983) is of great importance as it is an intercession into this discussion from an African critic's perspective. In *Manichean Aesthetics* and in several essays that followed it, JanMohamed offers a critical exploration of the relationship between hegemonic Eurocentric literature and the way that the forms of such literature can be appropriated for a counter-hegemonic framework. JanMohamed maintains that it is necessary to understand the influence of the racially divisive colonialist past on the antiracist discourses of the present. In this manner, JanMohamed demonstrates how African literary works take the themes of colonial texts and rewrite them in a way that destabilizes colonial history and allows for alternative narratives.

In My Father's House (1992) by Kwame Appiah offers a reading of African history that uses as its framework postmodernist cultural theory. Appiah argues that the "nativist" and "invention of Africa" discourses of figures such as Alexander Crummell, Edward Blyden, and George Padmore work to disrupt the race-centered labels that were created by slavery and opposition to slavery in nineteenth-century America. However, a very disruption of such labels depends on language that traps the critics within the race-based dialogue, and Appiah notes that the result of this kind of criticism is a focus on the reliance of African cultural structures on external influences. Appiah thus calls attention to the problematic nature of truly pure cultural formation in the face of the resilience of cultural interaction. As a postcolonial work that is impacted by postmodern theories about discourse, Appiah's work presents a complex theory about the way cultural relationships of opposition and recovery develop in relation to the colonial and postindependence eras of African history. Similarly, *The Invention of Africa* (1988) and *The Idea of Africa* (1995) by Zaïrean critic V. Y. Mudimbe chart the influence that theories about subjectivity and power structures have over the way such theories are applied to interaction and social identity across cultures. Although Mudimbe analyzes the effect that anthropological and missionary discourses have had over the structure of African identity, he also argues that there is a possibility for an independent African identity.

Critical works on African cultures also focus on the importance of noting local knowledge in their analyses. These works emphasize the study of the ideals and frameworks of the society that produces the texts under consideration, rather than in relation to Western ideas of textual analysis. As noted previously, it is also important for such a focus to take into account the kind of interaction that Mudimbe and Appiah note between African societies and European frameworks, as their influence upon one another cannot be ignored. It is due to this focus on connectivity in postmodernist and postcolonial theory that it is also important to note that some critics have voiced concern about the way that these theories of interaction might be detrimental to resistance and decolonization. It is the appearance of continual dependence on colonialist structures in postindependence social frameworks that such theories about the unavoidable connection between colonizer and colonized cause critics to be concerned about. In relation to this concern is the theory that opposition and resistance result in an inversion of colonial discourse that traps the oppositionist discourse in the very theoretical framework it attempts to overturn. More recent critics note that such oppositions and unequal cultural interactions are a part of the colonizing process that must be resisted with the knowledge that an unequal cultural interaction was part of the colonizing process, and makes resistance more complicated than simply reversing colonial frameworks. Stephanie Newell's *West African Literatures: Ways of Reading* (2006) takes into account West African cultural traditions, as she analyses poetry, fiction, and drama in relation to the political and cultural contexts of West Africa. Newell compares and contrasts literatures from before independence with those of contemporary authors who have moved from the earlier nationalist concerns to a more experimental mode. Gerald Gaylard shows similar concerns in his study of the effects of postcolonialism on African narrative structures and experimental techniques titled *After Colonialism: African Postmodernism and Magical Realism* (2006), which concludes that experimental techniques like magical realism can be useful for the contemplation of postcolonial Africa.

Feminist critics apply literary theory to African texts in order to rectify the patriarchal slant that has overlooked authors such as Efua **Sutherland**, Ama Ata **Aidoo**, and Flora **Nwapa**, and has provided negative criticism of more recently established authors such as Mariama **Bâ**, Bessie **Head**, and Buchi **Emecheta**. Feminist critics also note that postcolonial and decolonization theory needs to demonstrate the importance of gender difference in the analysis of colonial oppression in African literature. Rather, critics point out that a feminist analysis of African literature needs to take into account the double colonization of women, both as subjects of colonization and by the patriarchal

structures in African societies. Some critics point out that the patriarchal configuration of African societies may have been created or encouraged by the colonists, who approved methods of internal control. In addition, feminist critics like Nina Mba rewrite the histories that male novelists and historians have left women out of, in order to offer a rereading of African literature and history.

A need to redefine the terms of understanding oral literature in African literary theory is also of importance. European scholars such as Ruth Finnegan maintain that African oral literature can be studied in a literary rather than an anthropological framework, while African critics like Isidore **Okpewho** dispute the way that such literature is typically seen through European terms that relate to Classical literary history. A large number of critics, some of whom are Daniel P. **Kunene**, Richard Taylor, Karin Barber, and Elizabeth Gunner, stress the need to study oral literature alongside written literature without giving precedence to written literature. The connection between the written and the oral in the Yoruba culture of Nigeria is studied by Karin Barber, while Isabel Hofmeyr and others maintain that oral and written forms are interwoven in cohesive social contexts. These kinds of studies draw attention to the need to avoid relegating oral culture to the past and disconnecting it from written forms in African societies. These critics also draw attention to the importance of avoiding the assumption that the written word is a higher literary form than the spoken word.

Literary theory continues to be a difficult place of navigation in terms of its effect on African cultural and literary analysis, because of its association with repressive Western and colonial frameworks. As Biodun Jeyifo argues, literary theory can be viewed as a form of Western suppression of African cultures. In this sense it is important to ground theory in African cultural contexts while still taking into account their reaction to and connectedness with colonial forms. As is noted by Barbara Christian and Gerald Gaylard, African writers' use of narration and interaction with language rather than typical theoretical forms requires attention as well. Thus, a balance between critical theory and African cultural forms of resistance requires attentive negotiation in the theoretical analysis of African literature.

Further Reading

Anyidoho, Kofi. "Prison as Exile/Exile as Prison: Circumstance, Metaphor, and a Paradox of Modern African Literatures." In *The World behind Bars and the Paradox of Exile,* ed. K. Anyidoho. Evanston, IL: Northwestern Univeristy Press, 1997, 1–17.

Bulman, Stephen. "The Buffalo-Woman Tale: Political Imperatives and Narrative Constraints in the Sunjata Epic." In *Discourse and Its Disguises: The Interpretation of African Oral Texts,* ed. K. Barber and P. de Moraes Farias. Birmingham, AL: Center of West African Studies, University of Birmingham, 1989, 171–88.

Childs, Peter, Jean Jacques Weber, and Peter Williams. *Post-Colonial Theory and Literatures: African, Caribbean and South Asian.* Verlag, Germany: Wissenschaftlicher, 2006.

Gaylard, Gerald. *After Colonialism: African Postmodernism and Magical Realism.* Johannesburg: Witwatersrand University Press, 2006.

Gikandi, Simon. "Theory, Literature, and Moral Considerations." *Research in African Literatures* 32, no. 4 (2001): 1–18.

Haddour, Azzedine, ed. *The Fanon Reader.* London: Pluto Press, 2006.

Innes, Gordon, ed. *Sunjata: Three Mandinka Versions.* London: School of Oriental and African Studies, University of London, 1974.

Johnson, John William. "The Dichotomy of Power and Authority in Mande Society and in the Epic of Sunjata." In *In Search of Sunjata: The Mande Oral Epic as History, Literature, and Performance,* ed. R. A. Austen. Bloomington: Indiana University Press, 1999, 9–23.

Lazarus, Neil. "Representations of the Intellectual in *Representations of the Intellectual.*" *Research in African Literatures* 36, no. 3 (2005): 112–23.

Napier, Winston, ed. *African American Literary Theory: A Reader.* New York: New York University Press, 2000.

Newell, Stephanie. *West African Literatures: Ways of Reading.* Oxford: Oxford University Press, 2006.

Niane, Djibril Tamsir, ed. *Sundiata: An Epic of Old Mali.* Trans. G. D. Pickett. London: Longman, 1965.

Okpewho, Isidore. "African Mythology and Africa's Political Impasse." *Research in African Literatures* 29, no. 1 (1998): 1–15.

———. *Once upon a Kingdom: Myth, Hegemony, and Identity.* Bloomington: Indiana University Press, 1998.

Olaniyan, Tejumola (introduction). "Forum: African Literature and Theory." *Research in African Literatures* 36, no. 2 (2005): 95–131.

Priebe, Richard K. "Literature, Community, and Violence: Reading African Literature in the West, Post-9/11." *Research in African Literatures* 36, no. 2 (2005): 46–58.

Said, Edward W. *Representation of the Intellectual.* New York: Pantheon, 1994.

Wolfreys, Julian. "'A Self-Referential Density': Glyph and the '*Theory*' Thing." *Callaloo: A Journal of African Diaspora Arts and Letters* 28, no. 2 (2005): 345–57.

Little Karoo, The (1925)

Short stories by Pauline Smith. These stories are set at the turn of the nineteenth century in a region of South Africa's southwestern cape called the Little Karoo. Smith represents a community of Dutch settlers who are warm and caring despite their austerity and repression. She deals with subjects such as love, family, betrayal, and fate.

Livingstone, Douglas (1932–96)

A South African poet, Livingstone was born of Scottish parents in Kuala Lumpur. During the Japanese invasion of Malaysia in 1941 his father was taken prisoner, but the rest of the family managed to find its way to KwaZulu-Natal, South Africa, where he completed his schooling. After working in laboratories, he trained at the Pasteur Institute in Zimbabwe and from 1964 worked as a marine bacteriologist in Durban. He gained two doctorates from the University of Natal: one for his scientific work and an honorary one for his poetry. He produced five major volumes of verse: *Sjambok and Other Poems from Africa* (1964), *Eyes Closed against the Sun* (1970), *A Rosary of Bone* (1975, rev. 1983), *The Anvil's Undertone* (1978), and *A Littoral Zone* (1991). He also published *Selected Poems* (1984), three plays, and various translations. Collected editions include *A Ruthless Fidelity: Collected Poems of Douglas Livingstone* (2004), *Selected Poems* (2004). In addition to these collections, there is also a memoir titled *For Douglas Livingstone: A Reminiscence* by Walter Saunders (1996).

Livingstone was a lyrical poet of considerable range. He wrote many striking poems about animals and birds ("Gentling a Wildcat" is one of his best-known pieces), and the 1991 collection focuses on the sea coast. His poems cover many other topics and themes: people, especially individuals who are lonely or frustrated; places; incidents and stories, at times handled in mythic or phantasmagoric ways; and a wide range of seemingly more directly personal subjects (but one often senses the presence of a persona), including poems about love (*A Rosary of Bone* consists mainly of love poems). Since the mid-1970s some of his poems have also touched on political themes. Livingstone's poetry—energetic, remarkably varied, and inventive in texture and form—reveals a careful and cunning craftsman. Every poem has its own style, pace, and music; some poems are very dense and knotty, while a few are limpid and almost colloquial. The poems usually make some use of rhyme, often in unexpected ways; and a few poems exhibit, very successfully, surprisingly elaborate patternings of rhymes, half-rhymes, assonances, and alliteration.

Livingstone's lyrical style did not take easily to political themes. He was always opposed to **apartheid** and to totalitarianism. But in the 1970s, with the escalation of the antiapartheid struggle, a debate arose in literary circles about what kind of poetry could or should be written under conditions of political crisis. Livingstone quietly defended his position, but he also reacted warmly and sympathetically to much of the new poetry that expressed the anger and aspirations of the oppressed.

Further Reading

Brown, Duncan. "Environment and Identity: Douglas Livingstone's *A Littoral Zone*." *Critical Arts: A Journal of South North Cultural and Media Studies* 16, no. 2 (2002): 94–116.

Fazzini, Marco. "The Poetry of Moral Commitment in South Africa: The Life and Work of Douglas Livingstone." *Annali di Ca' Foscari: Rivista della Facolta di Lingue e Letterature Straniere dell' Universita di Venezia* 31, nos. 1–2 (1992): 89–107.

Klopper, Dirk. "A Libidinal Zone: The Poetic Legacy of Douglas Livingstone." *Scrutiny2: Issues in English Studies in Southern Africa* 2, no. 2 (1997): 43–48.

Morphet, Tony. "Littorally: A Note on Douglas Livingstone." *Pretexts: Studies in Writing and Culture* 6, no. 2 (1997): 205–11.

Looking on Darkness (1974)
A novel by André **Brink**. The narrator of this novel is Joseph Malan, a mixed-race man who is in prison, accused of the murder of his white lover, Jessica. Because of its depiction of interracial love, Malan's struggle for identity as a black South African, and the barriers to political action, this novel was banned by the censors.

Looming Shadow, The (1968)
Legson **Kayira**'s first novel. It depicts the Malawian rural experience before the modern central government took over. Its focus is more pastoral compared to Kayira's later novel, *The Detainee* (1974), which focuses on the treachery of the Banda regime.

Lubega, Bonnie (1929–)

A fiction writer and lexicographer, Lubega was born in Buganda province of Uganda, where he received his early education and qualified as a teacher. He worked as a journalist in the 1950s and published his own pictorial magazine, *Ssanyu*. He took a diploma in journalism in Germany, and then returned to Kampala and worked as a scriptwriter and radio producer. His first book, *The Burning Bush* (1970), depicts a herdsboy, Nakamwa-Ntette, whose narrative voice reveals the acuity of close observation. The major conflict in the novel is between Nakamwa-Ntette and the educated son of the village head and landlord. In *The Outcasts* (1971), Lubega presents the marginalized migrant *balaalo,* despised by the dominant Bugandans, for whom they herd cattle. But the hero, Karekyesi, penetrates his exploiters' psychology and outwits them. *The Great Animal Land* (1971) and *Cry, Jungle Children* (1974), although strongly didactic, assert Lubega's humanism as he refamiliarizes a youthful audience with Africa's threatened ecosystems. His Lugandan semantic dictionary, *Olulimi Oluganda Amakula* (1995), an original work, reflects an abiding cultural concern. He is also the co-author of *The Terrible Graakwa* (Luganda version by Janine Corneilse, 1998), and *One Dark Dark Night* (Luganda version by Lesley Beake, 1998).

Lubwa P'chong (1946–)

A playwright and poet, Lubwa P'chong was born in Gulu, Uganda, had his early education there and in Kyambogo. He taught for several years, and then studied literature and linguistics at Makerere University. He founded and edited *Nanga,* the magazine of the National Teachers College, Kampala, and edited *Dhana,* the Makerere literary magazine. His poetry has appeared in East African magazines and anthologies, but he is known mainly as a playwright. His plays *Generosity Kills* and *The Last Safari* (1975) were followed by *Words of My Groaning* (1976), a portrait of life in independent Africa. His other plays are *The Minister's Wife* (1982), *The Bishop's Daughter* (1988), *Do Not Uproot the Pumpkin* (1987), *Kinsmen and Kinswomen* (1988), and *The Madman* (1989). Lubwa has also published an article on "Okot p'Bitek: The Cultural Matrix of the Acholi in His Writings" in *Uganda: The Cultural Landscape,* edited by Eckhard Breitinger (1999).

M

Maclennan, Donald (Alasdair Calum) (1929–)

South African poet. Born in London, Maclennan came to South Africa in 1938; he was educated at the universities of the Witwatersrand and Edinburgh. His first collection, *Life Songs,* was published by Bateleur in 1977. It was followed by *In Memoriam Oskar Wolberheim* (1981), a collaboration that combines Maclennan's poetry with the music of Norbert Nowotny. In *Reckonings* (1983), Maclennan engages with the subject matter and themes that reappear in his subsequent collections: the nature of being, the limits of human understanding, and the rhythms and cycles of the natural world. *Collecting Darkness* (1988) and *The Poetry Lesson* (1995) return to these preoccupations, while *Letters* (1992) addresses absent family members, friends, lovers, and the poet himself. *Solstice* (1997), which won South Africa's 1997 Sanlam Literary Award, was praised for its simplicity of diction. The same qualities are evident in *Of Women and Some Men* (1998). Maclennan's fourteenth poetry collection, titled *Excavations* (2004), uses an imagery of land exploration in the Eastern Cape to explore his own inner life. Maclennan has also published such works as *Notes from a Rhenish Mission* (2001), *A Brief History of Madness in the Eastern Cape* with drawings by Siddis Firfield (2001), *The Road to Dromdraai* (2002), and *A Ruthless Fidelity: Collected Poems of Douglas Livingstone,* edited with Malcolm Hacksley (2004).

Madanhire, Nevanji (1961–)

Novelist Madanhire was born in Fort Victoria, now Masvingo, in Southern Rhodesia, now Zimbabwe. He was educated at the University of Zimbabwe. Madanhire taught for some years before he became a full-time journalist, and is editor-in-chief of *The Financial Gazette,* an important weekly. Madanhire's first novel, *Goatsmell* (1992), dramatizes the doomed romance between two students, a Shona and an Ndebele. As well, it offers a critique of politicians who exploit ethnic, regional, and racial differences in order to consolidate power. The novel anticipates that a new generation will allow a sense of nation to transcend local loyalties. *Goatsmell's* bold use of metaphorical language adds a new dimension to the already stylistically ambitious Zimbabwean novel in English. Madanhire's second novel is *If the Wind Blew* (1996).

Maddy, Yulisa Amadu (1936–)
(formerly Pat Yulisa or Pat Maddy)

A playwright and novelist, Maddy was born in Freetown, Sierra Leone, and educated in Sierra Leone and in the UK at Rose Bruford College and London University. He has worked as an actor and director and as a lecturer, instructor, and professor in Zambia, Nigeria, the UK, and the United States. His first play was *Obasai and Other Plays* (1971), which was followed by a novel, *No Past, No Present, No Future* (1973). He received the Sierra Leone National Arts Festival Award in 1973, the Gulbenkian Grant in 1978, and the Edinburgh Festival Award in 1979. His other plays are *Big Breeze Blow* (1984), *Take Tem Draw Di Rope* (1975), *Naw We Yone Dehn See* (1975), *Big Berrin* (1984), *A Journey into Christmas* (1980), *Drums, Voices and Worlds* (1985), *If Wishes Were Horses* (1963), a radio

play, and *Saturday Night Out* (1980), a play for television. *Yon Kon* (1982) examines money and its control of society. This theme is developed further in *No Past, No Present, No Future,* in which three men's friendship is called into question in a foreign land as they attempt to escape the social system of their native Sierra Leone. He writes mainly for an African audience, which he reaches by using Pidgin. In 1996 he co-authored with Donnarae MacCann *African Images in Juvenile Fiction: Commentaries on Neocolonialist Fiction,* and recently he has collaborated once again with MacCann on *Apartheid and Racism in South African Children's Literature, 1985–1995* (2001). Maddy has also co-authored (with MacCann) several critical articles on African children's literature, including "Anti-African Themes in 'Liberal' Young Adult Novels" published in *Children's Literature Association Quarterly* (2002), and "Ambivalent Signals in South African Young Adult Novels" published in *Bookbird: A Journal of International Children's Literature* (1998).

Further Reading

Palmer, Eustace. "*Yulisa Amadu Maddy,* No Past, No Present, No Future." *African Literature Today* 7 (1975): 163–66.

Madmen and Specialists (1971)

Play by Wole **Soyinka**. A satirical treatment of the Nigeria-Biafra war, this play follows the actions of Dr. Bero and his father, Old Man. Dr. Bero is an intelligence officer in the war, and his father expresses the violence of the war with irony. Four satiric sketches are interspersed through the play to parody the regime, and some hope is offered when Bero's sister and two aging Earth Mothers protect the traditional medicines.

Mafeking Diary of Sol T. Plaatje, The (1999)

Centenary edition of *The Boer War Diary,* Sol T. Plaatje (1973, 1990). Plaatje's diary follows the developments of the siege of Mafeking in 1900. He was able to record the events of the Anglo-Boer war from a black African perspective due to the information he garnered from his position as court interpreter for Robert Baden-Powell. His diary is multilingual and expresses a concern for the plight of the African people, as well as his personal interpretations of events.

Mafeking Road (1947)

Short stories by H.C. **Bosman**. The stories follow the backveld character Oom Schalk Lourens, who Bosman uses to ironically and sympathetically explore the Marico community. Despite the specific location, the themes of the stories deal with larger South African issues as well.

Magaia, Lina (1940?–)

A Mozambican short-story writer and novelist writing in Portuguese, Magaia was born in Maputo, Mozambique, to parents who moved north in search of secondary educational opportunities for their children. Although her education in the Portuguese colonial school system, designed like French colonial education to reproduce European manners and sensibilities in Africans, might have turned her into an *assimilado,* she rebelled and joined the Mozambican Liberation Front (Frelimo). She was put in jail for three months for her political activism. She graduated with a bachelor's in economics from the University of Lisbon in 1975 and works as an agricultural administrator in the Mozambique public service. She was a member of the Secretariat of the AEMO (Associação dos Escritores Moçambicanos), and a member of the Central Committee of the National Liberation Struggle Veterans' Association, and remains a writer, Parliamentarian, and long-time Mozambican activist.

During the war of independence, she served in the Mozambican Liberation Army, witnessing the atrocities of war and of the postwar period. Her first book, *Dumba nengue: histórias trágicas do banditismo* (1987; *Dumba Nengue, Run for Your Life: Peasant Tales of Tragedy in Mozambique,* 1988), is based on interviews with survivors of atrocities committed by the counterrevolutionary terrorist organization Renamo on July 22, 1987. *Dumba nengue* is also a local proverb that means "Run for your life" or "You have to trust your feet." The simple, journalistic style of her stories is evident from their titles (e.g., "Their Heads Were Crushed like Peanuts," "Pieces of Human Flesh Fell on Belinda's Yard"). Magaia has since published another collection of stories of war atrocities, *Duplo massacre em Moçambique: histórias trágicas do banditismo* (1989), and two novels, *Delehta: Pulos na vida* (1994) and *A Cobra dos Olhos Verdes* (1997).

Magona, Sindiwe (1942–)

A South African autobiographer and short-story writer, Magona grew up in a village in the Transkei and later in Guguletu, Cape Town. She has degrees from the University of South Africa and Columbia University and worked for the United Nations in New York. She published a two-part autobiography, *To My Children's Children* (1990) and *Forced to Grow* (1992), as well as a collection of short stories, *Living, Loving, and Lying Awake at Night* (1991). Another collection, *Push-Push and Other Stories,* appeared in 1996. Her first published novel, *Mother to Mother* (1999), is a response to the 1993 mob killing of American Fulbright scholar Amy Biehl in Guguletu. Magona has also been involved in several educational publications on the Xhosa language, which are titled *Xhosa* (2003), *Clicking with Xhosa: A Xhosa Phrasebook* (2001), *Teach Yourself Xhosa—Complete Course* (2000), both published in cooperation with Beverley Skorge Kirsch, and *Teach Yourself Xhosa Language* (1999), published with Beverley Kirsch and Silvia Skorge. Forthcoming is *Imida,* a book of Xhosa essays (2006).

Her most interesting work is a series of humorous and satirical short stories under the subtitle "Women at Work" in her 1991 collection. Sindiwe Magona retired from the United Nations' Department of Public Information, New York, in 2003. She returned to her homeland and lives in Cape Town, South Africa. Her short stories have been anthologized in many collections and have also appeared along with her articles in newspapers and magazines in Great Britain, South Africa, and the United States.

Mahfouz, Naguib (1911–)

Egyptian novelist, generally regarded as the creator of the modern Arabic novel. He is also author of many short stories and film scripts. He was awarded the Nobel Prize for Literature in 1988. He was born in Cairo and received his early education in a Koranic primary school. After taking a degree in philosophy in Cairo, he chose a literary career, while earning his living as a civil servant, first in the Ministry of Religious Endowments, and then as a film censor in the Ministry of Culture.

Mahfouz's literary career falls into a series of clearly marked periods. He wrote three historical novels set in ancient Egypt. He then wrote five novels concerned with the social problems of ordinary people in contemporary Cairo—*Midaq Alley* (1947; trans. 1966) and *The Beginning and the End* (1949; trans. 1985). In *The Cairo Trilogy,* which he called "a history of my country and of myself," he traces the fortunes of a family through three generations: *Palace Walk* (1956; trans. 1990), *Palace of Desire* (1957; trans. 1991), and *Sugar Street* (1957; trans.1992). Random House recently published a new edition of *The Cairo Trilogy* (with all three novels in one volume), translated by William M. Hutchins and with an introduction by Edward W. Said (2001).

The trilogy was completed in 1952. He then took a new direction with his religious allegory *Children of Gebelawi* (1959; trans.

1981). The controversies caused by this work provoked another silence, followed by six short novels, including *The Thief and the Dogs* (1961; trans. 1984), *Adrift on the Nile* (1966; trans. 1993), and *Miramar* (1967; trans. 1978); these use stream-of-consciousness technique and are full of existential problems.

Egypt's defeat in the Six Days War of 1967 caused a long silence. Then Mahfouz published *Mirrors* (1972; trans. 1977) and *Fountain and Tomb* (1975; trans. 1988). In his final period of activity he published *The Harafish* (1977; trans. 1994), in which he follows a Cairo family through more than ten generations. In *Arabian Nights and Days* (1979; trans. 1995) and *The Journey of Ibn Fattouma* (1983; trans. 1992) he demonstrates that his inspiration comes from classical Arabic models, and in *Al-A'ish fi'l-Haqiqa* (1985) he returns to the ancient Egypt with which he began his career.

In winning the Nobel Prize he became the target of certain extreme Islamic groups, surviving an assassination attempt in October 1994. This added to his popularity. He is regarded by most Egyptians to be the embodiment of all that is best in their country. Some of his most recent works (and republished works) include *The Day the Leader Was Killed* (2000); *Akenhaten: Dweller in Truth* (English translation, 1998); *The Beggar, The Thief and the Dogs, and Autumn Quail* (2000), a volume of three previously separately published novels that represent Mahfouz's thoughts about the struggles of post–Revolution Egypt; *Naguib Mahfouz at Sidi Gaber: Reflections of a Nobel Laureate, 1994–2001* from conversations with Mohamed Salmawy (2001); *Respected Sir; Wedding Song; The Search* (2001); *Mirrors,* illustrated by Seif Wanly and translated by Roger Allen (2001); and *Voices from the Other World—Ancient Egyptian Tales,* translated by Raymond Stock (2002). Interestingly, U.S. trumpeter and composer Dave Douglas titled a song on his 2001 album

Witness "Mahfouz"—the twenty-five-minute piece features singer Tom Waits reading an excerpt from Mahfouz's works.

Further Reading

Aboul-Ela, Hosam. "The Writer Becomes Text: Naguib Mahfouz and State Nationalism in Egypt." *Biography: An Interdisciplinary Quarterly* 27, no. 2 (2004): 339–56.

Hartman, Michelle. "Re-Reading Women in/to Naguib Mahfouz's *al-Liss wa' kilab (The Thief and the Dogs)*." *Research in African Literatures* 28, no. 3 (1997): 5–16.

Katner, Linda Beane. "Homage to Zola: The Question of Heredity in Naguib Mahfouz's *Cairo Trilogy* and *Midaq Alley*." *Excavatio: Emile Zola and Naturalism* 12 (1999): 201–6.

Kehinde, Ayo. "The Contemporary Arabic Novel as Social History: Urban Decadence, Politics and Women in Naguib Mahfouz's Fiction." *Studies in the Humanities* 30, nos. 1–2 (2003): 144–63.

Maina Wa Kinyatti (195?–)

Maina was is best known for his book *Thunder from the Mountains: Poems and Songs from the Mau Mau* (1980). He was imprisoned in 1982 by the Kenyan government for possession of seditious literature, and then released on October 17, 1988. He now lives in New York. In 1987 he published *Kenya Freedom Struggle,* and since his release from prison he has published *Mau Mau: A Revolution Betrayed* (1992), *A Season of Blood: Poems from Kenya Prisons* (1995), and *Mother Kenya: Letters from Prison, 1982–1988* (1997). His most recent work is *The Pen and the Gun* (2005), a collection of essays about the struggle for democracy in Kenya against a dictatorship and terrorism.

Man of the People, A (1966)

A novel by Chinua **Achebe**. Responsible leadership is replaced with corruption, selfishness, and greed in Achebe's novel about a postindependence country similar to Nigeria. Published just before Nigeria's first military coup d'état, Achebe's novel depicts negative leadership in the character of Chief Nanga, who is "a man of the people." The novel's outlook is grim, with a suggestion that such a corrupt society (where constitutional methods have failed) can only be given new hope through military intervention.

Man Who Lost His Shadow, The (1966)

A novel by Fathy **Ghanem**, translated from the Arabic by Desmond Stewart. The novel has four narrators who demonstrate the interconnected and ruthless nature of relationships in the Cairo newspaper world. The determined hero of the work is journalist Yusif Hamid, who is a narrator along with his father's second wife, an actress who Yusif lives with and then leaves, and a journalist who marries the cast-off actress.

Manaka, Matsemela (1956–98)

South African poet and playwright. Born at Alexandra, in the Johannesburg area, Manaka was active in the black theater movement that emerged after the Soweto riots of 1976, following the closure of opportunities for black artists and performers in mainstream South African theaters. Trained as a teacher, his original inspiration came from the heroism of the young schoolchildren who pitted themselves against the firepower of the **apartheid** regime. He founded the Soyikwa African Theatre group, whose members performed unscripted, workshop-generated plays in quick response to the events of the day, turning acts of repression into provocatively satirical farces. Manaka's own plays grew out of the same kind of workshop context. They include *Egoli: City of Gold* (1979), *Blues Afrika Café* (1980), *Vuka* (1981), *Mbumba* (1984), *Children of Asazi* (published in *Woza Africa! An Anthology of South African Plays,* ed. Duma Ndlovu, 1986), *Domba, the Last Prince* (1986) and *Pula (Rain)* (published in *Market Plays,* ed. Stephen **Gray**, 1986, and separately in 1990), *Size* (1987), *Taro* (1987), *Kama*

(1988), *Gorée,* a musical (with Motsumi Makhene and Peter Boroto, 1989), *Ekhaya: Coming Home* (1991), *Ekhaya: Museum over Soweto* (1991), and *Yamina* (1993). His plays promote black consciousness among the black township audiences. They were also successfully performed at overseas festivals in London, Edinburgh, Berlin, and Copenhagen. *Pula* and *Mbumba* won a Fringe Award at the Edinburgh Festival. Manaka also produced screenplays, including *Two Rivers* (co-authored with Ratshaka Ratshitanga, Mark Newman, and Eddie Wes) and *Kiba: The Beat Between.* Between 1979 and 1982, he was a member of the editorial collective of the literary magazine *Staffrider.* In 1987, he won the PEN International Freedom-to-Write Award. Manaka's plays continue to be staged, and recent productions of *Gorée* and *Pula* were produced at the African Bank Market Theatre and the Sanlam Studio, Baxter Theatre in Rondebosch (2004). In addition, Maakomele Manaka, Matsemela's son, is working on a movie script adaptation of *Gorée.*

Further Reading

Davis, Geoffrey V. *Voices of Justice and Reason: Apartheid and Beyond in South African Literature.* Amsterdam: Rodopi, 2003.

Fuchs, Anne, ed. *New Theatre in Francophone and Anglophone Africa.* Amsterdam: Rodopi, 1999.

Mangua, Charles (ca. 1940–)

Kenyan novelist Mangua was born in Nyeri, Kenya, and educated at the universities of Makerere and Oxford. He worked as an economist with the African Development Bank in Abidjan before returning to Kenya after the publication of his best-known novel **Son of Woman**. His later work includes *A Tail in the Mouth* and short stories.

Mapanje, Jack (1944–)

A Malawian poet, Mapanje was born of Yao and Nyanja parents in Kadango village, Malawi.

He attended Roman Catholic schools and then trained as a teacher. He took a bachelor's at Chancellor College, where he was a member of a group of aspiring writers that met regularly to discuss one another's work. He gained his master's in literature and his PhD degrees at London University and worked as a university lecturer in Malawi. He was placed in detention in 1987–91 by the Banda regime. After his release he moved to York, UK, where he has held a variety of teaching posts. He has made brief visits to Malawi since Banda's election defeat of 1994. These have enabled him to contribute to the vigorous debate about the future of the country. He is a Professorial Research Fellow in the School of English at the University of Leeds, and he was the recipient of the Fonlon-Nichols Award of the African Literature Association in 2002.

His two collections of poetry are *Of Chameleons and Gods* (1981), which includes work presented to the writers' group in the early 1970s, poems composed in London when he was doing his postgraduate degree, and verses written on "Re-entering Chingwe's Hole" on his return to Malawi with his master's degree. *The Chattering Wagtails of Mikuyu Prison* (1993) includes poems written in prison and following his release. Most recently he has edited *Gathering Seaweed: African Prison Writing* (2002), which is an anthology of African literature of incarceration, and has published *A Democracy of Chameleons: Politics and Culture in the New Malawi* (2002) with Harri Englund.

Recent work includes poems that follow up the trails begun in Mikuyu and responses to events in South Africa and Rwanda. As an academic he has shown continued concern with oral traditions and has embarked on an attempt to establish a theoretical basis for the critical examination of prison literature.

Marabi Dance, The (1973)

A novel by Modikwe **Dikobe**. The novel deals with class issues in the inner-city slumyard

Doornforntein in the 1930s. The protagonist, Martha, finds herself resisting the working-class slumyards in her hopes to acquire a middle-class status. Its depiction of urban growth emphasizes the adaptability of the working classes. The workshopped play *Marabi* (1981) is based on the novel.

Marechera, Dambudzo (1952–87)

Zimbabwean novelist and poet Marechera was born in Rusape and grew up amid racial discrimination, poverty, and violence. He attended St. Augustine's Mission, Penhalonga, where he clashed with his teachers over the colonial teaching syllabus; the University of Rhodesia, from which he was expelled during student unrest; and New College, Oxford, which also expelled him. In his short career he published a book of stories, two novels (one posthumously), a book of plays, prose, and poetry, and a collection of poetry (also posthumous).

He wrote *The **House of Hunger*** (1978) during a period of despair that followed his time at Oxford. The title story describes his brutalized childhood and youth in colonial Rhodesia. The book won the 1979 *Guardian* fiction prize. *Black Sunlight* (1980) explores the idea of anarchism as a formal intellectual position. *The Black Insider* (1990) is set in a faculty of arts building that offers refuge for a group of intellectuals and artists from an unspecified war outside, which subsequently engulfs them as well. The characters' conversation centers around African identity and the nature of art.

Marechera returned to the newly liberated Zimbabwe in 1982 to assist in shooting the film of *House of Hunger* but fell out with the director. He led a homeless existence in Harare before his death five years later. *Mindblast; or, The Definitive Buddy* (1984) was written the year after his return home. It contains three plays, a prose narrative, a collection of poems, and a park-bench diary. The book criticizes the materialism, intolerance, opportunism, and corruption of postindependence Zimbabwe, extending the political debate beyond the question of nationalism to embrace genuine social regeneration. The combination of intense self-scrutiny, cogent social criticism, and open, experimental form appealed to a young generation of Zimbabweans who were seeking new ways of perceiving their roles within the emergent nation.

Marechera's poetry was published posthumously under the title *Cemetery of Mind* (1992). These poems show the influence of modernist writers from Arthur Rimbaud and T. S. Eliot to Allen Ginsberg and Christopher **Okigbo**. His individualism, literary experimentation, and iconoclasm ensure that his work resists narrow definitions. Marechera's works have been included in such anthologies as *Nobody Ever Said AIDS: Stories and Poems from Southern Africa* (2004) and *Exile and African Literature: African Literature Today* (2000). Many of his works were republished, including *House of Hunger* (2004), *The Black Insider* (1999), and *Scrapiron Blues* (1999).

Further Reading

Pattison, David. *No Room for Cowardice: A View of the Life and Times of Dambudzo Marechera.* Trenton, NJ: Africa World Press, 2002.

Veit-Wild, Flora. *Dambudzo Marechera: A Source Book on His Life and Work.* London: Hans Zell, 2002.

Veit-Wild, Flora, and Anthony Chennells, eds. *Emerging Perspectives on Dambudzo Marechera.* Trenton, NJ: Africa World Press, 1999.

Marriage of Anansewa, The (1975)

A play by Efua **Sutherland**. The play is based on the Ananse storytelling tradition, and includes elements such as musical interludes and community participation. The audience is meant to gain self-reflection from the trickster figure and the plot, which has Ananse, the father of Anansewa, encouraging suitors for his daughter, and then eliminating all but her chosen one by announcing her death.

Marshall, Bill Okyere (1936–)

Ghanaian dramatist and novelist. Marshall was educated at Presbyterian schools and later attended the Guildhall School of Music and Drama in London. He spent a period in the United States, during which he composed the play *The Son of Umbele* (1973). On his return home, he wrote regularly for the press and from 1966 worked in the drama department of Ghana Television. In the 1970s he worked in advertising and subsequently set up his own media business, Studio Africain. During the early 1990s, he was both head of the National Film and Television Institute in Accra and lecturer at Legon's School of Performing Arts.

In addition to writing for the theater Marshall has written radio and television plays, and his novels include *Bukom* (1979) and *Permit for Survival* (1981). Both large-scale plays such as *Umbele* and "sittingroom dramas" such as *The Crows* (collected with *The Queue* and *Ali Dando* in *The Crows and Other Plays,* 1998) display his discipline, control, and awareness of the significance of color and sound. *The Oyster Man* (2000) follows the life of Kodzo, who is perceived as having mystical powers due to his birth in a canoe in the Volta river; *Stranger to Innocence* (2003) portrays the happiness and difficulties of an African priestly family; and *Shadow of an Eagle* (2003) depicts the life of a rural African family who deal with the return of one of the characters, Bimpo, from an absence in a foreign location.

In *Son of Umbele,* a drama of strong passions is played out before a fisherman's home. In *The Crows,* Marshall infuses a sense of authentic tragedy into a domestic drama that depicts the effect of a minister of religion's return from exile.

Martha Quest (1952)

The first of four novels in Doris **Lessing**'s *The Children of Violence* series. This novel, set in a British African colony based on Rhodesia, follows Martha from her teenage years into her young adult experience of city life. She escapes from her parents' farm to the social world of the city, only to find herself married and a mother. The other novels in the series build on this theme of freedom and imprisonment as they relate to an internal and external realization of self.

Master of Petersburg, The (1994)

A novel by J. M. **Coetzee**. The protagonist of the novel is a fictional Dostoevsky who searches for answers regarding his stepson's death in Dresden. The novel uses historical events and fictional characters to deconstruct the line between fiction, history, and reality.

Matigari (1989)

A novel by **Ngugi wa Thiong'o**, translated from Gikuyu (*Matigari,* 1986). This is a multigeneric interpretation of the novelistic form, which utilizes realism, oral narrative, performance, and myth to create a postmodern and experimental form.

Mattera, Umaruiddin Don (1935–)

South African poet, autobiographer, and short-story writer. Mattera was born in Western Native Township, Johannesburg, and was a founding member of the **Black Consciousness** movement. His publications include *Azanian Love Song* (1983), a book of poems that won a PEN award in 1983; *Gone with the Twilight: A Story of Sophiatown* (1987; published in the United States as *Sophiatown: Coming of Age in South Africa),* an autobiography; *The Storyteller* (1989), a collection of stories; and *The Five Magic Pebbles* (1992), a children's book. He works as a journalist for the *Guardian/Weekly Mail.*

Mattera's work focuses on the social and political world of South Africa. The spirit of reconciliation characterizes his autobiography, where he talks about the disintegration of his immediate family, his time as the leader of the youth gang the Vultures and the gang's shift from a kind of defense unit for street kids into one of the most violent and feared gangs in Johannesburg. Mattera was honored in 2004 by the Italian-South African Cultural Centre for his contribution for the liberation struggle. He has also won several international literary and humanitarian awards, including the World Health Organization's Peace Award from the Centre of Violence and Injury Prevention in 1997.

Matthews, James (1929–)

South African poet and short-story writer. Born in Cape Town, the son of a dock laborer and a charwoman, Matthews has held a variety of jobs, including newspaper boy, messenger, reporter for the *Golden City Post* and *Drum*, and night telephone operator. Of the generation of Es'kia **Mphahlele**, Lewis **Nkosi**, and Dennis **Brutus**, he began writing short stories in the 1950s, was one of the leading poets in the black literary renaissance of the 1970s, founded Blac Publishing House, which published some of his own work, and was detained without trial in Victor Verster prison in 1976. Matthews also established Realities in 2000, a publishing house based in Cape Town.

Undaunted when *Cry Rage!*, the anthology *Black Voices Shout!* (1974), and *Pass Me a Meatball, Jones* (1977) were banned, Matthews went on to publish *No Time for Dreams* (1981) and *Poisoned Wells and Other Delights* (1990). His early poems were passionate expressions of protest, attacking the inhumanity of **apartheid**, criticizing whites' lack of concern, and celebrating black survival. His short stories, twenty-four of which have been collected in *The Park and Other Stories* (1974), delineate the everyday sufferings of black people, making the reader aware of the wider context of social injustice. Stories such as "Azikwelwa" and "The Park" depict the beginnings of resistance. He sets his novel *The Party Is Over* (1997) in a "coloured" (mixed-race) area of Cape Town in the 1960s and deals with the frustration and despair of a writer trapped in a thwarting environment. Matthews is also the author of *Flames and Flowers* (2000) and *Poems from a Prison Cell* (2002).

Maunick, Edouard (1931–)

Mauritian poet, trained as a schoolteacher and a librarian. He published his first volume of poetry in Port Louis, *Ces Oiseaux de sang* (1954). He moved to Paris in the early 1960s to work for the French overseas radio as producer. He started at that time to publish in *Présence africaine*. In 1964 *Les manèges de la mer* was published. It was the first demonstration of his warm and sensual lyricism, found in all his following works: *Mascaret au Ie livre de la mer et de la mort* (1966), or in a more somber tone, influenced by the Nigeria-Biafra war, *Fusillez moi* (1970). He was appointed to UNESCO in 1970. He became Mauritian ambassador to the new South Africa in 1994. One of his most important works is *Anthologie personnelle* (1989), a personal anthology. He is also the author of *De sable et de cendr: poèmes* with illustrations by Robert Brandy (1996), translated as *Only the Poem* (2000); *It and Island—Poems of the Same Passion* (2002); *Poèmes (1964–1966–1970)* (ca. 2001); and *Mandela Dead and Alive 1976-200—Madela mort et vif* (2001). Maunick has been honored with le Grand Prix de la Francophonie 2003 by the French Academy, has received the Prix Apollinaire and the le Grand Prix international de Poésie Eugène Guillevic, is a member of the High Council of Francophonie and has been honored as a Chevalier of Arts and Lettres.

Mazrui, Ali A. (1933–)

Kenyan political scientist and essayist. Mazrui was educated in Great Britain and has taught at Makerere College (Uganda) and the University of Michigan. He holds the Albert Schweitzer Chair in the Humanities at Binghamton University, New York. Three of his many books are *Towards a Pax Africana* (1967), *A World Federation of Cultures* (1976), and *Cultural Forces in World Politics* (1990), but he is also well known for his novel, *The **Trial of Christopher Okigbo*** (1971). Recently, Mazrui has published *General History of Africa: Africa since 1935 Vol. 8* with Christopher Wondjie (1999); *The African Diaspora: African Origins and New World Identities* (co-editors Isidore Okpewho and Carole Boyce Davies, 1999); *Political Culture of Language: Swahili, Society and the State* (1999); *The Titan of Tanzania: Julius K Nyerere's Legacy* (2002); *Black Reparations in the Era of Globalization* (2002); and *The African Predicament and the American Experience: A Tale of Two Edens* (2004). Mazrui's work has also been anthologized by Ricardo René Laremont, Tracia Leacock Seghatolislami, Michael A. Toler, Fouad Kalouche, Toyin Falola, and Robert Ostergard in works such as *Power, Politics and the African Condition: Collected Essays of Ali Mazrui* (2004), *Africanity Redefined: Collected Essays of Ali Mazrui* (*Classic Authors and Texts on Africa*, 2002), and *Africa and Other Civilizations: Conquest and Counter-Conquest—Collected Essays of Ali A. Mazrui. Vol. 2* (2002).

Mazrui is currently the Director of the Institute of Global Cultural Studies, the Albert Schweitzer Professor in the Humanities, and a Professor of Political Science and of Africana Studies at the State University of New York at Binghamton. He is also the Chancellor for the Jomo Kenyatta University of Agriculture and Technology (Nairobi, Kenya), the Albert Luthuli Professor-at-Large for the University of Jos (Nigeria), a Senior Scholar in Africana Studies and Andrew D. White Professor-at-Large Emeritus at Cornell University (Ithaca), and the Ibn Khaldun Professor-at-Large in the School of Islamic and Social Sciences, Leesburg (Virginia). Mazrui has been honored with the Millennium Tribute for Outstanding Scholarship (2000), and with an

Honorary Doctorate of Letters, Nkumba University, Entebbe, Uganda (2000). He is also Vice-President of the International Political Science Association, and a consultant to the United Nations, the World Bank, the Organization of African Unity, UNESCO, and such broadcasting media as the BBC, PBS, ABC, NBC, and the Voice of America.

Further Reading

Mazrui, Alamin, and Willy Mutunga, eds. *Governance and Leadership: Debating the African Condition; Mazrui and His Critics, Volume Two.* Trenton, NJ: Africa World Press, 2003.

———, eds. *Race, Gender and Culture Conflict: Debating the African Condition; Mazrui and His Critics, Volume One.* Trenton, NJ: Africa World Press, 2004.

Mazrui, Alamin, and Ali A. Mazrui. *The Power of Babel: Language and Governance in the African Experience.* Chicago: University of Chicago Press, 1998.

Parviz, Morewedge, ed. *The Scholar between Thought and Experience: A Biographical Festschrift in Honor of Ali A. Mazrui,* Binghamton, NY: Institute of Global Cultural Studies Global Publications, Binghamton University, 2001.

Seifudein, Adem. *Paradigm Lost, Paradigm Regained: The Worldview of Ali A. Mazrui.* Provo, UT: Global Humanities Press, 2002.

Mbuli, Mzwakhe (1959–)

South African poet Mbuli was born in Sophiatown. During the 1970s he was involved in a number of dramatic and musical groups that promoted black creativity through **Black Consciousness**. Mzwakhe has produced a book of poems, *Before Dawn* (1989), and four albums, *Change Is Pain* (1986), *Unbroken Spirit* (1989), *Resistance and Defence* (1992), and *Africa* (1993). His poems, mainly in English, draw on a variety of influences, including praise poetry, Soweto poetry, rap music, dub, and the rhetoric of the political speech or pamphlet. His best-known poems are "Change Is Pain," "Triple-M," which satirizes Homeland leaders, and "Alone," which he composed while in solitary confinement. Mbuli was wrongly imprisoned from 1997 until 2003 for armed robbery and possession of a hand grenade. He recently published *Mbulism* (2004), a powerful work of poetry; *Mzwakhe Mbuli Greatest Hits: Born Free but Always in Chains* (1999), an album that includes four tracks recorded from the Pretoria Central Prison; *Umzwakhe Ubonga Ujehova* (1998); and *Kwazulu Natal* (1997).

Further Reading

Dube, Pamela Z. "Traditional Oral Texts in New Contexts: New Directions in South African Performance Poetry?" In *Across the Lines: Intertextuality and Transcultural Communication in the New Literatures in English,* ed. and introduction Wolfgang Klooss Amsterdam: Rodopi, 93–102.

McLoughlin, Timothy O. (1937–)

A Zimbabwean novelist, poet, and editor born of Irish parentage, McLoughlin was educated at St. George's School, Salisbury (now Harare) and obtained his bachelor's and PhD degrees at Trinity College, Dublin. He was exiled during the liberation war after refusing his call-up to combat the so-called terrorists. He returned to Zimbabwe at independence to be the Chair of English Literature in Harare.

He has produced a considerable body of academic criticism on English and Anglo-Irish eighteenth-century and postcolonial literature. McLoughlin stands out for two main achievements in the creative field: his novel *Karima* (1985) and his encouragement of Zimbabwean poets. *Karima* demonstrates the feelings and commitments of those on both sides of the struggle; in particular it depicts Shona customs and thought patterns. McLoughlin's contribution to the founding and editing of the literary magazine *Moto* gives young or new African writers the opportunity to express a forward-looking liberated culture in both poetry and short stories.

Mda, Zakes (Zanemvula Kizito Gatyeni) (1948–)

A prolific South African writer of plays, novels, poems, and articles for academic journals and newspapers, Mda's creative work also includes paintings and theater and film productions. He was born in the Eastern Cape, spent his early childhood in Soweto, and finished his school education in Lesotho after he joined his father in exile. As a poet, he published in magazines such as *Staffrider, The Voice,* and *Oduma,* and in the anthologies *New South African Writing* (1977), *Summer Fires* (1982), and *Soho Square* (1992). His first volume of poems, *Bits of Debris,* came out in 1986.

In 1978 Mda's play *We Shall Sing for the Fatherland,* written in 1973, won the first Arnstel Playwright of the Year Award. The following year he won this award again with *The Hill,* a play written in 1978. The publication of *We Shall Sing for the Fatherland and Other Plays* in 1980 enabled him to gain admission to Ohio University for a three-year master's degree in theater. His play *The Road,* written in 1982, won the Christina Crawford Award of American Theatre Association in 1984, by which time his plays were being performed in the USSR, the United States, and Scotland as well as in various parts of southern Africa.

Mda returned from the United States in 1984, joining the University of Lesotho as lecturer in the Department of English in 1985. In 1989 he was awarded a PhD by the University of Cape Town and his dissertation was later published as *When People Play People* in 1993, the same year as a collection of four plays, *And the Girls in Their Sunday Dresses.* In 1991 Mda was writer-in-residence at the University of Durham, where he wrote *The Nun's Romantic Story;* in 1992 as research fellow at Yale University he wrote *The Dying Screams of the Moon,* another play, and his first novel, *Ways of Dying* (1995). By 1994 he was back in South Africa as visiting professor at the University of the Witwatersrand. Currently Mda is Professor of Creative Writing and Literary Theory at Ohio University, and also runs a number of community projects and playwriting workshops in Africa. He is also a Founder and Trustee of the Southern African Multimedia AIDS Program, and he has won the 2001 Commonwealth Writers Prize, Africa Region, for *The Heart of Redness,* and the Olive Schreiner and M-Net Book Prizes for *Ways of Dying.*

Mda's plays are distinguished by the combination of a close scrutiny of social values with elements of magic realism that is even more pronounced in his novels, *Ways of Dying* and *She Plays with the Darkness* (1995), and in his novella *Melville 67* (1998). Mda is also the author of *Ululants* (1999); *Fools, Bells and the Habit of Eating: Three Satires* (2002); *The Heart of Redness* (2000); *The Madonna of Excelsior* (2002), which is based on the Immorality Act that made interracial sex illegal, and a 1971 trial; and *The Whale Caller* (2004), which is a kind of romantic comedy that reveals the changing attitudes of postapartheid South Africa.

Further Reading

Farred, Grant. "Mourning the Postapartheid State Already? The Poetics of Loss in Zakes Mda's *Ways of Dying." MFS: Modern Fiction Studies* 46, no. 1 (2000): 183–206.

Jacobs, J. U. "Zakes Mda and the (South) African Renaissance: Reading *She Plays with the Darkness." English in Africa* 27, no. 1 (2000): 55–74.

Liu, Yao-Kun. "Zakes Mda's *We Shall Sing for the Fatherland*: An Illustration of African Life Using European Dramatic Modes." *English in Africa* 30, no. 1 (2003): 123–34.

Salter, Denis. "When People Play People in (Post) Apartheid South Africa: The Theories and Practices of Zakes Mda." *Brecht Yearbook/Das Brecht-Jahrbuch* 22 (1997): 283–303.

Uwah, Chijioke. "The Theme of Political Betrayal in the Plays of Zakes Mda." *English in Africa* 30, no. 1 (2003): 135–44.

Woodward, Wendy. "Laughing Back at the Kingfisher: Zakes Mda's *The Heart of Redness* and Postcolonial Humour." In *Cheeky Fictions: Laughter and the Postcolonial,* ed. Susanne Reichl and Mark Stein. Amsterdam: Rodopi, 2005, 287–99.

Memmi, Albert (1920–)

A professor emeritus of sociology at the University of Paris, Nanterre, novelist and essayist in French, was born in the Jewish ghetto of Tunis, Tunisia. He was educated in Tunis and at the University of Algiers before his studies were interrupted by World War II. After the war, he completed his education in France before returning to Tunis, where he taught philosophy, worked as a journalist, and practiced as a psychologist. When Tunisia gained independence in 1956, he resettled in France, where he continues to reside.

His autobiographical first novel, *La Statue de sel* (1953; *The Pillar of Salt,* 1955), followed by *Agar* (1955; *Strangers,* 1960), established his early reputation as a provocative and controversial author. He draws on his own experience to provide insight into the plight of the dominated and oppressed within Tunisian society. The complexities of cultural division within his fiction also provide Memmi with the impetus for his study on colonialism and decolonization, *Portrait du colonisé* (1957; *The Colonizer and the Colonized,* 1965), which focuses on the destructive elements of oppression. A study of the Jewish condition, *Portrait d'un juif* (1962; *Portrait of a Jew,* 1962), was followed by *La Libération du juif* (1966; *The Liberation of the Jew,* 1966). After the publication of *L'Homme dominé* (1968; *Dominated Man,* 1968), he returned to fiction with *Le Scorpion* (1969; *The Scorpion,* 1971), a convoluted novel in which the protagonist becomes immersed in a metaphysical journey both to rediscover his past and to redefine his identity. His controversial study *Juifs et arabes* (1974; *Jews and Arabs,* 1975) was followed by *Le Désert* (1977), a novel set in the fifteenth century that provides Memmi with an imaginary venue to continue his quest for self-discovery.

Two more studies, *La Dépendance* (1979; *Dependence*, 1984) and *Le Racisme* (1982), were followed by *Le Pharaon* (1988), a novel similar in context to his early fiction in which the conflicted protagonist is forced to choose between the two cultures of his inheritance. In 2000 Memmi published *Racism*, translated by Stephen Martinot. *Racism* is a meditation on the subject of racism as a social mechanism, and explores how it can be overcome. The book contains three sections, "Description," "Definition," and "Treatment," which work through the causes, functions, and development of racism over centuries. New editions of *The Colonizer and the Colonized* (1991, 2001, 2003) have appeared recently, with introductions and afterwords from such influential persons as Jean-Paul Sartre, Homi Bhaba, and Susan Gilson Miller. Throughout his literary career, Memmi has maintained a unique commitment to his Tunisian heritage and his Jewish identity. He is the most prominent Tunisian novelist writing in French and one of the major theoreticians of Maghrebi literature.

Meniru, Theresa Ekwutosi (1931–)

Nigerian children's writer Meniru trained as a teacher in Nigeria and Britain, and after her return to Nigeria, she taught in schools and colleges in Nigeria, served as principal of St. Theresa's Training College, and worked for the Nigerian federal and state ministries of education before her retirement in 1984. Her three publications, *The Bad Fairy and the Caterpillar* (1970), *The Carver and The Leopard* (1971), and *The Melting Girl and Other Stories* (1971), are informed by popular Igbo folktales. She co-authored *Omalinze* (1971), another reconstructed Igbo tale. Her later works, including *Unoma* (1976), *Unoma at College* (1981), *Footsteps in the Dark* (1982), and *Drums of Joy* (1982), are adventure stories of brave and courageous boys and girls, as are *Ibe the Cannon Boy* (1987) and *The Last Card* (1987).

Mezu, S(ebastian) Okechukwu (1941–)

Nigerian novelist, poet, and literary critic Mezu was born in Owerri, Nigeria, and studied in Nigeria before continuing his education at Georgetown, La Salle, and Johns Hopkins Universities in the United States, where he earned a doctorate. He was a UNESCO fellow at the Sorbonne and Director of the African Studies and Research Program at the State University of New York, Buffalo. He established the Black Academy Press, through which he published several books. His book of poems, *The Tropical Dawn* (1970), which includes an elaborate essay entitled "Poetry and Revolution in Modern Africa," makes conscious use of elements from his cultural environment to create poetry with human concerns. His novel *Behind the Rising Sun* (1970) is about the Nigeria-Biafra war. The story examines the tribulations of a group of people desperate for survival and the subsequent effects of their interactions with dubious foreigners as well as dishonest compatriots. His critical works include *Léopold Sédar Senghor et la défense et illustration de la civilisation noire* (1968), *The Poetry of Léopold Sédar Senghor* (1973), and *The Philosophy of Pan-Africanism*. Mezu returned to Nigeria in the late 1970s and became involved in politics. When the military intervened he returned to publishing, and he has also become a successful businessman, now based in the United States, where he edits the revived *Black Academy Review*. Mezu also published *Black Nationalists: Reconsidering Du Bois, Garvey, Booker T. and Nkrumah* with Rose Ure Mezu (1999), which is a selection of academic papers edited by Okechukwu and Rose Mezu, and *The Life and Times of Saro-Wiwa* (1996). In addition, Mezu has contributed to such works as *Africa and the Diaspora: The Black Scholar and Society* (1999), *Black Leaders of the Centuries* (1970), and *The Meaning of Africa to Afro-Americans: A Comparative Study of Race and Racism* (1972).

Mhlophe, Gcina (1958–)

A South African children's writer, poet, and short-story writer, Mhlophe was born in Natal of a Xhosa mother and Zulu father and raised by her grandmother; she relates experiences of an eventful childhood in her autobiographical play, *Have You Seen Zandile?* (1988). After matriculating in the Eastern Cape and working for a year as a domestic in Johannesburg, she completed a journalism course and became a radio newsreader and writer for *Learn and Teach* magazine. Since 1983 she has been an actor, playwright, and director for the Market Theatre in Johannesburg.

Her short stories and poetry are regularly published in journals and anthologies, but she is primarily known for her folktales and children's stories: *The Snake with Seven Heads* (1989), *Queen of the Tortoises* (1990), *The Singing Dog* (1992), and *Hi, Zoleka!* (1994). Mhlophe is also the author of works such as *Fudukazi's Magic* (1999), *Nalohima, the Deaf Tortoise* (1999), *Nozincwadi Mother of Books* (2001), *African Mother Christmas* (2002), *Love Child* (ca. 2002), *Stories of Africa* (2003), *Molo Zoleka!* with Elizabeth Pulles (2003), and *Sawubona, Zoleka!* with Elizabeth Pulles (2003). Mhlophe has also released a storytelling CD titled *Fudukazi's Magic* (2000), and in 2001 her book *Nozincwadi Mother of Books* was produced as part of her nationwide reading road show to South African schools. Mhlophe has also received the BBC Africa Service Award for Radio Drama, the Fringe First Award at Edinburgh Festival, the Joseph Jefferson Award in Chicago, the OBBIE in New York, and honorary doctorates from London Open University and University of Natal.

Mhudi (1930)

A novel by Sol T. **Plaatje** (written between 1917 and 1920). Mhudi is the resilient female protagonist in Plaatje's narrative of the precolonial existence of the Barolong people.

Their encounters with European colonizers are followed in a manner that explores the effect of such contact on their future. The novel critiques racial segregation and the Land Act of 1913. Plaatje also relies on oral narrative techniques and uses more than one language to convey his message of shared humanity.

Miller, Ruth (1919–69)

A South African poet, Miller was born at Uitenhage in Cape Province, grew up in Pietersberg in the northern Transvaal, and spent her adult life in Belleville, Johannesburg, where she worked for many years as a clerk-typist and later as an English teacher. Her affection for the land accounts for the sense of awe in her poems; the loss of a fourteen-year-old son by electrocution may account for the pain that is often close to the surface.

Miller wrote poetry, short stories, and radio plays but is best remembered for her poetry, which was collected first as *Floating Island* (1965) and later in *Selected Poems* (1968). A selection of uncollected poems and other writing was published in *Ruth Miller: Poems, Prose, Plays* (1991), edited by Lionel **Abrahams**. Her poems, highly personal, are shaped by a wide reading of contemporary poets, a literary correspondence with Guy **Butler**, and a profound sense and experience of the violence to the individual body and psyche of Verwoerd's **apartheid** policies.

Further Reading

Pinnock, Don. *Ruth First: They Fought for Freedom.* Cape Town, South Africa: Maskew Miller Longman, 1995.

Millin, Sarah Gertrude (1888–1968)

South African novelist. Millin was barely a year old when her family moved from Lithuania, where she was born, to the Vaal River.

A contradictory figure, she was a friend of Jan Smuts and in many ways a liberal, yet the social commentaries in her fiction, intended for readers outside South Africa, were perceived internationally as overtly racist. Her best-known novel, *God's Step-Children* (1924), was acclaimed in the United States on the basis of what proved to be a misreading of its racist theme, but did not find an audience in South Africa. Two historical novels, *King of Bastards* (1949) and *The Burning Man* (1952), finally gained her the readership in South Africa she sought with *God's Step-Children*. Millin's *General Smuts* (volumes 1 and 2) have recently been republished by Simon Publications (2001). Critical debate about Millin continues. J. M. **Coetzee** argues that, like many serious writers, she was influenced by the scientific and social theories of her time, which were racist and sexist.

Mine Boy (1946)

A novel by Peter **Abrahams**, which uses the figure of the mine boy, Xuma, to explore the experience of the urban working classes. It also follows a number of other characters as they meet up at a shebeen run by a woman named Leah. The characters and their lives are both individualistic and representative portraits.

Mission to Kala (1958)

A novel by Mongo **Beti**, translated from the French (*Mission terminé*, 1957). First published in English as *Mission Accomplished,* this novel is set in colonial French Cameroon in the 1950s. The narrative is that of Jean-Marie Medza, whose father sends him on a mission to bring back his cousin's runaway wife from the town of Kala. With an exaggerated opinion of Jean-Marie's education and status, the townspeople treat him to extravagant celebrations, and he returns home married and with an appreciation for drink. The book's cynical language critiques the influence of colonialism on town life.

Mnthali, Felix (1933–)

A Malawian poet, novelist, and playwright, Mnthali was born at Shurugwi in the midlands of Zimbabwe (where his maternal grandfather had worked for Cecil Rhodes) and educated at Pius XII University College (now the University of Lesotho) and the University of Alberta (MA, PhD). Like many colleagues at the University of Malawi, he was jailed without charge in the 1970s. He is a professor of English at the University of Botswana.

Mnthali's publications include the poetry collection **When Sunset Comes to Sapitwa** (1980), two novels, *My Dear Anniversary* (1992) and *Yoranivyoto* (1999), a story about Malawi set between 1964 and the early 1990s, and several plays. Mnthali's verse is humanist in a traditional way that affirms life and diversity. The voices of **Okot p'Bitek**, **Ngugi wa Thiong'o**, Jack **Mapanje**, Christopher **Okigbo**, Chinua **Achebe**, and Ken **Lipenga** echo throughout verse that envisions a world beyond the ruin of youthful hopes for Malawi's independence.

Modisane, William "Bloke" (1923–86)

South African autobiographer and short-story writer Modisane grew up in Sophiatown, a black township in Johannesburg, where he saw one sister die of malnutrition and his father murdered and where his mother, called Ma-Bloke, ran a shebeen in order to support the family. He worked at Vanguard, a bookshop owned by a former trade unionist with radical sympathies, before becoming a journalist at *Drum,* during that magazine's glory years in the 1950s, as part of a team of writers that included Henry Nxumalo, Can **Themba**, Es'kia **Mphahlele**, and Lewis **Nkosi**. He also worked as jazz critic for the *Golden City Post,* the Johannesburg weekly tabloid and *Drum's* sister publication. Inspired by American cinema, he cultivated a debonair style that suited Sophiatown, home to jazz singers, shebeen queens, and *tsotsis* (gangsters). His nickname, Bloke, was inspired by the Leslie Charteris thriller novels featuring the Saint.

Drum published his short stories "The Dignity of Begging" (1951), about a beggar who prefers begging to working and who dreams of organizing a beggars' union, and "The Respectable Pickpocket" (1954), about a thief who pits his wits against society and the legal system. The title of another story, "The Situation," published in *Black Orpheus,* refers to the street slang for an educated African, like Modisane himself, who is "situated" above his fellows and finds he does not belong anywhere. Modisane was part of the African Theatre Workshop and played Shark in the first production of Athol **Fugard**'s play **No-Good Friday**. Some of Modisane's work is included in *The Anchor Book of Modern African Stories,* edited by Nadezda Obradovic and Chinua Achebe (2002).

In 1959 he left South Africa for England. There in 1963 he published **Blame Me on History**, his only book, which is remembered for its frankness and power. The book is at once a hymn to Sophiatown, destroyed in the late 1950s, and an analysis of what **apartheid** does to the soul of the educated black man. The volume was banned in South Africa in 1966. In exile, he worked as a writer, actor, and broadcaster and had a leading part in the London production of Jean Genet's *The Blacks* at the Royal Court Theatre. He died in Dortmund, West Germany.

Mofolo, Thomas (Mopoku) (1876–1948)

A novelist writing in Sesotho, Mofolo was born at Khojane in the Mafeteng region of Lesotho. He was schooled at Morija mission and graduated as a teacher in 1888. He gained international recognition through the publication, in translation, of his third novel, **Chaka**, in 1931.

His first novel, *Moeti oa Bochabela (Traveller to the East)* (1907) is an allegorical tale reminiscent of Bunyan's *The Pilgrim's Progress.* Despite its apparent simplicity, the novel shows the merging of traditional beliefs and Christian thought, thus pointing to a theme Mofolo develops more fully in his other novels. Another Sotho novel, *Pitseng* (1910), deals with the life of Katse and depicts the contrast between the ideal and the actual behavior of Christians as well as the conflict between traditional beliefs and Christian values. While still busy writing *Pitseng,* Mofolo started collecting historical data on the life of the Zulu conqueror Shaka. The results of his study were eventually published in 1925 as *Chaka,* a tragedy that describes the rise and subsequent fall of a hero whose pact with evil forces brings about one of the most brutal acts of destruction humankind has ever witnessed. The strength of the novel lies primarily in its characterization of the hero, portrayed as a man with noble possibilities that have gone tragically wrong. Mofolo offers adept psychological and philosophical insight into a remarkably complex personality.

Further Reading

Hooper, Myrtle. "Reading Africa: Mofolo's *Chaka* and the Subject of English, Current Writing." *Text and Reception in Southern Africa* 10, no. 2 (1998): 19–37.

Ricard, Alain. *The Languages and Literatures of Africa: The Sands of Babel.* London: James Currey Publishers, 2004.

Moore, Bai T(amia) J(ohnson) (1916–88)

Liberian poet, novelist, folklorist, and essayist. Moore was born in Dimeh, northwest of Monrovia, and originally trained as an agriculturist at Virginia Union University in the United States, from where he returned in 1941 as an administrator in the Liberian civil service. After a brief secondment to UNESCO, during which he served in the organization's education program within Liberia itself, he joined the government of President William S. Tubman as an under-secretary of state for cultural affairs.

Moore's poetry first appeared in *Echoes from the Valley: Being Odes and Other Poems,* which he co-edited with Ronald T. Dempster and T. H. Carey (1947). His main work includes a volume of poetry, *Ebony Dust* (1962, republished in 2001); a novella, *Murder in the Cassava Patch* (1963), which concerns a man betrayed by a lover (reproduced in *Liberian Writing*, 1970), with an introduction by President Tubman; and a popular novel, *The Money Doubler* (1976). He also contributed a story to *Four Stories by Liberian Writers*, edited by Wilton Sankawulo (1980). With Jangaba Johnson he published a collection of Liberian folktales, *Chips from the African Story Tree*.

Further Reading

"Bai Tamia Moore 1920–1988." *Liberian Studies Journal* 1920–1988 (Tribute) 1, no. 13 (1990): 5–9.

"Landsman: The Conversations of Bai T. Moore," with Dr. Arnold Odio. *Liberian Studies Journal* 15, no. 2 (1990): 32–49.

Liberian Studies Journal 15, no. 2, Special Issue in Memory of Bai Tamia Moore 1920–1988. Sewanee: Liberian Studies Association, 1990.

Mopeli-Paulus, A(twell) S(idwell)
(1913–60)

Poet and novelist. Mopeli-Paulus was resident in South Africa but born in Lesotho, a direct descendant of King Moshoeshoe's half-brother, Mopeli. He wrote both in Sesotho and in English; his Sesotho poetry is reflected best in *Ho tamaea ke ho bona (To Travel Is to Learn)* (1945), which contains accounts of his experience as a soldier in the Cape Corps during World War II. He is known for his novel **Blanket Boy's Moon** (1953, republished in 2000, written in collaboration with Peter Lanham). Although his second English-language novel, *Turn to the Dark* (1956, written in collaboration with Miriam Basner), did not enjoy the same popular success as *Blanket Boy's Moon,* his writing set the trend for many similar stories by black writers in the 1950s and 1960s.

Motsisi, (Karobo Moses) Casey "Kid"
(1932–77)

A South African journalist and short-story writer, Motsisi was born in Western Native Township (Johannesburg) and was trained as a teacher in Pretoria, where he edited the school magazine. He worked as a journalist at **Drum** magazine until 1962 and returned in 1974, having worked for *The World* in between. He is best known for his "On the Beat" column, which ran continuously from 1958 to 1962 and resumed in 1974. His style is a blend of American idiom and *tsotsitaal* (township slang) and his sketches draw freely on the Sophiatown shebeen culture with which he was thoroughly familiar, depicting a gallery of such township types as Aunt Peggy, the shebeen queen, and a variety of rogues such as "Kid Playboy" and "Kid Hangover." He also wrote a few stories for *The Classic,* a journal edited by Nat **Nakasa**. Of these, "Mita" (1963) is the most interesting: the story deftly evokes the Sophiatown milieu that inspired much of the black writing of the 1950s. A posthumous collection of his writings, *Casey and Co.: Selected Writings of Casey "Kid" Motsisi,* was published in 1978.

Further Reading

Tyler, Humphrey. *Life in the Time of Sharpeville: Wayward Seeds of the New South Africa.* Cape Town, South Africa: Kwela Books, 1995.

Mphahlele, Es'kia (Ezekiel) (1919–)

A South African novelist, short-story writer, and critic, Mphahlele was born in Pretoria. After a late start at school he qualified as a teacher, and in 1945 joined the staff of Orlando High School. Dismissed from teaching for his opposition to "Bantu education" in 1952, he joined the magazine **Drum** as political reporter and fiction editor. He gained a master's degree at the University of South Africa in 1956 and the following year began a period of exile that did not end until his return to South Africa in 1977. During his exile he taught at universities in Africa and the United States, gained a PhD at the University of Denver, and served as director of the Congress for Cultural Freedom in Paris. He retired in 1987 as professor of African literature at the University of the Witwatersrand. Es'kia is currently a Professor Emeritus at Witwatersrand University, has been awarded a University of Cape Town honorary doctorate of literature (2003), and the Titan Prize in Literature as Writer of the Century (2000).

Mphahlele's reputation as a writer has a great deal to do with his autobiography, **Down Second Avenue** (1959). Written in the mode of social realism interspersed with reflective passages, the book describes his childhood and the years leading up to his exile and is dominated by powerful female characters. The sequel to his autobiography, *Afrika My Music* (1984), was written and published on his return from exile and brings the story of his life up to date, recording in stream-of-consciousness fashion his reactions to the changing political face of Africa. The autobiographical novel *The Wanderers* (1968), which earned Mphahlele his doctorate and a nomination for the Nobel Prize for Literature, is set in countries modeled on Nigeria and Kenya and deals with the experience of exile. It has narrative features in common with his other novel, *Chirundu* (1979), which chronicles the downfall of a Zambian cabinet minister after his bigamy is exposed. The short story is also important to Mphahlele, who began his writing career with the collection *Man Must Live* (1946). Some of the stories that first appeared in *Drum* were included in his later collections, *The Living and Dead* (1961), *In Corner B* (1967), *The Unbroken Song* (1981), and *Renewal Time* (1988). He also wrote a novella for young readers, *Father Come Home* (1984).

He has expressed his thoughts and experiences in numerous critical articles and two seminal volumes, *The African Image* (1962, rev. 1974) and *Voices in the Whirlwind* (1972), which have been called his intellectual autobiographies. Both books have had a far-reaching effect on African writing, since Mphahlele was one of the earliest critics to question the applicability of value judgments to the emerging African canon and to argue for a new way of reading African literature. More recently Mphahlele has published *Es'kia: Es'kia Mphahlele on Education, African Humanism and Culture, Social Consciousness, Literary Appreciation,* with a foreword by Don Mattera (2003), and *Seasons Come to Pass: A Poetry Anthology for Southern African Students. Second Edition* (2002).

Mphahlele achieved notoriety with his criticism of negritude, which he argued failed to address the political needs of the African people and dismissed their revolutionary potential. Moreover he believes that only when black people can find their identity in the sum total of their experience of both traditional and Western society will the process of cultural and political decolonization begin. Like **Ngugi wa Thiong'o**, he has voiced doubts about the effectiveness of writing in English for an African audience, given his belief in literature's role in raising the political consciousness of people. It is this realization that forms the basis for the black aesthetic he has spent his life seeking to define. The testimony of Mphahlele's life and work is that it is only in relation to people and their social context that art has any validity.

Further Reading

Ruth Obee. *Es'kia Mphahlele: Themes of Alienation and African Humanism.* Athens: Ohio University Press, 1999.

Mpina, Edison (1942–)
Malawian poet and novelist. A Lomwe from Malawi's Mulanje district and a banker by profession, Mpina was educated at Zomba Catholic Secondary School but missed tertiary studies and thus remains relatively

uninfluenced by the University of Malawi's Writers' Workshop, which contributed to the development of fellow Malawian poets such as Ken **Lipenga** and Jack **Mapanje**. Indeed he did not begin to write until he reached middle age, after having experienced imprisonment without charge and personal tragedy. In 1981 his poem "Summer Fires of Mulanje Mountain" won a BBC award over literally thousands of others. His collection *Raw Pieces* and his long poem *Malawi Poetry Today* (both 1986) appeared after his experience at the Iowa International Workshop in 1982. With the fall of the Banda regime, his writing output increased and he set up a Malawian branch of PEN.

He writes about the land and the people of Malawi. *Malawi Poetry Today* wryly interrogates the context of most modern Malawian poetry. He founded the Lingadzi Writers' Workshop in Lilongwe. In the early 1990s he turned to prose, his novels *The Low Road to Death* and *Freedom Avenue* appearing in 1990 and 1991, respectively. The first attacks materialism, the second deals with the forced labor system on the tea estates of colonial Nyasaland.

Mtshali, (Oswald) Mbuyiseni (1940–)

South African poet Mtshali was born and went to school in the north of KwaZulu-Natal. He moved to Johannesburg, but was prevented by **apartheid** legislation from studying at the University of the Witwatersrand. He later went to the United States and completed master's degrees in creative writing and in education at Columbia University.

His first volume of poems, *Sounds of a Cowhide Drum* (1971), was a significant landmark in South African literature. In it he analyses the everyday experiences of black people living in an oppressive society. A number of black writers were inspired by Mtshali's example, which coincided with and partly provided an expression for the first strong stirrings of the **Black Consciousness** movement.

Many of the poets who followed Mtshali were more direct—more angry and/or more lyrical—than he had been. And as black politics became more militant in the next few years, Mtshali was often criticized for being too negative, and for not offering vigorous support to an alternative to apartheid oppression. His second volume of poems reveals a changed tone. Its strongest poems express a militancy that is immediate but that also looks back to the values of traditional African societies. *Fireflames* was banned by the government, but unbanned in 1986.

Further Reading

Gaylard, Rob. "Mtshali Then and Now: *Sounds of a Cowhide Drum* and *Fireflames* in Retrospect." *Scrutiny2: Issues in English Studies in Southern Africa* 5, no. 2 (2000): 33–38.

Mugo, Micere Githae (1942–)

A Kenyan poet, playwright, and literary critic, Mugo was born in Baricho, in Kirinyaga district. After primary and secondary education in Kenya, she gained university degrees at Makerere University in Kampala, Uganda (BA), and the University of New Brunswick, Canada (MA, PhD). She accepted a teaching position at the University of Nairobi in 1973, and in 1978 became the first female dean of the Faculty of Arts. Mugo is now a professor in the Department of African American Studies at Syracuse University in New York. The Mau Mau struggle of the 1950s impressed notions of self-liberation upon the adolescent Mugo, but an Anglocentric colonial education disparaged that history and the local culture. Her intuitions about the Mau Mau were rekindled by the anti-**apartheid** and American civil rights movements of the 1960s, which, along with her embrace of socialism, left a lasting impact on her poetry. Because of her political views, Mugo suffered arbitrary arrests by the Kenyan police and with the confiscation of her passport in 1982 had to go into exile. Since 1984 she has been a Zimbabwean citizen.

Mugo's first collection of poems, *Daughter of My People, Sing!* (1976), incisively questions the received ideas that constitute personal and cultural identities and reappreciates values, including "singing," that made it possible for her people to confront various hostile forces. Mugo's heightened sense of her people's history comes out in the play she co-authored with **Ngugi wa Thiong'o** in 1976, *The Trial of Dedan Kimathi,* while the vitality that she finds in oral forms is apparent in the lyrical flourish of *My Mother's Song and Other Poems* (1994). Mugo also wrote and edited plays and stories in Shona for an adolescent audience with the Zimbabwean writer Shimmer **Chinodya**. Mugo is the author of a critical work titled *African Orature and Human Rights in Gikuyu, Shona, and Ndebele Zamani Cultures* (2004), along with several critical articles and monographs. She is also the recipient of the Sojourner Truth Award for Black Woman Professor of the Year, National Association of Negro Business and Professional Women (2002), and is an active member of several committees, including the Southern African Institute for Development Studies.

Mulaisho, Dominic (1933–)

Zambian novelist Mulaisho was born in Feira, Zambia. After attending Canisius College, Chalimbana, he graduated from the University College of Rhodesia and Nyasaland. He entered public service in various ministries, including Education, and by 1965 was Permanent Secretary in the office of the President, Kenneth Kaunda. Later, he became Chairman of the Mining Industry, General Manager of the National Agricultural Marketing Board and the Managing Director of Indeco, as well as economic adviser to the Zambian government, and Governor of the Bank of Zambia. When there was a world shortage of copper

in the late 1970s, and Zambian mines were booming, he and his opposite numbers in Chile and Zaïre were able to combine for a period to extract good prices from the rich countries of the north. His novel *The Tongue of the Dumb* (1971) was launched by President Kaunda as the first Zambian novel. The book is about a power struggle between a councilor and Cruef; however, the book clearly draws on Mulaisho's experiences of the Zambian establishment. His next novel *The Smoke That Thunders* (1979) drew more obviously on his experience of public life. It is set during power struggles between the colonialists and the African nationalists in the period leading to the independence of the British colony of Musi-o-Tunya near Victoria Falls. Mulaisho is also the co-author of *Aid and Reform in Africa: Lessons from Ten Case Studies* with Lise Rakner and Nicolas van de Walle (2001).

Mungoshi, Charles (1947–)

A Zimbabwean poet, short-story writer, and children's writer, Mungoshe is best known for his novels in both English and Shona. Born in Manyene tribal trust land near Chivu, he attended the nearby Oaramombe primary school, then St. Augustine's High School near Mutare. He worked before Zimbabwe's independence for the forestry commission, as a clerk in a bookshop, and as an editor for the Literature Bureau. After independence he moved to the Zimbabwe Publishing House and in 1985 spent a year as writer-in-residence at the University of Zimbabwe. Mungoshi continues to work as a freelance writer, scriptwriter, and editor, and lives in Harare.

Mungoshi's first novel, the prize-winning *Makunun'unu maodzamwoyo* (1970), its title taken from the Shona proverb "Brooding breeds despair," was followed by his short-story collection, *Coming of the Dry Season* (1972), which was banned in Rhodesia. *Waiting for the Rain* (1975), a novel set in his home region, centers on young Lucifer, who visits his rural family home before leaving the country to take up a scholarship overseas. Conflict between younger and older generations and between rural and urban loyalties permeates much of Mungoshi's writing, as is evident in *Some Kinds of Wounds and Other Short Stories* (1980). His children's stories, largely adaptations from Shona, *Stories from a Shona Childhood* (1989) and *One Day Long Ago: More Stories from a Shona Childhood* (1991), are reminders of his grandmother's influence on him as a storyteller and his love for Shona oral traditions of narrative.

Mungoshi has won many awards for both his Shona and English works, including Commonwealth Writers Prizes (1988, 1998) and the Noma Award (1992). Versatile in the two languages, he explores the strengths of each as alternative modes of a Shona person's perception of the cultural complexities of Zimbabwe. His Shona novel of 1975, *Ndiko kupindana kwamazuva (How Time Passes)*, introduces new techniques to Shona narrative, while his fictional writing in English, sharpened by his spare and gently ironic poetry, is collected in *The Milkman Doesn't Only Deliver Milk* (1981). His translation of **Ngugi wa Thiong'o**'s *A Grain of Wheat* (1987) is further evidence of this curiosity in language across cultures. Mungoshi's earlier work was prohibited because it criticized the colonial regime, and his more recent work deals with similar issues regarding postcolonial oppression.

The stories in *Coming of the Dry Season* and *Some Kinds of Wounds* were reissued together as The *Setting Sun and the Rolling World* (1987). A new collection of stories, *Walking Still* (1997), won the 1998 Commonwealth Writers Prize (Africa Region) for fiction. Mungoshi's stories are also included in such collections as *Don't Read This! And Other Tales of the Unnatural* (2004) and *Writing Still: New Stories from Zimbabwe* (2003), which includes the story *The Sins of the Fathers*.

Munonye, John (1929–99)

Nigerian novelist Munonye is a graduate of English at University College, Ibadan, and an educationist of many years' standing. Born in Akokwa, Imo State, Nigeria, he is the author of six novels: *The **Only Son*** (1966), *Obi* (1969), ***Oil Man of Obange*** (1971), *A Wreath for the Maidens* (1973), *A Dancer of Fortune* (1974), and *Bridge to a Wedding* (1978). Munonye paints rural characters with sympathy and a folkloric imagination. His work reminds the reader that the novel as a genre deals with the particular in characters, locale, and sociocultural environment. His focus is usually on the fortunes of particular individuals, and he explores the environment and responses of his characters with depth and empathy. His fidelity to the Igbo cultural and social background contributes to the legitimacy of the actions and aspirations of his characters. Such themes as ancestral continuity, conflicting indigenous and Western religious sensibilities, the marriage institution as the bedrock of a stable and sane society, rural subsistence survival, and well-tested filial relationships recur in all his novels. Munonye also reveals a deep understanding of children's psychology. His unpretentious handling of the English language enables him to operate with ease at various levels of discourse involving character portraiture, descriptive narratology, and socio-anthropological information. His third novel, *Oil Man of Obange,* is a classic in the vivid depiction of the tragedy of the common person.

Further Reading

Purcell, William Fl. "Contested Translations: The Gospel versus Foreign Missionaries in John Munonye's *Obi*." *Christianity and Literature* 54, no. 1 (2004): 15–29.

Muntu (1975)

A play by Joe **de Graft** that the Nairobi assembly of the World Council of Churches commissioned. The work portrays a history of sub-Saharan Africa that emphasizes shared experiences. De Graft draws on the pageant form to portray characters from throughout history with equality and truthfulness.

Muriel at Metropolitan (1975)
A novel by Miriam **Tlali**. The narrative follows a young black woman named Muriel who works at a furniture company called Metropolitan that has both black and white staff. Muriel experiences what stands in for South African society as a whole, when her loyalties are split between the black and white employees and she ends up resigning. The novel draws specific attention to the unfair treatment of black workers in South Africa.

Mutloatse, Mothobi (1952–)
South African anthologist and short-story writer. Born in Western Native Township, Johannesburg, Mutloatse gained experience in journalism with the *Golden City Post*, *Weekend World*, and *The Voice* before founding the only South African publishing house exclusively devoted to black writing, Skotaville. Deeply interested in largely forgotten black literary and historical traditions, Mutloatse channels much of his energy into the documentation of black literature and historiography. He has compiled four anthologies of black writing: the first, *Casey and Co.: Selected Writings of Casey "Kid" Motsisi* (1978), a collection of articles for **Drum** and *The Classic*, celebrates the work of one of the older generation of black journalists. The others, which he refers to as his "Azanian trilogy," he provides with important introductions. He sees *Forced Landing: Africa South-Contemporary Writing* (1980) (banned on publication) as "cultural history penned down by the black man himself," and argues that the self-discovery of a people should find expression in new literary forms. *Reconstruction: Ninety Years of Black Historical Literature* (1981) focuses on hitherto ignored historical and journalistic texts by such writers as Tiyo Soga, Hope Dube, Noni **Jabavu**, and Sol T. **Plaatje** to give contemporary readers some sense of how earlier generations viewed their own history. Mutloatse presents the third book of the Azanian trilogy, *Umhlaba Wethu* (1987), as an exercise in nation-building and an alternative people's history, and it encompasses African music, autobiography, and women's struggles.

Mutloatse's own creative writing comprises short fiction and a work for the stage. The short story "The Truth, Mama" portrays the torment of a mother forced to explain to her children that their father is imprisoned for political activities, while the novella *Mama Ndiyalila* (1982) is a thinly disguised account of the transformative effect of events in Soweto in 1976 on the conflicting loyalties of the black middle class. His tribute to the jazz musician Ntemi Piliso, *Baby, Come Duze,* performed at the Market Theatre Warehouse in 1990, reconstructs the vibrant literary and musical scene of the 1950s. Mutloatse also adapted *Le Costume* for the stage with Barney Simon from the story *The Suit* by Can Themba in 2003 at the Young Vic Theatre in London. He has also written a children's book, *The Boy Who Could Fly* (1990), and a biographical account of Bob Gosani, one of the original *Drum* photographers, with Jacqui Masiza titled *Tauza—Bob Gosani's People* (2005).

Mutswairo, Solomon (1924–)
Zimbabwean storyteller and poet Mutswairo was born in Zawu, Mosowe district, central Zimbabwe, to Salvation Army missionaries and educated at Adams College, South Africa, Fort Hare University College, the University of Ottawa, Canada, and Howard University, Washington, DC. He won a Fulbright scholarship in 1960 and was the first ever writer-in-residence at the University of Zimbabwe. Mutswairo is also known because of his overwhelming support of the arts in

Zimbabwe, and he was the chairman of the Arts Board in 1992. His Shona-language fiction includes several novels, of which the first, *Feso* (1956; trans. 1974), prophetically describes a revolutionary war against white settler domination. His English-language novels, including *Mapondera, Soldier of Zimbabwe* (1978), and *Chaminuka, Prophet of Zimbabwe* (1983), also incorporate political protest. Mutswairo is also well known as the author of the lyrics for the Zimbabwean national anthem, in Shona titled "Simudzai mureza wedu weZimbabwe," which means "Blessed be the Land of Zimbabwe."

Mwangi, Meja (1948–)

Kenyan novelist. Born in Nanyuki, Kenya, Mwangi studied up to A level at Kenyatta College. He worked as a sound technician with the French Broadcasting Corporation in Nairobi and as a visual aids officer with the British Council before devoting his time to writing, and working as a journalist for radio and television, and film (including the film *Out of Africa*). He has twice won the Kenyatta Prize for Literature and has received the Afro-Asian Writers Award, the 1992 German youth book prize for *Kariuki,* and the Adolf Lotus Grimme Award.

Mwangi's work, more than any other Kenyan writer's, provides a representative view of the literature of the country as a whole, reflecting its main concerns and the direction of its evolution. He was the first to deal with the themes of the underworld in the postcolonial Kenyan city. *Kill Me Quick* (1973) exposes a hidden world of back streets and wretched humanity. Two other novels belong to the same tradition of social engagement. **Going down River Road** (1976) introduces the theme of the Kenyan working class to literature. A destitute crowd, assembled to work for a time on a building site, struggles for survival under conditions of near slavery with no prospects for improvement. *The Cockroach Dance* (1979) centers on the city slums as one more citadel of human degradation and on the strangely carefree subordination of the slum-dwellers to their surroundings. Two other novels, *Carcase for Hounds* (1974) and *Taste of Death* (1975), add to the corpus of literature dedicated to the Mau Mau anticolonial struggle in Kenya. In *The Bushtrackers* (1979) and *Bread of Sorrow* (1987), he sets aside his social and historical concerns and focuses on the thriller genre. *The Return of Shaka* (1989), set in contemporary Southern Africa, is a mythical tale of armed resistance, and *Weapon of Hunger* (1989), which has an American rock star turned philanthropist as its central character, tells of relief efforts during a famine in a drought-stricken area of Africa. In *Striving for the Wind* (1990) Mwangi once again turns to look at his society, this time focusing on the village, where he depicts life as a series of absurdities caused by individual human failings. The outcome of the story suggests that people are capable of suddenly realizing and rising above some of their major weaknesses, but it is an ambiguous hope, since the general level of inadequacy of life remains unchanged. *The Last Plague* (2001) is about a small town plagued by AIDS, and was nominated in 2002 by the Kenya National Library Service, Nairobi, for the International IMPAC Dublin literary awards, and in 2001 it won the Jomo Kenyatta Award for Literature. *Die Wilderer* was also published in 2001, and *The Mzungu Boy* (2005) is a young adult book about a boy named Kariuki and his interaction with both his village landscape and an English boy named Nigel.

Myth, Literature, and the African World (1976)

Essays by Wole **Soyinka**. The book is based on a number of lectures Soyinka gave while he was visiting fellow at Cambridge University in 1973. He analyzes works by authors such as Chinua **Achebe** and Ayi Kwei **Armah**, as well as his own poetry and drama.

In order to contextualize his analysis he provides background on Yoruba intellectual and religious culture as well.

Mzamane, Mbulelo (Vizikhungo)
(1948–)

A South African fiction writer, Mzamane was born in Brakpan and grew up in townships on the Witwatersrand. He attended secondary school in Swaziland, where he was taught by Can **Themba**, received his tertiary education at what was then the University of Botswana, Lesotho, and Swaziland, and taught at the Botswana and Lesotho campuses of the university. In 1979 he went to Sheffield, UK, for his doctoral studies, and from there to the United States, where he held posts at the universities of Georgia and Vermont. He returned to South Africa to take up an appointment at the University of Fort Hare in the Eastern Cape, where he was Vice-Chancellor. He also chaired and served on numerous boards, including the African Arts Fund (affiliated to the U.N. Centre against Apartheid), the Institute for the Advancement of Journalism (affiliated to the University of the Witwatersrand), the South African Broadcasting Corporation (SABC), the Heraldry Council of South Africa, and as the nonexecutive director of both the National Education Group and Nolwazi Publishers. He was appointed by Mandela and by current South African President Thabo Mbeki as a member of the Arts, Culture and Heritage Commission of the African Renaissance. Since leaving the University of Fort Hare, Dr. Mzamane has taken up fellowships at the Australian National University's Humanities Research Centre, the University of South Australia's Hawke Institute, and the Aboriginal Research Institute. He also held visiting posts at the University of California in San Diego, Saint Michael's College in Vermont, Brandeis University, and was the Professor and Interim Director of the Es'kia Mphahlele Institute of African Studies at the University of Venda for Science and Technology.

Mzamane's early exposure to the writings of black South Africans helps to explain why he turned naturally to the short-story form. Many of the stories in *Mzala* (1980, published outside South Africa as *My Cousin Comes to Jo'burg and Other Stories,* 1981) were written some years earlier and first published in magazines such as *Contrast, Izwi,* and *Staffrider.* He was the joint recipient (along with Achmat **Dangor**) of the Mofolo-Plomer Prize for his stories in 1976. In his stories he draws directly from life and he acknowledges his debt to his friends and relatives. The stories in the first part of *Mzala* reverse the usual Jim-comes-to-Jo'burg stereotype in their celebration of the ability of the narrator's country cousin Jola to survive and even thrive in the city. Other stories deal humorously with various township types and situations, and suggest the resilience and adaptability of the ordinary people from whom Mzamane derives his inspiration. Mzamane's most extended work of fiction is *The Children at Soweto* (1982), a thinly fictionalized account in three parts of the Soweto uprising of 1976. Mzamane foregrounds the response of the community to the unfolding events and the attempts of the activists to assert some kind of control. *The Children at Soweto* was banned shortly after its publication in 1982 and unbanned in 1987.

Mzamane's latest collection, *The Children of the Diaspora and Other Stories at Exile* (1996), builds upon his experience with South Africans abroad, most of whom, like Mzamane himself, have now returned home. Mzamane also wrote a paper on the "African renaissance" titled *Where There Is No Vision the People Perish: Reflections on the African Renaissance* (2001), and has assisted in the editing of *Multicultural Education in Colleges and Universities: A Transdisciplinary Approach* with Howard Ball (1998).

N

Nagenda, John (1938–)

Poet and novelist Nagenda was born in Gahini, Rwanda. He graduated in English from Makerere University, where he also edited *Penpoint* magazine. He has worked with Oxford University Press and as a radio and TV producer in New York, London, and Kampala. Nagenda also writes the Saturday column "One Man's Week" in Uganda's the *New Vision* newspaper. His poems, short stories, and articles have appeared in various journals and Nagenda has recorded his experiences with the Uganda Human Rights Commission and written a children's book entitled *Mukasa* (1973). He was also the recipient of the *Nalubaale Medal* (for civilian activists who assisted the NRA/NRM during the guerrilla war) in February 2004.

*The **Seasons of Thomas Tebo*** (1986) portrays an individual's involvement in the postcolonial struggle for political power in an African country. The story of the protagonist demonstrates that opposition to a repressive and corrupt regime may not necessarily be motivated by lofty ideals nor by a clear vision of an alternative; rather, it may be an impulsive rejection of inhumanity and an unconscious search for personal fulfillment.

Nakasa, Nat(haniel Ndazana) (1937–65)

South African journalist Nakasa was born in Durban and settled in Johannesburg to pursue a career in journalism. He was a regular contributor to ***Drum*** and *Golden City Post* and became the first black journalist on the *Rand Daily Mail,* for which he wrote a regular column. In 1963 he founded and edited the literary magazine *The Classic,* which sought to provide a publishing outlet for emerging black writers while promoting the principles of artistic freedom and multiracialism. He collaborated with white writers (including Nadine **Gordimer**) in his work

on the magazine and for newspapers, and his writing insistently rejected the hardening racial attitudes in the South Africa of the late 1950s and early 1960s. In 1964 he was awarded a Nieman Fellowship to study journalism at Harvard College in the United States. When his application for a passport was rejected he was forced to leave South Africa on an exit permit. He recorded his experiences of America in "Mr. Nakasa Goes to Harlem," commissioned by the *New York Times* in 1965. Here he wryly describes the mixed reception he was accorded as an African in black American society. He died after a fall from a high-rise building in New York. A selection of his writings has been posthumously collected by Essop Patel as *The World of Nat Nakasa* (1975). Nakasa's work has also been anthologized in James Clarke's *Laugh, Beloved Country* (2003), a compendium of South African humor. An award has been established in Nat Nakasa's name for Media Integrity, which is named each year in honor of Nakasa's role as the first black journalist to work at a white-owned South African newspaper, and is awarded by the South African National Editors' Forum (SANEF), Print Media South Africa, and the Nieman Society of Southern Africa.

Napolo Poems (1987)

These poems by Steve **Chimombo** attack injustice through the use of Malawian oral texts about the legendary figure of Mbona. They use irony and myth to critique modern repressive regimes.

Nazareth, Peter (1940–)

A critic and writer of fiction and drama, Nazareth was born in Uganda of Goan and Malaysian ancestry and educated at Makerere University, Kampala, Uganda, and at the universities of London and Leeds. Returning to Uganda after postgraduate study, he served as senior finance officer in Idi Amin's finance ministry until he was able to get out in 1973 to accept a fellowship at Yale University. As professor of English and African-American world studies at the University of Iowa, he has made important contributions to the fields of African and comparative literature through published criticism as well as through university teaching, appearances at conferences, and interviews with writers. Nazareth's first novel, *In a Brown Mantle,* is now on the curriculum at the University of Pretoria, and he also has many recent articles in *World Literature Today.* In his work with the International Writing Program at Iowa, he has encouraged writers from all over the world. Determined to bring the literature of his ancestral Goa to international attention, he has, for example, praised and publicized the work of Goan-Kenyan Violet Lannoy, whose writing was never published during her lifetime.

In a Brown Mantle (1972), forecast Idi Amin's coup and the subsequent expulsion of Asians from Uganda. *The General Is Up* (1991), his second novel, also deals with the Amin regime. He has written *Two Radio Plays* (1976) (*The Hospital* and *X* were produced for the BBC) as well as short stories. His critical writing includes *Literature and Society in Modern Africa* (1974; published in the United States as *An African View of Literature*); *The Third World Writer: His Social Responsibility* (1978); *In the Trickster Tradition* (1994), a study of Andrew Salkey, Francis Ebejer, and Ishmael Reed; and studies of single authors such as **Taban Lo Liyong**, **Ngugi wa Thiong'o**, and Joseph Conrad. In his role of professor at the University of Iowa, Nazareth is the creator and teacher of the popular course "Elvis as Anthology," which has received much media attention. Some scholarly works by Nazareth include "Elvis as Anthology" in Vernon Chadwick's *In Search of Elvis: Music, Race, Art, Religion,* two stories in Manohar Shetty's *Ferry Crossing: Short Stories from Goa,* and various critical analyses of Ishmael Reed in Bruce Dick's

Critical Responses to Ishmael Reed. He has also edited an anthology of East African fiction and one of Goan literature. His articles have appeared in journals in the United States and abroad. Recent critical works include such titles as *Elvis' Man Friday* with Gene Smith (1995) and *Critical Essays on Ngugi wa Thiong'o* (*Critical Essays on American Literature*) (2000). Nazareth is also included in *Half a Day and Other Stories: An Anthology of Short Stories from North Eastern and Eastern Africa* (2004).

Nazombe, Anthony (1955–2004)

Malawian poet. Nazombe was born in Nguludi, Malawi, and was educated at Pius XII Minor Seminary, the University of Malawi, and Sheffield University, where he completed his master's and PhD degrees in English, and was an Associate Professor of English at Chancellor College, University of Malawi until his death in February 2004. Among the second wave of writers who emerged in Malawi during the 1970s, he was deeply spiritual and wrote "in response to an inner urge to co-create with God." He edited *The Haunting Wind: New Poetry from Malawi* (1990), Malawi's second national anthology, in which only his attention to detail and his diplomacy prevented his running foul of Malawi's then notorious censorship laws. Nazombe's early association with the University of Malawi Writers' Workshop influenced his development as a poet. His work has been anthologized and has appeared in such journals as *Denga, Odi, Kunapipi, Marang, The Literary Half-Yearly, Caracoa,* and *Matatu.* His "In Memoriam" and "For a Singer" interrogate twin symptoms of life under the Banda regime: suicide as an escape for the poor and the raw vulnerability even of the professional class. "The Racket" (*The Haunting Wind*) indicts the West's show of aid and its literary establishment's contempt for African literature. In the post-Banda era he prepared another anthology, *Referendum*

Verse, and acted as secretary for foreign affairs in the political group AFORD. In 2004, before his death, he published *Operations and Tears: A New Anthology of Malawian Poetry,* which is the culmination of seven years of collecting and collating poetry from Malawi, and takes its most prominent inspiration from the political upheaval between 1992 and 1994.

Ndebele, Njabulo (Simakahle) (1948–)

South African short-story writer and essayist. Ndebele was born in Western Native Township near Johannesburg, educated at the University of Botswana, Lesotho and Swaziland (BOLESWA), Cambridge University, and the University of Denver, and since 1975 has been an academic and an administrator in southern African universities, including the University of the North, University of the Western Cape, University of the Witwatersrand, and National University of Lesotho. He has also been a Resident Scholar at the Ford Foundation's headquarters in New York, and he has been the Vice-Chancellor at the University of Cape Town since July 2000.

Ndebele's relatively small body of published work has had a great influence on South African literature. **Fools and Other Stories** (1983) won the Noma Award, and *Rediscovery of the Ordinary* (1991; published in the UK and the United States as *South African Literature and Culture: Rediscovery of the Ordinary*) collects his essays. The essay "Turkish Tales and Some Thoughts on South African Fiction," first published in *Staffrider* in 1984, contains many of his most influential thoughts. Ndebele focuses on "storytelling" in the place of "case-making" and praises writers who "give African readers the opportunity to experience themselves as makers of culture." He uses the example of the figure of the oral storyteller on the buses or trains who tells stories of a largely "apolitical" nature as tacit support for his own style of "rediscovering the ordinary."

In *Fools and Other Stories* Ndebele attempts to put his theories into fictional form. Ndebele is also the author of two children's books, *Bonolo and the Peach Tree* (1992) and *Sarah, Rings and I* (1993), and his stories *The Prophetess* (1992) and *Death of a Son* (1996) have been reissued as pamphlets. Ndebele has also published *The Cry of Winnie Mandela* (2004), which is composed of the stories of four ordinary South African women who are waiting for their husbands to return home, and then a dialogue with the imaginary and then real voice of Winnie Mandela. The book was given honorable mention from the Noma Award in 2005. Ndebele has also been anthologized in *Nobody Ever Said AIDS: Poems and Stories Southern Africa* (2004), edited by Nobantu Rasebotsa, Meg Samuelson, and K. Thomas; *Voices of the Transition: The Politics, Poetics and Practices of Social Change in South Africa* (2004), edited by Edgar Pieterse and Frank Meintjies; and *Telling Tales* (2004), edited by Nadine Gordimer.

Further Reading

Helgesson, Stefan. *Writing in Crisis: Ethics and History in Gordimer, Ndebele and Coetzee.* Scottsville: University of Kwazulu Natal Press, 2004.

Ndhlala, Geoffrey (1949–)

Zimbabwean novelist Ndhlala was born at St. Mary's Mission, Harare, and educated at St. Augustine Mission, Mutare, and at the University of Keele, UK. Since his return to Zimbabwe after graduating in 1973, he has worked as an advertising copywriter and a civil servant. His first novel, *Jikinya* (1979), portrays an idyllic rural African life in precolonial Zimbabwe that is shattered when white settlers invade the country and introduce materialistic values. His second novel, *The Southern Circle* (1984), explores the same theme but is more ambitious in scope, tracing three generations of an African family that becomes marginalized and dispossessed during the colonial period. Ndhlala uniquely fuses nineteenth-century realism with elements of fantasy associated with African folktales.

N'Djehoya, Blaise (1953–)

A novelist, N'Djehoya was born in Bangui, Central African Republic, of Cameroonian parents, went to France as a university student in 1973 and has remained there since. He is the author of *Bwanaland,* one section of *Un Regard noir* (1984), conceived as an anthropological study of Europe as seen by Africans. While the other section examines French beliefs in divination and magic, N'Djehoya's contribution, like his rather surrealistic novel, *Le Negre Potemkine* (1988), is marked by an extremely vigorous use of word play, in which standard French, slang, various African languages, and English are mixed with puns and allusions ranging from "Francois Meritand," president of France, through "grouchomarxisme," to a character named J.C. who is happy to be identified with Jesus Christ and John Coltrane. His alter ego in *Un Regard noir* is Ed Makossa wa Makossa, who lives on Chester Himes Avenue and observes the strange behavior and mating habits of the French. In *Le Negre Potemkine* a group of research students go in search of the *tirailleurs senegalais* who fought for France in two world wars and who have never received proper reward for their services to "DiGol" and "Zan Moulin" (Jean Moulin). Beyond the witty use of language, N'Djehoya's theme is the mistreatment of the African in Europe and the lack of knowledge of African culture by those who claim cultural superiority. In 2002 N'Djehoya wrote the preface for *Negres en images* or *Negros in images* by Chalaye Sylvie, and around 2000 he released the documentary *Cinq siècles de solitude—Los Palenqueros du Pacifique Colombien (Five Centuries of Loneliness—Los Palenqueros of the Colombian Pacific),* with

Sidiki Bakaba and through African Projection and Absynthe Production. The documentary received several awards, including the IUMOA in Fespaco (2001), the North-South Media award (2001), Side African Film Festival award (2001), the Images D'ailleurs award (2001), the Amiens award (2000), and the Black International Cinema Award 2000. N'Djehoya also helped create the Jazz Festival 2005 (Europe Jazz Network): *Banlieues Bleues Festival* 2005 (Seine-Saint-Denis).

Ndu, Pol Nnamuzikam (1940–76)

Nigerian poet Ndu was born in Eastern Nigeria and graduated from the University of Nsukka. After the Nigeria-Biafra war, which had a profound influence on him, he gained a PhD in Afro-American literature from the State University of New York and lectured in the United States for two years before returning to Nigeria in 1976. His first poetry appeared in *Black Orpheus.* In his short life, he produced two collections of poetry, *Golgotha* (1971) and *Songs for Seers* (1974), on the strength of which he was described as the heir apparent to the poetic mantle of Christopher **Okigbo**. The title poem of *Songs for Seers* is an elegy for Okigbo as Ndu's creative muse. Like his mentor, Ndu was a mythmaker.

Nervous Conditions (1988)

A novel by Tsitsi **Dangarembga**. The focus of this work is the role of women in African society. It follows the character Tambu, who moves from provincial poverty to the schoolteacher's middle-class space between the white authorities and the poor. A major message is the need for unity between African women of all ages and classes in order to effect social change.

Neto, Agostinho (1922–79)

Angolan poet Neto was born in Kaxikane, Angola. Trained as a physician in Portugal, he became involved in politics as a student and on his return to Angola in 1959 became involved in anticolonial movements. In 1975, he became the first president of the Republic of Angola.

Neto's works can be found in *Sagrada esperanca* (1974) and *A Renunica impossivel* (1983). A short story entitled "Nausea" was published in *Mensagem* in 1952, and various political writings have appeared posthumously. He writes protest poetry. It displays the struggle for independence and national identity. It uses urban and rural scenes and often employs the motif of mother as earth as Mother Africa or Mother Angola. Critical response to Neto's work ranges from analysis of its place in the context of Angolan history and lusophone literature to individual close readings. Neto has recently been included in the anthologies *Tricontinental Rebellion: Voices of the Wretched of the Earth from the 1960s to the 1980s,* edited by Ulises Estrada and Luis Subrez (2006) and *The African Diaspora and Autobiographics: Skeins of Self and Skin* from the San Francisco State University Series in Philosophy, Vol. 11 (2001).

Ngara, Emmanuel (1947–)

A literary theorist and poet, Ngara was born in Mhondoro, Southern Rhodesia, now Zimbabwe, and educated at St. Ignatius College, Chishawasha, University College of Rhodesia, and the University of London, where he gained a PhD. He was senior lecturer in English at the University of Lesotho until 1980, and after a short spell as Zimbabwe's deputy ambassador to Ethiopia and ambassador to the OAU, he joined the University of Zimbabwe, where he became professor of English and pro-vice-chancellor. He is Pro-Vice-Chancellor at the University of Natal in Durban, South Africa, and also currently holds the position of Deputy Vice-Chancellor for Students at the University of KwaZulu-Natal.

Ngara's studies of African literature are a consideration of its formal expression in fiction and poetry—and of the interactions between ideology and material reality. His first book, *Stylistic Criticism and the African Novel* (1982), explores the way that African novelists use English to express attitudes and ideas they produce from African experiences. *Art and Ideology in the African Novel* (1985) develops an explicitly Marxist theory, as does *Ideology and Form in African Poetry* (1990). In other theoretical and critical writing such as *Teaching Literature in Africa* (1984) he deals with the practical issues involved in literacy training, bilingualism, and teaching literature. His volume of poems, *Songs from the Temple* (1992), shows an energetic commitment to the pan-African past of Cheikh Anta Diop's historical research, Zimbabwe's liberation war, and the recovery of Great Zimbabwe. Ngara's bilingualism allows his poetry to appropriate and echo lines from T. S. Eliot, W. B. Yeats, Karl Marx, and the Christian scriptures in order to express his poetic vision of Africa.

Ngara is also the editor of critical collections on African writing: *Literature, Language and the Nation* (co-edited with Andrew Morrison, 1989), *New Writing from Southern Africa: Authors Who Have Become Prominent since 1980* (1996), *Socialism, Education and Development: A Challenge to Zimbabwe,* with Fay Chung (1995), and *The African University and Its Mission: Strategies for Improving the Delivery of Higher Education Institution* (1995).

Ngcobo, Lauretta (1931–)

A South African novelist and essayist, Ngcobo was raised by her Zulu mother and educated in the Ixopo district of southern Natal and at Fort Hare University College (BA, 1953). Her husband's detention in the aftermath of the Sharpeville massacre in 1960 eventually led to her escape into exile in 1963. After thirty-one years in exile she returned to Natal in 1994. Ngcobo currently works as an information officer for the Inkatha Freedom Party in KwaZulu-Natal, South Africa.

Ngcobo's rural background and the oppression of black South Africans under **apartheid** primarily inspire her work. In her first novel, *Cross of Gold* (1981), Ngcobo laments the lack of options open to young black South Africans. Set in the 1960s, the narrative traces the inexorable progress of a young Zulu man, Mandla, through his experience of institutionalized oppression to his violent end as a freedom fighter. The sequence of prisons, labor farms, and resettlement areas is relieved only by a brief, sensual glimpse of traditional rural life. *And They Didn't Die* (1990) portrays the women's rebellion in rural Natal in the late 1950s, and the way that apartheid and tradition cause Jezile physical and psychological suffering as she cares for herself and her children in the absence of her migrant laborer husband and with the help of the other women in her community. The novel records the sacrifice made by countless black country women, for so long the stoic, unheard, unseen victims of apartheid's migrant labor system and the pass laws.

In exile, Ngcobo published articles and spoke at conferences. She also edited *Let It Be Told* (1988), an anthology of writing by black women living in Great Britain, and also wrote a book for children, *Fiki Learns to Like Other People* (1994). Feminist Press (Center University) reissued *And They Didn't Die* in 1999 as part of the Women Writing Africa series, and such critical works as *New Women Writing in African Literature: African Literature Today,* No. 24 (2004) include work by Ngcobo.

Ngema, Mbongeni (1955–)

South African playwright, musician, choreographer, and director. Ngema was born in Verulam, South Africa. He started his career as a theater backing guitarist and later worked with Gibson **Kente** and discovered Stanislavsky, Brook, and Growtowski. Ngema was the recipient of the King Cetshwayo African Image Awards, and his name was set in a plaque at the City Hall in Durban—an area known as the "star walk," which was launched by President Thabo Mbeki in 2001. He has also initiated many social programs for change, some of which are Ingoba-makhosi, a nongovernmental organization that will ensure the elimination of race-related exploitation in the workplace in Durban, *Shout Africa,* which plans to establish twenty digital cinemas around the country in order to provide more affordable and accessible movies, and the Mbongeni Ngema Acting Academy based in Durban.

In 1979 he and fellow actor Percy Mtwa broke away from Kente's company to workshop *Woza Albert!* (1981), which is an episodic treatment of the gospels from a South African black theological perspective. Directed by Barney Simon for the Market Theatre (1980), the play toured the world, won more than twenty international awards, and was edited and recorded for the BBC. Ngema devised and directed a musical exploration of the township rent strikes for the Committed Artists in the award-winning *Asinamali!* (1984), which is a work he started in 1982. *Sarafina* (1987) celebrates the spirit of South African youth and was nominated for five Tony Awards and a Grammy after its successful transfer to New York. Ngema wrote and produced the soundtrack, co-wrote the screenplay with William Nicholson, and cochoreographed alongside Michael Peters for the film version of the play, which starred Whoopi Goldberg and Miriam Makeba. Ngema based *Township Fever!* (1990) on a railway strike in which scab workers were killed. The musical *Magic at 4 am!* (1993) was inspired by Muhammad Ali's 1974 fight against George Foreman in Zaire, premiered at Johannesburg's Civic Centre, and toured the world in 1994. *Sarafina 2!* (1996), a musical commissioned by South Africa's Ministry of Health to combat the spread of AIDS, turned out to be an expensive production. Four of Ngema's scripts have been published in *The Best of Mbongeni Ngema: The Man and His Music* (1995), and a CD titled *The Best of Mbongeni Ngema* was released in 1995, and rereleased in 2002. In February 2005 Ngema produced *Sing Africa Dance* in Johannesburg, which is a history of Africa showcased through song and dance, and in March 2005 he produced *House of Shaka*, which is a play based on the authorized biography of King Goodwill Zwelithini Zulu.

Further Reading

Banham, Martin, and Jane Plastow, eds. *Contemporary African Plays*. London: Methuen Publishing, 1999.

Jones, Laura. *Nothing Except Ourselves: The Harsh Times and Bold Theater of South Africa's Mbongeni Ngema*. New York: Viking, 1994.

Ngubiah, Stephen N. (1936–)

Kenyan novelist Ngubiah was born in the Gikuyu area north of Nairobi and worked as a teacher in the years preceding Kenyan independence before gaining a bachelor's at what was then University College, Nairobi. His only novel, *A Curse from God* (1970), emerged from the ambitious Students' Book-writing Scheme at University College, Nairobi. The book contributes to the postindependence debate over the relevance of traditional Gikuyu culture. Ngubiah paints a picture of almost unrelenting affliction in his tribal society. This perception squarely contradicted the position that the renowned Kenyan advocate of independence and prime minister Jomo Kenyatta had taken in his well-known *Facing Mount Kenya* (1938) and is likely Ngubiah's principal claim to a niche in Kenyan literary history. Eventually Ngubiah entered local politics in his home district.

Ngugi wa Thiong'o (1938–)

Kenyan novelist, playwright, and essayist (formerly known as James Ngugi). Ngugi was born in Kamiriithu village near Limuru in Kenya. He had his early schooling at the Church of Scotland mission primary school, studied English at Makerere University College, Kampala, where he graduated in 1964, and later did graduate work in West Indian literature at Leeds, UK. He taught at University College, Nairobi, and at Northwestern University in the United States and was the first African chair of the department of literature at the University of Nairobi. At the end of 1977 he was imprisoned for a year without trial for his outspoken criticism of the national government. Since the unsuccessful coup in Kenya in 1984, he has lived in exile in the UK, Sweden, and the United States, where he has taught at Yale University and New York University. Ngugi made his first public visit home to Kenya in twenty-two years in 2003, when Kenya's longstanding president, Daniel arap Moi, stood down in 2002 ahead of elections which saw the ruling Kanu party swept from power after four decades. He is currently a Distinguished Professor of English and Comparative Literature and Director of the International Center for Writing and Translation at the University of California at Irvine.

Ngugi's creative talent blossomed at Makerere: the first draft of his novel *The **River Between*** (1965) was completed in 1961 under the title "The Black Messiah." ***Weep Not, Child*** (1964) was written in 1962, as was the play *The Black Hermit* (1968). At Makerere Ngugi also emerged as a journalist and commentator on social and political affairs. He wrote his novel *A **Grain of Wheat*** (1967) at Leeds. The novel ***Petals of Blood*** (1977) and the play *Ngaahika Ndeenda* (1977; *I Will Marry When I Want*, 1982) attacked the Kenyatta regime and resulted in his detention, an experience that led to the publication of ***Detained*** (1981), which interprets the entire history of Kenya in terms of the Marxist dialectic. Following the publication in Gikuyu of the allegorical *Caitaani Mutharabaini* (1980; ***Devil on the Cross,*** 1982), which uses the motif of the journey, he developed another Gikuyu play, *Maitu Njugira* (1982; *Mother, Sing for Me),* for and with the active collaboration of the peasants; it was banned by the government and the people's open-air theater was dismantled. Other works of note by Ngugi are **Matigari** (1986; trans. 1989), written in Gikuyu, *Murogi wa Kagoogo,* also written in Gikuyu (1999), and *Ogi Wa Kagogo: Wizard of the Crow* (2004), which is the first volume of a satirical novel set in the imaginary country of Aburiria.

Ngugi's development as an artist and thinker has evolved through three stages. The first extends from 1960 to 1964, the year he graduated from Makerere, and is marked by the formative influences of Gikuyu social and cultural tradition, Christianity, and Western liberal thought. The second stage, from his arrival at Leeds in 1964 to his involvement in the Kamiriithu festival at Limuru in 1976, was influenced decisively by his introduction to Marxism, Frantz Fanon, pan-Africanism, and the cause of black solidarity through his study of West Indian writing and awareness of the Black Power movement in the United States. This period was characterized by his increasing disillusionment with bourgeois nationalism. In the third period, which extends from 1976 onward, the disillusionment is complete and Ngugi loses all hope of improving things in Kenya and in Africa except through total revolution brought about by the peasant masses. The turning point in his intellectual and emotional life was joining the Kamiriithu Cultural Centre in 1976. His theoretical leftism now assumes a concrete shape, and the change is nothing less than a spiritual conversion. His realization that he has nothing to teach and everything to learn from the Kenyan peasant he calls a "homecoming" that marks the end of the alienating influence of colonial education. One result of this change is his resolution to write only in the language of his people; another is an increasing reliance on the theater rather than the novel to create revolutionary awareness.

The River Between, Weep Not, Child, and *A Grain of Wheat,* along with the play *The Black Hermit* and the collection of stories *Secret Lives* (1975), are the work of a liberal and Christian humanist who believes in the virtues of conciliation, compromise, and love. There are militant characters such as Kabonyi and Boro, but they are not held up as models. Authorial approval goes to the conciliators like Waiyaki who, though he physically resembles Kenyatta, is a Christ figure. But *I Will Marry When I Want, Mother Sing for Me, Devil on the Cross,* and *Matigari* describe a different though familiar world. Ngugi's decision to write only in his mother tongue, which really meant writing primarily for his own people, resulted in a change in technique that led to a greater focus on allegory and fantasy. These works' dominant theme is the usurpation of power and wealth by the traitors and the people's persistent struggle to make them release it. Whether or not Ngugi has succeeded in winning the approval of the critics who had hailed his earlier work, there is no question that he has had tremendous success in winning the attention and adulation of his own people. These texts have acquired the status of folk epics and ballads and are read and heard in homes, taverns, and community centers.

Ngugi has also been an influential literary critic and cultural commentator, producing such works as *Homecoming: Essays on African and Caribbean Literature, Culture and Politics* (1972), *Writers in Politics* (1981; rev.1997), *Barrel of a Pen: Resistance to Repression in Neo-Colonial Kenya* (1983), *Writing against Neocolonialism* (1986), *Decolonising the Mind: The Politics and Language of African Literature* (1986), *Moving the Centre: The Struggle for Cultural Freedoms* (1993), *Penpoints, Gunpoints and Dreams* (1998), "Recovering the Original" in *World Literature Today* (2005), "Kamau Brathwaite: The Voice of African Presence" in *World Literature Today* (2005), and "Ngugi and the World of Christianity: A Dialectic" in the *Journal of Asian and African*

Studies (2004). Ngugi was awarded the 2001 Nonino Prize, delivered the Fourth Annual Steve Biko Freedom Lecture at the University of Cape Town in 2003, and was elected an Honorary Member in the American Academy of Arts and Letters in 2002. Ngugi has also contributed to such works as *Kinyira Njira! Step Firmly on the Pathway* (2004), *Fault Lines: A Memoir* (2003), *Black Linguists* (2003), *Resistance and Consciousness in Kenya and South Africa* (2002).

Further Reading

Bernth, Lindfors, and Bala Kothandaram. *The Writer as Activist: South Asian Perspectives on Ngugi wa Thiong'o.* Trenton, NJ: Africa World Press, 2002.

Gikandi, Simon. *Ngugi wa Thiong'o.* Cambridge Studies in African and Caribbean Literature. Cambridge: Cambridge University Press, 2000.

Killam, Douglas. *Literature of Africa.* Westport, CT: Greenwood Press, 2004.

Larson, Charles R., ed. *Under African Skies: Modern African Stories. 1997.* London: Canongate, 2005.

Lindfors, Bernth. *Blind Men and the Elephant: And Other Essays in Biographical Criticism.* Trenton, NJ: Africa World Press, 1999.

Lovesey, Oliver. *Ngugi wa Thiong'o.* Twayne's World Authors Series. Independence, KY: Twayne Publishers, 2000.

Mkandawire, Thandika, ed. *African Intellectuals: Rethinking Politics, Language, Gender and Development.* London: Zed Books, 2005.

Nazareth, Peter. *Critical Essays on Ngugi wa Thiong'o.* Critical Essays on American Literature. Independence, KY: Twayne Publishers, 2000.

Ricard, Alain. *The Languages and Literatures of Africa: The Sands of Babel.* Oxford: James Currey Publishers, 2004.

Simatei, Tirop Peter. *The Novel and the Politics of Nation Building in East Africa.* Bayreuth, Germany: Bayreuth University Press, 2001.

Nicol, Abioseh (1924–94)

Sierra Leonean poet, short-story writer, and critic. Nicol was born Davidson Sylvester Hector Willoughby Nicol in Bathurst village, Sierra Leone, had his early education in Nigeria, and gained a degree in science at Cambridge University in 1946. In the early 1950s he worked as a physician in the UK and by 1958 had received his PhD. He taught at the University of Ibadan, was the first Sierra Leonean principal of Fourah Bay College, and was vice-chancellor of the University of Sierra Leone. He was an economic director of UNITAR from 1972 to 1982, was the first black to be elected a fellow at Cambridge, and represented Sierra Leone as its ambassador in the United Kingdom.

Nicol was encouraged to write by Langston Hughes, who published one of his first stories in *An African Treasury* (1960). His two collections of stories, *The Truly Married Woman* (1965) and *Two African Tales* (1965), are reminiscent of Hughes's literary style. *The Devil at Yolahun Bridge* and *The Leopard Hunt* (published together as *Two African Tales)* show his fine handling of irony, wit, and dialogue. His stories, most of which draw on traditional sources, provide insights into the customs of the Creole people of Sierra Leone. His other publications are *Africa: A Subjective View* (1965), *Three Crowns* (1965), *Africanus Horton and Black Nationalism* (1969), *New and Modern Roles for Commonwealth and Empire* (1976), and *Nigeria and the Future of Africa* (1980). He also wrote scholarly and medical essays.

Nicol, Mike (1951–)

South African novelist and poet Nicol was born in Cape Town and educated at the University of the Witwatersrand in Johannesburg. He has worked as a journalist on *The Star, African Wildlife Magazine,* and *Leadership* and has published two volumes of poetry, *Among the Souvenirs* (1978), which won the Ingrid Jonker Prize, and *This Sad Place* (1993). He is best known for his novels, *The Powers That Be* (1989), *This Day and Age* (1992), and *Horseman* (1994). The setting for all three novels is an unspecified time and place, an obscurity that is also a feature of his poetry. He draws on South African history as his source for an actuality that is apocalyptic and bloody. *A Good-Looking Corpse* (1991) is a nonfiction account of the **Drum** generation of black writers that contains anecdotes, stories written by the writers themselves, and photographs. *The Waiting Country* (1995) is a meditation on the months surrounding the first democratic elections in South Africa that highlights random acts of violence and attempts to confront the possibility of forgiveness. *Africana Animals* (1982) is a children's book about African fauna, with illustrations from the work of early artists and travelers. Other works by Nicol include *Sea-Mountain, Fire City: Living in Cape Town* (2001), *The Invisible Line*, a book of photos and text that Nicol collaborated on with Ken Osterbroek (1998), *The Ibis Tapestry* (1998), and *Mandela: The Authorised Portrait* with Nelson Mandela (2005). He has also published several articles, such as "Seven Short Takes on the 'Civilised World'" (2002), "The New Bourgeois World" (1999), and "A Sort of Civil War" (2000), which are all available through the online magazine, Eurozine.

Night of Darkness (1976)
Malawian short stories by Paul Tiyambe **Zeleza**, who wrote and published them while an undergraduate. He treats a number of themes that are informed by oral narrative and history.

Nightwatcher, Nightsong (1986)
Poems by Frank **Chipasula**. This collection of poetry was written while Chipasula was in exile, and it openly criticizes the Banda regime. Chipasula places himself in the position of watchman over Malawi's dark night, and the poems portray history as nightmare.

Njami, Simon (1962–)
Cameroonian novelist Njami was born in Lausanne, Switzerland, of Cameroonian parents.

He has lived mainly in Europe. He studied in Switzerland and France and received a doctorate in law and also wrote a doctoral thesis on Boris Vian. Njami is based in Paris, but currently lives and works between Paris, New York, and Losanna. He is a curator, art critic, professor, and co-founder and editor of the Paris-based journal *Revue Noire,* a quarterly bilingual magazine devoted to black arts and literature. Recently he has curated exhibits such as *Africa Remix: Contemporary Art of a Continent* at the Museum Kunst Palast in Düsseldorf (2005), and was the artistic director of *Rencontres de la Photographie Africaine* in Bamako, Mali (2005). Njami has written two novels, *Cercueil et Cie* (1985; *Coffin and Company,* 1987) and *African Gigolo* (1989), as well as two books in Gallimard's Folio Junior collection for young people and a biography of James Baldwin. *Cercueil et Cie* is a *mise en abyme* involving the black detectives created by American novelist Chester Himes. *African Gigolo* is a story of the rootless life of a bright, handsome young African who wastes his time in Paris until, after traumatic experiences, he realizes he must return to Cameroon. A major theme of Njami's writing is the search for identity. Njami has also collaborated on several publications, including *Africa Remix: Contemporary Art of a Continent* (2005), *Looking Both Ways—Art of the Contemporary African Diaspora* (2004), *Zineb Sedira—Telling Stories with Difference* (2004), *Anthology of African Photography XIX and XX Century* (2004), *Africas: The Artist and the City: A Journey and an Exhibition* (2002), *Black Paris: The African Writers' Landscape* (2000), *Flash Afrique! Photography from West Africa* (2002), *Anthology of African Art: The Twentieth Century* (2002), and *Jane Alexander* (2002).

Njau, Rebeka (1932–)
(aka Marina Gashe)
A novelist, short-story writer, and playwright, Njau was born in Kanyariri, Kenya,

and educated in Kenya and at Makerere University, Uganda, where she gained a diploma in education. She has been a teacher, textile artist, researcher, and editor, writing only in her spare time. She has lived mostly in Kenya, and currently lives in Nairobi.

The Scar (1965), a poetic one-act play first performed at a Ugandan drama festival in 1960, marked Njau's debut as a writer. The play's heroine leads a movement of young women in a poverty-stricken Kenyan village against the traditional initiation ritual entailing genital laceration. She fails, not because of the opposition of the village's tradition-bound women, but because of a disclosure from her past by her erstwhile lover. Njau's second play, *In the Round,* first performed in 1964, represents some ambiguities about the Mau Mau political movement. She developed "Alone with the Fig Tree," which won first prize in an East African novel competition in 1964, into *Ripples in the Pool* (1975), in which the pool exercises a destructive influence on most of the characters. In *The Hypocrite and Other Stories* (1977), Njau retells a number of Kenyan folktales, and in *Kenyan Women Heroes and Their Mystical Power* (1984) she tells the stories of women who have been neglected in conventional historical records. Most recently Njau has published *The Sacred Seed* (2003), and as Kenya's first female playwright, she is a pioneer in the literary representation of women.

Nkosi, Lewis (1936–)

South African literary critic and novelist. Nkosi's move from *Ilanga lase Natal (The Natal Sun)* to **Drum** magazine in 1956 introduced him into that remarkable group of writers who began to articulate a contemporary black South African literary discourse within the **apartheid** state, a discourse that runs parallel to South Africa's white colonial discourse to this day. However, his acceptance of a Nieman Fellowship at Harvard University in 1961 obliged him to leave South Africa on a one-way exit permit. After a year at Harvard, where he wrote a play, *The Rhythm of Violence* (1964), he moved to London and worked as a journalist and literary critic. Nkosi's career as a Professor of Literature has included positions at universities in Africa (Zambia), the United States (Wyoming, California-Irvine), and Europe (Warsaw, Poland), and he is also a visiting professor at the universities of Cape Town and Durban-Westville, South Africa. He is currently a resident of Switzerland, where he has been doing research since his retirement in 1999 from teaching at the University of Wyoming.

In *Home and Exile* (1965) Nkosi criticized black writers who paid excessive lip service to European literary aesthetics. His readings in this vein of well-known South African texts render his carefully argued, skillfully crafted essays controversial. In *The Transplanted Heart* (1975), for example, Nkosi sees Athol **Fugard**'s The **Blood Knot** (1963) as subversively extolling white supremacy over black people, while in *Masks and Tasks: Themes and Styles of African Literature* (1981) he draws a distinction between black writers who invoke traditional African society *(masks)* and those who strive for new African orders *(tasks)*. Such premises are developed further in "Constructing the Cross-Border Reader" (in *Altered State? Writing and South Africa,* 1994, edited by E. **Boehmer** et al.), in which he suggests that a template of political, linguistic, and cultural boundaries obfuscates South African literary discourses. Nkosi has also written a book on *Nadine Gordimer* (2004), one titled *WeiÃŸe Schatten* (2003), a play titled *The Black Psychiatrist* (2001), and has collaborated on the publication *Come Back Africa* (2004).

The deeply embedded irony of his first novel, *Mating Birds* (1986), reinforces Nkosi's critical standpoint by revealing the sad state of European spirituality. In his own land, Sibya is accused of raping a white woman and condemned to death by a white court that safeguards those same European values that sanctioned the colonization of Africa. The novel *Underground People* (1993, republished in 2003), which was short-listed for a Boesman Prize in South Africa, focuses on the people oppressed by apartheid and the freedom fighter's accountability to his commitment in the armed struggle.

No Bride Price (1967)

David **Rubadiri** expresses his disappointment with the Banda regime's direction of independence in this novel. Malawi's ambassador to the UN, Rubadiri went into exile in Uganda when the novel was published.

No Longer at Ease (1960)

A novel by Chinua **Achebe**. Obi Okonkwo is the subject of this novel, which portrays his downfall. His story ends in disaster due to his arrogance derived from his overseas education, and a refusal to reconcile the conflict between his place in a modern Western context and the way that his Christianized family deals with Igbo traditions. Achebe sets the novel in the period preceding Nigeria's independence from colonial rule (1960), and its message warns of the difficulties that will result from independence.

No Sweetness Here (1970)

Short stories by Ama Ata **Aidoo**. Aidoo treats the themes of neo-colonialism, material wealth, class consciousness, and gender roles in these eleven stories. Aidoo conveys these themes through a narrative style that emphasizes the oral tradition and leads to a multiplicity of voices.

No-Good Friday (1958)

This play by Athol **Fugard** is set in a backyard in Sophiatown over one week. A number of characters interact with one another to demonstrate the lack of progress for black people in apartheid South Africa, despite their determination. The primary characters are Willie, the woman who lives with him named Rebecca, and the thug Shark. The play ends on Friday as Will awaits violence at the hands of Shark. The play was first staged at the Bantu Men's Social Centre in Johannesburg.

None to Accompany Me (1994)

A novel by Nadine **Gordimer**. Gordimer positions the personal narrative of her heroine parallel to the narrative of the transition of power to South Africa's majority. Vera Stark is a lawyer who is on the committee that has the challenge of drafting the country's new constitution. Her future is also undefined, as she escapes from her marriage and family to begin again.

Nortje, Arthur (1942–70)

South African poet Nortje was born in Oudtshoorn and educated at Paterson High School, Port Elizabeth, where he was taught by the writer Dennis **Brutus** (Nortje and Brutus were both prize-winners of the Mbari poetry competition in 1962), University College of the Western Cape, and Oxford University, where he received a scholarship. In 1967 he emigrated to Canada but returned to Oxford in 1970, where he died shortly afterward. His poems were published posthumously in the collections *Dead Roots* (1973) and *Lonely against the Light* (1973), and more recently in *Anatomy of Dark: Collected Poems of Arthur Nortje* (2000). July 2005 marked the first Arthur Nortje Memorial Lecture at Stellenbosch University. The lecture is an annual event organized by the Department of English, at which local and international scholars and writers present papers on the theme of "Literature, Exile and Identity."

The failure of relationships due to an inability to establish enduring attachments form the basis of much of Nortje's poetry, which is preoccupied with experiences of alienation and fragmentation. Classification as "coloured" (mixed-race) in **apartheid** South Africa encouraged Nortje to question the idea of self-identity. His exploration of the experience of alienation, though informed by his experiences of rejection and racial discrimination, leads him to the more disturbing insight that the construction of the psyche as such is an effect of difference. Exile is frequently cited as an important factor in explaining Nortje's sense of alienation. In his poetry, exile becomes the guiding metaphor of the themes of homelessness and marginality. His poetry shows a facility for inventive image making and passionate and elegant phrasing, which reveal an introspective poet who lived intensely and questioned deeply the conditions and circumstances of his existence.

Further Reading

Farred, Grant. *Midfielder's Moment: Coloured Literature and Culture in Contemporary South Africa*. Cultural Studies Series. Boulder, CO: Westview Press, 1999.

McLuckie, Craig, and Ross Tyner. *Arthur Nortje, Poet and South African: New Critical and Contextual Essays*. Pretoria: Unisa Press, University of South Africa, 2003.

———. "'Breathes There a Man?': A Note on Allusion in Arthur Nortje's 'Mirror Prison of the Self.'" *Notes on Contemporary Literature* 32, no. 3 (2002): 4–7.

Ntiru, Richard Carl (1946–)

A Ugandan poet, Ntiru was born in Kigezi, Uganda, and attended Makerere University College, Kampala, where he graduated with an honors degree, edited *The Makererean* and *Penpoint,* and managed the Makerere Travelling Theatre. He works as an editor for the International Centre for Research in Agro-Forestry in Nairobi. His only collection is *Tensions* (1971), which is rich in imagery reminiscent of the poetry of Christopher **Okigbo** and Pol **Ndu**. Ntiru deals with issues of contemporary East Africa, and while he acknowledges other poets in other literatures, he consciously explores the divisions within human society and critiques his society's attitudes toward the unfortunate. Apart from poetry he has also written a radio play and short stories, and his poems "If It Is True" and "The Miniskirt" are included in *The Penguin Book of Modern African Poetry* (1999).

Nwabueze, Emeka (1952–)

Dramatist Nwabueze was born at Awka, Nigeria, and studied at the University of Nigeria and Eastern Michigan and Bowling Green state universities in the United States, gaining a PhD in theater. Nwabueze has taught in several universities, is currently a Professor of Literature and Theatre in the Department of Dramatic Arts at the University of Nigeria-Nsukka, served as the visiting R-MWC Quillan Professor from 1998 to 1999, and has received many fellowships and academic honors around the globe. Nwabueze's published plays include a parable for the erosion of moral values titled *Spokesman for the Oracle* (1986); *Guardian of the Cosmos* (1990), which is a terse, rhythmic, and idiomatic commentary on the predicament of the social reformer in a corrupt and materialistic society; *A Dance of the Dead* (1991), which examines the moral crisis inflicted on society by conscienceless wealthy citizens; and a dramatized recreation of Chinua **Achebe**'s ***Arrow of God*** titled *When the Arrow Rebounds* (1991). Nwabueze has also published an article titled "Theoretical Construction and Constructive Theorizing on the Execution of Ikemefuna in Achebe's *Things Fall Apart*: A Study in Critical Dualism" in *Research in African Literatures* (2000), and a work titled *Heroes of Conscience* (1998).

Nwakoby, Martina Awele (1937–)

Nigerian writer of children's fiction and novelist. Nwakoby was born in Ogwashi-Ukn, Nigeria, and educated at schools in Nigeri and Birmingham, at the University of Pittsburgh, and at the University of Ibadan, where she gained a PhD in library studies. She is a lecturer at the Abia State University, Uturu, Nigeria. Nwakoby is the author of the children's books *Ten in the Family* (1975) and *A Lucky Chance* (1980) and the adult novel *A House Divided* (1985); she won the 1978 Macmillan children's book competition. *Quiz Time* (1980) is part of her efforts to encourage children to read and write. *Ten in the Family, A Lucky Chance,* and *A House Divided* are rooted in Nigerian social life and reflect the vices and virtues of both contemporary and traditional Nigerian life.

Nwankwo, Nkem (1936–2001)

Nigerian novelist. Nwankwo was born in Nawfia, Nigeria, and educated in schools and colleges in Lagos and at University College, Ibadan. After graduation he taught briefly and worked for **Drum** magazine before he started work for the Nigerian Broadcasting Corporation. He also served as a professor of English at Tennessee State University until his death in 2001. Winning an *Encounter* prize in 1960 for a play encouraged him to produce more creative writing, and he published two books for teenagers, *Tales Out of School* (1963) and *More Tales Out of School* (1965), that chronicle the adventures of two boys, Bayo and Ike. Nwankwo's best-known novel, *Danda* (1964), with its picaresque hero and loose narrative structure, enhanced his reputation as one of the major first-generation African literary voices. In Biafra he worked as a member of the Arts Council between 1967 and 1970, and after the Nigeria-Biafra war he worked as an editor of the *Daily Times* (Lagos). In 1973 he was appointed writer-in-residence at the African Studies Center at Michigan State University. His second novel, *My Mercedes Is Bigger Than Yours* (1975), is a political satire. In the 1970s Nwankwo embarked on further academic studies and obtained master's and doctorate degrees from the University of Indiana. His

third novel, *The Scapegoat* (1984), explores the underside of contemporary Nigerian society. Recent publications or republications of Nwankwo's work include *The Shadow of the Masquerade,* a memoir (2004), *Sex Has Been Good to Me,* essays (2004), and *The Scapegoat* (1984, 2002). Some of Nwankwo's work is also included in Herbert Igboanusi's *Igbo English in the Nigerian Novel* (2002).

Nwapa, Flora (1931–93)

Nigerian novelist Nwapa was born at Oguta in Imo State of eastern Nigeria and was the first Nigerian woman to write novels. Nwapa also wrote short stories and stories for children. She was the first Nigerian woman to be a publisher. With a bachelor's degree (1957) and a diploma in education (1958) she began her professional career as a civil servant and subsequently served her community as a commissioner in various ministries in the then East Central State post–Nigeria-Biafra war government. She established the Tana Press and Flora Nwapa Books in Enugu and received the Merit Award for Authorship/Publishing of the University of Ife Book Fair in 1985.

Nwapa is known best for her two novels, **Efuru** (1966) and *Idu* (1970), set in the early colonial period in the Oguta area of Igboland. The novels dramatize the problems of women in traditional society from different perspectives, particularly in relation to their ability to bear children. A short semiautobiographical novel, *Never Again* (1975), is based on her experiences during the civil war. Her last two novels, *One Is Enough* (1981) and *Women Are Different* (1986), have a modern urban setting; the former explores the themes of childlessness and women's economic independence, and the latter insists that women have options other than marriage and motherhood. As a short-story writer, Nwapa deals with women's experience. Her first collection of short stories, *This Is Lagos and Other Stories* (1971), focuses on the sexual exploitation of women, criminality, and violence, while in *Wives at War and Other Stories* (1980), women defend their rights to freedom from oppression. Nwapa began writing for children to satisfy her own children's needs for stories with which they could identify. The dual purpose of teaching and entertainment runs through the stories beginning with *Emeka-Driver's Guard* (1979) through *The Miracle Kittens* (1980), *Adventures of Deke* (1980), and *Journey to Space* (1980).

Further Reading

Nzegwu, Femi. *Love, Motherhood and the African Heritage: The Legacy of Flora Nwapa*. Dakar: African Resistance, 2001.

Nyamfukudza, Stanley (1951–)

Zimbabwean novelist and short-story writer. Nyamfukudza was born in Wedza, Zimbabwe, and educated in Zimbabwe and at Oxford University, where he gained a bachelor's in 1977. Nyamfukudza runs an editorial and information services consultancy in Harare, was formerly a managing editor with one of the major educational publishers in Zimbabwe, and has also ventured into scriptwriting for TV and film. The protagonist of his first novel, *The Non-Believer's Journey* (1980), both affirms and interrogates the viability of African nationalism, and the novel's ironic tone reveals the despair and disillusionment associated with African writing of the postindependence era. The same concern is apparent in *Aftermaths* (1983), a collection of eleven short stories that are critical of male characters and positively inclined toward the female characters. The ten stories in *If God Was a Woman* (1991) focus on ordinary characters and their relationships with the opposite sex. Nyamfukudza also contributed to *The Book Chain in Anglophone Africa,* which was compiled and edited by Roger Stringer (2002); he translated *How Chimpanzees Became Bald (Sei chimupanze ane mhanza)* for Mary-Rose Mbarga (2002); and his work is included in

such texts as *Walking Still: New Stories from Zimbabwe* (2003) and *Wenn Gott eine Frau ware* (2001).

Nyamubaya, Freedom (1958–)

Poet and prose writer Nyamubaya was born in Murehwa, Zimbabwe, and educated at primary and secondary schools. In Zimbabwe's liberation struggle in 1975 she achieved the rank of field operational commander and secretary for education for the political party ZANU. From 1982 to 1984 she studied social science at Ruskin College, Oxford, and has since then become director of a nongovernmental organization she founded to assist rural farmers in Zaire. Nyamubaya currently lives in a small town southeast of Harare. Her first publication, *On the Road Again* (1986), suggests that her strength lies in her invoking Shona proverbial expressions, folktale elements, myths, and traditional sayings, which she transforms into a poetic voice that expresses the tragedies of war and the resilience of the human spirit. The influence of African orature is also noticeable in her second collection of poems, *Dusk of Dawn* (1995), which contains a more reflective and somber tone. Recently, Nyamubaya's story "That Special Place" was anthologized in *Writing Still: New Stories from Zimbabwe* (2004). The writer's love for life, for Zimbabwe, and for Mozambique, which sheltered the fighters during the war, finds expression in her poetry, but her love is at the same time qualified by her recognition of the harsh and brutal side of life and history. Nyamubaya's writing is accessible, unique in texture and in orientation.

Nzekwu, Onuora (1928–)

A Nigerian novelist, Nzekwu was born in Kafanchan, Nigeria, of Igbo parents and was educated in several schools, including St. Anthony's School and St. Charles Higher Elementary Teacher Training College, Makurdi. His nine years of teaching in

Oturkpo, Onitsha, and Lagos provided much of the material that was to serve him in his writing career, and later he received Rockefeller Foundation and UNESCO fellowships that enabled him to travel widely. He became editorial assistant of *Nigeria Magazine* in 1956, rising to the position of editor in 1962, and his working relationship with historian Michael Crowder helped him to publish his first novel, *Wand of Noble Wood* (1961). His second novel, *Blade among the Boys* (1962), appeared the next year. Crowder and Nzekwu co-authored a novel for children entitled *Eze Goes to School* (1963), which made a tremendous impact on both schoolchildren and their teachers. Nzekwu's third novel, *Highlife for Lizards* (1965), examines polygamy. His career was interrupted by the Nigeria-Biafra war, and at its end he returned to public service. A sequel to *Eze Goes to School*, entitled *Eze Goes to College* (1988), also co-authored with Crowder, continues the story of the trials of Eze. Nzekwu, as one of the first generation of African writers in English, helped pioneer a new vision in African literature.

O

Obafemi, Olu (1948–)

Nigerian dramatist Obafemi was born in Akutupa, a small town in Kiriland, Nigeria, and had his university education in Zaria, Nigeria, and in Sheffield and Leeds, UK. Obafemi currently serves as the National President of the Association of Nigerian Authors (ANA) and is a professor at the University of Ilorin, Nigeria. He also served as chairman of the board for the National Commission for Museums and Monuments (NCMM) in 2004. His published plays include *Nights of a Mystical Beast* and *The New Dawn* (1986), *Suicide Syndrome*, and *Naira Has No Gender* (1993); he has had plays produced both in Britain, while he was on a fel-

lowship at the School of Drama, University of Leeds, and in Nigeria. A new edition of *Pestle and Mortar: A Play* (first published in 1974) was released in 1999 by Haytee Publishers. His novel, *Wheels* (1997), was serialized in the *Nigerian Herald*. He is a professor of English and the founder of the Ajon Players, an active drama society in Ilorin, Nigeria.

Obafemi belongs to the generation of Femi **Osofisan**, Niyi **Osundare**, Kole **Omotoso**, Tanure **Ojaide**, and Biodun Jeyifo, who brought politics into literature. *Nights of a Mystical Beast* uses folkloric and mythic images and icons to explore the primeval chaos that typifies the precolonial social form and the violence of colonialism. In *The New Dawn*, he envisions a new political consciousness emerging from the struggle to negate the history of colonialism and its exploitation and fragmentation. The dominant voice in *Suicide Syndrome* is that of an ideologue-artist who maneuvers character and actions, songs and dance to amplify his class sympathy. Obafemi's poems are included in the University Matriculation Examination syllabus, and his books are widely included in university and college courses. He also writes columns for several prominent newspapers in Nigeria, including the *Herald, Triumph, Punch, Tribune, Comet,* and *Post Express,* and helped develop the newspaper *Fore Runner* in Kwara.

Obafemi is also the author of two scholarly studies, *Nigerian Writers on the Nigerian Civil War* (1992) and *Contemporary Nigerian Theatre: Cultural Heritage and Social Vision* (1996); he has edited *New Introduction to Literature* (1994), and is the co-author of *Character Is Beauty: Redefining Yoruba Culture and Identity: (Iwalewa-Haus, 1981–1996)* with Wole Ogundele, Olu Obafemi, and Femi Abodunrin (2000).

Oculi, Okello (1942–)

A Ugandan novelist and poet, Oculi was born in Dokolo in northern Uganda and educated at Soroti College and St. Peter's College, Tororo, St. Mary's College, Kisubu, and Makerere University, Kampala, where he studied political science and worked as news editor of the *Makererean* and as a tutorial fellow. Currently he works at the National Centre for Women Development for Syntel-AZA Media Productions in Garki, Abuja Nigeria, and has worked with numerous organizations, including the International Human Rights Law Group and the Nigerian Ministry of Integration and Cooperation in Africa. Oculi has also written policy initiatives for the Pepoples Democratic Party (1999–2000), presented on the "Presidential System of Government and Policy-Making Processes: Implications for Nigeria" and "Strategic Policy Development under Presidential System of Government" at worldwide conferences in London and Lagos, proposed pro-women amendments to the 1999 Nigerian Constitution and conducted interviews with Nigerian volunteers for a report on "Communication Focus: VSO Nigeria, Voluntary Service Overseas, London" in 1999.

His poetry seeks to reassert the cultural heritage of Africa with a critique of foreign influences in East Africa. His first publication, *Orphan* (1968), is an allegory in verse and prose in which an orphan symbolizes Africans who either do not know or have forgotten their heritage. In *Prostitute* (1968), a novel, the central thread is the continuous deterioration of the slums, where the prostitutes live and operate. His other publications include *Koolokem* (1978), an episodic account of a victimized woman and her husband; *Malak* (1976), a long verse essay inspired by the regime of Idi Amin; *Kanti Riti* (1974); *Song for the Sun in Us* (2000), which explores the themes of ecology, ancestry, political and literary theory; and *Discourses on African Affairs: Directions and Destinies for the 21st Century* (1998, 1999, 2000), which is a collection of essays that ask pertinent political and social questions about the relationships

between Africa and the Western world. Oculi speaks with a communal voice invoking the collective symbols of Africa. Recently, Oculi has published articles titled "Decade of African Tourism," in *Crystal* (2000) and "On Nigeria's Skin War," and has presented lectures and papers titled "Challenges for Democracy in Nigeria" (2000), "Who is Ken Saro-Wiwa?", "Political Science and Women Development: A Nigerian Narrative," and "History and Literary Imagination" (1999).

Of Chameleons and Gods (1981)

Poems by Jack **Mapanje**. This collection of poetry seeks to find a poet's voice in order to deal with the realities of Malawian society. Mapanje uses Malawian oral traditions and beliefs to express his social and political concerns.

Ofeimun, Odia (1950–)

Nigerian poet Ofeimun was born in Irhukpen, Nigeria, and read political science at the University of Ibadan. He is a poet, essayist, political scientist, journalist, editorialist, polemicist, and political activist. He was private secretary to the late Chief Obafemi Awolowo, one of Nigeria's foremost politicians. He was an editor for the Lagos *Guardian*. As President of the Association of Nigerian Authors, he occupies an important position in the struggle to sustain a viable literary culture in Nigeria. He was the Secretary-General of the Association of Nigerian Authors (ANA) in 2003. He has also acted as the Chairman for the Editorial Board of Independent Communications Network Limited Publications (2001); was a personal secretary to Chief Obafemi Awolowo; was a writer for the *News*, a radical newspaper that contributed to the downfall of the last dictatorship in Nigeria, and was the Editorial Board Chairman of the *News* and *Tempo* magazines as of 2000.

Ofeimun's major poetry collections are *The Poet Lied* (1980), *A Handle for the Flutist and Other Poems* (1986), *Under African Skies*

(1990), *London Letter: And Other Poems* (2000), *A Feast of Return under African Skies: Poems for Dance Drama* (2000), and *Dreams at Work, and Other Poems* (2000). The publication of *The Poet Lied* generated literary and legal debate when Nigerian poet J. P. Clark **Bekederemo** threatened court action against the book's publisher, alleging that the title poem referred to him and injured his reputation. The case was finally settled out of court, but the controversy lingers on. Many critics see Ofeimun's *The Poet Lied* as a work that confronts certain aesthetic traditions and viewpoints expressed by a particular writer on the Nigeria-Biafra war. The speaker berates a fellow poet for abandoning truth. Ofeimun's poetry rejects the aloofness and abstractions of apolitical art and argues for a literature of social and political relevance.

Ogot, Grace (Emily) (1930–)

Kenyan short-story writer and novelist. Educated at Ng'iya Girls' School and Butere High School and trained as a nurse and midwife, Ogot later served as an announcer and scriptwriter for the BBC, a community development officer, a public relations specialist, a Member of Parliament, and a representative to the United Nations for Kenya. Ogot is involved in politics, is recognized locally for her broadcasting in the Luo language, and formerly acted as the Assistant Minister of Culture and Social Affairs. Considered by some critics to be the leading short-story writer in East Africa, she has published two novels, *The Promised Land* (1966, republished in 1999) and *The Island of Tears* (1980); two story collections, *Land without Thunder* (1968) and *The Other Woman* (1976); a novella, *The Graduate* (1980); and a retelling of Luo village myth, *Miaha* (1983). She often draws on her childhood and her work as a nurse as well as on African folktales and traditional practice for her plots and characters, which she sometimes blends with violent and macabre action. In *The Promised Land,* a young farmer and his wife who have migrated to Tanzania from Kenya become embroiled in jealousy and materialism. Short stories in the two collections draw on both urban and rural Kenyan experience, for example, in "The White Veil" from *Land without Thunder,* Otgot portrays a young female office worker who is vulnerable because of her age, her sex, and the prevailing attitudes about male-female relationships. Ogot's work is anthologized in *Under African Skies: Modern African Stories* (1997, 2005) and *Talking Gender: Conversations with Kenyan Women Writers* (2003).

Oguibe, Olu (1964–)

Nigerian poet Oguibe was born in Aba, Nigeria, and educated at the University of Nsukka, Nigeria, where he was expelled in 1989 for political activism, and the University of London, where he gained a PhD in art history. In 1995 he became an Assistant Professor of Art History at the University of Illinois; in 2001 he served as Senior Fellow of the Veral List Center for Art and Politics in New York; since 2003 he has taught at the University of Connecticut as an Associate Professor of Art and African American Studies; and in 2004 he was the Critic-in-Residence for Art Omi. Oguibe has also served on the boards of *Third Text, Social Identities, Atlantica,* and the literary journal, *Wasafiri.* In 1994 he co-founded *Nka: Journal of Contemporary African Art* in New York, and Oguibe has also been the co-editor of *aRude,* the publisher of the online art journal *Laundry,* and has curated many exhibitions for major institutions around the world. Oguibe also established the *Ugo Edemede Igbo Anyamele Oguibe* or the Anyamele Oguibe Prize for Writing in the Igbo Language, and he was awarded the distinction of Senior Fellowship of the Rockefeller Study and Conference Center in Bellagio (1999).

His first book of poetry, the lyrical long poem *A Song from Exile* (1990), explores the pain of exile. The poet's feelings of anger and despair at his powerlessness and separation from his country progressively merge with the greater sorrow of his community. *A Gathering Fear* (1992) was highly acclaimed in Africa, where it won the 1992 All-Africa Okigbo Prize and a mention by the 1993 Noma Award jury. A sense of loss and collective pain dominates these poems. A later collection, *Songs for Catalina* (1994), contains ten love poems. He also edited *Sojourners: New Writing by Africans in Britain* (1994), and has recently published *Authentic/ Ex-Centric: Conceptualism in Contemporary African Art* (2001, 2002), in conjunction with an exhibition of the same name and with Salah Hassan, *The Culture Game* (2004), a collection of essays that explore the obstacles and contradictions that non-Western artists must face, and *I Am Bound to This Land by Blood* (2005), which is an online article. Other recent articles by Oguibe include "Photography and the Substance of the Image" in *The Visual Culture Reader* (2002), "Connectivity and the Fate of the Unconnected" in *Relocating Postcolonialism* (2002), and "Finding a Place: Nigerian Artists in the Contemporary Art World" in *Art Journal* (1999). His contributions have also appeared in such works as *Art in Theory: 1900–2000, Theory in Contemporary Art: 1985 to the Present, The Dictionary of Art, Art History and Its Methods, The Third Text Reader on Art, Culture and Theory,* and *Black British Culture: A Reader.* Oguibe's work has been translated into Spanish and Catalan and has been published in Nigeria, Germany, Mexico, and Spain. Pitika Ntuli's interview with him has been published as a pamphlet entitled *The Battle for South Africa's Mind: Towards a Post-Apartheid Culture* (1995). Oguibe has also collaborated on such works as *Flash Afrique! Photography from West Africa* (2002) and *Reading the Contemporary: African Art from Theory to the Marketplace* (2000); is a contributor to *Black President: The Art and Legacy of Fela Anikulapo-Kuti* (2003); and

some books related to his exhibitions are *The African Sniper Reader* (2005), *Fresh Cream* (2000), *Cream: Contemporary Art in Culture* (1998), and *Site Matters: The Lower Manhattan Cultural Council's World Trade Center Artist Residency 1997–2001* (2004).

Ogunde, Herbert (1916–90). *See* Drama, West Africa.

Ogundipe-Leslie, Molara (1949–)
Nigerian literary critic and poet. Born in Lagos, Ogundipe-Leslie received her early schooling and university education in Nigeria. She then went on to further study at London, Oxford, Cambridge, Columbia, and Harvard. Since 2001 Ogundipe-Leslie has worked as a Professor in the Department of English, Theater and Mass Communications at the University of Arkansas at Pine Bluff, and her past positions include Visiting Professor, University of Maryland, College Park (2004), Professor in the Department of English and Modern Languages, Albany State University (2000–2001), and Professor, English Section, Ivy Tech State College, Fort Wayne, Indiana (1999). She is also the founder of the Pine Bluff Writers' Association at the University of Arkansas, and the Afrikana Students' Klub at the University of Arkansas at Pine Bluff. The recipient of many awards and academic honors, she has taught at universities in Canada and the United States and has initiated new courses in criticism, in African poetry and fiction, and in women's writing at several Nigerian universities. She has been honored with the Laurie New Jersey Chair in Women's Studies at Rutgers University, and she is also an Honorary Professor of English, Department of English at Rutgers; she was the appointed national reviewer for the 2004 Fulbright Global Millennium Award, and her book *Recreating Ourselves: African Women and Critical Transformations* was selected in First Nomination of 100 Best Books from Africa,

2000. Her critical writing includes *Gender and Subjectivity: Literary, Feminist, Cultural and Narratological Readings* (2005). She has contributed to such works as *No Condition Is Permanent: Nigerian Writing and the Struggle for Democracy* (2001) and *Feminism and "Race"* (Oxford Readings in Feminism, 2000). Ogundipe-Leslie's books in progress are *Inventing African Women: Making African Senses of Gender Discourses* (2008) and *The Politics of Motherhood: Mother and Child in African Arts* (2007). She is a founding member of several women's organizations, national and international, and in Nigeria has frequently been consulted by government ministries regarding women's issues.

She is the author of a volume of poetry, *Sew the Old Days* (1985). She is also an accomplished speaker, has been an actress and producer of plays, and appears frequently on radio. The diversity of her work contributes to the force of her activism and the quality of her writing, both critical and creative.

Ogunyemi, Wale (1939–2001)

Nigerian playwright. Ogunyemi was born in Igbajo, about 150 miles northwest of Lagos. Although he had no formal training in theater arts—he learned his craft through employment, from 1962, as an actor with the then Western Nigerian Television station, with the touring mini-Troupe Theatre Express, and with Wole **Soyinka**'s Orisun theater group. In 1967 he joined the Institute of African Studies at the University of Ibadan.

Ogunyemi was exceptionally prolific, and his sixteen published plays represent only a small portion of his total output for stage, television, and radio. His last work was a collaboration with advisers from the Manchester Education Authority, to devise a Yoruba version of *Macbeth* for performance in Manchester and Ibadan schools as part of the Commonwealth Games cultural program.

His most frequently performed play, *The Divorce* (1977), is a domestic comedy that has been criticized for its chauvinistic treatment of a wife's responsibilities. *Business Headache* (1966) is a comedy in Nigerian Pidgin, sharply observant of the economic realities most Nigerians confront in their daily lives. *Partners in Business* (1991), like *The Divorce*, deals with a marital crisis in a modern setting, but works through high melodrama rather than comedy. Most of his work deals with treatments of Yoruba myth, of relations between the Yoruba gods, and of Yoruba history. Plays such as *Eshu Elegbara* (1970) and *Obaluaye* (1972) deal with the problematic relationship between the gods and humankind. In these plays, as elsewhere, he works in a mode that comes close to total theater, with *gestus* and (especially) music playing as vital a part of the performance as does dialogue. *Eniyan*, Ogunyemi's adaptation of *Everyman* (1987; first performed 1969), is significant for the harshness with which the playwright, here as elsewhere, deals with impiety and social transgression. *Queen Amina of Zazzau* (1999) is a dramatic interpretation of the life of Queen Amina who was thought to have been the ruler of present-day Zaria between 1588 and 1589. Ogunyemi also contributed to *African Theatre in Performance: A Festschrift in Honour of Martin Banham* (2000).

Oil Man of Obange (1971)

A novel by John **Munonye**. This tragic narrative portrays the life of a poor man who attempts to gain a good education for his children, but fails. The protagonist, Jeri, tries to earn enough money to educate his children by working in the palm oil industry. A series of events prevents Jeri's goal, and the novel ends with his suicide.

Ojaide, Tanure (1948–)

Nigerian poet. Ojaide was educated at the University of Ibadan, Nigeria (BA) and at

Syracuse University (MA, PhD). Ojaide is currently a Professor of African American and African Studies at the University of North Carolina and is a former Fellow in Writing of the University of Iowa. He is a productive poet and has won several awards, including a commendation by the Commonwealth Writers Prize 2005 for his first novel *Sovereign Body,* and 2003 Association of Nigerian Authors Prize for Poetry. Ojaide's collections include *Children of Iroko* (1973), *Labyrinths of the Delta* (1986), which won a Commonwealth Poetry Prize, and *The Eagle's Vision* (1987), which won the Christopher Okigbo Prize. *The Endless Song* (1989) was specially mentioned by the Noma Award committee; *The Fate of Vultures and Other Poems* (1990) won the Association of Nigerian Authors' (ANA) Poetry Award; and the title poem of the latter volume received a BBC Arts and Africa Poetry Award. Other collections are *The Blood of Peace* (1991), *Invoking the Warrior God* (1995), which won the ANA's Poetry Award, *Cannons for the Brave* (1995), *Daydream of Ants* (1995), *The New African Poetry: An Anthology* (1999), *Invoking the Warrior Spirit: New and Selected Poems* (1999), *In the Kingdom of Songs: A Trilogy of Poems, 1995–2000* (2001), *Delta Blues and Other Home Songs* (1998, 2002), and *I Want to Dance and Other Poems* (2003). He has also published a book of short stories titled *God's Medicine-Men and Other Stories* (2004), and Ojaide's poetry is also included in such anthologies as *Ubangiji: The Conscience of Eternity* (2000), *The Palm of Time* (2002), and *Winging Words* (2004). He has been a Fellow of the Headlands Center for the Arts in Sausalito, California, and he teaches at the University of North Carolina at Charlotte. His scholarly publishing includes *The Poetry of Wole Soyinka* (1994) and *Poetic Imagination in Black Africa: Essays on African Poetry* (1996), *Culture, Society, and Politics in Modern African Literature: Texts and Contexts* (2002), *A Creative Writing Handbook for African Writers and Students* (2005), and

Poetry, Performance, and Art: Udje Dance Songs of the Urhobo People (2003). Ojaide has also recently published a novel, *Sovereign Body* (2004), written largely from a female perspective that describes an educated African woman's attempt to free herself from oppression and prejudice. The use of traditional African imagery, rhythm, and music and Nigerian English to express Nigerian/ African experience characterize Ojaide's poetry. In 1998 Ojaide published a personal memoir, *Great Boys: An African Childhood.*

Further Reading

Okome, Onookome, ed. *Writing the Homeland: The Poetry and Politics of Tanure Ojaide.* Bayreuth African Studies 60. Bayreuth: Eckhard Breitinger, 2002.

Olafioye, Tayo. *The Poetry of Tanure Ojaide.* Ikeja, Lagos State, Nigeria: Malthouse Press, 2000.

Okai, Atukwei (1941–)

Ghanaian poet. Okai was born in Accra, Ghana, and educated at the Gorky Literary Institute, Moscow (MA, 1967) and the University of London. Having taught Russian literature at the University of Ghana, he is a faculty member of the Institute of African Studies, Legon, and an executive of the Pan-African Writers' Association. He has published four volumes of poems, including one for children: *Flowerfall* (1969), *The Oath of the Fontomfrom and Other Poems* (1971), *Lorgorligi Logarithms* (1974), and *The Anthill in the Sea* (1988), subtitled "Verses and Chants for Children." He explores the plight of postindependence Africa, but a sense of cosmic balance tempers the gravity inherent in such reflections. *The Anthill in the Sea,* with its strong graphics, marks a singular departure in publishing for children in Ghana.

Okara, Gabriel (Imomotimi Gbaingbain) (1921–)

Nigerian poet Okara was born in Bumoundi, Western Nigeria. He received his secondary schooling in Umuahia and Lagos and worked as a bookbinder and a journalist after World War II. During the Nigeria-Biafra war (1967–70), Okara, then Head of Information Services for the Eastern Region, helped foster relief efforts by going on poetry recital tours in the United States. After the war, he took on the management of the Rivers State Broadcasting Corporation, which ran the first and only FM station in black Africa. He also edited a newspaper, *Nigerian Tide.* Upon retirement in 1975, he was appointed Writer-in-Residence of the Rivers State Council for Arts and Culture. Okara still writes and currently lives in retirement in Port Harcourt.

His widely anthologized poems, which first appeared in the magazine *Black Orpheus,* borrow imagery from his Ijo birthplace and from Dylan Thomas, William Blake, W. B. Yeats, and G. M. Hopkins to reflect on the tribulations of nation-building and the traumas that befall the self. The title poem of his slim but dense collection, *The Fisherman's Invocation* (1978), is his most ambitious, and the collection shared a Commonwealth Poetry Prize. Okolo has most recently published three poems in *World Literature Today:* "Welcome Home," "The Silent Voice," and "Waiting for Her Son" (2003). He speaks of his volume of poetry titled *The Dreams, His Vision* (2005) about a dreamer who "dreamt about the future of his country and joined the mass movement of the people, became a leader of the masses and was overthrown by the dictators" (quoted by Nwagbo Nnenyelike in the *Daily Sun,* March 16, 2004). In his poetic novel *The Voice* (1964), Okolo's quest through Sologa ends in self-sacrifice and death. The novel is a linguistic experiment sustained by the metaphorical opposition between Okolo's "straight words" in Ijo and political propaganda. Okara is also the author of two children's books: *Little Snake and Little Frog* (1981) and *An Adventure to Juju Island* (1981).

Okigbo, (Ifeanyichukwu) Christopher
(1932–67)

Nigerian poet. Born in Ojoto village in the former Eastern Region of Nigeria, baptized in the Roman Catholic religion, Okigbo was educated at the prestigious Government College, Umuahia, and University College, Ibadan, where he obtained a degree in classics in 1956. As an undergraduate at Ibadan, he edited the *University Weekly,* joined the Mbari Club, the literary society that published *Black Orpheus,* played jazz clarinet, and demonstrated talent as an athlete.

In the ten years following graduation in 1956, he held brief appointments with the Nigerian Tobacco Company, the United African Company, and the federal Ministry of Research and Information in Lagos; was Vice-Principal at Fiditi Grammar School; was appointed acting registrar of the new University of Nigeria at Nsukka; and represented Cambridge University Press in West Africa. The Nigeria-Biafra war (1967–70) forced him back to Eastern Nigeria, where he died at Nsukka while fighting as a major in the Biafran army. Although his life was brief, he exerted a profound influence on the African literary canon. For example, as Cambridge University Press representative in West Africa, he traveled widely in Africa and Europe, and he was an editor of *Transition.* In 1962 he attended the First African Writers Conference at Makerere University in Kampala, Uganda, where he made a controversial presentation entitled "What Is African Literature?" In 1965 he read his poetry at the Commonwealth Arts Festival in Edinburgh and in 1966 he declined to accept the Negro Festival Arts Prize for his poem *Limits* on the grounds that the award had "colour" or negritude connotations. In 1966, he co-founded with Chinua **Achebe** the short-lived Citadel Publishing Company.

Okigbo's major accomplishment as an artist is his poetry, which he described as "a necessary part of my being alive." His poetic works are **Heavensgate** (1962), which is organized into five sections that highlight the protagonist's religious experience; *Limits* (1964), which consists of two lyrics ("Siren Limits" and "Fragments out of the Deluge," both organized into twelve segments) that deal with the themes of art, religion, and culture; *Silences* (1965), which is composed of two protest poems ("Lament of the Silent Sisters," first published in *Transition,* 1963, and "Lament of the Drums") that treat national and international issues including the death of Patrice Lumumba and the imprisonment of Chief Awolowo; *Distances* (first published in *Transition,* 1964), which continues the themes of personal concerns—religion, art, and nature—explored in his earlier poetry; and the posthumous volumes **Labyrinths,** *with Path of Thunder* (1971) and *Collected Poems* (1986). The influences on his work of Igbo mythology and folklore and classical and modernist aesthetic practices, including those of Dante, Stéphane Mallarmé, G. M. Hopkins, T. S. Eliot, and Ezra Pound, lead some readers to describe it as impenetrable. Despite his reputation as a difficult poet, he remains widely popular with other poets and critics as well as readers, and *Labyrinths* was voted one of Africa's Best Books of the Twentieth Century.

Further Reading

Esonwanne, Uzoma. *Critical Essays on Christopher Okigbo.* Critical Essays on World Literature. New York: G.K. Hall, 2000.

Oko, Akomaye (1943–)

Nigerian poet and playwright, inspired by the Nigeria-Biafra war (1967–70). Born at Ibong, near Obudu, Cross River State, Oko enrolled at Ahmadu Bello University, Zaria, after his secondary education at Maryknoll College. Ogoja fled to the University of Nigeria, Nsukka, after the massacre of Easterners in Northern Nigeria in September 1966. During the war he was a member of a student delegation that toured Europe and America to promote the Biafran cause. His poetry, first published in *Nsukka Harvest* (1972), edited by Chukwuma Azuonye, and in the wartime German anthology *Gedichte aus Biafra* (1968), is mainly a record of his personal experience of war from the 1966 massacres to the end of the war in 1970. In his first collection, *Clouds* (1992), memories of war become a celebration of life in the midst of death. His play *The Cynic* (1992) is an allegorical conflict between the forces of good and evil with allusions to post–civil war Nigeria. It was first produced at the University of Benin (1978). He published a critical book, *The Tragic Paradox: A Study of Wole Soyinka and His Works,* in 1992.

Okome, Onookome (1960–)

Nigerian poet Okome was born on Nigeria's independence day, October 1, 1960, in Sapele, in present-day Delta State. He holds a bachelor's in English from the University of Nigeria, Nsukka, and master's and PhD degrees from the University of Ibadan. He is a member of the faculty of the Department of Theatre Arts at the University of Calabar; he was a Senior Lecturer of Theatre and Film Studies at the University of Calabar in Nigeria and Alexander von Humboldt Research Fellow at the Iwalewa Haus, University of Bayreuth, Germany; and he currently holds a position as an Associate Professor in the Department of English, University of Alberta. His poems first appeared on the pages of the *Guardian* (Lagos), a newspaper to which he regularly contributes articles on literature, culture, film, and politics. A selection from his unpublished collection of poems, "Chapters of Pain," features in the Association of Nigerian Authors (ANA) anthology of Nigerian poetry, *Voices from the Fringe* (1988), edited by Harry **Garuba**. His first collection of poems, *Pendants* (1993), is informed by disillusionment and outrage over the confused politics and pervasive moral bankruptcy in contemporary Nigeria. With Jonathan Haynes he has written a scholarly book, *Cinema and Social Change in West Africa* (1995), and as of October 2004 he was working on a book-length study on *Anxiety of the Local: From Traveling Theatre to Popular Video Films in Nigeria,* and *The Video-Film in Nigeria: Policy, Audience, and Producers* (mentioned in *NYFA Quarterly* in 2001). His recent scholarly publications include *Ogun's Children: The Literature and Politics of Wole Soyinka since the Nobel Prize* (2003), *Before I Am Hanged: Ken Saro-Wiwa, Literature, Politics, and Dissent* (1999), *Writing the Homeland: The Poetry and Politics of Tanure Ojaide* (2002), and *Nigerian Video Films* (2000), which he co-edited with Jonathan Hayes. Okome has also published scholarly articles like "Naming Suffering and Women in Nigerian Video Film: Notes on the Interviews with Emem Isong," which was published in *Calabar Journal of the Humanities* (2000).

Okot p'Bitek (1931–82)

Ugandan poet, born in Gulu, Uganda, and attended Gulu High School and King's College, Budo. He studied law at Aberystwyth, Wales, and social anthropology at Oxford, completing a bachelor's thesis on the traditional songs of the Acoli and Lango. In 1966 he returned to Uganda as Director of the Uganda Cultural Centre and later founded arts festivals at Gulu and Kisumu. Dismissed from his position for writing critically of the Amin government, he lived in exile in Kenya, where he was a faculty member of the literature department in the University of Nairobi. He was a Fellow in the International Writing Program at the University of Iowa in 1969–70 and a Visiting Professor at the University of Texas at Austin and the University of Ife in Nigeria in 1978. In 1979, after Idi Amin was overthrown, he returned to Uganda, where he was appointed a Professor of Creative Writing in the Department of Literature at Makerere University.

Okot p'Bitek's early Acoli-language novel *Lak Tar Miyo Kinyero Wi Lobo* (1953; *White Teeth,* 1989) was followed by the long poem **Song of Lawino**, first composed in Acoli rhyming couplets in 1956 and published in English in 1966. One of the most influential African poems of the 1960s, not only in Uganda but throughout Africa, *Song of Lawino* comprises a series of complaints by Lawino, an Acoli wife whose husband Ocol rejects her for a younger, more Westernized woman. *Song of Ocal* (1970) is the sophisticated, self-serving response of the unrepentant Ocol, who embraces the new culture as fervently as he does his new spouse. Another set of paired poems, *Two Songs,* was published in 1971: "Song of Prisoner" and "Song of Malaya" are dedicated to the memory of Patrice Lumumba, the prime minister of Congo who was murdered in 1961. These poems use the voices of a murderer and a street prostitute to reassert Okot's uncompromising position as a social critic. *Africa's Cultural Revolution* (1973) and *Artist, the Ruler: Essays on Art, Culture and Values* (1986) are collections of essays; *Horn of My Love* (1974) is a collection of oral verse translated from Acoli; *Hare and Hornbill* (1978) is a collection of folktales; and *Acholi Proverbs* (1985) is a collection of sayings. He also produced two scholarly works: *African Religions in Western Scholarship* (1971) and *Religion of the Central Luo* (1971). In 2001 Sudanese writer Taban Lo Liyong published a new translation of *The Defence of Lawino* from the Acholi, and other posthumous republications include *White Teeth: A Novel* (2000, 1996, 1989) and *Hare and Hornbill* (1999, 1978).

Further Reading

Imbo, Samuel Oluoch. *Oral Traditions as Philosophy: Okot p'Bitek's Legacy for African Philosophy.* Lanham, MD: Rowman & Littlefield, 2002.
Schatteman, Renee, and Sara Talis O'Brien. *Voices from the Continent, Vol. 2: A Curriculum Guide*

to Selected North and East African Literature. Trenton, NJ: Africa World Press, 2004.

Okoye, Ifeoma

Okoye is the most important Nigerian female novelist after Flora **Nwapa** and Buchi **Emecheta**. She was born in Anambra State in the former Eastern Nigeria and was educated at the University of Nigeria, Nsukka (1974–77), where she read English, and at Aston University in the UK (1986–87), where she gained a postgraduate degree in English. She teaches English at Nnamdi Azikiwe University, Nigeria, served as an Associate of the African Gender Institute in 2002, as a Senior Lecturer in English at the Nnamdi Azikiwe University in Awka, Nigeria, in 2000, and currently lives in Enugu, Nigeria, where she most recently published a work titled *The Trial and Other Stories* (2005), a collection about the difficulties of widows in Nigeria. Okoye was also the African Regional Winner for the Commonwealth Short Story Competition (1999).

Okoye's major novels are *Behind the Clouds* (1982), *Men without Ears* (1984), and *Chimere* (1992). She is also the author of a number of children's books. *Behind the Clouds* questions from a feminist perspective the conviction in African culture that women are to blame for childlessness. *Men without Ears* depicts the human greed occasioned by the Nigerian oil boom of the 1980s. *Men without Ears* was declared the best fiction of the year in 1984 by the Association of Nigerian Authors. In *Chimere,* a detective novel, a young woman who is mocked by fellow students for being fatherless sets out in search of her father against the will of her mother. Okoye is also the author of *No Where to Hide* (2000), and has been anthologized in such works as *Opening Spaces: An Anthology of Contemporary African Women's Writing* (1999) and *Winging Words* (2004).

Okpewho, Isidore (1941–)

Novelist and critic. Born in Abraka, Nigeria, Okpewho was educated at St. Patrick's College, Asaba, University of Ibadan, and University of Denver. Since 1991 Okpewho has held a position in the Department of Africana Studies at Binghamton University (SUNY) as a Professor of Africana Studies, English and Comparative Literature. He was named a distinguished professor by the State University of New York Board of Trustees in 2004, was named Guggenheim Fellow for 2003, and since 2002 has been the President for the International Society for Oral Literature in Africa. Besides editing a poetry anthology, *The Heritage of African Poetry: An Anthology of Oral and Written Poetry* (1985), Okpewho has published four novels: *The Victims* (1970), *The Last Duty* (1976), *Tides* (1993), and **Call Me by My Rightful Name** (2003); six scholarly studies: *The Epic in Africa* (1979), *Myth in Africa* (1983), *African Oral Literature* (1992), *Once upon a Kingdom: Myth, Hegemony, and Identity* (1998), *The African Diaspora: African Origins and New World Identities* (1999), and *Chinua Achebe's "Things Fall Apart": A Casebook* (2003). He has also contributed to *African Drama and Performance* (2004), and has published a large amount of literary criticism in such journals and critical works as *Research in African Literatures, African Folklore: An Encyclopedia, Oral Tradition, Journal of Folklore Research, Cambridge History of African and Caribbean Literature,* and *Meditations on African Literature.*

Okpewho concentrates on interactions between individual personalities and social forces in modern Africa's tragedy. *The Victims* takes the traditional literary archetype of a wife plotting against her rival and transforms it into a tragedy of individual failures occasioned by cultural resistance to change. The catastrophic denouement effectively integrates a moral tale into Okpewho's social criticism, as Nwabunor's poisoning of Ogugua's children also destroys her own child and brings ruin upon herself and her contemptible husband. The events in *The Last Duty* take place during the Nigeria-Biafra civil war (fictionalized as the Igabo-Simbi war) in an Igabo village where the presence of a Simbi woman married to an Igabo man unleashes a maelstrom of intrigues motivated by base opportunism and ethnic hatred. *Tides* addresses the problem of environmental pollution in the oil-producing areas of Nigeria. Ebika Harrison, a member of the otherwise peaceful Committee of Concerned Citizens, resorts to acts of violence in order to force the government to act on behalf of communities whose livelihoods are threatened by the devastating effects of a big dam. Okpewho demonstrates an accomplished prose style and a sensitive probing of the forces that undermine postcolonial Africa's quest for nationhood.

Okri, Ben (1959–)

Nigerian poet, novelist, and short-story writer. Born in Minna, Nigeria, Okri studied at Children's Home School, Sapele, Christ School, Ibadan, Urhobo College, Warri, and University of Essex, UK. Ben Okri is a Vice-President of the English Centre of International PEN, a member of the board of the Royal National Theatre, and was awarded an OBE in 2001. He currently lives in London and has honorary doctorates from the universities of Westminster (1997) and Essex (2002). Apart from writing, Okri has been poetry editor for *West Africa,* broadcaster for the BBC, and Visiting Fellow Commoner in Creative Arts, Trinity College, Cambridge. His novels include *Flowers and Shadows* (1980), *The Landscapes Within* (1981), *The Famished Road* (1991), which won the 1991 Booker Prize, *Songs of Enchantment* (1993), *Dangerous Love* (1996), which was awarded the Premio Palmi (Italy) in 2000 and is a reworking of *The Landscapes Within,* and *In Arcadia* (2002). His collections of short stories are *Incidents at the Shrine* (1986) and *Stars of the New Curfew* (1988, republished by Vintage Press in 1999); and his poetry

collections are *An African Elegy* (1992) and *Mental Fight* (1999). He has also published individual poems titled "Soul of the Nation" (1999) and "Children of the Dream" (2003) in the *Guardian* and "Draw" in the *Evening Standard* (2002), as well as "An African Elegy" in Debra Bricker Balken's book *Alfredo Jaar: Lament of the Images* (1999). His essays have been published as *Birds of Heaven* (1996) and *A Way of Being Free* (1997), and he has published articles such as "Our Work Is to Free Talent in the Project of Humanity" in the *Times Higher Education Supplement* (2003), "The New Dark Age" in the *Guardian* (2003), "The Neglect of Writers Is a Dangerous Thing for Any Country: Ben Okri Offers a Provocation" in the *Royal Society of Literature Magazine* (2003), "The Racial Colourist" in the *Cultural Breakthrough Exhibition* (2003), "Schools of the Future" in *Ode* (2003), also published in Dutch as "De universiteit van de toekomst" in *Ode* (2004), "Healing the Africa within Us" in *Ode* (2004), and "The Mysterious Anxiety of Them and Us: An Allegory of History" in *Global Agenda* (2005). He has won the Booker Prize, a Commonwealth Writers Prize, and the *Paris Review* Aga Khan Prize for fiction, and his work is anthologized in *Lament of the Images, Exhibition Catalogue* (1999), *The Art of the Story: An International Anthology of Contemporary Short Stories* (1999), *Colonial and Postcolonial Fiction in English: An Anthology* (1999), *Picador Book of African Stories* (2000), *Step into a World: A Global Anthology of the New Black Literature* (2000), and *Voices for Peace: An Anthology* (2001).

Okri is conscious of the postindependence realities of African societies, and his works are often satirical and critical of the various political and economic crises that have plagued African countries since the end of the colonial period. His first novel, *Flowers and Shadows,* examines the issue of corruption and its devastating effects on a family and a society. The short story "Laughter beneath the Bridge," in *Incidents at the Shrine*, focuses on the disastrous consequences of the Nigeria-Biafra war of 1967–70 on ordinary people. Okri's interest in the relationship between the natural and supernatural worlds leads to a negotiation between the two paradigms that characterizes his approach to the discussion of human existence. For example, the image of the *abiku*, the spirit child of Yoruba myth who dies soon after birth only to be reborn again and again, recurs in Okri's work, particularly in *The Famished Road* and *An African Elegy*. In *The Famished Road*, Azaro is the *abiku* child who shifts among worlds of the living, the dead, and the unborn, a trinity that is unique in the African worldview. In "Political Abiku," in *An African Elegy*, the *abiku* image represents Nigeria's attempts to fashion a sustainable political tradition because it represents the fact that from the time of independence in 1960, Nigerian governments have died in their early stages only to be reborn in other guises time after time. Okri writes with simple, lucid, and image-laden language in Nigerian English.

Further Reading

Fraser, Robert. *Ben Okri: Towards the Invisible City*. Devon: Northcote House, 2002.

Moh, Felicia Oka. *Ben Okri: An Introduction to His Early Fiction*. Enugu, Nigeria: Fourth Dimension Publishers, 2001.

Olafioye, Tayo Peter (1948–)

Nigerian poet and novelist Olafioye was born in Igbotako and educated at the University of Lagos in Nigeria and later at universities in the United States where he gained a PhD. He has taught at the University of Ilorin in Nigeria and at universities in California, and he is a Professor of English at National University and Southwestern College in San Diego, California. He has won the Golden Poet Award in San Francisco and the National Library Award of America, as well as many other prizes for his poetry in the United States and in Europe.

The combination in Olafioye's poetry and fiction of rural imagery and cosmopolitan themes reflects life in the riverine area of Ondo State and in Nigerian and American cities. His poetry and fiction incorporate myth, symbols, festival rites, and African gods, as well as proverbs and idioms, to express his despair over Africa's current condition. The poems of *Sorrows of a Town Crier* (1988) tell in elegiac tones of the abuse of power in Africa, continental disillusionment, and the devaluation of human values. In *Bush Girl Comes to Town* (1988), the characters forget their African background as they embrace the pleasures of life in California, a life that leaves them undefined and unfulfilled. His other publications include *The Excellence of Silence, A Stroke of Hope* (2000), **Arrowheads to My Heart** (1999), *A Carnival of Looters* (2000), *Ubangiji: The Conscience of Eternity* (2000), *The Parliament of Idiots* (2000), *Town Crier: Selected Poems, 1984–2002,* and *Tomorrow Left Us Yesterday* (2004), poems; *The Saga of Sego* (1982), a novel; *Grandma's Sun: Childhood Memoir* (2000), a semifictional autobiography; and three books of literary criticism: *Response to Creativity* (1988), *Critic as Terrorist: Views on New African Writings* (1989), and *Tanure Ojaide: Critical Appraisal* (2000). Forthcoming works by Olafioye include *Dining with the Gods: Stories from Africa* and *My Heart Swims in the Tears of Happiness*.

Old Man and the Medal, The (1969)

A novel by Ferdinand **Oyono**, translated from the French (*Le Vieux nègre et la médaille*, 1956). It narrates the story of an old man who holds more value in the appearance of power than actual power. It uses humor to demonstrate that the old man, Meka, sacrifices too much for a superficial goal, much like the society he lives in. After suffering through a medal ceremony Meka realizes that his privileging of the medal was ridiculous.

Oludhe Macgoye, Marjorie (1928–)

A novelist and poet, Oludhe Macgoye was born in Southampton, England, and moved to Kenya in 1954. She has published several novels and poetry such as that included in *Song of Nyarloka and Other Poems* (1977). Oludhe Macgoye's 1997 novel *Chira* was nominated by the Kenya National Library Service for the International IMPAC Dublin Literary Award 1999. Recently, Oludhe Macgoye has published works like *Coming to Birth* (1986, 2000) with J. Roger Kurtz, and *Moral Issues in Kenya* (1996, 2003).

Further Reading

Kuria, Mike, ed. *Talking Gender: Conversations with Kenyan Women Writers.* PJ Kenya, 2003.

Kurtz, J. Roger. "Crossing Over: Identity and Change in Marjorie Oludhe Macgoye's *Song of Nyarloka.*" *Research in African Literature* 33, no. 2 (2002): 100–118.

Omotoso, Kole (1943–)

A Nigerian novelist, playwright, and critic, Omotoso was born in Akure, Nigeria, and studied in Ibadan and in Edinburgh, where he gained a PhD. He has been actively involved in African writers' organizations, has taught at universities in Nigeria, and was a professor of African languages and literatures at the University of the Western Cape, South Africa, between 1991 and 2000. Kole Omotoso presently lives in South Africa and is a Professor of Drama at the University of Stellenbosch, South Africa. His body of work includes several novels, a number of plays, and books and articles on political and social issues.

Together with Femi **Osofisan**, Biodun Jeyifo, and Niyi **Osundare**, Omotoso belongs to a group of writers who have been critical of the first-generation African writers: Wole **Soyinka**, Chinua **Achebe**, Christopher **Okigbo**, and others. They pay respect to the elders, but they also claim that African literature should be more about contemporary social reality. Omotoso has experimented widely with literary styles and techniques to achieve his aim of reaching ordinary African people. He has written in the form of the allegory (his novel *The Combat,* 1972) and the detective novel (*Pella's Choice,* 1974) and combines fact and fiction in *Just before Dawn* (1988) and in his autobiographical novel *Memories of Our Recent Boom* (1990). His two plays, *The Curse* (1976) and *Shadows in the Horizon* (1977), reflect a radical vision of equality. *The Curse* critiques the perpetuation of corruption from one military coup to the next, while in *Shadows in the Horizon* the blaze that ends the play is the instrument for the redistribution of the wealth and property accumulated by the rich. Omotoso's journalistic column in *West Africa* during the 1980s was a respected literary forum. He has also written a critical study, *Achebe or Soyinka? A Study in Contrasts* (1996), and a book of commentary on Africa's crises, *Season of Migration to the South* (1994).

One Man One Wife (1959)

A novel by Timothy **Aluko**. Aluko uses humor to demonstrate the negative effects of the missionaries of the late nineteenth century on the farmers of Western Nigeria. The farmers' tradition of polygamy conflicts with the Christians' views of civilization, and uncovers the hypocrisy of characters like Pastor David and Royasin and their negative influence on the rural traditions.

Only Son, The (1966)

The first novel in a trilogy by John **Munonye**. The other two novels in the trilogy are *Obi* (1969) and *Bridge to a Wedding* (1978). The preservation of ancestral identity and the importance of the family home are focused on by Munonye in these novels. The first novel sees the character Nnanna brought up by his mother to honor tradition and in the image of his dead father. But Nnanna converts to Christianity, which his mother realizes threatens the Igbo emphasis on the preservation of ancestral identity. The second novel follows Nnanna (now called Joe)'s attempt to build a house in his ancestral village, his marriage, and his exile when he fails to marry another wife after his first appears unable to have children. The final novel reconciles the family after Joe, now Mr. Kafo, and his wife raise a large family in the city and see one of their daughters married.

Onwueme, Tess Akaeke (1955–)

Nigerian playwright, born in Ogwashi-Ukwu, Delta State, Nigeria. Onwueme holds degrees in literature and drama and currently holds a position at the University of Wisconsin Eau-Claire as Distinguished Professor of Cultural Diversity and Professor of English. She won the 1986 Association of Nigerian Authors Award in drama, the 1988 Distinguished Author Award from Obafemi Awolowo University, her alma mater, and the Drama Prize awarded by the Association of Nigerian Authors (ANA) for the plays, *Shakara: Dance-Hall Queen* (2001) and *Then She Said It* (2003). Her published works include the plays *A Hen Too Soon* (1983), *The Broken Calabash* (1984), *A Scent of Onions* (1985), *The Desert Encroaches* (1985), *Ban Empty Barn and Other Plays* (1986), *Mirror for Campus* (1987), *The Reign of Wazobia* (1988), *Legacies* (1989), *Parable for a Season* (1991), *Riot in Heaven* (1991), *Go Tell It to the Women* (1992), *Shakara: Dance-Hall Queen* (2000), *Then She Said It!* (2002), *The Missing Face* (2002), *What Mama Said* (an epic drama, 2003), *NO Vacancy* (2005), and *Riot in Heaven and Acadia Boys: Two Plays* (2005), as well as the novels *Why the Elephant Has No Butt* (2000) and *What I Cannot Tell My Father* (2005). The BBC World Drama Service recently featured *Shakara* as a major broadcast, while *The Missing Face* was performed off-Broadway in New York City, and *The Reign of Wazobia* was adapted into a film script. Her plays explore a wide range of themes such as poverty, elitism, corruption, hypocrisy, and cultural conflict. She is especially consumed with the unfulfilled potential of women in a patriarchal culture. Onwueme's plays often draw on Igbo mythology, operatic structures, and folklore to argue that the positive aspects of women's role in society were seriously eroded by the influences of cross-cultural patriarchal legacies characteristic of modern society. She has published the articles "Drumbeats in Black Women's Drama" in *Obsidian* (1999), "To the Would-Be African Female Writer: Husband Yourself First" in *The African Writers' Handbook* (1999), and "Buried in the Rubble: The Missing Face in African Literature" in the *African Literature Association Bulletin* (2002). Her most important plays, particularly the very polemical *Go Tell It to the Women,* argue that a universal feminist awareness must acknowledge and accommodate African gender sensibilities, values, and needs. *The Broken Calabash, Parables for a Season,* and *The Reign of Wazobia* have been collected in *Three Plays* (1993).

Further Reading

Akpewho, Lucky. "Tess Onwueme's Plays and Feminist Aesthetics in Nigerian Drama." Master's thesis, English Department, University of Port Harcourt, Rivers State, Nigeria, 2000.

Bradlette, Juliette. "Discourses on Power in Onwueme's Plays." PhD diss., English Department, Houston University, Houston, Texas, 2001.

Evwierhoma, Mabel. *Female Empowerment and Dramatic Creativity in Nigeria.* Ibadan, Nigeria: Caltop Publications, 2002.

Kamau, Oliver. "Revolutionary Theatre in Africa: The Example of Tess Onwueme's Plays." PhD diss., Theatre Department, University of Alberta, Edmonton, Alberta, Canada, 1999.

Uko, Iniobong. *Gender and Identity in the Works of Osonye Tess Onwueme.* Trenton, NJ: Africa World Press, 2004.

Onyeama, Dillibe (1951–)

An autobiographer, biographer, and novelist, Onyeama was born in Enugu, Nigeria, but educated mainly in England, where he lived between 1959 and 1981. His first book, *Nigger at Eton* (1972), deals with his experiences as a black student at the famous public school. His *The Return: Homecoming of a Negro from Eton* (1978) and *Notes of So-called Afro-Saxon* (1988), sequels to the first book, focus on the problems that he encountered as he tried to adjust to Nigeria. In *Chief Onyeama: The Story of an African God* (1982) he writes of the life and times of his late grandfather, a man who was reputed to be one of the most feared traditional rulers of his time. A foray into the supernatural produced *Juju* (1976) and *Godfathers of Voodoo* (1985), a book described by a commentator as "a supernatural thriller of love and African magic." His other books include *John Bull's Nigger* (1974), *The Book of Black Man's Humour* (1975), *Sex Is a Nigger's Game* (1976), *Secret Society* (1978), *Revenge of the Medicine Man* (1980), and the biographies *Modern Messiah: The Jim Nwobodo Story* (1983) and *African Legend: The Incredible Story of Francis Arthur Nzeribe* (1984).

Ordeal in the Forest (1968)

A novel by Godwin **Wachira**. This historical novel charts the resistance of the Kikuyu people of Kenya to colonialism. It portrays the progress of the group's understanding of foreign corruption, their feelings of oppression, and mounting anticolonial organization in the form of military and political protest. Wachira also demonstrates the complexity of such a community, and the inherent contradictions in character that make their success difficult and tempered with internal discord.

Osadebay, Dennis (Chukude) (1911–95)

Nigerian poet Osadebay was born in Asaba and was a journalist, a jurist, and a politician generally credited as one of the founders of the National Council of Nigeria and the Cameroon (NCNC) Party. He had his early education at the Hope Waddell Institute in Calabar before he traveled to England to study law. As a nationalist of the First Republic of Nigeria whose contemporaries included Nnamdi Azikiwe, Abubakar Tafawa Balewa, Obafemi Awolowo, Ahmadu Bello, Samuel Ladoke Akintola, and Anthony Enahoro, he along with these leaders inspired the London Constitutional Conference that led to Nigeria's independence in 1960. He held several important positions in his country, as he was president of the senate during the First Republic and also served as the first premier of the defunct Mid-West Region of Nigeria. As a poet Osadebay is generally grouped, along with Gladys **Casely-Hayford**, Raphael E. G. Armattoe, and Michael **Dei-Anang**, among the "pioneer poets" of West Africa who, while generally extolling African traditional values, vigorously assail European colonialism. *Africa Sings* (1952), published while he was in England, celebrates indigenous African cultural values and black pride (as in "Rise of Africa"), draws attention to the ironic glorification of Great Britain as a colonizing power (as in "Africa Speaks to England"), and celebrates nature (as in "Ode to the Palm Tree"). The poems show his knack for translation (some of his verse was translated from his native Igbo to English), and his diction is characterized by Pidgin and dialect. *Africa Sings* was reissued with later verse in *Poems of a Nationalist*.

Osahon, Naiwu (1937–)

Nigerian cultural critic and children's writer, born in Benin, Nigeria. Osahon obtained a master's degree in marketing and worked for the United African Company, but when his union activities led to his dismissal he established a publishing company, Di Nigro Press (known later as Third World First Publications and later still as Heritage Books), and started publishing his own writing. He is the leader of the International Pan African Movement (IPAM), and is an occasional columnist for the *Daily Sun*. His first book, *The*

Climate of Darkness (1971), was followed by *A Nation in Custody* (1973), *Black Power: The African Predicament* (1976), *Victim of UAC* (1977), and *Fires of Africa* (1973); these books expound his views on racism and the need for the assertion of an African identity. The book for which Osahon is best known is *Sex Is a Nigger* (1971), which details sexual escapades in Sweden; *Mr. Sugar Daddy* and *Lagos Na Waa, I Swear* are in a similar vein. However he is also the author of creative and critical works that include *No Answer from the Oracle* (1974) and *Poems for Young Lovers* (1974). In 1981 he published twenty-five books for children including five coloring books, five adventure stories, and fifteen storybooks. The variety of the stories indicates the influence of oral traditions, a didactic purpose, and a philosophical objective. Osahon has earned a reputation as a critic of corruption, demonstrated in *The Colour of Anger* (1991). His racial view of reality informs *God Is Black* (1993), in which he argues that internalized racial issues associated with religion must be eliminated. Osahon is also the author of *The Secrets of the Ages* (2001), which explores the origins of different religions in Africa.

Osiris Rising (1995)

A novel by Ayi Kwei **Armah**. Set in a fictional West African state, Armah's heroine is the African-American Ast, who is also an Egyptologist. Ast travels to Africa to search for her home, and becomes a member of the secret society of the Ankh, headed by her former partner Asar. Their goal is to place ancient Egypt at the center of African history, but a state security chief named Seth undermines them. Asar is killed and dismembered in a similar manner to Osiris, with a pregnant Ast looking on.

Osofisan, Femi (1946–)

A prolific Nigerian critic, poet, novelist, and playwright whose work attacks political cor-ruption and injustice. Osofisan was born in Erunwon village in the old Western Region of Nigeria and educated at the universities of Ibadan, Dakar, and Paris; he is a Professor of Drama at the University of Ibadan. He has also served as president of numerous literature companies, such as the international PEN Nigerian Chapter, the Pan African Writers Association/Westafrika, and the Association of Nigerian Authors. Among the literary awards and commendations he has won are prizes from the Association of Nigerian Authors (ANA) for both drama (1980) and poetry (1989).

Osofisan writes from the ideological left, and his work has generated controversy not only because he asserts that his work departs from the literary traditions of his contemporaries, particularly J. P. Clark **Bekederemo** and Wole **Soyinka** (his mentor), who, he claims, are too rooted in the past and to a celebration of imitative classical models, but because, unlike them, he primarily seeks new aesthetic forms. His only novel, *Kolera Kalej* (1975), written while he was a student in Paris, deals with corruption among students and faculty at a university. Under the pseudonym Okinba Launko, he has published four volumes of poetry: *Minted Coins* (1987), which explores topical themes as they relate to inequities; *Ire and Other Poems for Performance* (1998); *Dream Seeker on Divining Chain* (1993), which invokes traditional metaphors from Ifa, an oracle significant to the Yoruba people of southwestern Nigeria; and a collection of poetry titled *Pain Remembers, Love Rekindles* (2001). As a journalist and critic he has contributed insightful essays to several magazines and newspapers, including *West Africa, Daily Times, Newswatch,* and the Lagos *Guardian,* and he has also published and collaborated on several critical works, including *Contemporary African Plays* (1999), *African Theatre in Development* (1999), *African Theatre: Playwrights and Politics* (2001), *The Nostalgic Drum: Essays on*

Literature, Drama and Culture (2001), Insidious Treasons: Drama in a Postcolonial State (2001), Pressures of Freedom (2001), and African Theatre: Southern Africa (2004).

His strength as a writer is drama, and he has written more than a dozen plays, including A Restless Run of Locusts (1975), which deals with political corruption and violence; Once upon Four Robbers (1978), which examines the morality of armed robbery and public executions in Nigeria; Morountodun (1982), which employs myth, folklore, and history to address institutional oppression and armed revolt; and Aringindin and the Nightwatchmen (1991), which calls attention to the levels of despotism in the Nigerian polity. He is also the author of plays such as One Putting, Many Seasons (2001), Once upon Four Robbers (2001), Esu and the Vagabond Minstrels (2002), and Bishop Ajayi Crowther: The of Triumph and Travails of a Putting (2002). Recent productions of Osofisan's plays include Wèsóò Hamlet! (or The Resurrection of Hamlet) (2003), and The Trojan Women or The Women of Owu (2004). Several of his plays are collected in Birthdays Are Not for Dying and Other Plays (1990), The Oriki of a Grasshopper and Other Plays (1995), Kolera Kolej: A Novel and the Play (2001), Seasons of Wrath (five short plays) (2002), Restless Breed (four short plays) (2002), Major Plays 1: Many Colours Make the Thunder-King, Farewell to a Cannibal Rage, Oriki of a Grasshopper (2003), Major Plays 2 (2005), and Osofisan's work is included in the anthology A Melody of Stones (PEN) Anthology of New Nigerian Writing (2003). His writing employs a range of humor, irony, song, dance, folktale, and fable.

Further Reading

Jeyifo, Biodun, ed. Modern African Drama. New York: W. W. Norton & Company, 2002.

Richards, Sandra L. Ancient Songs Set Ablaze: The Theatre of Femi Osofisan. Washington, DC: Howard University Press, 1999.

Osundare, Niyi (1946–)

A poet, Osundare was born in Ikere-Ekiti, Nigeria, and gained degrees at the University of Ibadan (BA), the University of Leeds (MA), and York University, Canada (PhD). He was formerly Professor of English at the University of New Orleans, and currently teaches at the University of Ibadan, Nigeria. Osundare is also a columnist for Newswatch, a prominent Nigerian newsmagazine, and a frequent newspaper commentator on current affairs. A prolific poet, he published Songs of the Marketplace, his first book, in 1983. Some of his other collections include Village Voices (1984), The Eye of the Earth (1986), Moonsongs (1988), Midlife (1993), **Waiting Laughters** (1990), Selected Poems (1992), Songs of the Season (1999), Horses of Memory (1999), The Word Is an Egg (2000), Thread in the Loom: Essays on African Literature and Culture (2000), Pages from the Book of the Sun: New and Selected Poems (2002), The State Visit (2002) and Two Plays (2006). Osundare has also published volumes of poetry for children, some of which are titled Early Birds Book One: Poems for Junior Secondary Schools (2004), Early Birds Book Two: Poems for Junior Secondary Schools (2004), and Early Birds Book Three: Poems for Junior Secondary Schools (2004). The following anthologies include works by Osundare: The African Writers' Handbook (1999), Ibadan Mesiogo (2001), Essays on African Literature in Honour of Oyin Ogunba Kwesi (2003), Bola Ige: The Passage of a Modern Cicero (2003), Operations and Tears (2004), Winging Words (2004), and Emerging Perspectives on Niyi Osundare (2005). He struggled for a space for poetry in Nigerian newspapers, particularly the Sunday Tribune, where his poems began to appear in 1985 under the title "Songs of the Season." The Eye of the Earth won a Commonwealth Poetry Prize and Waiting Laughters won the Award.

Most of the poems in Songs of the Marketplace are concerned with the decay of social life in the poet's society and they focus on the contrasting images of poverty and affluence. *Songs of the Marketplace,* however, ends with the optimistic vision of a harmonic social order in a new world, a theme Osundare later explores more intensely in *Waiting Laughters. Village Voices* enriches rural tradition with local songs, myths, and panegyric verses. *The Eye of the Earth* portrays the shift from agrarian to capitalist production and mourns the destruction of a communal society due to individualism and plunder.

Oti, Sonny (1941–)

Nigerian playwright and songwriter. Born in Arochukwu, Abia State, Nigeria, Oti was a teacher in mission primary schools before he enrolled in the Department of English at the University of Ibadan at a time when the Theatre Arts Department was evolving from the traveling theater group organized by Geoffrey Axworthy. Under Axworthy's tutelage, Oti emerged as a nationally celebrated comic actor, playing Falstaff in episodes adapted from Shakespeare and more colorfully the picaresque hero of Nkem **Nwankwo**'s novel *Danda* (1964). Fleeing in the wake of the massacre of Easterners in Northern and Western Nigeria in 1966, he was among the zero-hour graduates of what for the brief moment between the Biafra declaration of independence on May 30, 1967, and the outbreak of the Nigeria-Biafra war on June 6, 1967, was the University of Biafra. In Biafra, he organized the Armed Forces Theatre Group, modeled on the Ibadan traveling theater, which toured military camps and war zones with a revue of songs, skits, and morale-boosting enactments often based on the events of the day. Shortly after the war, he enrolled in the Leeds University School of Theatre Arts, where he obtained a master's in 1972. Returning to Nigeria, he joined the faculty of the Department of Theatre Arts at the University of Jos, where he is a professor. He is the author of the farcical plays *The Carvers, The Drummers, Return Home and Roost Awhile* and *Dreams and Realities*

(1979) as well as *The Old Masters* (1977), *The Return of Jerome* (1981), and *Evangelist Jeremiah* (1982). Recordings of his songs have been available since the early 1970s.

Our Sister Killjoy (1977)

Ama Ata **Aidoo**'s first novel. It tells the story of Sissie as she wins a scholarship and travels from Ghana to Europe. The novel explores the importance of remembering and reinstating old African values as a way of overcoming oppression and finding subjectivity. It focuses on the African diaspora, slavery, and postindependence issues (to name a few) as it explores the importance of lost values.

Ovbiagele, Helen (1944–)

Nigerian novelist. Born in Benin City, Ovbiagele was educated at schools in Nigeria and at the University of Lagos, where she received a degree in education. She later studied in London, after which she taught at the Lagos City College, Yaba, and Corona School, Ikoyi. She is the women's page editor of the *Nigerian Vanguard* and has held that position since 1984. Her novels, all in Macmillan's Pacesetter series, utilize the romance formula, but her heroines are frequently older independent women, divorcees, and country-women-come-to-town who may yield even to prostitution, as in *Evbu My Love* (1980), in order to liberate themselves through better education. Her other novels are *A Fresh Start* (1982), *You Never Know* (1982), *Forever Yours* (1985), *Who Really Cares* (1986), and *The Schemers* (1991).

Owusu, Martin (Okyere) (1943–)

Ghanaian dramatist. Born in Agona Kwaman, Ghana, the son of a catechist, Martin Owusu received his secondary schooling at Mfantsipim School, Cape Coast, where he was influenced by his teacher Joe **de Graft**. He was trained as a teacher at the Presbyterian Training College, Akropong-Akuapem, and completed the diploma in theater studies at the School of Music and Drama in Legon. He has two postgraduate degrees: a master's from Bristol (1973) and a PhD from Brandeis (1979), both concerned with the classical influences on West African playwrights. He has held appointments at universities in Ghana and the United States and is a Senior Lecturer the School of Performing Arts at Legon.

Owusu is an actor, academic, teacher, and director, but he is best known for his published stage plays. The first of these were *Adventures of Sasa and Esi* (1968), playlets based on short stories about children encountering a giant and a witch. *The Story Ananse Told* (1970), originally prepared for the annual staff production at Mfantsipim, makes use of material from the body of stories known as *Anansesem. The Sudden Return and Other Plays* (1973) brings together experiments with various kinds of narrative drama. His most important play is a historical drama, *The Mightier Sword,* which was also published in *The Sudden Return and Other Plays.* The play is based on events that occurred during the first Ashanti-Denkyira war. Owusu's major contribution to the Ghanaian theater is as a director rather than as a playwright. His doctoral dissertation was published as *Drama of the Gods: A Study of Seven African Plays* (1983), and he has published another critical work titled *Analysis and Interpretation of Ola Rotimi's "The Gods Are Not to Blame"* (1998).

Oyebode, Femi (1954–)

Nigerian poet Oyebode was born in Lagos and trained in medicine and psychiatry in Nigeria and Britain. He currently works as a Professor of Psychiatry and the Head of the Psychiatric Department, University of Birmingham, UK, and as a consultant psychiatrist at the Queen Elizabeth Psychiatric Hospital in Edgbaston, Birmingham. Oyebode is a distinguished Honorary Research Fellow and Associate of CWAS (Centre of West African Studies), University of Birmingham, and has served as the Deputy Chief Examiner at the Royal College of Psychiatrists, and a PLAB examination board member for the GMC. Oyebode also writes for a number of medical journals, including *The British Journal of Psychiatry* and *The Mental Health Review.* His first poetry collection, entitled *Naked to Your Softness and Other Dreams* (1989), explores the varieties of the poet's experience in both his personal and public life. In the second collection of poems, *Wednesday Is a Colour* (1990), his personal experience of life in Britain reflects his impressions of the society and the people. *Forest of Transformations* (1991) draws upon the mythical and legendary world of the Yoruba, and *Selected Poems (Strategies for Communication in Southern Africa)* (2001) were selected, introduced, and analyzed by Onookome Okome.

Oyekunle, Segun (1944–)

Nigerian playwright Oyekunle was born in Kwara State, Nigeria, and is a graduate of Ahmadu Bello University, Zaria, whose drama unit was especially active and innovatory in the 1970s. During the 1980s, resident in Los Angeles, Oyekunle turned increasingly to filmscript writing. His best-known work is, however, the stage play *Katakata for Sofahead* (1983; first produced 1978). Written in a somewhat simplified Pidgin, *Katakata* is set in a prison cell and explores the "working" relationship between six prisoners as they establish a hierarchy among themselves and as they investigate the case history of Lateef, the newest arrival. Vivid and funny, the play has been produced successfully outside Nigeria (e.g., Johannesburg 1994), vindicating the Pidgin medium's ability to travel.

Oyono, Ferdinand (1929–)

Cameroonian novelist. After obtaining his high school diploma in Yaoundé, Oyono went to the *lycée* of Provins (France), where he received his *baccalauréat,* and studied law in Paris while attending the École Nationale d'Administration. After his return to Cameroon he worked in the Ministry of Foreign Affairs, became an ambassador, represented Cameroon at the United Nations, and eventually became Minister of Foreign Affairs. Oyono remains involved in politics, and is Cameroon's Minister of State in charge of Culture.

Of his three novels, *Une vie de boy* (1956; **Houseboy** 1966), *Le Vieux Nègre et la médaille* (1956; The **Old Man and the Medal,** 1969), and *Chemin d'Europe* (1960; *Road to Europe,* 1989), the first has become a classic. It tells the story of a teenager named Joseph Toundi who leaves his family to work for a white missionary, and relates his experiences among the colonizers in the form of a diary. The novel, which had a strong impact when it appeared, was considered an excellent representation of the wrongs brought by colonialism, but Oyono criticizes the system's morality more than its economic or cultural impact. In addition to its anticolonialist views, the novel evokes the Old Testament tale of Joseph and Potiphar's wife, the structure of a *bildungsroman* in its narrative treatment of Joseph's experience, and the scheme of a *Sô* initiation in some of its ethnographic detail. The latter pattern suggests that Oyono was not writing just for a white audience but also for other Cameroonians. The *Old Man and the Medal* ridicules Meka who believes he has become a friend of the whites because the French administration offers him a medal, and who ends up in jail instead. In *Road to Europe* Aki Barnabas hopes to go to France, but only when he joins a religious group can he fulfill his dream. Both novels use humor to show how easily people can be fooled.

Further Reading

Dunton, Christopher. *The Novels of Ferdinand Oyono.* Pueblo, CO: Passeggiata Press, 1997.

Oyono-Miha, Guillaume (1939–)

A Cameroonian dramatist writing in English and French, Oyono-Miha was born in Mvoutessi, Cameroon, and educated locally and then at the Collège Évangélique in Libamba. His first play, *Trois prétendants, un mari* (1964; *Three Suitors, One Husband,* 1968), was immensely successful when it was first performed and continued to be popular in Cameroon for many years. The play explores the consequences and complications of the practice in marriage of the dowry. He founded his first troupe in Libamba, where he held his first teaching post. He was awarded a British Council scholarship, which he held at the University of Keele in the UK, and won first prize in the BBC Africa Service's theater competition for his play *Until Further Notice* (1968), which was performed at the Edinburgh Festival in 1967. In this play the expectations of a village are raised by the return of a young couple from Europe. *His Excellency's Special Train,* a radio play, was first broadcast by the BBC in 1969. On his return to Africa he was appointed to a post in the English Department of the University of Yaoundé, and in the 1970s he worked for a period as Head of Cultural Affairs in the Ministry of Information and Culture. His later work includes three collections of tales, *Chroniques de Mvoutessi* (1971–72), first begun in 1964.

Oyono-Miha's plays inaugurated and inspired a tradition of Cameroonian theater that explores the confrontation between tradition and modernity with humor and to great comic effect. He has translated most of his writing into English and French so that it is accessible and widely known in both the anglophone and francophone regions of Cameroon.

P

Palangyo, Peter (1939–93)

A Tanzanian novelist, Palangyo was born in Nkoaranga, Tanzania, and educated at St. Olaf College, Minnesota (BA), Makerere

University College, Uganda (Dip. Ed.), Iowa State University (MA), and the State University of New York at Buffalo (PhD). He was also Tanzania's ambassador to Canada. Palangyo's novel *Dying in the Sun* (1968) was the first Tanzanian novel in English. It tells the story of Ntanya, a symbol of Africa caught between the past and the future, uncertain whether to retreat into a world of traditional cultural values undiluted by the advent of the white man or to meet the modern world directly. In the end Ntanya achieves peace, sensing that Africa should first be proud of itself and then seek to achieve things for the people.

Palm-wine Drinkard, The (1952)

Amos **Tutuola**'s first published novel tells a tale of a devoted drinker of palm wine who travels to the land of the dead in search of his tapster, who died while tapping palm wine. He must perform a number of tasks (such as the capture of death) before he can arrive at the town of the dead, and the juju he inherited from his father assists him. When he finds his dead tapster he learns that he may not be brought back to life, but the tapster gives the drinkard a magic egg that will help him obtain palm wine. Dylan Thomas's positive review added to the success of the novel.

Paradise Farm (1993)

A novel by Samuel **Kahiga**. The book combines reality, illusion, and the supernatural in order to uncover the resilience and steadfastness of love and humanity. Kahiga's novel boasts a very complex plot and meandering story line, which add to the challenge of the text. It received Special Honourable Mention in the Jomo Kenyatta Prize for Literature, 1995.

Path of Thunder, The (1948)

A novel by Peter **Abrahams**. Set in the Karoo, the novel depicts the battle of a black man named Lennie Swarts and his Afrikaans lover Sarie Villers to be together. They are killed in a gun battle with white racists, but Lennie kills three of their opponents before they die. The novel draws attention to the violence that results from interracial relations in South Africa, and calls for a more liberal outlook.

Paton, Alan (Stewart) (1903–88)

A South African novelist, poet, and biographer, Paton was born in Pietermaritzburg and had a distinguished academic career before beginning work as a teacher at Ixopo, where in later years he would set much of the action of **Cry, the Beloved Country** (1948). He made a momentous career change in 1935, taking on the post of director of a turbulent borstal for black youths, Diepkloof, near Johannesburg. Here he formed most of the important political ideas that were to shape his writing and his life.

Shortly after World War II Paton was sent on a tour of similar borstals in Scandinavia, Britain, and North America, during which he wrote *Cry, the Beloved Country*. He finished it in the United States, and it was immediately accepted by Scribner's. Its success was immediate and lasting; it is widely recognized today as one of the great novels of the twentieth century. With its message of hope and compassion and its evocation of a world that was startlingly exotic to most readers, but that the author obviously knew thoroughly, *Cry, the Beloved Country* conveyed a message of passionate protest at the treatment of blacks in terms that had a tremendous impact, not only in South Africa, but in countries such as the United States, where the civil rights movement was taking shape. The book's sales rapidly went into the millions, and it still sells more than fifty thousand copies a year.

Cry, the Beloved Country changed Paton's life, as the experience at Diepkloof had done. When the Nationalist government, which had come to power in the year of the novel's publication, decided that the director of Diepkloof was "soft on blacks," it removed him from his post. Paton became a full-time writer, turning out a stream of poems and a succession of biographies and novels. Paton's second novel *Too Late the Phalarope* (1953) focuses on the tragedy of the Afrikaner policeman in a country town who sleeps with a black woman. He is arrested and tried for the offense, and suffers the destruction of his reputation, his position in society, and much of his family as a result.

In pursuit of his nonracial ideals, Paton helped to found the South Africa Liberal Party and became its president. From then on his career became increasingly political and dedicated to helping all racial groups in South Africa. He was harassed by the Nationalist government, and only his international eminence saved him from imprisonment. He produced many poems that went unpublished in his own lifetime but were published posthumously as *Songs of Africa: Collected Poems* (1995), most of which contain a political message and satirical edge. He also produced two important political biographies, of his political mentor J. H. Hofmeyr (*Hofmeyr,* 1964), and of the Anglican bishop Geoffrey Clayton (*Apartheid and the Archbishop,* 1973). He saw these two very different men as representative of the roots of South African liberalism, and his biographies, like his novels, poems, and other writings, portray his consistent moral and political concerns. The same is true of his two volumes of autobiography, *Toward the Mountain* (1980) and *Journey Continued* (1988), in which he articulates his view of human life as a moral and spiritual pilgrimage. *Cry, the Beloved Country* was on Africa's top one hundred books list, and the first Scribner Classics edition was released in 2003. Also part of Paton's legacy is the Alan Paton Centre, which includes archives, a library, and a museum, with an annual newsletter titled *Concord.*

Further Reading

Killam, Douglas. *Literature of Africa*. Westport, CT: Greenwood Press, 2004.

Peck, Richard. *A Morbid Fascination: White Prose and Politics in Apartheid South Africa*. Westport, CT: Greenwood Press, 1997.

People of the City (1954)

A novel by Cyprian **Ekwensi**. Ekwensi uses the actions of a crime reporter for the Lagos newspaper and a part-time bandleader named Amusa Sango to capture the details of life in a modern African city. Through Sango, Ekwensi can demonstrate both the instability and happiness various characters experience in the city. He also attempts to understand and critique Lagostian society through his narrative.

Pepetela (1941–)
(pseudonym of Artur Carlos Maurício Pestana dos Santos)

Pepetela is currently a Professor of Sociology at the College of Architecture of Luanda, where he lives. He also served as Minister of Education and later became a Professor of Sociology at the University of Angola. He is a leading member of the Angolan Writers' Union (2002), and has received Brazil's Order of Rio Branco. In 1999 he was awarded the Dutch Prince Claus Prize, and in 1997 Pepetela was awarded the Camões Prize. His novel *A Geração Utopia* is on the list of the African one hundred best books of the twentieth century, and he has published several works, including *Jaime Bunda e a Morte do Americano* (2003), *Jaime Bunda, the Private Agent* (2002), *L'Esprit Des Eaux* with Michel Laban (2002), and *The Return of the Water Spirit* (1995). Some recent republications of Pepetela's works include *The Mountain of the Lilac Water, a Tale for All the Ages* (2002) and *A Geração da Utopia* (2000). Pepetela's article "The New Man and the Construction of Angolan Masculinities" was included in *Lusophone African Sexualities* (2004), edited by Hilary Owen and Phillip Rothwell.

Perpetua and the Habit of Unhappiness (1978)

A novel by Mongo **Beti** translated from French (*Perpétue, ou l'habitude du malheur*, 1974). Beti's novel realistically describes the city, but portrays Perpetua as a representative metaphor for Cameroonians who do not pursue agency.

Petals of Blood (1977)

A novel by **Ngugi wa Thiong'o**. The novel depicts the corruption of the Kenyan bourgeois class who cooperate with international capitalism to oppress the peasants. Ngugi utilizes the story of the burning death of three businessmen and the four accused suspects to explore the evolution of Kenyan society over the ages. In a narrative that focuses on the intricate human relations that result in oppression and ruin, Ngugi rejects Christian teaching and religious education for more political solutions.

Peters, Lenrie (Leopold Wilfred) (1932–)

Gambian poet and novelist. Peters was born in Bathurst (now Banjul) and educated at the universities of Cambridge and London, UK. He qualified as a surgeon in 1959 and has practiced in England, Sierra Leone, and since 1969 in his native Gambia. Peters currently works in the Westfield Clinic in Gambia, is Chairman of the Gambia Medical and Dental Association, writes for *The Gambia*, and has served as president of the Union of African Students in England.

Peters' poetry, first published as *Poems* (1964), owes little to the oral tradition and makes no use of indigenous mythology. Peters is a cosmopolitan poet whose themes are aging and death, the risks of love, and the loneliness of exile. In *Satellites* (1967), the poet-doctor's surgical detachment is a metaphor for the uprooted individual's painful existential isolation. Intellectual ideas about politics, evolution, science, and music orchestrate Peters's images in the form of debates. In his only novel, *The Second Round* (1965), a British-trained African physician, a victim of the "massacre of the soul" wrought by Westernization, returns to the capital city of his native land full of "noble ideas about progress in Africa." He ends by taking a post in a remote bush hospital, thus immersing himself deeper in the traditional experience. The new poems in *Selected Poetry* (1981) castigate the corrupt greed of tribalized leadership elites and balance nostalgia for a pastoral past with cautious assertions of hope for a future built on that past. Most recently Peters has published *The Way Through* (2005).

Plaatje, Solomon T(shekisho) (1876–1932)

South African journalist and novelist. Born on a Lutheran mission in the Orange Free State, Plaatje had no more than an elementary education. At the age of seventeen, after a number of years as a student teacher, he moved to Kimberley, where he was employed as a messenger in the colonial postal service. A talented linguist, Plaatje could speak at least nine languages fluently. In 1899, he moved to Mafeking, where he worked as court interpreter during the Anglo-Boer war (1899–1903). His diary of the siege of Mafeking was his first extended piece of writing. After the war, he edited the first Setswana newspaper, *Koranta ea Bechuana (The Friend of the Bechuana),* soon becoming known as a campaigner for the rights of his people. A political activist as well as a journalist, he was one of the founding members of the South African Natives National Congress (later the ANC) and headed two unsuccessful deputations to Britain to appeal for direct intervention on behalf of South Africa's native population against the Land Act of 1913. The effects of the Land Act on Africans are recorded in *Native Life in South Africa* (1916). Although by the time he died his political career had ended, he remained a respected figure among Africans and Europeans alike.

His other achievements include translating Shakespeare into Setswana; research into Setswana proverbs and phonetics, including the publication of the *Sechuana Reader* (1916), the first phonetic transcription of any African language; and the publication of the first anglophone novel, *Mhudi* (1930), by a black South African.

The Mafeking diary, written in 1900 but published posthumously as *The Boer War Diary of Sol T. Plaatje* (1973) and, in a new edition as *The Mafeking Diary of Sol T. Plaatje* (1999), is a personal document that reflects on the role Africans played during the siege and is the only record of the Anglo-Boer war from the perspective of a black man. Another posthumous publication of Plaatje's work is titled *Sol Plaatje: Selected Writings,* and is edited by Brian Willan (1997). In the diary Plaatje focuses on the effect of emergency regulations on the African population, foreshadowing major themes in his later work. The multilingual approach that denotes tasks associated specifically with one group of people reflects his ability to interpret accurately the mood and feelings of the different language groups, a technique later refined in *Mhudi.* Plaatje's reputation as a writer was established by *Native Life in South Africa,* which is an indictment of segregation and dispossession based on his observations during 1913 of the distribution of land in relation to the Land Act. *Mhudi* was generally favorably received, but critics failed to see its importance as an epic, commenting on its shortcomings as a realistic narrative. Modern scholars treat *Mhudi* as a major literary achievement that incorporates both the English written and the African oral traditions. The novel tries to reveal the underlying humanity of all nations while simultaneously providing a political allegory for modern South Africa.

Further Reading

Chrisman, Laura. *Rereading the Imperial Romance: British Imperialism and South African Resistance in Haggard, Schreiner, and Plaatje.* Oxford English Monographs. Oxford: Oxford University Press, 2000.

Plomer, William (Charles Franklyn)
(1903–73)

South African poet, novelist, and autobiographer. Plomer was born in Pietersburg, in the Transvaal, but spent much of his youth, including the period of World War I, at school in England. In the early 1920s he tried farming in the Eastern Cape, without much success, and trading in Zululand, but before the end of 1926 he had left South Africa permanently. His career as a writer falls into three distinct periods: in an early and precocious stage, primarily in South Africa, he attacked narrowness and complacency with creative passion; in the 1930s his writing was marked by tentativeness and dissatisfaction; and during and after World War II, increasing self-acceptance led to three productive decades of poetry.

Plomer's first novel, *Turbott Wolfe* (1926), published by Leonard and Virginia Woolf, grew out of his experience in Zululand and its treatment of race and sexuality aroused hostility in South Africa. A new edition of *Turbott Wolfe* from the Modern Library (2003) includes an introduction by Nadine Gordimer. Similarly his story "Via Masondo," in which a young black man experiences racial discrimination and insensitivity, prefigures cultural conflict as a recurring literary theme. During his last year in South Africa, Plomer collaborated with the poet Roy **Campbell** on the literary magazine *Voorslag.* Plomer, Campbell, and Laurens **van Der Post** produced most of what was published during the journal's short life. When *Voorslag* drew the same hostile responses as *Turbott Wolfe,* Plomer was persuaded that there was no place for him in South Africa.

Before settling finally in England in 1929, Plomer lived and taught in Japan. The writing from this period, his stories *Paper*

Houses (1929) and his novel *Sado* (1931), suggest that his lifelong sense of alienation was beginning to surface in his work, perhaps in connection with his acknowledgment of his homosexuality. Following his move to England, where he came increasingly in contact with well-known writers and publishers, he published two more novels, *The Case Is Altered* (1929), in which a young woman is murdered by her husband, and *The Invaders* (1934), in which the two characters must adjust to life as outsiders; and two biographies, *Cecil Rhodes* (1933) and *Ali the Lion* (1936). His own dissatisfaction with the novels and their lukewarm critical reception eventually led him away from prose. Although he had written poetry from the beginning, he concentrated his efforts in that direction from the 1940s on. The fifteen volumes of poetry he produced over his career range widely in time and subject, starting in 1927 with *Notes for Poems* and continuing throughout the period during and after World War II, when he wrote the accomplished, lyrical verse for which he is best known, including *In a Bombed House* (1942), *Borderline Ballads* (1955), *Taste and Remember* (1966), and a number of collections and selections. During this last period, he also collaborated with the composer Benjamin Britten, for whom he wrote the libretti for *Gloriana* (1952) and three "church" operas: *Curlew River, The Burning Firey Furnace,* and *The Prodigal Son.* The two volumes of his autobiography are entitled *Double Lives* (1943) and *At Home* (1958).

Poor Christ of Bomba, The (1971)

A novel by Mongo **Beti**, translated from the French (*Le Pauvre Christ de Bomba,* 1956). Beti questions the material nature of religion in a narrative that follows a white missionary named Father Drumont and his black attendant, Denis. Both experience a self-revelation when they travel to the Nyong and Sanaga regions of Cameroon. Denis learns that he can enjoy sexuality without confus-

ing the superficial with the meaningful, while Father Drumont questions his role as a sincere evangelist.

Popular Literature

EAST AFRICA

The development of popular fiction is of note, especially in Kenya. Earlier popular works were supported by government-funded presses, but after the 1980s obstacles in the publishing industry led authors to publish thrillers and adventure books on a large scale. Earlier popular works of note include John Karoki's *The Land Is Ours* (1970) and Stephen **Ngubiah**'s *A Curse from God* (1970), both of which offer a traditional reading of the trials of the rural community. **Ngugi wa Thiong'o** and others like Sam Githinji (who wrote *Struggling for Survival* in 1983) focus on the hardships of the rural inhabitants in their fiction. In contrast, city life is represented as morally questionable, and many works focus on the effects of anonymity and lawlessness in urban life. Readers are presented with a depiction of modern organizations and businesses in the work of G. Kalimugogo and Yusuf K. Dawood. Also of note is the relatively recent rise in women's writing that captures a middle-class female readership with new incarnations of the romance. These works explore the changing definitions of love, but they also explore the balance between individual identity and family-based roles. Although these kinds of romances are formulaic in their development of plot and character, they also offer a valuable realistic portrayal of daily life that captures the attention of readers.

Another early type of popular novel embraced rather than criticized immoral behavior. In *Son of Woman* (1971) by Charles **Mangua** the focus is on the immoral hero who pursues numerous vices along with all of the other characters in the book, which was banned in Tanzania. The rise of the middle class and ideas of individual freedom were supported by writers like Mwangi **Ruheni** in the 1970s. Similarly, David Maillu published a large number of romance novels after founding his own press. Maillu offers both moral instruction and romantic thrills in his novels, which were even published in a smaller size so they were easier to conceal. Some of Maillu's works include *After 4.30,* which explores the events in Nairobi office buildings after they have closed for the day, and *The Flesh* (Part 1) and *The Flesh* (*Part* 2), which were written in verse based on the format of **Song of Lawino** by **Okot p'Bitek**. The focus shifted after the 1980s to the punishment of imprudent heroes who fall into violence, prostitution, and drug use and are punished for their mistakes.

Also of importance are the formulaic novels that are published by international publishing companies and that target the whole African market. The skill of the writing varies in these works, and the focus is on dialogue and suspense, with occasional plot developments that specifically relate to the East African context (like smuggling or the question of the nation-state). Works about investigative journalists also uncover questions about corruption and improper power, and works that portray prison life are equally bleak. Juvenile romances also combine formulaic plots with concerns about social problems like unemployment and family divisions, so that series like the Macmillan Pacesetter series and Heinemann Kenya's Spear Books represent both escape and confrontation with daily life, as they take such issues and resolve them positively for the reader. The strong success of popular literature in this region contains possiblities for those who wish to see how different issues and topics are received by a large reading public.

SOUTH AFRICA

Popular literature is often defined based on book sales, although in South African literature this type of definition is problematic. One of the reasons for this misrepresentation is the fact that popular authors like Wilbur Smith also appeal more (although not only) to white South African readers. This minority of educated and higher-income readers has controlled the book marketplace in the past, while popular writing by South African black writers has been more centered on the short-story format rather than the novel, using affordable periodicals as a means of publication. Another reason for the short story as a form of popular literature is its connection to oral literature traditions, which also have a connection to the popular performance poetry of the **apartheid** period.

The popular literature published in magazines like **Drum** and *Staffrider* is sometimes defined as protest literature, but such works can also be defined as popular literature due to their appeal to a black urban popular culture and its focus on daily life. Writers like Casey **Motsisi** and Can **Themba** are important to a definition of black urban popular culture, while Njabulo **Ndebele** deals with a political view of everyday life. In this sense these works and the short story and poem format in general demonstrate how political views are expressed and brought to the surface through popular literature in South Africa. It is thus important to note that both the popular recreational literature of the white elite and the popular literature of South African black writers have shared a lack of literary attention in the past that is now being corrected by postmodern critics.

One genre that appears often within this definition of popular literature is that of the adventure story, a genre that is more strongly represented by male writers, perhaps because of its masculinist focus. Of the most successful of these kinds of works are Stuart

Cloete's novels, the most popular of which are a novel about the Great Trek of 1836 titled *Turning Wheels* (1937), and a novel set in the Anglo-Boer war, titled *Rags of Glory* (1963). South African writer Wilbur Smith is also well known for his work in this genre, as his novels combine sexual intrigue, action, and mainly African settings. Smith has published titles such as *When the Lion Feeds* (1964), *The Sunbird* (1972), and *Rage* (1987), along with more than twenty-five other titles, which have been translated into fourteen languages. Two of Sir Laurens **van Der Post**'s novels, *Venture to the Interior* (1952) and *The Hunter and the Whale* (1967), have their foundation in the adventure story, although they portray more philosophical and spiritual journeys. In another branch of the genre are works such as Antony Trew's *Smoke Island* (1964) and *Running Wild* (1982), which take place against a political background.

Crime novels are also an important form of popular fiction in South Africa. During the apartheid era some crime writers also undermined the formulaic nature of the genre in order to question legal and political institutions. South Africa's best-known crime writer is James McClure, who sets his novels in Trekkersburg (a fictional form of Piertermaritzburg) and whose detective character Tromp Kramer is Afrikans, while his detective sargeant character Michael Zondi is Zulu, resulting in racial tension. Mc-Clure's first novel *The Steam Pig* (1971) won a Golden Dagger award, and portrays the investigation of a murder that is indirectly related to South Africa's racial classification system and the Immorality Act. Similarly, the murder victim in *The Gooseberry Fool* (1974) works for the Bureau of State Security (BOSS). In South Africa, the first novel to use the thriller narrative as a way to undermine social norms was Herman Charles **Bosman**'s novel *Willemsdorp,* in which the crime is also motivated by the Immorality Act and inter-racial sex. Bosman wrote the novel before

he died in 1951, but it wasn't published until 1977. The novel *Junta* (1989) by June Drummond portrays a desire for progressive liberal change and takes as its setting the political atmosphere of South Africa. Drummond's novel *The Farewell Party* (1971) is the thriller by which she is best known (although she has a large number of published novels), and it is set in Durban. Wessel Ebersohn's *A Lonely Place to Die* (1979) begins a series of thrillers about Yudel Gordon, a South African Jewish prison psychologist. Ebersohn criticizes the South African state in his thrillers, which in addition to the above novel, also in include works such as *Divide the Night* (1981), *Closed Circle* (1990), and *Store up the Anger* (1980). *Store up the Anger* was banned because it is a mystery novel about the death of a **Black Consciousness** leader who closely resembles Steve Biko. Mike Nicol and Joanne Hichens's *Out to Score* (2006) is a crime thriller set in Cape Town during the abalone wars along the Cape coast, while Brian Reeve's *A Dangerous Game* (2005) is a thriller set in postapartheid South Africa and is about members of the old security apparatus who try to prevent the disclosure of their brutal crimes by any means necessary.

In postapartheid South Africa a number of thriller writers have begun to target primarily black readership. Of most importance in this category is Gomolemo Mokae, whose character Colonel Makena in *The Secret in My Bosom* (1996) is a detective living in Soweto. *Murder by Magic* (1995) by Nandi D'lovu features detective Jon Zulu.

The popular historical romance is less successful than the adventure or thriller genres in South Africa, but there are still a number of novels of this genre that are popular. Joy Packer's historical romances are often set in the Cape, and include titles such as *Valley of the Vines*, 1955, *The Man in the Mews*, 1964, and *Blind Spot*, 1967. Another popular writer in this genre is June Drummond, author of *The Blue Stocking* (1985) and *The*

Impostor (1993). Daphne Rooke's *A Grove of Fever Trees* (1950) won a major African literary prize, while her novels *A Lover for Estelle* (1961), *The Greyling* (1962), and *Diamond Jo* (1965) take as their backdrop the early days of Kimberley, and are more complex than other historical romances. Most recently award-winning author Dan Jacobson has added his name to this list, with *All for Love: A Novel* (2005), which is set in pre–World War I Europe. Miriam **Tlali** uses elements of the romance in her works ***Muriel at Metropolitan*** (1975) and ***Footprints in the Quag*** (1989), but she intertwines these elements with a critique of political institutions in order to communicate the importance of women's unity.

WEST AFRICA

Popular literature in West Africa is generally written by amateur authors, is not expensive, and is not difficult to read. It is usually written in either European languages or the vernacular, and is published in the form of dramas, novellas, self-help, essays (political or historical), and collections of folktales or proverbs. This kind of literature attempts to reach a large audience with the aim of entertainment and education. The Onitsha pamphlet literature in Nigeria is one illustration of this literary form, as it is about everyday people written by themselves and for their own entertainment. These works are short pieces that express the author's point of view in a small explanation of experience, and they are a result of the increase in urban population and literacy following World War II, as well as the dissemination of the locally owned printing press. Also important to the growth of this literature was the flowering of an ideal of democracy that focused on self-awareness and individual identity, as well as the reallocation of money that was previously maintained for the war into commercial, industrial, and technological development.

Further Reading

Abah, Oga S. "Perspectives in Popular Theatre: Orality as a Definition of New Realities." *Theatre and Performance in Africa,* ed. Eckhard Breitinger. Bayreuth: Breitinger, 2003, 79–99.

Barber, Karin. "Literacy, Improvisation, and the Virtual Script in Yoruba Popular Theatre." *African Drama and Performance,* ed. John Conteh-Morgan and Tejumola Olaniyan. Bloomington: Indiana University Press, 2004, 176–88.

Deumert, Ana. "Praatjies and Boerenbrieven Popular Literature in the History of Afrikaans." *Journal of Pidgin and Creole Languages* 20, no. 1 (2005): 15–51.

Erwin, Lee. "Genre and Authority in Some Popular Nigerian Women's Novels." *Research in African Literatures* 33, no. 2 (2002): 81–99.

Newell, Stephanie, ed. *Readings in African Popular Literature.* Bloomington: Indiana University Press, 2002.

Ryan, Cynthia. "'Am I Not a Woman?': The Rhetoric of Breast Cancer Stories in African American Women's Popular Periodicals." *Journal of Medical Humanities* 25, no. 2 (Summer 2004): 129–50.

Whitsitt, Novian. "Islamic-Hausa Feminism and Kano Market Literature: Qur'anic Reinterpretation in the Novels of Balaraba Yakubu." *Research in African Literatures* 33, no. 2 (2002): 119–36.

Prince Kagwema (1931–)
(pseudonym of Osija Mwambungu)

A novelist, Prince Kagwema was born east of Tukuyu, Tanzania, and studied at Makerere University College, Uganda, where he obtained a bachelor's, and at Cambridge University, UK. He worked in the civil service until his retirement in 1976. The characters in his novels *Married Love Is a Plant* (1983), *Chausiku's Dozen* (1983), and *Society in the Dock* (1984) discuss love, sex, and politics, his uninhibited approach to which caused the temporary banning of his novel *Veneer of Love* (1975) in Tanzania.

Pringle, Thomas (1789–1834)

Scottish poet, journalist and nonfiction writer. Regarded as the first published South African poet, Pringle was born on a farm near Kelso, Scotland, and educated at Edinburgh University. His early verse epistle, "The Autumnal Excursion," was adapted by James Hogg for inclusion in *The Poetic Mirror* and received praise from Sir Walter Scott. In 1820 Pringle and his family took advantage of the government's emigration scheme to settle British farmers in the Eastern Cape. Later he took up an appointment as sublibrarian of the Government (later South African) Library in Cape Town; he also opened a small private school. In 1824 he started the monthly *South African Journal,* and soon he was also co-editing a newspaper, *The Commercial Advertiser,* founded by Robert Greig. When Pringle published an article in the *Journal* critical of the government's handling of the grievances of the settlers, the governor used his influence to bring about Pringle's financial ruin, and he was forced to sell up and return to England, where he arrived after just six years in South Africa. His article on slavery at the Cape in the *New Monthly Magazine* (October 1826) led to his appointment as secretary of the Anti-Slavery Society soon after his arrival in London. Greig continued, and ultimately won, the campaign launched by Pringle to ensure freedom of the press in South Africa.

Pringle's poems are *Ephemerides: or Occasional Poems, Written in Scotland and South Africa* (1928) as well as the later *Poems Illustrative of South Africa,* which formed Part 1 of *African Sketches* (1834). Poems such as "The Bechuana Boy," "Afar in the Desert," "Makanna's Gathering," and "The Forester of the Neutral Ground" (the first South African poem to deal with miscegenation) illustrate Pringle's empathy with African victims of Boer oppression and British imperialism. Apart from pamphlets produced for the Anti-Slavery Society, Pringle edited George Thompson's *Travels and Adventures in Southern Africa* (1828), as well as a successful annual, *Friendship's Offering,* and his

prose *Narrative of a Residence in South Africa* was published as Part 2 of *African Sketches.*

Prison Literature in South Africa

The growth of a literature that portrays imprisonment, torture, and detention is related to the use of these same political forms of oppression in the **apartheid** era in South Africa. Prison-related works are most visible between 1960 and 1995, which reflects the political climate of the apartheid years (1948–94). Robben Island figures largely in many of these texts as a symbol of imprisonment and oppression, and for this reason can be seen as a subgenre of prison literature.

Early cases of banishment to Robben Island and other forms of imprisonment occur both before and during the colonial period (1652–1910), and form the basis for the beginnings of prison literature. In 1632 a Khoikhoi agent (named Autshumato, also known as Harry die Strandloper) of some English navigators who were using the Cape as a place to rest was banished to Robben Island until 1640. Later, Xhosa chiefs Maqoma (1857–69, 1871–73) and Makhanda, also known as Makhanda or Nxele (1819–20), were also exiled to Robben Island, while a Hlubi chief named Langalibalele was banished there from 1874–75. Although there are no written accounts from these prisoners, there are references to them in Zulu or Xhosa praise poems such as "Maqoma Son of Ngqika." Written prison accounts most likely exist before 1870, but they have not yet been uncovered as literary documents.

The /Xam narrative "//Kabbo's Capture and Journey to Cape Town—1871" (translated into English in *Specimens of Bushmen Folklore,* 1911) is the first written example of South African prison literature. //Kabbo's oral narrative was recorded in /Xam and in English by Wilhelm Bleek. Although the oral prison memoir is mediated in the written account, its indigenous perspective and the evidence of oral narrative style in elements like repetition are still apparent. Another early prison narrative is that of a Swazi prisoner named "Rooizak" whose story was recorded in 1875 by Nachtigal, a German missionary, and published by Peter Delius as *The Conversion: Death Cell Conversations of "Rooizak" and the Missionaries—Lydenburg 1875* (1984). Again, despite the mediation required to produce a written text from an oral narrative, the prisoner's traumatic experience is apparent through his account of solitary confinement, attempted suicide, and medical administration that amounted to psychological torture.

During the Anglo-Boer War (1899–1902) concentration camps were created by the British military to hold women, children, and indigenous "others" as part of the scorched-earth policy. The number of those who died of malnutrition, disease, or other causes was 27,000 out of the 118,000 who were incarcerated. A number of diaries, journals, and memoirs were published in Afrikaans, Dutch, and English (mainly in the 1930s and 1940s), and came out of the experiences of those who were held in the camps. Works of note that came out of this time period include the diary of 1901 Red Cross nurse Johanna Brandt-Van Warmeloo titled *Het Concentratie-Kamp van Iréne (The Concentration Camp at Irene)* (1905), the diary of A.D.L. (a chaplain in the camp at Bethulie in 1901) titled *Woman's Endurance* (1904), and *The Concentration Camps in South Africa during the Anglo-Boer War of 1899–1902* (1941) by Napier Devitt. Devitt wrote his work because he was concerned about the propaganda in use in the 1930s and 1940s regarding the camps. The conditions for 26,000 Anglo-Boer prisoners throughout exile camps in St. Helena, Ceylon, Bermuda, and India are discussed in several works as well. For example, G. S. Preller describes his experience in *Ons parool: dae uit die dagboek van'n krygsgevangene (Our Parole: Days from the Diary of a Prisoner-of-War)* (1938),

while Joubert Reitz confronts his yearning for his lost fatherland in his poem "The Searchlight." Henry Nxumalo's "Mr. Drum Goes to Gaol" (published in *Drum* in 1954) is the earliest work that speaks of prison conditions in South Africa under apartheid. The prison literature that has its foundation in the apartheid era has been published in many forms and languages.

The autobiographical form is one of the most prevalent forms of prison literature. Ruth First published *117 Days: An Account of Confinement and Interrogation under the South African Ninety-Day Detention Law* (1965) before she was assassinated in 1982, while Albie Sachs uses the diary form in *The Jail Diary of Albie Sachs* (1966). Other accounts of political imprisonment include *My Fight against Apartheid* (1982), which describes Michael Dingake's experience as a political prisoner on Robben Island for fifteen years; *And Night Fell: Memoirs of a Political Prisoner in South Africa* (1983) by Molefe Pheto; Indres Naidoo's narrative to Albie Sachs, *Prisoner 885/63: Island in Chains* (1982); *Bandiet: Seven Years in a South African Prison* (1974) by Hugh Lewin; followed by *Hell-Hole Robben Island: Prisoner 872/63* by Moses Dlamini (no date). Although their works are very different, Breyten **Breytenbach**'s *The True Confessions of an Albino Terrorist* (1984) and Nelson Mandela's *Long Walk to Freedom* (1994) are both very important to South African prison literature. When Breytenback was imprisoned he was a well-known Afrikaans author, and was caught up in political struggles, while Mandela was an immensely important political leader who was sentenced to life. Breytenbach's work is more fragmented and focused on the psychological survival of one individual, while Mandela's work (written partly by Richard Stengel) is linear and focuses on the possibilities associated with a collective goal of political freedom. Mandela concludes that a nation cannot be understood without an investigation into its jails, and that citizens were the victims of extreme mistreatment in South African prisons under apartheid.

Fictional works also touch on prison experiences for their inspiration. Herman Charles **Bosman** uses his real-life imprisonment on a charge of murder as inspiration for his *Cold Stone Jug* (1949). In 1967 Alex **La Guma** described his work *The Stone Country* as a tribute to "the daily average of 70,351 prisoners in South African gaols in 1964." D. M. Zwelonke published *Robben Island* in 1973, while "A Pilgrimage to the Isle of Makanua" by Mtutuzeli Matshoba came out in his work *Call Me Not a Man* in 1979. Wessel Ebersohn's work *Store up the Anger* (1980) is a fictionalized version of Steve Biko's last ten days that led to his death under the supervision of the security police. In his book *Mating Birds* Lewis **Nkosi** depicts a relationship between a black man and a white woman that ends in imprisonment, while Breyten Breytenbach's *Memory of Snow and Dust* (1988) is a fictionalized account of his time as a political prisoner.

The anthologies *One Day in June* (1986) and *The Return of the Amasi Bird* (1982) contain poems about prison experiences, while the English collections *Pass Me a Meatball, Jones* (1977) and *No Time for Dreams* (1981) by James **Matthews**, *Letters to Martha: Poems from a South African Prison* (1968) and *A Simple Lust* (1973) by Dennis **Brutus**, and *Inside* (1983) by Jeremy Cronin also deal with the subject. Dikobe wa Mogale's *Prison Poems* deal more with love than they do with political topics, while an annotated Afrikaans collection of poetry titled *Robbeneiland my kruis my huis (Robben Island My Cross My House)* (1983) was published by Frank Anthony. Breyten Breytenbach published five volumes of Afrikaans prison poetry containing four hundred poems: *Voetskrif (Footscript)* (1976), *Eklips (Eclipse)* (1983), *("YK") ("Ache")* (1983), *Buffalo Bill* (1984), and *Lewendood (Life and Death)* (1985), some of which is translated into English in *Judas Eye and Self Portrait/Deathwatch* (1988). Important dramatic literature that deals with imprisonment includes Jon Blai and Norman Fenton's *The Biko Inquest* (1978), Athol **Fugard**'s *The Island* (1973), and Strini Moodley's *Prison Walls* (1985).

Authors of prison literature have also explored didactic and epistolary forms. In *Learning from Robben Island: The Prison Writings of Govan Mbeki* (1991) by Govan Mbeki, the form is didactic and is related to the discussion on political education that came about on Robben Island. Similarly, Mosiuoa Patrick (Terror) Lekota wrote didactic letters about South African history to his daughter Tjhabi while he was imprisoned on Robben Island, and published them under the title *Prison Letters to My Daughter* (1991). *Voices from Robben Island,* compiled and photographed by Jurgen Schadeberg for Ravan Press, is a collection of photographs and recollections from several famous ex-political prisoners such as Nelson Mandela, Tokyo Sexwale, Govan Mbeki, and Walter Sisulu. *Reflections in Prison* includes essays by famous ex-Robben Island prisoners, with biographies and drawings of them. *Fischer's Choice: A Life of Bram Fischer* by Martin Meredith (Jonathan Ball) is a biography of the Afrikaner advocate who built underground networks for the African National Congress and the South African Communist Party while defending resistance leaders in court, while Richard Bartlett's *Halala Madiba: Nelson Mandela in Poetry* (2006) is a collection of poetry (from authors like Soyinka, Motion, Zephaniah, Brutus, Serote, and others) from 1963 (when Mandela was imprisoned) to 2005 (when he turned eighty-seven). In a similar vein, Zoe Wicomb's *David's Story: A Novel* (2001) is set in 1991 after Mandela's release, and follows the world of spies and activists involved in the liberation movement, and Jack Mapanje has edited an anthology titled *Gathering Seaweed: African Prison Writing* (2002).

Prisoners of Jebs (1988)

Collection of columns by Ken **Saro-Wiwa**. Saro-Wiwa bases his columns on the fictional creation of a prison island off the coast of Nigeria, where follies and vices are put on display. He comments on contemporary politics and society through the use of the island to satirize current events. He also questions the role of the satirist (himself) and has the courage to speak his mind in an antagonistic atmosphere.

Proper Marriage, A (1954)

A novel by Doris **Lessing**. This is the second novel in the *Children of Violence* series. In this narrative Martha Quest renews her political fervor and joins a group of white leftists after her husband leaves to fight in World War II. Lessing has Martha use an obsession with Communism to escape the British colonial family that she married into.

Q

Qabula, Alfred Temba (1942–2002)

South African poet. Qabula was born at Flagstaff, in what was then the Transkei, and experienced the hardships of migrancy and the homeland system at first hand. Qabula began in 1983 to compose and perform poems influenced by the praise poetry or *izibongo* he had heard in the Transkei. His poems deal mainly with issues of union organization and seek to adapt traditional Zulu and Xhosa poetic forms to new urbanized and politicized contexts. His best-known composition is "Praise Poem to FOSATU," in which he uses the form of *izibongo* (which mediates between ruler and subjects) to negotiate relations of power between workers and union. His other poems include "Tears of a Creator," and "Africa's Black Buffalo" or "Dear." These poems are increasingly narrative and reveal a greater concern with national issues than those of the shop floor. Recent criticism has emphasized the value of Qabula's work by placing it within the broader history of oral poetry in South Africa. Qabula published poems in *Black Mamba Rising: South African Worker Poets in Struggle* (1986) and in magazines, and wrote his autobiography, *A Working Life: Cruel beyond Belief* (1989).

Question of Power, A (1973)

A novel by Bessie **Head**. Head explores the internal identity of her heroine, Elizabeth, in this semiautobiographical novel. She depicts Elizabeth's thoughts as she declines into insanity and then recovers from her psychological illness. Head also portrays Elizabeth's involvement in co-operative gardening and her experiences of a Botswanian village.

R

Rabéarivelo, Jean-Joseph (1903–37)

Malagasy poet and novelist. Born into a noble but poor family, he was an illegitimate child and a self-taught literature student who dared compete with the masters of French Symbolist poetry. He became associated with literary and poetic circles in Malagasy working as a proofreader and was soon known for the variety of his talents. He wrote in Malagasy, translated his own works into French, corresponded with literary figures all over the world, wrote a novel, and kept a diary. In his poetry collections (*La coupes des cendres,* 1924; *Sylves,* 1927; *Volumes,* 1928) he expresses his longing for the old Malagasy ethos of the nobility as well as his aspiration to know the rest of the world. His verse conveys the volatility and subtlety of his feelings. He also attempted to translate his own work and published poems in both French and Malagasy (*Presque-songes,* 1934; *Traduit de la nuit,* 1935). When he couldn't get a passage to France he committed suicide. His mastery of language made his work one of the most remarkable achievements of French writing outside France. Two posthumous novels (*L'Interférence,* 1988; *L'Aube rouge,* 1998) have also been published. A diary remains to see the light of day. He was one of the first francophone poets to be translated in the Mbari publications (*24 Poems,* 1962) in Ibadan in the early 1960s.

Rabémanajara, Jacques (1913–2005)

Malagasy poet, dramatist, and politician. Born in Maroantsetra he became a well-known figure of Malagasy cultural life in the 1930s, to the extent that Jean-Joseph **Rabéarivelo** made him his spiritual heir in one of his last letters. Rabémanajara published poetry volumes and was also involved in colonial administration. During World War II he was in France and wrote literary dramas (*Les Dieux malgaches,* 1942). In 1945 he started to be involved in Malagasy nationalist politics, and became a *député* of Madagascar to the French National Assembly. In 1947 after the insurrection that was savagely put down by the French colonial army he was prosecuted and sentenced to death. This sentence was commuted to a term in jail, and while in prison he wrote several poetry collections, notably *Antsa* (1948, reissued in 1956 with a preface—dedicated "to his brother in Christ, unjustly jailed"—by well-known novelist and Nobel Prize–winner François Mauriac). Liberated in 1955 he was associated with the First Congress of Black Writers and Artists gathered at the Sorbonne in 1956 by Alioune Diop, and published several books (*Les Boutriers de l 'aurore,* drama, 1957; *Nationalisme et problèmes malgaches,* 1958). He reentered Malagasy politics at the time of independence, eventually rising to Vice-President of the Republic, until the 1972 revolution sent him back into exile; he lived in Paris and was closely associated with *Présence africaine* until his death in France on April 2, 2005, at the age of ninety-two.

Rainmaker, The (1975)

A play by Steve **Chimombo**. One of the landmarks of Malawian drama in English, Chimombo's play takes for its plot the mythic figure of Mbona. It was first staged at the opening of the University of Malawi's outdoor theater, and became a national favorite.

Rampolokeng, Lesego (1965–)

South African poet. Rampolokeng was born in Orlando West, Soweto, and as a poet and performer he is outstanding among an innovative group of younger South Africans. Early sources of his poetry were his grandmother, who taught him the art of *dithoko,* the recitations of the seSotho of South Africa, and the **Black Consciousness** poets, including Ingoapele Madingoane, Maishe Maponya, and others; later he incorporated elements of rap from poets such as Linton Kwesi Johnson and Mutabaruka, blending these elements into an urban performance poetry critical of contemporary South Africa both before and since the 1994 elections. He confronts the misuse of religion, sexuality, the violence that comes out of suppressed anxiety, and the corruption of politicians old and new in South Africa. Rampolokeng has six published volumes of poetry: *Horns for Hondo* (1990), *Talking Rain* (1993), *Bavino Sermons* (1999), *The Second Chapter* (2003), *Whiteheart: Prologue to Hysteria* (2004), and *Blackheart* (2004). He also has published music under the title of *The h.a.l.f. Ranthology* (2002) and two poems titled "Dedication" and "Koshun's Sac" in *New Coin Poetry* (2003).

Further Reading

Solberg, Rolf, ed. *South African Theatre in the Melting Pot: Trends and Developments at the Turn of the Millennium.* Grahamstown, South

Africa: South Africa Institute for the Study of English in Africa, 2003.

Raw Pieces (1986)

Poems by Edison **Mpina**. These poems celebrate Malawian identity. They depict Malawi's villages, gardens, fishing communities, and seasons. Mpina did not receive the formal training many other Malawian poets did at the University of Malawi Writers' Workshop.

Rediscovery (1964)

Poems by Kofi **Awoonor**. In this collection of poetry Awoonor demonstrates the importance of history to an understanding of the present. He incorporates indigenous Ewe beliefs and sets their restorative powers against the destruction caused by colonial and Western culture.

Reign of Wazobia, The (1988)

A play by Tess Akaeke **Onwueme**. Onwueme interprets Igbo mythology with a focus on women in this play. She depicts the Kingdom of Ilaa as a place where a woman may rule for three months as king-regent before the new king is enthroned. Wazobia uses this position to encourage revolt from the kingdom's women against the patriarchal structure of their society.

Religion and Literature

Literature often reflects the ways that religious belief defines cultural identity, and literary forms of expression rely on cultural history that is quite often tied to religious narratives and icons, which bring extra significance to a text. In Africa, religious imagery is part of the political, cultural, and social contexts, and as such it appears as an important identifying factor in much literature. Traditional African religious beliefs focus on the individual's relationship with religious forces in nature, all of which are overseen by God as the source of all life.

Human destiny is controlled by divinities and spirits who intercede with God on behalf of human life. Nature is important to the sustenance of human life within this religious structure, and as such, elements like rain and trees are viewed with reverence. However, these traditional beliefs were influenced by the advent of Islam and Christianity in Africa during the trans-Saharan and transatlantic slave trades. Both systems of monotheistic belief focused on drawing Africans away from traditional forms of belief, offering better education, employment, and cultural power in the event of conversion. These colonial interactions, although based on religious motives of salvation in both the Islamic and Christian faiths, also counted on conversion as a way to control the political and economic lives of Africans. Thus, anglophone works like Ayi Kwei **Armah**'s *Two Thousand Seasons* (1973) analyze colonialism through a depiction of both Arab-Islamic and Euro-Christian influences.

TRADITIONAL RELIGIONS AND LITERATURE

African literature quite often focuses on religious topics, due to the importance of religious belief in Africa, and also because of the involvement of foreign religions in the colonization of Africa. In his novels, Chinua **Achebe** responds to the way that colonial religions divide Africa through religious differences. Achebe's works demonstrate that African beliefs before Christianity should not be regarded as "savagery from which the first Europeans acting on God's behalf delivered them" ("The Novelist as Teacher," *New Statesman,* January 29, 1965). Rather, Achebe focuses on the fact that many African religious beliefs (like those of the Igbo people) demonstrate the existence of an African worldview that begins before the colonial era and continues long after it. Part of the previous aim is evident in Achebe's and other authors' portrayal of the religious importance of landscape and the nature gods in their literature. Nature gods depicted by Igbo authors include Idemili (god of water), Ani/Ala (earth goddess), and Amadioha (god of thunder), while Yoruba writers portray divinities such as Sango (god of thunder, lightning and electricity), Ogun (god of war and creativity), and Orunmila/Ifa (divinity of mysteries and wisdom). In *The Palm-wine Drinkard* (1952) by Amos **Tutuola**, the setting unites the worlds of the living, the dead, and spirits that reflects Yoruba metaphysics, while the interpreters in Wole **Soyinka**'s *The Interpreters* (1965) criticize the falling away of African traditional religion when they chastise those who are reverencing plastic plants instead of real nature.

Wole Soyinka and Ola **Rotimi** focus on traditional African religious beliefs in their dramatic works. Rotimi represents African rituals in his plays, which utilize an English that is close to the Yoruba language. Soyinka uses the rites of passage of the dead (especially the rituals of communication with the dead as they are administered by those in the masquerade cults) to structure his political play *A **Dance** of the Forests* (1963). *A Dance of the Forests* cautions against an unquestioning veneration of the past through its subversion of traditional masquerade rituals, while Soyinka's plays *The **Road*** (1965) and ***Death and the King's Horseman*** (1975) also use death rituals and masquerade to comment on contemporary issues. In a similar manner, Achebe depicts ancestor cult progressively in ***Things Fall Apart*** (1958), ***Arrow of God*** (1964), and *A **Man of the People*** (1966). In these works the depiction of the ancestor cult begins with heightened morality, but falls into a superficial entertainment that has been stripped of its mystical elements by the pervasiveness of Christian doctrines in the postindependence era of *A Man of the People*. Soyinka's *The **Trials of Brother Jero*** depicts the ways that these Christian doctrines are used by some Africans to control other Africans and gain power over them. Gary Jeffrey presents African traditional mythologies in graphic novel form in *African Myths* (2006), including the Yoruban creation myth, and an explanation of how all stories came to be owned by Anasi.

The relationship between poetry and religion in Africa is a strong one, as African rituals are performed in poetic and musical form. Praise poetry uses elements from nature to praise similar qualities in the person the poem is about, while court poetry supports the authority of the king through a combination of political and spiritual techniques. Cult poetry contains a very heightened sense of ritual in it, as traditional guilds in Africa are managed as cults with associated guild poetry that is only available to members. The principles and philosophies that determine the daily actions of the members of such cults are often depicted in the poetry. For example, the *Babalawo*, or the father of all cults in the Yoruba people of Nigeria, is the divine poet of a network of pharmacological, religious, and metaphysical doctrines called *Ifa*. In order to reflect an African aesthetic and to demonstrate the importance of poetry in African culture, many modern African poets (such as Kofi **Anyidoho**, Kofi **Awoonor**, Okinba Launko, Christopher **Okigbo**, and Wole Soyinka) have adapted elements of traditional poetry, especially cult poetry, for use in their own poems.

CHRISTIANITY AND LITERATURE

The majority of North Africa was Christian under Roman rule. Islam and Arab culture became more prevalent after the seventh century, when only Ethiopian and Coptic Christianity survived in Egypt and some other places. The Christian *Reconquista* of Spanish and Portuguese initiation in the fifteenth century had settlements in North and West Africa, and although the Spanish allowed Portuguese authority by the time of the Treaty of Tordessillas (1494), this authority was quickly questioned by French, British, and Dutch competition. By the late eighteenth and early nineteenth centuries, there was a very substantial growth of missionary work, and the end of the nineteenth century saw the foregrounding of Roman Catholic, Protestant, and other missionary groups vying for roles in the colonization of Africa (which by then included those of Belgium, Germany, and Denmark). In the 1950s independence movements started to develop, and they gained many of their aims up to and throughout the 1960s. Independent churches now exist in addition to the Christian and Islamic institutions.

Some of Africa's first literature comes from the writings of the early Christian church in Egypt, Ethiopia, Nubia, and Roman North Africa. The theological work of the Alexandrian church fathers in second-, third-, and fourth-century Egypt included works by Clement, Origen, Didymus the Blind, Athanasius, and Cyril the Great, while Valentinus's and Basilides' gnostic treatises date from second-century Egypt. Anthony and Pachomius were early third-century ascetics (those who practiced extremely rigorous self-discipline) who knew the Psalter and the Gospels in Coptic, and who inspired the early medieval monastic movement in Europe with the texts the *Rule of Pachomius* and Athanasius' *Life of Anthony*. Nubian kingdoms converted to Christianity in the sixth century, and produced religious records such as liturgical texts, fragments of scripture, and saints' lives. In North Africa, there are several literary texts from the third and fourth centuries that are of great importance, such as the *Passion of Saints Perpetua and Felicitas* (ca. 203), theological works by Tertullian, Cyprian, and those by Augustine, who was considered the father of Western Christianity and who wrote the *Confessions* (397),

and the *City of God* (411–26). By the eleventh century, Christianity was overtaken in importance by the development of Islam and Arab culture that began to spread through Egypt and across North Africa starting in the seventh century. In Egypt today the majority of the population is Muslim, with a minority of Coptic Christians. The consecration of Frumentius, Bishop of Aksum, by Athanasius marked the beginning of the Ethiopian Church, which possessed vernacular Old and New Testaments, liturgical texts, the *Rule of Pachomius,* the *Life of Anthony,* and an anthology of writings by Athanasius and Cyril the Great called *Qerellos* by the end of the sixth century. This period also brought forth the first version of Ethiopia's national religious epic, the *Kebra Nagast* (*The Glory of Kings*), which is a mythic narrative of Ethiopian Christianity's beginnings (and the establishment of Ethiopians as God's new chosen people and their land as Siyon) that was rewritten and expanded in the fourteenth century and begins with the union of the Queen of Sheba and King Solomon, and their son Menelik I's movement of the Ark of the Covenant from Jerusalem to Aksum. Due to the Muslim environment that Ethiopian Christianity developed within, some of the early writings focus on the need to make a strong effort to maintain identity, such as Zara Ya'iqob's *Mashafa Berhan* (*The Book of Light*) (ca. 1450), which is a collection of readings for sabbaths that encourages branding with marks of faith in order to ensure against falling into non-Christian habits. Portuguese Jesuit attempts to bring Roman Catholic doctrine to Ethiopian Christianity were not successful due to this strength of identity, as the sixteenth-century works *Confession of Faith* by Galawdewos and *Anqasa Amim* (*Door of the Faith*) by Enbaqom demonstrate. Another result of the isolation of Ethiopian Christianity was its lack of a missionary program. *Ethiopia Unbound* (1911) by Joseph Ephraïm **Casely-Hayford** depicts a combination of Ethiopian, European, and Fanti religious beliefs in reaction against modern colonial missionaries, while more recently the Amharic novel *The Thirteenth Sun* (1973) by Daniachew Worku illustrates the way that Ethiopian Christianity and local superstitions exist alongside one another in the difficult Ethiopian landscape.

It is also of extreme importance to note the interdependence between the missionaries and the slave trade. For example, in Portuguese Angola income was derived from the instruction and baptism of slaves, while slaves were also enlisted to serve as catechists and some gained additional education in Europe. A number of Latin poems that uphold Christian Spain as the new Ethiopia were written by a slave student named Juan Latino, who was enrolled at the cathedral school in Granada. Latino's poems include an epic titled the *Austriad* (1571), which rejoices over the victorious battle of Lepanto, won by Don Juan and the Holy League over the Turks. Some slaves returned to Africa and became missionaries themselves, such as the freed Dutch slave Jacobus Eliza Capitan (1717–47), who traveled to Ghana as an ordained missionary and who translated the Lord's Prayer, the Ten Commandments, and the Twelve Articles of Belief into Fanti. Although this is an amazing demonstration of missionary involvement in the slave trade, it is also important to note that missionary participation went as far as to insist that only Christian slaves should be traded, and only to Christians. For example, the Reverend Thomas Thompson (Africa's first Anglican missionary) was appointed to the Gold Coast in 1752 and in 1758 wrote *The African Trade for Negro Slaves Shown to Be Consistent with the Principles of Humanity and with the Laws of Revealed Religion* (1758).

During the British involvement in the slave trade several slaves spoke out against slavery through the written word. The *Letters* (1782) of Ignatius **Sancho** were published after his death, and follow his birth on a slave ship, how he was orphaned, and his move to England. Sancho criticizes English Christians for drinking on Sundays and for behaving inhumanely overseas. Ottobah **Cugoano** censures the English slave traders as un-Christian in his *Thoughts and Sentiments on the Evil of Slavery* (1787), while Olaudah Equiano makes a similar move in his work *The Interesting Narrative of the Life of Olaudah* **Equiano**; *or, Gustavus Vassa, the African, Written by Himself* (1789), which also exposes the hypocrisy of Christian Great Britain's participation in the slave trade. In response to works like these, along with the work of a number of prominent abolitionists in Great Britain, the African slave trade was abolished in 1807 and slavery was outlawed in the British Empire in 1833.

Christian missionaries were influential in many other aspects of African history as well. The early integration of Christianity into African culture is portrayed in the works of the baptized King Monso I of Kongo Mvemba Nzinga, whose writing was published under the title of *Correspondence de Dom Afonso, 1506–43* in 1974. The Crioulo language was formulated by the lusophone-African Christian upper classes in the Cape Verde islands, while colonialist Portuguese writing uncovers European racism in Africa. One example of such writing is Luiz Figueira's *Princesa negra: O presça da civilizaçao em Africa* (*Black Princess: The Price of Civilization in Africa,* 1932), which represents the marginalization of native Africans as romantic savages. The impact of Portuguese missionaries on Africa is apparent in works like those by Angolan poet Mario Antonio, and other luso-African authors who speak of the need to rediscover their native heritage in the face of colonial repression. Cultural conflict between native and Christian ideologies is dramatically represented in the plays of Martiniquan Lindo Longho, as well as in Angolan Domingos Van-Dúnem's play *Auto* de natal (*A Christmas Play*) (1972). Similarly, in José Luandino's short story "Dina" (*Vidas novas*, 1976) the title character is a prostitute whose parents were murdered as they sought asylum in the Mission of São Paulo. In a move that turns Christian scriptures against the actions of Christian missionaries, Mozambiquan Rui de Noronha's poem "Suge e ambula" ("Get up and Walk") uses a biblical miracle to explain the need for Africans to react to colonial repression.

After Portuguese power receded in the sixteenth and seventeenth centuries, Great Britain and France became more powerful in Africa. Evangelical revivals in the eighteenth and nineteenth centuries added new emphasis to missionary work, which resulted in new missionary groups that focused primarily on Africa. These organizations included those such as the British Baptist Missionary Society (1792), the London Missionary Society (1795), the British and Foreign Bible Society (1804), the American Board of Commissioners for Foreign Missions (1810), the Wesleyan Methodist Society (1817), the Societé des Missions Evangéliques (1822), the Berlin Mission (1824), the Bremen Mission (1836), the Plymouth Brethren (1830s), the Sudan United Mission (1870s), the Africa Inland Mission, the Gospel Missionary Union, the Christian and Missionary Alliance, and some evangelical high Anglicans. The Oxford Movement of the 1830s inspired many missionary foundations as well, and the Universities' Mission to Central Africa was established in 1859. An epistolary account of the period just following this boom in missionary organizations can be found in *Salt and Light: The Letters of Mamie and Jack Martin from Malawi* (2003), which is composed of the diary extracts and letters of a young missionary couple who moved from Scotland to Malawi in the 1920s. Other historical works that make use of primary materials are Kenneth R. Ross's *Christianity in Malawi: A Source Book* (1996), John McCracken's *Politics and*

Christianity in Malawi 1875–1940: The Impact of the Livingstonia Mission in the Northern Province (1977, 2000), and Eva Keller's *The Road to Clarity: Seventh-Day Adventism in Madagascar* (2005), which is based on the author's own involvement in the daily lives of the Seventh-Day Adventists in Madagascar. The Roman Catholic Society of Jesus was reestablished by the Vatican in 1814, while it also brought back Propaganda Fide in 1816 and established a French fundraising group titled Work for the Propagation of the Faith (1822). Roman Catholic aims in Africa were also enacted by social institutions like the Oblates of Mary Immaculate (1816), the Society of the Sacred Heart of Mary (1840), the Society of African Missions (1854), The English Society of St. Joseph, or Mill Hill Fathers (1866), and the Society of Missionaries of Africa, or White Fathers (1868).

Despite the use of missionary policies by European governments to gain economic and political influence, missionaries did help establish schools and develop orthographies for native languages. Missionaries translated Christian literature into indigenous languages and used the translations as educational textbooks, while Tiyo and John H. Soga (followers of Ntsikana) translated hymns, the Bible, and *Pilgrim's Progress* into Xhosha. Translations of such works into Sotho and Zulu were completed by 1895, while in West Africa Twi, Yoruba, Hausa, Ewe, Fanti, and Ga translations were made available. Yoruba orthography was developed by missionary Samuel Ajayi Crowther, a former slave who also translated the Bible and *Pilgrim's Progress*. In some cases, Christian missionaries helped to record African oral traditions. Missionary Paul M. B. Mushindo collected Bemba folktales in his book *Imilumbe ne ishimi: Shintu bashimika ku lubemba* (*Stories [with and without Songs]: The Ones They Tell in the Bemba Region*) (1957), while the Nigerian Efik riddle: "What is it that God our Father made but which we cannot sit on? Answer: A palm fruit with thorns" was given a Christian parable and is cited in O. R. Dathorne's book, *The Black Mind: A History of African Literature* (1974).

The writing and circulation of new poetry and fiction was encouraged by Christian missionaries who provided a Xhosa press in Lovedale, a Zulu press in Mariannhill, and a Sotho press in Morija in Basutoland, as well as other colonial possessions. Due to this influence, the first printed indigenous literatures demonstrate definite biblical influences. Thomas **Mofolo**'s *Moeti oa bochabela* (*Traveller to the East*) (1907) is a Sotho rendition of *Pilgrim's Progress* that follows the conversion of a despondent native African to Christianity. Henry Masila Ndawa's Xhosa novel *U-Hambo luka Gqoboka* (*The Journey of Gqoboka the Christian*) (1909) similarly follows the spiritual tribulations of his hero's search for Christian truth, while the Igbo novel *Omenuko* (1933) by Nigerian Pita Nwana also demonstrates the influence of Bunyan's work. Traditional spirit beings are portrayed alongside the Christian God in D. O. **Fagunwa**'s Yoruba novel *Ogboju-Ode Ninu Igbo Irunmale* (1938; *The* **Forest of a Thousand Daemons**, 1968), which brings its hero Akara-Ogun closer to a deeper understanding of Christianity with every magical escapade.

Pilgrim's Progress is not the only Christian text to influence early African literatures in indigenous languages. A Nigerian production of *King Elejigbo* (1904) was staged by Bethel African Church and St. Jude's Church who came together to form the Egbe Ife dramatic club. The Yoruba poems (1905, 1906) of J. Sobowale Sowande combine traditional chants with Christian themes, while *Mehla ea malimo* (*The Times of the Cannibals*) (1912), a collection of Lesotho stories by Edward Motsamai, comments on traditional culture from a Christian perspective (as do works by other authors such as E. L. Segoete and Z. D.

Mangoela). In his third novel, *Pitseng* (1910), Thomas Mofolo combines Christian ethics with Sotho traditions, while Malawian S. A. Paliani's Nyanja novel *1930 kunadza mchape* (*In 1930 Came a Witchdoctor*) (1930) observes the victory of Christian ideology over what is seen as native superstition. Another major concern in early African novels is the issue of marriage. Enoch S. Guma's heroine is rewarded with marriage to the man she loves in his Xhosa work *U-Nomalizo* (1918), while the Zulu hero of B. W. **Vilakazi**'s *Noma nini* (*For Ever and Ever*) (1935) attempts to find love and marriage. A woman acts against the demands of her father in her marriage choice when she is influenced by Roman Catholic thought in a Sotho novel titled *Lilahloane* (1951) written by Albert Nqueku, while an educational anxiety with Christian ethics is also expressed in Zimbabwean Paul Chidyansiku's Sholla novel *Nhoroondo dzukuwanana* (*Getting Married*) (1958).

Vernacular works that portray African identity are also infused with Christian references. Joseph Ghartey includes biblical diction in his Fanti poem "Nde ye ehurusi da" ("This Is the Day of Rejoicing") (1950), which celebrates the New Year. Abbé Alexis **Kagame** (a Roman Catholic cleric and poet) converts a Kinyarwanda praise song to the Rwandan king into a Christian pastoral epic addressed to God in his *Umulirimbyi wa nyili-ibiremwa* (*The Song of the Land of Creation*) (1952), which takes a Tutsi point of view and Christianizes all details of Rwandan life, even down to the cows that are important to Tutsi economy. Similarly, *Abapatili bafika ku babemba* (*The Catholic Priests Arrive among the Bemba*) (1956) by Zaïrean Stephen A. Mpashi and the Bemba novel *Ululumbi lwa mulanda kukakaata* (*The Fate of the Stubborn Poor Person*) (1956) by M. K. Chifwaila both attribute salvation from superstition and freedom from slavery among native Africans to the intervention of the Roman Catholic Church. Roman Catholic priest Patrick Chakaipa's preindependence Zimbabwean novel *Karikoga gumiremisere (Karikoga and His Ten Arrows)* (1958) and the Ndebele novel *Uvusezindala (In Days Gone By)* (1958) by David Ndoda reveal similar ideas.

The missionary influence on vernacular African literature was also very negative at times. The publication of Mofolo Morija's **Chaka** (1925; English trans. 1931) was held up for more than fifteen years because his masters (although they did not doubt his faith) did not agree with the uncritical representation of an unrepentant Zulu warrior and natural witchcraft in Mofolo's book. Samuel Edward Krune Loliwe Mqhayi (who is associated with Lovedale and the founding of Xhosa literature) published a poem on the 1925 visit of the Prince of Wales and the Duke of Kent to South Africa, which satirically pairs the Bible and brandy as colonial imports. A.C. **Jordan**'s Xhosa novel *Ingqumbo yeminyanya* (1940; *The Wrath of the Ancestors,* 1980) is also equivocal about the place of Christianity in the construction of African identity, while Zimbabwean Charles **Mungoshi**'s Shona novel *Ndiko KupindanaKwama (The Passing Days)* (1975) comments on the origins of religious nihilism.

Much contemporary African literature is defined by such skepticism toward Christianity and an ambiguous relationship between colonialism and Christianity. Prohibitions on traditional initiation, drumming, marriage and burial rites, dancing and singing, tribal naming, storytelling sessions, and African dress were backed by missionaries in both French and English colonial territories. New prophetic churches like the Harrisites (on the Gold Coast), and native African churches with lessened ties to established denominations like Dr. Mojola Agbebi's Native Baptist Church in Nigeria, or the South African Zionist churches that are more than two thousand in number, were created out of the need to break ties with European missionary influences. This complex relationship between colonialism and Christianity resulted in an African literary tradition that grew out of the influence of French colonialism, and one that was influenced by English colonialism. Early English- and French-language African drama demonstrates many Christian influences that originated from the mission school theatrical productions of biblical stories, which did not contain African references in the 1880s. However, secessionist native churches incorporated African instruments, dance, and song into these biblical representations, and early English-language theater in West and South Africa combines traditional elements with Christian morals. A Christian criticism of tribal magic and superstition is portrayed in South African Zulu dramatist Herbert I.E. **Dhlomo**'s *The Girl Who Killed to Save* (1935). Nigerian Herbert Ogunde started to put together performances of native song cycles to celebrate Easter and Christmas during World War II, and he also wrote a morality play that enacts Adam and Eve's rebellion against God titled *The Garden of Eden and the Throne of God* (1944). Similarly, a radio broadcast of Chawanda Kutse's dramatic works *The Creation, The Crucifixion,* and *The Resurrection* were thought to be acceptable for broadcast to an African audience.

Other playwrights choose to demonstrate the problems with dramatically representing Christian themes. Nigerian Wole **Soyinka** (a Nobel Prize laureate) represents the friction between indigenous and European Christian customs in his work, where Western church doctrine often gets reinterpreted into an African framework. In Soyinka's *The Road* (1965), for example, a denial of Western Christian doctrine results in a kind of conversion outside of church doctrine for his professor character. Patrick Ilboudo also criticizes Christian doctrine in his dark comedy *Le Procès du muet* (1987), which depicts a Muslim zealot named Imam Samba's opinion that Judas was actually the victim of Christ's trial. An even darker image is represented in South African Lewis **Nkosi**'s *The Rhythm of Violence* (1964), which represents the voice of a Zulu who calls on Christ to pick a side in South Africa. Aimé Césaire demonstrates the role of missionaries in the decline of morality in Zaire in her *Une saison au Congo* (1966), while Congolese Antoine Letembet-Ambily uses the story of Noah and his sons to provide an allegorical image of the immorality of Europe's colonization of Africa.

French and English poetry in Africa also represents a large range of attitudes toward Christianity. Protestant teachings were upheld in early poetry from the 1940s and 1950s by authors such as Sierra Leone's Crispin George, Ghana's Gladys **Casely-Hayford**, Michael **Dei-Anang**, and R.E.G. Armattoe, and Nigeria's Dennis **Osadebay**. For example, Crispin George's *Precious Gems Unearthed by an African* (1952) thanks an all-powerful God in a self-defacing manner, while there is contempt for traditional religious customs in Osadebay's *Africa Sings* (1952). In his *A Song out of Midnight* (1959), the Liberian poet Roland Dempster also ponders the place of Christianity in Africa, but with a much less moral-based voice than George or Osadebay. Chinua **Achebe**'s "Poems about War" are collected in *Beware, Soul Brother* (1972) and provide a number of significant images. One such image is that of a starved war baby alongside the healthy baby Jesus in the manger in "Christmas in Biafra." Poet Christopher **Okigbo**, who was killed in the Nigeria-Biafra war, utilizes several religious images (including Christian ones) in his poetry. Okigbo's "Easter Sequence" from **Heavensgate** (1962) is conceptualized as a mass but is presented to the stream (called "Mother Idoto") that cleans and sanctifies Okigbo's village, and the poem depicts the purification of the ancestral gods through their movement through the "stations of the cross." "Fireseed" is a parody of the parable of the mustard seed, in which Christian missionaries sow the fireseed that consumes African culture, while in *Limits* (1964) John the Baptist calls Roman Catholic teaching lifeless. In the final poem of Wole Soyinka's *A Shuttle in the Crypt* (1971) Okigbo's ghost has a conversation with Soyinka, in which Soyinka expresses the opinion that he'd rather die like Christ than suffer like Prometheus.

The uncertainty of the colonial condition is expressed in much of the work of L. S. **Senghor**, who was the father of the negritude movement. Senghor conveys appreciation to France for the Christian faith in *Hosties Noires* (1948), but later poems mourn the evil nature of the imperial nucleus and the ruin of Africa by the French. For example, the affliction of slaves offers a parallel to the affliction of Christ in Senghor's "Snow upon Paris" (1964), a parallel that Ivory Coast poet Bernard **Dadié** also expresses in his poem "Thank You God" (1964). In contrast, negritude poet and Senegalese Bernard Diop draws on the Roman Catholic rite of viaticum in "Viaticum" (1960) in order to denounce the rite as an empty superstition. David **Diop** depicts Christ as an African tramp in "Nigger Tramp" (1964), while in "The Vultures" he condemns missionary priests for their inability to criticize forced labor.

Other African poets who write in French similarly reflect on injustice. Zaïrean Felix Tchicaya U'Tam'si works oral rhythms into his work *Feu de brousse* (1957; *Bush Fire*, 1964), which criticizes churches for assisting colonial aims and compares the Congolese to the Israelites. Similarly, U'Tam'si's poem "The Scorner" compares a middle-class church to the crown of thorns that native Africans share with Christ. This message of inequality is also apparent in African poetry written in English. **Valley of a Thousand Hills** (1941) by Herbert Dhlomo represents the satanic acquisition of divine powers by whites, while a native African acts as a Christ figure. The title character in **Song of Lawino** (1966) by

Ugandan **Okot p'Bitek** offers a satirical account of African converts, Holy Communion, priests, and Christianity as a whole. In p'Bitek's *African Religions and Western Scholarship,* he questions authors like John Mbiti, who tries to bring together African and Christian religions. Job's revolt against God is repeated in South African Dennis **Brutus**'s poem "Our Aim Our Dreams Our Destinations" from his *China Poems* (1975). The uncovering of Christianity as a hypocritical agent for Western imperialism can also result in a lack of trust for any spiritual beliefs. Several African poets portray this ironic situation. J. P. Clark **Bekederemo**'s epic "Ivbie" in *A Reed in the Tide* (1965) uses images of Christian redemption, forgiveness, and love to mourn the loss of these ideals in African cultural traditions. Ghanaian Kwesi **Brew** uses many traditional tribal and Christian images in his poetry, but ideals are overcome by skepticism in his work *The Shadows of Laughter* (1968), while similar beliefs are elements of fellow Ghanaian Kofi **Awoonor**'s *Night of My Blood* (1971). In his collection *Silent Voices* (1972), Kenyan Jared **Angira** draws attention to the fact that Christians do not consider the situations of those Kenyans they attempt to convert, in his poem "He Will Come."

The majority of contemporary African poetry echoes Awoonor's message of loss in "Easter Dawn," which expresses a "final ritual" for the traditional gods. **Taban Lo Liyong** offers some hope in his collection *Another Nigger Dead* (1972), which portrays the position of those Africans who wish to categorize faith as a decision between beliefs. Despite the fact that Taban's poem "Bless the African Coups" satirically draws attention to the lack of distinction between white colonial oppression and black totalitarian rule, it also maintains hope for the revitalization of African culture. In his poem "Corpus Christi, 1977" Malawian poet Felix Mnthali contemplates whether Christian rituals that have been made African are really just surface performances, or if they actually do satisfy a desire for the idea of eternity. In this manner, Christianity is represented as another way that African spiritual identity and ideas about life and death can be expanded. More examples of the renegotiation of Christian images can be seen in the poetry of Sierra Leone poet Syl **Cheney-Coker**, whose work *The Blood in the Desert's Eye* (1990) utilizes many biblical and theological tropes. Cheney-Coker's poems "The Outsider," "Apocalypse," and "The Philosopher" call up images of the Passover, the Last Supper, and the crucifixion in order to ask God to rid Africa of the affliction that white colonial and black neo-colonial oppression has brought, and to plead for the help of Jeremiah to save Sierra Leone in the same manner that he saved Israel.

Christian themes are also prevalent in novels, short stories, and auto**biographies**. Ugandan prince Akiki K. Nyabongo's autobiography *The Story of an African Chief* (1935) tells of his experiences with the Bugandan aristocracy and also critically portrays the Christian missionaries and colonial administrators. However, a positive portrayal of Christian teachings was quite often the case in early novels. Thus, works like Ghanaian R. E. Obeng's *Eighteenpence* (1943) makes extensive use of biblical diction, while *Le Fils du fétiche* (1955) by Togo writer David Ananou also demonstrates a reliance on missionary didacticism. Nigerian Amos **Tutuola** demonstrates a move away from didacticism in *The **Palm-wine Drinkard*** (1953). This work is often thought of as the first modern African narrative of note in English, and it combines images of native folklore and Christian ideology in its narrative of the central character's journey to retrieve his tapster from the land of the dead. In Nigerian Chukwuemeka **Ike**'s *Toads for Supper* (1965) fanatical Christianity is treated satirically, while Legson

Kayira's *The Looming Shadows* (1967) features an evangelical character who is very difficult to read as a serious representation. In Stanlake **Samkange's** *The Year of the Uprising* (1978) the fictional representation of the 1896 Mhondoro cult uprising demonstrates how Christian zeal can really mean religious narrow-mindedness.

Cameroon author Mongo **Beti's** work *Le Pauvre Christ de Bomba* (1956; *The Poor Christ of Bomba,* 1971) represents a critical picture of the missionaries, as well as those Africans who gain prestige through conversion. *Le Roi miraculé* (1958; *King Lazarus,* 1960) by Mongo Beti also offers a representation of the questionable nature of missionaries in its representation of the colonial servant Father Le Guen. Hereditary concerns are addressed in Nigerian Onuora **Nzekwu's** *Blade among the Boys* (1962), whose primary character ends up rejecting his heritage and becoming a Roman Catholic priest. Similarly, the belittlement of native teachers by the European mission society is captured by Ghanaian Francis **Selormey** in his work *The Narrow Path* (1966). Nigerian writer John **Munonye's** work *The Only Son* (1966) depicts Christians as primarily evangelists who devalue African customs, while *Jingala* (1969) by Malawian Legson Kayira demonstrates how family ties are strained by the mission schools. In Stanlake Samkange's *The Mourned One* (1975) the false accusation and death sentence of a native teacher is effected by the missionary who takes the stand against him, while the Christian missionaries divide a Cameroonian village in Kenjo Jumbam's *The White Man of God* (1980) and the mission school Father Director is revealed as abusive in Zaïrean Ngandu Nkashama's *La Mort faite homme* (1986). In contrast, Peter **Abrahams** provides a more positive view of Christian missionaries in his work *The View from Coyoba* (1985), which features black American missionary Jacob Brown, who was a bishop in Liberia and Uganda.

The Christian tradition of marriage figures largely in works that contemplate the influence of such Christian rituals on African life. Beti's *Le Roi miraculé* represents a tribal chief who is a Christian convert and who bans polygamy, but does not disclose which wife he will maintain, while in *One Man, One Wife* by Nigerian T. M. **Aluko,** a Christian character resolves to have a second wife without acquainting his first wife with this decision. In contrast, Roman Catholic theology prevents a character in Gambian Lenrie **Peters's** work *The Second Round* (1965) from attaining a divorce from an unfaithful wife. An optimistic image of collaboration is portrayed in Samkange's *The Mourned One,* when the character Chibinha is married to a Roman Catholic teacher in a ceremony that combines Bantu and Christian traditions. However, in *Efuru* (1966) by Nigerian Flora **Nwapa** such a marriage to a Christian spells disaster for Efuru, while Stephen **Ngubiah's** *A Curse from God* (1970) criticizes polygamy from a Christian point of view.

The varied narratives of both French and English authors represent the equivocal place of Christianity in African culture. The missionaries both provide the educational opportunities for social movement, and at the same time undermine it with the prejudice they encourage against traditional spiritual beliefs. Authors like Peter Abrahams draw on these contradictions, as Abrahams does in his 1954 autobiography *Tell Freedom,* which positively represents Anglican teachers who were benevolent and not racist. However, Abrahams represents a questionable missionary education in his work A *Wreath for Udomo* (1956), which depicts both the hope of a missionary education and the simultaneous violence associated with that same education. The narrator of Malawian Aubrey Kachingwe's *No Easy Task* (1966) also benefits from a missionary education, but ends up so assimilated into Western habits that he loses the ability to communicate with his own people. The self-centered upper classes have appropriated both Christianity and Marxism in V. Y. Mudimbe's *Entre les eaux* (1973), which follows a native Zaïrean priest's discovery of this fact. A character in T. Obinkaram **Echewa**'s *The Land's Lord* (1976) commits suicide because he is torn between the position he gave up of the acolyte of the yarn god of his people (called Njoku) and Christianity. Similarly, Ugandan Timothy **Wangusa**'s *Upon This Mountain* (1989) tells the story of Mwambu, who is brought up as a Christian but who is also divided between church teachings and tribal traditions. Ama Ata Aidoo and others contemplate the future role of Christianity in Africa. In Aidoo's novel *Our Sister Killjoy* (1977), she translates the image of Dr. Christian Barnard's transplant of a black woman's heart into a white man to the image of the way that Western missionaries insist on the importance of a Christian name in order to be saved.

The Christian equation between materiality and spirituality is criticized by authors like Es'kia **Mphahlele**, who points out the church's focus on worldly things in his autobiography *Down Second Avenue* (1959). The Roman Catholic Church is represented as the means through which colonial propaganda is disseminated in Cameroon novelist Ferdinand **Oyono**'s *Le Vieux nègre et la médaille* (1956; *The Old Man and the Medal,* 1969), which depicts the ability of the church to ruin an individual. A similar message is portrayed in J. W. **Abruquah**'s fictional biography of his father titled *The Catechist* (1965), in which a man who is loyal to the church is rewarded with expulsion anyhow. Ghanaian Ayi Kwei takes a different route of criticism when he makes fun of biblical stories as oversimplified and childish tales in his work *Two Thousand Seasons*(1973). Another critical perspective focuses on the hypocritical sexual immorality of Christians, such as in Oyono's *Une vie de boy* (1960; *Houseboy,* 1966), which demonstrates the

connection between conversion, French civilization, and sexually transmitted diseases. Others who focus on this disconnect are Zaïrean author Thomas Mpoyi-Buatu, and Osija Mwambungu (**Prince Kagwema**), who broaches the topic of sexual promiscuity in his work *Veneer of Love* (1975). The role of the Roman Catholic Church in the colonization and exploitation of Africa is followed in the fictional prison journal that makes up the text of Mpoyi-Buata's book *La Réproduction* (1986), the time span of which is from the mid-nineteenth century to contemporary Kinshasa. The sexual acts in Mpoyi-Buata's work are picked up in a similar manner by another Zaïrean author, Thomas Bolya Baenga, who represents the desecration of Christian symbols through illicit sexual acts in his work *Cannibale* (1986).

Religious issues are taken up in a complex manner by authors like Wole Soyinka, whose novel *The Interpreters* (1965) takes inspiration from the stories of Lazarus and Barabbas in order to tell the story of Sekoni, a northern Nigerian Muslim man who marries a Christian. Soyinka returns to biblical images in *Season of Anomy* (1973), which also successfully intertwines biblical images into its narrative. In *Things Fall Apart* (1958) Chinua Achebe represents the generous and oppressive faces of Christianity and demonstrates the consequences of the conflict between Christian and Igbo customs. Such conflicts are picked up in *Arrow of God* (1964) as well, where the quarrel between a Christian missionary and a traditional priest demonstrates the result of such religious differences. Achebe uses the image of the python to heighten this conflict, as it can represent both a sacred native symbol, and the Christian image of original sin. **Ngugi wa Thiong'o** also depicts the ambiguous nature of Christianity in Africa in his novels. The teacher Isaka is killed because he denies that he has converted from Christianity to Mau Mau in Ngugi's *Weep Not, Child* (1964), which also draws on both Christian Old Testament and ancestral Gikuyu myths to demonstrate the rights of natives to reclaim the lands that were stolen from them by colonial invaders. Ngugi picks up on this theme of rightful land ownership in his novel *The River Between* (1965), which uses the image of God's gift of Canaan to the Israelites to depict the relationship between the Kemeno deity Murungu and the God of the Dutch Reformed Afrikaners, and the resulting space of disenchantment that arises from the conflict between the Christian missionaries and the traditionalists. Ngugi also obscures the divisions between Kenyan nationalist and Christian roles in his novel *A Grain of Wheat* (1967) through his representation of the Mau Mau rebel Kihika. Ngugi uses biblical images in his books *Matigari* (1983; trans. 1989) and *Caitaani Mutharabaini* (1980; *Devil on the Cross*, 1982) as well, and the use of these themes demonstrates the way that he utilizes familiar images (like that of the parable, or *Pilgrim's Progress*) for the purposes of questioning and instigating critical thought.

Christianity then assumes a very equivocal, and at times seemingly contradictory, role in African literature. Its complicity in the European oppression of African people links it to the ideologies of divine right of rule and "civilization" of Africa that colonizers used in an attempt to justify their presence. The denunciation of such ideologies is prevalent in contemporary African literature, and this negation of the objectification of others often has an ironically Christian basis that attempts to overthrow the very ideology it has helped to maintain. For example, *Trooper Peter Halket of Mashonaland* (1897) by Olive **Schreiner** calls on Christian morality to demonstrate the ungodly nature of Cecil Rhodes's racism. The use of Christian doctrine to validate racist or colonialist action (or to demonstrate its innocence) is most obvious in the way that the Great Trek of the Afrikaner Boers in the 1830s was characterized as a divine dispensation. Peter Abrahams's *Wild Conquest* and Jack Cope's *The Fair House* deal with this kind of Christian racism. Alan **Paton** denounces the hypocritical nature of a Christian religion that can advocate equality at the same time that it denies it to South African blacks in his ***Cry, the Beloved Country*** (1948). Similarly, in Bloke **Modisane's *Blame Me on History*** (1963) he demonstrates how the signs, rituals, and influence of the South African Christian Church are associated with the tyranny of **apartheid**. The biblical story of Jacob and Esau is used by Laurens **van Der Post** to depict the interactions between settler and bushman in his work *Heart of the Hunter* (1961), while *Kennis van die Aand* (1973; ***Looking on Darkness***, 1974) by Andre **Brink** questions the Afrikaner assumption that possession of the land is their god-given right.

Despite the manipulation of the Christian scriptures for colonial means, they do still motivate artistic representations of justice in ways that deviate from conventional European Christian images. For example, Bessie **Head** uses the image of the Garden of Eden in order to imagine democracy, freedom of expression, ideal morality, and human rights in her book *A **Question of Power*** (1974). Dambudzo **Marechera** also adapts a biblical image for secular expression in his Zimbabwean novel *The **House of Hunger*** (1978), which demonstrates how the moral authority of the Anglican Church is undermined by its conspiracy with Ian Smith's racist Rhodesian regime. *La Carte d'identité* (1980; *The Identity Card*, 1983) by Jean-Marie Adiaffi represents the important issue of respect (rather than belief or unbelief) in allegorical form. Thus, from as early as the Xhosa and English poetry and short stories of James J. R. Jolobe there has been literary subversion of colonial Christian ideology, and the theme continues to be one of importance in a negotiation of African identity that always requires new perspectives. For example, South African

Farida **Karodia** tackles the navigation of colonial and native African identity in relation to Mozambique's war of independence in her novel *A Shattering of Silence* (1993), while Imamu Amiri Baraka asks what Jesus Christ would have thought of the state of affairs in South Africa before Nelson Mandela was president in her preface to an anthology of African drama titled *Woza Afrika* (1986). This kind of questioning is the sort that is necessary given the long history of interaction between colonial or neo-colonial oppression and religious ideology.

ISLAM AND LITERATURE

During the seventh century, Islam spread throughout Africa (down the Nile and into East Africa, south to Mozambique and into West Africa). The contribution of Islam to literature in Africa has been great, although largely unstudied until the past few decades. *African Language Literatures* (1981) by Albert Gerard offers a study of contemporary literature and Islam, although it does not analyze the impact of African oral traditions. Due to the fact that those writers who come from Islamic areas tend to write in indigenous languages or Arabic, the influence of Islam on African anglophone literature has not been studied in depth. For example, Shehu Usman bn. Fodio is said to have written around 480 poems in Arabic, Hausa, and Fulfulde, along with a number of Arabic books. Novelists have tended to focus on an analysis of the role of Christianity rather than that of Islam, which is analyzed more fully by francophone authors like Senegalese writer Cheikh Hamidou Kane (*L'Aventure ambiguë*, 1961; *Ambiguous Adventure*, 1969) and from Mali, Yambo Ouologuem (*Le Devoir de violence*, 1968; *Bound to Violence*, 1971). Some anglophone novelists represent the impact of Islam in West Africa, like Ibrahim **Tahir** does in his novel *The Last Imam* (1984), which positively depicts Islamic values and decries the corruption of some imams who only have their own interests in mind. Tahir does not speak of the impact of Islam on traditional African beliefs.

The lack of historical and literary attention to the diversity of Islamic experiences (particularly in West Africa) is due to a number of reasons. One such reason is a disregard for the history of Islam in the colonial period due to a prevailing orientalist attitude, and another is the perception of a competition between Islam and Europe for colonialist hegemonic control over Africa that led to a barrier between European languages and Islamic tradition (especially in relation to the *a'jami* script and Islamic theological poetry). Kane's *L'Aventure ambiguë* (1961) was among the first African works to defend European thought. The work focuses on the battle between secular and religious institutions to control the interpretation of the word, and concludes by upholding the necessary role of Islam in the community. **Camara Laye** attempts to combine Islam with traditional rituals in his work, although aspects of Sufism are revealed through the tension that results from this combination. **Sembene Ousmane** depicts Islam as a barrier to the co-existence of soul and society, while Sophia Mustafa's *Broken Reed* (2005) is a narrative that follows the themes of love, imprisonment, and freedom through the experiences of Nureen, a Muslim woman who emigrates from India to Africa. Islam is perceived as an agent of colonization along the lines of the European Christian institution in works by Ghanaian novelist Ayi Kwei **Armah** and Senegalese poet Birago **Diop**. The works of Tayeb **Salih** depict complex Islamic communities, and portray Islamic traditions in the context of modern Africa.

Further Reading
Christianity and Literature
Binsbergen, Wim van. "'An Incomprehensible Miracle': Central African Clerical Intellectualism

versus African Historic Religion: A Close Reading of Valentin Mudimbe's Tales of Faith." *Journal of African Cultural Studies* 17, no. 1 (2005): 11–65.

Boulaga, Fabien Eboussi. *Christianity without Fetishes,* 2nd ed. Hamburg, Germany: Lit Verlag, 2002.

Brown, Duncan. "My Pen Is the Tongue of a Skilful Poet: African-Christian Identity and the Poetry of Nontsizi Mgqwetho." *English in Africa* 31, no. 1 (2004): 23–58.

Cooper, Brenda. "Landscapes, Forests and Borders within the West African Global Village." In *Mapping the Sacred: Religion, Geography and Postcolonial Literatures,* ed. Jamie S. Scott and Paul Simpson-Housley. Amsterdam: Rodopi, 2001, 275–93.

Dompere, Kofi Kissi. *Polyrhythmicity: Foundations of an African Philosophy.* London: Adonis & Abbey Publishers, 2006.

Fuchs, Anne. "From Dependence to Independence: Missions, Christianity and Theatre in Nineteenth- and Twentieth-Century South Africa." In *Colonies, Missions, Cultures in the English Speaking World: General and Comparative Studies,* ed. Gerhard Stilz. Tübingen: Stauffenburg, 2001, 276–86.

Kaschula, Russell H., and Samba Diop, eds. "Political Processes and the Role of the Imbongi and Griot in Africa." *South African Journal of African Languages/Suid-Afrikaanse Tydskrif vir Afrikatale* 20, no. 1 (2000): 13–28.

Lovell-Smith, Rose. "Science and Religion in the Feminist Fin-de-Siècle and a New Reading of Olive Schreiner's *From Man to Man.*" *Victorian Literature and Culture* 29, no. 2 (2001): 303–26.

Maithufi, Sope. "Black Christianity as Intellectual Resource in Njabulo Ndebele's *Fools and Other Stories.*" *English in Africa* 31, no. 1 (2004): 139–47.

Maxwell, David. "'Sacred History, Social History': Traditions and Texts in the Making of a Southern African Transnational Religious Movement." *Comparative Studies in Society and History* 43, no. 3 (2001): 502–24.

Ngwenya, Thengani H. "Ideology and Self-Representation in Autobiography: The Case of Katie Makanya." *Cross Cultures* 58 (2002): 143–56.

Sanneh, Lamin. "The African Transformation of Christianity: Comparative Reflections on Ethnicity and Religious Mobilization in Africa." In *Religions/Globalizations: Theories and Cases,* ed. Dwight N. Hopkins, Lois Ann Lorentzen, Eduardo Mendieta, and David Batstone. Durham, NC: Duke University Press, 2001, 105–34.

Sanneh, Lamin, and Joel A. Carpenter, eds. *The Changing Face of Christianity: Africa, the West and the World.* Oxford: Oxford University Press, 2005.

Stilz, Gerhard, ed. *Missions of Interdependence: A Literary Directory.* Amsterdam: Rodopi, 2002, 143–55.

Islam and Literature

Mahrouqi, Muhammad al-. "Religious Discourse in the Poetry of Abu Muslim al-Bahlani." *Journal of African Cultural Studies* 14, no. 1 (2001): 89–106.

Sato, Tsugitaka, ed. *Islam in History: Sufi Saints and Religious Factions. Acta Asiatica: Bulletin of the Institute of Eastern Culture* 86 (2004): iii-vi, 1–95.

Topan, Farouk. "Protecting Islam: Narrative in Swahili Poetry." *Journal of African Cultural Studies* 14, no. 1 (2001): 107–19.

Return to Beirut, The (1989)

A novel by Andrée Chedid, translated from the French (*La Maison sans racines,* 1985). The reunion between a child and her grandmother in Beirut and a planned peaceful protest come to a violent end in this novel, set in war-torn Lebanon in 1975. The granddaughter is killed on her way to meet her grandmother in the same square that a Christian and a Muslim woman decide to hold a women's peace demonstration. One of the women is also killed, and Chedid's ending reflects the arbitrary violence of the war.

Ripple from the Storm, A (1958)

The third novel in Doris **Lessing**'s *The Children of Violence* series. Martha Quest's commitment to Communism in the capital of a British colony based on Rhodesia during World War II leads her to become the mistress and then the wife of the leader of the Communist group she belongs to. Martha finds that she escaped a colonial culture, only to be similarly trapped by her involvement in Communism.

Rive, Richard (1931–89)
South African short-story writer and novelist. Rive was born in District Six, the multiracial, working-class area of Cape Town. He had a distinguished academic career in South Africa and overseas, including a Fulbright Fellowship in 1965 and a research fellowship at Oxford, where he wrote a doctoral thesis on Olive **Schreiner**, whose letters he would later edit. In an age of **Black Consciousness** Rive believed firmly in nonracialism. He was classified as "coloured" (mixed-race), but rejected the racial divisions of **apartheid** and refused to align himself with any literary or political organization in order to avoid compromising his objectivity as a writer.

Rive's early literary success is found in his short stories depicting the brutalization and humiliations of apartheid society. Many of his stories appeared in magazines such as *Drum* and *Fighting Talk*. He had his first collection of stories, *African Songs* (1963), published in East Berlin. He also edited two anthologies, *Quartet: New Voices from South Africa* (1963), which introduced work by fellow Western Cape writers James **Matthews**, Alex **La Guma**, and Alf Wannenburgh, and *Modern African Prose* (1964), a pioneering collection of writing from across the continent.

His first novel, *Emergency* (1964), is set against the background of the unrest that followed the Sharpeville shootings of 1960 and the subsequent declaration of a state of emergency. It addresses important issues through the moral and political dilemma of a young schoolteacher, Andrew Dreyer. An autobiography, *Writing Black* (1981), was followed by his second novel, *"Buckingham Palace," District Six* (1986), which celebrates

the community life of District Six, bulldozed in the name of apartheid. His last novel, *Emergency Continued* (1990), was published posthumously. Rive was brutally murdered at his home in Cape Town. The novel is a realistic representation of political events in Cape Town during the state of emergency of 1985 and a meditation on the nature of the political novel and the relationship of truth to fiction.

Further Reading
Davis, Geoffrey V. *Voice of Justice and Reason: Apartheid and Beyond in South African Literature.* Amsterdam: Rodopi, 2004.

Farred, Grant. *Midfielder's Moment: Coloured Literature and Culture in Contemporary South Africa.* Cultural Studies Series. Boulder, CO: Westview Press, 1999.

Marx, Lesley, and Loes Nas, eds. and introduction, and Chandré Carstens. *Juxtapositions: The Harlem Renaissance and the Lost Generation.* Cape Town, South Africa: University of Cape Town, 2000.

Willemse, Hein, ed. *More Than Brothers: Peter Clarke and James Matthews at Seventy.* Roggebaai, South Africa: Kwela Books, 2000.

River Between, The (1965)
A novel by **Ngugi wa Thiong'o**. The Christian and traditional religious factions occupying the ridges rising from the Honia River in 1930s and 1940s Kenya are the subject of this novel. It follows the actions of Waiyaki, who attempts to find a middle ground between the two groups and witnesses the destruction that results from his and others' attempts to do so. He falls in love with the daughter of the leader of the opposing Christian faction, and in midst of political and religious turmoil they are ushered off to their suggested deaths.

Road, The (1965)
A play by Wole **Soyinka**. Soyinka draws on Yoruba myth to depict the encounters with death that a group of characters from a

motor park experience in this play. It is set during the political crisis of the mid-1960s in Nigeria, and its characters represent the urban poor, including mechanics, criminals, a lay preacher, and a document forger.

Roberts, Sheila (1937–)

A South African short-story writer, novelist, and poet, Roberts was born in Johannesburg. She left South Africa in the late 1970s to settle in the United States, where she is Professor of English and co-ordinator of Creative Writing at the University of Wisconsin-Milwaukee.

Roberts's first volume of stories, *Outside Life's Feast* (1975), received the Olive Schreiner Prize and provides insight into white working-class society in South Africa. Her first collection of poems, *Lou's Life and Other Poems* (1977), appeared in a volume jointly with three other South African poets. Her first novel, *He's My Brother* (1977; published in North America as *Johannesburg Requiem*, 1980), was banned at the time for sexual explicitness. Her second novel is titled *The Weekenders* (1981), and was followed by a second collection of stories, *This Time of Year* (1983). She was awarded the Thomas Pringle Prize by the English Academy of South Africa for stories published in the literary periodical *Contrast*. Her critical study *Dan Jacobson* (1984) was followed by another collection of poems, *Dialogues and Divertimenti* (1985), the novel *Jacks in Corners* (1987), and more stories, *Coming In and Other Stories* (1993). She has most recently published *Christina* (2000), *Purple Yams* (2001), and is working on *Doris and the Dogs*. Roberts is best known for her short stories, in which she portrays the lives of the white underclass in South Africa.

Rotimi, Ola (1938–2000)

Nigerian dramatist Rotimi was born in Bendel State, Nigeria, to a Yoruba father and Ijo mother. After study in the United States, where some of his early plays were performed (including *Our Husband Has Gone Mad Again*, at Yale in 1966), he returned to Nigeria and in 1967 was appointed to the University of Ife (now Obafemi Awolowo University), where he was a founder of the Ori Olokun Theatre. Rotimi's plays from this period—*The **Gods Are Not to Blame*** (1971), *Kurunmi* (1971), *Ovonramwen Nogbaisi* (1974)—are very well known, frequently set as school texts, and are widely performed (especially *The Gods*). In 1977 Rotimi left Ife and joined the University of Port Harcourt, where he remained until 1992, returning then to Ife to establish a professional company, African Cradle Theatre. Rotimi held a position as Professor of Dramatic Arts at Obafemi Awolowo University, and founded "The Rotimi Foundation," which introduces people in the United States to African culture and the arts.

Although several radio plays, a large-scale historical play entitled *Akassa Youmi* (first performed in 1977), and a popular short Pidgin comedy, *Grip 'Am* (adapted from a Yoruba play by Agedoke Durojaiye), remain unpublished, the seven published plays demonstrate Rotimi's versatility. *Our Husband Has Gone Mad Again* (1974) is a political satire, as is *Holding Talks* (1979), which criticizes the use of language in power relations, while *The Gods Are Not to Blame* reworks Sophocles' *Oedipus* in the context of a precolonial Yoruba court. *Kurunmi* and *Ovonramwen Nogbaisi* are historical plays that deal with crises in nineteenth-century Yoruba and Benin history, respectively. *If* (1983), which depicts economic privation and political manipulation, and *Hopes of the Living Dead* (1988), which proposes strategies for collaboration against oppression, are Rotimi's most successful attempts to popularize literary drama. New editions of *Akassa You Mi A Historical Drama* (2001) and *Our Husband Has Gone Mad Again* (1999) have been released, as well as a project titled *Issues in African Theatre* (2001) put out by the

Department of Dramatic Arts at the Oba-femi Awolowo University (founded by Ola Rotimi), which consists of a collection of papers that detail the dramatist's final creative years and include contributions from Rotimi and others from his department.

Further Reading

Coker, Niyi. *Ola Rotimi's African Theatre: The Development of an Indigenous Aesthetic.* Lampeter, Dyfed, UK: Edwin Mellen Press, 2005.

Moore, David Chioni. "Theater and Teaching in Africa and America: An Interview with Ola Rotimi." In *Playwriting and Directing in Nigeria: Interviews with Ola Rotimi,* ed. Effiok B. Uwatt. Lagos: Apex Books, 2004.

Oyeleye, Lekan, and Olateju, Moji, eds. *Readings in Language and Literature.* Ife, Nigeria: Obafemi Awolowo Uniiversity Press, 2003.

Uwatt, Effiok Bassey, ed. *Playwriting and Directing in Nigeria.* Lagos: Apex Books, 2002.

Rubadiri, David (1930–)

Malawian poet and novelist Rubadiri was born in Liule and educated at Makerere University College, Uganda, and later at King's College, Cambridge. After serving as Malawi's first ambassador to the United States and the United Nations, he broke with the Banda regime and left the country to return to the academic world, where he remains. He served as Professor of Education at the University of Botswana until Banda fell from power. He was then reappointed Malawi's ambassador to the United Nations. He has retired from his position as Malawi's ambassador to the UN, as well as from his position as Vice-Chancellor of the University of Malawi. Rubadiri's only novel, *No Bride Price* (1967), reflects early disenchantment with Banda's postindependence regime. It was well received and, with Legson **Kayira**'s work, was among the first Malawian novels to be published. His play, *Come to Tea* (1965), was published in *New African.* He is best known as a poet, and his work has appeared in international journals such as *Transition, Black Orpheus,* and *Présence africaine,* as well as Gerald Moore's and Ulli Beier's pioneering anthology *Modern Poetry from Africa* (1963; rev. 1968). His poems indicated a new development among African writers, a combination of African influences and an awareness of European poetic modes. More recently he has published *An African Thunderstorm and Other Poems* (2004), which is a work that combines his more well-known poems with his newest poetry. Concerned passionately about the place of African literature in the continent's school and college syllabi, he emphasizes the importance of suitable teaching texts. Thus he edited *Poems from East Africa* (1971) with David Cook and *Growing up with Poetry: An Anthology for Secondary Schools* (1989) for Botswanan students.

Ruganda, John (1941–)

Ugandan playwright and novelist. Ruganda graduated from Makerere University, Kampala, was the senior fellow in creative writing at Makerere University, and later joined the Department of Literature at the University of Nairobi, and then the Department of English at the University of Swaziland. Currently Ruganda is Professor of Performing Arts at the Turfloop campus of Limpopo University, South Africa. He has won several playwriting competitions, and along with Robert **Serumaga** he is considered the main force behind the development of the theater in Uganda in the 1970s and 1980s. His first play, *The Burdens* (1972), explores the problems of society through family life. In his satire *Black Mamba* (1973), the figure of the prostitute is a symbol of the oppressed people of Africa. *Covenant with Death* (1973) is an investigation of social and psychological alienation. Other published plays include *Music without Tears* (1982), *Echoes of Silence* (1986), and *The Roods* (1980), which deals with the suffering of innocent victims at the hands of corrupt and incompetent governments. He is also the author of *Shreds of Tenderness* (2001), and *Igereka and Other African Narratives* (2002), which presents story telling from various perspectives and uses narrative to question perception and individual interpretation.

Ruheni, Mwangi (1934–)
(pseudonym of Nicholas Muraguri)

A novelist, born in Kenya. He holds a bachelor of science and master of science degrees from Makerere University College, Uganda, where he was also the editor of *St. Augustine's Newsletter,* produced by Catholic students. His second master's is from the University of Strathclyde, Scotland. He was the government chemist for Kenya for twenty-two years (retired in 1990), and holds a position in the Ministry of Health as a Medical Officer of Health for the Embu District of Kenya. Ruheni's first novel, *What a Life!* (1972), won him instant recognition and marked a new trend in Kenyan literature, which his subsequent novels, *The Future Leaders* (1973), *What a Husband!* (1974), and *The Minister's Daughter* (1975) consolidate. His chief preoccupation has been the difficult process of growing up and integrating in social life for young people. With *The Mystery Smugglers* (1975) and *The Love Root* (1976) Ruheni crosses the border to popular writing. He has also written a children's book, *In Search of Their Parents* (1973). *Random Thoughts Book I* (1995) contains a number of essays written around a variety of topics, ranging from religion and politics to publishing and soccer, and was published under Ruheni's real name, Nicholas Muraguri.

Ruhumbika, Gabriel (1938–)

Tanzanian novelist and short-story writer. Ruhumbika was born in Ukerewe Islands, Tanzania, and studied at the University of Makerere, Uganda, and the Sorbonne in Paris, where he gained a PhD in African literature (1964). Since 1970 he has taught literature at universities in East Africa and the United States, and acts as a Professor of Comparative Literature and Associate Head

at the University of Georgia. Ruhumbika's first novel, *Village in Uhuru* (1969), focuses on the problem of ethnic identities in the context of national unity. Ruhumbika, like **Ngugi wa Thiong'o,** abandoned English and published his subsequent books, a collection of stories and another novel, in Swahili. *Uwike Usiwike Kutakucha (Whether the Cock Crows or Not It Dawns)* (1978) examines the failures of Uhuru as promised by the elite. *Miradi Bubu ya Wazalendo (Invisible Enterprises of the Patriots)* (1991) is a historical novel about the plight of those who fought for Uhuru. Another of Ruhumbika's novels wrriten in Swahili is *Janga Sugu la Wazawa (Everlasting Doom for the Children of the Land)* (2002), and an English translation of Ruhumbika's *Myombekere and His Wife Bugonoka, Their Son Ntulanalwo and Daughter Bulihwali: The Story of an Ancient African Community* also appeared in 2002. In addition, Ruhumbika has been included in anthologies such as Simon Gikandi's *Encyclopedia of African Literature* (2002).

Rui, Manuel (1941–)

Rui was born in Nova-Lisboa, now Huambo, in Angola. He graduated from the University of Coimbra (Portugal), with a law degree and became a member of the Center of Literary Studies of the Academic Association of Coimbra, editor of the culture and art magazine *Vértice,* co-ordinator for the literary supplement *Sintoma,* and co-founder of *Mar Além (Sea Beyond),* out of which was born the *Magazine of Culture and Literature.* Rui is a regular contributor to radio, theater and film, and he writes and directs for theater. He is also the author of the Angolan national anthem, and has published a collection of chronicles titled *Maninha* (2003), *Um Anel na Areia (A Ring in the Sand)* (2003), *Saxofone e Metáfora (Saxophone and Metaphor)* (2001), and has made contributions to such works as *Communities of Youth Cultural Practice and Informal Learning* (2002).

Rumours of Rain (1978)

A novel by André **Brink**. The Afrikaner narrator of this novel, Mynhardt, is unreliable and Brink uses the irony of his first-person narrative to distance the reader from the narrator. Mynhardt portrays his experiences at the beginning of the Soweto riots, and attempts to explain away his guilty associations with apartheid. Despite his attempts to keep the different parts of his life separate, Mynhardt's best friend is convicted of "terrorism," his son rebels, he loses his mistress, and his farm is sold.

Rungano, Kristina (1963–)

Poet and short-story writer Rungano was born in Harare, Zimbabwe, and grew up near Kuatama Mission. She attended Catholic-run boarding schools in Selous and Harare, studied management in Britain, and obtained a diploma in Computer Science in England, where she currently lives. She is Zimbabwe's first published female poet, and *A Storm Is Brewing* (1984) is her first collection. She has since contributed poems to the anthologies *Daughters of Africa* (1992) and *The Heinemann Book of African Women's Poetry* (1995) and written short stories. Rungano's work is included in anthologies such as *The New African Poetry, African Women's Poetry,* and *The Penguin Book of Modern African Poetry* (1999). Although she views her poetry primarily as a means of self-release, her themes are resonant: self-exploration, aspects of womanhood, love, loneliness, alienation, and war are among her subjects, and she captures inwardly felt experience using a variety of personae.

S

Saadawi, Nawal el (1931–)

An Egyptian writer of fiction and nonfiction in Arabic, El Saadawi was born in the Egyptian village of Kafr Tahla and has worked in medicine, politics, government, literature, and cultural analysis for the equality of Muslim women in political, economic, and domestic life. Perhaps because of her reputation as a reformer, her accomplishments as a writer were long minimized, and her fictional works have only recently been available in English translation. She is the founder of the Arab Women's Solidarity Association, a founder of the Arab Organization for Human Rights, has been arrested and imprisoned, has lived under death threats by Muslim fundamentalists, and has had her books and appearances on radio and television banned in Egypt and other Middle Eastern countries. Saadawi also acted as Visiting Professor at Florida Atlantic University in Boca Raton, and was involved in the 2005 presidential election in Egypt (although she ultimately pulled out her candidacy). She was awarded the North-South Prize of the Council of Europe (2004), was nominated for the International Biographical Centre International Writer of the Year (2003), was awarded the Great Minds of the 21st Century Award from the American Biographical Institute (2003), and won the Premi Internacional Catalunya Literary Award (2003).

Despite this busy schedule she has managed to write twenty-seven books, including many works of fiction. *Memoirs from the Women's Prison* (1981; trans. 1986) is a vivid account of her own jail experiences. In the novel *Woman at Point Zero* (1975; trans. 1983) a female inmate on death row says "I was killed by revealing the truth, not in using the knife. They aren't afraid of the knife; it's the truth that terrifies them." Her short stories are terse, specific, and objectively told, and have appeared in several journals as well as in four collections, including *Death of an Ex-Minister* (trans. 1987) and *She Has No Place in Paradise* (trans. 1987). She often deals with traumas women feel from sequestration, from the veil, from sexual mutilation. Her seven novels depict both rural and urban life in contemporary Egypt and the abuses of power by a tyrannical government. Her novels include *God Dies by the Nile* (1975; trans. 1985), *The Circling Song* (trans. 1989), and *Searching* (trans. 1991). She was recognized in France through translations of her works by the Algerian writer Assia Djebar. Although Saadawi was known in the United States for her activism, her fiction did not appear in English translation until the 1980s. *A Daughter of Isis: The Autobiography of Nawal el Saadawi* (1999), covering the early years of her life, was translated from the Arabic by Sherif Hetata, and Hetata also translated *Walking through Fire: A Life of Nawal El Saadawi* (2002). El Saadawi has also recently published *Al Riwaya* (*The Fall of Imam*) in 2002. In addition to these works, there are also works that have not been translated, such as *Qad ̄ay ̄a al-mar'ah wa-al-fikr wa-al-siy ̄asah* (2001), *Adab Am Kellat Adab* (2000), and *Taw'am al-sultah wa-al-jins,* (1999), and works that exist in anthologies such as *Shattering the Stereotypes: Muslim Women Speak Out* (2005), and *Encyclopedia of World Literature in the 20th Century* (1999).

Further Reading

Royer, Diana. *A Critical Study of the Works of Nawal El Saadawi, Egyptian Writer and Activist.* Lampeter, Dyfed, UK: Edwin Mellen Press, 2001.

Salih, Tayeb (1929–)

A novelist writing in Arabic, Salih was born in the northern axis of central Sudan to an ethnic group reputed for the propagation of Islamic scholarship in the region. His primary education was religious, and it ignited his precocity to such an extent that by the time he entered secondary school in Khartoum he had already studied prominent Arab authors such as al Tahtawi, Muhammed Abdul, and Dr. Taha Husayn. After gaining an advanced degree in London, he worked for the BBC as the head of Arabic drama. On his return to Sudan, he became Director of Sudanese National Radio; later he accepted a secondment as Director General of the Ministry of Information of the Emirate of Qatar, where he makes his home.

Salih's writing is drawn from his experience of communal village life. He deals with themes of reality and illusion, the cultural dissonance between the West and the exotic orient, the harmony and conflict of brotherhood, and the individual's responsibility to reconcile his or her contradictions. These motifs and their contexts derive from both his Islamic cultural background and the experience of modern Africa, both pre- and postcolonial. His novels are *Al-Rajul al Qubrosi* (*The Cypriot Man,* 1978), *Urs al Zayn* (*The Wedding of Zein,* 1969), *Mawsim al-Hijra ila al-Shamal* (**Season of Migration to the North,** 1969), and *Daumat Wad Hamid* (*The Doum Tree of Wad Hamid,* 1985). He constructs an impervious unity of the social, religious, and political essence of the African or African Arab. His books have been translated into several languages, and he edited a volume of translated short stories titled *Sardines and Oranges: Short Stories from North Africa,* which was published in 2005. A Penguin Classics edition of *Season of Migration to the North* was released in 2003, and Salih has also been included in anthologies such as *The Anchor Book of Modern African Stories* (2002, and *African Fiction and Joseph Conrad: Reading Postcolonial Intertextuality* (2004).

Further Reading

Hassan, Waïl S. *Ideology and the Craft of Fiction.* Syracuse, NY: Syracuse University Press, 2003.

Sallah, Tijan M(omodou) (1958–)

Poet, born in Sere Kunda, Gambia. After attending St. Augustine's High School, he went to the United States, where he gained a bachelor's from Berea College, Kentucky, and a master's and a PhD from Virginia Polytechnic. He taught economics at Virginia

Polytechnic, Kutztown University, and the University of North Carolina before going to work for the World Bank, and he is currently a Senior Economist on Rural Development in the Middle East Department of the World Bank. His collections of poetry include *When Africa Was a Young Woman* (1980), *Kora Land* (1989), and *Dreams of Dusty Roads* (1993). His fourth publication, *Before the New Earth* (1988), is a collection of short stories. He focuses on the positive elements of African communal values, and distrusts the influence of Western modernity. His poetic style is epigrammatic poetry of simple diction, simple narration, and simple imagery, to mature poetry of description, imaginatively mixed metaphors, and satirically humorous or tragically engaging poetic narratives that often imitate the traditional art of the *griot*. His short stories are poetic and derive most of their imagery from nature, which is contrasted against negative images of modernity. Sallah is also the author/editor of some critical works such as *Chinua Achebe: Teacher of Light: A Biography,* with Ngozi Okonjo-Iweala (2003), and *New African Poetry: An Anthology,* with Tanure Ojaide (1999), and has a contribution in *Step into a World: A Global Anthology of the New Black Literature,* edited by Kevin Powell (2000).

Samkange, Stanlake (1922–88)

Zimbabwean journalist, historian, and historical novelist. Samkange was born in Zvimba, Zimbabwe, then Southern Rhodesia, the son of the Rev. Thompson Samkange, Methodist minister and nationalist politician, and his wife, Grace Mano, a Methodist evangelist. Thompson Samkange worked in both Matabeleland and Mashonaland during Samkange's childhood, and a characteristic of Samkange's writing is his refusal to adopt regional and ethnic perspectives. He was educated at Adams College in Natal, University College of Fort Hare, and the University of Indiana. After returning from Fort Hare

to teach in Southern Rhodesia in 1948 he began to plan Nyatsime College, a secondary school to be controlled by blacks rather than government or missionaries, which was finally opened in 1962. Samkange was deeply involved in the liberal politics of Southern Rhodesia during the 1950s and 1960s, but when it became clear that the white electorate would reject any multiracial option he moved to the United States, where he produced his most important literary work.

Samkange's first novel (which was banned in Rhodesia) was *On Trial for My Country* (1966), in which both Cecil Rhodes and Lobengula, the Ndebele ruler, are tried by their ancestors for their respective parts in obtaining and granting the various concessions that gave a spurious legality to Rhodes's occupation of Mashonaland. It was followed by *Origins of Rhodesia* (1968), a formal history covering the same ground as the novel, a partly autobiographical novel titled *The Mourned One* (1975), and a fictional reconstruction of the 1896 uprising titled *Year of the Uprising* (1978). He returned to Rhodesia in 1978 but retired from active politics to concentrate on his writing before the Lancaster House talks took place. With his wife, Tommie Anderson, he wrote *Hunuism or Ubuntuism* (1980), an attempt to systematize an African epistemology, and *African Saga* (1971), a popular history of Africa. His last novels were *Among Them Yanks* (1985) and *On Trial for That UDI* (1986), which put rebel Rhodesian Prime Minister Ian Smith and British Prime Minister Harold Wilson on trial.

In his historical fiction Samkange draws heavily on published documents and melds the historical and the imaginative. He evokes a white dialogue with a black voice, and determines a narrative strategy with radical implications in the Rhodesia of the 1960s and 1970s. In the three novels the black voice has access to rich mythic and spiritual sources whose authority is reproduced in a complex secular order, whether it is the Ndebele state in *On Trial for My Country* or village life in *The Mourned One.*

Sancho, Ignatius (1729–80)

Letter-writer, born in a slave ship between Africa and South America and died in England. He was baptized Ignatius by a bishop in South America and was sold to three Englishwomen at Greenwich after being separated from his parents around the age of two. These sisters, whom he detested, gave him the second name, Sancho, for the resemblance they saw between him and Don Quixote's servant, Sancho Panza. Often the three sisters taunted him with the prospect of selling him back into slavery in the Americas. While in the household of the Duchess of Montagu, where he was employed as a butler, he cultivated the friendship of the English novelist Laurence Sterne. He was well acquainted with the theater and made many friends as well among sculptors and painters, and a picture was made of him by Gainsborough. Among his other friends were Henry Fielding, David Garrick, and John Mortimer, who regularly consulted him on his views about painting.

Sancho is best known for his *Letters of the Late Ignatius Sancho, an African* (1782), which went into five editions. The letters, most often addressed to friends, contain lively details of domestic life and evidence of his affection for his six children, whom he calls the "Sanchonets," as well as observations and comments on a range of topics relevant to eighteenth-century city life. He also wrote music and his *Theory of Music,* dedicated to the Princess Royal, has not survived. Although his writing bears the styles and values of polite English society, the language of protest surfaces in discussions such as those focused on poverty and slavery.

Further Reading

Basker, James G., ed. *Amazing Grace: An Anthology of Poems about Slavery, 1660–1810.* New Haven, CT: Yale University Press, 2002.

Carey, Brycchan. "'The Extraordinary Negro': Ignatius Sancho, Joseph Jekyll, and the Problem of Biography." *British Journal for Eighteenth-Century Studies* 26, no. 2 (Spring 2003): 1–13.

———. "'The Hellish Means of Killing and Kidnapping': Ignatius Sancho and the Campaign against the 'Abominable Traffic for Slaves.'" In *Discourses of Slavery and Abolition: Britain and Its Colonies, 1760–1838,* ed. Brycchan Carey, Markman Ellis, and Sara Salih. Basingstoke, England: Palgrave/Macmillan, 2004, 81–95.

———. "Ignatius Sancho." In *The Encyclopedia of Life Writing: Autobiographical and Biographical Forms,* 2 vols, ed. Margaretta Jolly. London: Fitzroy Dearborn, 2001, II, 775–76.

Ellis, Markman. "Ignatius Sancho's Letters: Sentimental Libertinism and the Politics of Form." In *Genius in Bondage: Literature of the Early Black Atlantic,* ed. Vincent Carretta and Philip Gould. Lexington: University Press of Kentucky, 2001, 199–217.

Innes, C. L. "Black British Writing and Literary History." *The European English Messenger* 11, no. 2 (Autumn 2002): 13–16.

———. *A History of Black and Asian Writing in Britain, 1700–2000.* Cambridge: Cambridge University Press, 2002.

Nussbaum, Felicity A. "Being a Man: Olaudah Equiano and Ignatius Sancho." In *Genius in Bondage: Literature of the Early Black Atlantic,* ed. Vincent Carretta and Philip Gould. Lexington: University Press of Kentucky, 2001, 54–71.

Sandhu, Sukhdev. *London Calling: How Black and Asian Writers Imagined a City.* London: Harper Collins, 2003.

Smith, Johanna. "Slavery, Abolition, and the Nation in Priscilla Wakefield's *Tour Books for Children.*" In *Discourses of Slavery and Abolition: Britain and Its Colonies, 1760–1838,* ed. Brycchan Carey, Markman Ellis, and Sara Salih. Basingstoke, England: Palgrave/Macmillan, 2004, 175–93.

Saro-Wiwa, Ken(ule Beeson) (1941–95)

A Nigerian novelist, nonfiction writer, and television and film producer, Saro-Wiwa was educated at Government College, Umuahia, and the University of Ibadan. He held the political and administrative positions of Commissioner of Works, Land, and Transport, of Education, and of Information and Home Affairs in Rivers State between 1968 and 1973. During the Nigeria-Biafra war (1967–70) he served as administrator of the oil port of Bonny. In 1973 he published his first two books, *Tambari* and *Tambari in Dukana*, both intended for a youthful audience. Leaving government service the same year, he embarked on a successful business career in several fields, including publishing.

In 1985 he published a collection of his poetry, *Songs in a Time of War*, and the novel **Sozaboy**: *A Novel in Rotten English. Sozaboy* in particular received critical attention because of its creative mix of Pidgin, broken, and standard English. In the novel, Mene, the innocent and impoverished protagonist, joins the Biafran army for economic reasons and because of his romantic dream of being a *soza*, a soldier. *Sozaboy* is a compelling antiwar novel because of its portrayal of Mene's disillusionment as he witnesses the brutalities of warfare and the hypocrisy of those who precipitated the conflict. In the mid-1980s Saro-Wiwa turned to television production and his "Basi & Co." series was extremely popular, with more than 150 separate episodes finally being aired. Basi and his get-rich-quick schemes became the subject of *Basi and Company: A Modern African Folktale* (1987), a series of children's books featuring "Mr. B," *Basi and Company: Four Television Plays* (1988), and *Four Farcical Plays* (1989).

With the publication of *On a Darkling Plain: An Account of the Nigerian Civil War* (1989), Saro-Wiwa's autobiographical description of the conflict, his social activism on behalf of his people, the Ogoni, emerges. He portrays the Ibo as oppressors of the ethnic minorities in Eastern Nigeria, particularly the Ogoni, who are caught between the Yoruba, Ibo, and Hausa. Although he continued writing gentle satire and literature for children, his concerns about the injustice

and corruption he saw in Nigeria came to dominate, with some of his most compelling and critical comments appearing in *Prisoners of Jebs* (1988), *Nigeria: The Brink of Disaster* (1991), and *Similia: Essays on Anomic Nigeria* (1991). The books collect newspaper columns and articles written over the previous two decades covering a wide range of subjects and provide an overview of Saro-Wiwa's concerns. In *Genocide in Nigeria: The Ogoni Tragedy* (1992) he argues that the Ogoni are an exploited minority in Nigeria. Arrested and charged with treason, he was imprisoned briefly in 1993, an experience he describes in *A Month and a Day* (1995). Saro-Wiwa is also included in several anthologies, such as *Under African Skies: Modern African Stories* (1997), *Africa and the Middle East: A Continental Overview of Environmental Issues* (2003), *Heart Sounds* (2002), and *Gathering Seaweed: African Prison Writing* (2002). Upon his release he continued his efforts on behalf of the Ogoni, and through the organization Movement for the Survival of the Ogoni People charged Shell Oil and the Nigerian federal government with creating an ecological disaster in Ogoni lands. In 1995 he was accused of incitement to murder when some village heads were killed at a rally, and after a controversial trial was hanged. He is now best remembered for his reform efforts, advocacy of Ogoni rights, and for his creative use of language in his novel *Sozaboy*. In 2001 Ken Wiwa, Saro-Wiwa's son, published *In the Shadow of a Saint: A Son's Journey to Understand His Father's Legacy*. There are quite a number of works that deal with the continuing influence of Ken Saro-Wiwa, including Onookome Okome's *Before I Am Hanged: Ken Saro-Wiwa* (1999), *Ken Saro-Wiwa: Writer and Political Activist* (1999) co-authored by Craig W. McLuckie and Aubrey McPhail, Femi Ojo-Ade's *Ken Saro-Wiwa* (1999), A. Manguel's *God's Spies: Stories in Defiance of Oppression* (1999), as well as *Ken Saro-Wiwa and the Discourse of*

Ethnic Minorities in Nigeria (1999) by Imo Ubokudom Eshiet and Onookome Okome.

Sassine, Williams (1944–96)

Guinean novelist who wrote in French. He attributes his childhood stammering to a triple learning situation—catechism to please his Christian Lebanese father, the Koran to abide by his African mother's Islamic heritage, and the school system of a French colony. Dissatisfied with Sékou Touré's stranglehold over Guinean youth, Sassine fled Guinea in 1961 and survived in France as a student and immigrant for five years. From 1966 to 1988, he wrote four novels while making a living for his family—he had five children—as a mathematics teacher and headmaster in West African countries from Ivory Coast to Mauritania. He finally returned to Guinea. As chief editor of the satirical newspaper *Le Lynx,* he commented on Guinea's slow recovery from Sékou Touré's dictatorship.

In *Saint Monsieur Baly* (1973) and *Wirriyamu* (1976; trans. 1980) (the latter is the name of a village in an imaginary Portuguese colony) Sassine creates marginal characters whose fortitude give hope for survival after civil war. Symbolism and poetry lighten the novel's dark message that opponents to dictatorship are estranged even from those who should side with them. Sékou Touré's death in 1984 inspired Sassine with a renewed, humorous opposition style. *Le Zéhros n'est pas n'importe qui* (1985) is based on a pun about an exile called back to his country after the death of the PDG (Président-Directeur-Général) to serve as a "hero," even though his failures have confirmed him a "zero." Written before his return to Guinea, this novel foresees the dereliction of a country that has stagnated in poverty.

Schreiner, Olive (Emilie Albertina) (1855–1920)

Born one of twelve children in South Africa's northeastern Cape, Olive Schreiner rejected her missionary parents' religion from an early age. She left home at twelve, and began a lifetime of anxious wandering. Schreiner began working as a governess at fifteen. She read widely (including works by Emerson, Herbert Spencer, J. S. Mill, Darwin, and Carl Vogt), kept a journal from childhood, and began writing seriously in late adolescence. Her three novels, *The Story of an African Farm* (1883), *Undine* (1929), and *From Man to Man* (1926), were all under way while she was in her twenties.

She went to England in 1881. The commercial and critical success of *African Farm* provided the opportunity for acquaintance with Havelock Ellis, Karl Pearson, and Edward Carpenter. Despite her participation in the feminist and socialist intellectual activity of the time, she remained an outsider without conventional family or social ties. She returned to South Africa in 1889 and married Samuel Cronwright. Her baby, born in 1895, died and she did not have another. She focused her writing from this period on allegory and political analysis. She traveled again to England late in her life and there renewed her involvement in feminism and pacifism. She returned in 1920 to Cape Town, where she died. *Undine,* Schreiner's first major work (but published posthumously), is, by her own account, "exact autobiography." All her novels describe children with fragile family links whose unconventional behavior brings further alienation. Similarly her descriptions of the Eastern Cape countryside and the towns that emerged after the 1867 discovery of diamonds provide insight into the social context of her early life. By the time of *African Farm* she is more able to "paint what lies before her," as she enjoins local artists to do.

Schreiner's novels also provide valuable insights into the position of women under colonialism. Like Schreiner herself, female characters are denied a formal education, branded "odd" for their "manly" behavior, and hounded when they contravene the stifling sexual mores of insular Eastern Cape towns. Schreiner thus exposes how colonial society simultaneously afforded white women greater freedom and yet constrained them to uphold the family. The metaphor of seduction in *From Man to Man* represents the colonized land as feminized. Schreiner's interest in allegory, clear in her novels as well as in the collections *Dreams* (1870) and *Dream Life and Real Life* (1893), combine with her passion for politics in *Trooper Peter Halket of Mashonaland* (1897), a critique of the "civilizing" mission of the Chartered Company. Her idealization of rural Boer life in *Thoughts on South Africa* (1923) was intended as a strategic defense of the Afrikaner in the aftermath of the Jameson Raid. *An English South African's View of the Situation* (1899) aims to avert the impending Anglo-Boer conflict. Schreiner similarly intended to shock an intended British audience with *Trooper Peter Halket* and force a parliamentary reexamination of the affairs of the Chartered Company. *Closer Union* (1909) continues the critique of monopoly capitalism and segregation and proposes federalism for South Africa. *Woman and Labour* (1911) articulates Schreiner's theory that the exclusion of women from education and employment produces a condition of sex parasitism, which reduces women to the "passive performance of sex functions alone." The latter part of *Woman and Labour* addresses women's relation to war, reflecting her growing concern. "The Dawn of Civilisation" (1921) is a final discussion of gender and sex. Recent rereadings of Schreiner's work attentive to her position as a colonial woman writer in turn-of-the-century South Africa uncover a more nuanced portrait of her and are sensitive to her achievements as well as her limitations.

Further Reading

Burdett, Carolyn. *Olive Schreiner and the Progress of Feminism: Evolution, Gender, Empire.* Basingstoke, England: Palgrave/Macmillan, 2001.

Cardinal, Agnes, Dorothy Goldman, and Judith Hattaway, eds. *Women's Writing on the First World War.* Oxford: Oxford University Press, 2002.

Hackett, Robin. *Sapphic Primitivism: Productions of Race, Class, and Sexuality in Key Works of Modern Fiction.* New Brunswick, NJ: Rutgers University Press, 2004.

Heilman, Ann. *New Woman Strategies : Sarah Grand, Olive Schreiner, and Mona Caird.* Manchester, England: Manchester University Press, 2004.

Lessing, Doris. *Time Bites: Views and Reviews.* London: Fourth Estate, 2004.

Lewis, Simon. *White Women Writers and Their African Invention.* Gainesville: University Press of Florida, 2003.

Murphy, Patricia. *Time Is of the Essence: Temporality, Gender, and the New Woman.* SUNY Series, Studies in the Long Nineteenth Century. Albany: State University of New York Press, 2001.

Sanders, Mark. *Complicities: The Intellectual and Apartheid.* Durham, NC: Duke University Press, 2002.

Scully, William Charles (1855–1943)

A novelist, poet, and autobiographer, Scully was born in Dublin, Ireland, and came with his family to King Williamstown in the Eastern Cape in 1867. Scully was a prospector for diamonds in Kimberley, for gold in Lydenberg and Pilgrim's Rest; he worked as a Cape civil servant in 1876, eventually becoming a magistrate and civil commissioner in the Transkei, Namaqualand, and the Transvaal. He was an imperialist and he believed in and supported imperialism's aims and objectives. But he deplored the jingoistic excesses that precipitated the Anglo-Boer war of 1899–1902, and implicitly and overtly fostered racism through their paternalistic attitudes to African peoples.

Scully's writing shows a sympathetic interest in and understanding of the South African landscape, its peoples, and the impact of imperialism on the former. His work includes *The Wreck of the Grosvenor and Other South African Poems,* published anonymously in 1886, *Poems* (1892), and *Between Sun and Sand* (1898), a work that emphasizes the difficult lives of nomadic peoples in Namaqualand. *Lodges in the Wilderness* (1915) portrays the spirituality of the desert places in Namaqualand, while *Daniel Vallanda: The Life Story of a Human Being* (1923) retrospectively depicts Scully's sympathetic understanding of African values and experiences in both rural and urban settings from 1880–1920. He published three further collections of short stories, *Kafir Stories* (1895), *The White Hecatomb and Other Stories* (1897), and *By Veldt and Kopje* (1907); he also published *The Ridge of White Waters ("Witwatersrand"); or, Impressions of a Visit to Johannesburg* (1912), the autobiographical *Reminiscences of a South African Pioneer* (1913), and *Further Reminiscences of a South African Pioneer* (1913). Scully's short story *Ghamba* has been transcribed by Amazon Press (2001) and is available online.

Season of Anomy (1973)

A novel by Wole **Soyinka**. The novel takes as its subject the "anomy" of the pogroms in Northern Nigeria in 1966. Soyinka uses the myth of Orpheus and Euridice to create his characters Ofeiyi and Iriyese. The ideal society that Ofeiyi wishes to create is destroyed by the militaristic world of violence and selfishness that already exists.

Season of Migration to the North (1969)

A novel by Tayeb **Salih**. The two narrators of this novel contrast their experiences of a village in the Sudan with those in Europe. Mustafa Sa'id begins the narrative, which is composed of his violent sexual experiences in London, the murder of his wife, his imprisonment, and his return to the village to marry and have children, followed by his drowning death. The nameless narrator takes up the thread of the story and tells of the disastrous arranged marriage of Sa'id's widow, his guilt and love for her, and his thoughts of suicide.

Seasons of Thomas Tebo, The (1986)

A novel by John **Nagenda**. The life of the primary character unfolds parallel to that of an independent African country that has suffered under a number of brutal regimes. The plight of both nation and individual seem hopeless, but they both gain insight from their suffering and resolve to continue their battles.

Segun, Mabel (Dorothy) (1930–)

A poet and children's writer, Segun was born in Ondo, Nigeria, and studied at the University College of Ibadan. She has worked as an editor, broadcaster, teacher, and researcher at the University of Ibadan, and was founder and first president of the Children's Literature Association of Nigeria (CLAN). Segun retired from public life in 2003. In her children's literature she focuses on the need for intellectual alertness, emotional balance, and loyalty to cultural roots. Her poems, stories, and cultural commentary promote ideals such as collectiveness, patriotism, and self-reliance and critique narrow ethnicity, the romanticizing of the past, and the political, social, and economic contradictions in present-day Nigeria. Her style is always direct and full of irony, and at times she uses an oral technique that makes her poems sound like tales in verse. Her publications include *My Father's Daughter* (1965), *Youth Day Parade* (1983), *My Mother's Daughter* (1985), *Olu and the Broken Statue* (1985), *Sorry, No Vacancy* (1985), and *Conflict and Other Poems* (1986). *Friends, Nigerians, Countrymen* (1977) is a collection of her satirical radio broadcasts; her short fiction is collected in *The Surrender and Other Stories* (1995); and she is featured in the anthology *Ibadan Mesiogo* (2001), which is a collection of works celebrating Harlem.

Sekyi (William Essuman-Gwira) Kobina (1892–1956)

Ghanaian dramatist. Educated at Richmond College of West Africa, the University of London, and the Inns of Court, Sekyi became a member of the Inner Temple and the Aristotelian Society. In 1918 he returned to the then Cape Coast to embark on a legal career and became active in social and cultural clubs devoted to social reform and education. Sekyi's concern with reform and development is evident in his many essays and addresses, published in the 1930s and 1940s, and in poetry related to issues of nationalism, but his satirical play *The Blinkards* (not published until 1974) will arguably remain his greatest literary accomplishment. *The Blinkards,* first produced by the Cosmopolitan Club in Cape Coast in 1915, is an African comedy of manners written in Fanti and English. The play satirizes middle-class, Western-oriented Fantis who embrace Western culture. Sekyi reserves his greatest scorn for the likes of Mrs. Brofusem, who, in her not-quite-complete assimilation into the colonizer's culture, consistently misappropriates its most unseemly aspects. Sekyi seems to advocate a tempered modernity. A reading of the play raises questions about what Sekyi sees as inappropriate modernity. It is clear that Sekyi and *The Blinkards* in particular are critical manifestations of an important era of West African history.

Further Reading

Langley, J.A. "Biography of W.E.G. (Kobina) Sekyi of Ghana, 1852–1956." (forthcoming).

——. "William Esuman-Gwira Sekyi (Kobina Sekyi) of Ghana (1892–1956): Theory of Politics, Development and Cultural Identity." *Tinabantu (Journal of African National Affairs)* 1, no. 1 (2002): 81–103.

——, and Henry van Hein Sekyi. "Colonialism, Culture, and Development: The Political Thought of Kobina Sekyi of Ghana, 1892–1956." (forthcoming article).

Saint-André Utudjian, Eliane. "Uses and Misuses of English in *The Blinkards* by Kobina Sekyi." *Commonwealth Essays and Studies* 20, no. 1 (1997): 23–31.

Sellassie, Sahle (1936–)

An Ethiopian novelist, Sellassie was born in Wardena, Ethiopia, and educated in Ethiopia and at the University of Aix-Marseilles, France, and the University of California. His literary career began with *Shinega's Village: Scenes of Ethiopian Life* (1964), a fictionalized recollection of Ethiopian life during the 1940s, which was translated from Chaha, an Amharic dialect, into English. *The Afersata* (1969), his first novel in English, centers on an investigation by traditional collective means into the burning of a villager's hut. *Warrior King* (1974), a historical novel, is about Emperor Tewodros II, the nineteenth-century bandit who became an emperor. In *Firebrands* (1979) a man struggles to resist the corruption all around him in a society slowly crumbling during the reign of Haile Sellassie Mariam. Sellassie's novels describe the sociological realities of the lives of the urban elite and the rural poor in Ethiopia.

Selormey, Francis (1927–88)

A Ghanaian novelist, Selormey was born in a seaside village near Keta in what was then Gold Coast and was educated at a Roman Catholic primary school in his home area, St. Augustine's College, Cape Coast, the University of Ghana, Legon, where he studied physical education, and in Germany. He was chief physical education instructor at St. Francis Teacher Training College and later became the senior sports administrator in the Volta Region. He turned to writing initially as an avocation. In his autobiographical first novel, *The Narrow Path* (1966), a boy grows up to learn that his Christian father's harsh behavior toward him was a mark of his love. He also wrote two film scripts: "Towards a United Africa" and "The Great Lake," about

Ghana's Volta Lake. His patriotism and deep interest in African unity also influence some of his works.

Sembene Ousmane (1923–)

Pioneering Senegalese writer and filmmaker Sembene was born in Ziguinchor, in the southern Casamance region of Senegal, then French West Africa. Recently he requested a preference to be known simply as Sembene. His family was of the coastal Lebou branch of the Wolof people, and of the Muslim faith. As a boy, he was influenced by his maternal uncle, an Islamic scholar, and attended Koranic schools in the Casamance. At age twelve he traveled north to Dakar to attend French schools there, but dropped out after two years, turning to an apprenticeship in masonry, further Islamic engagements, immersion in traditional culture, fledgling union activity, and local theater. In 1942 he joined the French colonial military and fought in both Europe and Africa during World War II. Demobilized in 1946, he participated in the 1947–48 Dakar-Niger railway workers' strike against the French. In 1948 he left again for Europe, and he did not return for thirteen years. Though principally resident in France, he also traveled to Denmark, the USSR, China, North Vietnam, and elsewhere during this time.

Sembene's artistic career began in the early 1950s when he began writing poetry for French working-class periodicals. His first novel, *Le Docker noir* (*The **Black Docker**,* 1987), appeared in 1956 and describes the difficult life of African workers in the large French port city of Marseilles based on his own experience. His next novel, *O pays, mon beau peuple* (1988) tells a classic story of a young man who returns to Senegal after a stay in France and meets great difficulty. *Les Bouts de bois de Dieu* (**God's Bits of Wood**, 1962), appeared in 1960 and made him famous as one of Africa's most important writers. A realist historical novel, *Les Bouts de bois de Dieu,*

is a fictionalized account of the rail workers' strike in which Sembene took part. On his return to Africa in 1961 he realized how little impact the European-language literature he was writing had on the African populace. As a result he moved into film. Following a year of study at the Gorky studios in Moscow, Sembene released his first two films—*L'Empire Sonhrai* and *Borom Sarret*—in 1964, inaugurating a period of productivity in both literature and film that has continued for three decades. By 1997, Sembene had published several novels or novella collections and produced eleven films, the most important of which include the novel *Le Mandat* (1965; *The Money Order,* 1972), which was made into the film *Mandabi* (1968); another novel, *Xala* (1974; trans. 1976), made into a film with the same name (1975); and the film *Camp de Thiaroye* (1989). His work has also been anthologized in *Themes in African Literature in French,* edited by Sam Ade Ojo (2000), and he has been interviewed by Jared Rapfogel and Richard Porton in "The Power of Female Solidarity: An Interview with Ousmane Sembene," an article from the journal *Cineaste* (December 2004).

Sembene shifts from epics of nineteenth-century Islamic intrigue (the film *Ceddo,* 1976) to exposés of French colonial history (*Camp de Thiaroye;* the 1976 film *Emitai*) to tragic or savage depictions of postcolonial life (*Xala;* the 1981 novel *Le Dernier de l'empire; The Last of Empire,* 1983). His work is persistently committed to justice. Ordinary men and notably, throughout his work, women are depicted as heroic. His films are shot most often in the Wolof or Diola languages, with subtitles in French. Recent productions by Sembene include *L'heroisme au quotidian* (1999) and *Moolaadé* ("Protection," 2004). In addition, *Mandabi* (1970), *Xala* (1974), and *Black Girl* (1966) were all released on DVD in 2005. His film *Moolaadé* (2004) won the Philadelphia Liberty Bell Prize, the American Association of Film Critics—Best

Foreign Film of the Year, the Special Prize at the Marrakech Film Festival, Un Certain Regard Prize at Cannes, and the Fespaco Ministry of Health Prize.

Sembene's works have received much critical attention and are frequently taught in both English and French. *God's Bits of Wood* is widely regarded as one of the great rallying resistance novels of Africa's late colonial era. Here and in his other novels, he is seen as a narrator of the people, an inheritor of the *griots* (or traditional storytellers) who he strives to honor. Sembene is committed to social justice, resistance against both colonialism and neo-colonialism, and to African popular audiences. That he has produced novels and films with such commitment at the same time as he has maintained the highest artistic standards will ensure him an honored place in African literature and culture for many generations to come. In 2005 he was honored with a Lifetime Achievement Award at the Chicago International Film Festival, and the "Spirit of Saint-Louis" Prize awarded by the Washington, DC–based Human Rights Watch Group.

Senghor, L(eopold) S(edar) (1906–2001)

Senegalese poet, politician, and polemicist first of negritude and later *la francophonie.* Born in the coastal town of Joal, Senegal, he came from a relatively wealthy family of mercantile Christians belonging to the Serer tribe. He was educated at mission schools and later at the Sorbonne. He passed the *agrégation* in 1935 and taught until 1939, when he was called up. He was imprisoned by the Germans in 1940 but released two years later because of ill health. He entered Senegalese politics at the end of the war and in 1947 founded the *Bloc démocratique sénégalais.* In 1960 he was elected first president of Senegal, a position he held until 1980. He was the most powerful politician in francophone West Africa and enormously influential within francophone associations worldwide.

Senghor is best known in literary terms for his early promotion of and theoretical reflection on negritude with the West Indian writer Aimé Césaire and other black students and émigrés whom he met in Paris. His poetry of negritude was among the earliest francophone African poetry to be read and highly appreciated in France. His *Anthologie de la nouvelle poésie nègre et malgache* (1948) was one of the earliest works to introduce black writing in French from the colonies to a wide audience. It was highly influential because it was introduced by Jean-Paul Sartre's powerful essay "Orphée noir." The essay introduced a range of ideas that formed the foundations of diverse literary critical approaches to Senghor's own writings and the work of other francophone African writers. The possibility of finding synthesis at different levels—political, philosophical, linguistic—permeates all his writings, particularly the several volumes of his essays, *Liberté,* and these ideas are most visible in his notion of *la civilisation de l'universel.* However, it is in the dissonances, the ruptures, and the tensions of his *oeuvre* that Senghor emerges at his most subtle, powerful, and important as a writer.

Senghor wrote his nostalgic first collection, *Chants d'ombre,* before World War II but it was only published in 1945. In *Hosties noires* (1948) Senghor turns his focus from a lost Africa to the denunciation of many aspects of the West. The experience of Senegalese soldiers, the *tirailleurs sénégalais,* is important in the collection *Nocturnes* (1961; *Nocturnes: Love Poems,* 1969), which combines the personal and the public. Senghor's knowledge of oral traditions and of Wolof, Serer, Bambara, and Peuhl are most important in *Éthiopiques* (1956). His later collections, *Lettres d'hivernage* (1973) and *Élégies majeures* (1979), are more intellectual and touch on love, sexuality, and eroticism. Senghor's prose writings have aroused hostility from critics such as Marcien Towa

(*Essai sur la promblématique philosophique dans l'Afrique actuelle,* 1971 and *LS. Senghor: Négritude ou servitude?,* 1971), Stanilas Adotevi (*Négritude et négrologues,* 1972), and René Depestre (*Bonjour et adieu . . . la négritude,* 1980). Other commentators have sought to evaluate Senghor's negritude within a broader historical context (P. Hountondji, *Sur la philosophie africaine,* 1977) and argue that negritude was a necessary, if limited, counterideology at a moment when colonial structures needed to be challenged both intellectually and politically.

Further Reading

Harney, Elizabeth. *Senghor's Shadow: Art, Politics, and the Avant-Garde in Senegal, 1960–1995.* Objects/Histories. Durham, NC: Duke University Press, 2004.

Schwab, Peter. *Designing West Africa: Prelude to 21st Century Calamity.* London: Palgrave, 2004.

[Senghor, Léopold Sédar.] *Léopold Sédar Senghor et la Revue Presence Africaine.* Paris: Presence Africain Editions, 2001.

Sepamla, Sipho (Sydney) (1932–)

South African poet and novelist Sepamla was born in West Rand Consolidated Mines Township outside Krugersdorp and trained as a teacher at Pretoria Normal College. He has published six collections of poetry, ending with *Selected Works* (1984) and *From Gorée to Soweto* (1988), and several novels, including *The Root Is One* (1979), *A Ride on the Whirlwind* (1981) and *Rainbow Journey* (1996). In 1976 he was co-recipient (with Lionel **Abrahams**) of the Pringle Award and in 1985 received the Order of Arts and Literature from France. His achievement is not limited to his work as a writer; he has been an active encourager of art and culture for blacks in South Africa.

The philosophy of **Black Consciousness** awoke Sepamla's creative energies. He published *Hurry up to It!* (1975), a poetry collection, at about the same time as similar collections by Mongane **Serote** and Mafika **Gwala**, but his use of irony and satire set his poetry apart. His poems frequently include a combination of English, Afrikaans, and African languages to form a *tsotsi-taal* (township slang). As a novelist, he has explored what it means to be black in South Africa in an iconoclastic fashion, increasingly articulating his regret at the loss of community and respect for elders that has occurred since 1976. His work is also included in such anthologies as Stephen Grey's *Free-lancers and Literary Biography in South Africa* (1999). In 1978 Sepamla was instrumental in establishing the Federated Union of Black Artists (FUBA) Arts Centre, now known as the Fuba Academy of Arts. He briefly revived and edited the literary magazine *The Classic* under the title *New Classic,* and was editor of the theater magazine *S'ketsh'.* More recently he has served on the Arts and Culture Task Group, a think tank that advises government on artistic and cultural issues.

Seremba, George (1957–)

A playwright, Seremba was born in Kampala, Uganda, and educated in Buganda Province and at Makerere University. He was left for dead by soldiers loyal to Milton Obote. Seremba miraculously survived his execution and escaped to Kenya. He then lived in Canada for many years (beginning in 1984) and currently lives in Dublin, Ireland, after having acquired a PhD in Drama at the Samuel Beckett Centre in Trinity College. His play, *Come Good Rain* (1993), first produced in Toronto in 1992, reenacts his virtual execution and survival, telling the story of Nsimb'egwire, the girl of Bugandan folktale who is buried alive by her jealous stepmother. Seremba is also co-editor of *Beyond the Pale* (1996), an anthology of dramatic writing, and has been honored with a nomination in the Best Actor category of the ESB/Irish Times Theatre Awards (2005), as well as nominated for Best Male Performer in the ESB Dublin Fringe Festival (2004). His recently staged productions include *Come Good Rain* at the Cairde Summer Festival in Ireland (2005), and he acted in a production of Athol Fugard's play *Master Harold and the Boys* in Glór, Ireland (2005).

Serote, Mongane Wally (1944–)

A South African poet, Serote was born in Sophiatown but brought up in Alexandra, a black township on the north side of Johannesburg. After he left school he worked as a journalist and became an active participant in the cultural and political struggle against **apartheid**. In 1969 he was detained without trial for nine months. Four years later he won the Ingrid Jonker Prize for his first volume of poetry. In 1974 he went to the United States, where he won a master's degree in creative writing at Columbia University. He then returned to southern Africa and became one of the leading members of the exile community in Botswana. By this time his work was well known and admired in progressive literary circles within South Africa, and in 1983 he won the Ad. Donker Prize. In 1986 he moved to London, where he worked and traveled under the ANC's Department of Arts and Culture. He returned to South Africa in 1990, shortly after the unbanning of the liberation movements. In the first democratic election, in April 1994, he became an ANC Member of Parliament and he chairs the Parliamentary Committee on Arts, Culture, Science, and Technology. Serote is currently the CEO and Executive Chairperson of Freedom Park, a national heritage site in Pretoria (2005). He is also the Chairperson of the Parliamentary Portfolio of Art, Culture, Science and Technology, as well as the Chairperson of the Indigenous Knowledge Systems Secretariat. He was honored with the Pablo Neruda Award from the Chilean government in 2004.

Serote was one of a group of black poets who began to write and publish in the late 1960s and early 1970s. In his poems Serote succeeds in creating a new tone in South African poetry: part anger, part grief and despair, part yearning, and part quiet determination. While the apartheid regime lasted, Serote's poems evoked and defined both the outrage and a possible way to confront it. His first two volumes, *Yakhal'inkomo* (1972) and *Tsetlo* (1974), consist mainly of short lyrics, but *No Baby Must Weep* (1975) is a single poem of nearly sixty pages. The theme of personal fulfillment within an experience of true community is proposed in the long title poem of *Behold Mama, Flowers* (1978). His next two collections, *The Night Keeps Winking* (1982) and, another long poem, *A Tough Tale* (1987), were written during the period in which pressure on the South African regime was being intensified. Serote's tenth title is *History Is the Home Address* (2004). It is written in the form of a conversation between lovers, and examines the relationship between ancestry and African identity. He has produced three more long poems: *Third World Express* (1992), for which he won a Noma Award, *Come and Hope with Me* (1994), and *Freedom Lament and Song* (1997). In these poems he confronts some of the promises and dangers of a social order that is in a state of vigorous transition. In 1981 Serote published a novel, *To Every Birth Its Blood*. Written over a period of six years, it provides a self-conscious insight not only into life in a revolutionary society but also into the processes through which personal and political commitments develop. More recently he has written *Scatter the Ashes and Go* (2002), a novel about South Africans who return home only to feel out of place in a different country from the one they left behind; *Hyenas* (2001), about the African intellectual and a South African national identity; and *Gods of Our Time* (1999), which follows the later years of the liberation struggle in South Africa and the uncertain response of those who were experiencing them. He has also produced *Selected Poems* (1982) and a book of essays, *On the Horizon* (1990).

Further Reading

Pultz Moslund, Sten. *Making Use of History in New South African Fiction: Historical Perspectives in Three Post-Apartheid Novels.* Copenhagen: Museum Tusculanum, 2003.

Seruma, Eneriko (1944–)
(pseudonym of Henry S. Kimbugwe)

Ugandan novelist and short-story writer. Born in Uganda and educated in the United States, Seruma was very active in the East African literary world in the late 1960s and the 1970s. He was a public relations officer for the East African Publishing House, wrote short stories and poems for *Ghala, Busara, Zuka,* and *Transition* literary magazines, and is also included in the anthology *Half a Day and Other Stories: An Anthology of Short Stories from North Eastern and Eastern Africa* (2004), and in Simon Gikandi's *Encyclopedia of African Literature* (2002). He is an award winner of the East African Literature Bureau's and Deutsche Welle's creative writing competitions. The title of *The Experience* (1970) refers to "the impossible life of a black man in a white world" in America, and the short stories in *The Heart Seller* (1971) portray human characters and situations in Africa and America.

Serumaga, Robert (1939–80)

A Ugandan playwright and novelist, Serumaga attended Makerere University, Uganda, and Trinity College, Dublin, where he received a master's degree in economics. He was involved in drama at the BBC before returning to Uganda in 1966 to set up his own semiprofessional theater company, Theatre Limited. The Serumaga Foundation (established by Serumaga's children) works to promote his literary works and his life struggles along with self-sufficiency to struggling American communities. His novel *Return to the Shadows* (1969) deals with political and social upheaval in an African state, as the main character becomes involved in a political coup. Serumaga's reputation as a writer rests mainly on his plays, which include *The Elephants* (1971), *A Play* (1968), and *Majangwa* (1974). Most of his work shows his preoccupation with social and political change at the national level, as in *Return to the Shadows,* and at the interpersonal level in *The Elephants.* Serumaga was arrested in 1979 for allegedly attempting to overthrow the government of Idi Amin; he was later minister of commerce in Okello's government.

Shaihu Umar (1967)

A novel by Abubakar Tafawa Balewa, translated from the Hausa (*Shaihu Umar,* 1934). Abubakar Tafawa was the first prime minister of Nigeria from 1957–66. This is a historical novel, set in a period of unrest. The hero is an ideal character who exhibits traditional Islamic social values. This ideal morality also reflects the themes in Hausa poetry from the nineteenth century, and the Hausa concept of the good man. The novel was adapted for the stage in 1975.

Sibenke, Ben (1945–)

A Zimbabwean playwright, Sibenke was born in the midlands near Gweru in what was then Rhodesia and educated at Cyrene Mission School and Mutare Teacher Training College. Known also as a director and actor, he founded the Mashonaland Art, Drama, and Cultural Association in 1978 and the People's Theatre Company in 1982, and is deeply involved in the activities of the National Theatre Organization as a resource person on acting, writing, and directing. His first publication, *My Uncle Grey Bhonzo* (1982), originally written in Shona in 1974, won a National Theatre Award for promising comedies, while the playwright himself won the Bell Award for both acting and directing the same play. Other plays have been produced on stage, on radio, and on Zimbabwe television, including *Dr. Manzuma and the Vipers* and a number of plays in Shona. Sibenke's comedies are informed by traditional African values that are increasingly threatened by Western influences. Beneath the comedy, however, is a serious attempt to ascertain what the human character amounts to in life.

Simbi and the Satyr of the Dark Jungle (1955)

A novel by Amos **Tutuola**. The title character leaves the safety of her home to search for her kidnapped friends in this novel. An Ifa priest helps her get kidnapped herself, and she begins an adventure that includes enslavement, near death, marriage, the death of her children, and a number of battles with a satyr. She finally finds her kidnapped friends and returns to safety.

Sirens Knuckles Boots (1963)

Poems by Dennis **Brutus**. The poems in this collection convey a message of survival in the face of fear. The title recalls the fear of the police that the black or mixed-race South African during apartheid experiences. These images of fear are juxtaposed against ones of human compassion, the melancholy of exile, and the strength of survival.

Sithole, Ndabaningi. *See* Biography and Autobiography; Censorship

Sixth Day, The (1960)

A novel by Andrée **Chedid**, translated from the French (*Le Sixiéme jour*, 1960). This novel depicts a cholera epidemic in Cairo from the point of view of a washerwoman who attempts to hide her sick grandson for the critical six days of the disease. She does not want him to be taken to the city hospitals, where the dead are buried in mass graves and are not given traditional rites.

Sizwe Bansi Is Dead (1972)

A play by Athol **Fugard**. This play is set in a photographic studio run by Styles, who is making a long speech about how he can make images of people more attractive than they are in reality when he is interrupted by Sizwe Bansi posing as Robert Zwelinzima—a dead man who he and his friend Bantu found and whose passbook Sizwe takes to assume his identity. The implications for Sizwe's own identity, and the emphasis on the control of identity through the passbook and pass number system are the focus of the play. The play opened in Cape Town and then toured using private spaces to avoid the authorities, who saw it as subversive.

Slater, Francis Carey (1876–1958)

South African poet and anthologist. His first volume of poems, *Footpaths thro' the Veld* (1905), and a collection of stories, *The Sunburnt South* (1908), reflected the colonial verse expectations of the period. However, *The Karroo and Other Poems* (1924) revealed a more individual voice and a less Eurocentric perspective, and in 1925 he published the first major anthology of South African poetry, *The Centenary Book of South African Verse,* an authoritative collection that drew attention to a body of poetry comparable with that produced in other Commonwealth countries. Slater's successful long poem *Drought: A South African Parable* (1929) depicts physical desolation and spiritual drought caused by hatred. A second collection of stories, *The Secret Veld* (1930), was followed by his best volume of verse, *Dark Folk and Other Poems* (1935), in which he vividly evocates African life. *The Trek* (1938) is an epic poem on the Dutch voortrekkers that provides vignettes of Boer leaders. In 1945 he published a revised, updated anthology, the *New Centenary Book of South African Verse,* and in 1949 his last volume of poems, *Veld Patriarch and Other Poems.* Oxford University Press published a selection of his poetry in 1947, and in 1954 he produced an autobiography titled *Settler's Heritage.* He devoted his last years to a definitive edition, *The Collected Poems of Francis Carey Slater* (1957).

Further Reading

MacKenzie, Craig. *The Oral-style South African Short Story in English. A. W. Drayson to H. C. Bosman.* Cross/Cultures 37. Amsterdam: Rodopi Bv Editions, 1999.

Smith, Pauline (Janet) (1882–1959)

South African short-story writer and novelist. Born in Oudtshoorn in the Little Karoo region of the Cape, Pauline Smith enjoyed the beauty of the Karoo landscape and the kindness of the Dutch-Afrikaans farmers who made a deep impression on her. To console herself after the sudden death of her father, she began writing the sketches, stories, and poems based on her childhood memories that were later to be published as *Platkops Children* (1935). After settling with her mother and sister in Britain she began contributing stories and sketches of Scottish life to the *Evening Gazette* and *Aberdeen Free Press* under the name Janet Tamsen (1902–5). During her first return visit to South Africa with her mother in 1905, she kept a diary recording the places they revisited, as well as local stories, customs, and idiom of the Little Karoo and its people. After a chance meeting in 1909 the novelist Arnold Bennett, impressed by her "Platkops" sketches, became her mentor and for the next twenty-two years he encouraged and sometimes bullied her into drawing more deeply on her experience of and insight into the lives of the people of the Little Karoo. The success of *The Little Karoo* (1925) (it went into a fourth impression in the first year) encouraged her to complete a novel she had been working on, *The Beadle* (1926). *The Beadle* is set in Aangenaam Valley and explores the themes of self-righteousness and forgiveness.

During the next five years Smith wrote several more stories, two of them included in a new edition of *The Little Karoo* published in 1930, paid return visits to South Africa, and signed a contract for a new novel, the never-to-be-completed "Winter Sacrifice." After Bennett's death in 1931 she set about writing a memoir, *A.B. . . . "A Minor Marginal Note"* (1933), which not only pays tribute to Bennett but also offers a surprisingly objective and often wryly amusing account of their friendship. His death, however, robbed her of a prime motivating force. She made little progress with her novel, and her last major publication was *Platkops Children*. Yet her work won increasing recognition, and in the year before her death William **Plomer** and Roy Macnab presented her with an illuminated scroll signed by twenty-five South African writers as a tribute to her art. Although she produced only two major works, *The Beadle* and *The Little Karoo*, they have both remained in print as classics of South African prose. Recently, Pauline Smith's journal has been published under the title *Secret Fire: The 1913–14 South African Journal of Pauline Smith* (1997).

So Long a Letter (1981)

A novel by Mariama **BÂ**, translated from the French (*Une si longue letter*, 1979). BÂ critiques Senegalese Islamic society's treatment of women in this epistolary novel. The narrative is composed of a letter from the newly widowed Ramatoulaye to her childhood friend Aissatou. The subject of the narrative is the oppression that the women encountered in their polygamous marriages, and the suffering they endured. BÂ treats the roles of the women in their communities and Aissatou's choice to divorce her husband from a powerfully internal perspective.

Sofola, Zulu (1935–95)

Playwright, born to Igbo/Edo parents in Delta State, Nigeria. She began primary school in Nigeria and completed high school and university in the United States. Her first degree in English was from the Virginia Union Baptist Seminary in Nashville, Tennessee, and she later studied Drama at the Catholic University of America in Washington, DC. She then returned to Nigeria to teach at the University of Ilorin, and appeared several times on television and radio in Nigeria as a critic and theater practitioner with a deep commitment to Nigerian culture and values. She published criticism and opinion on African society and drama in journals in Africa, Europe, and America.

Sofola's plays are widely read and discussed in Nigeria, and a few often make the list of texts for the West African Examinations Council. Her plays view the past not in idyllic terms but as a basis upon which the present can be revised. They depict Nigeria's culturally diverse society, and draw from the traditional African roots of myth and ritual, as well as classical Western drama. The following of Sofola's plays have received the most attention: *The Disturbed Peace of Christmas* (1971), *Wedlock of the Gods* (1972), *The Sweet Trap* (1977), *The Deer and the Hunter's Pearl* (1969), *King Emene* (1974), *The Wizard of Law* (1975), and *Old Wines Are Tasty* (1981). Sofola has also been included in such anthologies as the 2004 (No. 24) volume of *African Literature Today* titled "New Women's Writing in African Literature." Sofola's dramatic practice focused on cultural conflict, human quirks, and social failings rather than more epic themes. Even in issues of gender, which animate many female African writers and critics, she is restrained and prefers to see such issues as part of a complex of temporary, transitional problems to be dealt with in Africa's contact with the West.

Further Reading

Kolawole, Mary Ebun Modupe. *Zulu Sofola: Her Life and Her Works.* Ibadan: Caltop Publishers, 1999.

Son of Woman (1971)

A novel by Charles **Mangua**. Mangua portrays the son of a Nairobi prostitute as he moves to Makerere, graduates, enters the civil service, and then turns to tax evasion and is imprisoned. He and his criminal girlfriend are married and plan to reform at the end of the novel.

Song of Lawino (1966)

A long poem by **Okot p'Bitek**. This is a lament in the voice of Lawino, whose Westernized husband Ocol has left her for a younger woman. Lawino is not only angry with Ocol, but also the new education, Christianity, and social trends in Uganda that drew him away from tradition. She also praises the Acoli traditions that Ocol rejects, and it is clear that he is the subject of p'Bitek's satire.

Sons and Daughters (1964)

A play by Joe **de Graft** that emphasizes jobs in the arts as a real alternative to the careers in law, engineering, and medicine that the Ghanan middle classes were favoring at the period. The play was a result of de Graft's work at Mfantsipim School in the Cape Coast, and it is a well-structured and conventional play.

Sony Labou Tansi (1947–95)

A Congolese novelist and playwright, Sony Labou Tansi was born in Zaïre (now Democratic Republic of Congo), where he spent part of his childhood. He studied at Brazzaville's École normale supérieure and taught English and French for some years before taking up employment with the Ministry of Culture. Made famous by the successes of the Rocado Zulu Theatre, a company he formed in 1979, he achieved critical and popular acclaim with numerous influential plays and novels. His plays include *Conscience de tracteur* (1979), *La Parenthèse de sang* (1981; *Parentheses of Blood, 1986)*, *Je soussigé cardiaque* (1981), *Antoine m'a vendu son destin* (1986), *Moi, veuve de l'empire* (1987), *Qui a mangé Madame d'Avoine Berghota?* (1989), and *Une chouette petite vie bien osée* (1992).

Based on universal themes yet going to the heart of the Congolese ambience, many of his plays were popular in Africa as well as Europe, where he often toured. He is also well known for his novels, which are challenging in their narrative style and content and always critical of the "barbaric attitude of man against man." They include *La Vie et demie* (1979), *L'État honteux* (1981), *L'Antépeuple* (1983; *The Antipeople,* 1988), *Les Sept solitudes de Lorsa Lopez* (1985; *The Seven Solitudes of Lorsa Lopez,* 1995), and *Les Yeux du volcan* (1988). His work has earned many literary awards and is included in the anthology *Nation-Building, Propaganda, and Literature in Francophone Africa* (2002).

Sowande, Bode (1948–)

Nigerian playwright and novelist. Born to Egba parents, Sowande was educated at Government College, Ibadan, and the Universities of Ife, Nigeria, and Sheffield, UK. A prolific author of novels, television and radio scripts, and newspaper articles as well as dramas, he has also kept alive a theater company, Odu Themes. He is a member of the Directors' Lab, Lincoln Center Theater, New York, and was a member of delegation of the Association of Nigerian Authors (ANA) in 1999. His work draws mostly on his Yoruba background. He brings cultures together in a Yoruba version of Moliere's *The Miser,* a drama about the mythological figure of Mammywater, and in *Ajantala-Pinocchio,* a study of two rebellious children, which opened in Italy in 1992. His reputation rests principally on two collections of plays, *Farewell to Babylon and Other Plays* (1979) and *Flamingo and Other Plays* (1986). Of the seven plays in the two collections, three—*The Night Before, Farewell to Babylon,* and *Flamingo*—comprise a trilogy that spans the period between Sowande's own undergraduate years and the late 1970s and scrutinizes the problems of living in Nigeria. Another, *Sanctus for Women,* written while he was a graduate student at Sheffield,

represents a deliberate attempt to use Yoruba folklore and mythology as a source for drama. Sowande's latest play, titled *Superleaf* (2004), combines mainstream theater technique with theater for development technique, and deals with herbal knowledge and genetic medicine to tackle issues regarding the search for a cure for hard-to-cure-diseases that plague humanity. He has also worked on a documentary film about sickle cell anemia (2003) in collaboration with a British company, and directed *Bandit and Beggars* (2001). Sowande recently produced *FOR AFRICA 05,* for which he brought out a company to work with the royal Court Young People's Theatre on an Amos Tutuola play. In his writing Sowande has responded to the increasing politicization of his society by repeatedly examining the problems faced by those who attempt to uphold humane values and high principles in a hostile environment.

Soyinka, Wole (1934–)

Nigerian playwright, poet, novelist, and essayist. The first African to be awarded the Nobel Prize (1986), Soyinka is a prolific writer whose work draws freely upon European models and is at the same time deeply rooted in Yoruba cultural practice. Born near Abeokuta, in southwestern Nigeria, Soyinka was educated at the universities of Ibadan and at Leeds in the UK. Several early plays, including *The Lion and the Jewel,* were written while he was still in Britain, where, between 1957 and 1959, he worked as playreader at the Royal Court Theatre, London. He returned to Nigeria in 1960, where he established two theater groups in succession, the 1960 Masks and Orisun Theatre Company, and taught at the universities of Ibadan, Ife (now Obafemi Awolowo), and Lagos.

In the mid-1960s, Soyinka's work began to reflect the sociocultural complexity and political contradictions of his country. The anxieties expressed in his independence play *A **Dance of the Forests*** (1963) are further developed in *The Road* (1965) and *Kongi's Harvest* (1967), in the poems of *Idanre and Other Poems* (1967), and in a documentary novel, *The Interpreters* (1965). He was imprisoned by Nigeria's military government for twenty-seven months between 1967 and 1969 during the Nigeria-Biafra war. The causes and prosecution of the war are investigated in the novel *Season of Anomy* (1973), in the poems in *A Shuttle in the Crypt* (1971), and in his play *Madmen and Specialists* (1971). *Death and the King's Horseman* is a play based on an incident in Nigeria's colonial history and deals with the individual and collective apprehension of death and the structure of cultural consciousness. Often highly successful in production (Chicago and Washington, 1979; Manchester, UK, 1990), this play has also served as a focal point for criticism of Soyinka's idealism and view of history, while his *Opera Wonyosi* (1981) is a musical satire based on Brecht's *The Threepenny Opera*, and vehemently attacks Africa's military dictators. In 1978 he founded the University of Ife Guerrilla Theatre Unit and in 1983 produced the satirical record *Unlimited Liability Company,* both examples of his use of theater and music for specific political goals. Through the 1980s his high profile in Nigeria was augmented by his much-publicized chairship of a Road Safety Corps and by virulent attacks on his work by critics such as **Chinweizu**. Retiring from full-time academic life in 1985 he continued to work in many literary genres. An active opponent of military dictatorship, in November 1994 he left Nigeria clandestinely after the seizure of his passport by the authorities.

Much of Soyinka's early life is described in three autobiographical works. *Aké* explores his childhood, with particular emphasis on the child's apprehension of the community around him. *Ibadan: The Penkelemes Years, a Memoir 1946–65* (1994) carries the story forward to events immediately preceding the civil war, and in the preface he identifies

his fear for the Nigerian state in the 1990s as one reason he wrote the book. *The Man Died* (1972) is a powerful account of his war internment. The essay collection *Art, Dialogue and Outrage* (1988) quarrels with other authors, but also offers fresh insight, while *Myth, Literature and the African World* (1976) theorizes African aesthetics and investigates performance in African theater in relation to central aspects of Yoruba thought. Here he focuses especially on the god Ogun, whose perilous embodiment of contradiction provides a key reference point in his apprehension of creative energy, and on the Yoruba concept of transition points in the life-death continuum. Some of his plays have been collected in *Contemporary African Plays,* which also contains plays by Percy Mtwa and Ama Aidoo (1999).

Soyinka's novels have been relatively neglected. Both *The Interpreters* and *Season of Anomy* suffer from being thematically grounded in overloaded symbolic structures. Yet *The Interpreters* also gives a startlingly concrete picture of life in southwestern Nigeria in the early 1960s. *Isarà: A Voyage Around "Essay"* (1983) has been classified as both a novel and a **biography**. Much more accessible than the first two novels, it is an affectionate account of the circle of friends that gathered around Soyinka's father from the 1920s to the 1940s. Between 1967 and 1989 Soyinka published four volumes of poetry (his best-known poem, the wryly satirical "Telephone Conversation," remains uncollected). The earlier poetry ranges in language and form from the precision and clarity of "Three Millet Stalks" (in *A Shuttle in the Crypt*) to the extreme complexity of the title poem of *Idanre and Other Poems,* in which he explores Yoruba myth, his own absorption in it, and its bearing on Nigeria's contemporary sociopolitical realities. *Ogun Abibiman* (1976) is his longest single poem, a five-hundred-line exploration of the nature and significance for contemporary Africa of two figures, the Yoruba god Ogun and the nineteenth-century Zulu emperor Shaka. The poem's political inspiration is stated in a prefatory note applauding Mozambican leader Samora Machel's declaration of hostilities toward white-ruled Rhodesia. The opening poems in *Mandela's Earth and Other Poems* (1988) address the condition of South Africa in what were to be the last years of **apartheid**; this wide-ranging collection also includes "Cremation of a Wormy Caryatid," a meditation on the historical fortunes of Yoruba culture. Recent works of poetry are *Samarkand and Other Markets I Have Known* (2002) and *Selected Poems: A Shuttle in the Crypt, Idanre, Mandela's Earth* (2002). Soyinka has also been included in anthologies such as *Under African Skies* (1997).

By the mid-1990s Soyinka had published seventeen individual plays as well as a collection of revue sketches, *Before the Blackout* (1971), while the later satirical sketches that were collectively titled "Priority Projects" remain unpublished. The most widely performed of the plays are those that are naturalistic in idiom, including the comedies *The **Trials of Brother Jero*** and *The Lion and the Jewel* (both 1963). *The Trials of Brother Jero,* like *Requiem for a Futurologist* (1985), satirizes religious charlatanism. In other plays he displays the brutal tyrannies of dictatorship, such as in *Kongi's Harvest, Opera Wonyosi, A Play of Giants* (1984), and *From Zia, with Love* (1992). *The Bacchae of Euripides* (1973) has been neglected. *A Dance of the Forests* has remained virtually unstaged since its 1960 Lagos première but has an intriguing dramatic scenario. *The **Strong Bread*** (1963) is a key text in understanding Soyinka's romantic projection of the isolated visionary hero. Most remarkable of all is *The Road,* premiered to enthusiastic recognition in London in 1965. Soyinka's most recent play, *King Baabu* (2002), is a satirical work concerning the dictatorial political regimes of Africa. Soyinka is also the author of numerous nonfiction works, among which are *Climate of Fear: The Quest for Dignity in a Dehumanized World* (2005), *Salutation to the Gut* (2003), *The Deceptive Silence of Stolen Voices* (2003), *The Burden of Memory, the Muse of Forgiveness* (1999), and *The Seven Signposts of Existence: Knowledge, Honour, Justice and Other Virtues* (1999).

Further Reading

Akporji, Chii. *Figures in a Dance: The Theatre of W. B. Yeats and Wole Soyinka.* Trenton, NJ: Africa World Press, 2003.

Banjo, Ayo, ed. *Bola Ige. The Passage of a Modern Cicero.* Stony Brook, NY: Bookcraft, 2003.

Ebewo, Patrick. *Barbs: A Study of Satire in the Plays of Wole Soyinka.* Kampala, Uganda: JAN Publishing Centre, 2002.

George, Olakunle. *Relocating Agency: Modernity and African Letters.* Albany: State University of New York Press, 2003.

Ibadan Mesiogo. Stony Brook, NY: Edited by Bookcraft, 2001.

Jeyifo, Biodun. *Wole Soyinka: Politics, Poetics, and Postcolonialism.* Cambridge Studies in African and Caribbean Literature. Cambridge: Cambridge University Press, 2003.

Kwesi Kwaa Prah, ed. *WS: A Life in Full.* Stony Brook, NY: Bookcraft, 2004.

Lindfors, Bernth. *Blind Men and the Elephant: And Other Essays in Biographical Criticism.* Trenton, NJ: Africa World Press, 1999.

Okome, Onookome. *Ogun's Children: The Literature and Politics of Wole Soyinka since the Nobel.* Trenton, NJ: Africa World Press, 2004.

Soyinka,Wole, and Biodun Jeyifo. *Conversations with Wole Soyinka.* Literary Conversations Series. Jacksonville: University Press of Mississippi, 2001.

Sozaboy: A Novel in Rotten English
(1985)

A novel by Ken **Saro-Wiwa** about a "soldier-boy" or Sozaboy volunteer in the Biafran army who returns to his home of Kukana in search of his wife and mother. Saro-Wiwa created the recruit's dialogue out of a combination of his first language, Kana, standard and "broken" forms of English, and Nigerian Pidgin. This combination of languages represents the clash of voices in post–civil war Nigeria.

Sport of Nature, A (1987)

A novel by Nadine **Gordimer** about a rebellious young woman named Hillela who is sexually and politically transgressive. Her white South African middle-class family disowns her for her behavior, and Hillela ends up marrying a black South African liberationist in Ghana and later the president of the OAU. The liberated sexuality of Hillela is directly associated with the freedom of independence.

States of Emergency (1988)

A novel by André **Brink**. Brink considers the possibility of writing a love story during a state of emergency in this self-reflexive and metafictional novel. He writes of a writer who attempts the project, but who abandons it—unlike Brink, who both writes and publishes the experiment in the form of this novel.

Stone Country, The (1967)

A novel by Alex **La Guma**. The stone country in the title refers to the prison, which La Guma experienced firsthand due to his political activism. The prison system in La Guma's account mirrors the apartheid system in South Africa, and the class hierarchy based on race means that violence and anger prevail. La Guma offers hope in the character of one of the inmates who remains compassionate and wishes that there could be unity among the inmates in order to overturn the system.

Story of an African Farm, The (1883)

A novel by Olive **Schreiner**. This well-known early example of South African fiction written in English is set in the Karoo region of South Africa in the 1860s. It follows three children

as they grow up on a farm in the area, and its narrative incorporates mystical allegories based on biblical stories. It weaves colonial, feminist, political, philosophical, and religious discourse into its plot and narrative.

Strong Bread, The (1963)

A play by Wole Soyinka that depicts the conflict when a schoolteacher named Eman comes into a community and criticizes its traditions in favor of those from his home town. When the villagers kill him, there is the promise of change for them. It is a clear, direct play that explores larger issues through its very specific plot.

Sutherland, Efua T(heodora) (1924–96)

Ghanaian playwright. Born Efua Theodora Morgue at Cape Coast in the Central Region of Ghana, Sutherland received her early education at St. Monica's School and Training College and taught for five and a half years before proceeding to Homerton College, Cambridge University, where she obtained her bachelor's in education. She spent another year at the School of Oriental and African Studies, London, where she studied linguistics, African languages, and drama. She returned to Ghana, then the Gold Coast, where she taught at her old school, St. Monica's, at Fijai Secondary School, Secondi, and later at Achimota School. In 1954, she married William Sutherland, with whom she had three children. She was the organizing energy behind the establishment of the Ghana Society of Writers in 1957, the Ghana Experimental Theatre Company a year later, and *Okyeame*, a literary magazine, in 1959. With funds from the Rockefeller Foundation and the Arts Council of Ghana, she founded the Ghana Drama Studio in 1960. The studio became part of the University of Ghana, where it was housed in the Institute of African Studies.

Sutherland's keen interest in the welfare of children translated into numerous projects, including Children's Drama Development of Ghana. As a direct outcome of her efforts for children in Ghana, the government established the Ghana National Commission on Children, with Sutherland as its first chair. In addition to essays, articles, short stories, and poems, she has published extensively in the genre of drama. Her best-known plays include *Foriwa* (1967), *Edufa* (1967), a Ghanaian rendition of Euripides' *Alcestis,* and *The Marriage of Anansewa* (1975), a veiled satiric comment on the early postindependent leadership in Ghana under Kwame Nkrumah, and by extension Africa as a whole. Her other published work includes *You Swore an Oath* (1964), *Vulture! Vulture* (and *Tahinta)* (1968), *The Original Bob: The Story of Rob Johnson, Ghana's Ace Comedian* (1970), *Anansegoro: Story-telling Drama in Ghana* (1983), and *The Voice in the Forest* (1983). *The Roadmakers* (1961), a pictorial presentation of Ghanaian life with photographs by Willis Bell, is for children. She published another picture book for children, *Playtime in Africa,* the following year, also in conjunction with Willis Bell. Sutherland's work is also included in the anthology *Athenian Sun in an African Sky: Modern African Adaptations of Classical Greek Tragedy* (2001). Although she studied widely in and outside of Africa, Sutherland's drama seeks an audience among children and adults in Ghana, both literate and nonliterate. Trained in the folklore of the Akan people of Ghana, she acknowledged the oral roots of her art in her choice of drama as her medium of expression. Her pioneering work in Ghanaian drama and theater has undoubtedly been a major influence on other Ghanaian dramatists such as Ama Ata **Aidoo**, Patience Henaku Addo, and Joe **de Graft**.

Sweet and Sour Milk (1979)

The first novel in a trilogy by Nuruddin **Farah** titled *Variations on the Theme of an African Dictatorship.* It is followed by *Sardines* (1981) and *Close Sesame* (1983). *Sweet and Sour Milk* uses the genres of political thriller and detective novel to depict the totalitarian regime. The regime uses traditional forms like oral culture and the family to secure its power in these novels, and the domestic upholds the political oppression. The aging grandfather who heads up an anticolonial family in *Close Sesame* presents a nonthreatening patriarchal image, but he is uselessly sacrificed in an unsuccessful attempt to assassinate a General.

T

Taban Lo Liyong (ca. 1939–)

A Ugandan poet, critic, novelist, and short-story writer, Taban Lo Liyong was born of Ugandan parents in southern Sudan. He received his early education at Gulu High School and the Sir Samuel Baker School, and subsequently studied at a teachers' college in Uganda, at Howard University (BA), and at the University of Iowa, where he was the first African to receive the MFA degree in creative writing and where he cultivated his unconventional writing style. He has taught at several universities, including the University of Papua New Guinea, the University of Nairobi in Kenya, where he co-founded the Department of Literature with **Ngugi wa Thiong'o**, and Juba University in Khartoum, Sudan. A former cultural affairs director in southern Sudan, he teaches at the University of Venda in South Africa, and also currently holds the position of Director of the Es'kia Mphahlele Institute for African Studies at the University of Venda.

Taban's work assimilates oral traditions, conscious and unconscious integration of heterogeneous sources, fragmented utterances, and a prosaic diction with little or no regard for a coherent logical sequence.

Fixions and Other Stories (1969) is filled with Luo mythology and folktales, an example of his experimentation with the short story as genre, while *Meditations in Limbo* (1970) creates a persona who acts antithetically with his father. Both demonstrate his strong sense of commitment to the indigenous culture and oral tradition as a viable source of literary imagery. The poems in *Frantz Fanon's Uneven Ribs* (1971), *Another Nigger Dead* (1972), *Thirteen Offensives against Our Enemies* (1973), and *Ballads of Underdevelopment* (1976) employ contrast, paradox, irony, innuendo, repetition, humor, cradle song, gossip, and surprise. More recenly Taban has published *The New Trumpet* (2000), *Poems from Perth* (2001), *The Defence of Lawino by Jane Okot p'Bitek* (translated by Taban, 2001), and is included in the poetry anthology, *Uganda Poetry—Anthology* (2000). Echoes of other writers reverberate in his work, especially in some of the title poems. For example, "The Marriage of Black and White" recalls Blake's "The Marriage of Heaven and Hell," while "Telephone Conversation Number Two" echoes Wole **Soyinka**'s "Telephone Conversation," demonstrating his affinity with other writers and his ability as an experimental poet to borrow and adapt and move with the times.

Tahir, Ibrahim (1940–)

Nigerian novelist Tahir was born in Bauchi, Nigeria, and educated at King's College, Cambridge University, where he obtained undergraduate and graduate degrees in social anthropology. As a student in England he contributed to the Hausa program of the BBC's Africa Service in London. When he returned to Nigeria he taught sociology and became department head at Ahmadu Bello University, Zaria, and later worked toward the formation of the National Party of Nigeria. When the military intervened in 1983 he was among the politicians detained. His novel *The Last Imam* (1984), which he had drafted in the 1960s, was published while he was in detention. Tahir criticizes the conservatism of his Muslim society through the story of Imam Usman. Tahir has been engaged in business and political activities since his release from detention.

Tejani, Bahadur (1942–)

Poet, novelist, and short-story writer. Of Gujarati origin and born in Kenya, Tejani is Ugandan by nationality. He studied at Makerere and Cambridge universities and gained a PhD in African literature from the University of Nairobi. He is an Associate Professor at the State University of New York. The *Rape of Literature and Other Poems* (1969) is a response to the poet's meeting with his ancestral home of India. The novel *Day after Tomorrow* (1971) projects a picture of a harmonious East African society born out of a deliberate and voluntary attempt by the African and Asian communities to integrate. Some of Tejani's short stories are oriented toward the American world and its materialism and technology, revealing a continuing preoccupation with multiculturalism and a humanist vision.

Tell Freedom (1954)

Peter Abrahams's autobiography. Abrahams explains the political developments from the 1930s to the date of publication and their effect on his literary identity. He demonstrates how his political beliefs motivate his fiction, and follows the development of South Africa alongside his writing.

Themba, (Daniel Canodoise) Can (1924–68)

South African short-story writer. Themba was born in Marabastad, outside Pretoria, but was to spend most of his productive literary life in Sophiatown, near Johannesburg, before it was bulldozed under the provisions of the Group Areas Act. He received a first-class degree in English and a teacher's diploma at Fort Hare University College. In the 1950s he wrote for **Drum** magazine after having won its first short-story contest; later he wrote for *The Classic* and *Africa South,* as well as the *Golden City Post,* also a *Drum* publication. In 1966, while he was working as a teacher in Swaziland, he was declared a "statutory communist" and his work was banned in South Africa. Only in the 1980s did it become freely available with the publication of two collections, The **Will to Die** (1972) and The *World of Can Themba* (1985). The work *Isutu* was republished by Juta & Co. Ltd in 2001, and Themba was recently included in the anthology *Come Back Africa,* edited by Lionel Rogosin and Peter Davis (2004).

Most of his stories, modeled on the romance or thriller genres, reveal an acute understanding of how life for people of color had been dominated by the **apartheid** legislation of the 1950s. His writing of the 1960s reveals his despair and frustration over the difficulties of living life as an outcast in his own country. He increasingly relied on alcohol. Introspective pieces such as "Crepuscle," "The Will to Die," and "The Bottom of the Bottle" are evidence of a growing darkness of sentiment and style. He died of alcoholism in Swaziland.

Things Fall Apart (1958)
Chinua **Achebe**'s first novel. Achebe uses the story of the novel's hero, Okonkwo, to demonstrate how British colonial Christianity destroyed traditional Igbo society in Eastern Nigeria at the turn of the twentieth century. The steadfastness of the religious beliefs of the Igbo community are represented in Okonkwo, who stays true to his culture's values and is killed as a result.

Thomas, Gladys (1934–)
A South African poet and playwright, Thomas was born to a mixed-race family and has lived most of her life in Cape Town. She left school at fifteen to work in a clothing factory. In 1983 she attended the International Writing Program in Iowa City. Much of her work was banned because it was critical of **apartheid**, and when a production of hers was praised by the *World* in 1979, her three plays were banned and she was detained. That year she received Kwanzaa honors for "writing under oppressive conditions." When the community of Crossroads was bulldozed in 1986 to make room for a white suburb, she interviewed the dispossessed children and told their stories in *Children of Crossroads* (1986). She based *The Wynberg Seven* (1987) on her interviews with parents whose teenagers were taken into Pollsmoor Prison. Her work has been published in newspapers, journals, **anthologies**, including *Cry Rage* (1972) and *Exile Within* (1986), and privately. She has also published *Spotty Dog and Other Stories: Stories for and of South African Township Children* (ca. 1983) and a play, *Avalon Court (Vignettes of Life of the Coloured People on the Cape Flats of Cape Town)* (1992).

Through a Film Darkly (1970)
A play by Joe **de Graft**. The film of the title is meant to replace the glass in the biblical reference, and has to do with the play's exploration of perception and racism. Through this image of skewed perception, de Graft explores the consequences of hate and a lack of understanding between cultures.

Time of the Butcherbird (1979)
A novel by Alex **La Guma**. The image of the butcherbird—a bird that traditionally eats ticks off the bodies of cattle and horses, but that La Guma uses to indicate the need for the overthrow of Afrikaner Nationalism—pervades this story set in the South African countryside. The novel demonstrates the violent end ahead as the character of Shilling Murile kills a man whose ancestors seized land in the Karoo and an Englishman who represents the English support of apartheid.

Tlali, Miriam (1933–)

South African novelist, was the first black woman writer to publish a novel in English inside South Africa. She was born in Doornfontein, grew up in Sophiatown, and lives in Soweto. Although she studied at the University of the Witwatersrand and then at Roma University in Lesotho, financial difficulties forced her to leave before taking a degree. Her experiences as a bookkeeper at a Johannesburg furniture store with a large African clientele prompted her to write her first, largely autobiographical novel, **Muriel at Metropolitan**. Although completed in 1969, it was only finally published (in expurgated form to circumvent censorship) by Ravan Press in 1975. When Longman published an international version in 1979 based on her original manuscript, both versions were banned. Tlali's life has been a relentless struggle to fulfill what she sees as her role as a writer: to "conscientize the people" and to tell the truth as she sees it, undeterred by **censorship** or the constraints of custom and tradition. She has played an active role in encouraging writing by women, was a regular contributor to *Staffrider,* served on the board of Skotaville Press, and edits a literary magazine for women, *Straight Ahead International.* Her frequent visits overseas brought her into contact with other writers and gave her a space for her own writing. She writes in English because it is a uniting factor and enables her to reach a wide audience.

Amandla (1980) was a great success by South African publishing standards: five thousand copies were sold in a few weeks before it was banned. The novel is one of several by black South African writers reflecting the 1976 Soweto uprising. The central character, Pholoso, is a student leader who witnesses the shooting of a friend. He is arrested and tortured, but escapes and flees the country, leaving behind his girlfriend Felleng. Through the interweaving of a number of stories, the impact of events on the wider community is registered. Although Tlali has said that in the novel women are represented as "mothers and militants at the same time," their role still seems largely supportive. Beginning with its first issue in March 1978, Tlali contributed a regular column to *Staffrider* entitled "Soweto Speaking," in which ordinary people spoke about their lives. Two of these pieces, as well as three travelogs and a short story, were reprinted in *Mihloti* (1984). Her most important contribution to date is collection of short stories, **Footprints in the Quag** (1989, published internationally as *Soweto Stories*). *Between Two Worlds: Broadview Encore Edition* includes a new introduction by Tlali that describes the circumstances under which she wrote the work. Tlali's recent work increasingly foregrounds the experience of women and their struggle to determine their own lives.

Further Reading

Hunter, Eva. "Miriam Tlali." *Dictionary of Literary Biography: South African Writers,* ed. Paul Scalon. Boston: Gale Group, 2000, 445–49.

Tomorrow Left Us Yesterday (2004)

Short stories by Tayo Peter **Olafioye**. Subtitled "African Short Stories," this collection contains stories about characters from throughout the continent. The author expresses concern over a fading sense of humanity in the world, and posits a chance for recovery in the younger generations of Africans who can help turn the world away from ambivalence.

Trial and Other Stories, The (2005)

Short stories by Ifeoma **Okoye** about the plight of widowhood in Nigeria. Okoye vividly describes the suffering and resilience of a number of different widows, who overcome prejudices, barriers, and painful situations in these short stories.

Trial of Christopher Okigbo, The (1971)

A novel by Ali **Mazrui**. Interspersed with quotations from Okigbo's poems, this tale of a court trial in the afterlife called "After-Africa" emphasizes pan-African unity to explore the relationship between nationalism and art, and the consequences of one's actions and decisions after death. Okigbo never shows up in the novel, because his defense attorney is charged with miscalculation, and his prosecutor with impatience.

Trials of Brother Jero, The (1963)

A play by Wole Soyinka that satirizes the popular preachers of Nigeria through the character of Brother Jero. The play centers around Jero's interactions with his assistant Chume, and it both exposes Jero as a hypocritic fraud and admits that he is a good businessman.

Tsodzo, T(hompson) K(umbirai) (1947–)
Playwright and novelist. Tsodzo was born in the Charter District of Southern Rhodesia, now Zimbabwe, and educated at the University of Zimbabwe and the University of Michigan. After Zimbabwean independence he became a senior official in the Ministry of Youth, Sport, and Culture. He lectures in the Department of English at the University of Zimbabwe. He holds the position of Permanent Secretary of Education, Zimbabwe, and is currently appointed as Principal Director in the Department of State for Public and Interactive Affairs in the Ministry of Youth Development and Employment Creation. From 2003–2004 he held the position of Secretary of the Ministry of Education, Sport and Culture, and from 2000–2001 and March 2004–April 2005 he served as Secretary of the Ministry of Youth Development and Employment Creation.

Tsodzo's novels and plays are satires addressing social and political concerns. Of the plays, *Babamunini Francis* (1977) deals with the lives of the wives of long-distance lorry drivers and has been criticized as sexist; *Rugare* (1982) examines the problems of urban migration; and *Tsano* (1982) the consequent crime among the cities' unemployed. In 1983 he turned his satire against the politicians of the newly independent state and in *Shanduko* exposes their failure to fulfill their promises. His first novel, *Pafunge* (1972), represents the failure of colonial education to relate to Zimbabwean experience, and *Tawanda, My Son* (1986) continues his critique of intellectual colonialism. The Shona novel *Mudhuri Murefurefu* (1992) considers the problem of retaining a stable identity amid the rapid economic and social changes of Zimbabwe, adding a new dimension to Shona literature.

Turbott Wolfe (1925)

A novel by William **Plomer**. The novel created a stir when it was published, due to its direct treatment of interracial relations. The characters in Plomer's novel are somewhat stereotypical as they take on representative positions in relation to his overall theme of interracial relations. A racist trader takes over Wolfe's trading post, Mabel van der Horst marries an African (a fact the book still seems uncomfortable with), and a missionary named Friston claims the end of the white man's control.

Tutuola, Amos (1920–97)
Nigerian fiction writer. Tutuola was born in Western Nigeria to Charles Tutuola, a cocoa farmer, and his wife Esther Aina. His education was limited to six years (from 1934 to 1939), after which he trained as a metalsmith. From 1944 until the end of World War II he worked as a coppersmith for the West African Air Corps of the Royal Air Force. Unable to establish himself in a trade or profession after the war, he joined the colonial service in 1948 as a messenger in the Labour Department, and began his career as a writer while working there. Despite his meager education he has earned a remarkable international

reputation. In 1979 he held a visiting research fellowship at the University of Ife (now Obafemi Owolowo University) at Ile-Ife, Nigeria, and in 1983 he was an associate of the International Writing Program at the University of Iowa. After he retired, he divided his time between residences at Ibadan and Ago-Odo. Tutuola has published two collections of short stories, a volume of Yoruba folktales, and nine folkloric narratives, of which *The Palm-wine Drinkard,* a kind of quest tale that incorporates traditional Yoruba folk material, is the best known. In each he has repeated the structure and style of the first, sometimes even reintroducing whole episodes and characters from earlier narratives in later ones. Despite similarities in plot, structure, style, and theme, the later texts do indicate Tutuola's recourse to **religion** and mythology as new sources (such as John Bunyan's *The Pilgrim's Progress, The Arabian Nights,* and Edith Hamilton's *Mythology*).

Simbi and the Satyr of the Dark Jungle (1955) and *The Brave African Huntress* (1958), Tutuola's third and fourth books, do depart somewhat from the general pattern, specifically in the choice of women as the principals. Adebisi, the brave huntress, is the more formidable of the two heroines. Having inherited her father's hunting profession along with all his powerful charms, Adebisi sets out to rescue her four older brothers, who had disappeared on a hunting trip into the fearful Jungle of the Pigmies. The critical reception abroad of Tutuola's work was initially enthusiastic, although it was mixed among fellow Nigerians put off by his incorrect English and haphazard plots. By the 1970s the enthusiasm had cooled, but Nigerian critical regard for his accomplishments increased. For example, in a 1970 article Molara **Ogundipe-Leslie** commended his accurate representation of an African (especially Yoruba) consciousness, and Chinua **Achebe** devoted a 1987 lecture to praising him as "the most moralistic of all" Nigerian writers.

Despite his successful career Tutuola has remained marginal among African writers, excluded from forums where the latter discuss literary and other issues and from the international lecture circuit that has become a prerequisite for African European-language writers of comparable reputation. His other works are *My Life in the Bush of Ghosts* (1954), *Feather Woman of the Jungle* (1962), *Ajaiyi and His Inherited Poverty* (1967), *The **Witch-Herbalist of the Remote Town*** (1981), *The Wild Hunter in the Bush of the Ghosts* (1982; rev. 1989), *Pauper, Brawler, and Slanderer* (1987), *The Village Witch Doctor and Other Stories* (1990), and the collection *Yoruba Folktales* (1986). Some of Tutuola's works appear in anthologies such as *Under African Skies: Modern African Stories* by Charles R. Larson (1997), *Black Water 2: More Tales of the Fantastic* by Alberto Manguel (2002), *Great Commonwealth Stories* from Klett Publishing (2000), and *Blind Men and the Elephant: And Other Essays in Biographical Criticism* by Bernth Lindfors (1999).

Further Reading

Gera, Anjali. *Three Great African Novelists: Chinua Achebe, Wole Soyinka and Amos Tutuola.* Creative New Literatures Series. New Delhi, India: Creative Books, 2001.

Oyekan Owomoyela. *Amos Tutuola Revisited.* Twayne's World Authors Series. Woodbridge, CT: Twayne Publishers, 1999.

Two Thousand Seasons (1973)

A novel by Ayi Kwei **Armah**. The message of communal action is foremost in this somewhat fantastical novel. Based on the lost ideal of balance between giving and receiving, the narrative follows a group of characters who are abducted onto a slave ship by their king, but escape and overtake a slave castle. With an emphasis on the oral community and myth, it posits the use of community in the face of villainous "predators" and "destroyers."

U

Udechukwu, Obiora (1946–)

Nigerian poet and playwright. Udechukwu is a professor of painting at the University of Nigeria, Nsukka, where he graduated in 1972. Udechukwu is the Dana Professor of Fine Arts at St. Lawrence University, Canton, New York, where he is also the Department Chair and the Coordinator of the African Studies Program. He is on the Advisory Board of *Nka: Journal of Contemporary African Art,* and is a contributing editor of *Okike: An African Journal of New Writing* (as of 2003). Recently he has been honored as Fellow of the-Pan African Circle of Artists (Le Cercle Pan-Africain des Artistes, 1999), and he is a member of the Nsukka Group associated with the Department of Fine and Applied Arts at the University of Nigeria-Nsukka. His book of poems, *What the Madman Said* (1990), won the Association of Nigerian Authors/Cadbury Poetry Prize (1990). He started writing poetry seriously during the Nigeria-Biafra war in 1967, and his English and Igbo poems have appeared in journals and anthologies. His poetry is marked by juxtaposition of African and European cultural elements. In *What the Madman Said,* artistic sensibility is sharpened by the sufferings of the war, and the first section titled "Totem of Lament" was written between 1967 and 1973 and contains images of physical ravages, while the second section, "What the Madman Said," continues the portrayal of distorted values. With members of Odunke Artists, he co-wrote two Igbo plays, *Ojadili* (1977) and *Onukwube* (1986). Udechukwu is also included in such anthologies as Nkiru Nzegqu's 1999 *Contemporary Textures: Multidimensionality in Nigerian Art.* He makes remarkable use of vivid diction and images, and some of his most recent exhibitions have been *Black President: The Art and Legacy of Fela Anikulapo-Kuti* (2005), Pendulum Art Gallery, Lagos display of Obiora and Ada Udechuckwu's work (2004), and *Lines of Migration,* paintings by Kenwyn Crichlow and Obiora Udechukwu (2003).

Ugah, Ada (1958–)

Novelist, essayist, and poet, born in Iga-Okpoya, Nigeria. He was educated in both Nigeria and France. He is a lecturer at the University of Calabar, Nigeria, and an active member of the Association of Nigerian Authors (ANA). His collection, *The Rainmaker's Daughter and Other Stories* (1992), which won an ANA prize in 1993, reveals his interest in tradition and in the plight of humanity in a rapidly changing world. He is perhaps best known for his experimental "novel in ballad," *The Ballads of the Unknown Soldier* (1989). He continues the experiment with the balladic narrative with even greater vigor in *Colours of the Rainbow* (1991), in which he employs aspects of Idoma mythology to bewail the failure of Africans to harness Africa's potential. Other works include *Naked Hearts* (1982), *Rêves interdits* (1983), and *Errance sans Frontières* (1996), poems; *Hanini's Paradise* (1985), a novel; *Anatomy of Nigerian Poetics* (1982) and *Reflections on a Republic* (1983), essays; and *In the Beginning: Chinua Achebe at Work* (1990), a biography.

Uka, Kalu (1938–)

Nigerian poet, novelist, and theater artist, born at Akaanu Ohafia, Abia State. After schooling at Hope Waddell Training Institution, Calabar and Methodist College, Uzuakoli (1951–57) he graduated with a bachelor's in English from University College, Ibadan, and a master's from the University of Toronto, Canada. He is a Professor of Theatre Arts at the University of Calabar. Uka's only collection of poetry, *Earth to Earth* (1971), mainly comprises poems inspired by the Nigerian crisis and the Nigeria-Biafra war (1967–70). His attempt to write similar poetry in Igbo (see "Ukpara Kititki" in *Aka Weta,* 1978, edited by Chinua **Achebe** and Obiora Ude-chukwu), was less successful. The textured language that characterizes the poetry does not seem to work well as a medium for prose narrative in his two published novels, also set in the Biafran war and its aftermath (*A Consummation of Fire,* 1978, and *Colonel Ben Brim,* 1985). More successful as a professor of theater arts and theater director, Uka founded the Oak Theatre at the University of Nigeria and produced a successful stage adaptation of Achebe's ***Things Fall Apart*** and ***Arrow of God*** under the title *A Harvest for Ants* (1979). He has also produced his own play, *Ikhamma* (1978).

Ulasi, Adaora Lily (1932–)

A Nigerian novelist, Ulasi has a bachelor's in journalism, has been a newspaper and magazine editor, and has worked for Voice of America and the BBC. Her major contribution to African literature, however, is as the first Nigerian detective novelist writing in English. Her first novel, *Many Thing You No Understand* (1970), and its continuation, *Many Thing Begin for Change* (1971), take place in 1935 in England. The theme of both novels is the confrontation between traditional Igbo authority and British colonial authority. Her third novel, *The Night Harry Died* (1974), is set in the southern United States. Her most accomplished detective novel is *Who Is Jonah?,* set in southeastern Nigeria. Her incorporation of aspects of the African occult in the Nigerian novels reflects the pervasiveness of black magic in Africa. *The Man from Sagamu* (1978) is her latest novel set in Western Nigeria.

Umelo, Rosina (1930–)

A writer of children's books, Umelo was born of British parents in Cheshire, England, and educated at Bedford College, University of London. She married a Nigerian and in 1971 became a Nigerian citizen. In Nigeria she has worked in education as a school principal and author of curriculum material for study in English literature and in publishing as an editor. As a creative writer she has won awards including a BBC story prize in 1966, the Nigerian Broadcasting Corporation short-story competition prizes in 1972 and 1974, the Cheltenham Literary Festival Prize in 1973, and the Macmillan Writer's Prize for Africa—Junior Award 2002 for *Who Are You?* Her collection of stories, *The Man Who Ate the Money* (1978), explores various aspects of Nigerian society, and the teenage novels *Felicia* (1978), *Finger of Suspicion* (1984), and *Something to Hide* (1986) address contemporary issues through effective narrative techniques. More recently Umelo has published *Newsbird (Mactracks)* (2001) and *No Problem Luganda (Hop, Step, Jump)* (2000).

V

Valley of a Thousand Hills, The (1941)

A poem by H.I.E. Dhlomo. In this long poem Dhlomo contrasts humanity and nature, and seeks to understand the position of the African soul. It draws both on a romanticism and an imagination of the past, present, and future to accomplish this depiction of nature, humanity, and the soul in an African context.

Vambe, Lawrence (1917–)

An autobiographer and journalist, Vambe was born in Chishawasha, Southern Rhodesia, now Zimbabwe, and educated at the Roman Catholic seminary at Chishawasha, although he chose to leave before ordination, and Francis College, Mariannhill, South Africa. In 1946 he joined Africa Newspapers and by 1953 was editor-in-chief of the group. He founded *African Parade,* one of the first publications to express in a popular form the life of the country's urban blacks and provide an opportunity for the publication of some of the first black-authored fiction, and the *Zimbabwean Review,* ZAPU's (Zimbabwe African People's Union) British newsletter. Vambe's autobiography titled *An Ill-fated People* (1972) uses anecdotes of his own and his family's experiences to reconstruct Shona culture before the colonial occupation and to write the early history of Rhodesia from the point of view of the colonized. His account registers complex attitudes toward the missionaries who occupied his people's ancestral land. *From Rhodesia to Zimbabwe* (1976) followed, again registering national history partly through personal experience. In addition to his autobiographies, Vambe's journalism is important to Zimbabwean literature. For more than forty years he has sought to negotiate a middle ground between the various extremes of national life. Vambe edits *Southern African Encounter.*

Van der Post, (Sir) Laurens (Jan)
(1906–97)

A South African novelist and travel writer, van der Post was born at Philippolis, Orange Free State, into a distinguished Afrikaans family. On his family's farms, van der Post got to know and admire the Khoisan people. He was educated at local schools, including Grey College, Bloemfontein. In the English-speaking, liberal atmosphere of the *Natal Advertiser,* where he began work as a reporter in 1925, he came into contact with a range of ideas alien to his deeply conservative upbringing; he also met the poet Roy **Campbell** and the novelist William **Plomer**, whom he joined in 1926 to edit the journal *Voorslag (Whiplash),* which was sharply critical of the "colour bar," as **apartheid** was then called. In 1928 he traveled to Europe, and in 1934 published his first novel, *In a Province.* The book depicts (for the time) radically unconventional ideas on race relations, friendship between blacks and whites, the destructive effects of Western ways on a tribal African,

and it maintains that love is stronger than the extreme politics being offered by left and right in the 1930s.

During World War II he served with the British forces, and his experiences as a prisoner of the Japanese were to result in *A Bar of Shadow* (1952), and in the film *Merry Christmas Mr. Lawrence* (1983). From 1948 on he lived in England, traveled tirelessly, and turned out twenty-five books in total by the time of his death. Van der Post made a number of trips to Africa during the 1950s, several of which resulted in books, notably *Venture to the Interior* (1951), an account of an expedition to East Africa, and *The Lost World of the Kalahari* (1958), describing his encounter with the Bushmen of what is now Botswana. These books were widely acclaimed and won several literary prizes, thus making a name for van der Post. Other notable volumes among his large output include *The Heart of the Hunter* (1961), *A Story like the Wind* (1972), and *A Far-off Place* (1974). In 1951 he met Carl Jung and became a confirmed Jungian. This strand of his thought shows most obviously in *Jung and the Story of Our Time* (1975) and in a television documentary he made on Jung in 1971, but Jung's ideas are evident everywhere in his writing from the mid-1950s on, combined with a late Romantic mysticism that is van der Post's own.

Further Reading
Hinshaw, Robert, ed. *The Rock Rabbit and The Rainbow: Laurens van der Post among Friends.* Einsiedeln, Switzerland: Daimon Books, 1999.
Jones, J.D.F. *Storyteller: The Many Lives of Laurens van der Post.* London: John Murray, 2001.
———. *Teller of Many Tales: The Lives of Laurens van der Post.* New York: Carroll & Graf, 2002.

Van Wyk, Christopher (1957–)
A South African poet, novelist, editor, and children's writer, van Wyk was born in Soweto and has worked as a clerk and for the independent South African Committee for

Higher Education (SACHED) as an educational writer of accessible literature for new readers. He was editor of *Staffrider* from 1981 to 1986 and in 1980 started the short-lived *Wietie* magazine with Fhazel Johennesse. He lives in Johannesburg and works as a writer and freelance editor. During the literary explosion among black writers that followed the Soweto uprising in 1976, van Wyk published a volume of poetry, *It Is Time to Go Home* (1979), that won the 1980 Olive Schreiner Prize. The book reflects the preoccupations of other Soweto poets such as Mongane **Serote**, Sipho **Sepamla**, and Mafika **Gwala** and employs the language of defiance and assertion in poetry that reveals the **Black Consciousness** of the era. It shows also the particular wit and humor that is present in all van Wyk's writing. In 1981 he received the Maskew Miller Longman Award for black children's literature for *A Message in the Wind* (1982), the story of two boys who travel in their homemade time machine to their shared tribal past of 1679. Other children's stories include *Peppy 'n Them* (1991) and *Petroleum and the Orphaned Ostrich* (1988). He has written books for adults, such as *The Murder of Mrs. Mohapi* (1995), *My Cousin Thabo* (1995), *Take a Chance* (1995), *My Name Is Selina Mabiletsa* (1996), and *Sergeant Dlamini Falls in Love* (1996); biographies of Sol **Plaatje** and Oliver Tambo for teenagers; and adaptations of works by Bessie **Head**, Sol Plaatje, and Can **Themba**. He won the 1996 Sanlam Literary Award for his short story "Relatives," published in *Crossing Over* (1995). *The Year of the Tapeworm* (1996) is an adult novel and warns of government control of the media. Van Wyk has also published a memoir titled *Shirley, Goodness and Mercy: A Childhood Memoir* (2004), and other recent books by van Wyk are *Freedom Fighters* (2003), *Now Listen Here—The Life and Times of Bill Jardine* (2003), and *Post-Traumatic: South-African Short Stories* (2003).

Vassanji, M(oyez) G. (1950–)

Novelist and short-story writer. Vassanji was born in Nairobi, Kenya, finished high school in Tanzania, and gained graduate degrees in physics at the Massachusetts Institute of Technology and the University of Pennsylvania. He subsequently moved to Canada, and for ten years pursued his scientific career. Vassanji currently lives in Toronto, is co-editor and co-founder of the *Toronto Review of Contemporary Writing Abroad* (formerly the *Toronto South Asian Review*), and he was made a Member of the Order of Canada in February 2005. When Vassanji turned to creative writing, it was to tell the full story of his people, the Indians of East Africa. His first novel, *The **Gunny Sack*** (1989), which won a Commonwealth Writers Prize, is about a young Tanzanian Asian's search for identity. With his unusual inheritance, a gunny sack full of ambiguous mementoes, as guide he seeks his community's past. *The **Book of Secrets*** (1994), winner of Canada's Giller Prize, views the history of the same Asian community from new perspectives. The narrative revolves around a British colonial administrator's 1913 diary, found in Dar es Salaam in 1988. The retired schoolteacher who attempts to explore its entries is overwhelmed by the way in which the past connects with the present. The same truth catches up with Nurdin of *No New Land* (1991), which is set in Canada. The short-story collection *Uhuru Street* (1992) deals with specific aspects of the Indian community's life in Dar es Salaam during the period between the 1950s and the 1980s. *Amriika* (1999) explores the immigrant experience of one character over several decades, while *When She Was Queen* (2005) is a collection of ten short stories that span Kenya, Tanzania, and Ontario. Vassanji's novel, *The In-Between World of Vikram Lall* (2003) won the Giller Prize (he is the first author to win the Giller Prize more than once), and it received nominations for the Commonwealth Writers Prize, the Libris Award,

Torgi Literary Award for Books in Alternative Formats, and the Trillium Book Award. Vassanji's work has also been included in such anthologies as *Passages: Welcome Home to Canada* (2002), *Half a Day and Other Stories: An Anthology of Short Stories from North Eastern and Eastern Africa* (2004), and *The Novel and the Politics of Nation Building in East Africa* (2001).

Vatsa, Mamman Jira (1944–86)
Nigerian poet. Vatsa was a major-general in the Nigerian army, minister of the new federal capital Abuja, and a member of the Supreme Military Council. He was executed following an abortive coup. Vatsa's eight poetry collections for adults and eleven for children were mostly didactic or nationalistic, with titles such as *Back Again at Wargate* (1982), *Reach for the Skies* (1984) (subtitled *Patriotic Poems on Abuja*) and *Verses for Nigerian State Capitals* (1973). His best books are about ordinary people's lives and simple creatures and include the Pidgin collection *Tori for geti bow leg* (1981), his cultural picture book in Hausa, *Bikin Suna*, and a charming picture storybook, *Stinger the Scorpion* (1979). He organized writing workshops for his fellow soldiers and their children and got their works published. He helped the Children's Literature Association of Nigeria with funds, built a Writers' Village for the Association of Nigerian Authors, and hosted or provided resources for their annual conferences (he was on the executive boards of both).

Vera, Yvonne (1954–2005)
Zimbabwean short-story writer and novelist, born in Bulawayo, Zimbabwe, and educated at Luveve and Mzilikazi Secondary Schools. She held a doctorate in literature from York University, Canada, and was a writer-in-residence at Trent University, Canada, in 1995. After her return to Zimbabwe, she devoted most of her time to creative writing.

She was Director of the National Gallery in Bulawayo from 1997–2003, and she received several awards and honors, including the 2004 Swedish PEN Tucholsky Prize for work dealing with taboo subjects, the 2003 Premio Feronia—Citta di Fiano, Italy (best foreign author category, for *Butterfly Burning*), the 2002 Initiative LiBeraturpreis, Germany (or German Literature Prize) for the best novel in German translation by a female writer from Asia, Latin America, Africa), the 2002 Macmillan Writer's Prize for Africa for *The Stone Virgins* (best unpublished manuscript), and the 1997 Commonwealth Writers Prize (Africa Region, Best Book) for *Under the Tongue*. Her first publication, *Why Don't You Carve Other Animals?* (1992), is a collection of short stories set in colonial Rhodesia during the liberation war. It depicts vulnerable people who are caught in the conflict, such as men anxious to hold onto the little they have and women dreaming about fulfillment and achievement for their children. Her second publication, *Nehanda* (1993), is a novel based on the 1893 uprising in Zimbabwe. Nehanda becomes the center of African resistance. Also implicit in Vera's creative reconstruction of the war is the central role women play in the shaping of Zimbabwean history. In *Without a Name* (1994), a woman is raped during the liberation war and later commits infanticide. *Under the Tongue* (1996), written in a highly lyrical style, deals with a young girl's intense, painful relationship with her father. Other works by Vera include *Butterfly Burning* (1998), *The Stone Virgins* (2002), *Opening Spaces: An Anthology of Contemporary African Women's Writing* (1999), and a novel titled *Obedience*, which she did not complete before her death in 2005.

Further Reading
Bull-Christiansen, Lene. *Tales of the Nation: Feminist Nationalism or Patriotic History? Defining National History and Identity in Zimbabwe.* Uppsala, Sweden: Nordic Africa Institute, 2005.

Emenyonu, Ernest N. *New Women's Writing in African Literature: African Literature Today.* No. 24. London: James Curry, 2004.

Grey, Stephen, ed. *The Picador Book of African Stories.* New York: Picador, 2000.

Hunter, Eva. "Zimbabwean Nationalism and Motherhood in Yvonne Vera's *Butterfly Burning.*" *African Studies* 59, no. 2: (2000): 191–202.

Muponde, Robert, ed. *Sign and Taboo: Perspectives on the Poetic Fiction of Yvonne Vera.* Harare, Zimbabwe: Weaver Press, 2002.

———, and Primorac, Ranka, eds. *Versions of Zimbabwe: New Approaches to Literature and Culture.* Harare, Zimbabwe: Weaver Press, 2005.

Stunton, Irene, ed. *Writing Still.* Harare, Zimbabwe: Weaver Press, 2003.

Vilakazi, B(enedict) W(allet) (1906–47)

Zulu poet. Vilakazi's works were originally written in the Zulu language and eventually translated into English. Like his fellow Zulu poet, Herbert I.E. **Dhlomo**, Vilakazi's poems were concerned with taking up the cause of the newly urbanized and consequently exploited mine workers. In this sense he, like Dhlomo, is an innovator in terms of South African poetry. Vilakazi produces a poetry that defines social conflict in terms of class, and he conveys his message in a direct and nonsubtle manner. Vilakazi's work *Amal'eZulu* was included in the list of Africa's one hundred best books of the twentieth century.

Visions and Reflections (1972)

Poems by Frank **Chipasula**. Chipasula published this book of poems while in exile in Zambia. Because he wrote them when he was a university student in Malawi, they depict his early literary sense of self and his experience of the liberation struggle in Malawi.

Vladislavic, Ivan (1957–)

A South African short-story writer and novelist, Vladislavic lives in Johannesburg, where he works as an editor. He has published a number of short stories, of which several have been translated into foreign languages. Individual stories, his collection *Missing Persons* (1989), and his novel, *The Folly* (1993), have won literary awards. He has recently been writing a series of short texts on Johannesburg, which was published under the title of *Portrait with Keys* (2005). Vladislavic is also the recipient of the Sunday Times Literary Award for *The Restless Supermarket* (2001) and was nominated for the international IMPAC Dublin literary award.

The Folly, situated in an apparently recognizable world, describes the building of a house, but the relevance extends to considerations of the imagination and to a satire of the political notion of constructing a new world. Vladislavic has most recently published *The Exploded View* (2004), which contains four stories that revolve around four men from Johannesburg; *Overseas* (2004), which he published with photographer Roger Palmer; *Blank: Architecture, Apartheid and After* (1999); and a compilation of written and photographic essays edited with Hilton Judin.

Voice, The (1964)

A novel by Gabriel **Okara**. Okara uses the character of Okolo (or Ijo, meaning the voice), to jumble English words in an attempt to fight their crooked nature. It is a poetic novel that traces Okolo's travels through the corrupt city of Sologa, or Lagos. Those in the city ignore Okolo's warnings about Nigeria's greed after independence, and send him away on the river.

W

Wachira, Godwin (1936–)

A novelist, Wachira was born and educated in Kenya before undertaking a bachelor of science at Berlin University, Germany. He has worked variously as a publisher (he founded Newsline Africa publishing in 1975), an editor, a journalist, and an ostrich farmer. His only novel, **Ordeal in the Forest** (1967), belongs to the body of historical fiction in Kenyan literature that deals with the Mau Mau struggle against colonialism. The book was written closely upon the events it describes and was a trial work. It presents a stereotypical image of the settler community and treats the experience of the common people under colonialism, the growth of anticolonial consciousness, and the formation of a resistance movement in a schematic manner. Its strength lies in the sobriety with which the novelist reveals the complexity of each fighter's story of participation in the liberation war.

Waciuma, Charity (1936–)

A novelist, Waciuma was born in Naaro village, Fort Hall, Kenya, and trained as a teacher in a college at Embu. She belongs among the pioneers of indigenous writing for children, having published *Mweru the Ostrich Girl,* her first book, in 1966. Her autobiographical novel of childhood and adolescence, *Daughter of Mumbi* (1969), gives a description of life among the Kikuyu people and a historical account of a decade and a half of colonial existence. The period ends with the worst years of the emergency and the Mau Mau uprising in the mid-1950s. What most impresses the child's sensibility is the experience of fear, uncertainty, and humiliation, and the rift that divided a once-united community.

Waiting for the Barbarians (1980)

A novel by J. M. **Coetzee**. Coetzee explores the characterization of the other as barbarian by colonizers. He follows an unspecified nation as its leaders move from a bureaucratized administration to a totalitarian regime. The narrator belongs to the bureaucratic regime, and he is not able to change the transition to totalitarianism. Coetzee highlights the constructedness of the bureaucrat's narrative by giving him a present-tense narration.

Waiting Laughters (1990)

Poems by Niyi **Osundare**. Split into four parts, this work contemplates the nature of both patience and humor. Osundare depicts the events that gained freedom for African peoples from Langa, Sharpeville, and Soweto, as well as those who helped accomplish that freedom. He counters these images with those that opposed freedom such as Hitler, Marcos, and Idi Amin. Although Osundare's Yoruba heritage provides inspiration for some of the work, many of the poems depict other people, places, and events as well.

Walk in the Night, A (1967)

A novella by Alex **La Guma**. La Guma draws attention to the way that community and happiness is jeopardized by the male anger and violence of the police state in this novella. Michael Adonis loses his job and expresses his anger, while the novella moves between his room and the other rooms in his apartment building, to a police van outside. The tension of impending violence makes the novella a political commentary on poverty and racism.

Wall of the Plague, The (1984)

A novel by André **Brink**. Brink uses the plague in medieval Europe as a metaphor for the apartheid system in South Africa. He equates writing with the walls that attempt to prevent the disease from spreading, and insinuates that it is a form of political resistance. The narrator of the novel takes over the voice of a mixed-race woman named Andrea, but at the end of the novel she plans to return to South Africa and reclaim her identity.

Wangusa, Timothy (1942–)

Ugandan poet and novelist Wangusa was born in Bugisu, in eastern Uganda, studied English at Makerere University and the University of Leeds, UK, and has been Professor of Literature at Makerere as well an administrator there and in the Ministry of Education. His collection of poems *Salutations: Poems*

1965–1975 (1977), reissued with additional poems as *A Patten of Dust: Selected Poems 1965-1990* (1994), reflects his rural origins. *Upon This Mountain* (1989), a novel, tells the story of Mwambu, who is determined to touch heaven. The novel combines African folktale and proverbs with Christian symbolism. Wangusa is currently working on the forthcoming work *African Epiphanies,* and is a visiting Research Professor of English in the Department of Education (Uganda Studies Program) at Uganda Christian University. In 2001 Ugandan President Yoweri Museveni appointed Wangusa as his literary advisor, and from 1969–2001 Wangusa was an Emeritus Professor at Makerere University; he is also an active lay leader in the Anglican Church of Uganda.

War Literature

EAST AFRICA

There is a focus on history in East African literature that is possibly due to the struggle with European influences. The battle against colonialism is the subject of many East African works of literature such as memoirs, autobiography, and the postindependence publications of nationalist leaders that present various points of view on the battle for national liberation. Examples of the these works include those such as Julius Nyerere's *Uhuru na Umoja/Freedom and Unity* (1967), Mutesa II, Kabaka of Buganda's *Desecration of My Kingdom* (1967), and Jomo Kenyatta's *Suffering without Bitterness* (1967). Documentary reports are also of note in this genre, which were written by those who took part in the liberation movement and participated in the Mau Mau uprising in the 1950s in Kenya. Waruhiu Itote's *"Mau Mau" General* (1967) and Gakaara wa Wanjau's *Mau Mau Author in Detention* (1988), the Gikuyu original of which won the 1984 Noma Award, are two examples of this kind of literature. The Mau

uprising is a major theme in many Kenyan historical works, three of which are the autobiographically based works *Land of Sunshine* (1958) by Muga Gakaru, Mugo Gatheru's *Child of Two Worlds* (1964), and Charity **Waciuma**'s *Daughter of Mumbi* (1969). All of these works deal with particular aspects of the uprising, such as its end in *Land of Sunshine,* political persecution in *Child of Two Worlds,* and the long-term effects of colonialism and the years of the emergency on people in *Daughter of Mumbi.*

The historical nature of fictional works is different from those that are autobiographical. Fictional works use historical material more freely because the author usually means to represent the feeling of the time, and to convey an idea of what the military circumstances were. Works with these aims include those such as *Ordeal in the Forest* (1967) by Godwin **Wachira**, *My Son for My Freedom* (1973) by Kenneth **Watene**, *Carcase for Hounds* (1974) and *Taste of Death* (1975) by Meja **Mwangi**, *The Long Illness of Ex-Chief Kiti* (1976) by Micere Githae **Mugo**, and *Passbook Number F. 47927: Women and Mau Mau in Kenya* (1985) by Muthoni **Likimani**. Texts that are centered around historical events or persons employ historical facts more carefully. For example, for the play *The Trial of Dedan Kimathi* (1976) **Ngugi wa Thiong'o** and Micere Mugo researched their topic, and so did Samuel **Kahiga** when he wrote *Dedan Kimathi: The Real Story* (1990). In contrast, a different way of representing history is demonstrated in the play *Dedan Kimathi* (1974) by Kenneth Watene, who depicts the blurred lines between historical reality and legendary figures in the cultural context.

Events outside Kenya that were similar to Mau Mau have also resulted in literary responses. The *utenzi* of Swahili literature took on the theme of resistance to foreign invasion, and while these poems are not well known they were written quite early and are of important historical and literary value. Such poems include Hemedi bin Abdallah bin Said Bin Abdalla bin Masudi el Buhry's *Utenzi wa Vita vya Wadachi kutamalaki Mrima 1307 A.H. (A Poem about the Conquest of the East African Coast by the Germans, 1891)* (1971), Mwenyi Shomari bin Mwenyi Kambi's *Kufa kwa Mkwawa (The Death of Mkwawa)* (1918), and Abdul Karim bin Jamaliddini's *Utenzi wa Vita vya Maji-Maji (A Poem about the Maji-Maji War)* (1957). The play *Kinjeketile* (trans. 1970) by the Tanzanian playwright Ebrahim N. Hussein also uses the Maji-Maji anticolonial uprising of 1905–7 in German East Africa as its backdrop. The first interactions between the Wameru and the white settlers, the growth of the colonial system, the peasant resistance movement, and the British government's removal of the Engare Nanyuki people from their ancestral lands are all events covered in the work *Blood on Our Land* (1974) by Tanzanian Ismael Mbise, which depicts events from the year 1896–1951.

Postcolonial events like the 1966 armed conflict between the forces of the Kabaka of Buganda and the forces of President Milton Obote in Uganda are also depicted in novels such as Robert **Serumanga**'s *Return to the Shadows* (1969). Similarly, John **Nagenda** uses a fictional setting that is reminiscent of the violent era of Idi Amin and the second presidency of Obote in his *The **Seasons of Thomas Tebo*** (1986). Marjorie Oludhe Macgoye uses history as both a realistic backdrop and an defining element for her characters. The story of self-realization of a peasant girl who develops alongside the Kenyan nation is related by Macgoye in her novel *Coming to Birth* (1986), while characters' memories of national history are major narrative elements in *The Present Moment* (1987) and *Homing In* (1994). M. G. **Vassanji** uses similar techniques that combine character development and historical narrative in his novels *The **Gunny Sack*** (1989) and *The **Book of Secrets*** (1994).

Ngugi wa Thiong'o has demonstrated a very intense interest with East African history in his literary work. In his novels ***Weep Not, Child*** (1964), *The **River Between*** (1965), and *A **Grain of Wheat*** (1967) Thiong'o analyzes a history that begins with anticolonial resistance and nationalist hero Waiyaki's death in the early 1890s, depicts Harry Thuku's campaign against colonial oppression in 1921–22, and follows the female circumcision controversy in 1929 that led to the institution of Gikuyu independent schools, all the way up to the Mau Mau emergency and independence. In the aforementioned works Ngugi provides a humanistic history by ensuring that the idea of a history of ordinary people is given privilege over pure historical data. However, Ngugi demonstrates a stylistic change in ***Petals of Blood*** (1975), which provides a macrohistorical perspective with complicated references to both the distant past and the African diaspora in order to confront the imperialist image of Kenya's past that neo-colonialist historians depict. On a more autobiographical note, Alephonsion Deng, Benson Deng, Benjamin Ajak, and Judy Bernstein's *They Poured Fire on Us from the Sky: The True Story of Three Lost Boys from Sudan* (2006) offers a nonfictional account of Benjamin, Alepho, and Benson Deng, who were raised among the Dinka of Suda and were forced to flee when the government-armed Murahiliin began to attack their villages, joining the group of child refugees known as the Lost Boys. Another important nonfictional account of war that maintains a narrative voice is Philip Gourevitch's *We Wish to Inform You That Tomorrow We Will Be Killed with Our Families: Stories from Rwanda* (1998), which tells of the realities of life in Rwanda, its history, and the roots of the genocide.

SOUTH AFRICA

South African literature has been influenced by three major wars: the Anglo-Boer war (1899–1902), World War II (1939–45), and the anti**apartheid** conflict in the 1970s and 1980s. Because the Anglo-Boer war obtained much public attention in England there was a large market for novels that depicted the war, most of which did so only superficially. The violent reality of the war is represented by Richard Dehan (pseudonym for Clothilde Graves) in his book *The Dop Doctor* (1910) despite its overall tendency to romanticize events. The work that is recognized as the most important literary text during the era is *Commando* (1929) by Deneys Reitz. In *Commando,* Reitz tells of his experiences in the commando raid led by General J. C. Smuts into the Cape Colony. Sol T. **Plaatje** also accurately represents the Anglo-Boer war in his work *The **Mafeking Diary of Sol T. Plaatje*** (1973; 1999), which provides the perspective of a black person during the war. Similarly, Douglas **Blackburn**'s *A Burgher Quixote* (1903) satirically demonstrates the lack of any honorable aim on both sides of the battle. Other literary works of note that depict the Anglo-Boer war are Robert Baden-Powell's *Sketches in Mafeking and East Africa* (1907), Edgar Wallace's *Unofficial Dispatches of the Anglo Boer War* (1901), and Winston Churchill's *Young Winston's Wars* (1972). More recently, Reza De Wet's *Breathing In* (2004) premiered at the Rhodes University Centenary, National Arts Festival in 2004, and tells the story of a wounded general at the end of the Second Anglo-Boer War, who meets a herbalist and her daughter, and is confronted with the ways these women survive in the face of war and disaster.

World War II also impacted many South African poets. Writers who thought of themselves as a part of the European literary scene were now faced with a revised sense of South African identity. Such a response is visible in noted poets Anthony Delius and F. T. Prince, and in works such as Guy **Butler**'s collection *Stranger to Europe* (1952), and *The Dream and the Desert* (1953) by Uys Krige. Theatrical productions like Arthur Ashdown's *Squadron* X (1943) and Madeleine Masson's *Passport to Limbo* (1942) and *Home Is the Hero* (1944) were funded by the South African Department of Defence.

The South African Defence Force was at war externally with SWAPO (South West African People's Organization) on the Namibia-Angola border and in the townships was involved in an undeclared civil war with the ANC (African National Congress) starting in 1972. The declaration of a state of emergency by the government in 1986 brought the internal conflict to its height. Both of these wars were essentially battles against apartheid and for liberation, which the literature from the era demonstrates in its division. Most of the literature of the 1970s and 1980s can thus be defined as war literature, especially since the experiences of activists and civilians are portrayed in novels, stories, poems, and plays from the period. Mongane **Serote**'s *To Every Birth Its Blood* depicts the experiences of those fighting alongside the ANC and its allies in guerilla warfare. Zakes **Mda** also portrays the feelings of participants in the war as well as the sacrifices made by everyday people caught up in it, in his plays *We Shall Sing for the Fatherland and Other Plays* (1980).

The negative representation of the liberation guerilla fighters as terrorists and white soldiers as heroes is upheld in the texts of some popular white writers of the period, such as Peter Essex who depicts this viewpoint in his work *The Exile* (1984). In contrast, more philosophical representations of the white experience of the war are explored in the anthology *Forces' Favourites* (1987), while the point of view of a guerilla fighter is portrayed in Paul Hotz's *Muzukuru: A Guerilla's Story* (1990). Other works of note that deal with the liberation war backdrop include many of Nadine **Gordimer**'s stories, her ***Burger's Daughter*** (1979) and *July's People* (1981), André **Brink**'s *A **Dry White Season*** (1979), and J. M. **Coetzee**'s *Life and*

Times of Michael K. (1983). Athol **Fugard** brings together a white soldier and a black nightwatchman in his play *Playland* (1992), which depicts the guilt that both the soldier and the nightwatchman are dealing with due to murders on both sides. The characters thus represent a kind of healing interaction that results from the confrontation of violence at the beginning of the postapartheid era in the 1990s. More recent novelists continue to deal with issues like guerrilla and civil war in modern-day South Africa, such as Lewis Desoto's *Blade of Grass* (2004), which explores the relationship between Afrikaners and black workers at a farm experiencing guerrilla violence on the South African border, and Peter Killian's *Dusklands* (2001), which follows the difficulties of four groups in the midst of a civil war.

SOUTH-CENTRAL AFRICA

From 1972 to 1980 the Zimbabwean war of liberation was fought against the white Rhodesian regime. The first novel about the war was *The Non-Believer's Journey* (written 1977, published 1980) by Stanley **Nyamfukudza**, and exhibits great cynicism about the nationalist armed struggle. When the conflict ended in independence in 1980, some romanticized images of freedom fighters were depicted in works such as Edmund **Chipamaunga**'s *A Fighter for Freedom* (1983), Garikai Mutasa's *The Contact* (1985), and Spencer Tizora's *Crossroads* (1985). The war struggles of the Zimbabwean people and their hope for future peace and equality are represented in the anthology *And Now the Poets Speak* (1981), as well as in the war poetry of Chenjerai **Hove**.

A large amount of political questioning of the war began in the mid-1980s, when a critical dialogue about it began to surface. For example, Chenjerai Hove sets his novels *Bones* (1988) and *Shadows* (1991) during the war and demonstrates its effects on his characters. Other authors who represent the effects of the war include Alexander Kanengoni and Isheunesu Mazorodze (who fought in the war), as well as Batisai Parwada who deals with the war in his short-story collection *Shreds of Darkness* (1987), and Gonzo Musengezi, whose Shona novel titled *Zvairwadza Vasara (It Hurts the Survivors)* represents the effect of the war on children. In his story "The Concentration Camp" in Dambudzo **Marechera**'s posthumous work *Scrapiron Blues* (1994), Marechera depicts the emotional and physical violence against those of the black population who were forced to live in villages called "keeps" by the Rhodesian army.

Gender issues have also been explored in relation to war in South-Central Africa. Former combatant Freedom **Nyamubaya** reflects on her disappointment at the lack of change in the Zimbabwean patriarchal social structure after the war in her poetry collection *On the Road Again* (1986). Women's support of the liberation war, and the cruelties performed against them by those on both sides of the battle, are explored in a collection of interviews conducted by Irene Staunton and published as *Mothers of the Revolution* (1990). Shimmer **Chinodya**'s *Harvest of Thorns* (1989) presents the psychological perspective of the guerilla warriors, as does Charles Samupindi's novel *Pawns* (1992). *Why Don't You Carve Other Animals?* (1992) by Yvonne **Vera** also takes on a women's point of view in its depiction of the war, and like many of the aforementioned works, questions the possibility of a national history in their deconstruction of a unified narrative and voice. The perspectives of the white soldiers who are fighting for a cause and society that they hold no faith in are represented by books like *Karima* (1985) by Tim McLoughlin, *White Man Black War* (1988) by Bruce Moore-King, and *Kandaya: Another Time, Another Place* (1993) by Angus Shaw.

WEST AFRICA

War has influenced a large amount of modern West African literature. Guerilla leader Amilcar Cabral wrote poetry associated with Guinea-Bissau's liberation war (1950s to 1974), while Cyprian **Ekwensi** depicts World War II in his stories "Land of Sani" and "Desterter's Dupe" (1947), as does Wole **Soyinka** in his play ***Death and the King's Horseman*** (1975). However, the Nigeria-Biafra war (1967–70) is the focus of much of the war literature in West Africa, and all genres represent a concern with the war, although the dramatic texts of most importance are Wole Soyinka's ***Madmen and Specialists*** (1971) and *Jero's Metamorphosis* (1973).

Biafra's first war novel, Victor Uzoma Nwankwo's *The Road to Udima* (*Der weg nach Udima*, 1969) and poetry like Odunke's *Gedichte aus Biafra* (1969) were published in Germany through the actions of the University of Biafra's Odunke Community of Artists and Pro-Afrika's Ruth Bowert. Chinua **Achebe** depicts life in Biafra in relation to the impact of the war on history in *Beware, Soul Brother and Other Poems* (1971), while *The Poet Lied* (1980) by Odia **Ofeimun** critiques J. P. Clark **Bekederemo**'s *Casualties* (1970) to the point that Bekederemo prevented it from being published by threatening libel for a number of years. Of the most notable poetry from this period is ***Idanre*** *and Other Poems* (1967) and *A Shuttle in the Crypt* (1971) by Wole Soyinka and "Path of Thunder: Poems Prophesying War" (***Labyrinths***, *with Path of Thunder,* 1971) by Christopher Okigbo. Okigbo has been honored by his contemporary poets due to his death while in the Biafran military, with works like the anthology *Don't Let Him Die,* edited by Chinua Achebe and Dubem Okafor (1978), and his stylistic influence continues to have an impact in works like Obiora **Udechukwu**'s *What the Madman Said* (1990).

A number of issues related to war are explored in prose as well. The anti-Igbo pogrom in northern and western Nigeria gave rise to Biafra's secession from Nigeria, and is represented by many Igbo writers, as are the internal inconsistencies in Biafra, neo-colonialism, and the struggles for healing after the war. Examples of these themes can be found in works such as *Behind the Rising Sun* (1970) by S. O. **Mezu**, *Girls at War and Other Stories* (1972) by Chinua Achebe, *A Wreath for the Maidens* (1973) by John **Munonye**, *The Anonymity of Sacrifice* (1974) by I.N.C. **Aniebo**, *Never Again* (1975) by Flora **Nwapa**, *Survive the Peace* (1976) and *Divided We Stand* (1980) by Ekwensi, *Destination Biafra* (1982) by Buchi **Emecheta**, and Ossie **Enekwe**'s *Come Thunder* (1984).

Non-Biafran fiction that focuses on war includes works such as Kole **Omotoso**'s *The Combat* (1972), which takes an allegorical approach; ***Heroes*** (1986) by Festus **Iyayi**; the mythologically themed ***Season of Anomy*** (1973) by Soyinka; and the extremely realistic *The Last Duty* (1976) by Isidore **Okpewho**. More recently Uzodinma Iweala's *Beasts of No Nation* (2005) offers a fictional account (given from the point of a nine-year-old boy) of the Nigerian civil war drawn from Uzodinma's work with refugees and the memories of his family members who fought in the war.

Further Reading

Adimora-Ezeigbo, Akachi. "From the Horse's Mouth: The Politics of Remembrance in Women's Writing on the Nigerian Civil War." *Matatu: Journal for African Culture and Society* 29–30 (2005): 221–30.

Feuser, Willfried F. "'Nothing Puzzles God!': Chinua Achebe's Civil War Stories." *Matatu: Journal for African Culture and Society* 23–24 (2001): 65–72.

Hlabane, D. M. "The War Poems of Mongane Serote: The Night Keeps Winking and A Tough Tale." *Literator: Tydskrif vir Besondere en*

Vergelykende Taal-en Literatuurstudie/Journal of Literary Criticism, Comparative Linguistics and Literary Studies 21, no. 3 (2000): 91–108.

Kièma, Alfred. "Allegory in *The Great Ponds* by Elechi Amadi." *Bridges: An African Journal of English Studies/Revue Africaine d'Etudes Anglaises* 9 (2003): 21–42.

Krebs, Paula M. "Narratives of Suffering and National Identity in Boer War South Africa." *Nineteenth-Century Prose* 32, no. 2 (2005): 154–72, 221.

McLuckie, Craig W. "Literary Memoirs of the Nigerian Civil War." *Matatu: Journal for African Culture and Society* 23–24 (2001): 21–39.

Pape, Marion. "Nigerian War Literature by Women: From Civil War to Gender War." *Matatu: Journal for African Culture and Society* 29–30 (2005): 231–41.

Ribeiro, Margarida Calafate. "Luso Love in the Time of War: Camões's Barbara Recast in *Jornada de Africa,* by Manuel Alegre." In *Sexual/Textual Empires: Gender and Marginality in Lusophone African Literature,* ed. Hilary Owen and Phillip Rothwell. Bristol, England: Department of Hispanic, Portuguese and Latin American Studies, University of Bristol, 2004, 83–97.

Seixo, Maria Alzira. "The Edge of Darkness, or, Why Saramago Has Never Written about the Colonial War in Africa." *Portuguese Literary & Cultural Studies* 6 (2001): 205–19.

Stevens, Mary. "Commemorative Fever? French Memorials to the Veterans of the Conflicts in North Africa." *French Studies Bulletin: A Quarterly Supplement* 97 (2005): 2–4.

Watene, Kenneth (1944–)

Kenyan playwright Watene was born in Central Province, Kenya, and is a graduate of the National Theatre Drama School. He has contributed prose and poetry to *Ghala* magazine, he wrote articles for *Kenya Weekly News* in 1966, and he was a commentator on theater for the *Daily Nation* in 1969. He has long since left the literary world and gone into business. Watene's most important plays, *My Son for My Freedom* (1973) and *Dedan Kimathi* (1974), deal with the Mau Mau anticolonial movement. The latter occupies a special place among Kenyan literary texts concerned with history. *Sunset on the Manyatta* (1974) explores a young man's quest for fulfillment and a restored sense of completeness in a life disrupted by foreign education and culture.

Watson, Stephen (1954–)

South African poet. Watson teaches English at the University of Cape Town, and he is currently the Director of the Department of English and of the Creative Writing Program. His poetry collections include *Poems 1977–1982* (1983), *In This City* (1986), *Cape Town Days* (1989), *Return of the Moon* (1991), *Presence of the Earth* (1995), and *The Other City: Selected Poems 1977–1999* (2000). He has also published a collection of essays, *Selected Essays: 1980–1990* (1990). Watson's regional poetry portrays Cape Town, the city in which he has lived most of his life. Watson's Cape Town is a somber city of cold, mist, and rain. The characters who exist in this environment reflect its mood of disappointment and muted hope. In *Return of the Moon,* subtitled "Versions from the /Xam," Watson draws on archival material, transcribed in the early years of the century by linguists who sought to record and preserve the culture of the /Xam (or Cape Bushmen). The poems seek to convey the essence of the lost world of the /Xam. Watson is also known for his analysis of contemporary South African literature.

Weep Not, Child (1964)

A novel by **Ngugi wa Thiong'o**. Ngugi explores the Kikuyu connection with the land, and the use of religious myths and legends and a Christian education to attempt reconciliation with the Christian faith. The novel narrates the events that preceded the first Emergency Situation in Kenya (Mau Mau) and their impact on one family. The primary character, Njoroge, believes he can reconcile Christian and traditional beliefs, but the novel follows his progressive disappointment.

Were, Miriam (1940–)

Kenyan novelist and biographer. Born to a devoutly Christian family in Lugola, Kakarnega District of northern Kenya, Were took degrees in the humanities and education at the universities of Pennsylvania (Philadelphia) and Makerere (Kampala, Uganda). She then trained as a physician at the University of Nairobi, where she is a Professor of Community Health. She represented Kenya at the 1985 UN Decade of Women Conference at Nairobi, is currently the Chair of the Kenya National AIDS Control Council, and was appointed to the AMREF International Board on October 5, 2001, and as Board Chair in March 2003. She was formerly the UNFPA/CSTAA Director in Ethiopia, the WHO representative and Chief of Mission to Ethiopia for three years, and the chief health and nutrition/senior advisor for UNICEF, also in Ethiopia. Were recently received the 2005 AMREF Gates Award for Global Health. Her novels, published as secondary school texts by the East African Publishing House, deal with the familiar postcolonial theme of conflict between European and indigenous African ways of life. *The Boy in Between* (1969) and *High School Gent* (1969) portray the struggles of an ambitious Kenyan boy. The heroine of *The Eighth Wife* (1972) becomes the eighth wife of a chief who competes for her love with his eldest son. Interethnic marriage provides the major conflict in *Your Heart Is Your Altar* (1984). Were also wrote the biography of a nurse, Margaret Owanyoni, in *The Nurse with a Song* (1978).

Whaley, Andrew (1958–)

A playwright, Whaley was born in Harare, Zimbabwe, and educated at Sir John Kennedy Primary in Kadoma and Prince Edward High School in Harare. He studied English literature at Bristol University, UK, and has since written and directed plays for both stage and screen. His first play, *Platform 5* (1987), recreates the plight of street children when the Zimbabwe government dispersed them in order to host conference delegates of the Non-aligned Movement in 1986. *Platform 5* won a prize as the best new play and the best production during the 1987 Zimbabwe National Theatre Festival and was staged later that year at the Edinburgh Cultural Festival. *The Nyoka Tree* (1988) assumes fable format to interrogate the semifeudal relations of colonial Rhodesia, mockingly dubbed "Paradise." *Chef's Breakfast* (1989) underlines how the politically powerful betray their former ideals, their comrades in war, and their own relatives. The play was inspired by the Sandura Commission, which investigated corruption in government circles in Zimbabwe in the late 1980s. *The Rise and Shine of Comrade Fiasco* (1991) dramatizes the liberation struggle and the reality of postindependent Zimbabwe. Recent works include *Brenda Remembered* (2004), and the screenplay and casting of *Yellowcard* (2000), as well as inclusion in anthologies such as Martin Banham and Jane Plastow's *Contemporary African Plays* (1999). In all of his plays Whaley uses theater as a social tool that can raise questions and underline issues.

Wheatley, Phillis (ca. 1753–84)

The poet Wheatley, the first black writer to publish a volume of poems, was taken from Africa to Boston in 1761 and became the slave of the Wheatley family. Frail but highly gifted, she made phenomenal progress in learning English and Latin. She became familiar with the Bible and the classics, which inspired her poetic imagination. She was the unofficial poet laureate of the Boston elite and addressed verses of sympathy and consolation to bereaved friends and families. Her first published poem, "On the Death of George Whitefield" (1770), was an immediate success. She also addressed poems to King George III (1768), William Legge, the Earl of Dartmouth (1772), and George Washington (1775). In 1773, she visited England and published her *Poems on Various Subjects, Religious and Moral.* Wheatley has survived negative criticism, exemplified by Thomas Jefferson's dismissal of her poetry as "beneath the dignity of criticism" (1782) and J. S. Redding's (1939) censure of "the negative, bloodless, unracial quality" of her poems. A fair assessment may be critical of her neoclassical and patriotic pretensions but it cannot ignore the fact that she was at heart an African; her work is one of the first examples of **African-American literature.** An anonymous volume of her poems and memoir appeared in 1834, and Charles Deane printed *The Letters of Phillis Wheatley* (1864). Collections of her work include Charles F. Heartman's *Poems and Letters* (1915) and Julian Mason's *Poems* (1966). Wheatley's work is also included in many anthologies, including *Old Glory: American War Poems from the Revolutionary War to the War on Terrorism,* edited by Robert Hedin and Walter Cronkite (2004); *In Praise of Black Women Vol. 2: Heroines of the Slavery Era* by Simone Schwartz-Bart (2002); *Amazing Grace: An Anthology of Poems about Slavery, 1660–1810* by James G. Basker (2002); and *Favorite American Poems* by Paul Negri (2002).

Further Reading

Borland, Kathryn Kilby, and Helen Ross Speicher. *Phillis Wheatley: Young Revolutionary Poet.* Young Patriots Series. Indianapolis: Patria Press, 2005.

Burke, Rick. *Phillis Wheatley.* Burke, Rick, American Lives. Chicago: Heinemann Library, 2003.

Gates, Henry Louis, Jr. *The Trials of Phillis Wheatley: America's First Black Poet and Encounters with the Founding Fathers.* New York: Basic Civitas Books, 2003.

Gregson, Susan R. *Phillis Wheatley.* Let Freedom Ring: American Revolution Biographies. Brookfield, CO: Capstone Press, 2001.

Kent, Deborah. *Phillis Wheatley: First Published African-American Poet.* Spirit of America, Our People. Chanassen, MN: Child's World, 2004.

Lasky, Kathryn. *A Voice of Her Own: The Story of Phillis Wheatley, Slave Poet,* 1st ed. Cambridge, MA: Candlewick, 2003.

McLeese, Don. *Phillis Wheatley.* Heroes of the American Revolution. Vero Beach, FL: Rourke Publishing, 2004.

Rinaldi, Ann. *Hang a Thousand Trees with Ribbons: The Story of Phillis Wheatley.* Great Episodes. Fairbanks: Gulliver Books Paperbacks, 2005.

Wheatley, Phillis. *Complete Writings.* Ed. Vincent Caretta. Penguin Classics. New York: Penguin, 2001.

When Sunset Comes to Sapitwa (1980)

Poems by Felix **Mnthali.** A Malawian poet, Mnthali explores the prevalent issues under the Banda regime. The poems depict suffering, the joy of life, resilience, and pride.

Why Are We So Blest? (1972)

A novel by Ayi Kwei **Armah.** The work is narrated by a Ghanaian student who goes to an American university and is disappointed with its perception of Africa; his girlfriend Aimée, who has a self-serving interest in African studies; and the interpreter Solo, who meets them when they move to North Africa. The couple is brutally murdered, and Solo narrates through his interpretation of their journals.

Wicomb, Zoë (1949–)

South African novelist and critic. Wicomb grew up in rural Cape Province and studied English literature at the University of the Western Cape (BA, 1968). In 1973 she left for exile in the UK, where she continued to study English literature and earned a master's degree (Strathclyde University, 1989). She is a founding editor of the *Southern Africa Review of Books,* has taught literature, women's studies, and literary linguistics in South Africa and Britain, has served as writer-in-residence at Glasgow and Strathclyde universities, and is also a Professor of English at the University of Strathclyde.

Irony characterizes Wicomb's single book-length fiction (**You Can't Get Lost in Cape Town**, 1987, republished by the Feminist Press in 1999, as well as translated into Swedish, Dutch, German, Italian, and French by Virago Modern Classics); two stories in anthologies (1990, 1991); and twelve critical essays (1988–94), in accord with her conviction that literature address power and its complexities. Wicomb insistently interrogates South African culture past and present; "Another Story" (1990), for example, creates descendants of a "coloured" (mixed-race) character that white South African Sarah Gertrude **Millin** created in **God's Step-Children** (1924). *You Can't Get Lost in Cape Town* establishes Wicomb as a postprotest writer committed to democratic ideals. Wicomb's own literary/cultural criticism illuminates her fiction.

Wilhelm, Peter (1943–)

South African novelist, poet, and journalist. Born in Cape Town, Wilhelm completed his schooling in the Transvaal, qualified as a teacher, and turned to journalism. He joined the *Financial Mail* in 1974 as political editor and film critic, and edited *Leadership* magazine, where he wrote on the personalities and trends of the South African transition to democratic government. *LM and Other Stories* (1975) comes out of his experiences in preindependence Mozambique; two other collections of stories and the novel *The Dark Wood* (1977) explore colonialism's legacy of violence and terror. His interest in science fiction is shown in some of the short stories and *Summer's End* (1984), a book for children. *The Mask of Freedom* (1994) is set in an indeterminate near future in which poverty, population growth, crime, and AIDS have determined social policy in a way that radically limits human freedom. Wilhelm's poetry has

been collected in *White Flowers* (1977) and *Falling into the Sun* (1993), some of his stories have been collected in *The Bayonet Field: Selected Stories* (2000), and collections of his columns have been published in *The State We're In* (2000). He has won awards for his writing and reporting, including the Science Fiction Society of South Africa's prize and the Pringle Prize for reviews, and his stories and poems have been widely anthologized.

Will to Die, The (1972)

Essays by Can **Themba**. This is a collection of essays that appeared in *Drum, Golden City Post,* and other Johannesburg journals in the 1950s and 1960s. Themba depicts black township life in Johannesburg in these essays. The collection also includes short stories, such as "The Suit," descriptions of the literary scene, his memorial to Nat Nakasa, and Lewis Nkosi's obituary for Can Themba himself.

Williams, Adebayo (1951–)

A novelist and journalist, Williams was born in Gbongan, Oyo State, Nigeria, and received his postsecondary education (BA, 1975; MA, 1979; PhD, 1983) at the University of Ife (now Obafemi Awolowo University), where he also taught for many years. He lives in Birmingham, UK, teaches in the United States at the Savannah College of Art and Design, and was the 2003 past Army Freeman Lee Chair in Humanities and Fine Arts at the University of the Incarnate Word, San Antonio, Texas.

Williams's first novel, *The Year of the Locusts,* won the Association of Nigerian Authors (ANA) literary award in 1988. His second novel, *The Remains of the Last Emperor* (1994), was a joint winner of the 1995 ANA-Spectrum Prize for prose fiction. More recent works published by Williams are *Governance and Democratisation in West Africa* (1999), a book that Williams co-edited with Dele Olowu, Kayode Soremekun, and Bayo

Williams and which documents and attempts to decipher political developments in West Africa; and *Bulletin from the Land of the Living Ghosts: Romance in the Reign of Commander Cobra* (2002), a book that covers many generations, worlds, and events that focuses on unrest in the West African country of Muleria. Essays by Williams also appear in works such as *Nigeria's Struggle for Democracy and Good Governance* (2004), edited by Adigun A. B. Agbaje; and in journals and newspapers such as *Africa Today: Voice of the Continent,* where he has published essays titled "Reconciliation Postponed, Truth Deferred" (2001), "Remembering Shehu Yar'Adua" (2001), "Riding out the Desert Storm" (2001), "Transition without Transformation" (2001), "Confessions at the Gate of Hell" (2000), and "The Autumn of the Literary Patriarch: Chinua Achebe and the Politics of Remembering" in *Research in African Literatures* (2001). Other scholarly articles have appeared in many prominent periodicals, including *Présence africaine, Okike,* and *Africa Quarterly.* He has been a columnist for *Newswatch* (1985–91) and *African Concord* (1992), an editor-at-large for *Africa Today* (since 1995), and he won the 1994 Diamond Award for Excellence in Journalism.

Witch-Herbalist of the Remote Town, The (1981)

A novel by Amos **Tutuola**. Based on a story about the Yoruba trickster Ajapa (the tortoise), Tutuola's hero travels to a witch-herbalist to remedy his wife's inability to have children. His disembodied first, second, and third minds assist him in his journey. He becomes pregnant after he eats some of the cure himself, against the orders of the witch-herbalist.

Wrath of Napolo: A Novel, The (2000)

Steve **Chimombo**'s novel begins as an investigation into the sinking of the *M. V. Vipya* on Lake Malawi in 1946, but it turns into a political and social commentary when Chilungamo Nkhoma, a reporter and the primary character of the novel, attempts to find out how it was grounded. He finds that some people will go to extremes in order to prevent the truth from being revealed. The narrative draws to a close as Nkhoma follows the ship's original course, and major political parties hold a rally on the shore of the lake.

Wrath of the Ancestors, The (1980)

A novel by A. C. **Jordan**, translated from the Xhosa (*Ingqumbo Yeminyanya,* 1940). The conflict between traditional Xhosa customs and modern educated Africans comes to the forefront in this novel. It tells of an heir to the chieftainship of the Mpondomise tribe who returns to claim his position after his education at the Lovedale Institution. The heir, Zwelinzima, refuses to marry who the ancestors choose for him, and when he marries a woman from the Lovedale Institution the community renounces her and forces him to take another. As a result both Zwelinzima and his wife commit suicide, and the ancestors prevail.

Y

Yirenkyi, Asiedu (1946–)

Ghanaian playwright. Yirenkyi became involved in theater through the Drama Studio Players, Accra, which he joined in the early 1960s. From there he went on to study drama at Legon and at Yale, in the United States, and to make a career as a lecturer in Nigeria and Ghana. He has been an actor, director, theater company manager, and author of screenplays, has held ministerial-level office, and currently serves as the chairman for the National Folklore Board for Accra, Ghana. Since 1986 he has taught playwriting and theater arts in the School of Performing Arts, Legon, but his most important contribution has been as a playwright. His collection *Ki-vuli and Other Plays* (1980) brings together texts written over an extended period and shows him working in a variety of styles, including an interest in drama based on the Ananse storytelling tradition.

You Can't Get Lost in Cape Town (1987)

Short stories by Zoë **Wicomb**. Each of the ten short stories in this collection stand alone in theme and narrative, but are connected by the narrative thread of Frieda Shenton as she grows up and returns to Cape Town to teach English. The stories treat the themes of the pretentiousness of anglophones, racism in South Africa, and general unrest.

You Must Set Forth at Dawn (2006)

Wole **Soyinka**'s sequel to his childhood memoir. In this memoir he explores the roles of the intellectual and the political in his life. Because of his involvement in the political struggles, his account of Nigeria's political disorder is very personal. He reminisces about his experiences of writing, exile, and prison against the backdrop of a number of Nigerian dictatorships. He also describes the political and social landscape of Nigeria as a whole, and describes his travels through other African landscapes as well.

Young Adult Literature

EAST, WEST, AND SOUTH-CENTRAL AFRICA

The term *young adult literature* is used here instead of *children's literature*, because a large amount of African and non-African writing complicates a boundary between childhood, adolescence, and even adulthood. In African literature, works that transcend the categories of children's literature and young adult literature are **Ngugi wa Thiong'o**'s *Weep Not, Child* and Ben Chirasha's *Child of War* (1985), which both demonstrate the need to avoid the

use of terms that limit based on age. In addition, there are problems with the definition of young adult literature, since traditionally children experienced storytelling as a part of the oral communication of culture. Traditional forms like folk legends, songs, riddles, ancestral sagas, cautionary anecdotes, and heroic panegyrics were all fundamental to community life and not just within the boundaries of childhood. Despite the lack of boundaries, there are a number of more recent developments that have led to a kind of narrative meant specifically for young adults. Some reasons for the emergence of a young adult literature are the focus on reading and writing in the Western-based reorganization of education into a formal process, the emphasis on written rather than spoken forms of narrative transmission, and the use of European languages and literary forms due to colonialism.

In the 1950s and 1960s a number of African writers reasserted the literary achievements of traditional narratives that had a history of more than three thousand years in North Africa, but had been obscured by colonialism. The education of children is one of the points of emphasis for many African authors, who discuss the social importance of inherited identity through education. Thus, many African authors take on public roles associated with education, publish practical treatises on teaching, provide personal narratives about childhood experiences (as does Wole **Soyinka** in his autobiographical *Ake: The Years of Childhood*, 1962), and communicate their opinions through literary works for African youth. Ama Ata **Aidoo**'s book of poetry *Birds and Other Poems* (1992) is targeted toward young adults, while she has also published books like *Changes* (rereleased by Harcourt Education in 2004), and *Yomi in Paris* (1966). The "bush of ghosts" novels by Amos **Tutuola** are a set of fantastic and magical stories that he wrote over a twenty-year period, while *Chike and the River* (1966) by Chinua **Achebe** is a children's story he published the same year as *A Man of the People.* After his work **Petals of Blood** (1977), Ngugi wa Thiong'o published *Nyamba Nene and the Flying Bus* (1986) and *Nyamba Nene's Pistol* (1986), which are children's works translated into English by Wangui wa Goro. Cyprian **Ekwensi** has also contributed greatly to young adult fiction in African literature, with the aim of providing African young adults and children with a view of the world that is other than Eurocentric.

In the last several decades, there has also been an effort to revive in written form the oral narratives that once held such an important place in the communal education of African children and young adults. A number of works offer collections of traditional oral tales and uphold rural tribal traditions, some of which include C. L. Vyas's *Folk Tales from Zambia* (1973) and L. Farrant's *Fables from Kenya* (1990). Sarah F. Oppong's *Around the African Fire* (1994) provides an unique example of such a collection, as it frames its narrative in contemporary England, where students from Uganda, Kenya, Cameroon, Nigeria, and Ghana tell tales that include figures such as Hare, Tortoise, and Spider. The tendency for young adult and folklore narratives like these to be collected as short stories may be a result of the episodic nature of oral storytelling, as well as the shortage of books in postcolonial schools—which led the teachers to read to classes out loud. The Ananse stories are well fitted to such a short-story approach, and have been collected in several anthologies such as S. Y. Manu's *Six Ananse Stories* (1993) and J. Osafoa Dankyi's anthologies *Ananse Searches for a Fool, The Pot of Gold Dust,* and *The Discovery of Palm Wine.*

Some writers have adapted the story elements of traditional oral narratives into novels or novellas that still maintain the structures of the stories. Examples of such texts are Cyprian Ekwensi's *An African Night's Entertainment* (1963), which frames the narrative with a storyteller who addresses the audience, and Clayton MacKenzie's *The Mbira Man* (1987) and *Adventure of the Dark Stone* (1993), which reflect the role of the traditional grandfather figure who recalls ancient central African tales told to young audiences in their modern narrators. In Peggy Appiah's *The Children of Ananse* (1990) there is a similar integration of Ghanaian folklore into the contemporary plot of the story.

Literary mythologies of ancient inheritance are thus passed down through the narrative and structural adaptations of contemporary authors, who are concerned with a renewal of indigenous culture in the face of colonialism. This renewal is difficult given the urban growth and removal of many from the reality of village story folklore, which results in the tendency in much contemporary African literature to represent an urban community looking back at its rural beginnings. West African city life is portrayed in such a manner in Comfort Blay's *Esuon in the City* (1989), which depicts the adventures of a young girl who stays with her aunt in the city and has both positive and negative experiences, as well as Mahamed Chaaban's *The Secrets of Biri Forest,* which follows two police detectives who visit the rural east of Zimbawe, while Marjorie Oludhe Macgoye's *Growing up at Lina School* narrates the experiences of a character who returns to rural Kenya after spending time in urban England. These narratives tend to remind their young readers of the importance and closeness of a rural past that needs to be reinforced in the face of urbanization. Recent works continue to combine folklore elements with contemporary social issues. Baba Wague Diakite's *Hunterman and the Crocodile: A West African Folk Tale* (1997) is an example of one such work, where the hero Donso learns to live in harmony with nature. Similarly, Anton Auintana's *Baboon King* (1999) tells of a boy born to a Kikuy mother and a Masai father who must learn tolerance when he's banished and becomes the leader of a troop of baboons. Isaac O. Olaleye's *In the Rainfield: Who Is the Greatest?* (2000) recounts a Nigerian folktale about a competition between the wind, rain, and fire. In a similar vein is James Rumford's *Calabash Cat and His Amazing Journey* (2003), which chronicles the journey of the calabash cat on a quest to find out where the world ends, during which each of the animals show him their homes; the book also has Arabic writing in it. Works with a more contextual theme relating to contemporary society or education of the past are Velma Maia Thomas's *Lest We Forget: The Passage from Africa to Slavery and Emancipation* (1997); Sonia Levitin's *Dream Freedom* (2000), which describes how slavery in modern Sudan affects everyone; Benjamin Zephaniah's *Refugee Boy* (2002), which tells of Alem's struggles to survive the civil war between Ethiopians and Eritrians and become a refugee in England; as well as Joelle Stolz and Catherine Temerson's *The Shadows of Ghadames* (2004), a story about how as eleven-year-old Malika approaches marriageable age she begins to appreciate the women's community in her culture.

In contrast, some authors focus exclusively on the contemporary cultural contexts for young people in Africa. *The Smugglers* (1966) by Barbara **Kimenye** follows three young people who encounter danger on their way to Kampala, and more recently she has published *Beauty Queen* (1997) and *Prettyboy, Beware* (1997). The novels of Juma Bustani, titled *Adventure in Nakuru, Adventure in Mombasa,* and *Adventure in Nairobi* (1988, 1990), portray male and female heroes who must battle city crimes such as industrial pollution, drug trafficking, and murder. V. Asare Agyeman focuses on a less dark theme in *Mansa and Asana* (1988), which follows a group of girls on holiday in West Africa. More serious themes are taken up by the On Stage series created by the College Press of Zimbabwe, which presents plays such as Cont Mhlanga's *Workshop Negative* (1992), Tsitsi

Dangarembga's *She No Longer Weeps* (1987), and Dorras and Walker's *The Big Wide World* (1987). In these plays relevant adolescent themes such as race relations, teenage pregnancy, and unemployment are dealt with. Nancy Farmer offers a futurist view of an extremely technologically advanced Harare in the year 2245 in her *The Eye, the Ear and the Aim* (1994), while in 1996 Farmer published *A Girl Named Disaster.* Nigerians Anne Akpabot (*Aduke Makes Her Choice,* 1966, and *Sade and Her Friends,* 1967) and Niyi Osundare (*Early Birds Book One: Poems for Junior Secondary Schools, Early Birds Book Two,* and *Early Birds Book Three,* 2004) are important young adult authors. As is Rosina Umelo, who is the author of *Newsbird* (*Mactracks*), published by Macmillan Education (2001), *No Problem Luganda (Hop, Step, Jump)* Macmillan Education (2000), and *Striped Paint: Langi Y'Emisittale (Ya Mutoogo)* Macmillan Education (1992, 2000). Theresa Meniru has published five works for young adults: *Ibe the Camon Boy* (Ibadan: Ibadan University Press), *Last Card* (Ibadan: Macmillan), *The Lion on the Hill* (Ibadan: Macmillan), *The Mysterious Dancer* (Ibadan: Macmillan), and *Uzo: A Fight with Fate* (Ibadan: Evans). Charles Mungoshi is the author of *Don't Read This! And Other Tales of the Unnatural* (2004), while Mary-Rose Mbarga wrote and Mashet Ndhlovu Illustrated *How Chimpanzees Became Bald (Sei chimupanze ane mhanza),* originally written in Shona and translated by Stanely Nyamfukudza (2002). Driss Chraïbi is the author of *L'âne Khal invisible* (2000) and *L'âne Khal à la television* (2000), while Mohammed Ben-Abdallah has written a play for children titled *Ananse and the Golden Drum: A Play for Children* (1994). Also out of Ghana, Amu Djoleto is the author of *Girl Who Knows about Cars* (1996), *Kofi Loses His Way* (1996), and *Akos and the Fire Ghost* (1998). T. Obinkaram Echewa is the author of *Mbi, Do This! Mbi, Do That: A Folktale from Nigeria* (1998/1999), while

Cyprian Ekwensi (also from Nigeria) is the author of at least six works for young adults: the 1966 *Juju Rock, The Red Flag* (a story of Uzo and the day he ran into the sea when the red flag was flying, 1996), *Masquerade Time* (1991), which tells the story of a threatening local masquerade seen by a black American boy, *The Drummer Boy* (1991), *Gone to Mecca* (1991), which describes a pilgrimage to Mecca and the payment of debts, and most recently *Motherless Baby* (2001), a new title that tells the story of an adolescent school girl who has an unwanted baby. Namibian writer Dorian Haarhoff is the author of a young adult work titled *Grandpa Enoch's Pipe* (2002), while the University of Calabar Department of English and Literary Studies has published a book called *Children and Literature in Africa* (1992). Other recent and readily available works on young adult literature include Osayimwense Osa's *African Children's and Youth Literature* (1995) and Meena Khorana's *Critical Perspectives on Postcolonial African Children's and Young Adult Literature* (1998). Authors Margy Burns Knight and Mark Melnicove, and illustrator Anne Sibley O'Brien, educate children and adolescents about Africa in their young adult book titled *Africa Is Not a Country* (2000), which takes the reader across Africa in one day to witness the different cultures and customs across the continent.

Historically, indigenous publications have come up against many difficulties and despite the number of current publications for young adults, this genre is no different. During colonial occupation, educators imported Eurocentric texts that demonstrated the importance of Westernized values and ideologies to the educational system, and under these restrictions the publication of indigenous literatures was limited. During the postcolonial era, indigenous young adult literature did not immediately prosper due to the economic restrictions associated with the provision of universal primary education.

Not only were indigenous young adult literatures not widely available, it was difficult for the schools to afford such resources. The rise of a number of indigenous African-based printing houses and commercial publishers starting in the 1960s made the production of children's literature a more viable reality. African state support has helped to encourage not only indigenous subsidiaries of international publishing groups like Longman, Macmillan, and Oxford University Press, but also independent publishing companies such as East African Educational Publishers (created as a division of Heinemann in 1992) and Longhorn Kenya (established in 1994 as a division of Longman). Such publishing houses have been extremely important to the local production of relatively low-cost texts that are geared to a local readership.

Locally produced and focused texts for young people have been very successful. The novel *Woman in Struggle* (1984) by Irene Mahamba was published by Mambo Press (Zimbabwe), and depicts the Rhodesian civil war in a way that is specifically directed at young readers who were experiencing its aftermath. Phoenix Publishers in Kenya started the Phoenix Young Readers Library; the Spellbinder series is published by the Macmillan subsidiary College Press; Longman Zimbabwe publishes the Storyline series; the extensive Junior Readers list includes names such as Ekwensi, Achebe, Charles **Mungoshi**, and Ngugi and is published by East African Educational Publishers; the Anchor Readers series is a product of Longhorn Kenya; and Macmillan in Africa publish the young adult–targeted Pacesetters books. Series like these create a system of educational and publishing expectations for young adult literature, the result of which is a large base of indigenous writing for young adults that offers a counter to foreign literature. Thus, young adult literature has developed with a much stronger indigenous publishing focus than have other genres of African literature.

SOUTH AFRICA

Young adult and children's literature in South Africa grew out of a number of different beginnings. While European examples in French, English, German, and Dutch provided the basis for English and Afrikaans young adult literature, African young adults experienced oral storytelling. In the nineteenth century, young adults were exposed to European classics and a small number of local texts, which did not get much attention. However, more recently the oral literary tradition has made its way into books for young adults and children.

Indigenous texts that were published in the nineteenth century—such as Harriet Ward's *Hardy and Hunter* (1858) and *In the Land of the Lion and the Ostrich* (undated) by Gordon Stables—still reiterated the accepted colonial perceptions of Africa. Similarly, the oral narratives collected by Wilhelm Bleek (and other explorers) in the nineteenth century were not intended as literary examples, but as scientific specimens. Local folklore is bowdlerized in H. Rider Haggard's *King Solomon's Mines* (1885), which also relies on colonial perceptions of African identity. Although colonial influences remain embedded in Sir Percy **Fitzpatrick**'s animal tale, *Jock of the Bushveld* (1907), a large amount of local detail is also included in the text. Other animal tales of note include the English and Afrikaans narratives published by brothers C. G. and S. B. Hobson, and the Afrikaans hunting stories of P. J. Schoeman. Books by Enid Blyton became very popular after World War II, when the South African book market was overcome by books from Britain. The first local picture book with full-color illustrations was Penny Miller's *The Story of Rory* (1963), while oral tales were collected and retold by Phyllis Savory in reaction to a revival of African folklore in the 1960s. Savory's tales were the standard until the publication of Marguerite Poland's collection

of Bushman tales titled *The Mantis and the Moon* (1979).

Until the 1980s, there were not many attempts to produce young adult literature in South Africa outside of folklore. In 1987, however, the first Conference on Children's Literature was held in Cape Town, and authors began to pay attention to the young adult audience. Of note is Niki Daly's *Not So Fast, Songololo* (1985), which demonstrates a new focus in South African literature for young people. Black authors also began to publish books aimed at younger audiences, and works such as Gcina **Mhlophe**'s *The Queen of the Tortoises* (1990) and *Hi, Zoleka!* (1994), Michael Williams's *The Genuine Half Moon Kid* (1992), and Chris van Wyk's *Message in the Wind* (1982) made a superior place for themselves in the young adult market. Well-known authors such as Mothobi **Mutloatse**, Gladys **Thomas**, and Miriam Mabetoa also produced young adult literature. Important racial issues and representations of the oppressed were addressed by young adult authors during this period as well, with works such as *The Strollers* (1987) and *A Cageful of Butterflies* (1989) by Lesley Beake, and Brenda Munitich's *The Scar* (1987). Historical fiction author Jenny Seed depicts the conditions experienced by a black youth during the siege of Mafeking in *The Hungry People* (1992), while Elana Bregin addresses interracial marriage in *The Red-haired Khumalo* (1994). Estelle Bryer provides a picture of the life of a child with Down syndrome in *Jason and the Grey Witch* (1991), and the protagonists in Dianne Hofmeyr's *Boikie You Better Believe It!* (1994) are outsiders who are alienated from their environment on the eve of South Africa's first democratic election.

More recently, (Alu)Remi Aduke's *Moonlight Stories* published by Heinemann Educational books in 1999 contains ten short stories that are based on ancient folktales. The book *Hunterman and the Crocodile: A West African Folk Tale* (1997), written and illustrated by Baba Wague Diakite, describes how a West African hunter learns the importance of living in harmony with nature. *In the Rainfield: Who Is the Greatest?* (2000) by Isaac O. Olaleye relates a Nigerian folktale about the wind, fire, and rain. T. Obinkaram Echewa's *Mbi, Do This! Mbi, Do That: A Folktale from Nigeria* was published either in 1998 or 1999, and Cyprian Ekwensi is sometimes categorized as a writer of folktales (although he is also a writer of novels and popular fiction). Ellen Kuzwayo's *African Wisdom: A Personal Collection of Setswana Proverbs* (1998) could also be considered a type of folklore. Gcina Mhlophe is a prolific contemporary young adult writer, and is the author of the following new works: *Sawubona, Zoleka!* (with Elizabeth Pulles, 2003), *Molo Zoleka!* (with Elizabeth Pulles, 2003), *Stories of Africa* (2003), *Love Child* (republication in English, 2002), *African Mother Christmas* (2002), *Have You Seen Zandile?* (republication, 2002), *Nozincwadi Mother of Books* (published along with a CD, 2001), *Fudukazi's Magic* (storytelling CD, 2000), *Nalohima, the Deaf Tortoise* (1999), and *Fudukazi's Magic* (1999). Reggie Finlayson wrote a biography of Nelson Mandela (*Nelson Mandela*) for young readers in 2002, while Pauline (Janet) Smith's *The Little Karoo* went through republications in 1990 and 1997. Another biography for young readers is Don Pinnock's *Ruth First: They Fought for Freedom* (1995), which tells the story of the antiapartheid activist Ruth First who was killed in 1982 by a parcel bomb. Other works that deal with postapartheid and contemporary issues are Rachel Isadora's *At the Crossroads* (1991), which tells of South African children who gather together to welcome their fathers who have been working in the mines, Elinor Batezat Sisulu's *Day Gogo Went to Vote: South Africa, April 1994*, which follows six-year-old Thembi as she watches her great-grandmother leave the house for the first time in years to vote,

and Anton Ferreira's *Zulu Dog* (2002), telling of eleven-year-old Vusi Ngugu, a post-apartheid Zulu, and his dog Gillette who make friends with the daughter of a privileged white farmer.

Z

Zeleza, Paul Tiyambe (1955–)

Zimbabwean short-story writer and novelist. Zeleza was born in Salisbury, now Harare, and educated at the University of Malawi (BA), the University of London (MA), and Dalhousie University, Canada (PhD). As an undergraduate he participated in the University of Malawi's Writers' Workshop. After doctoral studies he went to work at the University of the West Indies rather than return to Malawi. He was a Professor of History at Trent University, Canada, until 2002, when he held a position as Professor of History and African Studies and Director of the Center for African Studies at the University of Illinois at Urbana-Champaign. Since 2003 he has been affiliated with Pennsylvania State University. In 1994 he won the prestigious Noma Award for his book *A Modern Economic History of Africa* (1993). Zeleza's early short-story collection, **Night of Darkness** (1976), melds the boundaries between history and literature in a form that draws on traditional oral material. In 1992 he published his first novel, *Smouldering Charcoal*, about postcolonial Malawi, and then in 1994 a second collection of short stories, *The Joys of Exile*. Zeleza's short story "Blood Feuds" was published in *The Picador Book of African Stories* (2000), and his story "Foggy Seasons" was published in *Fiery Spirits and Voices: Canadian Writers of African Descent* (2000). Recent research publications by Zeleza include *Sacred Spaces and Public Quarrels: African Cultural and Economic Landscapes* (1999), *Women in African Studies Scholarly Publishing* (2001),

Rethinking Africa's Globalization Volume 1: The Intellectual Challenges (2003), *Leisure in Urban Africa* (2003), *In Search of Modernity: Science and Technology in Africa* (2003), *The Encyclopedia of Twentieth Century African History* (2003), *African Universities in the 21st Century Volume 2: Knowledge and Society* (2004), and *Human Rights, the Rule of Law and Development in Africa* (2004).

Zimunya, Musaemura Bonas (1949–)

Zimbabwean poet and short-story writer. Zimunya was born in Mutare in the then Southern Rhodesia, now Zimbabwe, and educated in Rhodesia and at Kent University, UK, where he gained an MA in literature in 1979. From 1980 to 1999 he was a teacher of literature at the University of Zimbabwe. In 1999 Zimunya left his position as Professor of Literature at the University of Zimbabwe, and he is currently a Director and Visiting Professor in the Black Studies Program at Virginia Tech and State University. Zimunya began publishing poems before he was an undergraduate at the University of Rhodesia in local literary periodicals, and later in journals and anthologies in Britain, the United States, and Yugoslavia, as well as in Kizito Muchemwa's *Zimbabwean Poetry in English* (1978) and in the collection he co-edited with Mudereri Khadani, *And Now the Poets Speak* (1981). The poems show an imagination keen to capture the beauty of nature almost in the tradition of the English romantics. *Thought Tracks* (1982) fuses Western literary techniques and African oral tradition to articulate the way a generation felt itself uprooted from its cultural past and marginalized by the colonial dispensation. In *Kingfisher, Jikinya, and Other Poems* (1982), the poet broadens his horizon and celebrates life, nature, and love. The tone changes in *Country Dawns and City Lights* (1985), in which he demythologizes rural life as idyllic and also portrays the city as a nightmare for the newly urbanized African. Zimunya followed *Country Dawns* with the sombre *Perfect Poise* (1993) and *Selected Poems* (1995) as well as his first collection of short stories, *Nightshift* (1993), in which satire, pathos, and allegory underline the vulnerability and misery that haunt a once-colonized people. He has also published a volume of literary criticism, *Those Years of Drought and Hunger: The Birth of African Fiction in English in Zimbabwe* (1982), and publishes scholarly articles like the one titled "Zimbabwean Poet Reviews—Rhodesian Poets—Part 1," which appeared in the *Herald* (Zimbabwe) in 2000.

Further Reading
Wilhardt, Mark, ed. "Musaemura Zimunya." *The Routledge Who's Who in 20th Century World Poetry*. New York: Routledge, 2001.

Zungur, Sa'ad (1915–58)

Nigerian poet. The first Northerner to gain admission to Yaba College, Lagos, he represented an early radicalism among the Western-educated emirate elite. His charismatic personality influenced the political thought of the first generation of Hausa intellectuals in the immediate postwar years, notably Aminu Kano, who formed the NEPU opposition party in the North and later wrote a memoir of Zungur (1973). In particular, two of Zungur's poems ensured his reputation: "Maraba da Soja" ("Welcome to the Soldiers") (1946), where the discourse is of political values, and the influential "Arewa: Jumhuriya ko Mulukiya?" ("The North: Republic or Monarchy?") (ca.1949), in which he warned the Hausa-Fulani emirs to improve their governance or face political subjugation by the non-Hausa, non-Muslim Southerners.

Further Reading
Yakubu, A. M. *Sa'adu Zungur: An Anthology of the Social and Political Writings of a Nigerian Nationalist*. Kaduna: Nigerian Defence Academy Press, 1999.

SELECTED BIBLIOGRAPHY

Amadiume, Ifi. *Male Daughters, Female Husbands: Gender and Sex in an African Society*. London: Zed Books, 1987.

Arndt, Susan. *African Women's Literature: Orality and Intertextuality*. Beyreuth, Germany: Eckhard Breitinger, 1998.

———, ed. *Dynamics of African Feminism*. Eritrea: Africa World Press, 2002.

Arnfred, Signe, Babere Kerata Chacha, and Amanda Gouws, eds. *Gender, Activism, and Studies in Africa*. Senegal: Codesria, 2004.

Attwell, David, and Barbara Harlow, eds. "South African Fiction after Apartheid." *MFS: Modern Fiction Studies* 46, no. 1 (2000): 282–95.

Balderston, D. *Encyclopedia of Latin American and Caribbean Literature 1900–2003*. London: Routledge, 2004.

Banham, Martin, Errol Hill, and George Woodyard, eds. *The Cambridge Guide to African and Caribbean Theatre*. Cambridge: Cambridge University Press, 1994.

Barnard, Ian. *Queer Race: Cultural Interventions in the Racial Politics of Queer Theory*. New York: Peter Lang, 2004.

Black, Ayanna, ed. *Fiery Spirits, Canadian Writers of African Descent*. Toronto: HarperCollins, 1994.

———, ed. *Voices, Canadian Writers of African Descent*. Toronto: HarperCollins, 1992.

Boehmer, Elleke. *Stories of Women: Gender and Narrative in the Postcolonial Nation*. Manchester, England: Manchester University Press, 2005.

Bogues, Anthony. *Black Heretics, Black Prophets: Radical Political Intellectuals*. New York: Routledge, 2003.

Boyce Davies, Carole, and Anne Adams Graves, eds. *Ngambika: Studies of Women in African Literature*. Trenton, NJ: Africa World Press, 1986.

Braxton, Joanne M., and Maria I. Diedrich, eds. *Monuments of the Black Atlantic: Slavery and Memory*. Münster: LIT, 2004.

Carey, Brycchan, Markman Ellis, and Sara Salih, eds. *Discourses of Slavery and Abolition: Britain and Its Colonies, 1760–1838*. Basingstoke, England: Palgrave/Macmillan, 2004.

Carretta, Vincent, and Philip Gould. *Genius in Bondage: Literature of the Early Black Atlantic*. Lexington: University Press of Kentucky, 2001.

Chapman, Michael, Colin Gardner, and Es'kia Mphahlele, eds. *Perspectives on South African English Literature*. Johannesburg: Ad. Donker, 1992.

Chevannes, Barry. *Rastafari and Other African-Caribbean Worldviews*. London: Macmillan Press, 1995.

Childs, Peter, Jean Jacques Weber, and Peter Williams. *Post-Colonial Theory and Literatures: African, Caribbean and South Asian*. Germany: Wissenschaftlicher, 2006.

Chinweizu, Onwucheckwa Jemi, and Ihechuckwu Madubuike, eds. *Towards the Decolonization of African Literature*. Enugu: Fourth Dimension; Washington, DC: Howard University Press, 1980.

Clarke, Austin. "In the Semi-Colon of the North." *Canadian Literature* 95 (1982): 30–37.

Clarke, George Elliott, ed. *Fire on the Water, Volumes One and Two*. Lawrencetown Beach, Nova Scotia: Pottersfield Press, 1991.

———, ed. *Odysseys Home: Mapping African-Canadian Literature.* Toronto: University of Toronto Press, 2002.

Collins, Patrica Hill. *Black Feminist Thought: Knowledge, Consciousness, and the Politics of Empowerment.* New York: Routledge, 2000.

Cuder-Domínguez, Pilar. "African Canadian Writing and the Narration(s) of Slavery." *Essays on Canadian Writing* 79 (2003): 55–75.

Dash, J. Michael. *The Other America: Caribbean Literature in a New World Context.* Virginia: University of Virginia Press, 1998.

Davis, Geoffrey V. *Voices of Justice and Reason: Apartheid and Beyond in South African Literature.* Amsterdam: Rodopi, 2003.

De Caires Narain, Denise. *Contemporary Caribbean Women's Poetry: Making Style.* London: Routledge, 2002.

DeCorse, Christopher R., ed. *West Africa during the Atlantic Slave Trade: Archaeological Perspectives.* London: Leicester University Press, 2001.

De Lange, Margreet, and Ampie Coetzee. *The Muzzled Muse: Literature and Censorship in South Africa.* Amsterdam: Benjamins, 1997.

Elimimian, Isaac. *Theme and Style in African Poetry.* Lewiston, Lampeter, Dyfed, UK: Edwin Mellen Press, 1991.

Emenyonu, Ernest N. *New Women's Writing in African Literature: African Literature Today.* No. 24. London: James Curry, 2004.

Evwierhoma, Mabel. *Female Empowerment and Dramatic Creativity in Nigeria.* Ibadan: Caltop Publications, 2002.

Frank, Heike. *Role-Play in South African Theatre.* Bayreuth: Thielmann & Breitinger, 2004.

———. "'That's All Out of Shape': Language and Racism in South African Drama." In *The Politics of English as a World Language: New Horizons in Postcolonial Cultural Studies,* ed. Christian Mair. Amsterdam: Rodopi, 2003, 305–14.

Gafaiti, Hafid. "Between God and the President: Literature and Censorship in North Africa." *Diacritics: A Review of Contemporary Criticism* 27, no. 2 (1997): 59–84.

Gaylard, Gerald. *After Colonialism: African Postmodernism and Magical Realism.* Witwatersrand University Press, 2006.

Gibbons, Rawle. "Theatre and Caribbean Self-Definition." *Modern Drama* 38, no. 1 (1995): 52–59.

Gikandi, Simon. "Theory, Literature, and Moral Considerations." *Research in African Literatures* 32, no. 4 (2001): 1–18.

Gilroy, Paul. "The Black Atlantic as a Counterculture of Modernity." In *Theorizing Diaspora: A Reader,* ed. Jana Evans Braziel and Anita Mannur. Malden: Blackwell, 2003, 49–80.

Graham, Shane. "The Truth Commission and Post-Apartheid Literature in South Africa." *Research in African Literatures* 34, no. 1 (2003): 11–30.

Gruesser, John Cullen. *Confluences: Postcolonialism, African American Literary Studies, and the Black Atlantic.* Athens: University of Georgia Press, 2005.

Habekost, Christian. *Verbal Riddim: The Politics and Aesthetics of African-Caribbean Dub Poetry.* Atlanta: Rodopi, 1993.

Harris, Claire. "Poets in Limbo." In *A Mazing Space: Writing Canadian Women Writing,* ed. Shirley Neuman and Smaro Kamboureli. Edmonton: Longspoon/Newest, 1986, 115–25.

Hill, Alan. "The *African Writers Series.*" *Research in African Literatures* 2 (1971): 18–20.

hooks, bell. *Ain't I a Woman: Black Women and Feminism.* London: Pluto Press, 1982.

Horrell, Georgie. "Post-Apartheid Disgrace: Guilty Masculinities in White South African Writing." *Literature Compass* 2, no. 1 (2005).

Hudson-Weems, Clenora. *Africana Womanism.* Troy: Bedford Publishers, 1993.

Jenkins, Lee M. *The Language of Caribbean Poetry: Boundaries of Expression.* Gainesville: University Press of Florida, 2004.

John, Catherine A. *Clear Word and Third Sight: Folk Groundings and Diasporic Consciousness in African Caribbean Writing.* North Carolina: Duke University Press, 2003.

Keizer, Arlene R. *Black Subjects: Identity Formation in the Contemporary Narrative of Slavery.* Ithaca, NY: Cornell University Press, 2004.

Kibble, Matt. "The *African Writers Series* Reborn: An Electronic Edition." *Wasafiri: The Transnational Journal of International Writing* 46 (2005): 66–68.

Killam, G. D. *Literature of Africa.* Westport, CT: Greenwood Press, 2004.

———, ed. *The Writing of East and Central Africa.* Nairobi: Heinemann, 1984.

Kinnahan, Linda A. *Lyric Interventions: Feminism, Experimental Poetry, and Contemporary Discourse.* Iowa City: University of Iowa Press, 2004.

Le Roux, Elizabeth, ed. *Gender, Literature and Religion in Africa.* Senegal: Codesria, 2005.

Miller, Margaret. "Forms of Resistance: South African Women's Writing during Apartheid." *Hecate* 5, no. 1 (1998): 118–44.

Mkandawire, Thandika, ed. *African Intellectuals: Rethinking Politics, Language, Gender and Development.* London: Zed Books, 2005.

Moslund, Sten Pultz. *Making Use of History in New South African Fiction: An Analysis of the Purposes of Historical Perspectives in Three Post-Apartheid Novels.* Copenhagen: Museum Tusculanum, 2003.

Muponde, Robert, and Primorac, Ranka, eds. *Versions of Zimbabwe: New Approaches to Literature and Culture.* Weaver Press, 2005.

Napier, Winston, ed. *African American Literary Theory: A Reader.* New York: New York University Press, July 2000.

Newell, Stephanie. *West African Literatures: Ways of Reading.* Oxford: Oxford University Press, 2006.

Ngugi wa Thiong'o. *Decolonizing the Mind: The Politics of Language in African Literature.* London: James Currey; Portsmouth, NH: Heinemann, 1981.

———. "License to Write: Encounters with Censorship." *Comparative Studies of South Asia, Africa and the Middle East* 23, nos. 1–2 (2003): 54–57.

Nussbaum, Felicity A. *The Limits of the Human: Fictions of Anomaly, Race, and Gender in the Long Eighteenth Century.* Cambridge: Cambridge University Press, 2003.

Okpewho, Isidore. *Once upon a Kingdom: Myth, Hegemony, and Identity.* Bloomington: Indiana University Press, 1998.

Okyerefo, Michael Perry Kweku. "The Cultural Crisis of Sub-Saharan Africa as Depicted in the *African Writers Series:* A Sociological Perspective." *European University Studies, XII: Sociology* 348 (2001): 208.

Oyewumi, Oyeronke, ed. *African Gender Studies: A Reader.* London: Palgrave, 2005.

Pape, Marion. "Nigerian War Literature by Women: From Civil War to Gender War." *Matatu: Journal for African Culture and Society* 29–30 (2005): 231–41.

Pieterse, Cosmo, and Donald Munro, eds. *Protest and Conflict in African Literature.* New York: Heinemann, Africana Publishing Corp., 1969.

Priebe, Richard K. "Literature, Community, and Violence: Reading African Literature in the West, Post-9/11." *Research in African Literatures* 36, no. 2 (2005): 46–58.

Puri, Shalini. *The Caribbean Postcolonial: Social Equality, Post-Nationalism, and Cultural Hybridity.* New York: Palgrave Macmillan, 2004.

Reyes, Angelita. *Mothering across Cultures: Postcolonial Representations.* Minneapolis: University of Minnesota Press, 2002.

Ricard, Alain. *The Languages and Literatures of Africa: The Sands of Babel.* London: James Currey, 2004.

Sanneh, Lamin, and Carpenter, Joel A., eds. *The Changing Face of Christianity: Africa, the West and the World.* Oxford: Oxford University Press, 2005.

Singh, Jaspal. "Representing the Poetics of Resistance in Transnational South Asian Women's Fiction and Film." *South Asian Review* 24, no. 1 (2003): 202–19.

Smith, Ann. "Queer Pedagogy and Social Change: Teaching and Lesbian Identity in South Africa." In *Lesbian and Gay Studies and the Teaching of English: Positions, Pedagogies, and Cultural Politics,* ed. William J. Spurlin. Urbana, IL: National Council of Teachers of English, 2000, 253–71.

Solberg, Rolf, ed. *South African Theatre in the Melting Pot: Trends and Developments at the Turn of the Millennium.* Grahamstown: South Africa Institute for the Study of English in Africa, 2003.

Spitczok von Brisinski, Marek. "Rethinking Community Theatre: Performing Arts Communities in Post-Apartheid South Africa." *South African Theatre Journal* 17 (2003): 114–28.

Stanford, Ann Folwell. *Bodies in a Broken World: Women Novelists of Color and the Politics of Medicine.* Chapel Hill: University of North Carolina Press, 2003.

Trengove Jones, Tim. "Fiction and the Law: Recent Inscriptions of Gayness in South Africa." *MFS: Modern Fiction Studies* 46, no. 1 (2000): 114–36.

Welsh, Sarah Lawson. *The Routledge Reader in Caribbean Literature.* London: Routledge, 1996.

Wisker, Gina. "Redefining an African Sky: South African Women's Writing Post-Apartheid." *Kunapipi: Journal of Post-Colonial Writing* 24, nos. 1–2 (2002): 140–54.

INDEX

Abisong, E. B., 14
Abrahams, Lionel, 36, 86, 98, 140, 197, 243, 285
Abrahams, Peter, 55, 198, 265
Abruquah, Joseph Wilfred, **2**
Achebe, Chinua, **2–4,** 5, 49, 60, 188, 198, 206, 219, 220, 229, 235, 256, 257, 263, 297, 300, 302, 312, 318–19
Achmat, Dangor, 61
Acholonu, Catherine Obianuju, **4**
Adair, Barbara, **4**
Adali-Mortty, G., 38
Adedeji, (Alu) Remi Aduke, **4–5**
Adichie, Chimamanda Ngozi, **5**
Adu, Raulf, 15
Africa Is People (Achebe), 3, **5**
African-American Literature, **8–12,** 314
African-British Literature, **13–16**
African-Canadian literature, **16–20**
African-Caribbean literature, **23–26**
The African Child (Camara), **5–6**
The African Image (Mphahlele), **6**
African Music and Drama Association, 112
African Research and Educational Puppetry Programme, 114
An African Tragedy (Dhlomo), **6,** 105
African Writer Series, **6–8**

Afrika, Tatamkhulu Ismail, **27–28,** 61, 137
Afrocentrism ideal, 17
Age of Iron (Coetzee), **28,** 92
Aidoo, Ama Ata, **28–29,** 33, 39, 45, 106, 117, 120, 129, 136, 219, 240, 266, 295, 318
Aiyejina, Funso, **29**
Ajayi, Christie Ade, **29**
Ajayi, Tolu(walogo), **29**
Ajibade, Yemi, 116
Ajose, Audrey, **29**
Akassa You Mi: A Historical Drama (Rotimi), **30**
Ake: The Years of Childhood (Soyinka), **30,** 60, 318
Akello, Grace, **30**
Akenhaten: Dweller in Truth (Mahfouz), **30**
Alford, Gwen, **30**
Alkali, Zaynab, **30**
All for Love: A Novel (Jacobson), **31,** 155
All for Oil (Bekederemo), **31,** 51
Aluko, Timothy Mofolorunso, **31,** 235, 265
Amadi, Elechi, **31,** 94, 143
Anduru, Agoro, **32**
Angelou, Maya, 11, 72
Angira, Jared, **32,** 34, 173, 264
Aniebo, I.N.C., **32–33,** 157, 312
Anowa (Aidoo), **33,** 117
Anthills of the Savannah (Achebe), 3, **33**
anthologies, **33–39,** 297; of East Africa, **33–35;** of South Africa, **35–37;** of

South-Central Africa, **37–38;** of West Africa, **38–39**
Anyidoho, Kofi, **39–40,** 257
apartheid, 35, **40–43,** 64, 74, 75, 78, 81, 92, 101, 111, 119, 132, 134, 140, 154, 155, 164, 183, 188, 197, 199, 213, 220, 248, 251, 286, 293, 297, 303, 309
Appiah, Kwame, 180
Armah, Ayi Kwei, 29, **44–45,** 49, 133, 147, 150, 206, 238, 268, 315
Armattoe, R.E.G., 263
Arrowheads to My Heart (Olafioye), **45,** 234
Arrow of God (Achebe), 3, **45,** 220, 257, 266, 302
Atta, Sefi, **45–46**
Attridge, Derek, 36
Attwell, David, 42
Awoonor, Kofi (Nyedevu), 38, **46–47,** 136, 172, 256, 257, 264

Bâ, Amadou Hampâté, **47**
Bâ, Mariama, **47–48,** 158, 289
The Bacchae of Euripides (Soyinka), **48**
Bailey, Jim, 118
Baldwin, James, 9
Baldwin, William Charles, 58
Balewa, Abubakar Tafewa, 118, 287
Banana, Canaan, 84
Bandele-Thomas, Biyi, **48–49**
Bangirana, Alex, 34
Banjo, Ayo, 61

Bantu Dramatic Society, 111
Barber, Karin, 115, 181
Bavino Sermons
    (Rampolokeng), **49**
*The Beautification of Area
    Boy* (Soyinka), **49**
*The Beautyful Ones Are Not
    Yet Born* (Armah), 29,
    45, **49**
*The Beggar, The Thief and the
    Dogs, and Autumn Quail*
    (Mahfouz), **49–50**
Bekederemo, J. P. Clark, 31,
    50–51, 53–54, 116, 225,
    238, 264
Bell, Vera, 23
Ben, in the World
    (Lessing), **51**
Ben-Abdallah, Mohammed,
    52–53
Benge, Okot, 34
Ben Jelloun, Tahar, **51–52**
Beold, Robert, 35
Beti, Mongo (Alexandre
    Biyidi), **53,** 136, 168,
    245, 265
Betrayal in the City
    (Imbuga), 81
Beyala, Calixthe, 129
Biko, Steve, 34, 65, 249
The Bikoroa Plays
    (Bekederemo), **53–54**
biography and autobiography,
    54–61, 264, 292; of East
    Africa, **54**; of North Africa,
    54; of South Africa, **54–57**;
    of South-Central Africa,
    57–59; of West Africa,
    59–61
Bitter Eden (Ismail), **61**
Bitter Fruit: A Novel
    (Achmat), **61,** 101
Black, Stephen, **61–62,**
    111, 148
Black Atlantic, **62–63**
Blackburn, Douglas,
    67–68, 310
Black Community
    Programmes, 65

Black Consciousness
    movement, 10, 40, 41, 70,
    113, 145, 161, 191, 193,
    202, 249, 255, 270, 285; in
    South Africa, **64–67**
The Black Docker (Sembene),
    67, 283
Blackheart (Rampolokeng), **68**
Black People's Convention, 65
Black Thoughts, 101
Black Women's Federation, 65
Blame Me on History
    (Modisane), **68,** 199, 267
Blanket Boy's Moon (Mopeli-
    Paulus), **68,** 200
Blay, J. Benibengor, **68**
Blind Moon (Hove), **69**
The Blood Knot (Fugard), **69,**
    134, 218
Bloodlines (Boehmer), **69**
Bloom, Harry, **69**
Boehmer, Elleke, **69–70,** 218
Boesman and Lena (Fugard),
    70, 134
Boetie, Dugmore, **70**
Bontemps, Ama, 9
Booker Prize, 73
The Book of Secrets
    (Vassanji), **70–71,** 304
Bosman, Herman Charles, 1,
    71, 139, 142, 186, 249, 253
Boundaries (Karodia), **72**
Brand, Dionne, 17–18
Brandt, Johanna, 55
Brathwaite, Kamau, 24–25
Brettel, N. H., **72**
Brew (Osborne Henry)
    Kwesi, **72**
Breytenbach, Breyton, 34, 57,
    72–73, 82, 156, 252
Brink, Andre, 36, **73–74,** 82,
    119, 153, 156, 183, 267,
    274, 294, 307, 310
Brodber, Erna, 25
Broken Reed (Mustafa), **74**
Brookes, Gwendolyn, 9
Brown, Claude, 10
Brown, Wellis, 9
Bruner, Charlotte H., 39

Brutus, Dennis, **74–75,** 82,
    161, 169–70, 192, 219, 253,
    264, 288
Bukenya, Austin, **75**
Bulpin, T. V., 55
Bunn, David, 36
Burger's Daughter
    (Gordimer), **75,** 82,
    140, 310
Burton, Nefertiti, 114
Butler, Frederick Guy, 35, 55,
    75–76, 197, 310
By the Sea (Gurnah), **76**

The Cairo Trilogy (Mahfouz),
    76, 187
Call Me by My Rightful Name
    (Okpewho), **76–77,** 232
Call Me Woman (Kuzwayo),
    56, **77,** 154, 165
Camara Laye, **77–78,** 268
Campbell, A. A., 58
Campbell, Roy(ston), 55,
    78–79, 98, 246, 303
Campion Medal, 3
The Captain's Tiger
    (Fugard), **79**
Carnival of Looters
    (Olafioye), **79**
Casely-Hayford, Adelaide, 79,
    129, 258–59
Casely-Hayford, Gladys,
    38, 263
Casely-Hayford, Joseph
    Ephraim, **80**
Catherine T. MacArthur
    Foundation, 11
censorship, 40, 298; in East
    Africa, **80–81**; in North
    Africa, **81**; in South Africa,
    81–83; in South-Central
    Africa, **83–84**; in West
    Africa, **84–85**
Censorship and
    Entertainment Control
    Amendment Act (1983), 84
Chaka (Mofolo), **86,** 199, 262
*Chaos Theory of the Heart
    and Other Poems Mainly*

since 1990 (Lionel Abrahams), 1, **86**
Chapman, Michael, 176
Chedid, Andrée, **86–87,** 269, 288
Cheney-Coker, Syl, 18, **87,** 168, 264
Chestnutt, Charles Waddell, 9
Children of Gebelawi (Mahfouz), **87–88,** 187
Childress, Alice, 10
Chimombo, Steve, **88,** 255
Chingono, Julius, **88**
Chinodya, Shimmer, 7, 59, **88–89,** 203, 311
Chinweizu, **89,** 172, 178, 292
Chipamaunga, Edmund, **89–90**
Chipasula, Frank, **90,** 217, 306
Chraïbi, Driss, **90–91**
Christianity, and literature, **257–68**
Churchill, Winston, 55
Clark, Ebun, 115
Clarke, Austin, 17
Clarke, George Elliot, 20
Clayton, Cherry, **91**
Cleaver, Eldridge, 10
Cliff, Michelle, 11
Clifton, Lucille, 10
Cloete, (Edward Fairlie) Stuart (Graham), **91,** 248–49
Clouts, Sydney (David), **91**
Cochlovius, Karen, **92**
Coetzee, Ampie, 35
Coetzee, J. M., 28, 36, 42, 55, **92–93,** 120, 153, 170, 176, 191, 307, 310–11
Coleman, Wanda, 12
The Collector of Treasures (Head), **93,** 147
Collen, Lindsay, **93–94**
Collins, Merle, 23
Combrinck, Lisa, **94**
The Concubine (Amadi), **94**
Congress of South African Writers (COSAW), 101
The Conservationist (Gordimer), **94,** 140

Conteh, Fatmata, 34
Conton, William (Farquhar), **94**
Cook, David, 33, 38, 272
Cook, Méira, **94–95**
Cope, Jack (Robert Knox), 35, **95,** 156
Couchoro, Félix, **95–96**
Couto, Mia, **96**
Crail, Archie, 19
Creider, Jane Tapsubei, 19
Cripps, A. S., 37, **97**
Cromwell, Liz, 19
Cry, the Beloved Country (Paton), 55, **97,** 243, 244, 267
Cugoano, Ottobah, **97–98**
Cullen, Countee, 9
Cullinan, Patrick (Roland), **98**
Currey, Ralph Nixon, **98–99**

Dadié, Bernard, **99,** 263
A Dance in the Sun (Jacobson), **100,** 155
A Dance of the Forests (Soyinka), **100,** 116, 257, 291
Dangarembga, Tsitsi, 37, **100,** 211, 320
Dangor, Achmat, 35, 41, **101,** 207
Dathorne, O. R., 24, 261
Daughter of Mumbi (Waciuma), **101,** 308
Daughters of Twilight (Karodia), **101,** 159
Dawes, Kwame, 19
Daymond, Margaret, 36
Death and the King's Horseman (Soyinka), **102,** 257, 312
Dedan Kimathi (Watene), **102,** 110, 308, 313
De Graft, Joe (Joseph Coleman), 80, **102,** 204–5, 240, 290, 295, 297
Dei-Anang, Michael Francis, **102–3,** 263
Delany, Martin Robinson, 8, 9

Desai, Ashwin, 57
Detained: A Writer's Prison Diary (Ngugi wa Thiong'o), **103,** 214
Devil on the Cross (Ngugi wa Thiong'o), 81, **103–4,** 214, 267
Dhlomo, H.I.E., 35, 41, **104,** 111, 139, 176, 262, 302, 306
Dhlomo, R.R.R., 6, **104–5**
Dib, Mohammed, **105**
Diescho, Joseph, **106**
Dikobe, Modikwe, **106**
The Dilemma of a Ghost (Aidoo), 28, **106,** 117
Diop, Alioune, **107,** 171
Diop, Birago, **107–8,** 171, 268
Diop, Cheikh Anta, **108–9,** 171
Diop, David, **109,** 146, 263
The Divorce (Ogunyemi), 109
Djoleto, (Solomon Alexander) Amu, **109–10**
Douglass, Frederick, 8
Down Second Avenue (Mphahlele), **110,** 266
drama, **110–18**; of East Africa, **110–11**; of South Africa, **111–15**; of West Africa, **115–18**
Drayton, Geoffrey, 23
Driver, Dorothy, 36
Drum (literary magazine), **118–19,** 146, 192, 199, 200, 208, 248, 297
A Dry White Season (Brink), 74, 82, **119,** 310
Dube, Hope, 205
Dubois, W.E.B., 9
Dugmore, H. H., 55
Dunbar, Paul Laurence, 9
Dunton, Christ, 116
Duodu, Cameron, **119–20**
Du Plessis, Menán, **119**
Durban Workers Cultural Local (DWCL), 113
Dusklands (Coetzee), 92, **120**

Easmon, Raymond Sharif, 115, **120**

East Africa: anthologies of, **33–35**; biographies/ autobiographies of, **54**; censorship in, **80–81**; drama of, **110–11**; popular literature of, **247–48**; war literature of, **308–9**; young adult literature of, **318–21**

Ebersohn, Wessel, 249

Echeruo, Michael J. C., **120–21**

Echewa, T. Obinkaram, **121**, 266

Edufa (Sutherland), 115, **121**, 295

Efuru (Nwapa), **121**, 128, 221, 265

Egbuna, Obi Benedict, **121–22**

Eisenstein, Zillah, 129

Ekwensi, Cyprian, 96, **122**, 244, 312, 319

Elliot, Lorris, 20

Ellison, Ralph, 9

Emecheta, Buchi, 14, 60, **123**, 129, 152–53, 157, 159, 232, 312

Enekwe, Ossie, **124**, 312

Eppel, John, **124**

Equiano, Olaudah, 4, 8, 13, 17, 59, **125**, 153, 259

Essop, Ahmed, **125**

Essuman-Gwira, WIlliam, **282**

Etherton, Michael, 115

Everett, Percival, 11

The Experience (Seruma), **126**

The Eye of the Earth (Osundare), **126**

Fagunwa, Daniel O., **126**, 133, 168, 261

Fall, Malick, **127**

The Famished Road (Okri), 14, **127**, 233

Fanon, Frantz, 17

Farah, Nuruddin, **127**, 133

feminism and literature, **128–29**, 178

Fettouma, Touati, **130–31**

Fiawoo, Ferdinand Kwasi, **131**

Figueira, Luiz, 259

Finn, D. E., 37

First Physical Theater Company, 114

The Fisherman's Invocation (Okara), **131**, 229

Fitzpatrick, (Sir) J. Percy, **131–32**, 322

Fixions and Other Stories (Tabon Lo Liyong), **132**, 296

Fools and Other Stories (Ndebele), **132–33**

Footprints in the Quag (Tlali), **133**, 250, 298

Forest of a Thousand Daemons (Soyinka), 126, **133**, 168, 261

Foriwa (Sutherland), **133**, 295

Fragments (Armah), 45, **133**

Fraser, Robert, 61

Freedom of Expression Institute, 83

From a Crooked Rib (Farah), **127**, 133

Fugard, Athol, 42, 56, 69, 70, 79, 112, **133–35**, 134, 142, 199, 218, 253, 288, 311

Fugard, Sheila Meiring, **135**

Garba, John Mamman, 60

Garuba, Harry, 38, **135–36**, 230

Gates, Henry Louis, Jr., 12

gay and lesbian sexuality, in literature, **136–37**

Gaylard, Gerald, 181

Gbadamosi, Gabriel, 14

Gbaingbain, Imomotimi. *See* Okara, Gabriel

George, Crispin, 263

Gerard, Albert, 268

Ghana Drama Studio, 115

Ghanem, Fathy, **138**, 188

Gibb, James, 40

Gibbon, Perceval, **138–39**

Gibbons, Rawle, 24

Gikandi, Simon, 172

Gilroy, Paul, 63

The Girl Who Killed to Save: Nongquase the Liberator (Dhlomo), **104**, 111, 139, 262

Githinji, Sam, 247

Glynn, Martin, 15

Goal, Réshard, 19

The Gods Are Not to Blame (Rotimi), **139**, 165, 271

God's Bits of Wood (Sembene Ousmane), **139**, 283

God's Step-Children (Millin), 139, 198, 316

Going Down River Road (Mwangi), **140**

Golden, Marita, 11

Goldswain, Jeremiah, 55

Gordimer, Nadine, 7, 36, 42, 75, 82, 129, **140–41**, 143, 149, 157, 208, 219, 294, 310

Gordone, Charles, 12

Graham-White, Anthony, 115

A Grain of Wheat (Ngugi wa Thiong'o), **142**, 204, 214, 267, 309

The Grass is Singing (Lessing), **142**

Gray, Stephen, 35, 71, **142–43**, 176, 188

The Great Ponds (Amadi), **143**

Greig, Robert, 35

Griggs, Sutton, 9

A Guest of Honor (Gordimer), 140, **143**

Gunner, Elizabeth, 181

The Gunny Sack (Vassanji), **143–44**, 304

Gurnah, Abdulrazak, 7, 14–15, 76, **144**

Gwala, Mafika, 41, 66

Gwala, Mafika Pascal, **144–45**

Haarhoff, Dorian, **145**

Hadeja, Mu'azu, 136

Haggard, H. Rider, 58

Hakim, Te[a?]wfiq (Husayn) al-, **145**

Haley, Alex, 10

Hammer Blows (Diop), 109, **146**

Hansberry, Lorraine, 9

Harlem Renaissance, 9

Harlow, Barbara, 42

Harper, Ellen Watkins, 9

Harris, E. Lynn, 12

Hartley, Aidan, 54

Head, Bessie, 7, 40, 93, 129, **146–47**, 254, 267, 304

The Healers (Armah), 45, **147**

Heavensgate (Okigbo), **148**, 230

Helena's Hope (Black), 111, **148**

Hello and Goodbye (Fugard), 134, **148**

Henshaw, James Ene, 115, **148**

Heroes (Iyayi), **148**

Hill, Lawrence, 18

Hope, Christopher (David Tully), **148–49**

Houseboy (Oyono), **149**, 242

The House Gun (Gordimer), 140, 149

House of Hunger (Marechera), 149, **190**, 267

Hove, Chenjerai, 69, **149–50**, 311

Howell, William Dean, 9

Hughes, Langston, 9, 62, 79, 103, 216

Hurston, Zora Neale, 9

Hussein, Ebrahim N., **150**

Ibadan: The Pankelemes Years, a Memoir 1946–1965 (Soyinka), **151**, 292

Idanre (Soyinka), 151

Ike, (Vincent) Chukwuemeka, **151–52**, 264

Ikiddeh, Ime, 116

Imbuga, Francis, 81, 111, **152**

Incidents at the Shrine (Okri), **14**, 153, 233

An Instant in the Wind (Brink), 73, **153**

The Interesting Narrative of the Life of Olaudah Equiano; or, Gustavus Vassa, the African, Written by Himself, 8, 13, 17, 59, 125, **153**, 259

The Interpreters (Soyinka), 136, **153**, 266, 292

In the Ditch (Emecheta), **152–53**

In the Fog of the Season's End (La Guma), **153**, 166

In the Heart of the Country (Coetzee), 92, **153**

Iroh, Eddie, **153**

Irungu, James, 110

Islam, and literature, **268**

I Will Marry When I Want (Ngugi wa Thiong'o), **151**

Iyayi, Festus, 148, **154**, 312

Jabavu, Noni (Helen Nontando), 129, **154**, 205

Jackman, Oliver, 24

Jacobson, Daniel, 31, 100, **155**

Jeffrey, Gary, 257

Jeyifo, Biodun, 223, 235

Johnson, James Weldon, 9

Johnson, Lemuel A., **156**

Johnson, Lincoln Kwesi, 15

Jolly, Rosemary, 36

Jonker, Ingrid, **156–57**

Jordan, Archibald Campbell, **157**, 262, 317

The Journey Within (Aniebo), **157**

The Joys of Motherhood (Emecheta), 123, 157

July's People (Gordimer), 140, **157**

Ka, Aminata Maiga, **158**

Kadhani, Mudereri, 37

Kagame, Alexis, **158**, 261

Kaggia, Bildad, 54

Kagwema, Prince, 80

Kahiga, Samuel, **158–59**, 162, 308

Kamau, Oliver, 117

Kariara, Jonathan, 34

Kariuki, Joseph, 34, 54

Karodia, Farida, 19, 72, 101, **159**, 268

Karoki, John, 247

Karone, Yodi, **160**

Kassam, Arnin, 33

Katiyo, Wilson, 84, **160**

Kaunda, Kenneth, 34

Kayira, Legson, **160–61**, 265, 272

Kente, Gibson, 82, 112, 137, **161**, 213

Kentridge, William, 114

Kenyatta, Jomo, 54

Kgositsile, Keorapetse, **161**

Kibera, Leonard, **162**

Kimbugwe, Henry S. *See* Seruma, Eneriko

Kimenye, Barbara, **162**, 320

Kincaid, Jamaica, 11

Knox, Robert. *See* Cope, Jack

Konadu, (Samuel) Asare, **162–63**

Kongi's Harvest (Soyinka), **163**, 292

Kourouma, Ahmadou, **163**

Kunene, Daniel P., 82, 161, **164**, 181

Kunene, Mazisi (KaMdabuli), **164–65**

Kurunmi (Rotimi), 116, **165**

Kuzwayo, Ellen, 56, 77, 154, **165**

Labyrinths (Okigbo), **167**

Ladipo, Duro, 167

La Guma, Alex, 7, 153, **166**, 253, 270, 294, 297, 307

Laing, Bernard Kojo, **167–68**

Lament for an African Pol (Beti), **168**

Landlocked (Lessing), **168**, 169

Langbodo (Ogunyemi), **168**

The Last Harmattan of Alusine Dunbar (Cheney-Coker), 18, 87, **168**

Launko, Okinba, 257

Leipoldt, Louis, 55

Leroux, Ètienne, 82

Lessing, Doris, 37, 38, 51, 58, 84, 142, **168–69**, 191, 254, 269–70

Letters to Martha and Other Poems from a South Africa Prison (Brutus), 75, **169–70**, 253

Life and Times of Michael K (Coetzee), 92, **170**

Likimani, Muthoni, **170**, 308

Liking, Werewere, 129

Limits (Okigbo), **170**, 229

The Lion and the Jewel (Soyinka), **170–71**

Lionel, Abrahams, 1

Lipenga, Ken, **171**, 198, 202

literary criticism, **171–80**; of South Africa, **176–77**; of West Africa, **177–80**

literary theory, **180–82**

The Little Karoo (Smith), **182**, 289

Livingstone, Douglas, 72, **182–83**

Locke, Alain, 9

Looking on Darkness (Brink), **74**, 82, **183**, 267

The Looming Shadow (Kayira), **160**

Luandino, José, 260

Lubega, Bonnie, **184**

Lubwa P'chong, Cliff, 111, **184**

Maclennan, Donald (Alasdair Calum), **184–85**

Macnab, Roy, 36

Macoye, Margorie Oludhe, 34

Madanhire, Nevanji, **185**

Maddy, Yulisa Amadu, 137, **185**

Madmen and Specialists (Soyinka), **185**, 292, 312

The Mafeking Diary of Sol T. Plaatje (Plaatje), **185–86**, 246, 310

Mafeking Road (Bosman), **186**

Magai, Lina, **186**

Magona, Sindiwe, **186–87**

Mahfouz, Naguib, 7, 30, 34, 49–50, 76, 87–88, 140, **187–88**

Maillu, David G., 80

Maimane, Arthur, 40

Maina Wa Kinyatti, **188**

Manaka, Matsemela, 66, 113, 161, **188–89**

Mandela, Nelson, 34

Mangua, Charles, 80, **189**, 247, 290

Manim, Mannie, 112

A Man of the People (Achebe), 3, **188**, 257, 319

The Man Who Lost His Shadow (Ghanem), 138, **188**

Mapanje, Jack, 2, 7, 173, **189**, 198, 202, 224

Mapfumo, Thomas, 84

Maponya, Maishe, 113, 161, 173

The Marabi Dance (Dikobe), 106, **189–90**

Marechera, Dambudzo, 84, 149, 173, **190**, 267, 311

Marke, Ernest, 14

The Marriage of Anansewa (Sutherland), 115, **190**, 295

Marshall, Bill Okyere, **191**

Marshall, Paule, 25

Martha Quest (Lessing), 169, **191**

Masinde, Elijah, 110

The Master of St. Petersburg (Coetzee), 92, **191**

Mathews, James, 35

Matigari (Ngugi wa Thiong'o), 80, **191**, 215, 267

Matshikiza, Todd, 40, 82

Matshoba, Mtutuzeli, 66

Mattera, Umaruiddin Don, 56, **191–92**

Matthews, James, 40, 82, 137, 145, **192**, 253, 270

Maunick, Edouard, **192**

Mazrui, Ali A., **192–93**, 299

Mboya, Tom, 54

Mbuli, Mzwakhe, 41, **193–94**

Mbure, Samuel N., 34

McKay, Claude, 9

McLaren, Robert, 112

McLoughlin, T. O., 37, **194**

Mda, Zakes (Zanemvula Kizito Gatyeni), **194–95**, 310

Meintjes, Sheila, 36

Memmi, Albert, **195–96**

Meniru, Theresa Ekwutosi, **196**

Mezu, Sebastian Okechukwu, **196**, 312

Mhlophe, Gcina, 129

Mhudi (Plaatje), **197**, 246

Midaq Alley (Mahfouz), 187

Miller, Ruth, **197**

Millin, Sarah Gertrude, 56, 139, **197–98**, 316

Mine Boy (Peter Abrahams), 1, **198**

Mission to Kala (Beti), 53, **198**

Mitford, Bertram, 58

Mnthali, Felix, **198**

Modisane, William "Bloke," 40, 55, 57, 68, 118, **198–99**, 267

Mofolo, Thomas (Mopoku), 85, 164, **199**, 261

Molema, Leloba, 36

Moore, Bai Tamia Johnson, **199–200**

Moore-King, Bruce, 59

Mopeli-Paulus, Atwell Sidwee, 68, **200**

Morrison, Toni, 10, 11, 129

Motsisi, (Karobo Moses) Casey "Kid," 40, 118, **200**, 248

Mphahlele, Es'kia, 6, 35, 40, 55, 82, 118, 161, 172, 176, 192, 198, **200–201,** 266

Mphlophe, Gcina, **197,** 322

Mpina, Edison, **201–2,** 256

Mtshali, (Oswald) Mbuyiseni, 145, **202**

Mtwa, Percy, 112

Mugo, Micere Githae, 110, 175, **202–3,** 308

Mulaisho, Dominic, **203**

Mumonye, John, 265

Mungai, Joseph, 54

Mungoshi, Charles, 37, 84, **203–4,** 262, 320

Munonye, John, **227,** 265, 312

Muntu (De Graft), 80, 102, **204–5**

Muraguri, Nicholas. *See* Ruheni, Mwangi

Muriel at Metropolitan (Tlali), 82, **205,** 250, 298

Mushindo, Paul M. B., 260

Mustafa, Sophia, 74

Mutasa, Garikai, 84

Mutiga, Joseph G., 34

Mutloatse, Mothobi, 36, 41, 82, **205,** 322

Mutswairo, Solomon, 84, **205–6**

Mwambungu, Osija, 80

Mwangi, Meja, 140, 173, **206,** 308

Myambo, Melissa Tandiwe, 39

Myth, Literature and the African World (Soyinka), 116, 172, **206–7,** 292

Mzamane, Mbulelo, 36, 41, 82

Nagenda, John, **208,** 281

Naipaul, V. S., 23

Nakasa, Nathaniel Ndazana, 40, 82, 118, 200, **208**

Napolo Poems (Chimombo), 88, **208**

Nazareth, Peter, 34, 175, **208–9**

Nazombe, Anthony, **209–10**

Ndebele, Njabulo, 41, 132–33, **210,** 248

Ndhlala, Geoffrey, **210–11**

N'Djehoya, Blaise, **211**

Ndu, Pol Nnamuzikam, **211**

Nervous Conditions (Dangarembga), **211**

Neto, Agostinho, **211–12**

Newell, Stephanie, 181

Ngara, Emmanuel, **212**

Ngcobo, Lauretta, **212–13**

Ngema, Mbongeni, 112, 114, 161, **213–15**

Ngubiah, Stephen, 247, 265

Ngugi wa Mirii, 80

Ngugi wa Thiong'o, 2, 33, 34, 54, 80, 81, 103, 110, 111, 142, 150, 151, 172, 174, 198, 200, 203, 204, 209, **214–16,** 245, 247, 266, 267, 270, 273, 295, 308, 318

Nicol, Abioseh, **216**

Nicol, Mike, **216–17**

Niesewand, Peter, 59

Nigerian Afro Beat, 15

Night of Darkness (Zeleza), **217,** 323

Nightwatcher, Nightsong (Chipasula), 90, **217**

Njami, Simon, **217**

Njau, Rebeka, 111, 136, 137, **217–18**

Nkosi, Lewis, 40, 82, 118, 172, 192, 198, **218,** 253, 263

No Bride Price (Rubadiri), **219,** 272

No Longer at Ease (Achebe), 3, **219**

No Sweetness Here (Aidoo), **219**

No-Good Friday (Fugard), 112, 134, 199, **219**

None to Accompany Me (Gordimer), 140, **219**

North Africa: biographies and autobiographies of, **54;** censorship in, **81**

Nortje, Arthur, 19, **219–20**

No Sweetness Here (Aidoo), 28, **219**

Ntiru, Richard Carl, **220**

Nwabueze, Emeka, **220**

Nwakoby, Martina Awele, **220–21**

Nwankwo, Nkem, **221, 240**

Nwapa, Flora, 129, 159, **221–22,** 232, 265, 312

Nxumalo, Henry, 198

Nyamfukudza, Stanley, **222,** 311

Nyamubaya, Freedom, **222**

Nzekwu, Onuora, **222–23,** 265

Obafemi, Olu, 38, 118, **223**

Oculi, Okello, **223–24**

Of Chameleons and Gods (Mapanje), **224**

Ofeimun, Odia, **224–25**

Ogot, Grace (Emily), **225**

Oguibe, Olu, **225–26**

Ogunde, Hubert, 115, **226.** *See also* drama, of West Africa

Ogundipe-Leslie, Molara, **226–27,** 300

Ogunyemi, Wale, 109, 116, 117, 168, **227**

Ohaeto, Ezenwa, 34

Oil Man of Obange (Munonye), **227**

Ojaide, Tanure, 38, 223, **227–28**

Okai, Atukwei, **228**

Okara, Gabriel (Imomotimi Gbaingbain), 131, **228–29**

Okigbo, (Ifeanyichukwu) Christopher, 38, 148, 167, 170, 198, 211, **229–30,** 235, 257, 263

Okike: Journal of New African Writing, 3

Oko, Akomaye, **230**

Okola, Lennard, 33

Okome, Onookome, **230–31**

Okot p'Bitek, 263–64, 290

Okoye, Ifeoma, **232,** 298–99

Okpewho, Isidore, 76–77, 178, 181, **232–33,** 312

Okri, Ben, 14, 153, **233–34**

Olafioye, Tayo Peter, 79,
    234, 298
The Old Man and the Medal
    (Oyono), **234,** 242
Olive Schreiner Prize, 28
Oludhe Macgoye,
    Marjorie, **235**
Omotoso, Kole, 117, 136, 173,
    223, **235,** 312
One Man One Wife (Aluko),
    235, 265
The Only Son
    (Mumonye), 265
Onoge, Omafume, 178
Onwueme, Tess Akaeke, 117,
    236, 256
Onyeama, Dillibe, **236–37**
Ordeal in the Forest
    (Wachira), **237,** 307
Order of the Federal
    Republic, the
    Commonwealth Poetry
    Prize, 3
Orine, David, 15
Osadebay, Dennis (Chukude),
    38, **237,** 263
Osahon, Naiwu, **237–38**
Osiris Rising (Armah),
    45, **238**
Osofisan, Femi, 38–39,
    117, 173, 223,
    235, **238–39**
Osundare, Niyi, 126, 223, 235,
    239–40, 307
Otek p'Bitek, 2, 111, 132, 137,
    173, 174, 198, **231**
Oti, Sonny, **240**
Ouologuem, Yambo, 137
Our Sister Killjoy (Aidoo), 28,
    136, **240,** 266
Ovbiagele, Helen, **240**
Owusu, Martin (Okyere),
    240–41
Oyebode, Femi, **241**
Oyekunle, Segun, **241**
Oyono, Ferdinand, 53,
    149, 234
Oyono-Miha,
    Guillaume, **242**

Packer, Joy, 249
Palangyo, Peter, **242–43**
The Palm-wine Drinkard
    (Tutuola), 171, **243,** 257,
    264, 300
Pam-Grant, Sue, 114
Pan-Africanism, 17, 18
Paradise Farm
    (Kahiga), **243**
Parnwell, E. C., 36
The Path of Thunder (Peter
    Abrahams), 2, **243**
Paton, Alan (Stewart), 41, 55,
    97, **243–44,** 267
People of the City (Ekwensi),
    122, 244
People's Experimental Theater
    (PET), 113
Peptela (Artur Carlos
    Mauricio Pestana dos
    Santos), **244**
*Perpetua and the Habit of
    Unhappiness* (Beti),
    53, **245**
Petals of Blood (Ngugi wa
    Thiong'o), 214, **245,** 309
Peters, Lenrie (Leopold
    Wilfred), 38, **245,** 265
Peters, Peter, **1–2**
Philip, Marlene Nourbese,
    17, 18, 25
Plaatje, Sol T., 40, 55, 176,
    185–86, 197, 205,
    245–46, 304, 310
Plomer, William (Charles
    Franklyn), 55, 156,
    246–47, 299, 303
The Poor Christ of Bomba
    (Beti), 53, **247,** 265
popular literature, **247–50;**
    of East Africa, **247–48;** of
    South Africa, **248–50;** of
    West Africa, **250**
Prince Kagwema (Osija
    Mwambungu), **250,** 266
Pringle, Thomas,
    35, **250–51**
Prisoners of Jebs
    (Saro-Wiwa), **254**

prison literature, in South
    Africa, **251–53**
A Proper Marriage (Lessing),
    169, 254
Puppets against AIDS
    project, 114

Qabula, Alfred Temba,
    57, **254**
A Question of Power (Head),
    147, **254,** 267

Rabéarivelo, Jean-Joseph,
    254–55, 255
Rabémanajara, Jacques, **255**
The Rainmaker (Chimombo),
    88, **255**
Raji, Wumi, 38
Rampolokeng, Lesego,
    49, 68, **255**
Raven-Hart, R., 55
Raw Pieces (Mpina), **256**
Reddy, Vasu, 137
Rediscovery (Awoonor),
    46, **256**
The Reign of Wazobia
    (Onwueme), **256**
religion and literature, **256**
religions, traditional, and
    literature, **256–57**
The Return to Beirut
    (Chedid), **269**
Ricard, Alain, 115
Richards, Sandra L., 61
A Ripple from the Storm
    (Lessing), 169, **269–70**
Rive, Richard, 36, 56,
    172, **270**
The River Between (Ngugi wa
    Thiong'o), 214, 267,
    270, 309
Roach, Eric, 23
The Road (Soyinka), 116,
    257, **270–71,** 291
Roberts, Sheila, **271**
Ross, Kenneth R., 260
Rotimi, Ola, 30, 115,
    116, 139, 165,
    257, **271–72**

Rubadiri, David, 33, 34, 219, **272**

Ruganda, John, 33, 81, 111, **272–73**

Ruheni, Mwangi, 248, **273**

Ruhumbika, Gabriel, **273**

Rui, Manuel, **273**

Rumours of Rain (Brink), 73, **274**

Rungano, Kristina, **274**

Saadawi, Nawal el, **274–75**

Salih, Tayeb, 268, **275**, 281

Salkey, Andrew, 24

Sallah, TIjan Momodou, **275–76**

Samkange, Stanlake, 59, 84, 265, **276–77**

Sancho, Ignatius, 13, 17, 59, 259, **277**

Saro-Wiwa, Ken(ule Beeson), 85, 254, **277–79**, 293–94

Sartre, Jean-Paul, 171

Sassine, William, 136, **279**

Schreiner, Olive, 129, 153, 267, 270, **279–80**, 294

Scott, Dennis, 24

Scully, William Charles, 55, **280–81**

Season of Anomy (Soyinka), 137, 266, **281**, 292

Season of Migration to the North (Salih), 275, **281**

The Seasons of Thomas Tebo (Nagenda), **281**, 309

Sebuliba, Catherine, 54

Segun, Mabel, 60, **281**

Sekyi, Kobina, 115

Sekyi, (William Essuman-Gwira) Kobina, 115, **282**

Sellassie, Sahle, **282**

Selormey, Francis, 265, **282–83**

Selvon, Samuel, 23

Sembene Ousmane, 67, 139, 173, 268, **283**

Senghor, Leopold Sedar, 38, 127, 171, 263, **284–85**

Senkoro, F.E.M.K, 18

Sepamla, Sipho (Sydney), 41, 66, 82, **285**

Seremba, George, **285–86**

Serote, Mongane (Wally), 41, 66, 145, **286**, 310

Seruma, Eneriko, 34, 126, **287**

Serumaga, Robert, 110, 111, 272, **287**, 309

Shaihu Umar (Balewa), **287**

Shange, Ntozake, 10

Shimanyula, James, 110

Sibenke, Ben, **287–88**

Simbi and the Satyr of the Dark Jungle (Tutuola), **288**, 300

Simon, Barney, 70, 112, 205

Sirens Knuckles Boots (Brutus), 75, **288**

Sithole, Ndabaningi, 84

The Sixth Day (Chedid), **288**

Sizwe Bansi Is Dead (Fugard), 134, **288**

Skelton, Kenneth, 59

Slabolepzsy, Paul, 114

Slater, Francis Carey, 35, 55, **288–89**

Small, Adam, 156

Smit, Bartho, 156

Smith, Angela, 34

Smith, Pauline (Janet), 129, 182, **289**

Snelling, John, 37

Sofola, Zulu, 116, 117

Soga, Tiyo, 205

So Long a Letter (Bâ), **289**

Song of Lawino (Okot p'Bitek), 248, 263–64, **290**

Son of Woman (Mangua), **290**

Sons and Daughters (De Graft), 102, **290**

Sony Labou Tansi, 7, 136, **290–91**

South Africa: anthologies of, 35–37; biographies/ autobiographies of, 54–57; black consciousness in, **64–67**; censorship in, 81–83; drama of, **111–15**; literary criticism of, **176–77**; popular literature of, **248–50**; prison literature in, **251–53**; war literature of, **309–11**; young adult literature of, **322–23**

South-Central Africa: anthologies of, **37–38**; biographies/ autobiographies of, **57–59**; censorship in, 83–84; war literature of, **311**; young adult literature of, **318–21**

Sowande, Bode, **291**

Soyinka, Wole, 7, 14, 30, 38, 49, 60, 100, 116, 126, 133, 136, 137, 140, 151, 163, 168, 170–71, 172, 206–7, 227, 235, 238, 257, 262, 266, 270–71, 281, **291–93**, 294, 299, 312, 318

Sozaboy: A Novel in Rotten English (Saro-Wiwa), **293–94**

A Sport of Nature (Gordimer), 140, **294**

States of Emergency (Brink), **74, 294**

The Stone Country (La Guma), 253, **294**

The Story of an African Farm (Schreiner), 153, 279, **294**

The Strong Bread (Soyinka), 293, **294**

Sutherland, Efua Theodora, 102, 115, 133, 190, **294–95**

Sweet and Sour Milk (Farah), 127

Taban Lo Liyong, 34, 132, 137, 174, 175, 204, 209, 231, 264, **295–96**

Tahir, Ibrahim, 268, **296**

Taylor, Jane, 36

Taylor, Richard, 181

Tejani, Bahadur, 33, **296**

Tell Freedom (Peter Abrahams), 2, 265, **296**

Terry, Lucy, 8

Theater Council of Natal (TECON), 113

Themba, (Daniel Canodoise) Can, 40, 118, 173, 198, 205, 207, 248, **296, 304**, 316

Things Fall Apart (Achebe), 3, 45, 49, 257, 266, 297, 302

Thomas, Dylan, 171

Thomas, Gladys, **297**, 322

Thompson, Thomas, 259

Through a Film Darkly (De Graft), 102, 297

Time of the Butcherbird (La Guma), 166, **297**

Tlali, Miriam, 41, 66, 82, 129, 133, **205**, 250, **298**

Tomorrow Left Us Yesterday (Olafioye), **298**

Toomer, Jean, 9

The Trial and Other Stories (Okoye), **298–99**

The Trial of Christopher Okigbo (Mazrui), 193, **299**

The Trials of Brother Jero (Soyinka), 257, **299**

Tsodzo, Thompson Kumbirai, **299**

Turbott Wolfe (Plomer), **299**

Turner, Darwin, 8

Tutuola, Amos, 126, 171, 243, 257, 264, 288, **299–300**, 317, 318

Two Thousand Seasons (Armah), 45, **300**

Tyne, Maxine, 18

Udechukwu, Obiora, **301**, 312

Udensi, Uwa, 116

Ugah, Ada, **301**

Uka, Kalu, 116, **301–2**

Ulasi, Adaora Lily, **302**

Umelo, Rosina, **302**

Uwatt, Effiok Bassey, 115

Valley of a Thousand Hills (Dhlomo), 263, **302**

Vambe, Lawrence, 59, 84, **302–3**

Van Der Post, Laurens, 55, 246, 249, 267, **303**

Van Wyk, Christopher, 41, 56, **303–4**

Vassanji, Moyez G., 7, 19, 32, 34, 70–71, 143–44, **304–5**

Vatsa, Mamman Jira, **305**

Vera, Yvonne, 19, **305**, 311

Vilakazi, Benedict Walter, 176, 261, **306**

Visions and Reflections (Chipasula), 90, **306**

Vladislavic, Ivan, **306**

The Voice (Okara), **306**

Wachira, Godwin, 237, **306–7**, 308

Waciuma, Charity, 101, 307, 308

Waiting for the Barbarians (Coetzee), 92, **307**

Waiting Laughters (Osundare), 239, **307**

Walcott, Derek, 23, 24

Walker, Alice, 128

A Walk in the Night (La Guma), 166

The Wall of the Plague (Brink), **307**

Wally, Mongane, 82

Wangusa, Timothy, 266, **307–8**

Wanjala, Chris L., 33

Ward, Baha'i Frederick, 18

war literature, **308–13**; of East Africa, **308–9**; of South Africa, **309–11**; of South-Central Africa, **311**; of West Africa, **312**

Watene, Kenneth, 102, 110, 308, **313**

Watson, John, 7

Watson, Stephen, **313**

Webb, Frank, 9

Weep Not, Child (Ngugi wa Thiong'o), 214, 266, 309, **313–14**, 318

Were, Miriam, **314**

West Africa: anthologies of, **38–39**; biography and autobiography, **59–61**; censorship in, **84–85**; drama of, **115–18**; literary criticism of, **177–80**; popular literature of, **250**; war literature of, **312**; young adult literature of, **318–21**

Whaley, Andrew, **314**

Wheatley, Phillis, 8, **314–15**

When Sunset Comes to Sapitwa (Mnthali), 198, **315**

Why Are We So Blest? (Armah), 45, **315**

Wicomb, Zoë, **315–16**, 318

Wilhelm, Peter, 176, **316**

Willemse, Hein, 35

Williams, Adebayo, **316–17**

The Will to Die (Themba), 297, **316**

The Witch-Herbalist of the Remote Town (Tutuola), 300, **317**

The Wrath of the Ancestors (Jordan), 317

Wright, Richard, 9

Yakubu, A. M., 38

Yirenkyi, Asiedu, 117–18, **317–18**

You Can't Get Lost in Cape Town (Wicomb), 316, **318**

You Must Set Forth at Dawn (Soylinka), 318

Young adult literature, **318–23**; of East Africa, **318–21**; of South Africa, **322–23**; of South-Central Africa, **318–21**; of West Africa, **318–21**

Yulisa, Pat. *See* Maddy, Yulisa Amadu

Zake, Mda, 115

Zeleza, Paul Tiyambe, 217, **323–24**

Zephaniah, Benjamin, 15

Zimunya, Musaemura Bonas, 37, 38, **324**

Zindi, Frederick, 84

Zungur, Sa'ad, 136, **324**

About the Authors

DOUGLAS KILLAM is Professor Emeritus of Commonwealth Literature at the University of Guelph. His previous books include *Literature of Africa* (Greenwood, 2004).

ALICIA L. KERFOOT is a Ph.D. candidate in the Department of English and Cultural Studies at McMaster University.